A Century of Doctorates

DATA ANALYSES OF GROWTH AND CHANGE

U.S. PhD's—Their Numbers, Origins, Characteristics, and the Institutions from Which They Come

LINDSEY R. HARMON, *Project Director*

A Report to the
NATIONAL SCIENCE FOUNDATION
to the
NATIONAL ENDOWMENT FOR THE HUMANITIES
and to the
UNITED STATES OFFICE OF EDUCATION
from the
BOARD ON HUMAN-RESOURCE DATA AND ANALYSES
Commission on Human Resources
National Research Council

NATIONAL ACADEMY OF SCIENCES
Washington, D.C. 1978

NOTICE: This report is based on research conducted by the National Research Council with the support of the National Science Foundation, the U.S. Office of Education, and the National Endowment for the Humanities under Contract No. NSF-C310, Task Order 314. However, any opinions, findings, conclusions, or recommendations expressed herein are those of the authors and do not necessarily reflect the views of the sponsoring agencies.

LIBRARY OF CONGRESS CATALOGING IN PUBLICATION DATA

National Research Council. Board on Human-Resource Data and Analyses.
A century of doctorates.

Includes bibliographical references and index.
1. Degrees, Academic--United States. 2. Doctor of philosophy degree. I. United States. National Science Foundation. II. National Endowment for the Humanities. III. United States. Office of Education. IV. Title.
LB2386.N32 1978 378'.24'0973 78-5644
ISBN 0-309-02738-1

Available from

Printing and Publishing Office
National Academy of Sciences
2101 Constitution Avenue, N.W.
Washington, D.C. 20418

Printed in the United States of America

Preface

How many PhD holders are there in the United States? How many new PhD's are granted each year, and how has this changed over time? What are the characteristics of this group--such as age, racial/ethnic identification, family backgrounds, geographic origins? Where do they go, and what do they do, after they graduate? What about the institutions from which they came? Questions such as these concern those in graduate education, in government at state and national levels, and the professional societies to which many PhD's belong. These queries were the main motivating force for the publication of the present volume.

This book is the seventh in a series published by the National Academy of Sciences (NAS) on doctorate cohorts and the baccalaureate and doctorate institutions of U.S. PhD's. (The term PhD is used generically here, referring to all third-level earned degrees.) The first book, published in 1948, concerned only the science doctorates of the period 1936-1945. This volume's immediate predecessor concerned the recipients of doctorates granted in all fields over the period 1958-1966. The present volume goes back to the beginnings of the doctorate in the United States, over a century ago, and brings the data forward to 1974. The general content of the book, as well as the limitations on its scope, was agreed to by the sponsors and the Commission on Human Resources prior to the awarding of the contract and represents their primary areas of concern.

The principal sources of data for this volume were the Doctorate Records File (DRF) of the Commission on Human Resources of the National Research Council (NRC), supplemented in part by data from the Comprehensive Roster of Doctoral Scientists and Engineers, also maintained by the Commission on Human Resources, and, to a limited extent, data from the

U.S. Office of Education. The more recent periods have been emphasized in the analyses not only because of the greater practical concern with data of greatest present relevance but also because of greater data availability. The DRF, with individual data, begins with 1920; data beyond degrees held, dates, and the institutions granting them, however, became available from 1957 on. The Commission on Human Resources receives completed Doctorate Survey questionnaires continually from the graduate schools of the United States, with extensive data on all new PhD's, and uses the responses in numerous statistical tabulations. The Comprehensive Roster entails biennial follow-ups of a carefully stratified sample of PhD's to determine current employment information. Both resources have been used as the basis for numerous other publications and are currently used as data sources for statistical studies by members of the academic community and others. In these researches, individual identity of the PhD's is carefully protected. Statistical tabulations are provided by the NAS to anyone on a cost reimbursement basis.

Many hands have contributed to the preparation of this volume. The National Science Foundation (NSF) was the chief sponsor of this project. The U.S. Office of Education and the National Endowment for the Humanities were cosponsors. The staffs of these agencies, particularly Dr. Charles Dickens of NSF, have offered valuable advice and suggestions. Members of the Board on Human-Resource Data and Analyses and the Board on Fellowships and Associateships have served as advisers, planners, and reviewers. Particularly deserving of mention are Lee Grodzins, who together with Winton Manning, Elizabeth Gantt, and Monroe Donsker, shepherded the book through the draft stages, and Michael Pelczar, Lewis Slack, and Wade Ellis, who offered valuable suggestions in review of the draft. Robert Alberty, William Kelly, and Dorothy Gilford provided not only administrative support but also valuable comments on drafts of the book. The Data Processing Section of CHR, under the leadership of Herbert Soldz, provided computer programing and data tables. Norma Melendez and Susan Henry not only prepared computer tables and typed text but also performed the endless other chores without which such a book cannot be produced.

However, there is one person, above all others, whose special talents and professional expertise were instrumental in the production of this volume. That person is Lindsey Harmon, Project Director for this book. His meticulous editing and attention to detail in the preparation of both text and figures for the final manuscript will make the masses of statistical data presented in this report accessible to those involved either directly or indirectly in graduate education. All of us involved in graduate education are indebted to Lindsey Harmon for this synthesis of the first 100 years of graduate education in the United States.

MICHAEL J. PELCZAR, JR., *Chairman*
Board on Human-Resource Data and Analyses

Contents

List of Tables

List of Figures

A Century of Doctorates

DATA ANALYSES OF GROWTH AND CHANGE

Introduction

Since 1948 the National Academy of Sciences (NAS) has published a series of seven books having to do with doctorates granted in the United States, the baccalaureate origins of these doctorate recipients, and some of their more important educational and employment characteristics. These books are listed in the selective bibliography at the end of this book. From 1946 to the present a file has been built up within the NAS that contains data on all PhD's (or equivalent third-level research degree holders) from U.S. universities since 1920. This file is called the Doctorate Records File (DRF). It has been the focal point for many studies and a starting point for many others. The series of seven books, of which this is the latest, have described the numbers of PhD's and their origins, characteristics, educational backgrounds, and plans at the time of PhD graduation. The present book goes farther back and extends the data forward to 1974, tracing the growth of PhD graduations from the beginning over a century ago. It provides a wider context regarding the relationship of PhD's to the rest of the U.S. population. It does not attempt to trace the origins of graduate education, the development of policies, or the influence of individuals; it is limited to a presentation of data on degrees awarded and certain characteristics of those receiving degrees. No attempt is made to evaluate the quality of the degrees; in the statistics herein presented we are concerned only with a count of numbers.

The four chapters of this book describe the numbers of PhD's over the past century and how these numbers have varied; the characteristics of PhD's, particularly with regard to education, citizenship, age, and migration; the plans of the PhD's at the time of graduation, and something of how these plans were carried out in actuality, with regard to further education or employment; and, finally, some data regarding the institutions from which the PhD's came--the numbers of schools, growth in numbers since 1920, and geographic distribution and the undergraduate institutions in which the PhD's earned their bachelor's degrees. Additional data, too voluminous and detailed for this book, will be made available on a cost reimbursement basis for those who wish to pursue research in this area. The highlights of the findings reported in this book are given below.

HIGHLIGHTS

Historically, PhD's were first conferred by Yale in 1861. Over the period since 1875 the growth in numbers of PhD's has been at an average rate of about 7 percent per annum. This results in approximately doubling the output each decade. This growth rate has fluctuated widely, particularly as a result of World Wars I and II and also as a result of the great economic depression of the 1930's, as well as for reasons that cannot be accurately determined, particularly in the early years of this century. About 100 years ago, in the late 1870's, the number of PhD's graduating each year was about 40; by 1900 this number had risen to about 300; by 1925 it was about 1,200; in the mid-1970's it had stabilized at about 33,000.

Education of the U.S. Population

The PhD's represent an increasing fraction of an increasingly well-educated U.S. population. Over the past century, the average educational level of the general population has increased at a rate of one grade level each 15 years. The PhD's have come predominantly from families at the leading edge of this educational wave; their parents were, on the average, about two grade levels ahead of the general public. The women PhD's come from slightly better-educated families than do their male colleagues, but their mothers had less education than their fathers--which is typical of the general public also. Field variations in the level of education of the parents of PhD's are pronounced, but have become less so over the past 2 decades. The pattern of these changes is described in Chapter 2.

The Population of PhD's

The above data refer to graduations. By taking into account the age at graduation, the proportions of men and women in each field, and age-specific death rates (which are much lower for PhD's than for the general population), it is possible to construct a computer model of the number of PhD's by field, sex, and age in the U.S. population. Such checks as have been made to date have indicated that this model provides rather accurate information on the population of living PhD's of U.S. origin. Projections of these numbers can be made, based on projections of anticipated output of new PhD's into the future. Over the period since 1940, the PhD populations in most fields have followed parallel growth trends, growing at an average rate of about 7 percent per year. Three fields have grown considerably more rapidly than the average. These are education, which has grown at a rate of about 11 percent per annum, and engineering and psychology, which have grown at about 8 percent per annum. It is worthy of note that these three fields have a large "applied" component, relative to that typical of the slower-growing fields.

Women and the Doctorate

American society until recently has regarded graduate education as predominantly for men, but trends have varied. At the turn of the century, about 9 percent of the new PhD's were women. In the 1920's this shifted markedly, the percentage of women rising to about 15 percent of PhD graduations in the early 1920's, then declining, first gradually, then more rapidly during the period of World War II and its aftermath, to a low of about 10 percent in the early 1950's. Since that time, the proportion of women has increased, first slowly, then much more rapidly, until in 1974 it was over 20 percent of PhD's granted and still rising. Changes in the sex ration have been accompanied, in recent years, with a shift in the overall field mix: the natural sciences, particularly the physical sciences and engineering, have dropped, while the behavioral sciences, the humanities, and education have been rising. The latter fields have typically had higher proportions of women than have the natural sciences, which have historically claimed about half of the male PhD production. Only about one-fourth of the women have graduated in the natural sciences, while another one-fourth have been in education, which has included only about one man in six.

Racial/Ethnic Identification

Only recently has information on the racial/ethnic composition of the doctorate population become available. The data presently available--which apply only to the recent graduates and, for a longer period of time, to the science fields--indicate that about 88 percent of recent PhD's are white, 3.4 percent are black, ½ of 1 percent are American Indians, 1.2 percent are of Hispanic origin, and 7.2 percent are of Oriental origin. Blacks and American Indians tend to be concentrated in education, and Orientals in the engineering, mathematics, and physical science (EMP) fields. These data include all citizenship categories, foreign as well as U.S.

U.S. and Foreign Citizens among the PhD's

In those fields of greatest immediate significance to developing countries, such as agricultural sciences, engineering, and the medical sciences, the proportion of non-U.S. citizens is relatively high, from one-fifth to one-third of the total of all U.S. PhD's. In those fields which are most closely bound up with the culture, such as education and psychology, the proportion of foreign citizens is quite low--about 1 in 20. There are important sex differences, varying by field, in foreign citizenship also. Overall, about 15 percent of the male PhD's are foreign citizens, compared with about 10 percent of the female PhD's.

Age at Completion of PhD

Most PhD's attain the doctorate at about 30 years of age--earlier in the physical sciences, particularly chemistry, and later in the nonscience fields. In education, age 40 is more nearly typical. Most of this age difference is accounted for in the baccalaureate-to-doctorate time lapse, although there are age differences at the baccalaureate level also. Over the past half-century, the time in graduate school has increased; a part of the change was that induced by the effects of World War II, which interrupted the process of education for so many. However, even in recent years there has been a tendency toward longer time in graduate school, in spite of the effects of programs of support for those in graduate training.

Master's Degrees

In all fields except chemistry, over half of the PhD's have master's degrees. In chemistry, the proportion is 41 percent; while in physics it is 64 percent; in the biomedical sciences, 65 percent; psychology, 77 percent; the earth sciences, 78 percent; mathematics, 79 percent; the social sciences, 83 percent; humanities, 87 percent; engineering, 89 percent; the agricultural sciences, 90 percent; and education, 97 percent. The significance of the master's degree varies not only by field but also by the institution granting the degree. In some departments it is a routine landmark for those making progress on their way to the doctorate; in others it is a much more definitive credential in its own right. There are sex differences in the proportion of PhD's who take master's degrees; the percentage is typically higher for women than for men except in the earth sciences, engineering, and the agricultural sciences.

Field-Switching Patterns

Although the major source of PhD's in any given field is the same field at the baccalaureate level, a significant portion of PhD's switch fields between the bachelor's and doctor's degrees, and the switches follow rather pronounced patterns. The net result within the sciences is principally a flow from mathematics, physics, chemistry, engineering, and the agricultural sciences into the biosciences and earth sciences. There is also a flow from all science fields into the humanities and education. The remaining fields have an approximate balance in proportions at the bachelor's and doctor's levels. Each field may be considered in terms of its donor/receptor characteristics: the extent to which it "donates" its baccalaureate recipients to various doctorate-level "receptor" fields. The patterns of these field switches is described in Chapter 2.

Migration

Regional shifts from the region in which the bachelor's degree is earned to that in which the doctorate is earned have changed over time, as the spread of doctorate-granting institutions has progressed. In the early days, doctorate education was concentrated heavily in the Northeast and in California; more recently, a more even distribution over the United States has brought doctorate-level training nearer home for baccalaureate graduates in other areas. This has resulted in changes over time in the regional migration patterns, which have been shown to be a complex function of the relative strength of each region at the secondary, higher-education, and graduate levels. Patterns of migration are explored to some extent in Chapter 2; a more comprehensive analysis of these matters is available in *Migration of PhD's, Before and After the Doctorate*, published by the NAS in 1971.

After the Doctorate: Employment or Further Education?

Postdoctoral education has historically been restricted to a relatively few outstanding scholars or scientists and has frequently been undertaken some years after the doctorate, during which time the individual has been engaged in teaching and/or research in higher education. More recently, immediate postdoctoral education (following directly upon PhD graduation) has become more common. Currently, up to 40 percent of PhD's in the biomedical sciences, but fewer than 1 in 20 in the nonscience fields, undertake such education.

Employment

The traditional employment for new PhD's has been in universities, particularly those with strong research programs. These universities now offer fewer opportunities, while production of new PhD's remains high. Nonacademic employment has not taken up the slack of cutbacks in university hiring. As a result, the new PhD's who are caught in this squeeze are far less sure of their eventual employment and increasingly have taken a variety of postdoctoral appointments as interim employment while seeking permanent jobs better suited to their training and interest. Follow-up via the Comprehensive Roster of Doctoral Scientists and Engineers shows that, by and large, plans for the first year following the doctorate, which are given in the Survey of Earned Doctorates (a form completed by each new PhD), are largely realized. These data are limited at present to the science and engineering fields but will shortly be extended to include the humanities fields also.

Geography

Geographic movement following the doctorate depends on plans for further training or immediate employment, among other things. Those who plan to take postdoctoral education tend to favor the Pacific Coast or the Middle Atlantic States if they move from the region in which they took the doctorate. Interregional migrants who plan immediate employment after the doctorate tend to favor the East North Central States or Middle Atlantic States if they enter academe, or the South Atlantic and Middle Atlantic States, in that order, if they take nonacademic jobs. Thirteen percent of those who seek further training, 5 percent of those who seek academic employment, and 11 percent of those entering nonacademic employment go abroad. Foreign citizens predominate among these groups.

The PhD-Granting Institutions

In 1974 there were 307 regionally accredited institutions granting the doctorate, including as separate institutions medical schools and separately administered branches of large state systems. This was an increase from a total of only 61 institutions in the 1920-1924 period. In the early 1940's there were 107, and in the early 1960's 208, doctorate-granting institutions. This represents an accelerating growth curve, with no present indications of leveling off, although there are administrative and economic forces at work that may reduce this rate of increase in the future.

The Lion's Share is Shrinking

More than half of the PhD degrees granted over the 55-year period from 1920 through 1974 were granted by institutions that began awarding doctorates prior to 1920. Those institutions that began to turn out PhD's in the 1920's account for about one-fifth of the total, while all the others, who began granting PhD's in 1930 or later, account for only one-fourth of the total. The proportions, however, are shifting. When institutions are grouped according to the decade in which they began to grant the doctorate, the institutions of the 1930's, 1940's, 1950's, and 1960's are currently almost equal in PhD's granted, and those beginning in the 1970's are rapidly rising in their share of the total.

The northeastern corner of the country might be termed the "cradle of PhD education," and it still remains the leading region. Now, however, it has almost been overtaken by the Midwest. Meanwhile the West (the Pacific Coast and the Rocky Mountain States) has risen quite rapidly since the end of World War II but has in turn almost been overtaken by the even more rapid rise of the South, where doctorate-level education was almost nonexistent in 1920.

1

Historical Trends

HIGHLIGHTS

- The number of PhD's awarded in the United States has approximately doubled in each decade over the past century. Quarter-century landmarks show that in 1900 the annual output was about 300; in 1925, about 1,200; in 1950, about 6,000; and in 1974, about 33,000.
- World Wars I and II have produced the major fluctuations in the rate of growth of PhD production--first a dramatic drop, then an enormous rate of increase. The Great Depression of the 1930's had a less dramatic but nonetheless pervasive effect in lowering the rate of growth of PhD graduations.
- The proportion of women among PhD's rose in this century from about 9 percent in 1900 to about 15 percent in the early 1920's, declined (except for World War II) to a low of 10 percent in the early 1950's, then rose sharply to over 20 percent in 1974.
- The natural sciences claim about one-half of the PhD's among men; among women it is about one-fourth. Another one-fourth of the women are in education, which claims only about one-sixth of the men.
- Proportions of PhD's in the various fields and field groups have varied over time; since 1970 the proportion in the natural sciences has diminished, and the proportion in education has increased markedly.
- The number of living PhD's in the United States has increased since 1920 by a factor of 50, while the general population has approximately doubled.
- Among living PhD's, the fields of engineering, education, and psychology--fields with a large "applied" component--have grown most rapidly; the other fields have grown at a more modest rate.

GROWTH OF PhD AWARDS

From the time the first earned PhD was granted in the United States--by Yale University in 1861--to the present day, the number of PhD's granted annually has increased at an average rate of about 7 percent per year, doubling every decade. The term PhD is used here to include equivalent third-level research degrees, such as ScD, EngD, and EdD, but excludes such professional degrees as MD, DDS, DVM, or JD. The records of the U.S. Office of Education (USOE) for the years prior to 1920 are a bit uncertain and lacking in detail but are the best available. The data for the period since 1920 have been assembled from the Doctorate Records File (DRF) maintained by the Commission on Human Resources of the National Research Council (NRC). All data are in terms of calendar year unless otherwise noted. No attempt is made here to assess the quality of these degrees. We have simply counted the numbers as if each degree were equal to the others within the categories used here, such as field, sex, and cohort of graduation.

The growth in PhD's can be envisioned in a number of ways--in terms of numbers of degrees granted, in terms of the fluctuations in the growth of numbers of degrees granted, and in terms of the resulting numbers of the PhD population. In this chapter, all of these approaches will be used, with a number of graphic techniques to aid in visualization of the data.

A linear plot of the number of degrees granted annually over the past century averaged over 5-year intervals is given in Figure 1.

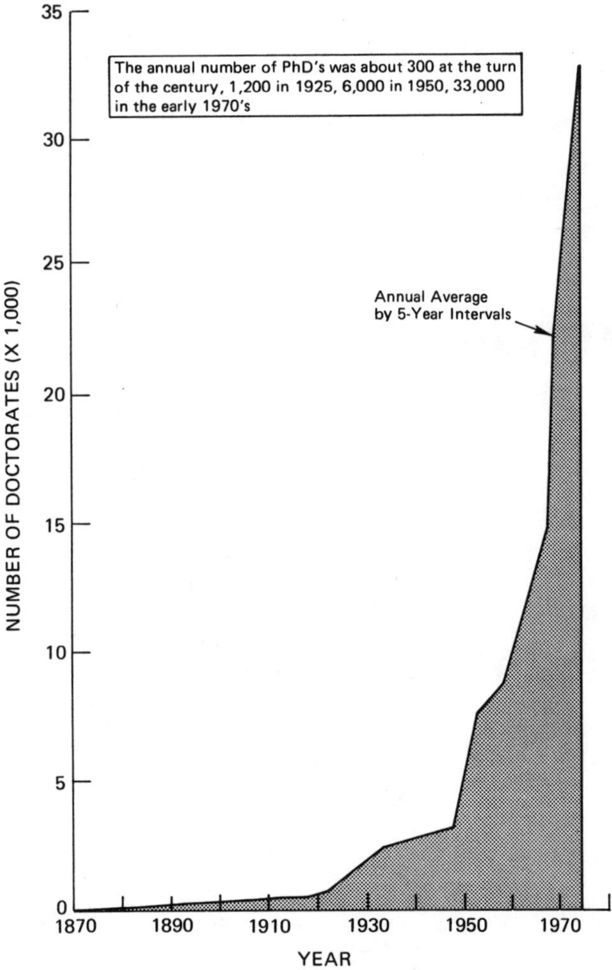

SOURCE: NRC, Commission on Human Resources

FIGURE 1 Doctorates granted annually.

While dramatic, this graph has a number of drawbacks from the standpoint of interpretation. The data cover a period in which the annual number of degrees increased a thousandfold. It is easier to visualize such an exponential growth process by plotting the data on a semilogarithmic scale. This is done in Figure 2, which shows the average number of degrees granted per year for each 5-year period from 1875 through 1974. A straight line drawn through the "stair steps" of the graph depicts a steady 7 percent annual growth rate over this century. The deviations from this steady growth are informative, but one must allow for a greater degree of uncertainty of the data and the effects of small numbers in the years prior to the twentieth century. A slowing down is apparent for 15 years after 1895, and the year-by-year data of Table 1 show a particularly sharp decline during World War I. A growth spurt follows in the 1920's, then a slowing down during the years of the economic depression of the 1930's. Again, year-by-year data show a very sharp drop in PhD's granted during World War II and an upswing later that is even more dramatic than the huge step in Figure 2 at the beginning of the 1950's. Another slowing down appears after 1950; the growth of the "GI period" (about 1945-1950) was obviously not sustainable, and a secondary effect of World War II appeared in the late 1950's. This was a lean period due to the interruption and postponement of undergraduate education by the war; the gap moved on to the PhD level about 1957. Following this there is a steady increase through the 1960's, which experienced the highest sustained growth in PhD output since the beginning of graduate education. The early 1970's show a sharp break in the growth curve.

The output of PhD's, depicted graphically in Figures 1 and 2, is shown numerically in Table 1, which provides both annual data and 5-year summaries. As noted earlier, the data prior to 1920 are from the USOE, except for the years 1917 and 1919, which had to be filled in from NRC sources, since the USOE data became biennial after 1916.

A third way of looking at PhD growth is shown in Figure 3, which depicts the 5-year summaries in PhD graduation numbers as successive tree rings, each ring adding to the previous number of doctorates granted. In Figure 3, the *area* of each new ring is proportional to the number of new degrees granted in the 5-year

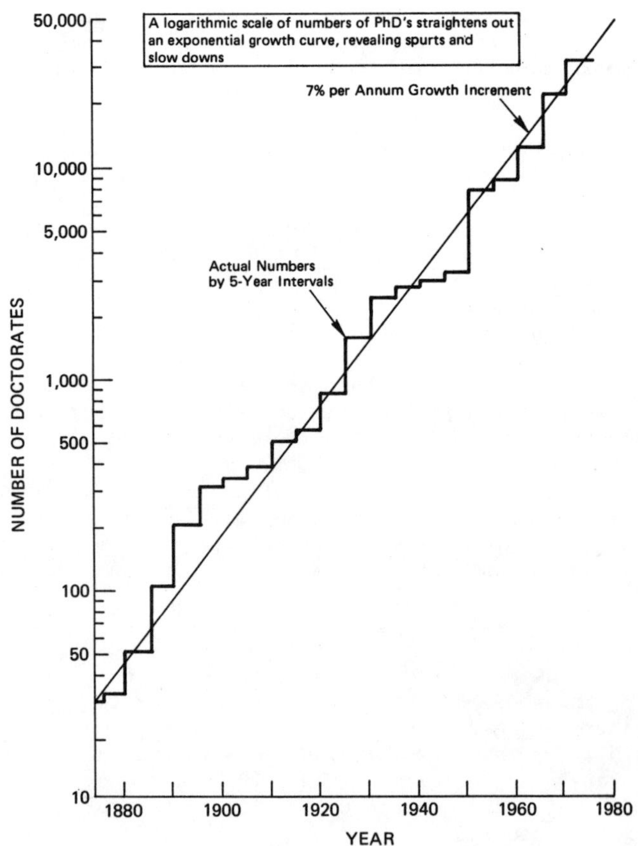

SOURCE: NRC, Commission on Human Resources

FIGURE 2 Doctorates granted annually (logarithmic scale).

TABLE 1
DOCTORATES GRANTED ANNUALLY BY U.S. UNIVERSITIES, 1875-1974,* WITH 5-YEAR SUMMARIES
(Calendar Year Data)

Year	PhD Total	Year	PhD Total	Year	PhD Total	Year	PhD Total
1875	23	1900	382	1925	1,206	1950	6,535
1876	31	1901	365	1926	1,441	1951	7,331
1877	39	1902	293	1927	1,540	1952	7,717
1878	32	1903	337	1928	1,632	1953	8,380
1879	36	1904	334	1929	1,917	1954	8,708
1875-1879	161	1900-1904	1,711	1925-1929	7,736	1950-1954	38,671
1880	54	1905	369	1930	2,075	1955	8,905
1881	37	1906	383	1931	2,344	1956	8,516
1882	46	1907	349	1932	2,400	1957	8,611
1883	50	1908	391	1933	2,462	1958	8,838
1884	66	1909	451	1934	2,696	1959	9,370
1880-1884	253	1905-1909	1,943	1930-1934	11,977	1955-1959	44,240
1885	77	1910	443	1935	2,529	1960	9,998
1886	84	1911	497	1936	2,713	1961	10,827
1887	77	1912	500	1937	2,752	1962	11,975
1888	140	1913	538	1938	2,754	1963	13,515
1889	124	1914	559	1939	2,950	1964	14,951
1885-1889	502	1910-1914	2,537	1935-1939	13,698	1960-1964	61,266
1890	149	1915	611	1940	3,277	1965	17,110
1891	187	1916	667	1941	3,484	1966	19,202
1892	190	1917	664	1942	3,404	1967	21,216
1893	212	1918	556	1943	2,592	1968	24,328
1894	279	1919	371	1944	1,967	1969	27,417
1890-1894	1,017	1915-1919	2,869	1940-1944	14,724	1965-1969	109,273
1895	272	1920	562	1945	1,634	1970	31,489
1896	271	1921	662	1946	1,990	1971	33,163
1897	319	1922	780	1947	2,951	1972	34,458
1898	324	1923	1,062	1948	3,940	1973	33,472
1899	345	1924	1,133	1949	5,389	1974	33,165
1895-1899	1,531	1920-1924	4,199	1945-1949	15,904	1970-1974	165,747

*Preliminary data received too late for further analysis indicate that in 1975 there were 33,146 PhD's granted; 33,200 were estimated for 1976; 32,000 for 1977.

SOURCE: NRC, Commission on Human Resources.

period so that the total area shows cumulative numbers of degrees. This provides a beginning for consideration of the PhD population, as distinct from graduation numbers, a topic that is taken up in more detail later in this chapter.

Most of the data available with respect to doctorate output and the characteristics of PhD's comes from the period since 1920, which marks the beginning of the DRF of the Commission on Human Resources of the NRC. Although data collection for the DRF began only in 1946, it was possible to go back to the universities and obtain graduation records, permitting the beginning of a name file, with individual data on each graduate. A decade later a further step was taken, with the initiation of a questionnaire, the Survey of Earned Doctorates, which was filled out by each graduate and forwarded to the NRC. This permitted more information and more accurate information with respect to the graduate, including his or her own statement as to the fields of specialization at the time of all degrees earned and where and when the degrees were earned. This in turn permitted study of baccalaureate-to-doctorate time lapse, the switching of fields between baccalaureate and doctorate, geographic migration, and a number of other topics described in later chapters.

Growth of PhD output during the 1920-1974 period is depicted graphically on a linear plot in Figure 4. The data here are 3-year moving

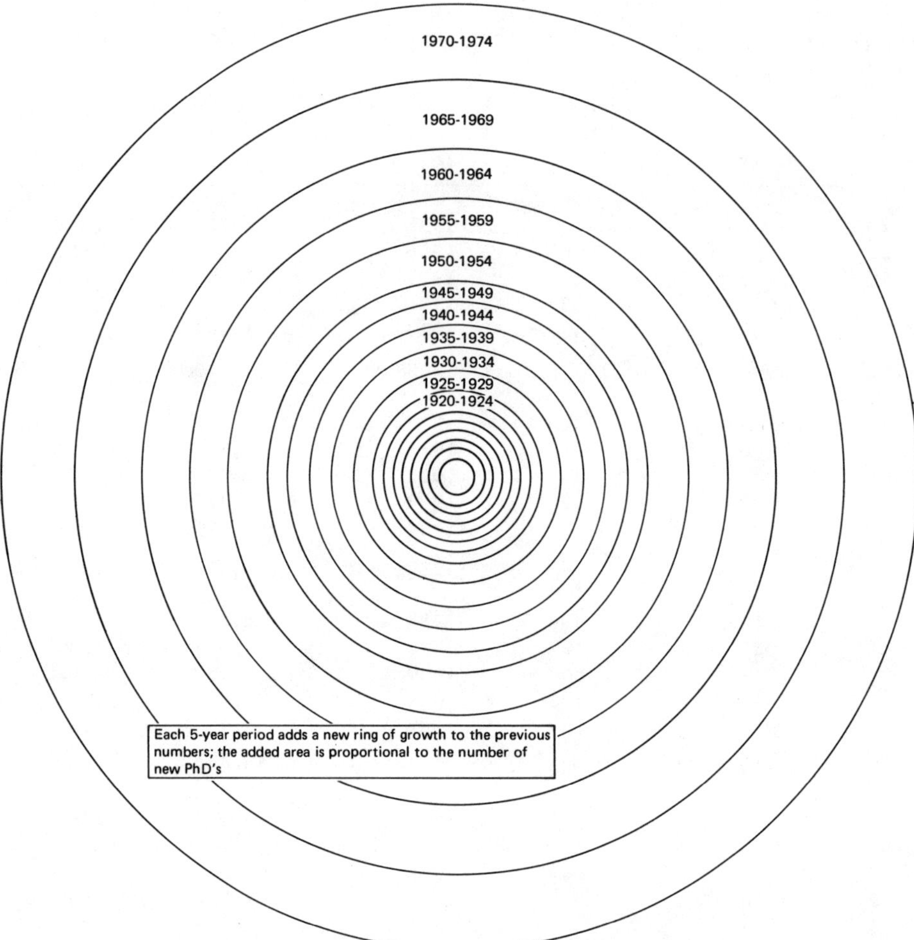

SOURCE: NRC, Commission on Human Resources

FIGURE 3 Growth in doctorates depicted as tree rings.

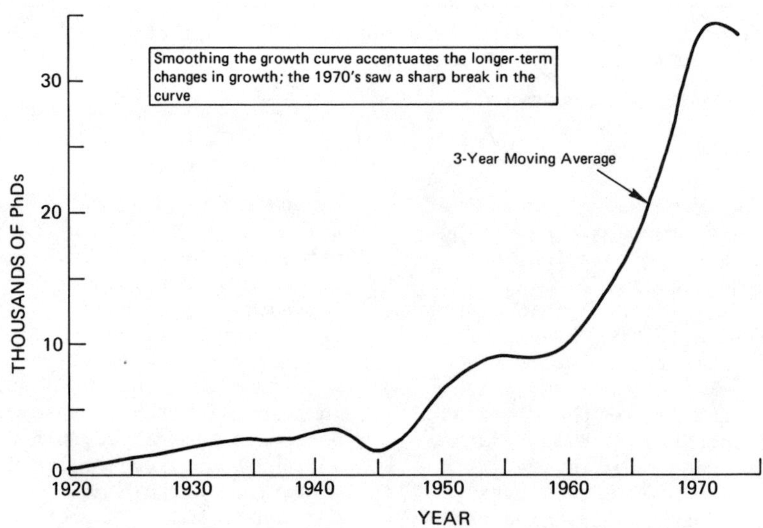

SOURCE: NRC, Commission on Human Resources

FIGURE 4 Growth in doctorates since 1920.

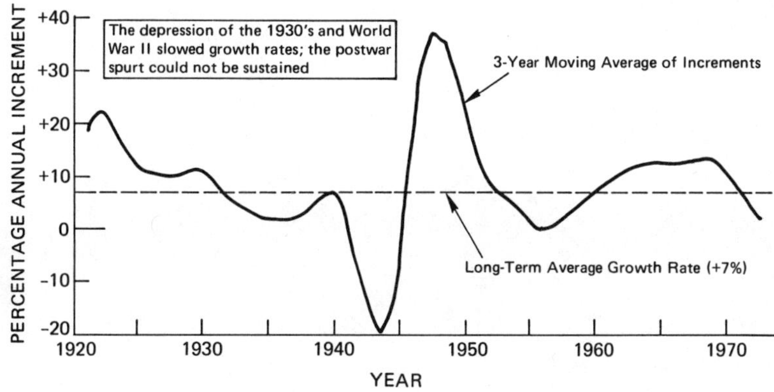

SOURCE: NRC, Commission on Human Resources

FIGURE 5 Growth increments in doctorates granted.

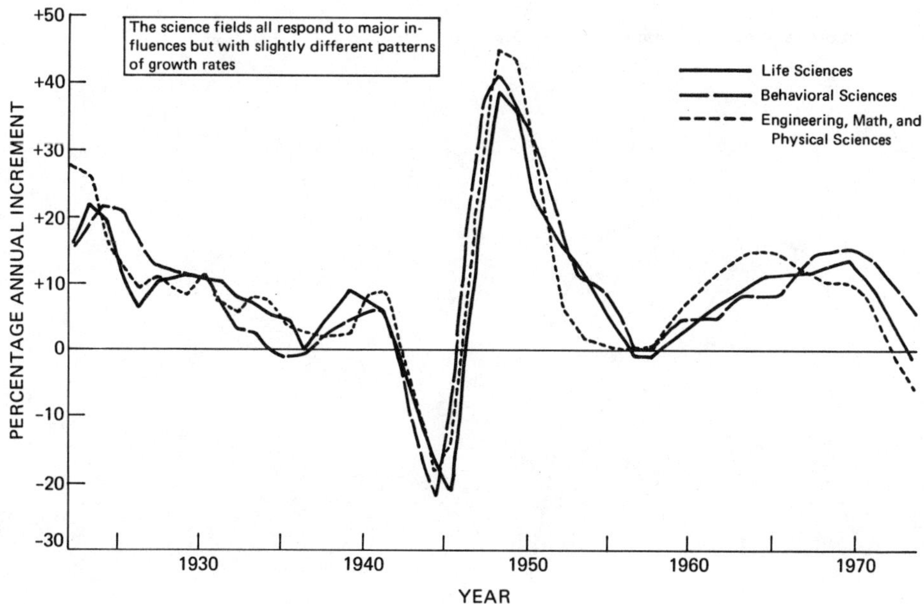

SOURCE: NRC, Commission on Human Resources

FIGURE 6 Growth increments in doctorates granted in three science fields.

averages, which show chronological changes more faithfully than the 5-year summary data. Such averages iron out the year-to-year changes that are to a certain extent random, depending on minor factors such as universities' policies with respect to when graduations occur or the month in which all requirements are finally met. In Figure 4, the flattening of the growth curve during the depression of the 1930's is shown, as is the deep decline in output during World War II. The long steep rise of the 1960's is followed by a sharp change in the 1970's, including an acutal drop in output for the first time since 1957.

GROWTH INCREMENTS

Changes in rate of output of PhD's are more readily visualized in a graph of percentage increments or decrements. These data, calculated on an annual basis, are somewhat unstable and are best viewed after smoothing by means of a moving average. Figure 5 shows such a graph for the period from 1920 through 1974. Here the changes due to wars become dramatically apparent and the depression of the 1930's shows a gradual decline. The drop during the 1970's, following the prosperous 1960's, is even more evident than in the linear output graph of Figure 4.

Figure 5 shows total output figures; some breakdown by fields may be useful in considering the possible causes and consequences of the changes that have occurred. Figure 6 shows the analogous curves for three field groups:

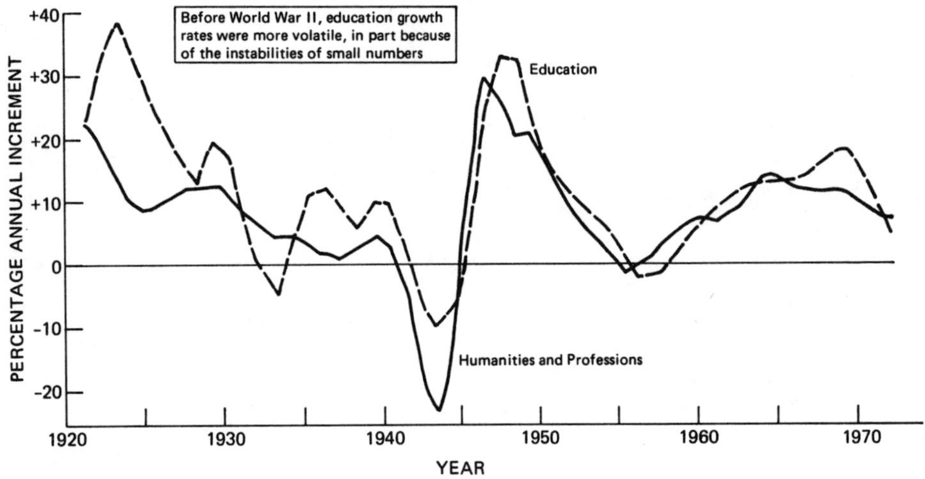

SOURCE: NRC, Commission on Human Resources

FIGURE 7 Growth increments in doctorates granted in nonscience fields.

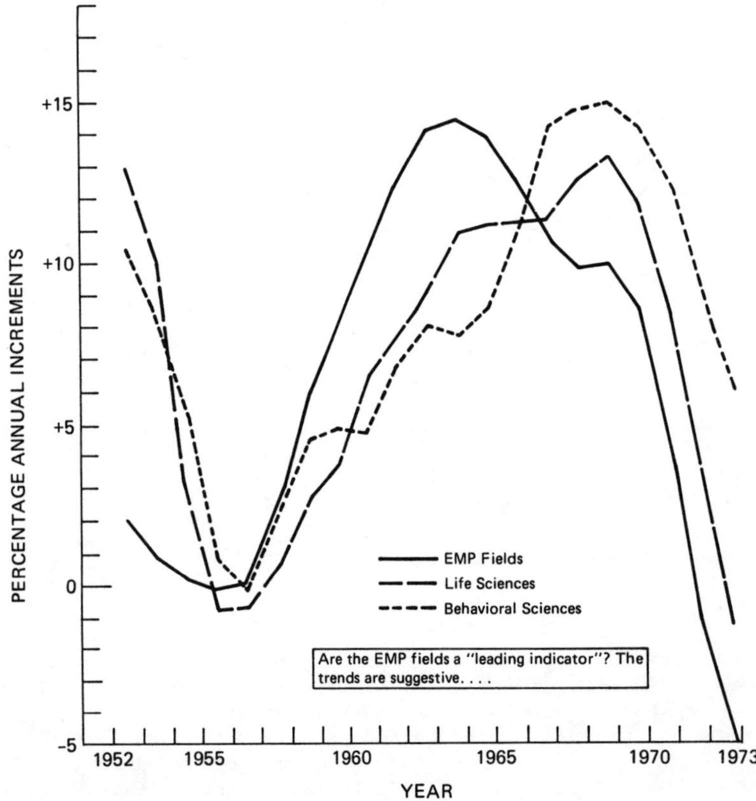

SOURCE: NRC, Commission on Human Resources

FIGURE 8 Increments in doctorates granted in three science fields 1952-1974 (moving averages).

(1) EMP fields, (2) life sciences, and (3) behavioral sciences. Figure 7 shows the same kind of data for the remaining major field groups: humanities, professions, and education.

Data on growth by field by year, with 5-year summaries, are given in Table 2. The numerical data for the series of increment graphs are given in Table 3, for those who wish to examine the data in more detail. The most intriguing data, however, relate to the performance of the science fields for the most recent period, as shown in Figure 8.

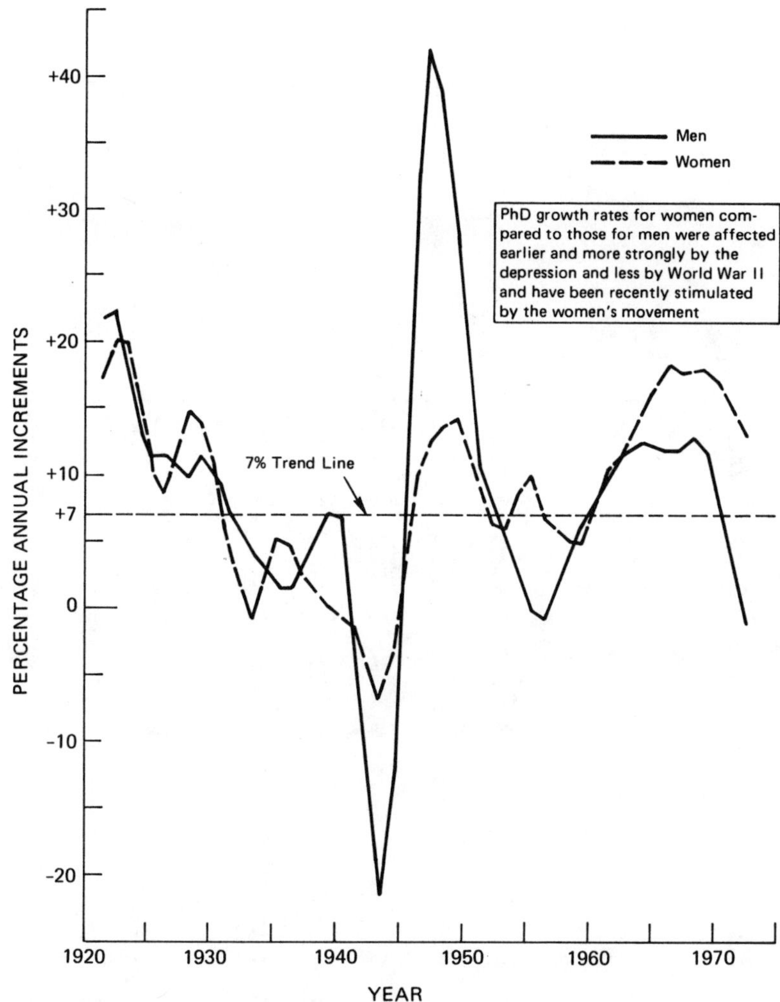
+40
+30
+20
+10
+7
0
-10
-20
PERCENTAGE ANNUAL INCREMENTS
Men
Women
PhD growth rates for women compared to those for men were affected earlier and more strongly by the depression and less by World War II and have been recently stimulated by the women's movement
7% Trend Line
1920
1930
1940
1950
1960
1970
YEAR

SOURCE: NRC, Commission on Human Resources

FIGURE 9 Growth increments in doctorates by sex.

the three science field groups shown in Figure 8 is striking. The EMP fields behave like a "leading indicator"--to borrow a term from the jargon of economics. The fluctuations in the life sciences output are closer to the general average of all PhD fields, while the behavioral sciences show a lag, moving downward, upward, and downward again later than the other fields. These variations cannot be accounted for directly from the data at hand; a number of studies have been made and are being made of the determinants of doctorate output. As the results are as yet inconclusive, no attempt will be made here to account for the rather striking curves of Figure 8.

One factor affecting the time trends in output of PhD's that is evident in the preceding graphs is the economic climate. Another is the effect of wars. These two influences affect the two sexes differently, and the result of these, as well as other influences, is shown in Figure 9, which shows the incremental changes since 1920 for men and for women separately. (The graph here is not a 3-year moving average, but a 4-year center-weighted moving average, which is somewhat more stable, though slightly less sensitive. This center-weighted average doubles the data for the 2 middle years and divides the sum by 6. It was chosen to iron out the random fluctuations that occur with small numbers, as, for example, with women in the earlier years of this period.) It is clear from Figure 9 that the effect of World War II and its aftermath was greater for men than for women, as expected. The figure also suggests that the earning of doctorates by women is highly sensitive to the economic climate, as shown in the 1930's; during the depression the curve for women dropped earlier and more steeply than did that for men; in the most recent period, the drop in increment started earlier for women in the "academic depression," which began in 1968. It was not so severe as the drop in the curve for men for a number of reasons, probably the principal one being the different "field

TABLE 2A
DOCTORATES AWARDED ANNUALLY IN ENGINEERING, MATHEMATICS, AND NATURAL SCIENCES, 1920-1974, WITH 5-YEAR SUMMARIES

	Total, All Fields	Physics	Chemistry	Earth Sciences	Physical Sciences Total	Mathematics	Engineering	EMP Fields, Total	Basic Medical Sciences	Other Biosciences	Biosciences, Total	Medical Sciences	Agricultural Sciences	Environmental Sciences	Life Sciences	Natural Sciences, Total
1920	562	31	77	21	129	19	7	155	38	67	105	12	17		134	289
1921	662	37	125	12	174	15	10	199	34	57	91	27	15		133	332
1922	780	55	140	22	217	17	15	249	42	69	111	19	27		157	406
1923	1062	60	185	40	285	34	14	333	67	102	169	28	45		242	575
1924	1133	62	224	44	330	29	14	373	50	100	150	34	32		216	589
TOTAL 1920-24	4199	245	751	139	1135	114	60	1309	231	395	626	120	136		882	2191
1925	1206	51	211	27	289	28	16	333	69	110	179	30	36		245	578
1926	1441	87	252	42	381	48	27	456	77	120	197	33	29		259	715
1927	1540	81	217	45	343	51	33	427	103	121	224	24	42		290	717
1928	1632	95	255	31	381	42	51	474	98	155	253	20	56		329	803
1929	1917	97	251	48	396	68	41	505	108	164	272	39	60		371	876
TOTAL 1925-29	7736	411	1186	193	1790	237	168	2195	455	670	1125	146	223		1494	3689
1930	2075	106	302	66	474	76	64	614	103	169	272	46	61		379	993
1931	2344	113	334	42	489	82	67	638	130	225	355	52	62		469	1107
1932	2400	115	328	55	498	74	68	640	132	201	333	40	83		456	1096
1933	2462	133	382	74	589	75	92	756	153	205	358	44	75		477	1233
1934	2696	124	415	68	607	91	119	817	175	246	421	64	91		576	1393
TOTAL 1930-34	11977	591	1761	305	2657	398	410	3465	693	1046	1739	246	372		2357	5822
1935	2529	133	365	66	564	75	111	750	126	233	359	47	80		486	1236
1936	2713	138	443	71	652	76	70	798	150	275	425	45	60		530	1328
1937	2752	155	504	54	713	74	98	885	163	254	417	26	59		502	1387
1938	2754	156	409	70	635	62	75	772	218	258	476	51	68		595	1367
1939	2950	160	468	62	690	93	69	852	242	267	509	36	69		614	1466
TOTAL 1935-39	13698	742	2189	323	3254	380	423	4057	899	1287	2186	205	336		2727	6784
1940	3277	144	534	59	737	102	107	946	260	303	563	47	95		705	1651
1941	3484	179	647	64	890	96	122	1108	244	274	518	53	92		663	1771
1942	3404	158	590	66	814	76	98	988	271	296	567	60	102		729	1717
1943	2592	132	511	43	686	44	53	783	228	218	446	43	75		564	1347
1944	1967	65	475	19	559	44	65	668	175	130	305	39	47		391	1059
TOTAL 1940-44	14724	678	2757	251	3686	362	445	4493	1178	1221	2399	242	411		3052	7545
1945	1634	43	290	23	356	36	68	460	120	97	217	31	54		302	762
1946	1990	73	326	38	437	54	104	595	91	147	238	31	45		314	909
1947	2951	145	421	59	625	115	120	860	146	258	404	41	81		526	1386
1948	3940	230	615	70	915	119	258	1292	218	314	532	61	101		694	1986
1949	5389	314	935	118	1367	146	451	1964	288	386	674	86	183		943	2907
TOTAL 1945-49	15904	805	2587	308	3700	470	1001	5171	863	1202	2065	250	464		2779	7950
1950	6535	422	1052	130	1604	176	469	2249	324	442	766	97	254		1117	3366
1951	7331	501	1034	148	1683	205	586	2474	404	437	841	95	271		1207	3681
1952	7717	520	1063	149	1732	204	570	2506	439	496	935	113	309		1357	3863
1953	8380	522	1008	167	1697	224	568	2489	549	599	1148	115	332		1595	4084
1954	8708	524	1018	160	1702	247	563	2512	539	596	1135	150	370		1655	4167
TOTAL 1950-54	38671	2489	5175	754	8418	1056	2756	12230	2255	2570	4825	570	1536		6931	19161
1955	8905	511	1013	180	1704	243	649	2596	575	540	1115	164	368		1647	4243
1956	8516	485	981	157	1623	228	579	2430	488	487	975	193	356		1524	3954
1957	8611	464	1041	187	1692	256	589	2537	619	513	1132	155	345		1632	4169
1958	8838	504	958	199	1661	237	658	2556	609	511	1120	139	325		1584	4140
1959	9370	523	1077	235	1835	301	712	2848	576	534	1110	155	362		1627	4475
TOTAL 1955-59	44240	2487	5070	958	8515	1265	3187	12967	2867	2585	5452	806	1756		8014	20981
1960	9998	574	1107	251	1932	289	825	3046	636	559	1195	146	429		1770	4816
1961	10827	601	1138	261	2000	362	1006	3368	697	509	1206	172	433		1811	5179
1962	11975	767	1192	257	2216	411	1288	3915	723	621	1344	208	510		2062	5977
1963	13515	829	1356	326	2511	537	1453	4501	813	667	1480	209	472		2161	6662
1964	14951	936	1370	325	2631	620	1804	5055	957	715	1672	278	537		2487	7542
TOTAL 1960-64	61266	3707	6163	1420	11290	2219	6376	19885	3826	3071	6897	1013	2381		10291	30176
1965	17110	1065	1480	395	2940	734	2186	5860	1074	815	1889	319	567		2775	8635
1966	19202	1187	1712	434	3333	803	2437	6573	1230	881	2111	314	604		3029	9602
1967	21216	1361	1793	418	3572	849	2621	7042	1367	991	2358	355	647		3360	10402
1968	24328	1447	1824	481	3752	1046	2985	7783	1628	1182	2810	409	689		3908	11691
1969	27417	1575	2129	499	4203	1131	3360	8694	1740	1312	3052	452	892		4396	13090
TOTAL 1965-69	109273	6635	8938	2227	17800	4563	13589	35952	7039	5181	12220	1849	3399		17468	53420
1970	31489	1715	2284	534	4533	1282	3603	9418	1823	1504	3327	544	1012		4883	14301
1971	33163	1743	2248	564	4555	1274	3654	9483	1890	1589	3479	607	1109	29	5224	14707
1972	34458	1697	2007	636	4340	1341	3493	9174	1971	1556	3527	604	1064	69	5264	14438
1973	33472	1412	1831	575	3818	1215	3259	8292	1820	1427	3247	583	1002	105	4937	13229
1974	33165	1360	1800	574	3734	1155	3039	7928	1807	1396	3203	611	1083	116	5013	12941
TOTAL 1970-74	165747	7927	10170	2883	20980	6267	17048	44295	9311	7472	16783	2949	5270	319	25321	69616
GRAND TOTAL	487435	26717	46747	9761	83225	17331	45463	146019	29617	26700	56317	8396	16284	319	81316	227335

SOURCE: NRC, Commission on Human Resources.

TABLE 2B
DOCTORATES AWARDED ANNUALLY IN THE BEHAVIORAL SCIENCES, TOTAL OF ALL SCIENCES, AND NONSCIENCE FIELDS, WITH 5-YEAR SUMMARIES

	Psychology	Economics and Econometrics	Anthropology and Sociology	Political Science, etc.	Other Social Sciences	Behavioral Sciences Total	Total, Sciences	History	English and American Language and Literature	Foreign Language and Literature	Other Humanities	Total Humanities	Professional Fields	Education	Other and Unknown	Total, Nonsciences
1920	35	22	15	12	3	87	376	23	23	42	31	119	18	48	1	186
1921	28	38	14	24	7	111	443	38	30	42	40	150	34	33	2	219
1922	34	33	14	17	3	101	507	56	34	45	44	179	32	59	3	273
1923	65	40	15	22	8	150	725	61	44	48	69	222	45	68	2	337
1924	55	52	20	29	5	161	750	60	57	65	46	228	52	102	1	383
TOTAL 1920-24	217	185	78	104	26	610	2801	238	188	242	230	898	181	310	9	1398
1925	71	64	29	28	13	205	783	63	55	57	60	235	56	128	4	423
1926	74	81	26	33	13	227	942	71	71	55	76	273	64	161	1	499
1927	76	91	29	45	17	258	975	88	63	64	88	303	88	170	4	565
1928	84	85	25	52	11	257	1060	94	70	68	83	315	77	173	7	572
1929	122	103	59	37	24	345	1221	107	69	94	112	382	85	211	18	696
TOTAL 1925-29	427	424	168	195	78	1292	4981	423	328	338	419	1508	370	843	34	2755
1930	101	107	45	33	27	313	1306	128	96	95	96	415	75	268	11	769
1931	119	119	50	57	18	363	1470	118	108	103	124	453	107	303	11	874
1932	105	122	57	58	20	362	1458	123	129	137	115	504	124	309	5	942
1933	92	108	52	68	27	347	1580	148	114	140	109	511	103	261	7	882
1934	128	113	52	65	24	382	1775	148	137	166	74	525	103	280	13	921
TOTAL 1930-34	545	569	256	281	116	1767	7589	665	584	641	518	2408	512	1421	47	4388
1935	112	90	52	61	26	341	1577	156	136	174	81	547	134	254	17	952
1936	114	103	56	53	12	338	1666	135	144	185	98	562	103	355	27	1047
1937	112	108	74	65	10	369	1756	144	161	169	80	554	80	358	4	996
1938	116	125	61	56	10	368	1735	159	159	172	84	574	83	362		1019
1939	117	112	75	60	14	378	1844	177	173	164	106	620	109	377		1106
TOTAL 1935-39	571	538	318	295	72	1794	8578	771	773	864	449	2857	509	1706	48	5120
1940	129	125	73	82	25	434	2085	167	174	180	107	628	94	470		1192
1941	113	158	91	72	13	447	2218	182	189	178	127	676	111	478	1	1266
1942	126	138	77	70	13	424	2141	168	177	150	126	621	148	493	1	1263
1943	92	82	58	50	13	295	1642	122	124	115	81	442	105	402	1	950
1944	68	61	41	36	14	220	1279	60	74	70	66	270	103	314	1	688
TOTAL 1940-44	528	564	340	310	78	1820	9365	699	738	693	507	2637	561	2157	4	5359
1945	65	59	32	28	5	189	951	71	74	72	62	279	108	294	2	683
1946	82	84	60	39	9	274	1183	119	112	70	79	380	79	347	1	807
1947	122	135	92	61	17	427	1813	169	165	120	111	565	116	455	2	1138
1948	190	143	82	109	19	543	2529	146	167	135	154	602	142	666	1	1411
1949	266	183	118	147	41	755	3662	224	179	154	152	709	173	844	1	1727
TOTAL 1945-49	725	604	384	384	91	2188	10138	729	697	551	558	2535	618	2606	7	5766
1950	360	243	168	166	41	978	4344	274	235	211	213	933	219	1038	1	2191
1951	488	299	189	165	54	1195	4876	339	298	201	257	1095	250	1110		2455
1952	581	313	178	157	37	1266	5129	298	262	180	286	1026	247	1315		2588
1953	656	311	214	164	58	1403	5487	350	333	202	338	1223	242	1425	3	2893
1954	667	350	250	186	50	1503	5670	364	344	216	347	1271	260	1507		3038
TOTAL 1950-54	2752	1516	999	838	240	6345	25506	1625	1472	1010	1441	5548	1218	6395	4	13165
1955	734	375	229	213	53	1604	5847	333	327	216	340	1216	270	1572		3058
1956	629	316	220	248	88	1501	5455	267	347	221	310	1145	275	1638	3	3061
1957	714	305	175	202	55	1451	5620	340	369	200	361	1270	334	1384	3	2991
1958	773	320	235	225	76	1629	5769	314	310	207	391	1222	343	1503	1	3069
1959	800	338	242	230	62	1672	6147	351	346	230	395	1322	356	1544	1	3223
TOTAL 1955-59	3650	1654	1101	1118	334	7857	28838	1605	1699	1074	1797	6175	1578	7641	8	15402
1960	752	376	224	252	80	1684	6500	364	368	206	531	1469	390	1632	7	3498
1961	861	434	236	262	64	1857	7036	362	447	231	503	1543	440	1801	7	3791
1962	888	408	280	271	81	1928	7905	395	453	275	504	1627	494	1951	8	4070
1963	974	497	309	318	109	2207	8869	433	489	300	569	1791	547	2296	12	4646
1964	968	534	296	346	101	2245	9787	547	581	337	602	2067	586	2494	17	5164
TOTAL 1960-64	4443	2249	1345	1449	435	9921	40097	2101	2338	1349	2709	8497	2447	10174	51	21169
1965	1072	572	322	410	97	2473	11108	626	684	434	697	2441	654	2892	15	6002
1966	1164	689	413	420	107	2793	12395	725	759	489	784	2757	804	3229	17	6807
1967	1373	718	492	559	156	3298	13700	702	847	556	832	2937	853	3659	67	7516
1968	1606	722	569	578	260	3735	15426	820	995	672	966	3453	1031	4333	85	8902
1969	1843	779	617	591	401	4231	17321	934	1035	682	1073	3724	1063	5086	223	10096
TOTAL 1965-69	7058	3480	2413	2558	1021	16530	69950	3807	4320	2833	4352	15312	4405	19199	407	39323
1970	2119	842	785	719	555	5020	19321	1092	1227	796	1206	4321	1404	6305	138	12168
1971	2181	864	883	893	620	5441	20148	1143	1285	886	1230	4544	1415	6898	158	13015
1972	2386	991	904	925	673	5879	20317	1236	1413	969	1431	5049	1627	7318	147	14141
1973	2512	901	1017	916	741	6087	19316	1221	1410	1008	1726	5365	1425	7331	35	14156
1974	2741	904	1031	857	800	6333	19274	1201	1333	955	1589	5078	1486	7219	108	13891
TOTAL 1970-74	11939	4502	4620	4310	3389	28760	98376	5893	6668	4614	7182	24357	7357	35071	586	67371
GRAND TOTAL	32855	16285	12022	11842	5880	78884	306219	18556	19805	14209	20162	72732	19756	87523	1205	181216

SOURCE: NRC, Commission on Human Resources.

TABLE 3
THREE-YEAR MOVING AVERAGES OF ANNUAL PhD GROWTH INCREMENTS, 1920-1974, BY FIELD AND TOTAL

Year	Mathematics	Physics	Chemistry	Earth Sciences	Engineering	TOTAL, EMP	TOTAL, Life Sciences	Psychology	Social Sciences	TOTAL, Behavioral Sciences	TOTAL Sciences	Humanities	Professions	Education	GRAND TOTAL
1921*	-3.9	34.0	37.2	20.2	46.5	26.8	8.7	0.7	20.2	9.3	16.1	23.2	41.5	23.8	17.8
1922	30.7	25.7	35.5	40.7	28.7	29.1	23.8	30.9	22.4	22.4	25.1	23.2	41.2	21.0	23.9
1923	32.9	20.3	21.7	58.4	14.4	23.6	20.5	32.4	10.8	15.6	20.3	15.0	16.8	48.0	20.2
1924	27.3	-1.8	15.8	17.7	2.5	11.7	18.9	10.9	26.0	27.7	16.9	9.9	21.3	30.3	16.4
1925	17.8	18.7	11.6	9.0	27.7	12.7	2.9	6.0	21.8	15.1	9.4	7.1	12.5	33.8	10.9
1926	24.8	15.3	-0.1	8.0	35.1	6.6	10.3	12.0	19.9	17.2	9.4	10.3	19.8	19.0	10.9
1927	20.0	27.0	7.7	10.5	48.5	13.8	10.3	5.8	9.4	8.0	10.8	10.4	13.1	21.8	10.8
1928	16.9	4.2	0.7	10.3	19.0	3.7	12.6	19.5	14.3	15.8	9.1	13.4	11.8	9.8	10.1
1929	18.7	9.6	12.1	20.4	30.3	13.0	9.5	12.8	6.4	8.2	10.3	11.7	9.5	16.9	10.6
1930	27.2	6.0	9.8	18.6	13.7	10.7	12.9	15.3	13.0	13.6	15.9	13.2	14.0	20.7	12.9
1931	3.3	5.9	9.7	10.7	20.8	3.6	7.7	-3.7	5.2	2.1	10.6	8.6	15.9	14.0	7.9
1932	-0.2	8.0	8.4	9.7	13.8	7.4	8.5	-2.1	6.5	3.9	11.1	7.0	14.5	-0.1	6.0
1933	4.3	3.6	7.8	19.1	22.0	8.8	7.5	5.0	1.4	1.9	6.6	5.2	-0.3	-2.1	4.8
1934	1.7	5.4	4.4	7.8	19.3	6.0	3.3	4.7	-3.7	-1.6	3.2	3.5	4.4	-6.3	1.9
1935	1.7	1.4	6.0	-1.1	-4.8	2.1	4.8	9.5	-4.1	-0.5	2.2	4.4	2.3	12.7	3.5
1936	-6.3	7.8	7.7	-6.4	-1.2	3.0	-3.9	-4.2	0.9	-0.8	-0.1	1.1	-5.1	10.6	0.8
1937	-5.8	5.6	5.5	4.4	-6.8	1.5	7.4	1.2	3.5	2.7	3.3	0.7	-13.9	14.7	3.0
1938	10.4	5.2	3.1	-1.9	2.8	2.8	5.5	0.9	5.5	3.9	3.5	1.9	4.3	2.1	2.9
1939	14.9	-2.3	3.2	4.5	7.9	2.9	12.2	4.9	6.2	5.7	6.1	4.3	7.1	10.1	6.1
1940	18.0	5.6	16.6	-2.6	20.4	12.9	4.0	-0.4	10.0	6.8	8.6	5.6	11.9	10.1	8.2
1941	-5.6	0.7	8.8	2.3	16.5	5.8	6.3	3.1	5.2	4.2	5.3	0.3	12.5	9.8	5.0
1942	-23.2	-1.3	-0.3	-7.7	-17.2	-4.9	-6.2	-9.3	-11.1	-10.8	-6.8	-9.7	7.4	-4.8	-6.6
1943	-21.7	-26.3	-9.1	-29.9	-14.3	-15.6	-14.7	-13.9	-22.8	-20.4	-16.3	-25.4	0.8	-12.3	-16.9
1944	-19.5	-33.5	-20.0	-21.7	-6.2	-22.3	-25.3	-19.2	-25.1	-23.3	-23.7	-21.8	-9.0	-15.9	-21.8
1945	9.9	-4.9	-11.3	10.2	26.7	-5.6	-16.1	-1.4	4.0	2.0	-7.8	2.1	-7.7	-2.9	-6.2
1946	48.3	44.9	1.9	51.2	24.0	15.0	16.6	23.5	32.1	29.1	17.4	29.8	7.9	13.6	18.0
1947	53.5	74.3	28.9	45.2	61.1	40.8	34.0	41.1	42.9	41.8	39.0	30.8	13.8	32.3	34.3
1948	47.1	65.3	43.1	51.8	68.8	49.7	44.8	49.7	37.6	41.2	45.8	22.6	30.0	34.7	39.8
1949	15.7	43.1	36.2	32.6	65.2	38.6	28.6	43.7	26.7	31.9	34.3	18.5	23.6	32.3	30.4
1950	20.6	31.2	21.8	33.9	34.9	26.5	21.1	39.5	26.7	31.3	25.2	22.4	21.2	18.9	23.9
1951	11.6	18.1	4.2	7.3	8.7	8.2	12.8	28.5	12.5	18.7	12.0	14.2	13.0	15.9	12.6
1952	8.6	7.6	-1.3	27.2	7.3	3.6	12.7	22.5	6.9	13.0	8.1	10.1	3.7	11.4	8.7
1953	6.5	1.5	-0.5	21.2	-1.3	0.5	11.3	11.1	6.0	7.9	5.2	5.7	1.4	10.8	5.9
1954	6.2	-0.6	-1.6	25.1	4.7	1.2	6.9	8.3	8.4	8.3	4.5	6.2	3.1	6.2	4.9
1955	0.8	-2.4	-0.9	-1.5	1.2	-0.7	-1.4	-0.8	5.4	2.5	-0.4	-2.1	4.4	4.7	0.6
1956	1.5	-4.0	0.8	6.3	2.1	0.5	-0.3	3.2	-3.7	-1.0	-0.5	0.3	9.1	-2.3	-0.3
1957	-0.4	-0.3	-1.7	4.2	0.8	-0.4	-1.1	2.5	0.3	0.8	-0.7	0.5	8.7	-0.9	-0.2
1958	10.6	2.7	3.5	14.5	7.2	5.5	2.3	8.4	0.8	3.9	4.1	5.1	9.3	-1.4	3.2
1959	5.2	7.4	2.4	10.4	11.9	6.4	2.9	1.9	8.3	5.2	5.0	5.3	5.4	5.7	5.1
1960	16.1	6.1	6.0	9.6	15.3	9.7	4.6	4.0	5.2	4.5	6.8	8.3	8.8	6.4	7.0
1961	11.6	14.0	3.4	3.1	21.9	11.3	8.3	3.9	6.1	4.9	8.8	7.3	10.8	8.0	8.5
1962	23.2	13.5	7.1	9.8	20.9	13.9	7.0	9.1	10.0	9.5	10.9	6.9	12.0	12.1	10.6
1963	19.9	16.2	6.5	8.3	21.7	14.5	11.3	4.1	8.9	6.7	11.7	10.4	10.0	11.4	11.3
1964	21.5	11.6	7.6	16.0	19.4	14.4	10.5	6.6	10.6	8.8	12.0	14.6	10.5	14.2	12.7
1965	14.4	12.7	8.2	10.4	19.0	13.5	12.0	6.2	9.9	8.3	13.2	15.5	13.9	12.1	12.4
1966	11.2	13.3	9.5	9.2	13.4	11.7	10.6	12.4	14.7	13.7	13.2	12.6	13.5	13.6	12.4
1967	12.8	10.8	7.4	7.1	11.0	9.9	12.1	14.5	15.0	14.8	12.9	12.7	16.7	14.4	12.5
1968	12.3	9.9	7.7	5.0	11.4	9.8	13.2	16.6	13.7	14.9	11.8	11.5	10.0	16.4	12.6
1969	14.9	8.0	8.6	8.6	11.2	10.2	13.3	15.6	14.8	15.1	12.1	13.9	18.7	19.9	14.1
1970	7.0	6.4	7.5	5.4	7.1	6.9	10.2	10.8	15.4	13.4	9.4	9.3	12.0	16.9	10.9
1971	6.0	2.6	-1.7	8.3	1.4	1.9	6.2	8.9	13.7	11.6	5.5	10.0	16.0	13.1	8.0
1972	-1.8	-5.9	-7.0	2.9	-3.2	-4.1	0.4	5.7	7.3	6.6	0.1	7.2	1.2	5.2	2.1
1973*	-2.4	-9.7	-9.7	1.6	-5.5	-6.5	-2.7	7.3	4.7	5.8	-1.4	8.6	1.5	3.2	0.5

*Data for 1921 and 1973 are 2-year averages.

SOURCE: NRC, Commission on Human Resources.

mix" of men and women PhD's. Men are concentrated more heavily in the sciences, particularly the physical sciences and engineering; women are concentrated more heavily in education, which has shown a remarkable increase in recent years. In addition, of course, the women's movement has in recent years been an important factor in higher education and advanced training. All these factors, as well as others, have kept the output of women PhD's at a high level.

BACCALAUREATE DEGREES

One of the basic factors involved in numbers of PhD's, quite obviously, is number of baccalaureate-level graduates. The trend in these degrees is shown in Figure 10, the figures for which come from the USOE. (For the period prior to 1961, the USOE data are for "baccalaureate and first professional" degrees; after 1961, the two degree types are separated. In Figure 10, a correction

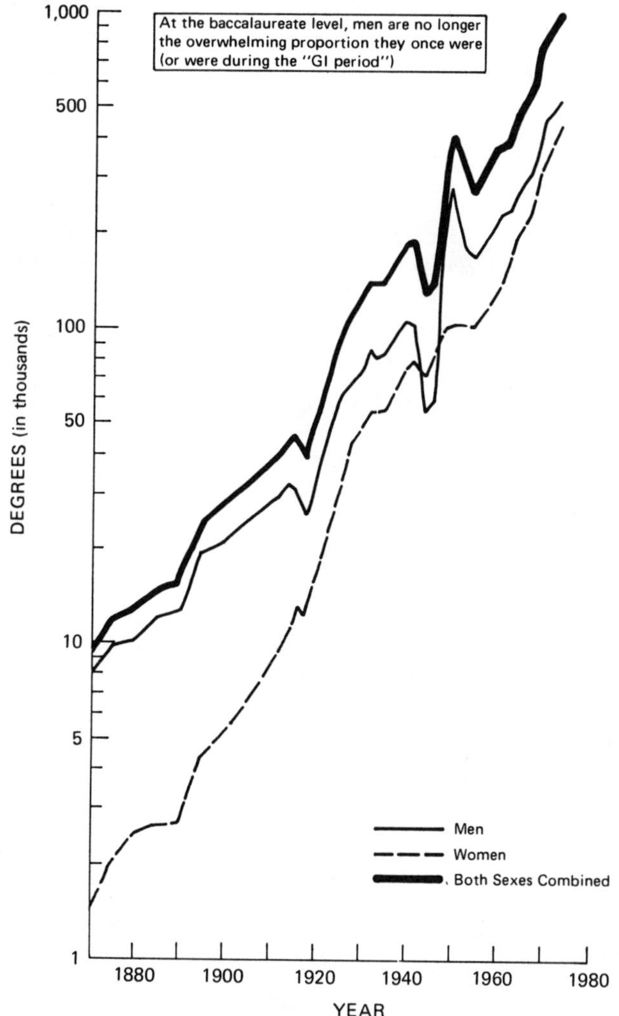

SOURCE: NRC, Commission on Human Resources

FIGURE 10 U.S. baccalaureates conferred annually.

was introduced for the period of the 1950's; before that time the number of first professional degrees is too small to warrant a correction in the graphic display; the shape of the curve is not changed in any case.) In Figure 10, it is apparent that the curve for baccalaureate degrees granted to women is converging with that for men; this is an obvious source of influence for the corresponding but weaker tendency, somewhat later, at the doctorate level. Because BA-PhD time lapse varies by field and by time period, and because people switch fields between the baccalaureate and doctorate, it is not possible to demonstrate a close linkage between baccalaureate output in a given period and PhD output at some later time. General trends only are shown in Figure 10; their significance may well be very important a generation later, as indicated in Chapter 2; no more definitive interpretation will be attempted here.

Another factor frequently invoked to help to account for the changes in numbers of doctorates granted is that of financial support to research and development. There have been a number of attempts to relate such support to output in particular fields, as, for example, the biomedical sciences, but there is no real consensus on the importance and timing of the effects in variations in federal support for research. There are a number of reasons why the impact is neither immediate, direct, nor unambiguous. One is the differing impact of expenditures for basic research as distinct from development. A much higher proportion of basic research funds go to universities, as compared to development funds, in which the business and industry sector participates more heavily. Another reason why funds for research do not have an unambiguous effect is that they go, in an undetermined proportion, for salary of the principal investigator, equipment expenses, overhead, etc., and in some other proportion for the support of training of research personnel who also participate in the research. Figure 11, here reproduced from a National Science Foundation (NSF) report (NSF 77-311), depicts graphically the changes in federal obligations to universities and colleges over the period FY 1963-1975. The top graph shows total dollars, interpreted also in terms of constant 1972 dollars, using the GNP deflator. The bottom graph shows a breakout of the current dollar amounts into several categories. Figure 12, also from the NSF (NSF 76-310), shows the trends in funding, both federal and nonfederal, from 1953 through 1976 (the last 2 years estimated). In both Figure 11 and Figure 12, whether current dollars or constant dollars are concerned, the long upward trend in federal support ceased in 1967, and a decline, in constant dollar terms, set in. During the 1970's, the trends have been mixed, in constant dollar terms, with little net change in federal obligations to universities and colleges but a net drop in total federal funds for research and development (R&D), taken up in part by increases in nonfederal sources, as shown in Figure 12.

A factor that cannot be shown by either of these charts is the fact that universities have their homeostatic mechanisms for adjusting to varying kinds and amounts of financial support. Historians have discovered evidence for such adjustments as far back as the early 1800's, in the correspondence of Thomas Jefferson, concerned with support for the University of Virginia in its early days. Federal support for science, for example, may result in shifts of support from other sources toward the nonscience fields; each university finds its own means for maintaining balance despite fluctuations in "soft money" from federal sources. The effect of federal funds, therefore, while important, is diffuse. No doubt many students felt that, even though they had scant prospects of a typical academic job, nevertheless their prospects were better after attaining the doctorate than before, and they therefore persisted despite diminishing prospects in the faculty job market. Examination of these factors in student decision making and institutional adjustments, interesting as they are, cannot be further pursued in this report.

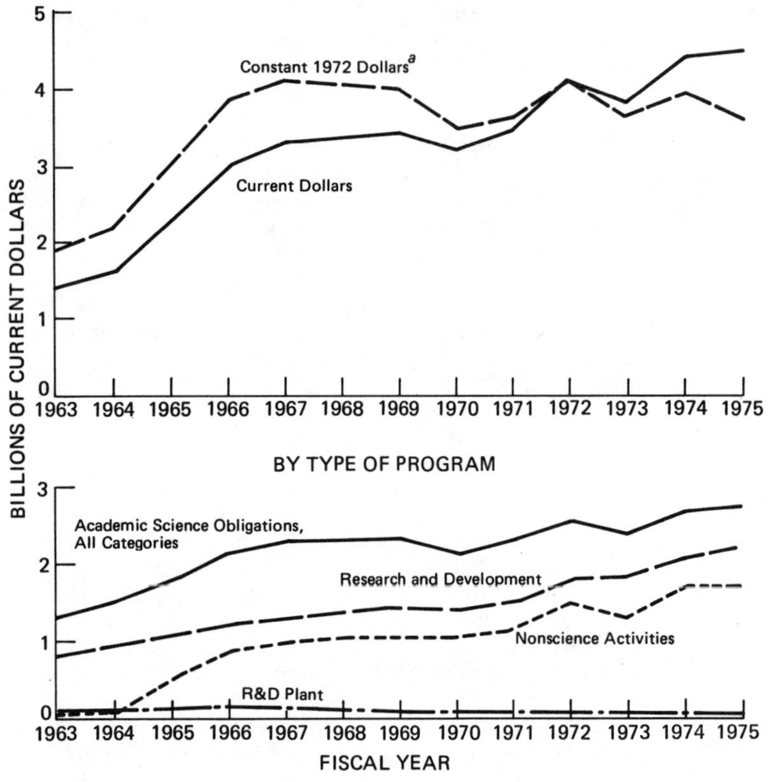

[a]Based on GNP implicit price deflator
SOURCE: National Science Foundation

FIGURE 11 Federal obligations to universities and colleges, FY 1963-1974; growth by type of program.

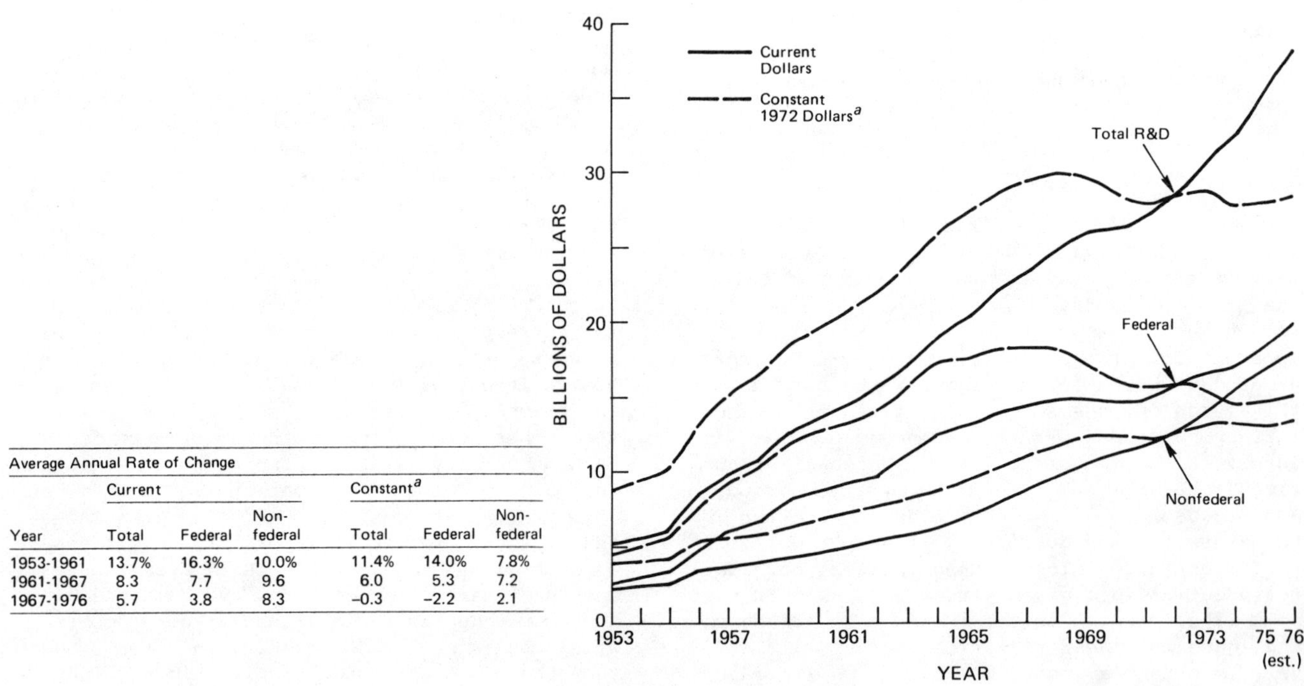

Average Annual Rate of Change						
	Current			Constant[a]		
Year	Total	Federal	Non-federal	Total	Federal	Non-federal
1953-1961	13.7%	16.3%	10.0%	11.4%	14.0%	7.8%
1961-1967	8.3	7.7	9.6	6.0	5.3	7.2
1967-1976	5.7	3.8	8.3	–0.3	–2.2	2.1

[a]Based on the GNP implicit price deflator
SOURCE: National Science Foundation

FIGURE 12 R&D funding trends: 1953-1976.

THE ROLE OF WOMEN

The fluctuations in the growth of PhD output and the differing trends of the growth increments for the male and female segments of the PhD graduating classes have been mentioned. This aspect of doctorate production needs more attention (since the changes shown are in part a function of the changing "field mix" over time and are in part a cause of this change) because men and women typically differ greatly in their field preferences. To begin with the basic proportions, we see in Figure 13 and in Table 4 the changes in the overall proportion of PhD's who are women from 1900 to 1974. In both figure and table, the data are given for 5-year periods, except for the last 5 years, where the explosive growth in proportions of women, year by year, is shown in detail. This proportion, combined with the increasing numbers of PhD's during the past quarter-century, results in varying numbers of women, as depicted in "tree ring" format in Figure 14. Here we see the increasing segment attributable to women since 1950, together with the widening rings, as the number of doctorates expands. Looking back toward the center of the graph, we note that there was a rather wide wedge representing women in the 1920's and 1930's, gradually shrinking in the 1940's, but drastically shrinking during the "GI" period after World War II.

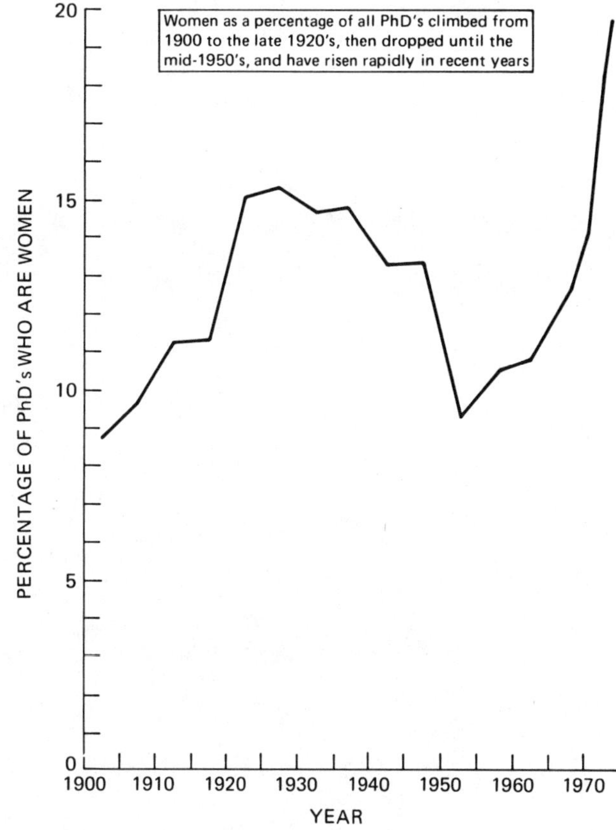

SOURCE: NRC, Commission on Human Resources

FIGURE 13 Women PhD's, 1900-1974.

SEX DIFFERENCES IN FIELD MIX

The differing field mix of men and women doctorates is shown graphically in Figure 15, in which the outer ring depicts the total number of doctorates granted to men since 1920, while the inner ring shows the number of doctorates granted to women. The area of each ring is proportional to the number of doctorates, while the segments within each ring represent the proportions of the several major fields of specialization. Figure 15 also incorporates small tables showing the numbers of male and female PhD's, together with percentages, and also the relative proportions of the male and female populations in the several fields.

The most obvious sex difference is in the natural science segment. The outer ring (men) is approximately half (50.4 percent) natural sciences, including mathematics and engineering, shown as the shaded portion. The inner ring has only about one-quarter shaded, showing that the natural sciences, mathematics, and engineering

TABLE 4
PERCENTAGE OF U.S. PhD's WHO ARE WOMEN, 1900-1974

Period	Women *N*	Women Percent	Period	Women *N*	Women Percent	Period	Women *N*	Women Percent
1900-1904	150	8.8	1930-1934	1,755	14.7	1960-1964	6,606	10.8
1905-1909	188	9.7	1935-1939	2,026	14.8	1965-1969	13,520	12.4
1910-1914	286	11.3	1940-1944	1,984	13.5	*Single Years*		
1915-1919	324	11.3	1945-1949	2,139	13.4	1970	4,378	13.9
1920-1924	634	15.1	1950-1954	3,617	9.4	1971	4,985	15.0
1925-1929	1,193	15.4	1955-1959	4,647	10.5	1972	5,723	16.6
						1973	6,371	19.0
						1974	6,785	20.5

SOURCE: NRC, Commission on Human Resources.

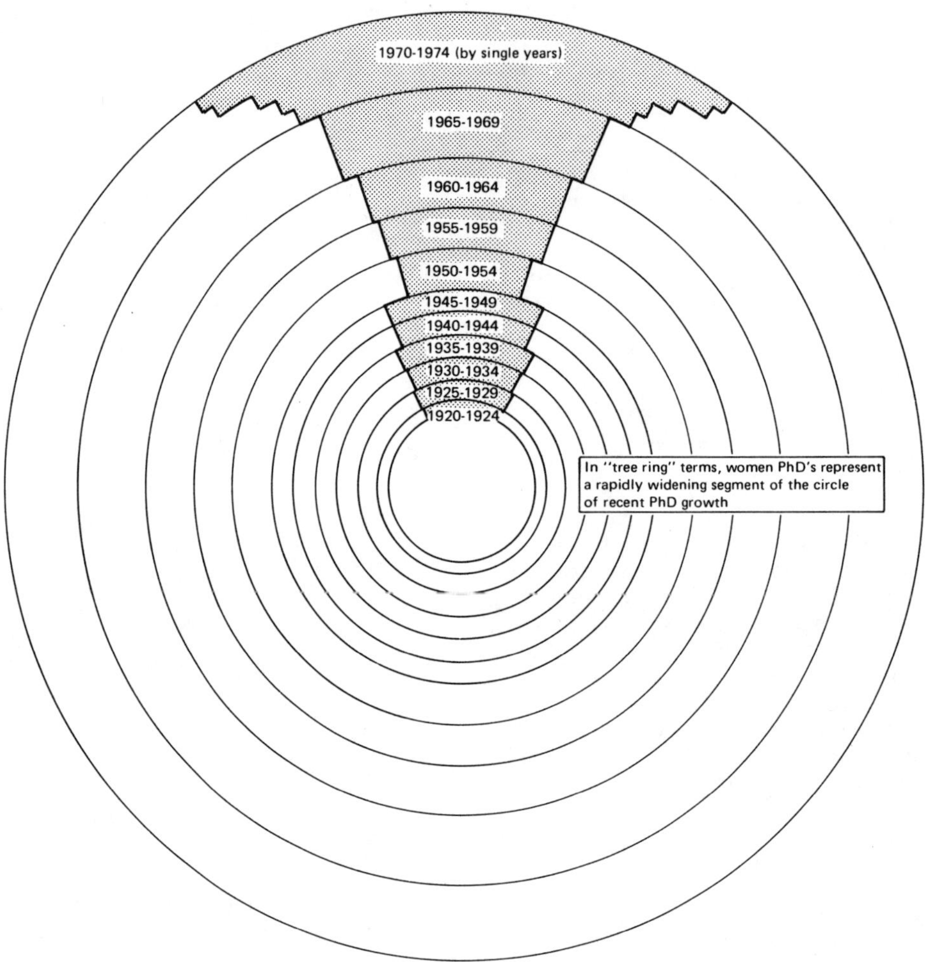

SOURCE: NRC, Commission on Human Resources

FIGURE 14 Proportion of women PhD's depicted as tree rings.

attract only 24.5 percent of the women. Another prominent sex difference is in education. About one man in six among the doctorate recipients has his degree in education; among the women this proportion is almost doubled (27.9 percent). Languages and literature are smaller segments and hence less conspicuous, but the sex difference is actually larger proportionately: 5.7 percent for the men versus 15.2 percent for the women. In psychology, we find 6.0 percent of the men and 11.2 percent of the women. In the life sciences, the proportions are almost in balance, 16.8 percent of the men and 15.9 percent of the women. In the EMP fields, the disparities are greater, ranging from 3.8 percent versus 2.0 percent in mathematics to 10.8 percent versus 0.4 percent in engineering.

DOCTORATES GRANTED IN FIELD GROUPS

The various fields and field groups have not grown uniformly over time, as has been shown. More detail with respect to the different growth rates, and the consequences in terms of field mix, are explored below. Figure 16 gives an overall picture of the changing output numbers by general field groups. The heavy line shows the growth of the EMP group. The largest single group shown in Figure 16, it also depicts the general growth curve, with a slowing down in the depression and World War II periods, the sharp postwar spurt, the secondary slowing down, then the extended high growth during the 1960's, and, finally, a slower growth during the 1970's--a familiar picture shown in a different form earlier in this chapter. The vertical axis in Figure 16 is average number of degrees granted annually over each 5-year period.

Although the other field groups in Figure 16 do not follow exactly the same growth pattern, the major effects of circumstances are similar. The other four fields originally are quite different in numbers of doctorates granted, then merge indistinguishably for a period of about 15 years in the 1950's and 1960's, to emerge later in a different rank order. In 1920 the

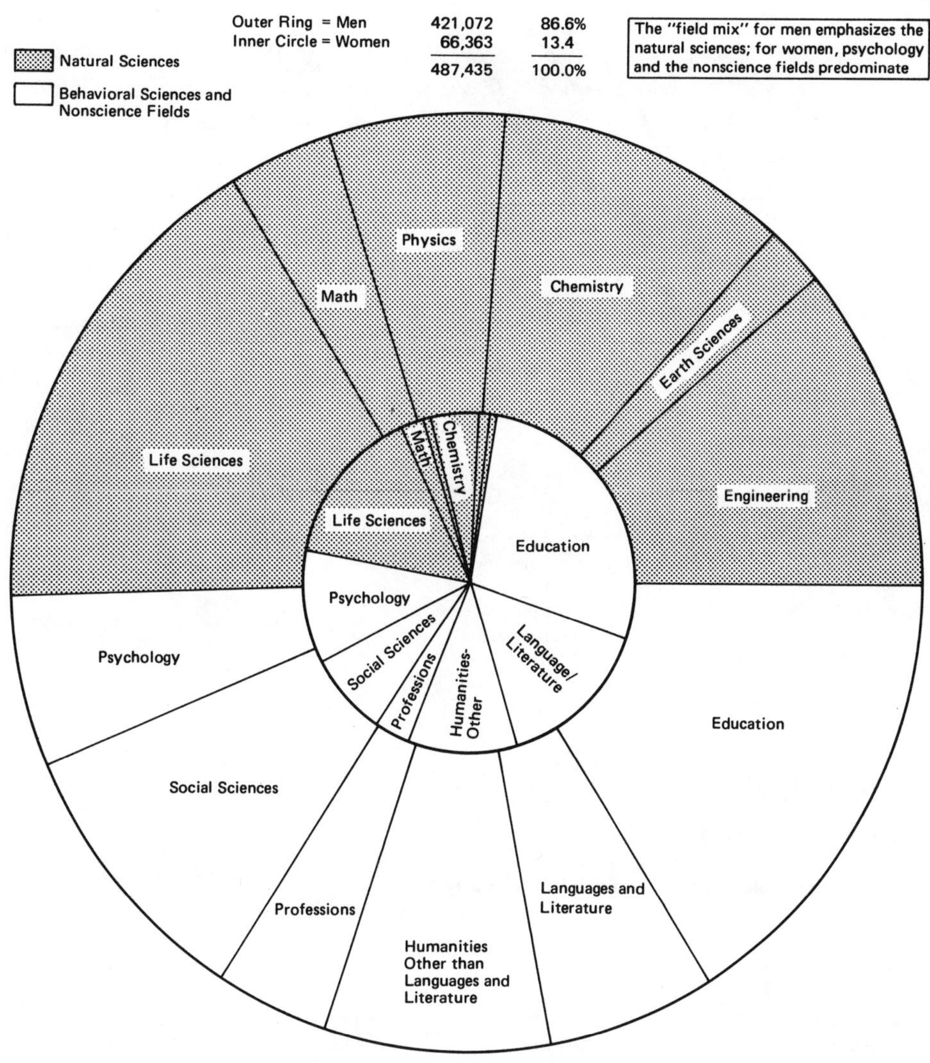

Field	Male	Female
Life Sciences	16.8	15.9
Math	3.8	2.0
Physics	6.2	1.2
Chemistry	10.5	4.6
Earth Sciences	2.3	0.4
Engineering	10.8	0.4
TOTAL, Natural Sciences	50.4	24.5

Field	Male	Female
Education	16.2	27.9
Languages and Literature	5.7	15.2
Other Humanities	7.8	9.9
Professions	4.1	3.5
Psychology	6.0	11.2
Social Sciences	9.6	7.8
TOTAL, Social Sciences, Arts, and Education	49.4	75.5

SOURCE: NRC, Commission on Human Resources

FIGURE 15 Field mix by sex, 1920-1974.

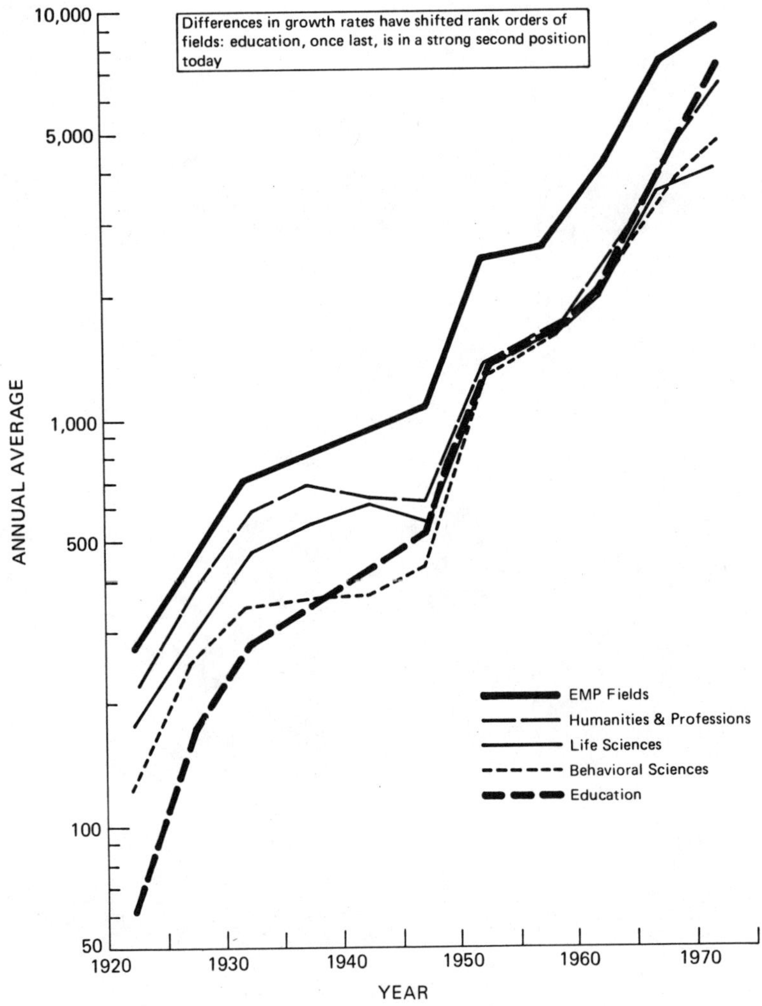

FIGURE 16 Growth curves of field groups, 1920-1974, by 5-year periods.

rank order of these field groups was EMP, humanities and professions, life sciences, behavioral sciences, and education. In 1974 the rank order was EMP, education, humanities and professions, behavioral sciences, and life sciences. The humanities and professions group (here combined to avoid cluttering the graph further) were originally the second largest of the field groups. But this field group underwent a prolonged period of slow growth and negative growth, to emerge again in recent years below education, which moved up from a poor fifth position to second after the EMP group. Even during World War II education continued to grow, a function of two factors: the large proportion of women in the field and the relatively advanced age at doctorate in the education field, both factors diminishing the effect of the draft. The continued growth of the EMP fields during the World War II period was due to a quite different reason--the vital importance of these fields to the war effort. The life sciences, third in the period from 1920-1950, grew relatively slowly from 1950 to 1974, finally appearing as the smallest of the field groups shown. The behavioral sciences generally remained one of the smaller field groups until the last 5-year period, when they grew rather rapidly, overtaking the life sciences fields (see Figure 8). For those interested in the finest detail of subfields, Appendix 1 provides data for the entire 1920-1974 period by fine field, with additional columns for the 1960-1969 period and annual data for the 1970's.

CHANGING PROPORTIONS OF FIELD GROUPS

The shifting growth patterns depicted above result in varying proportions of the PhD total, as shown in Figure 17, here reduced to four general field groups for the sake of simplicity. The brackets at the sides of the figure show the percent that each of these groups represents in the 1920's and in the 1970's. Although the EMP group has remained relatively constant through most of the half-century depicted here, and actually increased for a time, the recent sharp drop in output has cut the proportion to

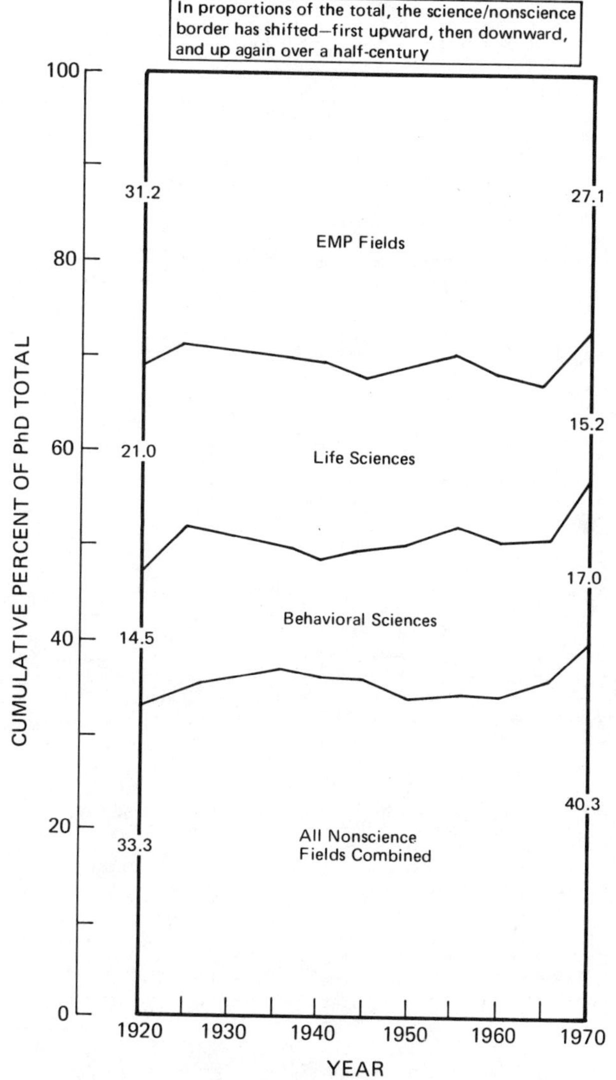

SOURCE: NRC, Commission on Human Resources

FIGURE 17 Changing proportions of four general field groups.

27.1 percent of the total during the first half of the 1970's, from 31.2 percent in 1920. The life sciences as a group have gradually shrunk from 21.0 percent at the beginning to 15.2 percent at the end. The behavioral sciences, which include psychology and the various social sciences, after a quick expansion in the early 1920's, shrank gradually as a proportion of the total, then expanded during World War II and the subsequent period, shrank again during the 1960's, and finally expanded sharply in the most recent period. Nonscience fields show the clearest trend, rising, then falling again until the 1950's, and expanding rapidly in recent years.

The overall changes shown in Figure 17 are best understood by examining in more detail the various subfields. In Figure 18, the six fields that compose the natural sciences are shown as proportions of the natural science total. Although the changes in the fields at the top and bottom of the graph are most easily visualized, the changes for all fields over the 50-year span are shown by the numbers in brackets at the sides. The proportion attributable to mathematics has almost doubled; the proportion within physics has shrunk, then expanded again to about its original size; chemistry has shrunk, except for the period of the 1930's, and now is considerably less than half its original proportion (34.3 percent down to 14.6 percent); the earth sciences have diminished gradually from 6.3 percent to 4.1 percent, while engineering has expanded enormously--by a factor of 9, actually--from 2.7 percent in the 1920's to 24.8 percent in the 1970's. Life sciences, as indicated above, have gradually shrunk from 40.3 percent to 35.9 percent, but show some signs of revival in the latest period. The numbers for Figure 18 are found in Table 5.

The nonscience fields are shown in Figure 19. At the top, the languages and literature group is shown, with an almost steady decrease in proportion of the total of the nonsciences, from the 1930's to present. The other fields within

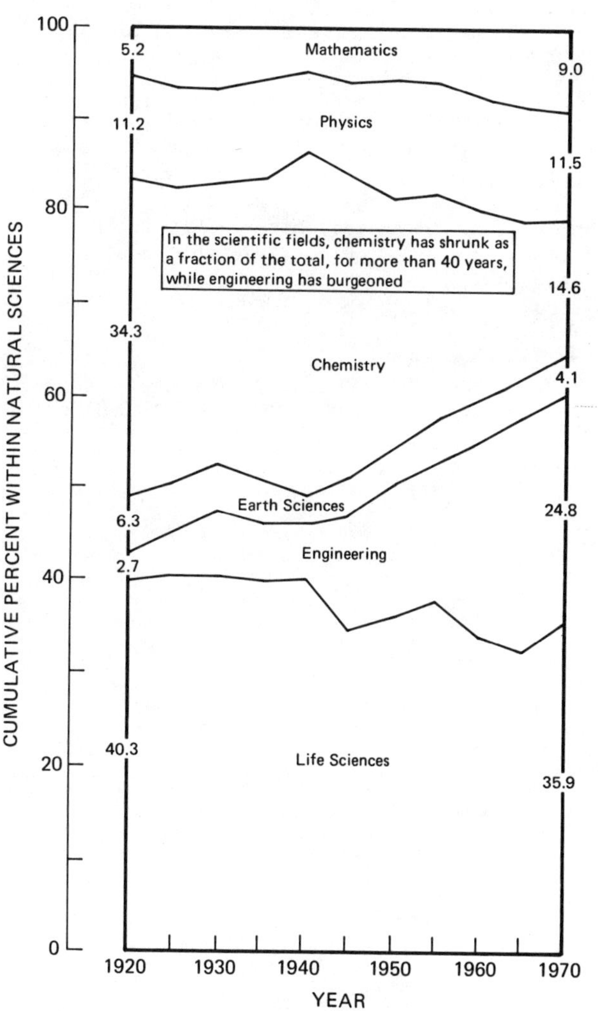

SOURCE: NRC, Commission on Human Resources

FIGURE 18 Changing proportions of six science fields.

TABLE 5
CHANGING PROPORTIONS OF SIX FIELDS IN THE NATURAL SCIENCES AND ENGINEERING, 5-YEAR PERIODS, 1920-1974

	EMP Field Group						
Period	Math	Physics	Chem-istry	Earth Sci-ences	Engi-neering	Life Sci-ences	Total
1920-1924	5.2	11.2	34.3	6.3	2.7	40.3	100.0
1925-1929	6.4	11.1	32.1	5.2	4.6	40.5	100.0
1930-1934	6.8	10.2	30.2	5.2	7.0	40.5	100.0
1935-1939	5.6	10.9	32.3	4.8	6.2	40.2	100.0
1940-1944	4.8	9.0	36.6	3.3	5.9	40.4	100.0
1945-1949	5.9	10.1	32.5	3.9	12.6	35.0	100.0
1950-1954	5.5	13.0	27.0	3.9	14.4	36.2	100.0
1955-1959	6.0	11.9	24.2	4.6	15.2	38.2	100.0
1960-1964	7.4	12.3	20.4	4.7	21.1	34.1	100.0
1965-1969	8.5	12.4	16.7	4.2	25.4	32.7	100.0
1970-1974	9.0	11.5	14.6	4.1	24.8	35.9	100.0

Percentages may not total 100.0 because of rounding.

SOURCE: NRC, Commission on Human Resources.

the humanities have also diminished, but not as spectacularly, while the professions, always a small group, have fluctuated somewhat but without any marked change in overall proportion. The graph is dominated, however, by the high percentages in education, a field that has increased, with the exception of a single 5-year period, throughout the half-century shown, until it is half of the nonscience total. Table 6 provides the figures.

These data on proportions are all brought together and are combined with data on actual numbers of doctorates per 5-year period, in the tree ring graph of Figure 20, in which the field groups are shown as segments of the whole circle. Because the natural science fields are shown on

TABLE 6
RELATIVE PROPORTIONS OF TWO GENERAL GROUPS, 1920-1974, 5-YEAR PERIODS: (A) BEHAVIORAL SCIENCES AND (B) HUMANITIES, PROFESSIONS, AND EDUCATION

	A. Behavioral Sciences		B. Humanities, Professions, and Education				
Period	Psy-chology	Social Sciences	Language and Literature	Other Human-ities	Profes-sions	Educa-tion	Total
1920-1924	35.6	64.4	30.8	34.1	12.9	22.2	100.0
1925-1929	33.0	67.0	24.2	31.7	13.4	30.6	100.0
1930-1934	30.8	69.2	27.9	28.0	11.7	32.4	100.0
1935-1939	31.8	68.2	32.0	24.7	10.0	33.3	100.0
1940-1944	29.0	71.0	26.7	22.5	10.5	40.3	100.0
1945-1949	33.1	66.9	21.7	22.4	10.7	45.2	100.0
1950-1954	43.4	56.6	18.9	23.3	9.3	48.6	100.0
1955-1959	46.5	53.5	18.0	22.1	10.2	49.6	100.0
1960-1964	44.8	55.2	17.4	23.0	11.6	48.1	100.0
1965-1969	42.7	57.3	18.3	21.4	11.3	49.1	100.0
1970-1974	41.1	58.9	17.0	19.9	11.0	52.1	100.0

Percentages may not total 100.0 because of rounding.

SOURCE: NRC, Commission on Human Resources.

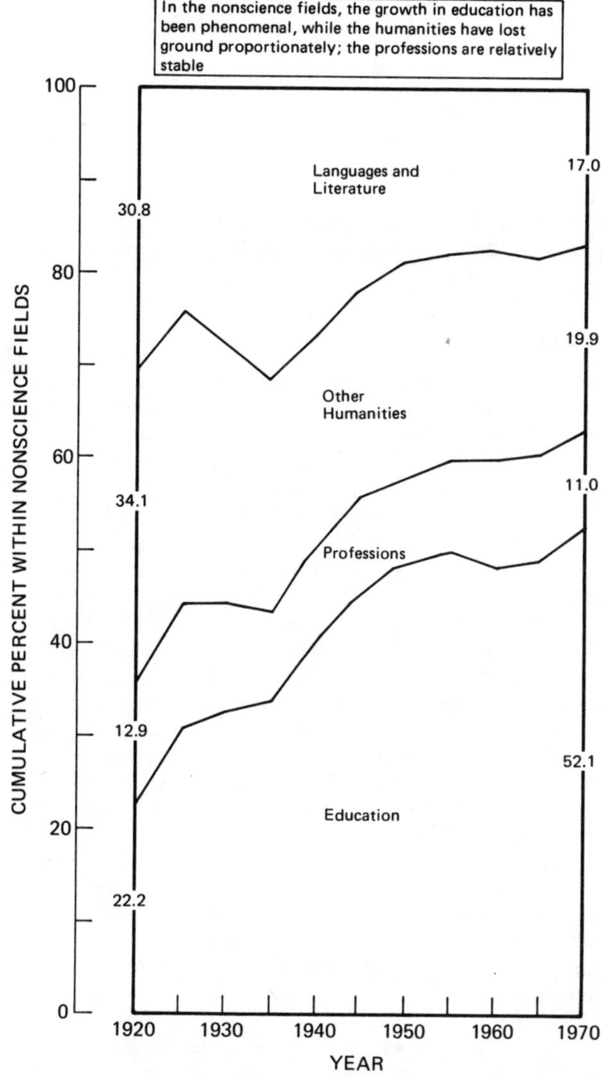

SOURCE: NRC, Commission on Human Resources

FIGURE 19 Changing proportions of nonscience fields.

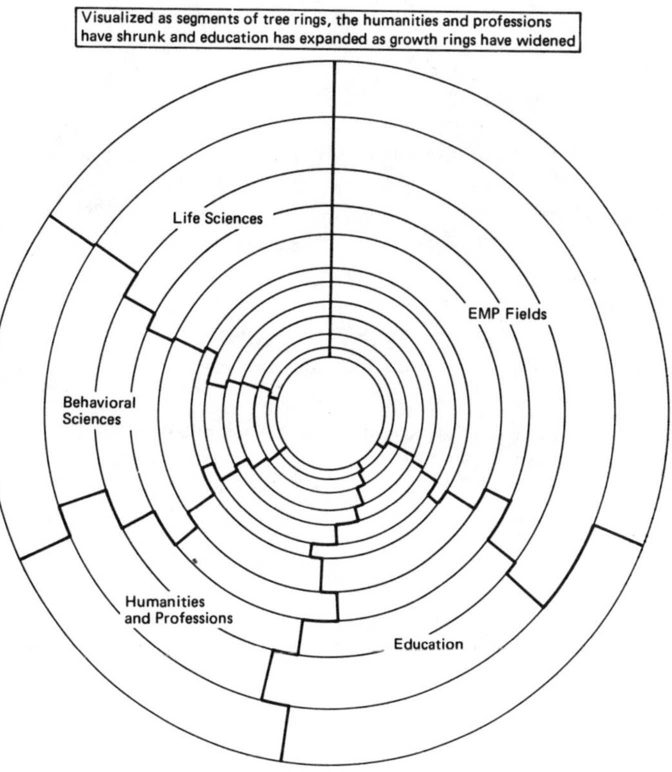

SOURCE: NRC, Commission on Human Resources

FIGURE 20 Changing field mix depicted as tree ring segments.

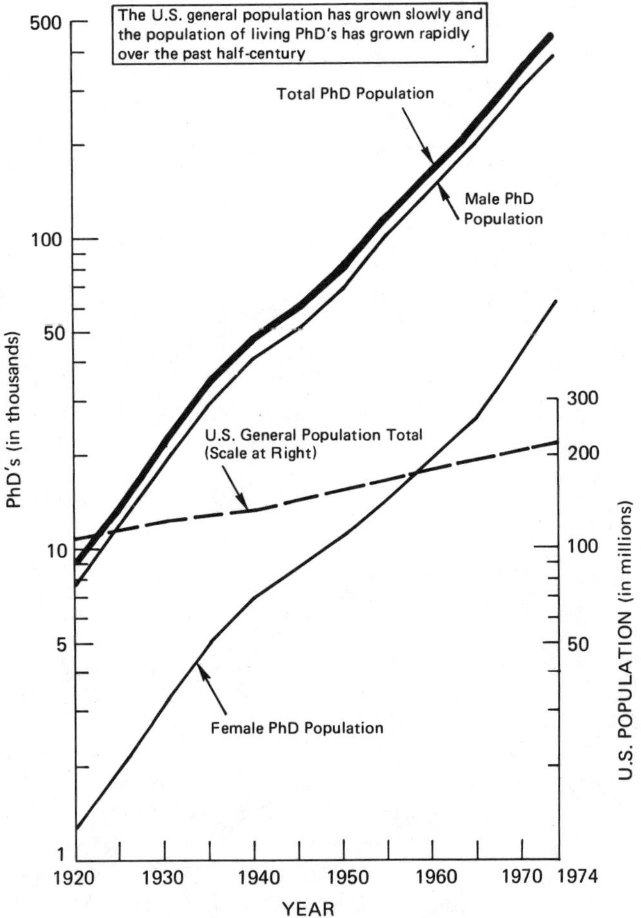

SOURCE: NRC, Commission on Human Resources

FIGURE 21 Estimated living U.S. PhD population compared with U.S. general population.

either side of the vertical radius, they are most easily visualized as entities. The fluctuations shown here are a function both of the growth in total numbers and of the proportions shown in Figure 17. The other fields are shown as less regular segments, but the rapidly increasing numbers and proportions in education, for example, are unmistakable. The behavioral science segment has remained roughly constant, while the humanities and professions sector has shrunk.

THE DOCTORATE POPULATION

What is the size of the living doctorate-level population? The first approximation to an answer to this question is shown in Figure 21, which shows the size of the total and sex-differentiated living doctorate-level populations in the United States from 1920 to 1974. This figure is based on a computer model[1] using graduations and the application of age-specific death rates to the graduation data; emigration and immigration of the doctorate-holding population has been excluded. The death rates, which are significantly lower than those for the U.S. general population, were taken from actuarial data of the Teachers Insurance and Annuity Association. The assumption that all the graduates from U.S. universities remain in the United States is not true, of course; many go abroad after graduation. But this number is to some extent offset by immigrations; in the model shown here the assumption is made that immigration balances emigration. The precise accuracy of this assumption cannot be tested from data currently available, but it is believed to be good enough so that the conclusions are not materially affected.

Figure 21 is semilogarithmic--that is, the vertical scale is logarithmic and the horizontal scale (time) is linear. It is the logarithmic nature of the scale that results in the compression that makes the data for both sexes slightly different from that for men alone. Overall, the proportion of women in the PhD population is about 13.6 percent at present; it has varied from nearly 15 percent in 1940 to less than 12 percent in 1960. The logarithmic scale results in a compression of these numbers by a factor of about 8, when the male and total data are com-

[1]The computer program that produces PhD population estimates begins with data on the distribution of age at completion of the PhD, separately for each sex, field, and time period of graduation--a rather extensive data set. It then calculates survivorship of each age-sex-field group in each year from graduation until all are deceased, using age-specific death rates based on data from Teachers Insurance and Annuity Association. (These rates, quite different from general population age-specific death rates, have been independently verified through application to a known population of scientists.) The program then accumulates data across cohorts to provide a table, by age, of the living PhD's of a given field and sex, in any given year. Data are provided for each of 10 fields of PhD and may be accumulated in field and sex groupings as desired. Projections to future years are possible, based on assumed PhD graduation rates.

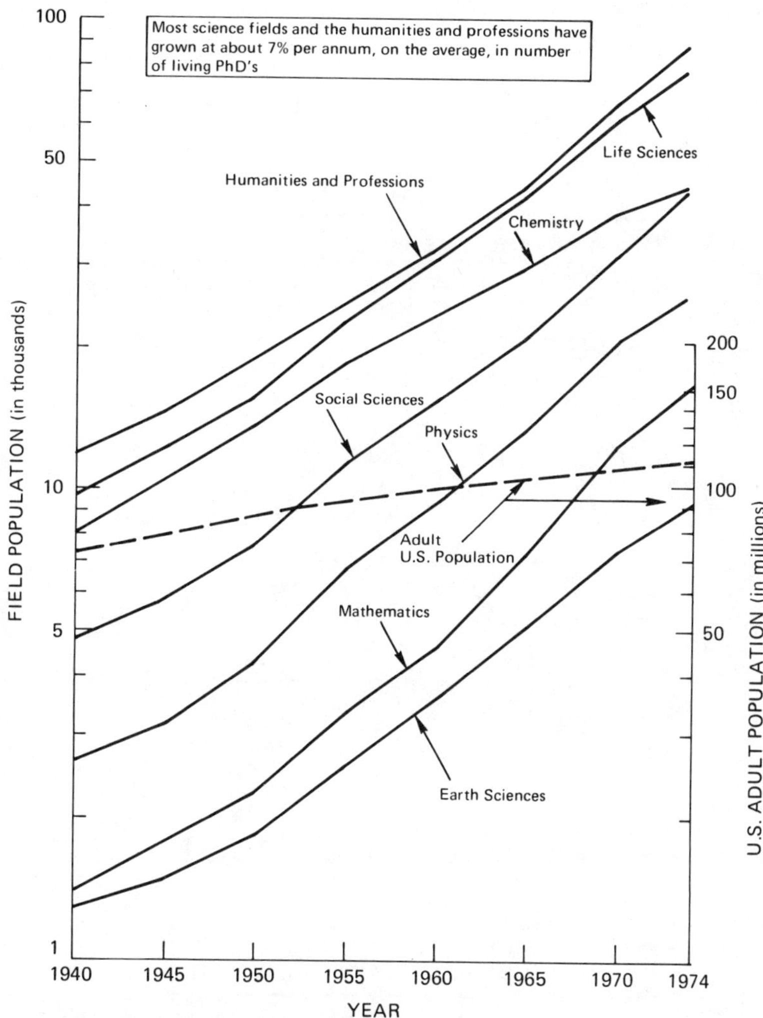

SOURCE: NRC, Commission on Human Resources

FIGURE 22 Estimated living U.S. PhD population in seven fields compared with U.S. population age 25 and over.

pared. Table 7 presents the total data by sex, and Table 8 presents the data by field of doctorate but with reference data on the general U.S. population. In all of these population data, field of doctorate, rather than field of present specialization, is presented. Switching of fields after the doctorate is not taken into account in these figures. Field switching has been described in a separate report,[2] as far as scientists and engineers are concerned, and will be discussed further in Chapter 2.

In Figure 21, the growth of the total U.S. population is shown for comparison with the growth in the PhD population. The scale for the U.S. population is shown in the right margin; it uses the same scale as the PhD population scale on the left but is multiplied by 10,000. Over the period from 1920 to 1974, the U.S. population approximately doubled, going from about 105 million to over 210 million. But over the same period, the PhD population increased by a factor of 50, going from 8,830 to 448,900. In terms of proportion, the PhD's increased from less than 1 per 10,000 of the general population in 1920 to about 21 per 10,000 in 1974.

Figure 22 depicts the growth of 7 of the 10 doctoral field populations, over the period 1940-1974. In this set of fields, the growth is rather regular, and the curves run approximately parallel. There are differences in growth rate, ranging from an average annual increment of 5.0 percent in chemistry to 7.5 percent in mathematics. As expected on the basis of doctoral graduations, the growth has been steepest over the past 15 years and, for most fields, slowest during the World War II period. The smallest of the fields shown in Figure 22, earth sciences, increased from about 1,300 in 1950 to about 9,000 in 1974, averaging

[2]Commission on Human Resources, NRC, *Field Mobility of Doctoral Scientists and Engineers* (Washington, D.C.: NAS, 1976).

TABLE 7
ESTIMATED POPULATION OF LIVING U.S. PhD's, BY SEX, 1920-1974, COMPARED WITH U.S. POPULATION

Year of Estimate	Male PhD's	Female PhD's	Total PhD's	U.S. Population	PhD's per Million
1920	7,580	1,250	8,830	106,466,000	83
1925	11,550	1,950	13,500		
1930	18,630	3,150	21,780	123,188,000	177
1935	28,900	4,900	33,800		
1940	40,700	6,920	47,620	132,122,000	360
1945	51,000	8,690	59,690		
1950	67,950	10,930	78,880	151,683,000	520
1955	103,000	14,530	117,530		
1960	140,300	19,000	159,300	179,323,000	888
1965	196,800	25,800	222,600		
1970	297,700	41,000	338,700	203,200,000	1,667
1974	388,400	60,500	488,900	213,000,000 (estimate)	2,108

SOURCE: NRC, Commission on Human Resources.

TABLE 8
ESTIMATED PhD POPULATION, BY FIELD, 1940-1974, COMPARED WITH U.S. POPULATION 25 AND OVER

PhD Field	Reference Year 1940	1945	1950	1955	1960	1965	1970	1974
Mathematics	1,460	1,630	2,200	3,260	4,480	7,020	11,940	16,190
Physics	2,600	3,110	4,200	6,650	9,010	12,960	19,900	25,160
Chemistry	7,900	10,260	13,380	18,190	22,880	28,750	37,580	43,640
Earth sciences	1,260	1,440	1,800	2,520	3,450	4,880	7,080	8,970
Engineering	1,230	1,630	2,990	5,870	9,140	16,720	31,450	43,260
Life sciences	9,580	12,040	15,340	22,380	29,870	40,260	58,570	75,200
Psychology	2,140	2,560	3,520	6,530	10,050	14,580	22,340	30,390
Social sciences	4,710	5,710	7,500	11,090	14,990	20,410	30,650	42,000
Humanities and professions	11,770	14,370	17,880	24,390	31,660	42,670	63,550	84,870
Education	5,190	6,940	10,080	16,660	23,800	34,380	55,660	79,240
TOTAL	47,620	59,690	78,880	117,530	159,300	222,600	338,700	448,900
U.S. population Age 25 and over (in thousands)	74,775		86,484		99,465		109,899	113,000

The data have been rounded, and hence may not add exactly to the totals given.

SOURCE: NRC, Commission on Human Resources.

a growth rate of 6.3 percent per year. The largest field, humanities and professions, had almost 12,000 in 1940 and grew to over 84,000 in 1974, averaging a growth rate of 5.9 percent annually. The growth rates for the other fields, over the period shown, averaged 7.0 percent for physics, 6.3 percent for the life sciences, and 6.5 percent for the social sciences.

In Figure 22, the PhD population by field is compared with the U.S. population age 25 and

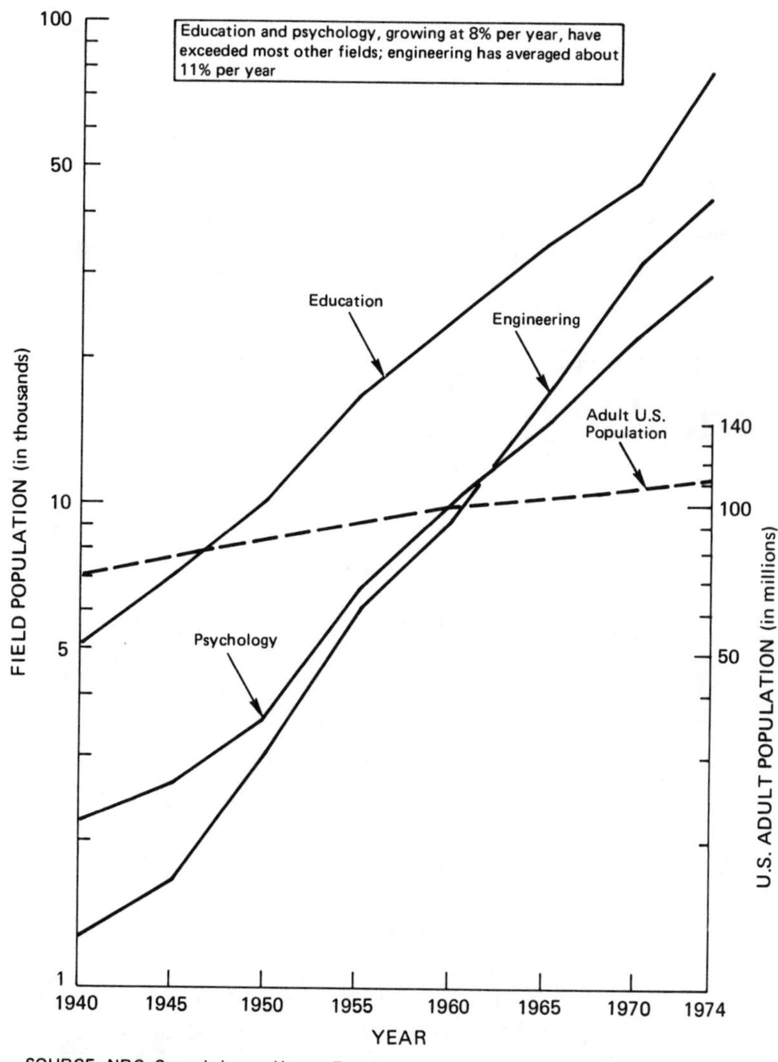

SOURCE: NRC, Commission on Human Resources

FIGURE 23 Three fast-growing PhD populations.

over. This is a more relevant reference group than the total U.S. population shown in Figure 21, since almost all PhD's are over the age of 25. Again, the general population scale is at the right, and again it is multiplied by a factor of 10,000 as compared with the PhD's. About the same relative difference is apparent in the slopes of the PhD populations, as compared with the U.S. 25-and-over totals. However, the percentage differences vary. In 1940, there were about 6 PhD's per 10,000 of the population 25 and over; in 1950 this ratio increased to slightly over 9; in 1960, to 16; in 1970, to almost 31; and in 1974 the ratio was almost 40 per 10,000 U.S. population of comparable age. Since slightly more than half of the general population over 25 is female, while about 86 percent of the doctorate population is male and 14 percent female, the PhD/population ratio for males is about 70 per 10,000; for females about 10 per 10,000.

Figure 23 depicts the growth of the remaining three fields of doctorates. These are all faster growing than those shown in Figure 22 and, if superimposed, would cross the lines of that figure repeatedly. The three fields are education, psychology, and engineering. Education, with an average annual growth rate of 8.4 percent, grew from about 5,140 in 1940 to about 78,800 in 1974. Psychology, with an average growth rate of 8.2 percent, rose from about 2,200 to 30,300 over the 34-year period. Engineering, with a growth rate averaging 11 percent per annum, moved from the position of smallest field (about 1,260) in 1940 to one of the largest (43,200) in 1974. As in Figure 22, the total U.S. population age 25 and over is shown for comparison.

The detailed data, showing the numbers in each field by sex and by single years of age, for each year from 1920 through 1974, are available in computer tape form and are the basis for additional analyses described in Chapter 2 relating to demographic data.

2

Characteristics of Doctorate Recipients

In the first chapter, we were concerned with the numbers of PhD's, as they varied over time, by field, and by sex. We turn now to the characteristics of the doctorate recipients themselves--those characteristics that can be tabulated from the data of the DRF. These appear to be of primary importance regarding the education and employment of these people--particularly to the educational institutions and to the agencies that provide support for graduate education. These characteristics, in the order in which they will be described, concern:

1. The educational background of the families from which they come.
2. Citizenship and racial/ethnic identification.
3. Age and the time lapse between baccalaureate and doctorate degrees.
4. Master's degrees.
5. Field switching between the baccalaureate and doctorate levels.
6. Geographic migration, region by region within the United States, from high school to PhD.

HIGHLIGHTS

- *Educational Background*. The general population of the United States has become steadily better educated over the past century, at the rate of a little less than two grade levels per generation. The PhD's have come from families at the leading edge of this educational wave--from families that were, on the average, one generation ahead of the general population. There are significant sex differences: The women PhD's come from slightly better-educated families than do the male PhD's. Field differences also exist but are decreasing in magnitude. The pattern of all of these changes makes a fascinating mosaic.
- *Citizenship*. One in seven PhD's awarded in the United States is to a non-U.S. citizen. The proportion varies profoundly by field: foreign citizenship is highest in male-dominated agricultural sciences (33 percent), engineering (28 percent), and medical sciences (21.5 percent), and lowest in education (5.4 percent) and psychology (5.2 percent), in which the proportion of women is much higher. Thus the field differences can be said to explain a large part of the overall sex differences: 15 percent of the male PhD's and 10 percent of the female PhD's are non-U.S. citizens.
- *Racial/Ethnic Identification*. Data on racial/ethnic composition of the doctorate recipients has only recently become available. It varies by field, and hence, to some extent, by sex. Overall, including U.S. and foreign citizens but omitting those for whom racial/ethnic data are unavailable, 87.7 percent of recent PhD's are white, 3.4 percent are black, 0.5 percent are American Indians, 1 percent are Spanish Americans, Mexican Americans, or Chicanos, 0.2 percent are Puerto Ricans, and 7.2 percent are Orientals. Blacks and American Indians tend to be concentrated in education, and Orientals in the EMP fields.
- *Age*. The typical PhD is about 30 years old at graduation--younger in the sciences, older in the nonsciences, particularly education. Age at baccalaureate and age at doctorate tend to show the same pattern of field differences, but there

is less spread at the BA level. Age at PhD is therefore determined principally by time lapse between the baccalaureate and doctorate. BA-PhD time lapse has increased over the past half-century, but the major fluctuations were those induced by World War II and its interruption of the educational progress of both men and women, but particularly the men.

• *Master's Degrees*. Except in chemistry, most PhD's also have master's degrees. In chemistry, 41 percent have the degree; in physics, 64 percent; in the biosciences and the medical sciences, 65 percent; in psychology, 77 percent; in the earth sciences, 78 percent; in mathematics, 79 percent; in the social sciences, 83 percent; in the professions, 86 percent; in the humanities, 87 percent; in engineering, 89 percent; in the agricultural sciences, 90 percent; and in education, 97 percent. The percentages are typically higher for women than for men, the exceptions being the earth sciences, engineering, and agricultural sciences.

• *Fields at BA and PhD*. Field switching, for the doctorate-bound population, results principally in flows from mathematics, physics, chemistry, engineering, the agricultural sciences, and the humanities to the biosciences, the earth sciences, and education. The other fields are in relatively close balance overall, but for the women there is a particularly strong movement out of the professions[1] and the medical sciences.[2] In this report each field is considered in terms of its donor/receptor characteristics: the extent to which it "donates" its baccalaureate recipients to the various "receptor" fields at the doctoral level.

• *Interregional Migration*. Most PhD's earn their doctorates in the same geographic regions in which they graduated from high school and from college. The regional shifts have varied over time and are a function of the relative strength of each region at the secondary, higher education, and graduate levels and population. Patterns of migration are explored in terms of "donor" and "receptor" regions, at the HS-PhD level and BA-PhD level.

SOCIOECONOMIC BACKGROUNDS OF DOCTORATE RECIPIENTS

Potentially, there are a number of indicators that could be used to describe the socioeconomic backgrounds of doctorate recipients. However, as a practical matter, the only indicator available in the DRF is the level of education attained by the parents of the PhD's. Fortunately, this is an important indicator for this particular group, distinguished as it is from the general population primarily by its educational attainment.

It is of course to be expected that PhD's come mostly from the better-educated families. The extent of the difference in the educational spectrum from which PhD's come, as compared with the general population, was explored in *Profiles of PhD's in the Sciences*, published by the NAS in 1965. That study compared the educational levels of the general population with those of the parents of the PhD's who graduated over the period from 1935 to 1960. Because PhD's are, on the average, about 30 years old at the time they take the doctorate, and because their parents are, on the average, assumed to be about 30 years older than that, the time differential between the birth of the parents and the year in which the PhD's graduate is assumed to be 60 years. It is this time differential that was used to compare the PhD's and the general population in the 1965 study.

UPDATE AND NORMATIVE FRAMEWORK

It is now possible to update and extend the earlier study. A sample of 10,000 PhD's was used in the 1965 study, drawn from the graduation cohorts of 1935, 1940, 1945, 1950, 1955, and 1960. At the present time, complete data are available for the more recent graduates, here divided into four cohorts, the PhD's of 1963-1965, 1966-1968, 1969-1971, and 1972-1974. Census data from the decennial censuses for 1940-1970 provide information on the educational levels attained by the general population, typically divided into 10-year age cohorts. Educational level is recorded at nine steps of attainment: no formal education; grades 1-4; grades 5-7; grade 8; 1-3 years of high school; high school graduation; 1-3 years of college; college graduation; and postcollege training. In the tables and graphs to follow, some discontinuities, showing up as jagged lines in percentile graphs of educational attainment, will be found. This is in part a result of the particular steps of attainment that were employed, but it is also due to the fact that, historically, generally accepted termination points of formal education have been eighth grade, high school graduation, and college graduation.

In the case of the PhD's in the DRF, a slightly different set of educational attainment points was used (third grade instead of fourth; sixth grade instead of seventh; and an additional level at the top, differentiating master's degrees and the doctorate). However, the data sets are compatible, and meaningful comparisons are provided, using the assumption described above to define the birth cohorts of the parents of PhD's. In examining the graphs, particularly Figures 27 and 28, a slight truncation of the norm for the general population will be noted for the most recent cohort. This is because data were available in 1970 for persons age 25 and up, but some of them (more men than women) had not completed their formal education at that time. The limitation is slight and does not interfere with the usefulness of the data, except for post-baccalaureate degrees.

[1]The professions include business administration, home economics, journalism, theology, law, social work, library science, and the speech and hearing sciences.

[2]The medical sciences include medicine and surgery, dentistry, veterinary medicine, hospital administration, parasitology, pathology, pharmacy, and pharmacology.

TABLE 9
EDUCATIONAL ATTAINMENT OF THE UNITED STATES POPULATION, BY BIRTH COHORT AND SEX
(Averaged Data from Censuses of 1940, 1950, 1960, and 1970)*

Educational Level Attained		Year of Birth: Before 1866	1866-1875	1876-1885	1886-1895	1896-1905	1906-1915	1916-1925	1926-1935	1936-1940
Males										
No education	%	10.13	8.28	6.73	5.40	2.79	1.46	1.02	0.95	0.91
	C%†	10.13	8.28	6.73	5.40	2.79	1.46	1.02	0.95	0.91
Grades 1-4	%	18.63	18.48	16.44	14.29	9.75	6.33	3.85	2.49	1.52
	C%	28.76	26.76	23.37	19.69	12.53	7.80	4.87	3.44	2.43
Grades 5-7	%	23.03	22.84	22.18	21.73	19.92	15.41	9.90	7.30	4.93
	C%	51.79	49.60	45.54	41.42	32.45	23.20	14.77	10.74	7.36
8th grade	%	33.00	30.18	29.69	28.11	26.48	19.74	12.60	8.79	5.95
	C%	84.79	79.78	75.23	69.53	58.92	42.95	27.36	19.52	13.31
High school, 1-3 years	%	4.80	6.72	8.91	11.53	15.94	20.25	21.19	19.74	17.90
	C%	89.59	86.49	84.13	81.06	74.86	63.20	48.55	39.26	31.12
High school graduate	%	4.99	6.55	8.06	9.32	12.54	20.26	29.37	31.77	37.13
	C%	94.58	93.04	92.19	90.36	87.40	83.46	77.92	71.03	68.24
College, 1-3 years	%	2.53	3.22	3.62	4.74	6.08	7.96	10.05	11.50	13.44
	C%	97.11	96.26	95.81	95.12	93.47	91.42	87.97	82.53	81.69
College graduate	%	2.01	2.52	2.88	3.14	3.84	4.31	6.20	8.67	8.64
	C%	99.12	98.78	98.69	98.26	97.32	95.73	94.16	91.20	90.33
Graduate/professional school	%	.87	1.22	1.31	1.73	2.69	4.26	5.83	8.80	9.67
	C%	100.00	100.00	100.00	100.00	100.00	100.00	100.00	100.00	100.00
Median		7.27	7.51	7.65	7.81	8.16	9.54	11.55	11.84	12.01
Mean		6.39	6.77	7.17	7.65	8.59	9.67	10.76	11.53	12.01
Females										
No education	%	9.44	6.91	5.87	5.19	2.62	1.23	0.82	0.86	0.81
	C%	9.44	6.91	5.87	5.19	2.62	1.23	0.82	0.86	0.81
Grades 1-4	%	14.88	14.18	13.02	11.13	7.80	4.56	2.65	1.70	1.18
	C%	24.32	21.08	18.89	16.32	10.42	5.79	3.47	2.56	1.99
Grades 5-7	%	21.54	21.52	20.83	20.27	18.32	13.90	8.59	5.65	4.04
	C%	45.86	42.60	39.72	36.59	28.73	19.69	12.06	8.21	6.03
8th grade	%	35.26	32.24	29.99	27.76	24.68	18.53	11.66	7.19	5.12
	C%	81.12	74.84	69.70	64.35	53.41	38.22	23.72	15.40	11.15
High school, 1-3 years	%	6.34	8.78	11.43	13.75	17.11	21.13	21.93	21.90	20.22
	C%	87.46	83.62	81.13	78.10	75.52	59.35	45.65	37.30	31.37
High school graduate	%	8.01	10.25	11.53	12.50	16.77	24.91	37.62	42.41	45.26
	C%	95.47	93.87	92.65	90.60	87.29	84.26	83.27	79.71	76.63
College, 1-3 years	%	2.81	3.82	4.53	5.89	7.73	9.19	10.06	11.38	12.86
	C%	98.29	97.69	97.19	96.49	95.02	93.45	93.33	91.09	89.49
College graduate	%	1.50	1.98	2.32	2.62	3.56	4.03	4.42	5.89	7.29
	C%	99.79	99.66	99.50	99.11	98.58	97.48	97.74	96.99	96.78
Graduate/professional school	%	0.21	0.36	0.51	0.89	1.42	2.52	2.27	3.02	3.22
	C%	100.00	100.00	100.00	100.00	100.00	100.00	100.00	100.00	100.00
Median		7.62	7.73	7.84	7.98	8.36	10.17	11.62	11.80	11.91
Mean		6.75	7.25	7.60	7.99	8.89	9.91	10.73	11.30	11.67

*See text for censuses contributing to each average.
†C% = cumulative percent.

The general population educational attainment data are shown in Table 9. The percentage completing each level, and the cumulative percentage up to that level, is shown for each birth cohort, for men and for women. Additionally, means and medians, by cohort and sex, are given.[3] The data on mean educational levels from this table are plotted in Figure 24, which also shows comparable data for the educational levels of the parents of PhD's, for the birth cohorts for which data are available. In the case of both the general population (shown as heavy lines) and the PhD population (shown as lighter lines), the data for males are given in solid lines and the data for females in dashed lines. It is apparent

[3]For those who may wish to compare the data of Table 9 with other sources, it should be noted that the columns of this table usually combine data from two or more censuses to obtain more stable percentages. This is particularly important at the extremes of the distributions, where data are sparse. The census data available were from rather small samples, rather than complete figures. The pre-1866 data were taken solely from the 1940 census; 1866-1875 and 1876-1885 data from the 1940 and 1950 censuses; 1886-1895 data from the 1940, 1950, and 1960 censuses; 1896-1905 and 1906-1915 data from the censuses of 1950, 1960, and 1970; 1916-1925 data from the censuses of 1960 and 1970; and the rest from the 1970 census alone.

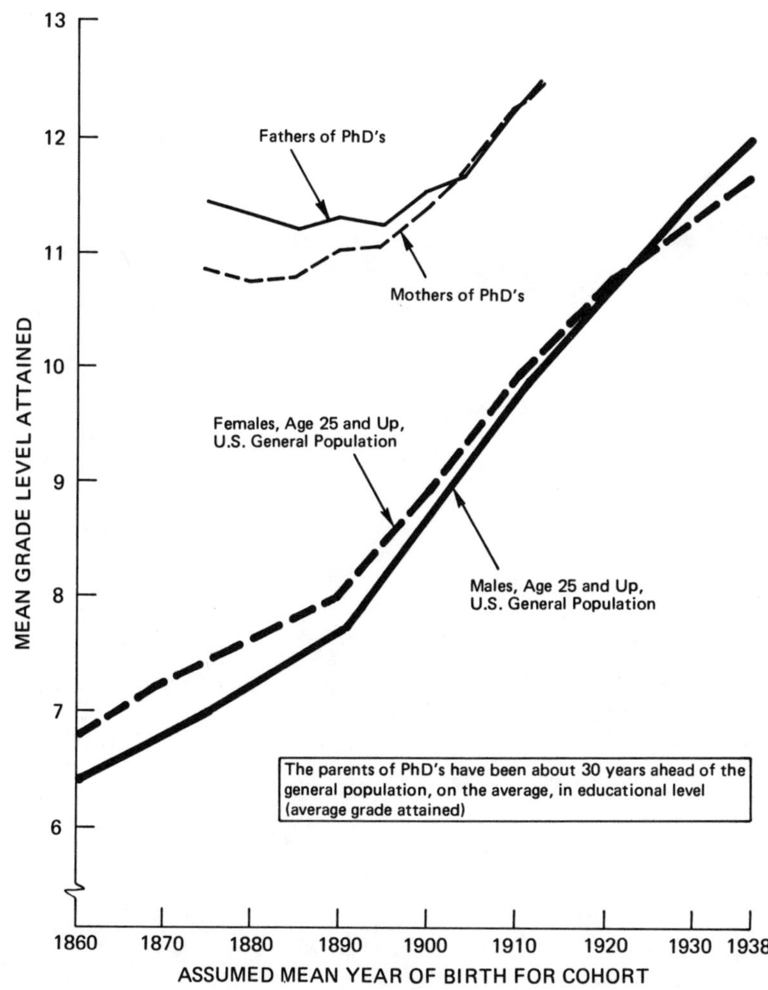

SOURCE: NRC, Commission on Human Resources

FIGURE 24 Educational level of parents of U.S. native PhD's compared to U.S. general population, by year of birth.

that over the 75 years shown here, there has been a steady progression of educational attainment. The trend for the two sexes is similar, but prior to 1920 the mean for women was higher than that for men, whereas the reverse is true for the more recent cohorts.

PARENTS AND POPULATION NORMS

The educational level of the parents of PhD's is in marked contrast to that of the general population, as far as the means in Figure 24 are concerned. From the earliest cohort shown until the beginning of the twentieth century, the parents of native-born U.S. PhD's averaged just under high school graduation as their highest level of educational attainment.[4] Meanwhile, the general population norm moved up from about the seventh grade to about the eighth grade. From the beginning of the present century, the average of parents of PhD's moved up approximately parallel to the change in the general population norm. It is interesting to note that, prior to 1900, the mean educational level of the mothers of PhD's was below that of the fathers, but in the more recent cohorts the difference in means has vanished. The difference in distribution of educational attainments has not vanished, as will be seen, thus illustrating a limitation of mean values to describe a population characteristic.

[4]Parents of U.S. natives only are included here, both because of the difficulty in equating educational levels across cultural lines and because of field and cohort differences in percentage of persons of foreign origins. Had they been included, some marked distortions would have been produced.

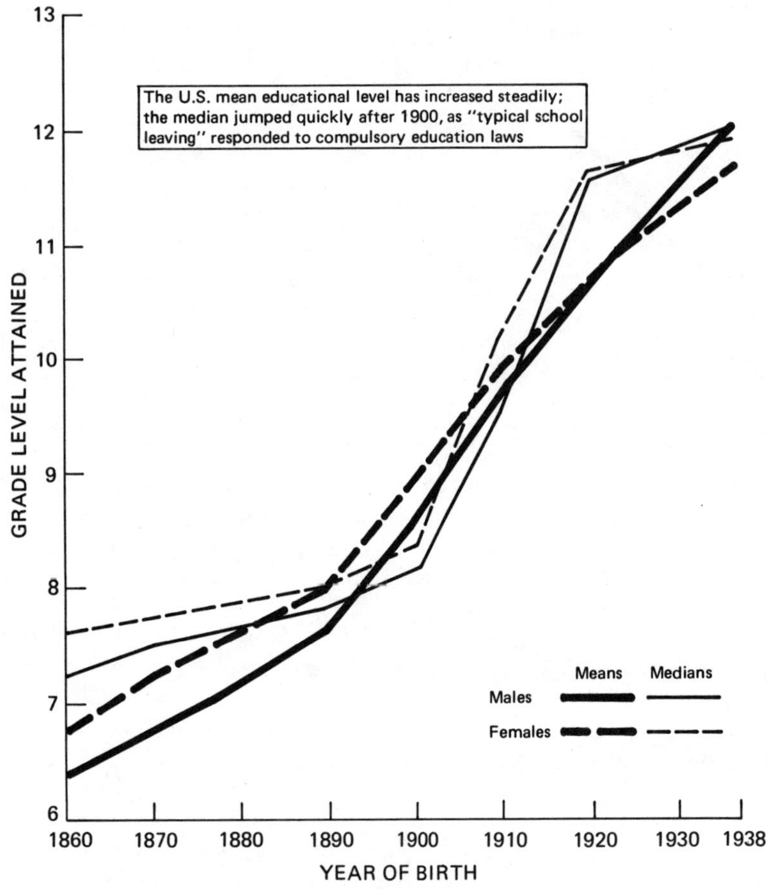

SOURCE: U.S. Decennial Censuses of 1940, 1950, 1960, and 1970

FIGURE 25 Changing educational level of U.S. population: means versus medians.

A CHANGING EDUCATIONAL SPECTRUM

The difference between means and medians may be noted in examining the data of Table 9. It is illustrated graphically in Figure 25 for the general population. Here we see again the progression of means over the same period as shown in Figure 24. Median data are also shown and, by contrast to the means, show sharp changes during the first 20 years of the present century. The medians rise at a very modest rate until the beginning of the twentieth century, when they shoot up rapidly, then rise slowly after 1920. This is an effect due to the quite rapid change of the middle section of the population--a move

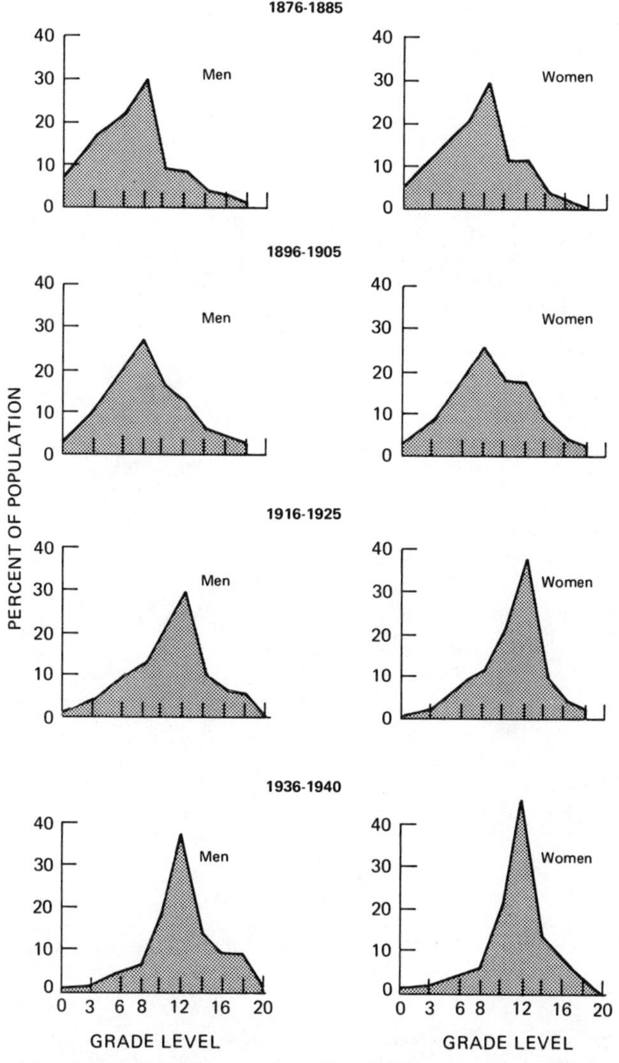

SOURCE: NRC, Commission on Human Resources, based on Bureau of Census data

FIGURE 26 Distributions of educational attainment of general population age 25 and up, by birth cohort and sex.

from a norm of eighth grade graduation to a norm of high school graduation. The median is affected by changes around the midpoint only, whereas the mean is affected by changes at any point in the educational scale. Figure 26 shows frequency diagrams of the percentage of the population, by sex, at each educational level recorded in the census statistics, for selected birth cohorts, from those born between 1876 and 1885 to those born between 1936 and 1940. The peaks of the distributions shift, in the first 2 decades of the twentieth century, from eighth grade to twelfth grade. In the 1936-1940 cohort the grade level range has been extended by incorporation of data calculated from DRF to supplement the census data.

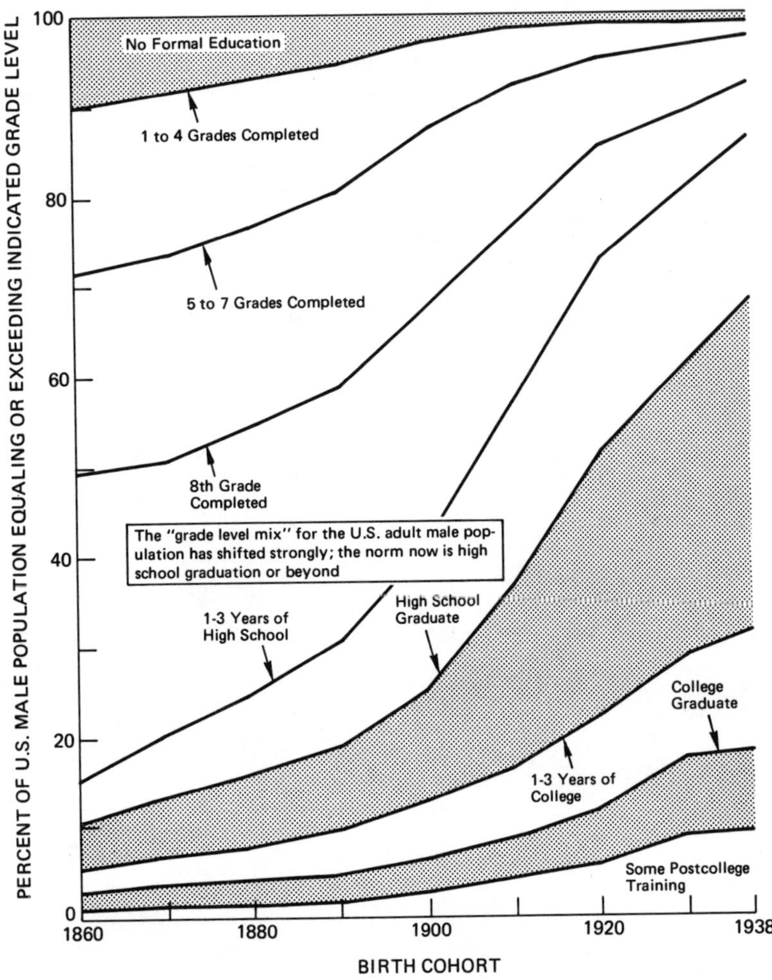

SOURCE: NRC, Commission on Human Resources, based on Bureau of Census data

FIGURE 27 Changing educational spectrum of U.S. male population.

GROWTH CURVES OF EDUCATIONAL ATTAINMENT

A sex difference is visible in the frequency polygons of Figure 26 chiefly by way of a larger proportion of men who have gone to college. The changes over time in educational attainment are not as easy to see in Figure 26 as in the next graphs, which show time changes in the various levels of educational attainment. The proportion of the population which has had no formal education decreases, for both men and women, from about 10 percent to about 1 percent in Figures 27 and 28, which are taken from the data of Table 9. The proportion who are high school graduates, but who go no farther than high school, is shown as the shaded area in the center of the graph. For the men, this area increases gradually and rather regularly; for the women there is an almost explosive growth after the beginning of the twentieth century. The shaded area near the bottom of the graph in both pictures indicates those who have completed baccalaureate degrees but no more. This is somewhat larger for men than for women, but it is the portion beyond the baccalaureate that shows the greatest sex difference. In the most recent cohort (where data were incom-

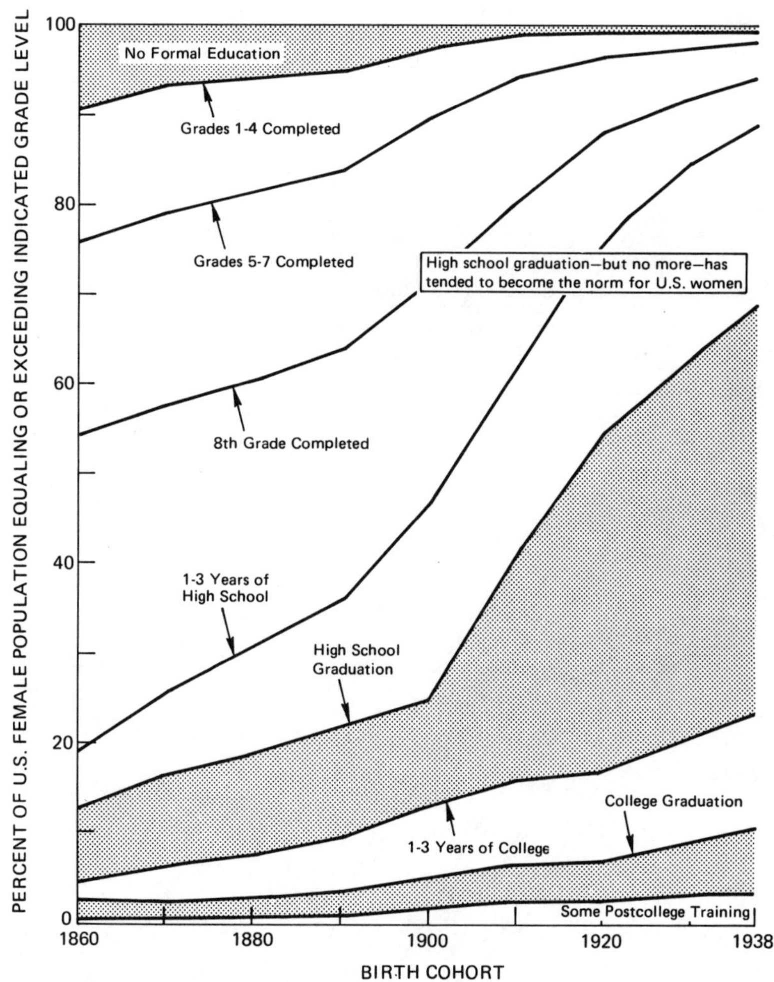

SOURCE: NRC, Commission on Human Resources, based on Bureau of Census data

FIGURE 28 Changing educational spectrum of U.S. female population.

plete in the 1970 census), the proportion of men is almost 10 percent; for women it is only slightly over 3 percent. The curves for all educational levels progress rather smoothly, with the exception of the very rapid shift in high school graduations after 1900. This is probably the effect of changes in the compulsory education laws.[5] These state laws, enacted mostly during the last half of the nineteenth century, began to have a marked effect at the high school level in the beginning of the twentieth century. At that point most state laws required attendance only up until age fourteen; by 1920, age sixteen was a more typical school-leaving minimum. Because these state laws were not all enacted simultaneously, and because of inevitable lags in enforcement, the effects were not sudden--although as noted earlier, the expansion of the women, high-school-graduate-only group is quite rapid, because a much smaller proportion of women than of men go on to college.

[5]See A. W. Steinhilber and C. J. Sokolosky, *State Law on Compulsory Attendance*, Publication OE 23044, Circular 793 (Washington, D.C.: USOE, 1966). (Superintendent of Documents Catalog FS 5.223:23044.)

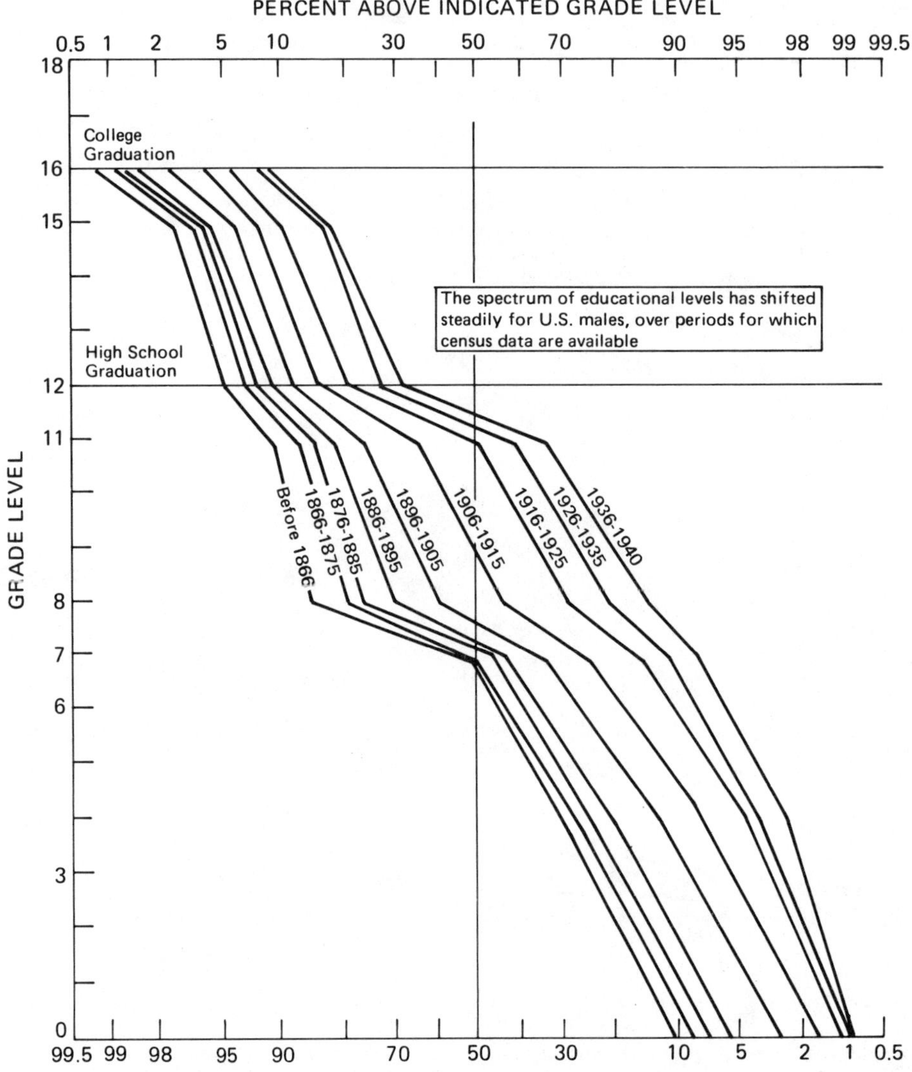

SOURCE: NRC, Commission on Human Resources, based on Bureau of Census data

FIGURE 29 Percentile graphs of educational levels attained by U.S. males age 25 and over, by decade of birth.

PERCENTILE NORMS OF EDUCATIONAL ATTAINMENT

Up to this point, we have considered means, medians, frequency distributions, and growth curves of the educational levels of the general population. In order to put the data into a form that will facilitate comparison with the educational spectrum of the fathers of PhD's, Figure 27 has been recast into percentile terms, with one percentile curve for each birth cohort, in Figure 29. A similar set of curves could be drawn for the general population of women, as a normative frame for the mothers of PhD's. In both cases, the progression of the birth cohorts is seen as a march of the curves across the page from left to right. The curves for women (not shown because they are so similar as to be redundant) vary only in that smaller percentages achieve the higher levels of education, although at the elementary education levels, the percentage of women at each grade level is slightly higher than that for men. The percentile data are plotted with normal probability spacing, which provides for equal intervals in terms of standard deviation units. This compresses the percentages around the middle of the distribution and expands the percentages at the extremes. In spite of this midrange compression, the greatest

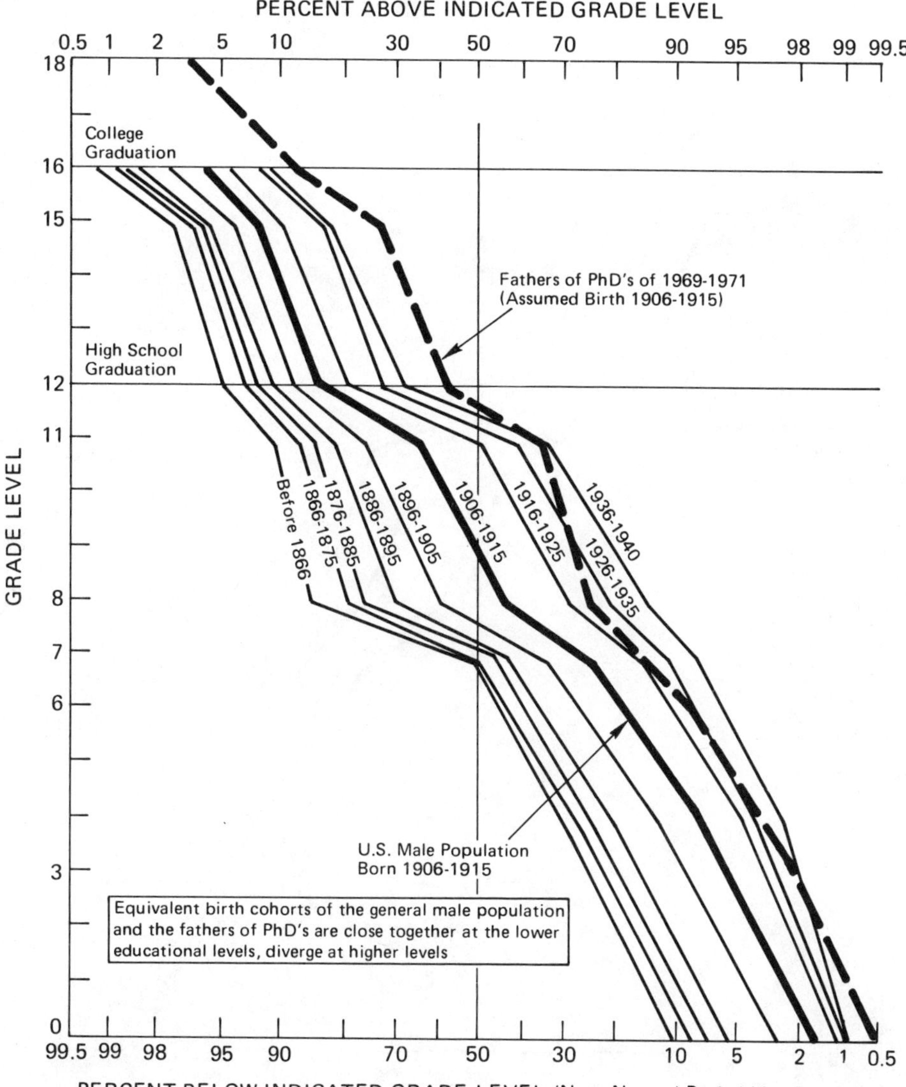

SOURCE: NRC, Commission on Human Resources

FIGURE 30 Educational attainment of fathers of PhD's, by birth cohort, compared with the norms of Figure 29.

changes are shown at about this point between the eighth and twelfth grades. Because it is the upper educational levels that are the primary concern with respect to the parents of PhD's, this method of normal probability spacing permits a clearer view of the changes where they are most relevant to the present study. If the percentiles had been plotted as equal intervals, the result would have been a tight compression at both extremes of the distribution, minimizing the most relevant data.

Figure 29 provides a normative frame for interpreting the data on the educational attainment spectrum for the fathers of PhD's. This is done in Figure 30, where a heavy black line has been used to represent the general population curve for the birth cohort of 1906-1915, and a dashed line to represent the fathers of PhD's who were their contemporaries--the fathers of the PhD's of 1969-1971. A similar comparison could be made for the mothers of PhD's of the same era, compared to the general population of women, but the data are too nearly redundant to justify a separate graph. In both cases, in spite of minor sex differences, one may say as a rough generalization that the parents of PhD's are about one generation ahead of the general population in educational attainment.

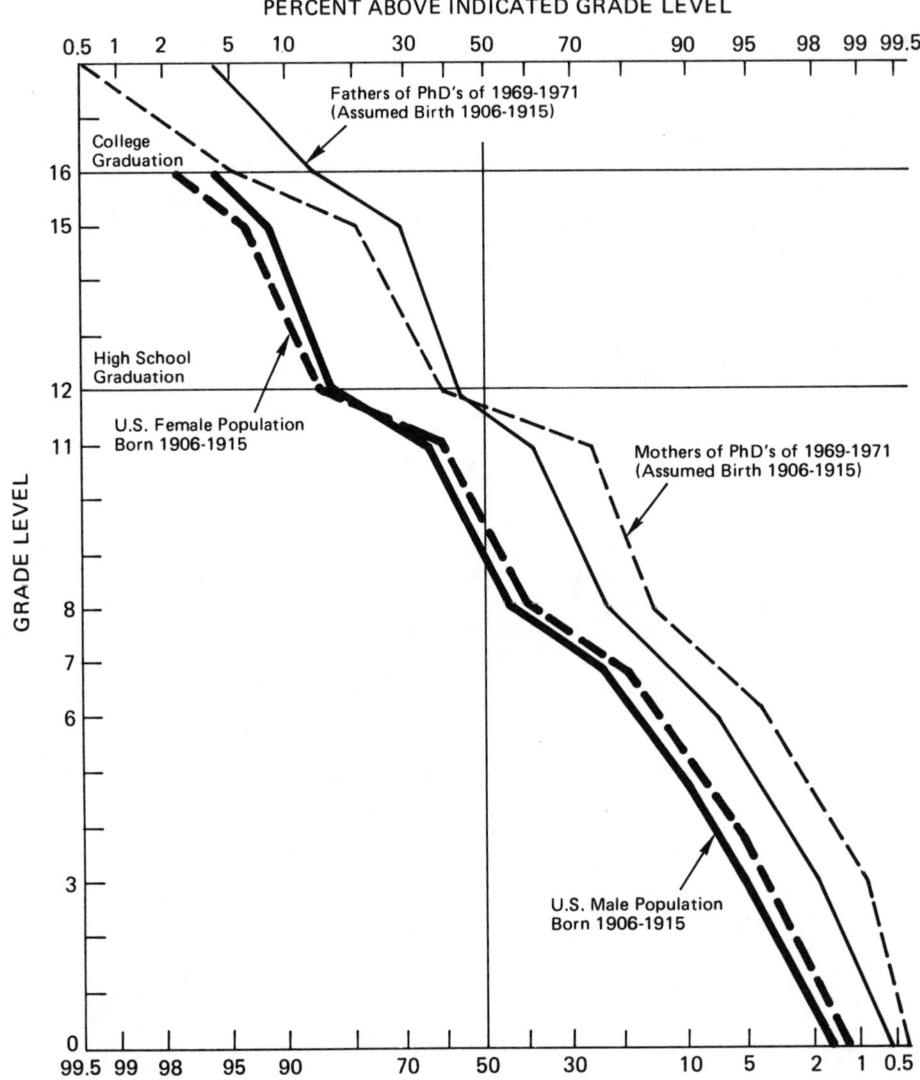

SOURCE: NRC, Commission on Human Resources

FIGURE 31 Comparison of educational attainment spectra of males and females in general population and parents of PhD's.

SEX DIFFERENCES IN EDUCATIONAL ATTAINMENT

To summarize the comparison of the data on parents of PhD's as compared to the general population, and to present data for both males and females, Figure 31 shows four percentile curves. The heavy lines are those for the general population, the lighter lines for the parents of PhD's, and, in both cases, solid lines represent data for men, dashed lines data for women. For both the general population and for parents of PhD's, there is a crossing-over of the men and women's graphs at the high school level. The difference, however, is greater for the parents of PhD's than it is for the general population. In both comparisons, the curve for men is above that for women at the higher education level but below at the elementary school level.

The data for the various grade levels for fathers of PhD's are given in Table 10 and for mothers in Table 11. In both tables, data are given separately for the female PhD's and the male PhD's and for both combined. At the bottom of the table, the summary statistics are provided: means, standard deviations, and the percentile points 10, 25, 50, 75, and 90. The sex differences here provide an interesting study and will be examined in more detail in the graphs to follow. The interesting new information shown here is that the progression of the cohorts continues, for both the mothers and the fathers of the PhD's, for the recent cohorts. The mean data shown here are shown graphically in Figure 24. The data of Tables 10 and 11 show that the same progression given for the means holds also for the other portions of the educational spectrum.

TABLE 10
DISTRIBUTION OF EDUCATIONAL LEVELS OF FATHERS OF PhD's OF U.S. ORIGIN, BY COHORT AND SEX OF PhD

Father's Education		PhD Year and Sex: 1963-1965 Male	1963-1965 Female	1963-1965 Total	1966-1968 Male	1966-1968 Female	1966-1968 Total	1969-1971 Male	1969-1971 Female	1969-1971 Total	1972-1974 Male	1972-1974 Female	1972-1974 Total	Total, 1963-1974 Male	Total, 1963-1974 Female	Total, 1963-1974 Total
NONE	N	312	30	342	329	41	370	348	47	395	285	64	349	1274	182	1456
	V1	1.0	.8	1.0	.8	.7	.7	.6	.5	.6	.5	.5	.5	.7	.5	.6
	V3C	1.0	.8	1.0	.8	.7	.7	.6	.5	.6	.5	.5	.5	.7	.5	.6
GRADES 1-3	N	490	60	550	672	77	749	846	106	952	840	170	1010	2848	413	3261
	V1	1.6	1.6	1.6	1.5	1.3	1.5	1.4	1.0	1.3	1.4	1.2	1.4	1.5	1.2	1.4
	V3C	2.6	2.4	2.6	2.3	2.0	2.2	2.0	1.5	1.9	1.9	1.7	1.9	2.2	1.7	2.0
GRADES 4-6	N	2361	247	2608	2942	365	3307	3500	519	4019	3108	666	3774	11911	1797	13708
	V1	7.6	6.5	7.5	6.8	6.0	6.7	5.8	5.1	5.7	5.3	4.7	5.2	6.2	5.3	6.0
	V3C	10.2	8.9	10.1	9.1	8.0	8.9	7.8	6.6	7.6	7.2	6.4	7.1	8.4	7.0	8.0
GRADES 7-8	N	6155	626	6781	7539	916	8455	9515	1356	10871	8264	1591	9855	31473	4489	35962
	V1	19.8	16.5	19.4	17.3	15.0	17.1	15.7	13.4	15.4	14.2	11.2	13.6	16.3	13.1	15.8
	V3C	30.0	25.4	29.5	26.4	23.0	26.0	23.5	20.0	23.0	21.4	17.6	20.7	24.7	20.1	23.8
H.S. 9-11	N	3543	370	3913	4777	611	5388	6256	884	7140	5771	1168	6939	20347	3033	23380
	V1	11.4	9.8	11.2	11.0	10.0	10.9	10.4	8.7	10.1	9.9	8.2	9.6	10.5	8.9	10.3
	V3C	41.4	35.2	40.7	37.4	33.0	36.9	33.9	28.7	33.1	31.3	25.8	30.3	35.2	29.0	34.1
H.S. GRAD(12)	N	6399	784	7183	9765	1182	10947	14830	1959	16789	14801	2939	17740	45795	6864	52659
	V1	20.6	20.7	20.6	22.5	19.4	22.1	24.5	19.3	23.8	25.4	20.7	24.5	23.7	20.1	23.1
	V3C	62.0	55.9	61.3	59.9	52.4	59.0	58.4	48.0	56.9	56.7	46.5	54.8	58.9	49.1	57.2
COL.1-3(13-15)	N	3775	512	4287	5649	845	6494	8184	1504	9688	8154	2073	10227	25762	4934	30696
	V1	12.1	13.5	12.3	13.0	13.9	13.1	13.5	14.8	13.7	14.0	14.6	14.1	13.3	14.4	13.5
	V3C	74.1	69.4	73.6	72.9	66.3	72.1	71.9	62.8	70.6	70.7	61.1	68.9	72.2	63.5	70.7
COL GRAD (16)	N	4395	608	5003	6392	1128	7520	8984	1941	10925	8894	2772	11666	28665	6449	35114
	V1	14.1	16.0	14.3	14.7	18.5	15.2	14.9	19.1	15.5	15.2	19.5	16.1	14.8	18.8	15.4
	V3C	88.2	85.4	87.9	87.6	84.8	87.3	86.8	81.9	86.1	85.9	80.6	85.0	87.0	82.3	86.1
MA,ETC.(17-18)	N	2628	396	3024	3913	632	4545	5666	1288	6954	5884	1903	7787	18091	4219	22310
	V1	8.5	10.5	8.7	9.0	10.4	9.2	9.4	12.7	9.9	10.1	13.4	10.7	9.4	12.3	9.8
	V3C	96.7	95.9	96.6	96.6	95.2	96.5	96.2	94.6	96.0	96.0	94.0	95.7	96.4	94.6	95.9
PHD,P-DOC (20)	N	1037	156	1193	1502	294	1796	2290	546	2836	2355	841	3196	7184	1837	9021
	V1	3.3	4.1	3.4	3.5	4.8	3.6	3.8	5.4	4.0	4.0	5.9	4.4	3.7	5.4	4.0
	V3C	100.0	100.0	100.0	100.1	100.0	100.1	100.0	100.0	100.0	100.0	99.9	100.1	100.1	100.0	99.9
TOTAL KNOWN	N	31095	3789	34884	43480	6091	49571	60419	10150	70569	58356	14187	72543	193350	34217	227567
	V1	100.0	100.0	100.0	100.1	100.0	100.1	100.0	100.0	100.0	100.0	99.9	100.1	100.1	100.0	99.9
	V2	96.2	94.9	96.0	96.9	95.6	96.7	95.3	94.4	95.2	92.7	92.1	92.5	95.0	93.7	94.8
	V3C	100.0	100.0	100.0	100.1	100.0	100.1	100.0	100.0	100.0	100.0	99.9	100.1	100.1	100.0	99.9
UNKNOWN	N	1238	203	1441	1412	282	1694	2992	597	3589	4629	1212	5841	10271	2294	12565
	V2	3.8	5.1	4.0	3.1	4.4	3.3	4.7	5.6	4.8	7.3	7.9	7.5	5.0	6.3	5.2
GRAND TOTAL	N	32333	3992	36325	44892	6373	51265	63411	10747	74158	62985	15399	78384	203621	36511	240132
	V2	100.0	100.0	100.0	100.0	100.0	100.0	100.0	100.0	100.0	100.0	100.0	100.0	100.0	100.0	100.0
MEAN		11.61	12.17	11.67	* 11.90	12.47	11.97	* 12.15	12.90	12.26	* 12.36	13.11	12.50	* 12.07	12.83	12.18
STD. DEV.		4.30	4.31	4.30	* 4.21	4.26	4.22	* 4.10	4.17	4.12	* 4.06	4.13	4.09	* 4.16	4.20	4.17
10 PCTILE		6.43	6.63	6.49	* 6.61	6.78	6.63	* 6.78	7.01	6.81	* 6.89	7.15	6.93	* 6.71	6.96	6.74
25 PCTILE		8.00	8.45	8.04	* 8.34	9.11	8.38	* 8.93	10.23	9.09	* 9.59	11.21	9.86	* 8.62	10.16	8.82
50 PCTILE		11.92	12.22	11.95	* 12.06	12.38	12.10	* 12.16	12.91	12.21	* 12.24	13.22	12.31	* 12.13	12.70	12.18
75 PCTILE		15.57	15.85	15.60	* 15.65	15.97	15.70	* 15.70	16.14	15.78	* 15.79	16.21	15.89	* 15.70	16.11	15.77
90 PCTILE		16.92	17.37	16.98	* 17.05	17.50	17.11	* 17.18	17.77	17.29	* 17.32	17.89	17.46	* 17.16	17.75	17.27

N = number of cases; V1 = vertical percentage on known total; V3C = cumulative percentage; V2 = percent of grand total.

SOURCE: NRC, Commission on Human Resources.

TABLE 11
DISTRIBUTION OF EDUCATIONAL LEVELS OF MOTHERS OF PhD's OF U.S. ORIGIN, BY COHORT AND SEX OF PhD

Mother's Education		PhD Year and Sex: 1963-1965 Male	1963-1965 Female	1963-1965 Total	1966-1968 Male	1966-1968 Female	1966-1968 Total	1969-1971 Male	1969-1971 Female	1969-1971 Total	1972-1974 Male	1972-1974 Female	1972-1974 Total	Total, 1963-1974 Male	Total, 1963-1974 Female	Total, 1963-1974 Total
NONE	N	266	24	290	261	52	313	224	34	258	202	50	252	953	160	1113
	V1	.9	.6	.8	.6	.9	.6	.4	.3	.4	.3	.4	.3	.5	.5	.5
	V3C	.9	.6	.8	.6	.9	.6	.4	.3	.4	.3	.4	.3	.5	.5	.5
GRADES 1-3	N	240	30	270	303	32	335	323	62	385	321	68	389	1187	192	1379
	V1	.8	.8	.8	.7	.5	.7	.5	.6	.5	.5	.5	.5	.6	.6	.6
	V3C	1.7	1.4	1.6	1.3	1.4	1.3	.9	.9	.9	.8	.9	.8	1.1	1.1	1.1
GRADES 4-6	N	1299	157	1456	1547	224	1771	1887	275	2162	1633	343	1976	6366	999	7365
	V1	4.2	4.1	4.2	3.6	3.7	3.6	3.1	2.7	3.1	2.8	2.4	2.7	3.3	2.9	3.2
	V3C	5.9	5.5	5.8	4.9	5.1	4.9	4.0	3.6	4.0	3.6	3.3	3.5	4.4	4.0	4.3
GRADES 7-8	N	4851	566	5417	5792	768	6560	7018	1028	8046	5860	1198	7058	23521	3560	27081
	V1	15.7	14.9	15.6	13.4	12.6	13.3	11.6	10.1	11.4	10.0	8.4	9.7	12.2	10.4	11.9
	V3C	21.6	20.4	21.4	18.3	17.7	18.2	15.6	13.7	15.4	13.6	11.7	13.2	16.6	14.4	16.2
H.S. 9-11	N	3645	422	4067	4966	646	5612	6294	1008	7302	5553	1266	6819	20458	3342	23800
	V1	11.8	11.1	11.7	11.5	10.6	11.3	10.4	9.9	10.3	9.5	8.9	9.4	10.6	9.7	10.5
	V3C	33.4	31.5	33.1	29.8	28.3	29.5	26.0	23.6	25.7	23.1	20.6	22.6	27.2	24.1	26.7
H.S. GRAD(12)	N	9817	1025	10842	14741	1671	16412	22034	2887	24921	22286	4340	26626	68878	9923	78801
	V1	31.8	27.0	31.3	34.0	27.4	33.2	36.4	28.4	35.3	38.1	30.5	36.6	35.7	28.9	34.6
	V3C	65.2	58.5	64.4	63.8	55.7	62.7	62.4	52.0	61.0	61.2	51.1	59.2	62.9	53.0	61.3
COL.1-3(13-15)	N	5495	761	6256	7737	1255	8992	10766	2189	12955	10604	2923	13527	34602	7128	41730
	V1	17.8	20.1	18.1	17.8	20.6	18.2	17.8	21.5	18.3	18.1	20.5	18.6	17.9	20.8	18.3
	V3C	83.0	78.6	82.5	81.6	76.3	80.9	80.2	73.5	79.3	79.3	71.6	77.8	80.8	73.8	79.6
COL GRAD (16)	N	4037	589	4626	6028	1024	7052	8625	1851	10476	8566	2695	11261	27256	6159	33415
	V1	13.1	15.5	13.3	13.9	16.8	14.3	14.3	18.2	14.8	14.6	18.9	15.5	14.1	18.0	14.7
	V3C	96.1	94.1	95.8	95.5	93.1	95.2	94.5	91.7	94.1	93.9	90.5	93.3	94.9	91.8	94.3
MA,ETC.(17-18)	N	1134	198	1332	1874	388	2262	3060	744	3804	3222	1239	4461	9290	2569	11859
	V1	3.7	5.2	3.8	4.3	6.4	4.6	5.1	7.3	5.4	5.5	8.7	6.1	4.8	7.5	5.2
	V3C	99.8	99.3	99.6	99.8	99.5	99.8	99.6	99.0	99.5	99.4	99.2	99.4	99.7	99.3	99.5
PHD,P-DOC (20)	N	83	19	102	115	42	157	223	92	315	234	125	359	655	278	933
	V1	.3	.5	.3	.3	.7	.3	.4	.9	.4	.4	.9	.5	.3	.8	.4
	V3C	100.1	99.8	99.9	100.1	100.2	100.1	100.0	99.9	99.9	99.8	100.1	99.9	100.0	100.1	99.9
TOTAL KNOWN	N	30867	3791	34658	43364	6102	49466	60454	10170	70624	58481	14247	72728	193166	34310	227476
	V1	100.1	99.8	99.9	100.1	100.2	100.1	100.0	99.9	99.9	99.8	100.1	99.9	100.0	100.1	99.9
	V2	95.5	95.0	95.4	96.6	95.7	96.5	95.3	94.6	95.2	92.8	92.5	92.8	94.9	94.0	94.7
	V3C	100.1	99.8	99.9	100.1	100.2	100.1	100.0	99.9	99.9	99.8	100.1	99.9	100.0	100.1	99.9
UNKNOWN	N	1466	201	1667	1528	271	1799	2957	577	3534	4504	1152	5656	10455	2201	12656
	V2	4.5	5.0	4.6	3.4	4.3	3.5	4.7	5.4	4.8	7.2	7.5	7.2	5.1	6.0	5.3
GRAND TOTAL	N	32333	3992	36325	44892	6373	51265	63411	10747	74158	62985	15399	78384	203621	36511	240132
	V2	100.0	100.0	100.0	100.0	100.0	100.0	100.0	100.0	100.0	100.0	100.0	100.0	100.0	100.0	100.0
MEAN		11.68	12.01	11.72	* 11.95	12.30	11.99	* 12.19	12.69	12.26	* 12.35	12.90	12.46	* 12.10	12.63	12.18
STD. DEV.		3.42	3.52	3.44	* 3.30	3.51	3.33	* 3.18	3.31	3.20	* 3.11	3.23	3.14	* 3.23	3.35	3.26
10 PCTILE		7.03	7.09	7.04	* 7.27	7.29	7.27	* 7.53	7.76	7.56	* 7.76	8.11	7.82	* 7.42	7.67	7.45
25 PCTILE		9.37	9.71	9.41	* 10.27	10.59	10.31	* 11.20	11.55	11.30	* 11.55	11.65	11.56	* 10.89	11.53	11.01
50 PCTILE		12.02	12.18	12.04	* 12.10	12.30	12.12	* 12.16	12.43	12.19	* 12.20	12.47	12.25	* 12.14	12.40	12.17
75 PCTILE		14.16	14.94	14.25	* 14.41	15.33	14.53	* 14.61	15.58	14.79	* 14.76	15.68	15.03	* 14.54	15.57	14.73
90 PCTILE		16.04	16.22	16.06	* 16.11	16.32	16.14	* 16.18	16.40	16.22	* 16.22	16.48	16.28	* 16.16	16.41	16.20

N = number of cases; V1 = vertical percentage on known total; V3C = cumulative percentage;
V2 = percent of grand total.

SOURCE: NRC, Commission on Human Resources.

TABLE 12
MEAN EDUCATIONAL LEVEL OF FATHERS AND MOTHERS OF U.S. NATIVE PhD's, BY COHORT AND FIELD

	1935-1960 Cohorts from Career Patterns Studies											
	1935		1940		1945		1950		1955		1960	
	Mother	Father	Mother	Father	Mother	Father	Mother	Father	Mother	Father	Mother	Father
Mathematics	10.60	10.63	10.68	10.72	11.71	12.56	10.67	11.13	11.67	11.58	11.68	12.08
Physical sciences	11.45	12.16	11.45	11.97	11.58	12.38	11.84	12.21	11.57	11.63	12.04	12.19
Engineering	10.72	11.44	9.88	10.33	10.24	10.97	11.26	11.57	11.21	12.22	11.16	10.95
EMP TOTAL	11.23	11.86	11.10	11.55	11.34	12.12	11.57	11.93	11.47	11.80	11.73	11.79
Biosciences	10.54	10.69	10.57	11.29	10.38	10.61	10.89	11.26	10.69	11.01	11.42	11.57
Agricultural sciences	10.41	9.34	10.14	9.91	10.94	10.26	11.26	10.37	10.48	10.49	10.68	10.49
Medical sciences*	11.14	13.01	10.90	12.38	11.71	12.50	12.26	13.32	11.07	11.67	11.29	11.72
LIFE SCIENCE TOTAL	10.55	10.66	10.53	11.18	10.52	10.64	11.03	11.12	10.70	10.99	11.27	11.37
Psychology	10.83	12.22	11.44	13.05	11.43	10.79	10.42	10.63	10.75	10.83	11.42	11.85
Economics	11.19	12.47	11.21	11.64	11.88	11.44	10.22	10.86	10.92	10.64	11.09	11.85
Other social sciences	11.15	12.22	11.32	12.04	10.83	11.65	10.81	11.29	11.07	11.10	11.40	11.67
BEHAVIORAL SCIENCE TOTAL	11.07	12.26	11.32	12.16	11.18	11.41	10.58	11.01	10.92	10.91	11.35	11.77
HUMANITIES AND PROFESSIONS	10.72	11.22	10.57	11.11	10.81	11.20	11.24	12.07	11.45	11.80	11.58	11.69
EDUCATION	9.33	10.45	9.27	9.55	9.39	9.93	9.90	9.36	10.63	10.29	10.48	10.39
GRAND TOTAL												
Males	10.74	11.37	10.56	11.09	10.62	10.96	11.03	11.21	11.05	11.17	11.34	11.52
Females	11.17	11.84	12.26	13.33	11.49	12.24	10.79	12.41	11.51	12.05	11.86	11.75
Total	10.81	11.44	10.75	11.34	10.80	11.21	11.01	11.32	11.09	11.25	11.39	11.54

	1963-1974 Cohorts from DRF									
	1963-1965		1966-1968		1969-1971		1972-1974		Total 1963-1974	
	Mother	Father	Mother	Father	Mother	Father	Mother	Father	Mother	Father
Mathematics	12.32	12.56	12.90	13.09	12.97	13.31	13.08	13.40	12.88	13.16
Physical sciences	12.13	12.27	12.50	12.64	12.61	12.79	12.82	13.10	12.54	12.73
Engineering	12.06	11.97	12.10	12.10	12.38	12.41	12.59	12.77	12.30	12.34
EMP TOTAL	12.13	13.21	12.41	12.51	12.58	12.73	12.79	13.04	12.51	12.66
Biosciences	11.99	11.95	12.20	12.31	12.64	12.82	12.93	13.15	12.53	12.67
Agricultural sciences	11.40	10.59	11.69	11.01	11.92	11.24	12.20	11.65	12.87	11.20
Medical sciences	11.47	11.48	11.84	11.99	12.18	12.16	12.44	12.44	12.08	12.11
LIFE SCIENCE TOTAL	11.82	11.64	12.08	12.07	12.47	12.47	12.75	12.82	12.37	12.36
Psychology	11.69	11.81	12.08	12.28	12.58	12.81	12.75	13.02	12.41	12.63
Economics	11.89	11.66	12.33	12.16	12.80	12.96	13.00	13.28	12.59	12.63
Other social sciences	11.76	11.76	12.28	12.41	12.67	12.79	12.85	12.99	12.57	12.68
BEHAVIORAL SCIENCE TOTAL	11.75	11.77	12.20	12.30	12.64	12.82	12.82	13.04	12.50	12.65
HUMANITIES AND PROFESSIONS	12.01	12.13	12.27	12.39	12.62	12.83	12.91	13.19	12.56	12.75
EDUCATION	10.71	10.38	10.92	10.49	11.26	10.82	11.50	11.11	11.21	10.81
GRAND TOTAL										
Males	11.68	11.61	11.95	11.90	12.19	12.15	12.35	12.36	12.10	12.07
Females	12.01	12.17	12.30	12.47	12.69	12.90	12.90	13.11	12.63	12.83
Total	11.72	11.67	11.99	11.97	12.26	12.26	12.46	12.50	12.18	12.18

*Numbers small; means unreliable.

SOURCE: NRC, Commission on Human Resources.

FIELD DIFFERENCES

In the tables and graphs above, we have examined the data for all fields of PhD's combined--as if they were a homogeneous set. However, there are marked differences between the fields, as shown in Table 12 and in Figures 32 and 33. Table 12 provides data on the mean educational level of the fathers and mothers of the PhD's, by field, with summaries into general field groups. Figure 32 shows the data on fathers' education for a set of these fields; Figure 33 shows corresponding data with respect to the educational levels of the mothers. The general average of all fields is shown for reference, as a heavy line in each figure. These average lines are the same as those shown earlier in Figure 24, but here the chart has an expanded

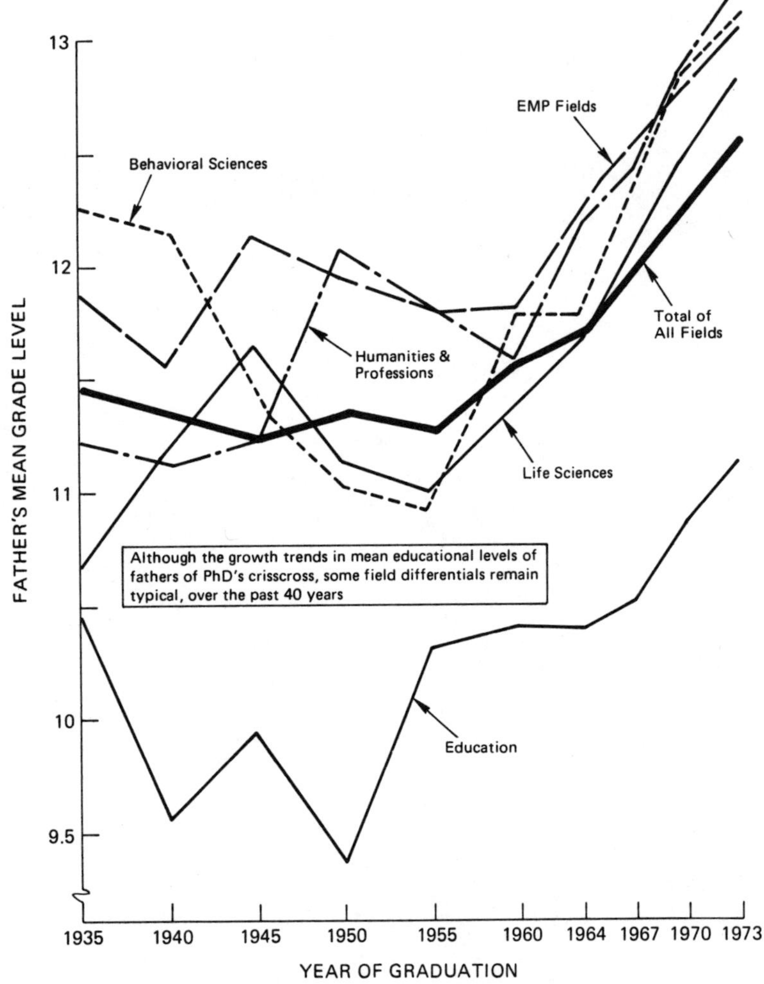

SOURCE: NRC, Commission on Human Resources

FIGURE 32 Field differences in educational level of fathers of PhD's.

scale, since only the parents of PhD's, and not the general population, are involved.

Although the field differences are pronounced, it is of interest to note that the lines for the several field groups show a marked convergence over time, with respect to both fathers' and mothers' education. This narrowing of differences between fields is true also of differences within fields.

An exception to the convergence of field lines is that for education. Both the fathers and the mothers of those who attain doctorates in education are at a much lower educational level than the parents of doctorate recipients in the sciences and humanities. Within the science fields, the parents of life scientists in the early cohorts were on the average less well educated than the parents of other scientists. This difference has greatly diminished in the more recent cohorts, probably reflecting the effects of urbanization. Many life scientists in the early years came from rural families: this differential is undoubtedly decreasing as a smaller and smaller proportion of the population lives on farms. The decreasing differential may also represent the effects of changes within the bioscience fields--the increased emphasis on analytic methods as compared with the earlier primarily descriptive science.

It is interesting to compare the differences

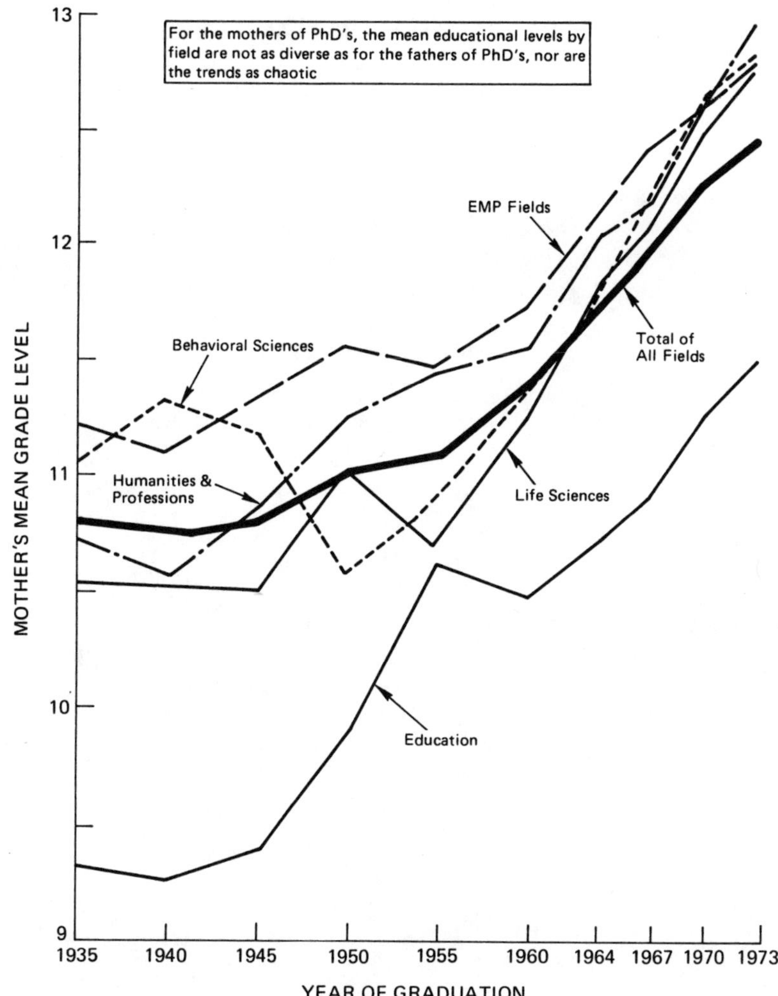

SOURCE: NRC, Commission on Human Resources

FIGURE 33 Field differences in educational level of mothers of PhD's.

shown here with the differences between fields shown by earlier studies[6,7] of the high school backgrounds of doctorate recipients. In those studies, data were secured from the high schools from which the PhD's graduated, with respect to their grades and their scores on standardized tests of academic aptitude. The general hierarchy of fields that was found there was similar to that shown in the current data. Another similarity to the present data concerned the ability levels of the male PhD's as compared to the females. Across all fields taken together, and within each of the fields separately, the women PhD's in the earlier studies showed higher academic ability than the male PhD's at the high school level, in terms of both grades and intelligence test scores. For more detail, see the reports referenced above. The general thrust of those findings is similar to the differences shown in Tables 10 and 11. More detailed data, showing mean educational levels for the fathers and mothers of men and women PhD's separately, are provided in Table 13, by field and cohort, with field summaries and summary data also for the entire 1963-1974 period.

[6]L. R. Harmon, High school backgrounds of science doctorates, *Science* 133(3454):679-788.
[7]L. R. Harmon, High school ability patterns, a backward look from the doctorate, in *Scientific Manpower Report 6* (Washington, D.C.: NAS/NRC, August 20, 1965).

TABLE 13
EDUCATIONAL LEVEL OF FATHERS AND MOTHERS OF NATIVE U.S. PhD's, BY SEX, FIELD, AND COHORT

Field and Sex of Doctorate Recipient	Cohort 1963-1965		Cohort 1966-1968		Cohort 1969-1971		Cohort 1972-1974		Total 1963-1974	
	Father	Mother	Father	Mother	Father	Mother	Father	Mother	Father	Mother
Mathematics										
Male	12.51	12.29	13.06	12.87	13.24	12.92	13.34	13.04	13.10	12.84
Female	13.42	12.88	13.68	13.47	14.26	13.66	13.98	13.41	13.94	13.43
Physical sciences										
Male	12.26	12.11	12.62	12.47	12.74	12.58	13.06	12.78	12.69	12.51
Female	12.79	12.53	13.31	13.20	13.75	13.29	13.72	13.36	13.51	13.19
Engineering										
Male	11.97	12.05	12.09	12.10	12.40	12.37	12.76	12.59	12.33	12.30
Female	--	--	--	--	13.11	12.72	13.99	12.87	13.94	13.01
TOTAL EMP										
Male	12.19	12.11	12.49	12.39	12.69	12.55	13.00	12.76	12.62	12.48
Female	12.99	12.67	13.44	13.27	13.86	13.37	13.81	13.35	13.64	13.25
Biosciences										
Male	11.83	11.91	12.18	12.11	12.64	12.53	12.99	12.81	12.50	12.42
Female	12.81	12.54	12.99	12.62	13.74	13.21	13.77	13.40	13.48	13.07
Agricultural sciences										
Male	10.58	11.39	11.00	11.69	11.22	11.90	11.58	12.15	11.17	11.84
Female	--	--	--	--	12.55	13.02	13.53	13.62	13.07	13.31
Medical sciences										
Male	11.36	11.38	11.94	11.75	12.10	12.10	12.35	12.48	12.02	12.02
Female	12.75	12.32	12.44	12.57	12.53	12.71	12.81	12.30	12.66	12.47
TOTAL LIFE SCIENCES										
Male	11.51	11.74	11.94	12.00	12.30	12.36	12.64	12.64	12.19	12.26
Female	12.79	12.52	12.94	12.62	13.60	13.15	13.64	13.27	13.39	13.02
Psychology										
Male	11.65	11.61	12.02	11.92	12.59	12.41	12.77	12.56	12.38	12.23
Female	12.51	12.06	13.27	12.70	13.49	13.11	13.64	13.21	13.41	12.96
Economics										
Male	11.59	11.86	12.11	12.32	12.89	12.77	13.16	12.90	12.54	12.53
Female	13.18	12.45	13.15	12.56	13.74	13.15	14.51	13.92	13.87	13.27
Other social sciences										
Male	11.71	11.72	12.31	12.23	12.66	12.58	12.78	12.69	12.52	12.45
Female	12.18	12.12	13.04	12.57	13.54	13.14	13.77	13.44	13.47	13.12
TOTAL BEHAVIORAL SCIENCES										
Male	11.65	11.70	12.14	12.11	12.67	12.54	12.83	12.67	12.46	12.37
Female	12.47	12.10	13.19	12.65	13.52	13.12	13.74	13.33	13.45	13.03
Foreign literature and languages										
Male	11.79	11.63	11.96	12.01	12.52	12.13	12.55	12.39	12.29	12.11
Female	12.39	12.03	13.13	12.75	14.04	13.31	14.43	13.65	13.89	13.24
Other humanities										
Male	12.05	11.98	12.27	12.18	12.63	12.52	12.95	12.75	12.55	12.43
Female	12.72	12.45	13.05	12.72	13.39	13.08	13.80	13.35	13.43	13.06
Professions										
Male	11.59	11.66	11.84	11.85	12.08	12.07	12.00	12.15	11.93	11.99
Female	12.01	11.85	11.76	12.03	12.18	12.12	12.54	12.76	12.22	12.31
Education										
Male	10.19	10.56	10.33	10.81	10.62	11.12	10.85	11.30	10.58	11.05
Female	11.21	11.36	11.17	11.38	11.62	11.82	11.87	12.06	11.61	11.80
TOTAL NONSCIENCES										
Male	11.06	11.22	11.22	11.44	11.45	11.68	11.67	11.87	11.42	11.62
Female	11.81	11.78	11.97	11.96	12.39	12.35	12.71	12.62	12.39	12.33
GRAND TOTAL										
Male	11.61	11.68	11.90	11.95	12.15	12.19	12.36	12.35	*12.07*	*12.10*
Female	12.17	12.01	12.47	12.30	12.90	12.69	13.11	12.90	*12.83*	*12.63*

SOURCE: NRC, Commission on Human Resources.

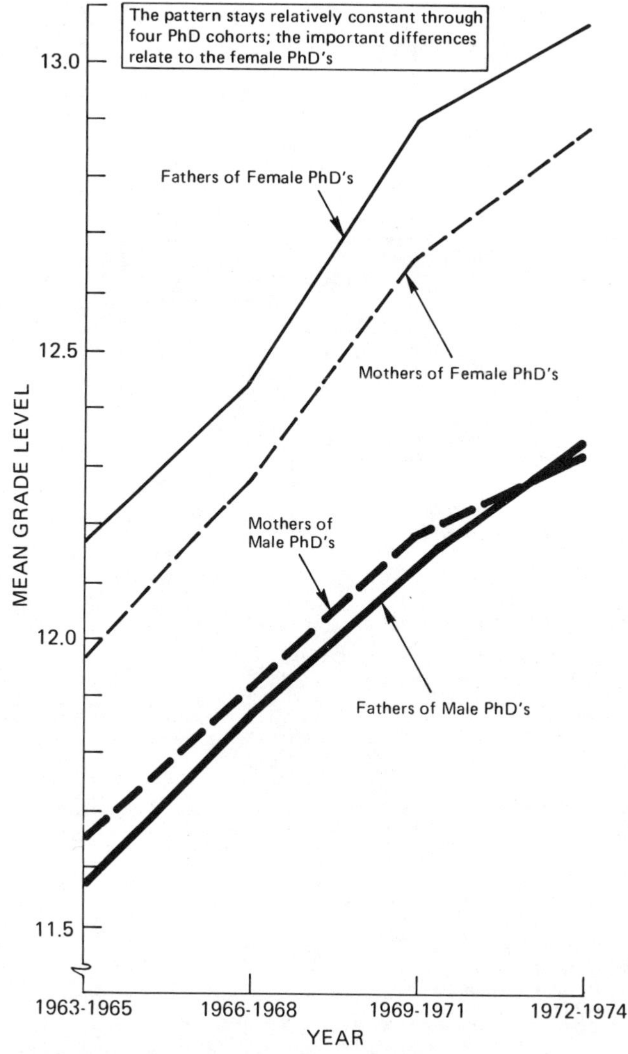

SOURCE: NRC, Commission on Human Resources

FIGURE 34 A tetrad pattern: Educational level of fathers and mothers of male and female PhD's (U.S. native PhD's only, 1963-1974).

TETRAD PATTERNS

Figure 34 illustrates the pattern of mean educational levels of parents of PhD's, that is, of fathers and mothers of male and female PhD's; hence the brief term "tetrad patterns." The overall pattern, for all fields combined, is rather constant across the four cohorts illustrated, but it is definitely *not* the characteristic pattern for each field separately. The bottom two lines of Table 13 provide the data for Figure 34. Examination of the other rows quickly shows the importance of controlling for field, because of field differences. If one considers the rank order of the means for the four parental groups as defining the tetrad patterns, there are three distinct patterns, as well as some that are mixed or less distinct. These patterns, shown in Table 13 for the several fields, are described below.

The most frequent tetrad pattern is that illustrated by the set of four means in the top left corner of Table 13--those for mathematics in the 1963-1965 cohort. Beginning with the highest educational level and proceeding downward, we have, in rank order: (1) fathers of women PhD's, (2) mothers of women, (3) fathers of men, and (4) mothers of men. This will be termed tetrad pattern A. Examination of the rest of the table shows that pattern A characterizes all of the EMP fields in all cohorts, psychology and "other humanities" in all cohorts, and the biosciences, the "other social sciences," and the behavioral science total in all but the earliest cohort. It is clearly the dominant tetrad pattern in Table 13.

A contrasting pattern, here termed pattern Z, characterizes the field of education in all cohorts and is found also in agricultural sciences, where data are available only for two cohorts, and in the professions for the 1972-1974 cohort and the total. In tetrad pattern Z, the order of educational levels is (1) mothers of women, (2) fathers of women, (3) mothers of men, and (4) fathers of men. A third pattern is found chiefly in the field group totals, and in the grand total, and is hence designated pattern T. It is the pattern illustrated in Figure 34: (1) fathers of women, (2) mothers of women, (3) mothers of men, and (4) fathers of men. It is clearly the resultant of the mixture of widely varying patterns, since it is seldom characteristic of individual fields, being found only in cohort 1963-1965 in the biosciences, medical sciences, "other social sciences," and in cohorts 1963-1965 and 1966-1968 in economics and the professions. As noted above, it does typify a number of the field group totals. Other patterns, perhaps random ones determined by the small numbers of cases, are found in the medical sciences. The patterns are intriguing and cause one to reflect on the pattern of parents' education as a determining factor in the eventual attainment of a doctorate degree--and perhaps as an influencing factor too on the field in which the degree is earned. The relation of pattern of grades in high school to later field of doctorate was also examined--and with interesting results--in the high school backgrounds study.[8]

[8]Ibid.

TABLE 14
PROPORTION OF POPULATION HOLDING ADVANCED DEGREES, BY COHORT AND SEX

Cohort Birth Years	From Census* Of	Sex	Population Age 25 And Up	Masters and Professional Degrees: Number	Masters and Professional Degrees: Percent	PhD Degrees Granted in the Decade: Corresponding PhD Years	Number† (from DRF)	Per Million Population Age 25 And Up
1886-1895‡	1940	M	7,962,019	107,941	1.36	1916-1925	6,527	820
		F	7,550,052	46,224	0.61		1,189	157
		Total	15,512,071	154,165	0.99		7,716	497
1896-1905	1940	M	9,164,794	156,938	1.71	1926-1935	17,922	1,956
		F	9,168,426	83,720	0.91		3,114	340
		Total	18,333,220	227,308	1.24		21,037	1,147
1906-1915	1940	M	10,520,974	216,152	2.05§	1936-1945	23,553	2,239
		F	10,818,052	86,040	0.80§		3,974	367
		Total	21,339,026	302,216	1.42§		27,503	1,289
1916-1925	1960	M	11,757,900	590,594	5.02	1946-1955	55,542	4,724
		F	12,336,433	224,778	1.83		6,304	420
		Total	24,094,333	815,372	3.38		61,874	2,568
1926-1935	1970	M	11,273,090	890,602	7.90	1956-1965	101,442	8,999
		F	11,865,637	345,966	2.91		12,269	1,034
		Total	23,138,727	1,236,060	5.34		113,713	4,983
1936-1945	1970	M	12,162,643	926,285	7.61§	1966-1975	243,324	20,005
		F	12,676,202	400,401	3.16§	(1975	46,586	3,675
		Total	24,838,845	1,326,686	5.34§	estimated)	289,873	11,670

*The 1950 census provided no data on postcollege degrees. Where a later census provided larger figures, for either population or degree holders, the later and larger figure was used.

†PhD data were from the DRF, supplemented by USOE data for 1916-1919 (sex breakout estimated) and an estimate for 1975, for which complete data were unavailable.

‡Data for birth cohorts prior to 1886 were deemed too inaccurate for use because of deaths by 1940, the earliest date for which postcollege degree data were available.

§The data for these years in the census indicated are probably underestimates by 50-75 percent for the graduate degrees other than the PhD. Differences of this magnitude appeared with successive censuses (1960 vs. 1970) for the same cohorts, where the cohorts were under age 35 at the time of the census.

SOURCE: NRC, Commission on Human Resources, based on Census, USOE, and Commission on Human Resources data.

POPULATION WITH ADVANCED DEGREES

Time and space does not permit following out the implications of these patterns of parental education to a definitive conclusion, but one additional set of data is available: The proportion of the population, by birth cohort, which holds advanced degrees, is shown in Table 14. This table combines data from two sources--the U.S. census and the DRF. The census provided data for numbers of persons with education beyond the baccalaureate, and the DRF provided data on the number of PhD's. By subtraction, the number of degrees at the master's and professional level was derived and expressed in terms of percentage of the cohort, by sex, holding such degrees. Because of the lesser frequency of doctorate degrees, the numbers were expressed in terms of PhD's per million in the population age 25 and up, also by birth cohort.

The data from the censuses are truncated in the case of the youngest cohort from each census, since many persons who would eventually attain postbaccalaureate degrees had not yet attained them. By comparison of cohorts that appeared in two censuses, one 10 years later than the other, it was possible to estimate roughly the extent of such truncation. The extent is noted in the footnotes to Table 14 and is to be taken as a rough indication only. It is worthy of consideration, however, that a great number of master's degrees are earned in the field of education, where it is typically a prolonged process, so that many such degrees are earned when the student is in middle and late 30's; the doctorate is earned more typically at about age 40.

Can the educational level of the parents be used to account for the proportion of any generation going on to graduate school and eventual doctorates? Probably much more information than is provided here is needed to answer the question. All the growth curves--master's/professional and doctorate, separately by sex and with the sexes combined--show a constant upward trend in the data shown here. There does not appear to be any intergenerational point at which one can say that aspiration to the doctorate is triggered, but rather there seems to be a regular tendency for a higher proportion of the children to seek further education as the educational level of the parents rises. As noted earlier, the time lag of the general educational level of the population

TABLE 15
PERCENTAGE OF NON-U.S. CITIZENS AMONG U.S. PhD's, 1960-1974, BY FIELD AND COHORT

	Men				Women				Both Sexes Combined			
	1960-1964	1965-1969	1970-1974	Total	1960-1964	1965-1969	1970-1974	Total	1960-1964	1965-1969	1970-1974	Total
Mathematics	16.3	15.0	20.4	17.8	15.0	21.1	21.0	20.2	16.2	15.3	20.4	17.9
Physics	14.3	15.3	21.2	17.6	29.6	29.3	40.8	35.9	14.5	15.6	21.9	18.1
Chemistry	12.1	13.1	17.0	14.4	21.6	24.9	29.4	26.5	12.6	13.9	18.2	15.3
Earth sciences	16.0	18.4	20.5	18.8	16.7	20.4	16.7	17.8	16.0	18.5	20.3	18.7
Engineering	21.4	23.7	34.0	28.0	58.1	43.8	45.8	47.1	21.6	23.8	34.1	28.1
EMP TOTAL	16.3	18.2	25.2	20.9	22.7	25.3	29.2	27.0	16.5	18.4	25.4	21.1
Agricultural sciences	25.9	32.0	36.0	32.6	67.7	61.4	51.6	55.5	26.5	32.5	36.6	33.1
Medical sciences	19.3	22.2	22.6	21.9	23.9	22.6	16.9	19.1	19.7	22.3	21.6	21.5
Biosciences	16.8	16.7	15.4	16.1	15.6	15.2	14.3	14.8	16.7	16.4	15.2	15.9
LIFE SCIENCE TOTAL	19.4	20.7	21.1	20.6	17.9	17.1	16.4	16.8	19.2	20.2	20.4	20.1
Psychology	4.7	4.5	5.2	4.8	6.2	6.2	6.2	6.2	4.9	4.9	5.4	5.2
Social sciences	18.6	19.9	19.4	19.4	12.3	11.3	11.8	11.7	18.1	19.0	18.2	18.4
BEHAVIORAL SCIENCE TOTAL	12.7	13.8	14.0	13.7	8.3	8.2	8.6	8.4	12.1	12.9	12.9	12.8
SCIENCE TOTAL	16.2	17.8	21.3	19.1	14.5	14.9	14.7	14.7	16.1	17.6	20.5	18.7
Humanities	5.8	8.0	8.9	8.0	6.7	8.4	9.1	8.6	6.0	8.1	8.9	8.1
Professions	12.3	14.0	15.6	14.5	15.1	15.6	10.1	12.6	12.7	14.2	14.9	14.3
Education	5.0	4.9	5.8	5.4	6.3	6.1	5.0	5.5	5.2	5.2	5.6	5.4
NONSCIENCE TOTAL	6.2	7.2	8.1	7.5	7.2	7.8	7.0	7.2	6.4	7.3	7.8	7.4
GRAND TOTAL	13.0	14.3	16.4	15.1	10.4	10.9	10.2	10.5	12.7	13.9	15.3	14.4

SOURCE: NRC, Commission on Human Resources.

behind that of the parents of the PhD's appears to be roughly on the order of one generation. So we are left with a question, rather than an answer: What is the influence of parents' education?

CITIZENSHIP

The proportion of PhD's who are of non-U.S. citizenship has been increasing. The data on citizenship of doctorate recipients is limited to the last 15 years or so, but longer-term data on foreign origins of PhD's is available from analysis of baccalaureate origins. These data show a long-term upward trend in doctorate recipients who earned their baccalaureate degrees abroad, varying between 7 percent and 9 percent until the 1960's, when the trend was sharply upward, moving up to about 15 percent in the most recent period. The proportion of foreign origin PhD's varies by field, the highest proportions being in the natural sciences and engineering. The behavioral sciences (except economics), the humanities, and education are much more intimately bound up with the culture than are the natural sciences; hence U.S. doctoral education in these fields is much less attractive to those of foreign origins than to those who have been immersed in the American culture from the beginning of their education.

In the period since 1960, the proportion of U.S. PhD's who are foreign citizens has continued to increase, as shown by Table 15 and Figure 35. In Figure 35, the fields have been separated into two groups to simplify the graphic presentation. On the left-hand portion of the page, the EMP fields are depicted; all the other fields are on the right. It is striking that the two fields attracting the largest proportions of non-U.S. PhD's are engineering and agricultural sciences--two applied fields of great economic impact. The third field in terms of proportion of non-U.S. citizens is the group included in medical sciences--also important in terms of the health of the populations to which the results of these sciences are applied.

Within the physical science group, the differences in proportion of non-U.S. citizenship are not large; the lines cross and recross and vary from 12-16 percent in the 1960-1964 period to 18-22 percent in 1970-1974, a distinct increase that applies to all fields, although the growth rates are not all the same. In the remaining fields, the changes have not been large, and in some fields--for example, the biosciences--there has been a decline of a few points over the 15-year period. In the professions (a field in which many are employed in applications rather than basic research) and in the humanities there has been a small increase. In the social sciences, psychology, and education there has been no significant time trend. In the latter two fields the proportion of foreign citizens is only about 5-6 percent; in the humanities it is slightly higher, moving up from 6 percent to 9 percent over the time period shown.

There are sex differences in the proportion, by field, in citizenship. These are shown in Table 15, which also shows the time trends, by field and field group, and 15-year totals. The really striking percentages among the women PhD's might be dismissed as due to the unreliability of small numbers, were it not for the consistency of the time trends and the fact that the total

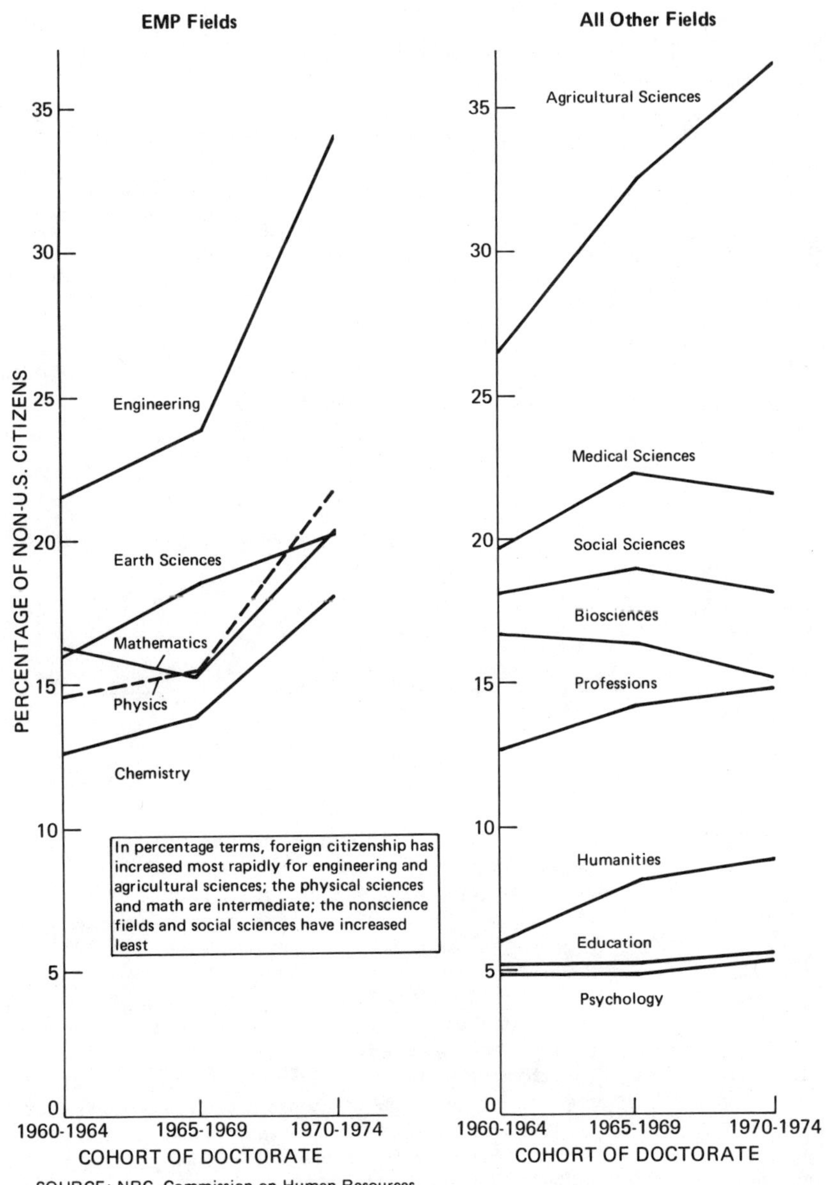

FIGURE 35 Percentages of non-U.S. citizen PhD's by field.

across all time periods results in substantial numbers, even in the fields of engineering and agricultural sciences. In these two fields, the very high proportion of non-U.S. citizens may best be thought of in terms of the very small proportion of U.S. women entering these fields, rather than in terms of high proportions among foreign citizens. The same is true, although to a lesser extent, in the other fields of physical science and medical sciences. Another sex difference is the fact that, except for physics and chemistry, the proportion of foreign citizens among the women has increased slightly, or not at all, and in some cases has decreased. This is more likely due to the upswing in the proportion of women among U.S. PhD's than to any great change in the trends of foreign citizens entering the United States, since the upward trend in proportion of non-U.S. citizens has continued in the case of men.

TABLE 16
RACIAL/ETHNIC GROUPS IN THE DRF, 1973-1975, BY FIELD OF PhD, BOTH SEXES AND ALL CITIZEN CATEGORIES COMBINED

PhD Field		White	Black	American Indian	Spanish American, Mexican American, Chicano	Puerto Rican	Oriental	Other	Unknown	Total
MATHEMATICS	N	2128	38	9	21	4	301	6	467	2974
	H	71.6	1.3	.3	.7	.1	10.1	.2	15.7	100.0
	V	3.5	1.7	2.5	3.1	3.2	6.1	8.1	3.4	3.6
PHYSICS	N	2402	21	10	23	3	404	7	647	3517
	H	68.3	.6	.3	.7	.1	11.5	.2	18.4	100.0
	V	4.0	.9	2.8	3.4	2.4	8.2	9.5	4.7	4.3
CHEMISTRY	N	3183	61	9	28	4	541	4	711	4541
	H	70.1	1.3	.2	.6	.1	11.9	.1	15.7	100.0
	V	5.3	2.7	2.5	4.1	3.2	11.0	5.4	5.2	5.5
EARTH SCIS	N	1039	7	9	10	3	91	2	255	1416
	H	73.4	.5	.6	.7	.2	6.4	.1	18.0	100.0
	V	1.7	.3	2.5	1.5	2.4	1.9	2.7	1.8	1.7
ENGINEERING	N	4609	70	18	48	11	1328	21	1626	7731
	H	59.6	.9	.2	.6	.1	17.2	.3	21.0	100.0
	V	7.7	3.1	5.0	7.0	8.9	27.1	28.4	11.8	9.4
EMP TOTAL	N	13361	197	55	130	25	2665	40	3706	20179
	H	66.2	1.0	.3	.6	.1	13.2	.2	18.4	100.0
	V	22.2	8.6	15.3	19.0	20.2	54.3	54.1	26.9	24.5
AGRIC SCIS	N	1690	65	7	46	3	338	6	452	2607
	H	64.8	2.5	.3	1.8	.1	13.0	.2	17.3	100.0
	V	2.8	2.9	1.9	6.7	2.4	6.9	8.1	3.3	3.2
MEDICAL SCIS	N	971	30	4	13	3	130	3	291	1445
	H	67.2	2.1	.3	.9	.2	9.0	.2	20.1	100.0
	V	1.6	1.3	1.1	1.9	2.4	2.6	4.1	2.1	1.8
BIOSCIENCES	N	6087	149	35	78	12	600	3	1426	8390
	H	72.6	1.8	.4	.9	.1	7.2		17.0	100.0
	V	10.1	6.5	9.7	11.4	9.7	12.2	4.1	10.3	10.2
LIFE SCI TOT	N	8748	244	46	137	18	1068	12	2169	12442
	H	70.3	2.0	.4	1.1	.1	8.6	.1	17.4	100.0
	V	14.6	10.7	12.8	20.0	14.5	21.8	16.2	15.7	15.1
PSYCHOLOGY	N	5195	119	29	39	12	81	2	964	6441
	H	80.7	1.8	.5	.6	.2	1.3		15.0	100.0
	V	8.6	5.2	8.1	5.7	9.7	1.7	2.7	7.0	7.8
SOCIAL SCIS	N	6487	228	34	61	15	401	6	1576	8808
	H	73.6	2.6	.4	.7	.2	4.6	.1	17.9	100.0
	V	10.8	10.0	9.5	8.9	12.1	8.2	8.1	11.4	10.7
BEHAV SC TOT	N	11682	347	63	100	27	482	8	2540	15249
	H	76.6	2.3	.4	.7	.2	3.2	.1	16.7	100.0
	V	19.4	15.2	17.5	14.6	21.8	9.8	10.8	18.4	18.5
HUMANITIES	N	10053	220	64	154	24	250	5	1978	12748
	H	78.9	1.7	.5	1.2	.2	2.0		15.5	100.0
	V	16.7	9.7	17.8	22.4	19.4	5.1	6.8	14.3	15.5
PROFESSIONS	N	2693	79	8	14	2	125	2	675	3598
	H	74.8	2.2	.2	.4	.1	3.5	.1	18.8	100.0
	V	4.5	3.5	2.2	2.0	1.6	2.5	2.7	4.9	4.4
EDUCATION	N	13536	1192	123	151	28	318	7	2730	18085
	H	74.8	6.6	.7	.8	.2	1.8		15.1	100.0
	V	22.5	52.3	34.3	22.0	22.6	6.5	9.5	19.8	22.0
NON-SCI TOT	N	26282	1491	195	319	54	693	14	5383	34431
	H	76.3	4.3	.6	.9	.2	2.0		15.6	100.0
	V	43.8	65.4	54.3	46.5	43.5	14.1	18.9	39.0	41.8
GRAND TOTAL	N	60073	2279	359	686	124	4908	74	13798	82301
	H	73.0	2.8	.4	.8	.2	6.0	.1	16.8	100.0
	V	100.0	100.0	100.0	100.0	100.0	100.0	100.0	100.0	100.0

*N = number of persons; H = horizontal percent; V = vertical percent.

SOURCE: NRC, Commission on Human Resources.

RACIAL/ETHNIC GROUPS[9]

Data regarding minority groups, particularly racial groups, are relatively scarce because for many years the collection of these data was forbidden to public institutions or projects funded by the federal government. However, in recent years this situation has been reversed, and data are now routinely collected in the Doctorate Survey regarding racial/ethnic identification. Three books have been published by the NAS[10,11] and the National Board on Graduate Education,[12] which draw heavily on the DRF and the Comprehensive Roster of Doctoral Scientists and Engineers. The present report will therefore be relatively brief and limited to data collected in the DRF for FY 1973 and 1974 and the first half of FY 1975--the only years for which any racial/ethnic data were available in the DRF in time for this analysis. The data for both FY 1973 and 1975 are incomplete; the combined data for the entire period will be presented without chronological breakdown. Because these data include non-U.S. citizens, they are not suitable as a base for affirmative action programs. Readers are referred to the other publications listed in the footnotes for more detailed tables.

Table 16 provides the essential information by racial/ethnic groups and field for the 1973-1975 period, for both sexes and all citizenship categories combined. Table 17 provides data in the same format by sex. We will examine the field differences first for the combined sex group and then for each sex. One of the factors to be remembered in all of these data is that there is a correlation between racial/ethnic identification and foreign citizenship: the foreign citizen PhD's include a lower percentage of whites and higher percentages of the minority groups, with the exception of American Indians. This affects particularly those applied science fields of engineering, agricultural sciences, and medical sciences, which are relatively more important to the developing countries; these countries also have a smaller percentage of whites than does the United States.

In Tables 16 and 17 the racial/ethnic groups of the Doctorate Survey are arranged in columns, and the fields of doctorate in rows. In Table 17, the data for men are presented in the left half of the table, and the data for women in the right half. In both tables, both horizontal and vertical percentages are given. Horizontal percentages show the percentage of each racial/ethnic group as a proportion of the total for that field; the vertical percentages show the field mix for each racial/ethnic group. Both sets of percentages are important for an understanding of the data. Scanning first down the column for whites, it is apparent that this group largely determines the field mix percentages for the total of all groups, since whites constitute three-fourths of the total. The only field group that is significantly lower for whites than for the total is engineering; the reason for this lower percentage is the heavy predominance of engineering as a field of choice for Orientals.

The second column is for blacks. Here we note a lower-than-average percentage in all the natural science fields, particularly the EMP fields. The reasons for the lower percentages in so many fields is apparent in the final field--education. Here we find over half of the blacks as compared with 22 percent for all racial/ethnic groups combined; this concentration

[9]The categories of racial/ethnic identification used here are those adopted by the federal government and control all data collection funded by federal sources.

[10]Commission on Human Resources, *Minority Groups among United States Doctorate Level Scientists, Engineers, and Scholars, 1973* (Washington, D.C.: NAS, December 1974).

[11]Dorothy M. Gilford and Joan Snyder, *Women and Minority PhD's in the 1970's: A Data Book* (Washington, D.C.: NAS/NRC, November 1977).

[12]National Board on Graduate Education, *Minority Group Participation in Graduate Education* (Washington, D.C.: June 1976).

TABLE 17
RACIAL/ETHNIC GROUPS IN THE DRF, 1973-1975, BY FIELD OF DOCTORATE AND SEX, U.S. AND FOREIGN CITIZENS COMBINED

PhD Field		Men									Women								
		White	Black	American Indian	Spanish American, Mexican American, Chicano	Puerto Rican	Oriental	Other	Unknown	Total	White	Black	American Indian	Spanish American, Mexican American, Chicano	Puerto Rican	Oriental	Other	Unknown	Total
MATHEMATICS	N	1916	33	9	21	4	263	4	436	2686	212	5				38	2	31	288
	H	71.3	1.2	.3	.8	.1	9.8	.1	16.2	100.0	73.6	1.7				13.2	.7	10.8	100.0
	V	4.0	2.0	3.2	3.6	4.3	6.2	5.9	3.8	4.0	1.8	.8				5.9	33.3	1.3	1.8
PHYSICS	N	2317	20	9	22	3	367	7	619	3364	85	1	1	1		37		28	153
	H	68.9	.6	.3	.7	.1	10.9	.2	18.4	100.0	55.6	.7	.7	.7		24.2		18.3	100.0
	V	4.8	1.2	3.2	3.8	3.2	8.6	10.3	5.4	5.1	.7	.2	1.3	.9		5.8		1.2	1.0
CHEMISTRY	N	2890	59	8	28	4	451	4	648	4092	293	2	1			90		63	449
	H	70.6	1.4	.2	.7	.1	11.0	.1	15.8	100.0	65.3	.4	.2			20.0		14.0	100.0
	V	6.0	3.5	2.8	4.8	4.3	10.6	5.9	5.6	6.2	2.4	.3	1.3			14.1		2.7	2.8
EARTH SCIS	N	987	7	8	10	3	89	2	245	1351	52		1			2		10	65
	H	73.1	.5	.6	.7	.2	6.6	.1	18.1	100.0	80.0		1.5			3.1		15.4	100.0
	V	2.1	.4	2.8	1.7	3.2	2.1	2.9	2.1	2.0	.4		1.3			.3		.4	.4
ENGINEERING	N	4545	70	18	48	11	1314	21	1607	7634	64					14		19	97
	H	59.5	.9	.2	.6	.1	17.2	.3	21.1	100.0	66.0					14.4		19.6	100.0
	V	9.5	4.1	6.4	8.3	11.7	30.8	30.9	14.0	11.5	.5					2.2		.8	.6
EMP TOTAL	N	12655	189	52	129	25	2484	38	3555	19127	706	8	3	1		181	2	151	1052
	H	66.2	1.0	.3	.7	.1	13.0	.2	18.6	100.0	67.1	.8	.3	.1		17.2	.2	14.4	100.0
	V	26.3	11.2	18.4	22.2	26.6	58.2	55.9	31.0	28.8	5.9	1.4	3.9	.9		28.3	33.3	6.5	6.7
AGRIC SCIS	N	1627	64	7	46	3	308	6	435	2496	63	1				30		17	111
	H	65.2	2.6	.3	1.8	.1	12.3	.2	17.4	100.0	56.8	.9				27.0		15.3	100.0
	V	3.4	3.8	2.5	7.9	3.2	7.2	8.8	3.8	3.8	.5	.2				4.7		.7	.7
MEDICAL SCIS	N	763	27	4	12	2	104	3	245	1160	208	3		1	1	26		46	285
	H	65.8	2.3	.3	1.0	.2	9.0	.3	21.1	100.0	73.0	1.1		.4	.4	9.1		16.1	100.0
	V	1.6	1.6	1.4	2.1	2.1	2.4	4.4	2.1	1.7	1.7	.5		.9	3.3	4.1		2.0	1.8
BIOSCIENCES	N	4777	107	26	69	10	458	3	1164	6614	1310	42	9	9	2	142		262	1776
	H	72.2	1.6	.4	1.0	.2	6.9		17.6	100.0	73.8	2.4	.5	.5	.1	8.0		14.8	100.0
	V	9.9	6.3	9.2	11.9	10.6	10.7	4.4	10.1	9.9	10.9	7.1	11.7	8.5	6.7	22.2		11.3	11.2
LIFE SCI TOT	N	7167	198	37	127	15	870	12	1844	10270	1581	46	9	10	3	198		325	2172
	H	69.8	1.9	.4	1.2	.1	8.5	.1	18.0	100.0	72.8	2.1	.4	.5	.1	9.1		15.0	100.0
	V	14.9	11.7	13.1	21.9	16.0	20.4	17.6	16.1	15.4	13.1	7.8	11.7	9.4	10.0	30.9		14.0	13.7
PSYCHOLOGY	N	3647	82	23	30	10	49	1	668	4510	1548	37	6	9	2	32	1	296	1931
	H	80.9	1.8	.5	.7	.2	1.1		14.8	100.0	80.2	1.9	.3	.5	.1	1.7	.1	15.3	100.0
	V	7.6	4.9	8.2	5.2	10.6	1.1	1.5	5.8	6.8	12.9	6.3	7.8	8.5	6.7	5.0	16.7	12.8	12.2
SOCIAL SCIS	N	5280	192	29	52	8	350	5	1376	7292	1207	36	5	9	7	51	1	200	1516
	H	72.4	2.6	.4	.7	.1	4.8	.1	18.9	100.0	79.6	2.4	.3	.6	.5	3.4	.1	13.2	100.0
	V	11.0	11.4	10.3	9.0	8.5	8.2	7.4	12.0	11.0	10.0	6.1	6.5	8.5	23.3	8.0	16.7	8.6	9.6
BEHAV SC TOT	N	8927	274	52	82	18	399	6	2044	11802	2755	73	11	18	9	83	2	496	3447
	H	75.6	2.3	.4	.7	.2	3.4	.1	17.3	100.0	79.9	2.1	.3	.5	.3	2.4	.1	14.4	100.0
	V	18.6	16.2	18.4	14.1	19.1	9.3	8.8	17.8	17.7	22.9	12.3	14.3	17.0	30.0	13.0	33.3	21.4	21.8
HUMANITIES	N	6988	153	46	107	16	186	4	1406	8906	3065	67	18	47	8	64	1	572	3842
	H	78.5	1.7	.5	1.2	.2	2.1		15.8	100.0	79.8	1.7	.5	1.2	.2	1.7		14.9	100.0
	V	14.5	9.1	16.3	18.4	17.0	4.4	5.9	12.2	13.4	25.5	11.3	23.4	44.3	26.7	10.0	16.7	24.7	24.3
PROFESSIONS	N	2331	55	7	13	2	109	2	589	3108	362	24	1	1		16		86	490
	H	75.0	1.8	.2	.4	.1	3.5	.1	19.0	100.0	73.9	4.9	.2	.2		3.3		17.6	100.0
	V	4.9	3.3	2.5	2.2	2.1	2.6	2.9	5.1	4.7	3.0	4.1	1.3	.9		2.5		3.7	3.1
EDUCATION	N	9962	818	88	122	18	220	6	2044	13278	3574	374	35	29	10	98	1	686	4807
	H	75.0	6.2	.7	.9	.1	1.7		15.4	100.0	74.3	7.8	.7	.6	.2	2.0		14.3	100.0
	V	20.7	48.5	31.2	21.0	19.1	5.2	8.8	17.8	20.0	29.7	63.2	45.5	27.4	33.3	15.3	16.7	29.6	30.4
NON-SCI TOT	N	19281	1026	141	242	36	515	12	4039	25292	7001	465	54	77	18	178	2	1344	9139
	H	76.2	4.1	.6	1.0	.1	2.0		16.0	100.0	76.6	5.1	.6	.8	.2	1.9		14.7	100.0
	V	40.1	60.8	50.0	41.7	38.3	12.1	17.6	35.2	38.0	58.1	78.5	70.1	72.6	60.0	27.8	33.3	58.0	57.8
GRAND TOTAL	N	48030	1687	282	580	94	4268	68	11482	66491	12043	592	77	106	30	640	6	2316	15810
	H	72.2	2.5	.4	.9	.1	6.4	.1	17.3	100.0	76.2	3.7	.5	.7	.2	4.0		14.6	100.0
	V	100.0	100.0	100.0	100.0	100.0	100.0	100.0	100.0	100.0	100.0	100.0	100.0	100.0	100.0	100.0	100.0	100.0	100.0

*N = number of individuals; H = horizontal percentage; V = vertical percentage.

SOURCE: NRC, Commission on Human Resources.

forces lower percentages elsewhere. The American Indian column shows percentages that seldom deviate far from the average of all groups, considering the unreliability of percentages based on small numbers. The American Indians are low in the EMP fields, except the earth sciences, and high on education, although not to the extent that characterizes the black population. The fourth column combines Spanish Americans, Mexican Americans, and Chicanos, and the fifth column the other Spanish-speaking group, Puerto Ricans. The data for these two columns are similar, except that the former group has a higher percentage in the agricultural sciences. Again, the unreliability due to small numbers must be noted.

Orientals include those of both east Asian and south Asian origins--a limitation of the data that complicates interpretation. As noted earlier, this group is very high in engineering and high also in the other EMP fields and, to a lesser extent, in the life science fields. The natural sciences combined claim over three-fourths of the Oriental group; the remaining fields are correspondingly depleted in terms of percent as compared with the total of all racial/ethnic groups, particularly in psychology and education--two fields in which the cultural component is very high. The column labeled "other" usually does not deviate very far from the total of all groups, but is a bit high in mathematics, physics, engineering, agricultural sciences, and medical sciences and relatively low in the fields most closely tied to the American culture. This seems to be a function of the foreign origins of a substantial portion of this group--many of whom could not readily fit their racial/ethnic identification into the DRF categories. Finally, the unknown group has field percentages that never deviate importantly from the total of all groups--an indication that there is no substantial bias hiding in the "unknown" category.

SEX DIFFERENCES

Table 17 contains the same data as does Table 16 but they are separated into tables for men and for women. Here we note that the pattern of sex differences is, in the main, that which is typical of the general PhD population--there are relatively fewer women in the sciences, particularly the EMP fields and the professions, while there are relatively more women in education and psychology. This pattern applies in general across all the racial/ethnic groups; the small numbers make separate consideration of particular groups hazardous, but the data are presented for whatever uses readers may wish to make of them.

OF AGE AND THE DOCTORATE

There is an old expression among those who have studied the rate of academic progress in elementary schools: "the lockstep of the grades." As one consequence, students graduate from high school at age 18, with only a small spread on either side of this figure. If they then go on to college, as a high proportion do, they typically graduate in 4 years, again with a small spread on either side of a median age of 22 years. But, for a variety of reasons, the spread is greater than at high school graduation; the standard deviation, for those who go on to the doctorate at least, is typically 2 or 3 years. The attainment of the doctorate is another matter entirely; the lockstep is thoroughly broken, and the distribution of ages is very wide--the standard deviation is 7 years. The "4-year plan" for the doctorate actually holds for only a small percentage of students. The typical age is a function of field of PhD and sex. Women, who are younger at the baccalaureate, are typically older at the doctorate, for a variety of reasons.

The typical age at which one receives the PhD degree is about 30 in the science fields and mid-to-late 30's in the nonscience fields. The sex differences occur mostly in the behavioral science and nonscience fields. The field differences are vast, ranging from a mean age of 29 in chemistry to around 40 in education. These age differences reflect primarily the typical educational practices in the different fields, but to some extent they may also reflect student selection or self-selection differences. This is indicated by the fact that there are systematic age differences at the baccalaureate degree level, paralleling those at the PhD. Perhaps even more interesting than the mean differences by sex and field are the differences in the distributions about those means. The distributions are highly skewed--particularly at the doctorate level but also at the baccalaureate. At the younger end of the distribution there is not much difference by sex or field. But at the older end of the distribution the differences are great--by both sex and field.

Figure 36 presents, in diagrammatic fashion, the distributions of age at baccalaureate and doctorate for the two sexes separately for several field groups. (Table 18 shows data for more detailed field breakouts.) The fields shown in Figure 36 are those in which strong differences are evident; where the differences are smaller, the fields are grouped. The EMP fields--engineering, mathematics, and the physical sciences--do not vary greatly in age statistics and have been grouped as shown on the top lines of Figure 36. Here we note that there is a sex difference. The women, shown with the dotted line with an arrow marking the mean age, are younger than are the men on the average. At the baccalaureate level they are younger at all percentile points in the age distribution, but at the doctorate level the 90th percentile for women is higher than that for men. In a similar manner, the pattern of all field groups and both sexes may be examined. As one does so, the field differences, the sex differences, and the pattern of mean time lapse between baccalaureate and doctorate become apparent.

The second pair of lines in Figure 36 shows the data for the life sciences, and again, as in the EMP fields, the women are younger than the men at the baccalaureate level, except at the 90th percentile. At the doctorate level, on the other hand, the age distributions are higher for women than for men. Something is intervening to lengthen the time it takes women to complete graduate school. In the behavioral sciences, the pattern of the life sciences is repeated but with greater emphasis. In the humanities fields, this pattern is further developed, and it becomes extreme in the professional fields and in education. Next to the bottom, these latter three fields are grouped into a nonscience total. Finally, the total of all fields, sciences and nonsciences combined, is shown with broader lines to set it off from the separate field groups. The marked sex difference evident in the total is due in large part to the higher proportion of women in those

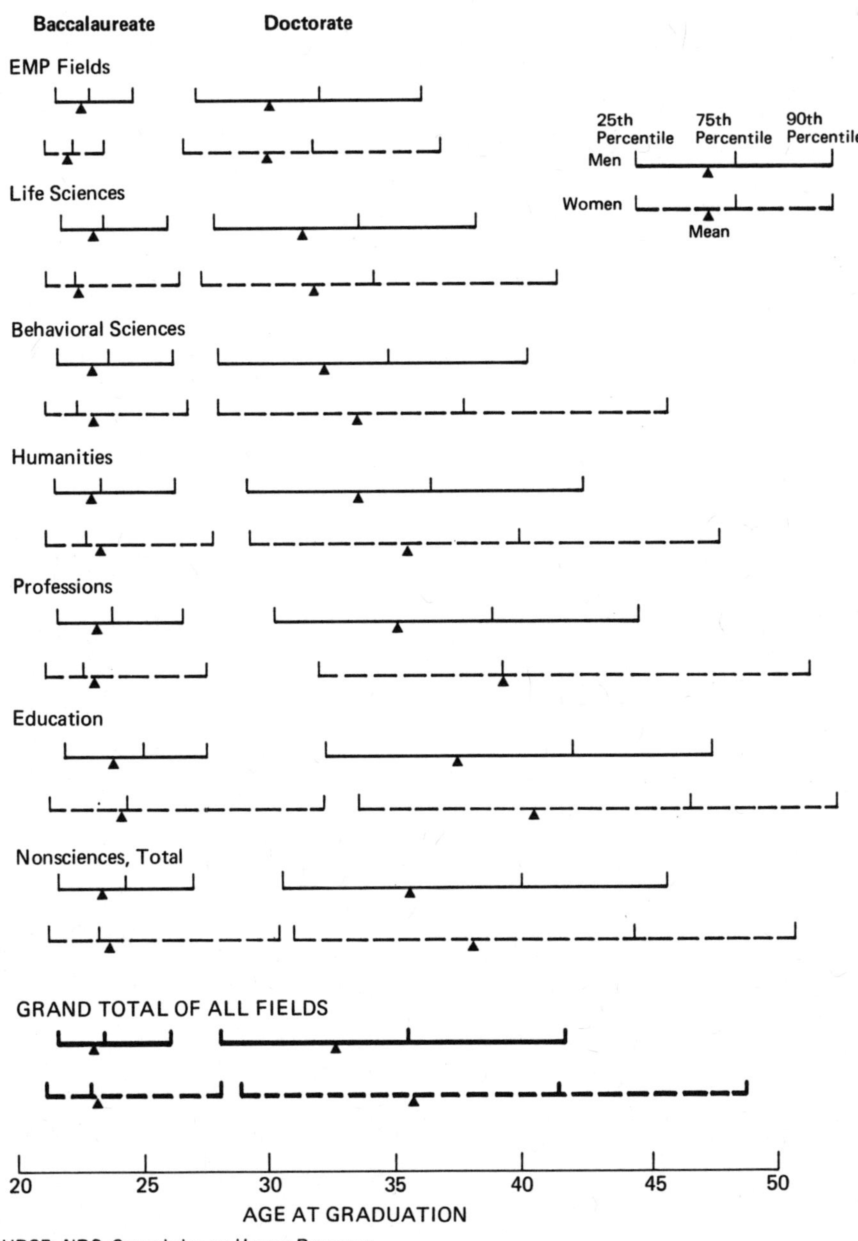

SOURCE: NRC, Commission on Human Resources

FIGURE 36 Age distributions at baccalaureate and doctorate.

fields in which the sex differences are most pronounced.

More detail is shown in Table 18. The five fields of the EMP group are given separately, as well as in combination. The first pair of columns (for men and women separately) gives mean age; the standard deviation is given in the second pair of columns, and the 25th, 50th, 75th, and 90th percentiles in the remaining columns. Age at baccalaureate is shown in the top half of the table, and age at doctorate in the bottom half.

One notes immediately that the standard deviations of age are greater for women than for men--with only two exceptions at the doctorate level and none at the baccalaureate level. This is to be expected if there are more factors that slow the rate of progress of women; the size of the standard deviation is largely determined by the numbers in the older age ranges. We have seen earlier that women come from better-educated families on the average, and previous studies have shown that they have higher average academic aptitude (those who attain the doctorate--not women in general). It is no surprise, therefore, that they complete undergraduate work at a younger age. But the greater spread about the mean age, and the skewness of the distributions, seem to indicate that for a significant portion of women there are forces at work--marriage,

TABLE 18
AGE AT BACCALAUREATE AND DOCTORATE, BY SEX AND FIELD OF PhD, 1960-1974

	Age at Baccalaureate											
	Mean		Std. Dev.		25th Percentile		50th Percentile		75th Percentile		90th Percentile	
Field of PhD	Men	Women	Men	Women	Men	Women	Men	Women	Men	Women	Men	Women
Mathematics	22.2	22.0	1.88	2.16	21.4	20.9	22.0	21.7	22.6	22.4	24.1	23.7
Physics	22.3	21.8	1.76	1.87	21.5	20.9	22.0	21.7	22.6	22.3	24.1	23.3
Chemistry	22.4	22.2	1.71	2.01	21.6	21.3	22.1	21.9	22.8	22.5	24.2	23.6
Earth science	22.9	22.6	2.21	2.54	21.7	21.6	22.3	22.1	23.5	22.7	25.7	24.0
Engineering	22.7	22.3	1.95	1.96	21.7	21.3	22.3	22.1	23.3	23.0	24.9	24.3
EMP TOTAL	22.5	22.1	1.88	2.06	21.6	21.2	22.2	21.9	23.0	22.4	24.5	23.6
Agricultural science	23.4	22.4	2.63	2.75	21.9	21.3	22.6	22.0	24.4	22.8	26.6	24.3
Medical science	23.0	23.9	2.34	4.58	21.7	21.6	22.5	22.3	23.7	23.8	25.8	30.0
Biosciences	22.9	22.4	2.31	2.75	21.7	21.3	22.3	21.9	23.4	22.4	25.7	24.1
LIFE SCIENCE TOTAL	23.1	22.6	2.41	3.02	21.8	21.3	22.4	21.9	23.6	22.5	26.0	25.5
Psychology	23.1	23.0	2.70	4.24	21.7	21.2	22.3	21.9	23.5	22.6	26.1	25.6
Social science	23.3	23.2	3.04	4.43	21.7	21.2	22.3	21.9	23.9	22.7	26.5	27.2
BEHAVIORAL SCIENCE TOTAL	23.2	23.1	2.91	4.32	21.7	21.2	22.3	21.9	23.8	22.6	26.3	26.9
SCIENCE TOTAL	22.8	22.7	2.33	3.59	22.2	21.7	22.3	22.4	23.2	23.0	25.9	25.7
Humanities	23.1	23.3	3.01	4.69	21.7	21.2	22.3	21.9	23.5	22.8	26.2	28.0
Professions	23.3	23.1	3.22	4.24	21.7	21.1	22.4	21.9	23.9	22.8	26.6	27.6
Education	24.0	24.3	3.40	5.49	22.0	21.3	22.9	22.1	25.1	24.5	27.6	32.2
NONSCIENCE TOTAL	23.6	23.8	3.27	5.12	21.8	21.3	22.5	22.0	24.4	23.4	27.0	30.6
GRAND TOTAL	23.1	23.3	2.72	4.56	21.7	21.2	22.3	22.0	23.6	23.0	26.0	28.2
	Age at Doctorate											
	Mean		Std. Dev.		25th Percentile		50th Percentile		75th Percentile		90th Percentile	
	Men	Women	Men	Women	Men	Women	Men	Women	Men	Women	Men	Women
Mathematics	29.7	30.6	4.37	5.64	26.6	26.7	28.6	28.9	31.5	32.9	35.2	38.5
Physics	29.8	29.7	3.87	3.85	27.2	26.9	28.9	28.8	31.3	31.2	34.6	34.6
Chemistry	29.1	29.7	3.86	4.78	26.5	26.6	28.1	28.3	30.6	31.1	33.8	36.0
Earth science	31.8	32.3	5.09	6.02	28.2	28.0	30.6	30.4	34.1	36.0	38.6	41.8
Engineering	31.1	30.8	4.89	4.73	27.7	27.7	29.9	29.4	33.2	32.8	37.5	37.0
EMP TOTAL	30.2	30.1	4.52	5.00	27.1	26.7	29.1	28.7	32.1	31.7	36.1	37.0
Agricultural science	32.5	32.1	5.34	5.85	28.6	28.2	31.2	30.7	35.1	34.1	39.8	39.1
Medical science	32.5	35.4	5.44	8.12	28.6	28.7	31.3	32.8	35.2	41.1	39.8	47.8
Biosciences	31.0	31.3	4.71	6.07	27.7	27.1	29.8	29.3	33.0	33.5	37.1	40.1
LIFE SCIENCE TOTAL	31.5	31.8	5.00	6.42	27.9	27.3	30.3	29.5	33.7	34.3	38.2	41.5
Psychology	31.1	33.1	5.33	7.53	27.3	27.5	29.5	30.5	33.2	37.1	38.2	44.7
Social science	33.0	34.6	6.14	7.74	28.6	28.7	31.5	32.2	35.8	38.9	41.8	46.4
BEHAVIORAL SCIENCE TOTAL	32.3	33.7	5.92	7.65	28.0	28.0	30.7	31.2	34.9	37.9	40.5	45.6
SCIENCE TOTAL	31.0	32.4	5.09	6.96	26.7	27.9	30.2	30.5	33.6	35.8	38.2	39.0
Humanities	33.6	35.5	6.26	8.11	29.1	29.3	32.1	33.1	36.6	40.0	42.4	47.6
Professions	35.2	39.3	6.82	8.58	30.1	32.1	33.5	38.8	38.9	45.4	44.6	51.2
Education	37.6	40.5	6.93	8.50	32.2	33.6	36.6	39.9	42.1	46.6	47.4	52.3
NONSCIENCE TOTAL	35.8	38.3	6.93	8.69	30.5	31.0	34.5	36.9	39.8	44.3	45.6	50.8
GRAND TOTAL	32.7	35.8	6.22	8.51	28.1	28.9	31.0	33.4	35.6	41.4	41.7	48.5

SOURCE: NRC, Commission on Human Resources.

children, economics, and perhaps others--that prevent the rate of academic progress typical of their male counterparts.

The effect of cases at the extremes of the distributions, particularly at the range beyond the 90th percentile, account for the high standard deviations in the several field and sex groups where they have been noted. To get a better picture of the numbers who graduate in the upper age ranges, at both degree levels, we have the data of Table 19. In the EMP fields, few persons of either sex are over 30 at the time the baccalaureate degree is earned, as shown in the top left pair of columns in Table 19: 0.89 percent for men and 1.52 percent for women. As we go down the column, however, to

TABLE 19
PERCENTAGE OF DOCTORATE POPULATION IN SUCCESSIVE "OVER-AGE" BRACKETS AT BACCALAUREATE AND DOCTORATE, BY SEX AND GENERAL FIELD OF PhD, 1960-1974

	Age at Baccalaureate						Age at Doctorate					
	30 and Over		40 and Over		50 and Over		40 and Over		50 and Over		60 and Over	
Field Group	Men	Women	Men	Women	Men	Women	Men	Women	Men	Women	Men	Women
EMP Fields	0.89	1.52	0.03	0.05	0.01	0.00	4.52	6.19	0.43	0.59	0.02	0.00
Life sciences	2.10	3.81	0.10	0.47	0.01	0.01	7.37	12.47	0.67	2.23	0.03	0.10
Behavioral sciences	3.31	7.00	0.35	1.68	0.03	0.09	11.35	20.97	1.72	4.68	0.12	0.30
Science total	1.77	4.89	0.13	0.96	0.01	0.05	6.88	15.31	0.80	3.08	0.05	0.18
Humanities	3.29	8.35	0.48	1.93	0.07	0.21	15.15	26.03	2.39	6.98	0.23	0.90
Professions	4.15	7.69	0.57	1.16	0.06	0.12	22.51	44.75	4.05	12.84	0.26	0.86
Education	5.38	13.87	0.69	2.82	0.03	0.14	34.77	50.62	5.89	15.92	0.26	1.11
Nonscience total	4.46	11.18	0.60	2.34	0.05	0.17	25.99	40.52	4.37	11.98	0.25	1.01
GRAND TOTAL	2.71	8.49	0.29	1.75	0.03	0.12	13.50	29.72	2.04	8.17	0.12	0.65

SOURCE: NRC, Commission on Human Resources.

the life sciences, behavioral sciences, and especially to the nonscience fields, the proportion over 30 increases quite markedly, particularly in the case of women. Almost one in seven of the women who earn the doctorate in education is over 30 at the time she earns the baccalaureate degree. The proportion over 40 at the time of the baccalaureate is smaller but still surprisingly high and follows the same general pattern of sex and field differences. Finally, there are some--very few, to be sure, but still some cases in all fields--who are over 50 at the time the baccalaureate degree is earned. The field and sex differences persist, indicating that this is a real phenomenon, not a figment of random errors in the tabulation processes.

At the doctorate level, the ages represented in the three sets of columns have been moved up a decade, to indicate percentages earning PhD's at the age of 40 or over, 50 or over, and 60 or over. In the case of the nonscience fields, the percentages of both men and women who are beyond the half-century mark at the time the doctorate is awarded is surprisingly high, ranging from over 2 percent for men in the humanities to almost 16 percent of women in education. Taking all fields together, as shown at the bottom line in Table 19, we see that at least 1 man in 50, and 1 woman in 12 is at least 50 years old when the doctorate is awarded. The numbers who are 40 or over are larger, of course, and the proportions are indeed surprisingly large; even in the EMP field group, 4.5 percent of the men are over 40 at the time of the doctorate; in the nonscience fields the proportion is 1 in 4 for the men and 4 in 10 for the women.

TIME TRENDS IN AGE AT DOCTORATE

Have the field and sex differences in age at PhD been constant for the entire 15-year period under examination? Table 20 provides some of the answers. Sex differences and field differences have been decreasing over the last 15 years. Convergence has begun, but there is still a long way to go before the differences are insignificant.

BACCALAUREATE-TO-DOCTORATE TIME LAPSE

As we have seen, the primary determiner of age at doctorate is the time lapse between the baccalaureate and doctorate degrees, although age at BA is also a contributing factor. This time lapse, and that portion of it represented by time registered in graduate school, has been the subject of a number of studies, including the previous volume in this series, *Doctorate Recipients from United States Universities*, published by the NAS in 1967. Our primary concern here will be with field and time differences in the total time lapse, disregarding the differentiation into registered time and time not in study status.

TABLE 20
MEAN AGE AT PhD, BY FIELD, SEX, AND 5-YEAR COHORTS, 1960-1974

	1960-1964		1965-1969		1970-1974	
Field of Doctorate	Men	Women	Men	Women	Men	Women
Mathematics	30.2	31.9	29.2	30.4	29.8	30.4
Physics	29.9	31.7	29.6	29.2	29.9	29.5
Chemistry	29.2	29.9	28.9	29.7	29.2	29.6
Earth sciences	31.6	--	31.7	32.8	32.0	31.8
Engineering	31.0	31.0	31.0	30.9	31.3	30.7
EMP TOTAL	30.2	30.7	30.0	30.0	30.4	30.0
Agriculture	32.4	32.7	32.6	31.4	32.4	32.0
Medical sciences	33.1	36.0	32.5	35.6	32.3	35.2
Biosciences	31.5	32.8	31.0	31.3	30.6	31.0
LIFE SCIENCES TOTAL	31.9	33.0	31.5	31.8	31.3	31.5
Psychology	31.9	34.8	31.1	33.6	30.7	32.5
Social sciences	33.9	36.7	33.1	35.7	32.7	33.8
BEHAVIORAL SCIENCES	33.1	35.4	32.3	34.4	32.0	33.0
SCIENCE TOTAL	31.3	33.7	30.9	32.5	31.0	32.0
Humanities	34.1	36.8	33.6	35.8	33.4	35.0
Professions	35.4	40.0	35.5	40.2	34.9	38.6
Education	38.4	42.5	37.8	41.3	37.2	39.6
NONSCIENCE TOTAL	36.3	40.1	35.9	38.9	35.6	37.6
GRAND TOTAL, ALL FIELDS	32.9	37.3	32.5	36.1	32.7	35.3

SOURCE: NRC, Commission on Human Resources.

TABLE 21
MEAN BACCALAUREATE-TO-DOCTORATE TIME LAPSE, BY FIELD, TIME PERIOD, AND SEX

	Males					Females					Both Sexes Combined				
Field of Doctorate	1920-1944	1945-1949	1950-1959	1960-1974	1920-1974	1920-1944	1945-1949	1950-1959	1960-1974	1920-1974	1920-1944	1945-1949	1950-1959	1960-1974	1920-1974
Mathematics	7.46	8.89	8.13	7.41	7.56	9.45	9.35	10.79	8.61	8.98	7.74	8.93	8.26	7.49	7.66
Physics and Astronomy	7.04	7.98	7.38	7.48	7.43	8.85	7.81	8.52	8.01	8.22	7.12	7.98	7.40	7.49	7.45
Chemistry	5.89	7.04	6.52	6.73	6.54	8.43	8.02	8.23	7.51	7.80	6.04	7.09	6.60	6.69	6.62
Earth sciences	7.85	9.47	8.13	8.89	8.64	8.11	--	10.13	9.78	9.57	7.86	9.56	8.17	8.91	8.67
Engineering	7.31	8.27	8.05	8.37	8.29	--	--	--	8.57	9.06	7.31	8.29	8.07	8.38	8.30
EMP TOTAL	6.53	7.73	7.32	7.72	7.52	8.68	8.56	8.92	8.01	8.27	6.65	7.77	7.36	7.73	7.55
Life sciences	7.69	9.36	8.09	8.36	8.25	9.01	10.12	10.02	9.27	9.37	7.88	9.46	8.27	8.48	8.39
NATURAL SCIENCE TOTAL	6.97	8.26	7.59	7.92	7.76	8.89	9.54	9.64	8.84	8.98	7.14	8.36	7.70	7.99	7.85
Psychology	8.07	9.11	8.04	8.00	8.04	9.38	10.08	11.52	10.31	10.38	8.42	9.32	8.55	8.55	8.56
Social sciences	9.32	11.64	10.50	9.83	9.96	11.48	12.25	13.10	11.73	11.89	9.56	11.70	10.70	10.06	10.18
BEHAVIORAL SCIENCE TOTAL	8.98	10.87	9.44	9.12	9.22	10.36	11.12	12.14	10.88	11.00	9.20	10.91	9.73	9.42	9.50
Humanities	9.71	11.99	11.37	10.81	10.81	12.09	14.26	15.15	12.89	13.08	10.23	12.44	11.91	11.25	11.26
Education	13.56	15.53	14.81	13.71	13.95	14.61	17.01	17.72	16.74	16.73	13.78	15.86	15.34	14.36	14.53
TOTAL, ALL FIELDS	8.58	10.36	9.65	9.62	9.54	11.25	13.19	13.98	12.68	12.70	8.97	10.75	10.08	10.05	9.96

Source: NRC, Commission on Human Resources

MEAN TIME LAPSE, BY FIELD AND SEX

Table 21 provides an overview of the mean BA-to-PhD time lapse, by field and field group, in terms of four general time intervals. The earliest interval represents PhD graduations in the quarter-century from 1920 to 1944. Although this includes most of the World War II period, most of the people earning doctorates during the war years had completed the major portion of their graduate work earlier. Only the last four years of this period could have been affected by the war. The second time period is 1945-1950, during which the returning veterans and the "GI Bill" played an important part in the campus scene. The third period is 1950-1959, during which time the effect of the war period and Veterans Administration programs was diminishing. The fourth period is the most recent 15 years, which has been examined in some detail in previous sections.

As in the previous tables relating to age, sex differences are evident, and time trends in these differences are of some interest. In the EMP fields, for instance, although women are relatively few, it is clear from Table 21 that during the 1945-1949 period they took less time to attain the doctorate than in either the preceding or the following period. For the men graduating during this period, exactly the opposite is true, because this period includes the graduations of the greatest number of those whose educational careers had been interrupted by military service. In the 1950's, the mean time lapse for men went down, whereas for the women it went up. In the most recent period, the time trends are again reversed, going up for the men and down for the women, with the net effect that the disparity between the data for men and women is at a minimum in the recent past--particularly, as we have seen in the age data, in the last third of this 15-year period.

TIME TRENDS IN TIME LAPSE

The data of Table 21 are means and neglect the important matter of variations. These variations can be expressed in two ways. The first is percentile distributions. One of the best ways to visualize variations over a period of time is to examine changes in the percentile points. Figure 37 does this for chemistry, which represents the field with the minimum time lapse. Figure 39 does this for the life sciences, an intermediate field, and Figure 41 does this for education, the field with the greatest BA-to-PhD time lapse. An alternative view of the same data is provided by a set of isochrons--lines of equal time lapse taken by varying proportions of the population. Figures 38, 40, and 42 provide such data for the same three fields.

Percentiles and Isochrons

When one compares Figures 37 and 38, representing changes in baccalaureate-to-doctorate time lapse in chemistry from 1920 through 1974, by 5-year intervals, one notes that in Figure 37 the lines of percentile trends are crowded close to the bottom of the figure. In Figure 38 by contrast, the isochrons, representing changes over time in the percentage of persons requiring a constant amount of time for the BA-to-PhD interval, are crowded toward the top of the figure. Chemistry has for 50 years or more been the field with the shortest average time lapse. During the 1920's and 1930's, the median time lapse was about 5 years. This was even improved slightly in the early 1940's, but the delays occasioned by World War II raised the median time to over 6 years, from which it dropped a bit until the most recent 5-year period, when another increase is seen. The other percentile points can be traced in a similar manner. It is noteworthy, however, that the time required by

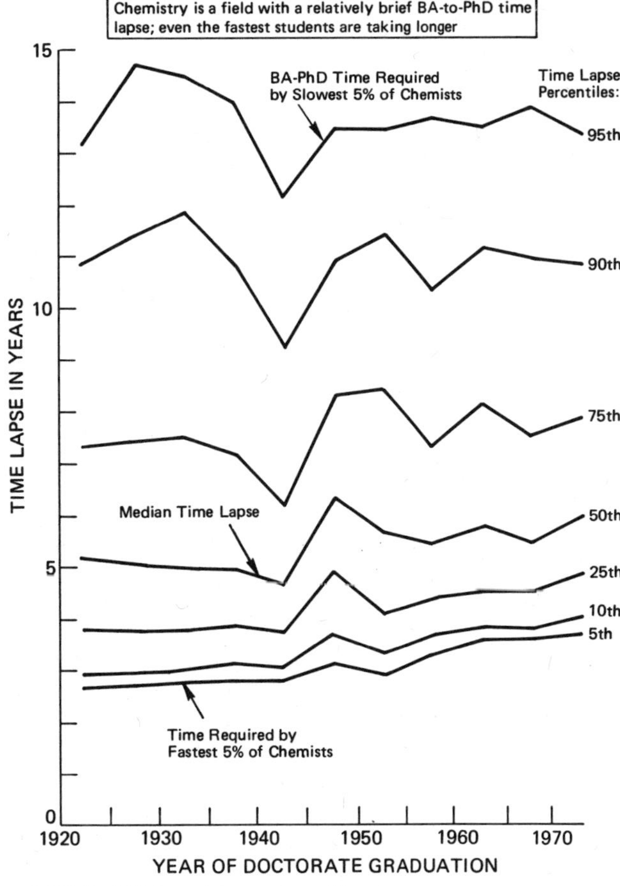

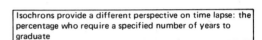

FIGURE 37 BA-to-PhD time lapse percentiles: chemistry.

the fastest 10 percent, or even 5 percent, has drifted gradually upward over almost the whole of the 1920-1974 period, with a slight perturbation at the time of World War II. At the slow end of the time scale--the curves for the slowest 5 percent and the slowest 10 percent--the variations from one era to another were larger, but there is no consistent upward slope to the curves.

The same data are interpreted somewhat differently by the isochrons of Figure 38. Here we see, in the bottom line, that the proportion of chemists taking only 4 years between the BA and PhD degrees has declined rather steadily (except for the World War II period), from about 20 percent in 1920 to about 2 percent in the recent past. The proportion requiring 5 years or less has declined from 40 percent in the early 1920's to about 17 percent recently. The proportion requiring 6 years or less went up from about 57 percent in the early 1920's to 65 percent in the late 1940's, then plummented during the World War II period to about 35 percent, recovered to about the 50 percent point, and has subsequently declined to between 40 percent and 45 percent. At the top of the graph, representing those who require 15 years or longer, the proportion is small, but has varied only slightly over the years.

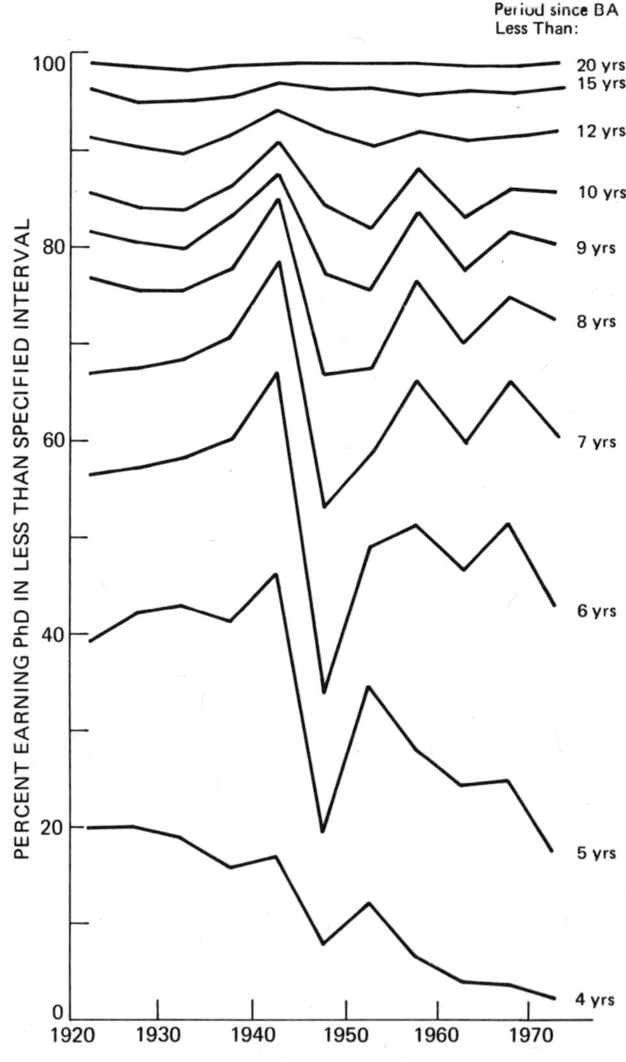

FIGURE 38 Isochrons of BA-to-PhD time lapse: chemistry.

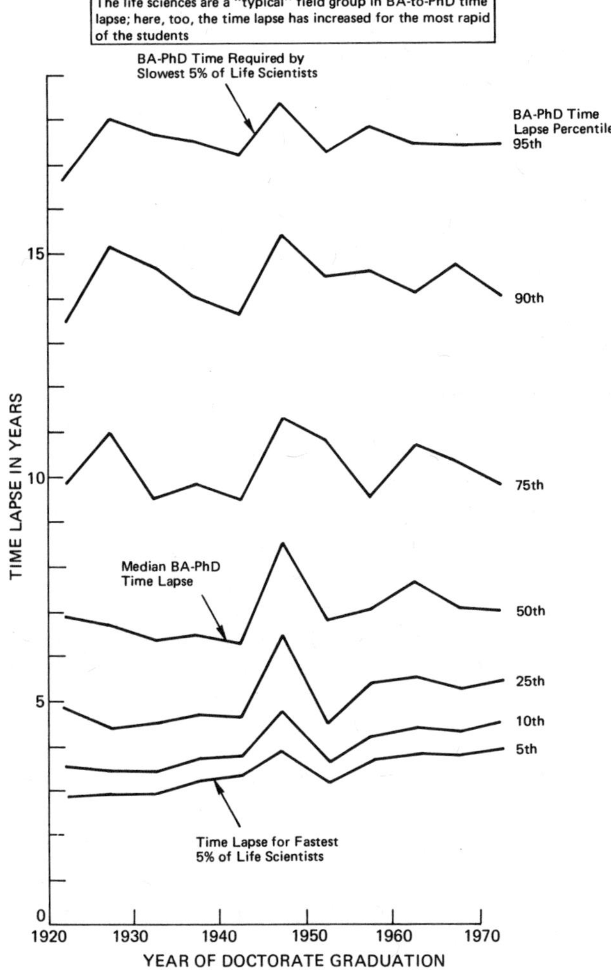

FIGURE 39 BA-to-PhD time lapse percentiles: life sciences.

The Life Sciences

Similar data are provided for the life sciences in Figures 39 and 40. The life sciences as a group have been slower than the EMP fields and faster than the behavioral sciences in time lapse and were powerfully affected by World War II. Perhaps the greater effect of the war was that there was little perceived immediate application of the life sciences in the conduct of the war. In physics and chemistry, applications were evident and abundant; in psychology the applications were also touted, as, for example, in the useful and popular book *Psychology and the Fighting Man*. Perhaps the life sciences other than in medical applications were expected to have a more long-term, rather than immediate, payoff. Decreased support during World War II no doubt had the effect of increasing the stretch-out of the BA-to-PhD interval. As in chemistry, there was an upward drift in the percentile curves, a given percentage of the graduates taking longer and longer to complete the doctorate. The isochrons show a corresponding decrease in the proportions finishing in the shorter time intervals and an increase in the proportion taking longer times.

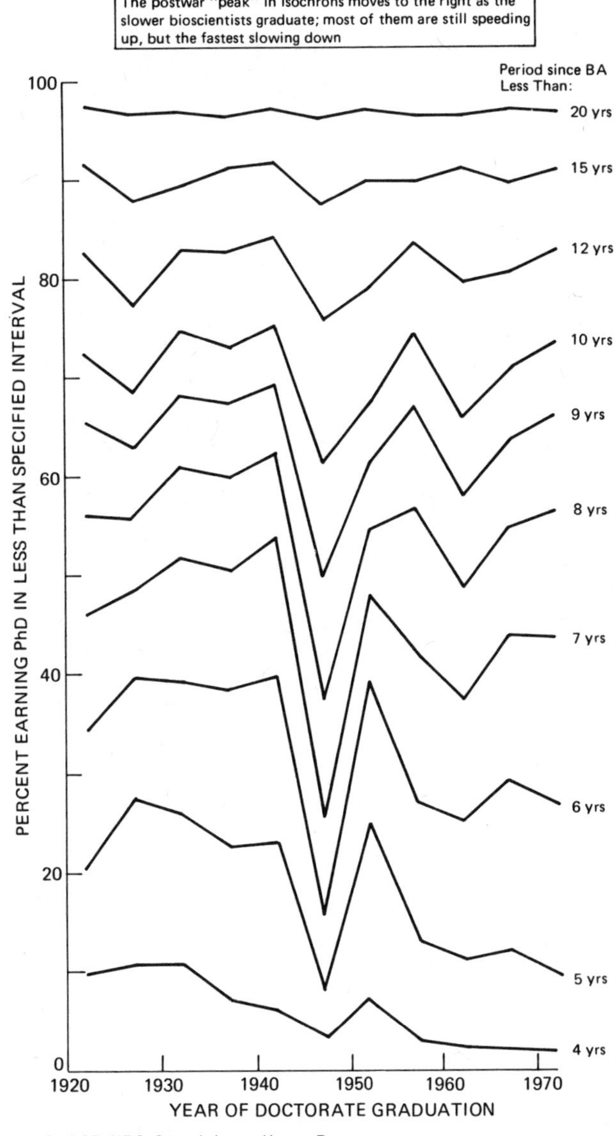

FIGURE 40 Isochrons of BA-to-PhD time lapse: life sciences.

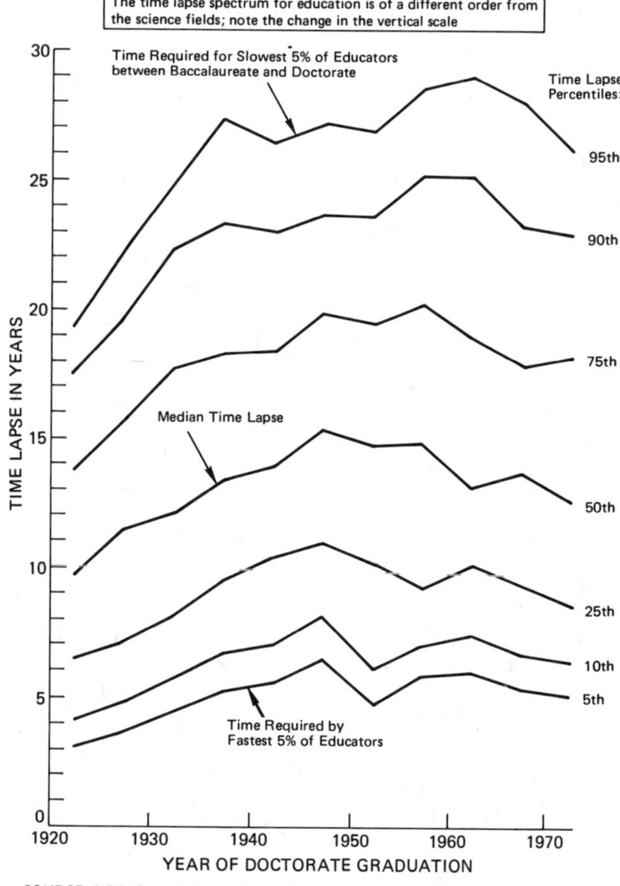

FIGURE 41 BA-to-PhD time lapse percentiles: education.

Education

The final pair of graphs depict the time intervals for those with doctorates in education. On Figure 41 it has been necessary to compress the vertical scale, since a large proportion take longer than the 95th percentile of the other fields. The time trends are generally upward, from 1920 to the "GI period," and generally downward since. It is noteworthy that the effect of World War II is less spectacular than it is in the other fields. This is a function of the longer average time span--the effects are less concentrated in those graduating in a given period and are diffused over a wider range of cohorts. A gradual shifting of the "hump" denoting the effects of World War II is noted as we move up the percentile lines, until the 95th percentile, where it is evident in the last 10-15 years. These are the people who are taking well over 20 years to complete the doctorate.

Other Fields

In the interest of brevity, percentile graphs and isochron graphs are not presented for the remaining fields. The full set are available from the Commission on Human Resources for those wishing more detail. A few comments, however, may be in order with respect to the time lapse variations by field. In the case of psychology, there was a shortening of the time lapse in the immediate postwar period, perhaps due primarily to the government support of training in clinical psychology, which was seen to be important not only for the rehabilitation of World War II veterans, but more generally, so that support was provided by both the Veterans Administration and by the National Institutes of Health. The latest period shows an average time lapse in psychology lower even than in the 1920-1944 period. This is true of only one other field--mathematics.

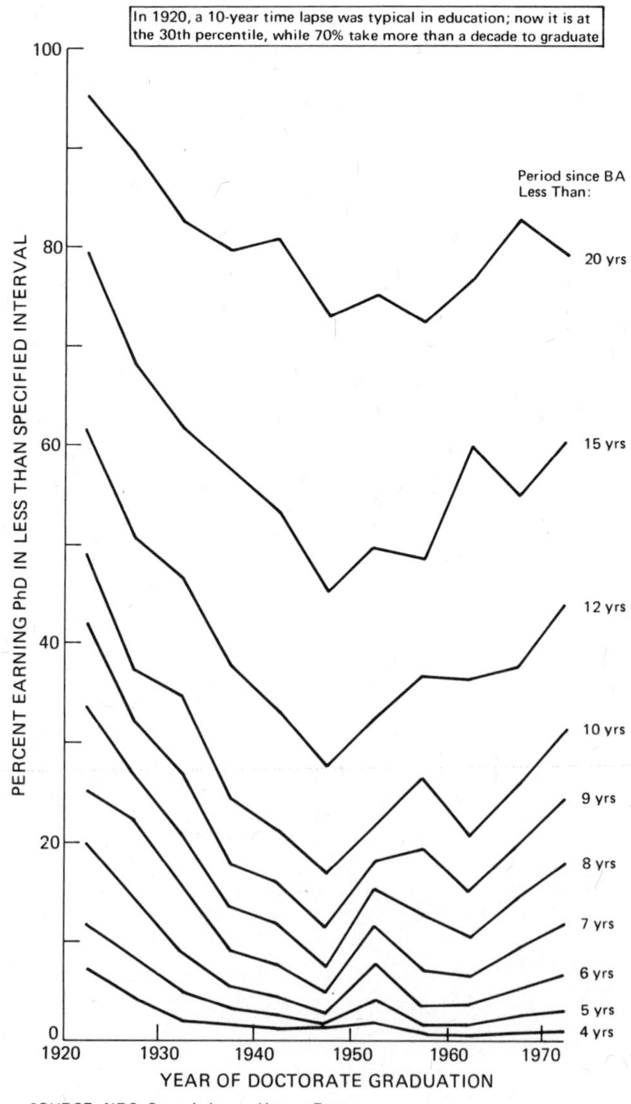

FIGURE 42 Isochrons of BA-to-PhD time lapse: education.

TABLE 22
PERCENTAGE OF PhD's WITH MASTER'S DEGREES, BY FIELD AND SEX, 1960-1974 TOTAL

	Men			Women			Both Sexes Combined		
Field of PhD	Yes	No	Total	Yes	No	Total	Yes	No	Total
Mathematics	9,565	2,564	12,129	785	135	920	10,350	2,699	13,049
	78.9	21.1	100.0	85.3	14.7	100.0	79.3	20.7	100.0
Physics	11,393	6,366	17,759	369	141	510	11,762	6,507	18,269
	64.2	35.8	100.0	72.4	27.6	100.0	64.4	35.6	100.0
Chemistry	9,469	13,879	23,348	929	994	1,923	10,398	14,873	25,271
	40.6	59.4	100.0	48.3	51.7	100.0	41.1	58.9	100.0
Earth sciences	4,949	1,397	6,346	137	47	184	5,086	1,444	6,530
	78.0	22.0	100.0	74.5	25.5	100.0	77.9	22.1	100.0
Engineering	32,923	3,865	36,788	196	29	225	33,119	3,894	37,013
	89.5	10.5	100.0	87.1	12.9	100.0	89.5	10.5	100.0
EMP TOTAL	68,299	28,071	96,370	2,416	1,346	3,762	70,715	29,417	100,132
	70.9	29.1	100.0	64.2	35.8	100.0	70.6	29.4	100.0
Agricultural sciences	9,728	1,044	10,772	241	37	278	9,969	1,081	11,050
	90.3	9.7	100.0	86.7	13.3	100.0	90.2	9.8	100.0
Medical sciences	3,222	1,814	5,036	531	244	775	3,753	2,058	5,811
	64.0	36.0	100.0	68.5	31.5	100.0	64.6	35.4	100.0
Biosciences	19,885	10,145	30,030	3,699	2,490	6,189	23,584	12,635	36,219
	66.2	33.8	100.0	59.8	40.2	100.0	65.1	34.9	100.0
LIFE SCIENCE TOTAL	32,835	13,003	45,838	4,471	2,771	7,242	37,306	15,774	53,080
	71.6	28.4	100.0	61.7	38.3	100.0	70.3	29.7	100.0
Psychology	13,595	4,103	17,698	4,409	1,333	5,742	18,004	5,436	23,440
	76.8	23.2	100.0	76.8	23.2	100.0	76.8	23.2	100.0
Social sciences	22,949	4,857	27,806	3,336	629	3,965	26,285	5,486	31,771
	82.5	17.5	100.0	84.1	15.9	100.0	82.7	17.3	100.0
BEHAVIORAL SCIENCE TOTAL	36,544	8,960	45,504	7,745	1,962	9,707	44,289	10,922	55,211
	80.3	19.7	100.0	79.8	20.2	100.0	80.2	19.8	100.0
SCIENCE TOTAL	137,678	50,034	187,712	14,632	6,079	20,711	152,310	56,113	208,423
	73.3	26.7	100.0	70.6	29.4	100.0	73.1	26.9	100.0
Humanities	31,949	5,063	37,012	10,216	1,340	11,556	42,165	6,403	48,568
	86.3	13.7	100.0	88.4	11.6	100.0	86.8	13.2	100.0
Professions	10,611	1,820	12,431	1,671	107	1,778	12,282	1,927	14,209
	85.4	14.6	100.0	94.0	6.0	100.0	86.4	13.6	100.0
Education	48,509	1,687	50,196	13,771	477	14,248	62,280	2,164	64,444
	96.6	3.4	100.0	96.7	3.3	100.0	96.6	3.4	100.0
NONSCIENCE TOTAL	91,069	8,570	99,639	25,658	1,924	27,582	116,727	10,494	127,221
	91.4	8.6	100.0	93.0	7.0	100.0	91.8	8.2	100.0
KNOWN TOTAL	228,747	58,604	287,351	40,290	8,003	48,293	269,037	66,607	335,644
	79.6	20.4	100.0	83.4	16.6	100.0	80.2	19.8	100.0

SOURCE: NRC, Commission on Human Resources.

MASTER'S DEGREES

The majority of PhD's hold master's degrees although the proportion varies substantially by field of PhD and to some extent by sex. The data showing the numbers and percentages of each field, by sex and for the combined total of both sexes, are provided in Table 22 and shown graphically in Figure 43. These data relate to the entire 1960-1974 period, without cohort breakouts.

The comments in the next two paragraphs should be read with several caveats in mind. The requirements for the master's degree vary markedly from school to school, from field to field, and may not even be uniform within a given school, since some departments may require a thesis while others may not.

In the EMP field group, engineering PhD's with 89.5 percent for men and 87.1 percent for women is highest in percentage of master's degrees, followed by mathematics (78.9 percent and 85.3 percent), earth sciences (78.0 percent and 74.5 percent), physics (64.2 percent and 72.4 percent), and chemistry (40.6 percent and 48.3 percent) in that order. Chemistry is the only field in which fewer than half of the PhD's have received master's degrees. It is also the field in which the BA-to-PhD time lapse is least.

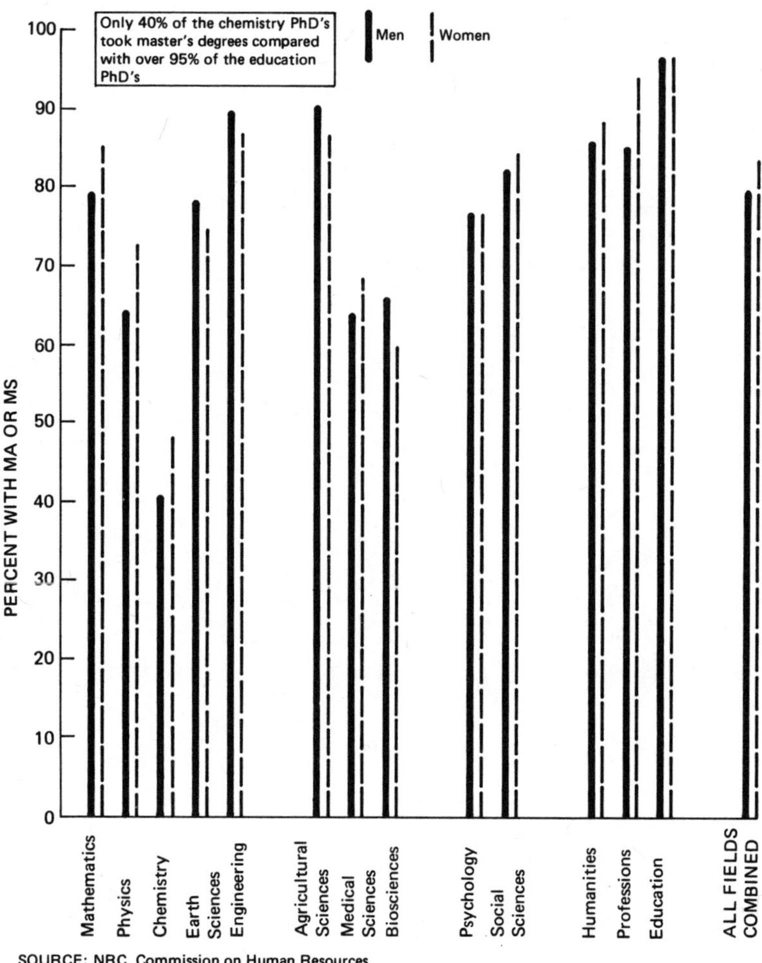

SOURCE: NRC, Commission on Human Resources

FIGURE 43 Percentage of PhD's with master's degrees.

Higher percentages of women than men have master's degrees in mathematics, physics, and chemistry; in the earth sciences and engineering, a higher percentage of women have master's degrees. Within the life sciences group, the agricultural sciences lead by a wide margin, 90.3 percent of the men and 86.7 percent of the women having master's degrees. In the medical and biological sciences, about two-thirds of both sexes in both fields have master's (64.0 percent of the men and 68.5 percent of the women). In psychology, there is no sex difference; 76.8 percent have the degree. In the social sciences the percentages are higher: 82.5 percent for the men and 84.1 percent for the women. In the humanities, the percentages are still higher: 86.3 percent for the men and 88.4 percent for the women. In the professions, there is a notable sex difference--the percentages are 85.4 percent for the men and 94.0 percent for the women. In education, however, the peak is reached: over 96.6 percent of each sex holds the master's degree. Combining across all fields, we note that 79.6 percent of the male PhD's and 83.4 percent of the female PhD's hold the master's degree.

FIELDS OF SPECIALIZATION

There are some students who maintain a particular direction with respect to their interests and field of specialization from the time they enter college as freshmen to the time they complete graduate training. Many others switch fields once or more during their careers in higher education. Typically, a student tends to specialize more as he advances, but, perhaps more often than we have supposed, he also switches from one major field to another. This may represent a growing awareness of one's deeper interests, a better knowledge of what is actually involved in the work of a given field, a testing of abilities, or the discovery that one does not have the talents for outstanding work in the field of first choice but can compete very effectively in a different field. Or it may represent a changing perception of the opportunities, scientific, academic, or financial, in the various fields open to the student. In the current study, we have no data on the reasons for the changes that are observed, but we do have considerable data on changes that have actually occurred. Field

TABLE 23
RATIOS OF DOCTORATES TO BACCALAUREATES, BY FIELD, SEX, AND COHORT, 1960-1974 PhD's*

	Men				Women				Both Sexes Combined			
Field	1960-1964	1965-1969	1970-1974	Total	1960-1964	1965-1969	1970-1974	Total	1960-1964	1965-1969	1970-1974	Total
Mathematics	0.86	0.80	0.70	0.76	0.59	0.57	0.50	0.53	0.84	0.78	0.68	0.74
Physics	1.02	0.93	0.85	0.92	0.82	0.88	0.78	0.81	1.02	0.93	0.85	0.91
Chemistry	0.86	0.83	0.78	0.81	0.62	0.58	0.55	0.57	0.84	0.80	0.75	0.79
Earth sciences	1.19	1.20	1.39	1.27	1.06	1.16	1.33	1.25	1.19	1.20	1.37	1.27
Engineering	0.88	0.88	0.88	0.88	0.66	0.49	0.83	0.69	0.88	0.87	0.88	0.88
EMP TOTAL	0.92	0.88	0.84	0.87	0.64	0.62	0.59	0.61	0.90	0.87	0.83	0.85
Agricultural sciences	0.74	0.72	0.88	0.79	0.74	1.05	1.32	1.15	0.74	0.73	0.89	0.80
Medical sciences	0.90	1.10	1.33	1.15	0.44	0.54	0.50	0.51	0.83	0.97	1.02	0.97
Biosciences	1.37	1.37	1.19	1.28	1.35	1.32	1.18	1.24	1.37	1.35	1.19	1.28
LIFE SCIENCE TOTAL	1.08	1.11	1.11	1.10	1.15	1.16	1.02	1.08	1.09	1.12	1.10	1.10
Psychology	1.16	1.03	0.95	1.02	1.39	1.20	1.12	1.18	1.19	1.06	1.00	1.05
Social sciences	1.05	1.05	1.03	1.04	0.94	0.88	0.98	0.95	1.04	1.03	1.03	1.03
BEHAVIORAL SCIENCE TOTAL	1.10	1.04	1.00	1.03	1.19	1.05	1.06	1.08	1.11	1.05	1.01	1.04
Humanities	0.69	0.74	0.72	0.72	0.67	0.77	0.77	0.76	0.68	0.75	0.74	0.73
Professions	0.96	1.04	1.03	1.02	0.81	0.78	0.75	0.76	0.94	1.00	0.98	0.98
Education	1.77	1.79	1.82	1.80	1.64	1.59	1.61	1.61	1.74	1.74	1.78	1.76
NONSCIENCE TOTAL	1.02	1.09	1.13	1.10	1.00	1.04	1.06	1.05	1.02	1.09	1.11	1.09
KNOWN TOTAL	1.00	1.00	1.00	1.00	1.00	1.00	1.00	1.00	1.00	1.00	1.00	1.00

*Only those whose baccalaureate and doctorate fields were known are included in this table.

SOURCE: NRC, Commission on Human Resources.

switching from the field of baccalaureate to field of doctorate will be the subject investigated in this section.

Doctorate Fields as Destinations

From the perspective of the baccalaureate degree, the fields of doctorate specialization can be viewed as destinations. Most mathematics BA majors may be expected to go on in mathematics if they seek the doctorate. But just how big a majority? And if not mathematics, what other fields do they enter? Each field of baccalaureate may thus be examined as a point of departure to see what destinations are actually reached by those who have taken baccalaureates in the various fields and gone on to the doctorate.

As background for consideration of the specific field-to-field switches, it is useful to consider the relative number in each field who do switch. This number may be expressed as a ratio of doctorates to baccalaureates within the PhD recipient groups in each general field. Table 23 provides these ratios by field, sex, and 5-year cohort for the period 1960-1974. In calculating these ratios, only the cases where both field of baccalaureate and field of doctorate were known were used. Figure 44 shows the changes over time for the combined-sex total. In Figure 44, fields have been set forth in three groups to make the graph more legible: the EMP fields, the biosciences/behavioral fields, and the nonscience fields. The horizontal line at 100 represents the balancing point, where the losses to a given field just balance the gains.

DONOR AND RECEPTOR FIELDS

The switches from field to field are not necessarily symmetrical, as can be readily seen in Figure 44 and Table 23. Some fields--those with fewer PhD's than BA's--may be considered "donor" fields, since some of their baccalaureates are "given" to other fields. Others may be considered "receptor" fields, since they receive more people whose baccalaureates were in other fields than they contribute to those other fields. It is this proportion that describes the vertical axis in Figure 44. Over the past 15 years mathematics, physics, chemistry, engineering, the agricultural sciences, and the humanities have been donor fields, inasmuch as a substantial portion of those who earn baccalaureates in these fields switch to other fields for their doctorate degrees. Receptor fields include the earth sciences, biosciences, and education. This leaves a third group in which the switches for the total of the 15-year period are approximately in balance: psychology, the social sciences, the medical sciences, and the professions.

Changes over Time

Of the various reasons mentioned above for making field switches, the perception of career opportunities is perhaps the one that varies most over time. The time trends in the PhD/BA ratios may reflect market conditions, and the slopes in the curves in Figure 44 would seem to be most readily interpreted in terms of the condition of the market--academic and nonacademic--over the

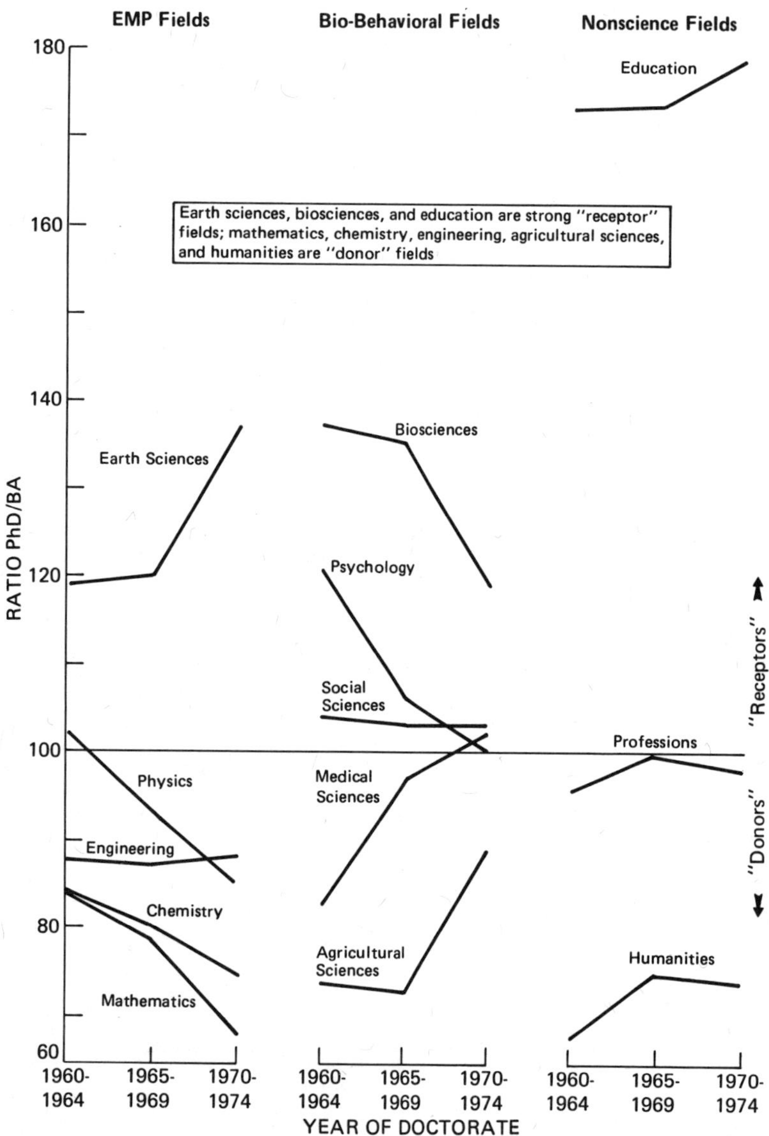

SOURCE: NRC, Commission on Human Resources

FIGURE 44 Ratio of doctorate degrees in each field to BA degrees in that field held by PhD's of 1960-1974.

past 15 years. Thus, physics, chemistry, mathematics, the biosciences, and psychology show declining trends. The fields with ascending curves are the earth sciences, the agricultural sciences, and the medical sciences; perhaps the employment and career opportunities in these fields have been relatively better than in the remaining groups. Engineering, the social sciences, and the professions have been relatively stable in their PhD/BA ratios. The heterogeneity of these three fields may well explain their "middling" position; subfields may well show ascending and descending curves.

SEX AND FIELD DIFFERENCES

The PhD/BA ratios in Figure 44 are for both sexes combined and reflect predominantly, of course, the situation with respect to the men. Data for women PhD's are also given in Table 23, and it is easy to see that they are in many cases different from those for men. The ratios vary much more. That is, the ratios for the donor fields are lower, in general, for the women than the men, the exceptions being agricultural sciences, psychology, and the humanities.

The question may be raised as to the factors that are most important in determining the long-term differences between the donor and receptor fields--averaging across extended time periods to rule out the effects of market fluctuations. Perceived or demonstrated ability to compete is probably one of the more important factors. We might expect the more demanding fields to "donate" their less successful students to another field where their chances of graduation would be

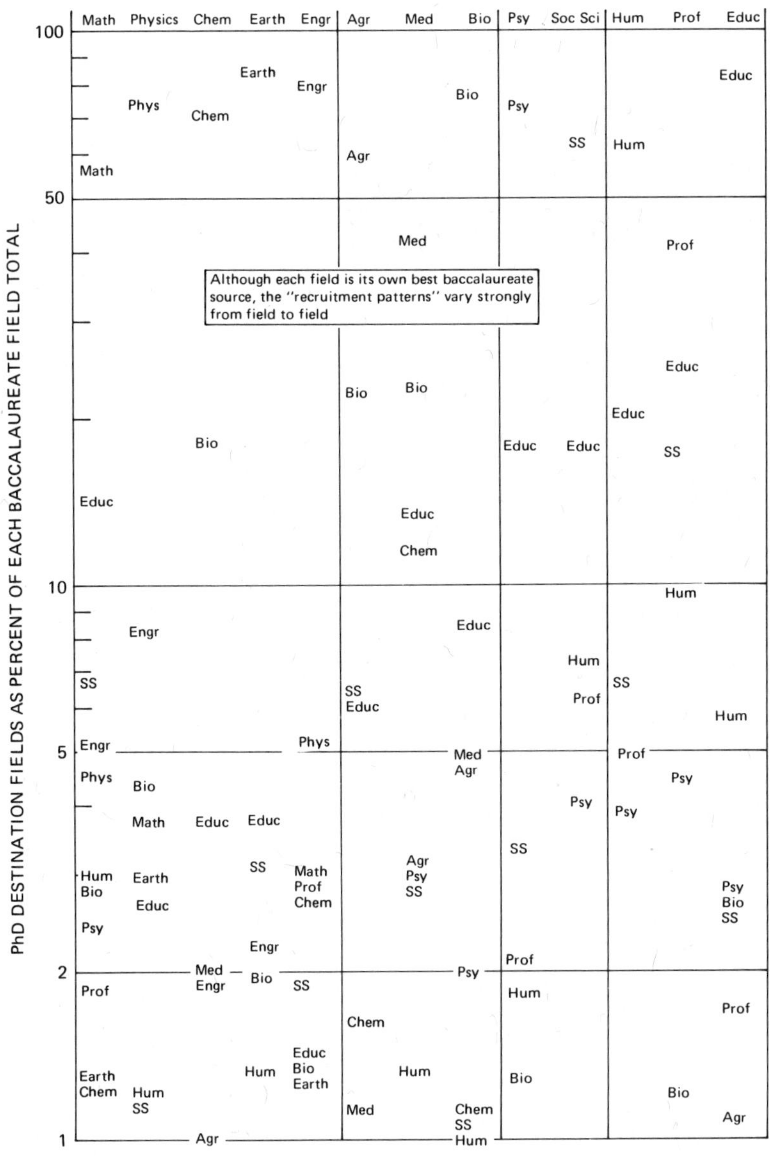

SOURCE: NRC, Commission on Human Resources

FIGURE 45 Relative frequency of PhD field as discipline destinations for various BA field sources.

better. The overall pattern of donor and receptor fields seems to fit this concept reasonably well. For a more detailed analysis, particularly with respect to the sex differences, it would be necessary to examine the field-to-field changes, by sex and cohort, which can be provided by the Commission on Human Resources. For the present, it will probably be most useful to consider data first for both sexes combined, and for the entire 15-year period, as shown in Table 23.

MATRIX OF FIELD-TO-FIELD SHIFTS

A matrix of the shifts from each baccalaureate field to each doctorate field, in percentage terms, with source fields (baccalaureate) on the vertical axis and destination fields (PhD) on the horizontal axis, is provided in Table 24. To show these changes more graphically, two charts have been prepared, one from the standpoint of the baccalaureate fields as sources (Figure 45) and the other from the standpoint of the PhD fields that draw selectively upon these sources (Figure 46). We will examine the data of Figure 45 first.

Because the majority of baccalaureates in each field remain in that field (with two minor exceptions, which will be noted), while many fields take up small percentages, it has seemed appropriate to represent the scale of PhD desti-

TABLE 24
BA-PhD FIELD SWITCHING, 1960-1974

BA Fields	%	PhD Fields: Math	Physics	Chem-istry	Earth Sci-ences	Engi-neering	Agricul-tural Sci-ences	Medi-cal Sci-ences	Bio-Sciences	Psychol-ogy	Social Science	Human-ities	Pro-fes-sions	Educa-tion	Total	Total N
Mathematics	H	*56.4*	4.5	1.2	1.3	5.1	0.2	0.2	2.8	2.4	6.6	2.9	1.8	14.5	100.0	17,033
	V	*73.7*	4.1	0.8	3.5	2.3	0.3	0.6	1.3	1.7	3.6	1.0	2.2	3.8	5.1	
Physics	H	3.7	*73.0*	0.9	3.0	8.3	0.2	0.3	4.3	0.8	1.1	1.2	0.6	2.6	100.0	19,248
	V	5.4	*76.9*	0.7	8.9	4.3	0.3	1.0	2.3	0.7	0.7	0.5	0.8	0.8	5.7	
Chemistry	H	0.4	0.8	*69.2*	0.9	1.8	1.0	2.0	17.9	0.7	0.6	0.8	0.5	3.7	100.0	31,250
	V	0.9	1.4	*85.6*	4.1	1.5	2.7	10.5	15.4	1.0	0.6	0.5	1.1	1.8	9.3	
Earth sciences	H	0.5	0.7	0.3	*84.1*	2.2	0.8	0.2	1.9	0.6	3.1	1.3	0.5	3.7	100.0	4,950
	V	0.2	0.2	0.1	*63.8*	0.3	0.4	0.1	0.3	0.1	0.5	0.1	0.2	0.3	1.5	
Engineering	H	3.1	5.2	2.6	1.2	*78.7*	0.3	0.2	1.3	0.6	1.8	0.8	2.8	1.4	100.0	40,842
	V	9.8	11.5	4.2	7.4	*86.8*	1.2	1.3	1.5	1.1	2.4	0.7	8.0	0.9	12.2	
Agricultural sciences	H	0.2	--	1.6	0.6	0.7	*59.9*	1.1	22.3	0.2	6.4	0.3	0.7	6.0	100.0	13,470
	V	0.2	--	0.8	1.2	0.2	*73.0*	2.7	8.3	0.1	2.7	0.1	0.7	1.3	4.0	
Medical sciences	H	0.1	0.1	11.5	--	0.2	3.2	*41.0*	22.9	3.0	2.8	1.3	0.8	13.1	100.0	5,051
	V	0.1	--	2.3	--	--	1.5	*35.6*	3.2	0.7	0.4	0.1	0.3	1.0	1.5	
Biosciences	H	0.1	0.1	1.0	0.9	0.2	4.6	5.0	*75.4*	2.0	1.0	1.0	0.4	8.3	100.0	27,022
	V	0.3	0.1	1.1	3.5	0.2	11.3	23.4	*56.3*	2.3	0.8	0.5	0.8	3.5	8.1	
Psychology	H	0.2	--	0.1	--	0.1	--	0.4	1.3	*72.8*	3.3	1.8	2.1	17.8	100.0	21,482
	V	0.3	--	0.1	0.1	--	0.1	1.6	0.8	*66.8*	2.2	0.8	3.2	5.9	6.4	
Social sciences	H	0.4	--	--	0.2	0.2	0.6	0.3	0.6	4.0	*62.5*	7.1	6.1	17.8	100.0	29,224
	V	0.9	0.1	--	1.0	0.2	1.6	1.7	0.5	5.0	*57.5*	4.3	12.6	8.1	8.7	
Humanities	H	0.4	0.3	0.4	0.2	0.5	0.2	0.3	1.3	3.8	6.7	*61.0*	4.9	20.2	100.0	63,224
	V	1.9	1.1	1.0	1.7	0.9	1.0	2.9	2.2	10.3	13.3	*79.4*	21.6	19.8	18.8	
Professions	H	0.5	0.2	0.2	0.2	0.7	0.6	0.5	1.2	4.4	17.1	9.6	*40.2*	24.6	100.0	13,718
	V	0.5	0.1	0.1	0.4	0.3	0.8	1.2	0.5	2.6	7.4	2.7	*38.8*	5.2	4.1	
Education	H	0.7	0.2	0.6	0.2	0.1	1.1	0.3	2.7	2.8	2.6	5.8	1.7	*81.1*	100.0	35,527
	V	2.0	0.5	0.8	0.9	0.1	3.4	1.6	2.7	4.3	2.9	4.2	4.3	*44.7*	10.6	
Unknown	H	3.8	5.4	4.7	1.7	7.5	2.0	6.7	12.7	6.0	11.9	18.0	5.6	14.1	100.0	13,603
	V	3.9	4.0	2.5	3.5	2.8	2.5	15.7	4.8	3.5	5.1	5.0	5.3	3.0	4.1	
Grand Total	N/10	1,305	1,827	2,527	653	3,701	1,105	581	3,622	2,344	3,177	4,857	1,421	6,444	33,564	
	H	3.9	5.4	7.5	1.9	11.0	3.3	1.7	10.8	7.0	9.5	14.5	4.2	19.2	100.0	335,644

N = number of cases; H = horizontal percentage; V = vertical percentage.

SOURCE: NRC, Commission on Human Resources.

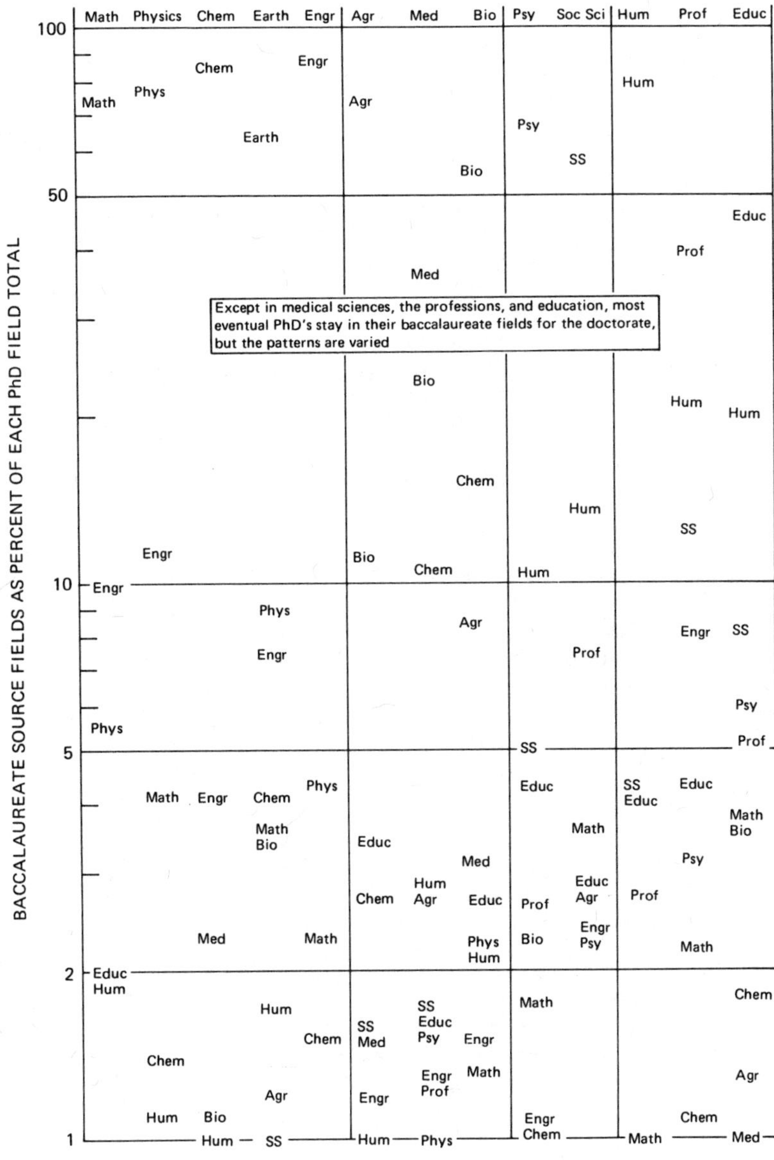

SOURCE: NRC, Commission on Human Resources

FIGURE 46 Relative frequency of various BA source fields, for each PhD field.

nations in logarithmic form, to spread out those that would otherwise be too close together for legibility. Thus, in the case of mathematics, in column 1 of Figure 45, mathematics as a PhD destination appears near the top but still is only at the 56 percent point. Moving down the column, we note that about 15 percent of mathematics baccalaureates take doctorates in education, about 7 percent in the social sciences, 5 percent each in physics and engineering, 3 percent each in the humanities and biosciences, 2 percent each in psychology and the professions, and 1 percent each in the earth sciences and chemistry.

In a similar manner, one may look down each succeeding column and note the percentage who remain in the field of undergraduate major and the percentage who switch to other fields. By reference to Table 24, a more exact statement of the percentages is available. Mathematics, as it turns out, is one of the lowest of the baccalaureate fields in retention of its graduates through to the doctorate. Alternatively, it can be described as one of the best as a basis for getting a PhD in a variety of fields. High proportions of mathematics majors go into other fields, partly as a function of the transferability of skills, and partly as a function of the relative size of the various fields. The contrasting sizes of the fields of earth sciences and chemistry, both near the bottom of the mathematics column, brings the latter consideration into focus.

Looking at the other fields of baccalaureate as contributors to their own fields at the PhD level, one sees that the earth sciences and education retain a high proportion (over 80 percent) through to the doctorate. Engineering (79 percent), the biosciences (75 percent), physics and psychology (73 percent each), and chemistry (69 percent) are intermediate, and the other fields are much lower in retention rate. It must be recognized that "retention rate" is a function of the breadth of the field and that in important ways fields designated here are not uniform in "breadth," although there is no way that one can define breadth objectively and quantitatively. The transferability of skills learned in undergraduate training is an important factor. No doubt the ubiquitousness of the need for mathematical skills accounts in large part for the number of persons leaving mathematics as a specialty and moving to other fields where their mathematics skills can be utilized. Another factor in this particular case is the fact that mathematicians *per se* have little other than the academic area for employment, whereas by switching, they find more fields of application. The relatively high proportion of math BA's going into education undoubtedly represents a recognition that opportunities to teach mathematics and do research in mathematics are limited at the university level. If one majors in education, more opportunities open up in colleges, junior colleges, and even in high schools--perhaps for those with teaching skills and interests but less aptitude for research in mathematics.

Physics as a baccalaureate source field contributes, not unexpectedly, to engineering about 8 percent of its graduates. Bioscience (4 percent) comes next, in large part, no doubt, because of the development of the growing field of biophysics. Mathematics and physics have a great deal of overlap in terms of skills learned and required, and mathematics absorbs almost 4 percent of physics majors. Other destination fields include the earth sciences and education (3 percent each) and the social sciences and humanities (1 percent each).

Chemistry contributes a high proportion of its baccalaureates to the biosciences (18 percent)--a tribute to the size of the biochemistry field. Almost 4 percent of BA-level chemists go into education and 2 percent or fewer into engineering and medical sciences; 1 percent or less enter other fields. The earth sciences, as noted earlier, have the highest retention rate, but still contribute 4 percent of their graduates to education, 3 percent to the social sciences, 2 percent each to the biosciences and engineering, and 1 percent to the humanities. Engineering and physics, as noted earlier, have a reciprocal relationship, and physics is the major nonengineering destination field (5 percent) for engineering graduates; approximately 3 percent go into mathematics, chemistry, and the professions and between 1 percent and 2 percent into four other fields: earth sciences, biosciences, social sciences, and education.

The agricultural sciences have an understandably close relation to the biosciences: 22 percent finish with bioscience PhD's. The social sciences get 6 percent, perhaps because of a certain degree of ambiguity regarding the classification of agricultural economics. Education also claims 6 percent--undoubtedly primarily as teachers of agriculture. No other field takes over 2 percent. The medical sciences contribute 12 percent of their number to chemistry as a PhD destination field, probably concentrated mainly in pharmaceuticals. Bioscience gets 23 percent; education, 13 percent; and psychology, the agricultural sciences, and the social sciences, 3 percent each. The net result is that only 41 percent of those with baccalaureates in the medical science fields take doctorates in this field. A certain degree of ambiguity attends this finding, however, since the coding of foreign pre-PhD degrees in this field involves some uncertainty and in the early 1960's MD degrees were coded here in a combined "baccalaureate and first professional" category.

The biosciences have a high retention rate, but still about 8 percent go into education at the doctorate level, followed by 5 percent each to the agricultural sciences and the medical sciences, and 2 percent to psychology. Psychology, as might be expected, is closely related to education; about 18 percent of psychology majors end up with education doctorates. About 3 percent go into the social sciences, and 2 percent each into the humanities and the professions. The social sciences contribute about as many of their graduates to education (18 percent) as does psychology but a much higher proportion (7 percent) to the humanities, 6 percent to the professions, and 4 percent to psychology (an almost even exchange).

Of the humanities baccalaureates, over 20 percent finish in education, about 7 percent in the social sciences, 5 percent in the professions, and 4 percent in psychology. The "professions" are a very diverse set of fields, including theology, business administration, home economics, law, journalism, speech and hearing sciences, social work, and library science. The PhD field destinations are also diverse, including only 40 percent to the "professions," 25 percent to education, 17 percent to the social sciences, 10 percent to humanities, and 4 percent to psychology. Education, as noted earlier, has a high retention rate, but still 6 percent of education majors complete doctorates in the humanities, and about 3 percent each in the biosciences, the social sciences, and psychology. The psychology-education exchange is predominantly a one-way street.

There is an additional row on the baccalaureate side of Table 24 that is not shown on the chart of Figure 45. That row is for unknown baccalaureate fields. These range from about 2.5 percent to a little over 5 percent entering each PhD field, with the exception of the medical sciences. As noted earlier, there is some ambiguity about the medical sciences at the "baccalaureate" level, and this is probably the reason for the deviation of the medical sciences from all the others in the row for "baccalaureate field unknown."

BACCALAUREATE SOURCE FIELDS

As mentioned earlier, one may look at the field-switching phenomenon from an entirely different perspective: backwards from the doctorate fields to see what source fields contribute to each of the PhD disciplines. This is shown in diagrammatic fashion in Figure 46. Here it is immediately apparent that each field is its own best supplier by a much higher margin than one would expect from the data of Figure 45. Mathematics supplies three out of four of its own PhD's, taking 10 percent from engineering, 5 percent from physics, and 2 percent each from the humanities and education. The transferability of skills is undoubtedly a major factor in this pattern--fields other than engineering and physics are unlikely to require the development of mathematical skills sufficient to permit their graduates to switch to mathematics as a doctorate-level discipline. A few make it, but undoubtedly because of special interests and choice of electives, rather than by reason of required training.

A similar and reciprocal set of relationships is found for the source fields for physics. Engineering contributes about 12 percent, mathematics about 4 percent, and chemistry and the humanities 1 percent each. Chemistry is even higher than mathematics and physics in the extent to which it draws on its own baccalaureate field for future doctorate recipients. It does, however, draw also on engineering (4 percent), medical sciences (2 percent), biosciences (1 percent), and the humanities (1 percent). The earth sciences, which had the highest retention rate from BA to PhD, is lower than any other natural science field as a source field for its own doctorates--no doubt because, as an undergraduate field, it is very small. It draws extensively from the other sciences, physics (9 percent), engineering (7 percent), math, the biosciences, and chemistry (about 4 percent each), and less on other fields (humanities, 2 percent; social sciences, 1 percent; agricultural sciences, 1 percent). Engineering is highly self-contained, but does draw about 4 percent of its doctorates from physics, 2 percent from mathematics, a little less than 2 percent from chemistry, and about 1 percent from the humanities.

Agricultural sciences as a PhD field draws about three-fourths of its members from undergraduate majors in agricultural sciences, but it also draws heavily on the biosciences (11 percent). Education and chemistry each contribute 3 percent, and the medical and social sciences about half of that.

The ambiguities in the medical sciences as a first-level field do not apply at the doctorate. This field includes veterinary medicine, parasitology, pharmacology, pharmacy, pathology, environmental health, public health and epidemiology, hospital administration, and nursing, as well as "other" and "general." It is not surprising, therefore, that the source fields for the medical sciences are diverse: 11 percent come from chemistry, 23 percent from the biosciences, 3 percent each from the agricultural sciences and the humanities, 2 percent each from psychology, the social sciences, and education, and 1 percent each from physics, engineering, and the professions.

The biosciences as a doctorate field draw heavily from the undergraduate fields of chemistry (15 percent) and agricultural sciences (8 percent) and less from others--3 percent each from medical sciences and education and 2 percent each from physics, engineering, and the humanities. Psychology draws a surprisingly high 10 percent from the humanities, 5 percent from the social sciences, 4 percent from education, 3 percent from the professions, and 2 percent each from the biosciences and mathematics. The social sciences draw heavily (13 percent) from the humanities, somewhat less so from the professions (7 percent), 4 percent from mathematics, 3 percent each from the agricultural sciences and education, and 2 percent each from engineering and psychology.

The humanities draw 4 percent of their PhD's from the social sciences, an equal percentage from education, 3 percent from the professions, and not over 1 percent from any other field; 79 percent of the humanities doctorates had undergraduate training in the same field group. The professions, by contrast, are a very miscellaneous set, and their undergraduate sources show it. The humanities contribute 22 percent; the social sciences, 13 percent; engineering, 8 percent; education, 4 percent; psychology, 3 percent; and mathematics, 2 percent. Education is also very broad in its undergraduate origins: humanities, 20 percent; social sciences, 8 percent; psychology, 6 percent; professions, 5 percent; mathematics, 4 percent; biosciences, 4 percent; chemistry, 2 percent; and agricultural and medical sciences, 1 percent each.

THE GEOGRAPHY OF DOCTORATE ORIGINS

The major change in the geography of doctorate production has been the rise of the South and Rocky Mountain States in the output of PhD's. In this section we look at these data from a different perspective--the regional interchanges between the baccalaureate and doctorate degrees and, going farther back, the regional interchanges from the level of high school graduation to doctoral graduation. The map in Figure 47 shows the states in each region, and the accompanying table (Table 25) shows the 1970 population in each region.

One of the simpler ways of looking at the data of regional interchanges is to consider the ratio of the number of doctorate-bound baccalaureates a region produces to the number of doctoral degrees granted in that region. One may think of this ratio as a donor/receptor ratio, since all regions "give" students at one level to all other regions and "receive" students from all regions for graduate education. If this giving and receiving were equal, the ratio would be 1.00. If a region gives more than it receives

TABLE 25
DONOR-RECEPTOR RATIOS* AT TWO EDUCATIONAL LEVELS, BY SEX, FOR EACH U.S. REGION, 1960-1974

	High School to PhD			Baccalaureate to PhD		
Region	Men	Women	Total	Men	Women	Total
New England	0.84	0.81	0.83	1.12	1.07	1.11
Middle Atlantic	1.40	1.24	1.37	1.16	1.07	1.15
East North Central	0.85	0.86	0.85	0.88	0.91	0.88
West North Central	1.22	1.31	1.23	1.21	1.27	1.22
South Atlantic	0.84	0.89	0.85	0.84	0.88	0.85
East South Central	1.26	1.40	1.28	1.28	1.32	1.29
West South Central	1.08	1.20	1.10	1.08	1.17	1.10
Mountain	0.83	0.72	0.82	0.91	0.75	0.89
Pacific	0.79	0.77	0.79	0.84	0.85	0.84

*Donor regions are those with ratios over 1.00; receptor regions have ratios under 1.00.

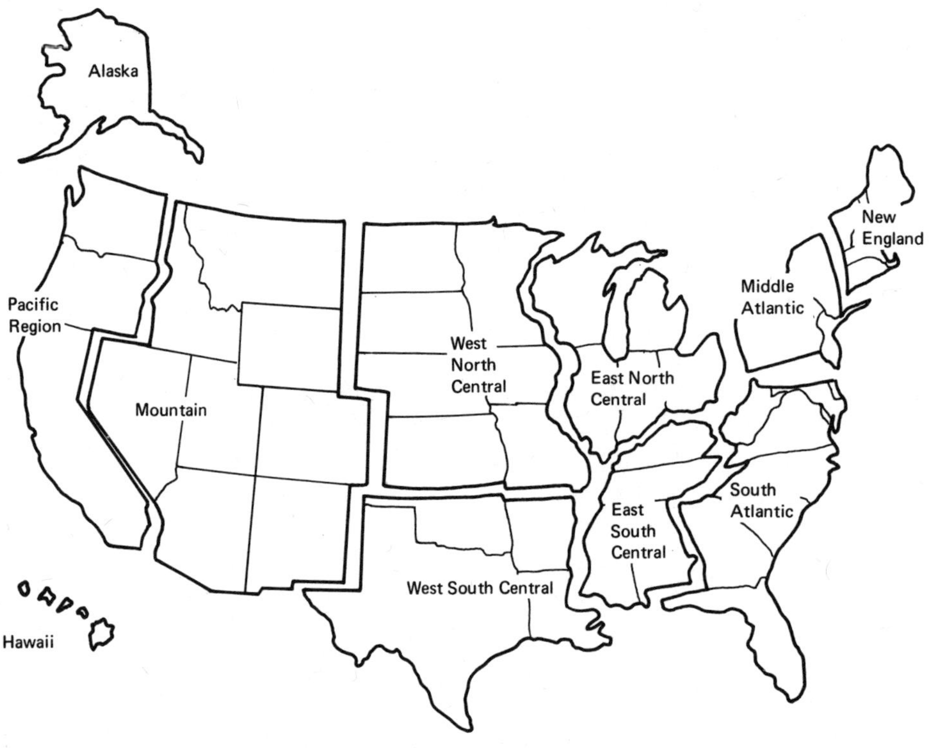

States in Each Region:

1. New England: Maine, Vermont, New Hampshire, Massachusetts, Rhode Island, Connecticut
2. Middle Atlantic: New York, New Jersey, Pennsylvania
3. East North Central: Ohio, Indiana, Illinois, Michigan, Wisconsin
4. West North Central: Minnesota, Iowa, Missouri, North Dakota, South Dakota, Nebraska, Kansas
5. South Atlantic: Delaware, Maryland, D.C., Virginia, West Virginia, North Carolina, South Carolina, Georgia, Florida
6. East South Central: Kentucky, Tennessee, Alabama, Mississippi
7. West South Central: Arkansas, Louisiana, Oklahoma, Texas
8. Mountain: Montana, Wyoming, Colorado, New Mexico, Arizona, Utah
9. Pacific: Washington, Oregon, California, Alaska, Hawaii (plus Puerto Rico and Panama Canal Zone)

1970 Population by Census Region (in thousands)

New England	11,842	East South Central	12,803
Middle Atlantic	37,199	West South Central	19,321
East North Central	40,252	Mountain	8,282
West North Central	16,319	Pacific	26,523
South Atlantic	30,671	TOTAL U.S.	203,212

SOURCE: NRC, Commission on Human Resources

FIGURE 47 The nine census regions of the United States.

TABLE 26
TIME CHANGES IN DONOR/RECEPTOR RATIOS AT TWO EDUCATIONAL LEVELS, 1960-1974

	High School to PhD			Baccalaureate to PhD		
Region	1960-1964	1965-1969	1970-1974	1960-1964	1965-1969	1970-1974
New England	0.77	0.82	0.88	1.01	1.13	1.15
Middle Atlantic	1.26	1.37	1.43	1.06	1.15	1.18
East North Central	0.81	0.87	0.86	0.84	0.89	0.89
West North Central	1.23	1.26	1.21	1.21	1.25	1.21
South Atlantic	0.93	0.84	0.84	0.93	0.84	0.84
East South Central	1.60	1.31	1.18	1.63	1.29	1.20
West South Central	1.21	1.12	1.05	1.22	1.11	1.05
Mountain	1.14	0.84	0.74	1.25	0.90	0.81
Pacific	0.76	0.74	0.83	0.81	0.79	0.89

SOURCE: NRC, Commission on Human Resources.

from other regions, its ratio is higher than 1.00; if it grants more doctorates than it contributes to other regions at the undergraduate level, its ratio would be lower than 1.00. We can thus think of the regions with high ratios as donor regions and those with lower ratios as receptor regions. In these very simplified terms, the regions with older, well-established doctorate-granting institutions are the prime receptor regions. This group includes the East North Central States, the South Atlantic region, the Pacific Coast, and, for the most recent decade, the Mountain States. Prior to 1965, the Mountain States were in the donor category, but they have made a dramatic shift and are now in the receptor category. No other region has shifted across the balancing line of a 1.00 ratio, although the southern states have moved strongly in the same direction. Rather surprisingly, New England is in the donor category--apparently because its excellent undergraduate institutions attract many high school graduates from other regions, so that it donates more doctorate-bound baccalaureates than it graduates PhD's.

At the high school to PhD interchange, New England exhibits a sharp contrast to its performance at the baccalaureate level. Because of its relatively small population, it produces fewer high school graduates that eventually attain the doctorate than it does either baccalaureates or doctorates. It is the only region that shifts from the receptor to the donor category between the high school and undergraduate levels of education. Tables 25 and 26 provide the information with respect to the relevant ratios. Table 25 shows the data for the entire 1960-1974 period, by sex, for both the high school/doctorate shifts and the baccalaureate/doctorate shifts. Table 26 shows the time changes, by 5-year cohorts, at both levels, for the combined total of both sexes. Tables 27 and 28 show all the regional interchanges for the entire 1960-1974 period. More detailed tables, by field, sex, and time period, are available from the Commission on Human Resources. Note that foreign areas are excluded in Tables 25 and 26 but given in Tables 27 and 28.

Sex differences in the donor/receptor ratios are quite distinct although usually not as dramatic as the changes over time. The patterns of sex differences are similar at the high school and baccalaureate levels, although the magnitude of the differences, and the range of the donor/receptor ratios, is greater at the high school level than at the baccalaureate level. The regions in which the HS/PhD ratios and the BA/PhD ratios are higher for men than for women are the Rocky Mountain States and the New England and the Middle Atlantic States. In the other five regions--the Pacific Coast, the South Atlantic States, and all the Central State regions, the ratios are higher for women than for men. That is, the tendency to "donate" relatively more men than women is stronger in the central regions and the Pacific Coast, while the East Coast and the Rocky Mountain States have a stronger tendency to "donate" women destined for the doctorate degree. This may be in part a result of field differences that have not been examined, since there are substantial sex and regional differences in the field mix at both the baccalaureate and doctorate levels, and they may be related in such a way as to produce the sex differences that have been noted in the donor/receptor ratios.

TABLE 27
REGIONAL INTERCHANGES BETWEEN BACCALAUREATE AND DOCTORATE DEGREES, PhD's OF 1960-1974, BOTH SEXES COMBINED

Region of BA		Region of PhD: New England	Middle Atlantic	East North Central	West North Central	South Atlantic	East South Central	West South Central	Mountain	Pacific and Insular	Total
NEW ENGLAND	N*	10306	5874	4258	892	2265	231	449	560	2905	27740
	V	34.9	9.3	5.4	3.1	6.2	2.1	1.9	3.1	6.2	8.3
	H	37.2	21.2	15.3	3.2	8.2	.8	1.6	2.0	10.5	100.0
MIDDLE ATLANTIC	N	5982	31391	9030	1787	5569	541	989	1143	3818	60250
	V	20.3	49.9	11.4	6.2	15.3	5.0	4.2	6.3	8.2	18.0
	H	9.9	52.1	15.0	3.0	9.2	.9	1.6	1.9	6.3	100.0
EAST NORTH CENTRAL	N	3107	5484	33716	4180	3592	827	1466	2234	4648	59254
	V	10.5	8.7	42.6	14.6	9.9	7.7	6.2	12.3	10.0	17.7
	H	5.2	9.3	56.9	7.1	6.1	1.4	2.5	3.8	7.8	100.0
WEST NORTH CENTRAL	N	1002	1825	5913	12565	1460	445	1718	2378	2516	29822
	V	3.4	2.9	7.5	43.9	4.0	4.1	7.3	13.1	5.4	8.9
	H	3.4	6.1	19.8	42.1	4.9	1.5	5.8	8.0	8.4	100.0
SOUTH ATLANTIC	N	1403	3200	3829	791	13568	1538	1109	589	1324	27351
	V	4.8	5.1	4.8	2.8	37.2	14.3	4.7	3.2	2.8	8.1
	H	5.1	11.7	14.0	2.9	49.6	5.6	4.1	2.2	4.8	100.0
EAST SOUTH CENTRAL	N	372	665	2190	515	2296	4862	1179	244	405	12728
	V	1.3	1.1	2.8	1.8	6.3	45.2	5.0	1.3	.9	3.8
	H	2.9	5.2	17.2	4.0	18.0	38.2	9.3	1.9	3.2	100.0
WEST SOUTH CENTRAL	N	587	881	2488	1376	1568	1103	12552	1092	1226	22873
	V	2.0	1.4	3.1	4.8	4.3	10.3	53.4	6.0	2.6	6.8
	H	2.6	3.9	10.9	6.0	6.9	4.8	54.9	4.8	5.4	100.0
MOUNTAIN	N	463	878	2073	1101	622	140	685	5886	2694	14542
	V	1.6	1.4	2.6	3.8	1.7	1.3	2.9	32.4	5.8	4.3
	H	3.2	6.0	14.3	7.6	4.3	1.0	4.7	40.5	18.5	100.0
PACIFIC AND INSULAR	N	1730	2394	3794	1250	1190	184	713	2191	18843	32289
	V	5.9	3.8	4.8	4.4	3.3	1.7	3.0	12.1	40.5	9.6
	H	5.4	7.4	11.8	3.9	3.7	.6	2.2	6.8	58.4	100.0
FOREIGN	N	4417	9187	11401	3995	4062	788	2438	1731	7566	45585
	V	15.0	14.6	14.4	14.0	11.1	7.3	10.4	9.5	16.2	13.6
	H	9.7	20.2	25.0	8.8	8.9	1.7	5.3	3.8	16.6	100.0
UNKNOWN	N	143	1126	452	182	273	99	187	122	626	3210
	V	.5	1.8	.6	.6	.7	.9	.8	.7	1.3	1.0
	H	4.5	35.1	14.1	5.7	8.5	3.1	5.8	3.8	19.5	100.0
TOTAL	N	29512	62905	79144	28634	36465	10758	23485	18170	46571	335644
	V	100.0	100.0	100.0	100.0	100.0	100.0	100.0	100.0	100.0	100.0
	H	8.8	18.7	23.6	8.5	10.9	3.2	7.0	5.4	13.9	100.0

SOURCE: NRC, Commission on Human Resources

*N = number of persons; V = vertical percent; H = horizontal percent.

TABLE 28
REGIONAL INTERCHANGES BETWEEN HIGH SCHOOL GRADUATION AND DOCTORATE DEGREE, PhD's OF 1960-1974, BOTH SEXES COMBINED

Region of High School		Region of PhD: New England	Middle Atlantic	East North Central	West North Central	South Atlantic	East South Central	West South Central	Mountain	Pacific and Insular	Total
NEW ENGLAND	N*	6702	3977	3098	707	1868	218	371	517	1656	19114
	V	22.7	6.3	3.9	2.5	5.1	2.0	1.6	2.8	3.6	5.7
	H	35.1	20.8	16.2	3.7	9.8	1.1	1.9	2.7	8.7	100.0
MIDDLE ATLANTIC	N	7267	31117	11053	2202	6681	778	1297	1535	4695	66625
	V	24.6	49.5	14.0	7.7	18.3	7.2	5.5	8.4	10.1	19.8
	H	10.9	46.7	16.6	3.3	10.0	1.2	1.9	2.3	7.0	100.0
EAST NORTH CENTRAL	N	2922	4325	30685	4229	3417	830	1512	2366	4627	54913
	V	9.9	6.9	38.8	14.8	9.4	7.7	6.4	13.0	9.9	16.4
	H	5.3	7.9	55.9	7.7	6.2	1.5	2.8	4.3	8.4	100.0
WEST NORTH CENTRAL	N	1140	1725	5645	11727	1451	459	1757	2473	2824	29201
	V	3.9	2.7	7.1	41.0	4.0	4.3	7.5	13.6	6.1	8.7
	H	3.9	5.9	19.3	40.2	5.0	1.6	6.0	8.5	9.7	100.0
SOUTH ATLANTIC	N	1701	3027	3940	824	11946	1570	1126	556	1496	26186
	V	5.8	4.8	5.0	2.9	32.8	14.6	4.8	3.1	3.2	7.8
	H	6.5	11.6	15.0	3.1	45.6	6.0	4.3	2.1	5.7	100.0
EAST SOUTH CENTRAL	N	425	663	2140	497	2184	4444	1207	279	520	12359
	V	1.4	1.1	2.7	1.7	6.0	41.3	5.1	1.5	1.1	3.7
	H	3.4	5.4	17.3	4.0	17.7	36.0	9.8	2.3	4.2	100.0
WEST SOUTH CENTRAL	N	675	893	2467	1374	1556	1030	11645	1110	1412	22162
	V	2.3	1.4	3.1	4.8	4.3	9.6	49.6	6.1	3.0	6.6
	H	3.0	4.0	11.1	6.2	7.0	4.6	52.5	5.0	6.4	100.0
MOUNTAIN	N	517	770	1914	977	560	129	603	4771	2696	12937
	V	1.8	1.2	2.4	3.4	1.5	1.2	2.6	26.3	5.8	3.9
	H	4.0	6.0	14.8	7.6	4.3	1.0	4.7	36.9	20.8	100.0
PACIFIC AND INSULAR	N	1578	2084	3433	1185	1105	196	681	2171	15670	28103
	V	5.3	3.3	4.3	4.1	3.0	1.8	2.9	11.9	33.6	8.4
	H	5.6	7.4	12.2	4.2	3.9	.7	2.4	7.7	55.8	100.0
FOREIGN	N	5051	10603	13344	4646	4911	948	2953	2063	9218	53737
	V	17.1	16.9	16.9	16.2	13.5	8.8	12.6	11.4	19.8	16.0
	H	9.4	19.7	24.8	8.6	9.1	1.8	5.5	3.8	17.2	100.0
UNKNOWN	N	1534	3721	1425	266	786	156	333	329	1757	10307
	V	5.2	5.9	1.8	.9	2.2	1.5	1.4	1.8	3.8	3.1
	H	14.9	36.1	13.8	2.6	7.6	1.5	3.2	3.2	17.0	100.0
TOTAL	N	29512	62905	79144	28634	36465	10758	23485	18170	46571	335644
	V	100.0	100.0	100.0	100.0	100.0	100.0	100.0	100.0	100.0	100.0
	H	8.8	18.7	23.6	8.5	10.9	3.2	7.0	5.4	13.9	100.0

SOURCE: NRC, Commission on Human Resources

*N = number of persons; V = vertical percent; H = horizontal percent.

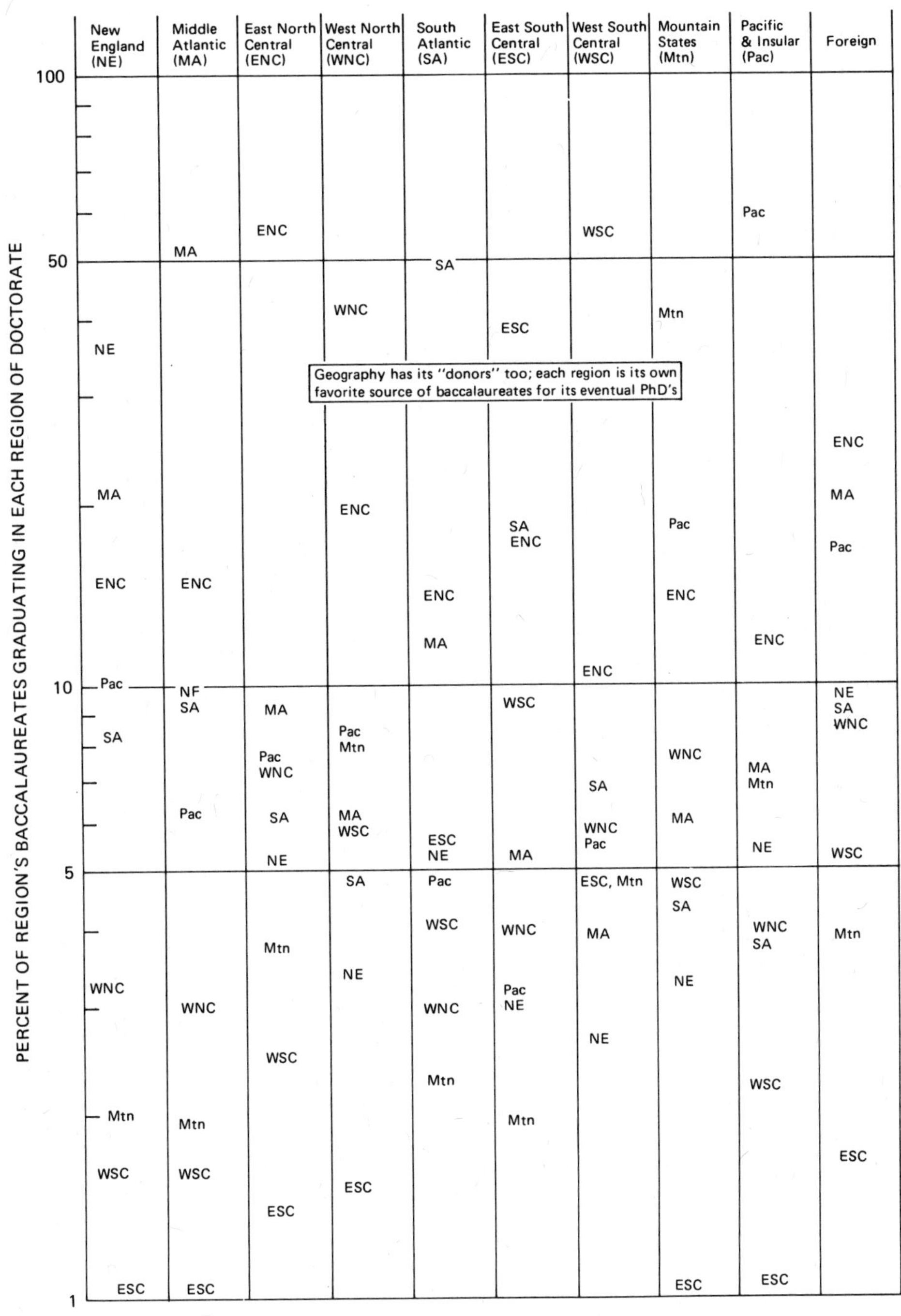

SOURCE: NRC, Commission on Human Resources

FIGURE 48 Graph of baccalaureate regional "donor" percentages.

REGIONAL DONOR PERCENTAGE DIAGRAMS

To provide a visual picture of the regional interchanges, Figures 48, 49, 50, and 51 show the individual region-to-region percentage changes at both the baccalaureate-to-doctorate levels and the high-school-to-doctorate levels. At both levels, each region is considered from both the donor and receptor points of view; hence there are four figures in all. By examining these four figures (or the data of Tables 27 and 28) it is possible to develop a sense of the interregional interchanges that are occurring to move people from the high school and baccalaureate levels to the doctorate level. It should be noted, in examining Figures 48 through 51, that the vertical scale is logarithmic. This was done to bring into sharper focus the smaller

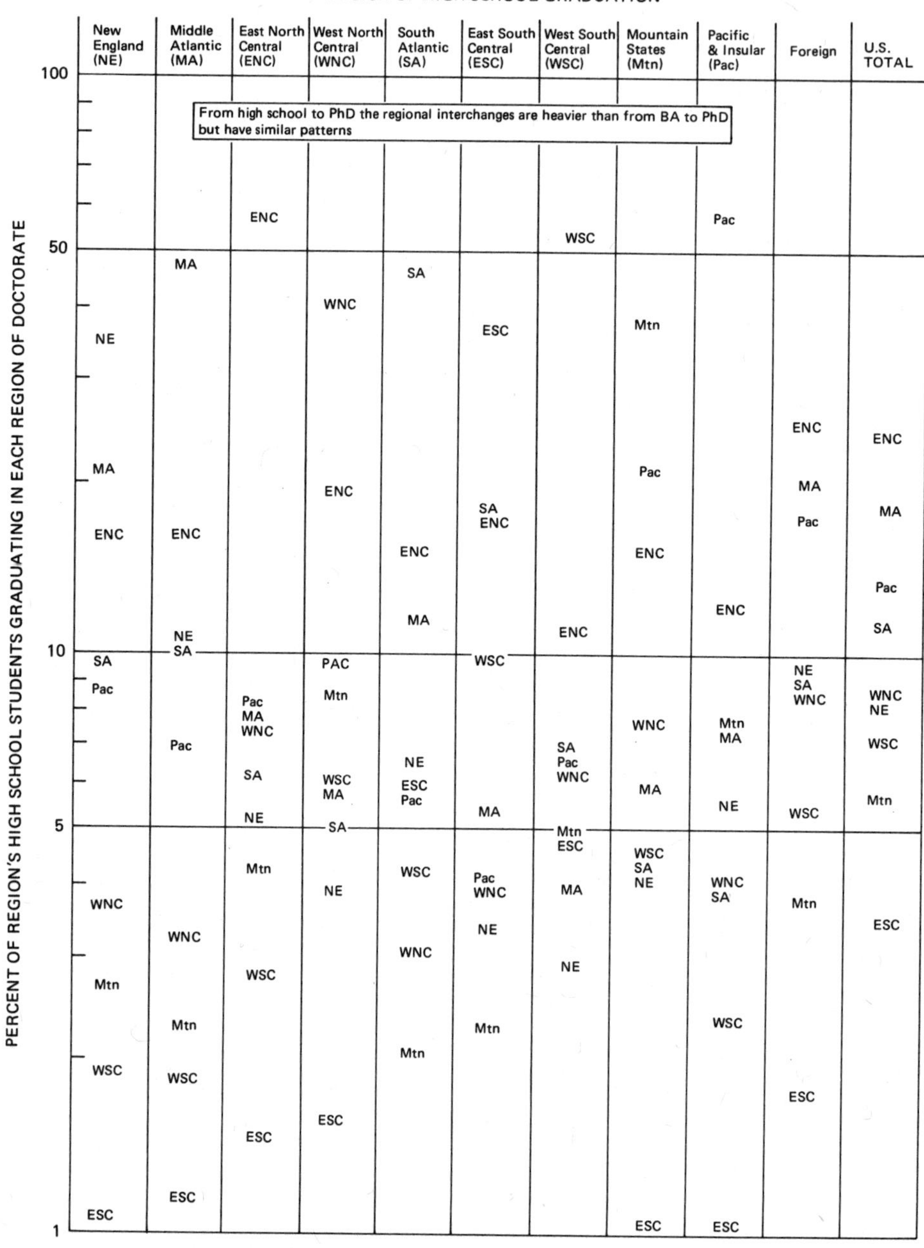

SOURCE: NRC, Commission on Human Resources

FIGURE 49 Graph of high school regional "donor" percentages.

percentages that characterize the interregional changes, in contrast to the "in-breeding" ratios (the diagonal data of Tables 27 and 28). Each region is, by a good margin, its own best source of doctorates--with the single exception of New England at the high school level. New England gets more doctorate-bound high school graduates from the nearby Middle Atlantic States than it does from its own high schools.

We will begin an examination of Figure 48--the baccalaureate donor percentage diagram--with the column for New England. Here we see that New England contributes about 37 percent of its own doctorates, the smallest self-contribution figure for any of the regions. It contributes 21 percent of its BA's to the contiguous Middle Atlantic region, and 15 percent to the East North Central region. Next in order is the Pacific region, distant as it is geographically, closely followed by the nearby South Atlantic region. Far down--below 4 percent--are the other four regions, all more distant and with fewer vigorous doctoral institutions. In a similar manner the donor characteristics of the other regions may be examined. It is noteworthy that for each of the regions, its contribution to its own doctor-

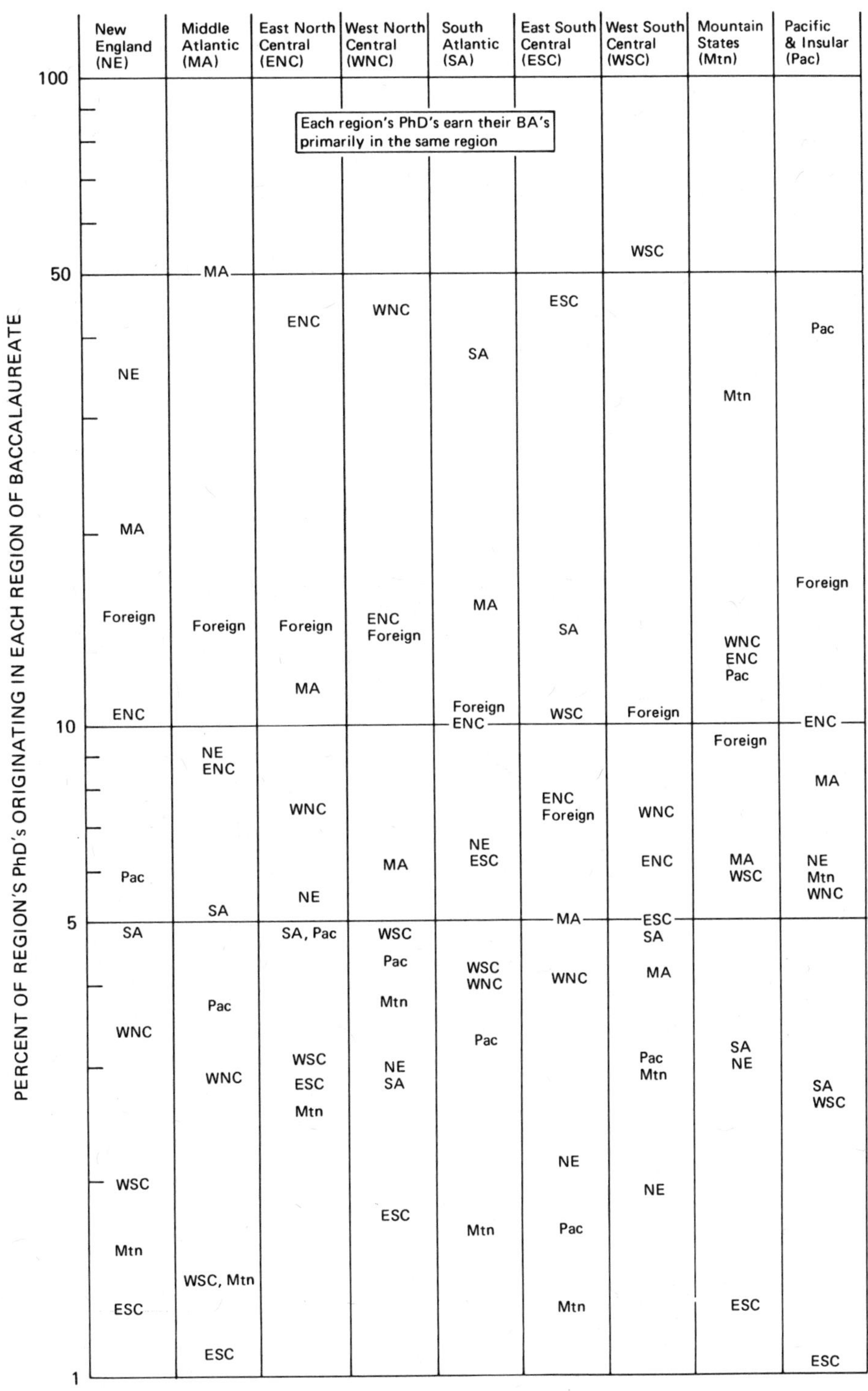

FIGURE 50 PhD regional "receptor" percentages from each region of baccalaureate.

ate production ranges somewhat above or below the 50 percent line but that no region contributes more than 21 percent of its baccalaureates to any other single region. Typically, the interchanges that rank highest are between nearby regions but this is not always the case, particularly with regard to the West Coast. Finally, to the right is a column for the total of all foreign regions of baccalaureate. The foreign regions, taken as a totality, contribute one-

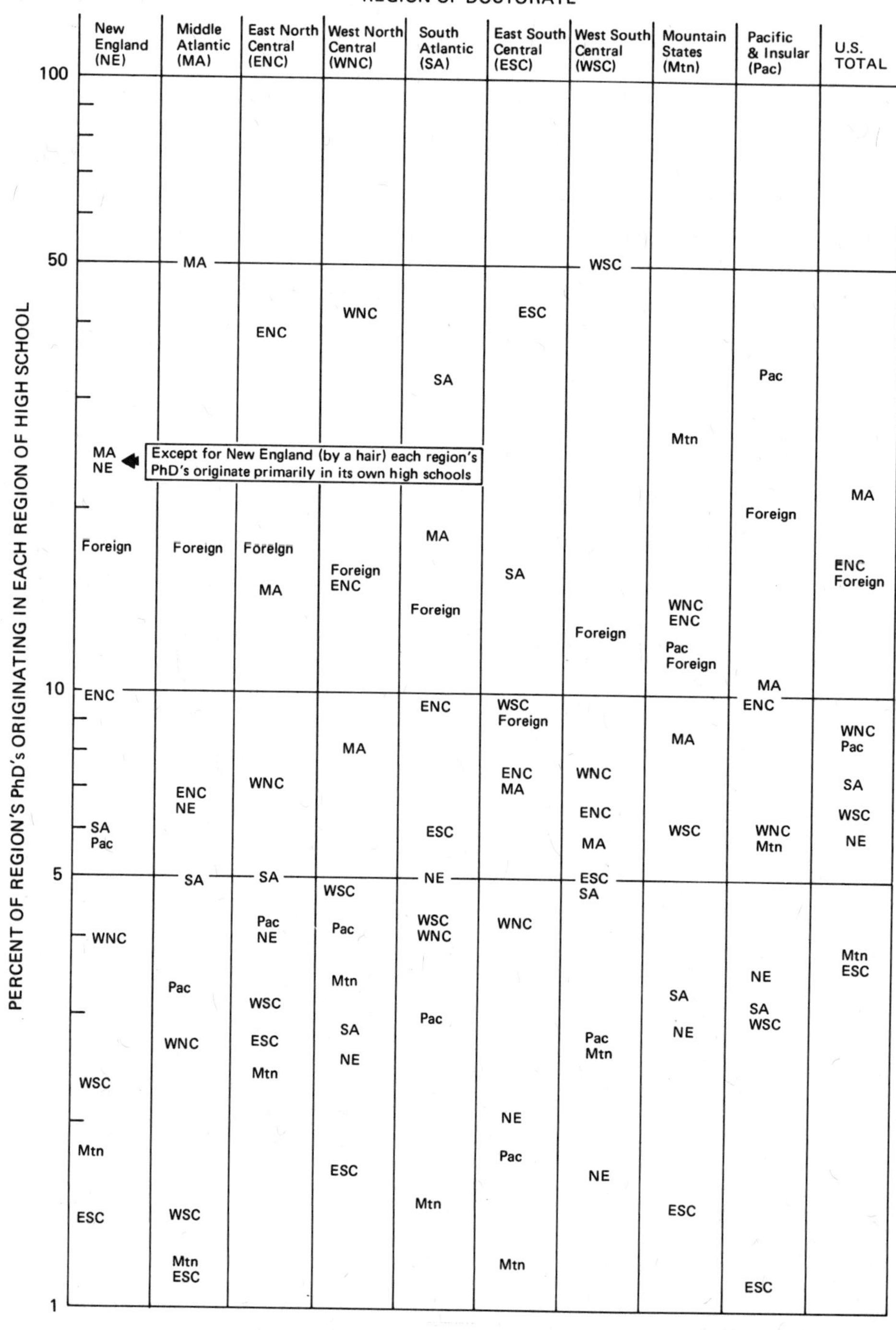

SOURCE: NRC, Commission on Human Resources

FIGURE 51 PhD regional "receptor" percentages from each region of high school.

fourth of their number to the East North Central region, one-fifth to the Middle Atlantic, one-sixth to the Pacific region, and less than 10 percent to each of the other regions.

Going back one educational level, we see, in Figure 49, the analogous contributions of each region of high school graduation to the several doctoral regions. New England contributes 35 percent of its doctorate-bound high school graduates to itself, 21 percent to the Middle Atlantic States, 16 percent to the East North Central States, and less than 10 percent to each other region. The pattern is very similar to the baccalaureate donor pattern but not exactly so. In comparing the regions at or near the bottom of the page, it may be noted that the

East South Central region, although it is typically low except for the other southern regions, is never off the scale, as it is in the case of the baccalaureate origins. At the far right, beyond the foreign origin column, is a column for the total United States. What this column tells is the doctoral destinations for the entire U.S. doctorate-bound high school graduation population. The regions are, therefore, shown in terms of their relative outputs of doctorates of U.S. origin, which can be compared with their relative standing in output of doctorates from foreign secondary school sources, shown in the adjoining column.

REGIONAL RECEPTOR PERCENTAGE DIAGRAMS

The data of Table 25 can be examined in graphic form in Figures 49 and 50. Turning first to Figure 50, we see the pattern of baccalaureate receptor percentages--the percentage of each regions's PhD's that have been received from each of the regions of baccalaureate origin. New England receives 35 percent of its PhD's from New England undergraduate sources, 20 percent from the Middle Atlantic colleges and universities, 15 percent from foreign sources, a bit over 10 percent from the East North Central region, and so on down the column. The Middle Atlantic States, shown in the second column, get half their doctorates from Middle Atlantic undergraduate schools, 15 percent from foreign sources, and less than 10 percent from any of the other regions. Each of the regions, as we scan across the diagram, is seen to be its own best undergraduate source, with the proportions ranging from about one-third to one-half of the region's doctorates. Foreign sources range downward from about 16 percent to about half of that for each of the regions of PhD. In no region except New England does another U.S. region contribute more than 15 percent to a region's PhD output.

The pattern of secondary school sources for the various receptor regions, shown in Figure 51, is similar to that of Figure 50 but with some subtle yet pervasive differences. For example, the foreign area contributions, region by region, are higher at the high school than the baccalaureate level, because some people with secondary education in foreign countries come to the United States for their undergraduate education. As mentioned earlier, the East South Central States never run off the bottom of the chart at the high school level, as they occasionally do at the baccalaureate level. The pattern of these differences suggests that a more intensive study than is possible in this book may well be rewarding. Such a more intensive examination, should scholars in this area be interested in pursuing it, could follow the movement, by sex and field, from high school to college to graduate school and eventually on to employment. Many of the data necessary for such a study were published in the book *Mobility of PhD's*, published by the NAS in 1971; an update that takes into consideration the rather profound changes during the late 1960's and early 1970's--the period of "the new depression in higher education"--might be very revealing. It might be particularly revealing if it would take into account the educational backgrounds from which the migrants and nonmigrants come, the nature of the jobs they eventually take, and some measures of career achievements. The necessary data for further studies of this nature, by university researchers or others, are available at cost from the DRF and Comprehensive Roster of the Commission on Human Resources.

3

After the Doctorate

The typical employment of new PhD's has been found in the nation's colleges and universities, which offered an opportunity for a combination of teaching and research responsibilities. Postdoctoral education, when it was undertaken, was typically in preparation for such employment. During the past decade, a transition has been in evidence, as mounting numbers of new PhD's have come near to saturating the academic market, diminished by a reduced flow of new students. In view of these developments, what have been the plans of the new graduates, as expressed in the Survey of Earned Doctorates? This chapter seeks answers to the marketplace response of the graduating PhD's.

HIGHLIGHTS

- Postdoctoral study, historically restricted to a few outstanding scholars or scientists, has become "the thing to do" for substantial numbers of new PhD's--up to 40 percent in the life sciences, but under 5 percent in the nonscience fields.
- Faculty jobs, traditional domain of most PhD's other than chemists and engineers, now offer fewer opportunities, while PhD output remains high.
- Nonacademic employment, which might be expected to take up the slack as colleges and universities reach the saturation point, has so far failed to do so.
- PhD's, at graduation, caught in the squeeze of increased numbers and decreased opportunities, are less sure of their eventual employment and increasingly take a variety of postdoctoral appointments as interim employment while seeking permanent jobs suited to their training and interests.
- Follow-up via the Comprehensive Roster of Doctoral Scientists and Engineers shows that, by and large, the plans for the first postgraduation year, stated on the Survey of Earned Doctorates, are realized.
- Geographic destinations following PhD graduation vary according to plans for further training or type of employment. Redistribution of this trained talent favors the Pacific Coast and Middle Atlantic States, in that order, for postdoctoral training, the East North Central and Middle Atlantic States for academic employment, and the South Atlantic and Middle Atlantic States, in that order, for nonacademic employment.
- Thirteen percent of those seeking further training plan to go abroad, as compared with 5 percent of those seeking academic jobs and 11 percent of those seeking nonacademic jobs.

POSTDOCTORAL STUDY

Historically, the doctorate has been the highest recognized level of education. But education beyond the doctorate has also had a long history, in the form of postdoctoral study, either formally via a postdoctoral fellowship, or less formally in the course of a sabbatical year. As a rule, the objective is to obtain research experience under the guidance of a mentor recognized for his or her achievements and ability to communicate matters of knowledge, technique, or approach to other scholars or scientists. Training at this level in the sciences received perhaps its first significant formal recognition in the establishment in 1919 of the National Research Fellowship program by the National Research Council, supported by a grant from the Rockefeller Foundation. Over the ensuing quarter century or so, well over 1,000 young scientists, selected for their especial promise as researchers, received postdoctoral education in this program. Following World War II, new programs supported by government agencies as well as private foundations grew rapidly, particularly in the science fields. For students who chose this path, the objective was primarily better preparation for academic careers of research and teaching.

A number of studies have been made of the process and results of postdoctoral training, particularly in the sciences, two of them by the National Research Council.[1,2] These studies showed the rapid growth of postdoctoral training over the post-World War II period, particularly during the 1960's. They also showed that people who undertook postdoctoral study were, on the average, better prepared intellectually for research work and, apart from excellent initial ability, apparently profited from the additional training by an increased research productivity. Meanwhile, another phenomenon appeared that to some extent changed the direction and extent of the postdoctoral experience. This was the advent of what has been called "the new academic depression." Because new PhD's were experiencing greater difficulty in obtaining academic jobs, and because those with postdoctoral training were favored for such positions as were available, a year or more of postdoctoral experience became "the thing to do" for an increasing portion of the new PhD generation. To some extent, this postdoctoral year--sometimes more than a year--became a "holding pattern" for young men and women for whom jobs that fully employed their research skills were not available. For others, the postdoctoral year afforded an opportunity to switch fields, from that of the dissertation research to something else that offered greater possibilities, either because it accorded better with their developing interests, or because more opportunities were thought to be available in the new field. At a time when the traditional disciplinary lines in the sciences were changing, and new fields developing, this postdoctoral period afforded an excellent means of transition. The names under which such transitional education took place were numerous. To the traditional fellowship there was added the postdoctoral traineeship, usually supported by a grant from a government agency, and various types of postdoctoral associateships, which might be either publicly or privately supported and which also bore a variety of designations on different campuses. For the present purpose, there is no distinction between these categories; the data herein include all types of postdoctoral education experience.

Comprehensive data going back to the 1930's are available but are not as reliable as the more recent data based on the DRF. The pre-1960 data come primarily from surveys conducted many years after PhD graduation and include postdoctoral training at various stages, from appointments immediately following graduation to senior postdoctoral study which may be undertaken even decades later. Comparability is therefore not possible, but the trends within the various data series can be pieced together to indicate a relatively consistent historical pattern. One important factor to note is that while immediate postdoctorals are characteristic of the natural sciences, in the behavioral sciences, the humanities, and the professions they are atypical; characteristically persons in these latter fields have undertaken postdoctoral education many years after graduation, and typically after having taught several years in a university. Data from the Career Patterns studies[3] of the NAS indicate that in all the science fields there was a gradual increase in the proportion of each successive cohort who undertook postdoctoral training of some sort. This general trend was interrupted by World War II but was later resumed. More recent data, from the DRF, is given in Table 29, and refers to plans for training in the first postdoctoral year. (As will be shown later, these plans are a very good indicator of the actual experience, as verified by follow-up.) Figure 52 shows these data graphically for four general summary fields but with greater chronological detail. It is noteworthy that in most fields for most periods the proportion of women taking postdoctoral training is greater than the proportion of men taking such training. The exceptions, in Table 29, are mathematics, medical sciences, and economics, and, in the 1970's, chemistry and engineering.

[1]National Research Council, *The Invisible University, Postdoctoral Education in the United States* (Washington, D.C.: NAS, 1969).

[2]National Research Council, *Postdoctoral Training in the Biomedical Sciences, An Evaluation of the NIGMS Postdoctoral Traineeship and Fellowship Programs* (Washington, D.C.: NAS, 1974).

[3]See Commission on Human Resources, *Profiles of PhD's in the Sciences, Summary Report on Follow-up of Doctorate Cohorts, 1935-1960*, Publication 1293 (Washington, D.C.: NAS, 1965).

TABLE 29
PERCENTAGE OF PhD's, BY FIELD AND SEX, WHO PLANNED POSTDOCTORAL STUDY IN EACH OF FIVE COHORTS FROM 1960 TO 1974

	Men						Women						Both Sexes Combined					
Field of Doctorate	1960-1964	1965-1968	1969-1970	1971-1972	1973-1974	Total, 1960-1974	1960-1964	1965-1968	1969-1970	1971-1972	1973-1974	Total, 1960-1974	1960-1964	1965-1968	1969 1970	1971-1972	1973-1974	Total, 1960-1974
Mathematics	8.5	6.3	8.3	9.2	8.9	8.1	5.4	4.1	4.4	12.5	7.4	7.0	8.3	6.2	8.1	9.4	8.8	8.0
Physics	16.6	23.7	37.1	42.8	44.4	31.3	8.6	16.8	41.7	42.9	44.8	33.1	16.5	23.6	37.2	42.8	44.4	31.4
Chemistry	25.0	29.7	36.7	49.6	46.4	35.4	29.1	33.5	37.9	45.4	45.0	38.1	25.2	30.0	36.8	49.3	46.3	35.6
Earth sciences	8.2	11.7	20.6	21.5	21.8	15.9	11.1	8.8	28.9	34.2	23.2	22.8	8.2	11.6	20.9	21.9	21.8	16.0
Engineering	4.9	5.2	8.3	12.9	13.1	8.6	11.8	8.3	7.1	4.8	11.8	9.3	4.9	5.3	8.3	12.9	13.1	8.6
EMP TOTAL	13.8	15.1	20.9	26.5	25.6	19.7	20.2	22.3	28.9	33.8	30.1	27.3	14.0	15.3	21.2	26.8	25.9	20.0
Agricultural sciences	7.2	9.2	12.0	14.4	14.9	11.3	12.5	17.9	27.9	26.8	24.7	23.4	7.3	9.4	12.3	14.8	15.3	11.6
Medical sciences	16.8	22.4	29.5	31.7	30.1	25.9	19.4	25.2	27.6	34.5	24.4	26.8	17.0	22.7	29.2	32.1	28.9	26.1
Biosciences	28.0	34.3	45.1	46.6	46.0	39.4	30.4	38.2	49.5	49.0	54.9	45.2	28.3	34.9	45.8	47.1	48.0	40.4
LIFE SCIENCE TOTAL	21.7	27.6	35.8	37.3	36.6	31.3	29.0	36.6	46.3	46.4	49.1	42.4	22.4	28.7	37.2	38.7	38.8	32.8
Psychology	10.4	13.2	13.4	12.4	12.2	12.3	10.0	10.9	13.1	13.4	14.2	12.6	10.3	12.7	13.3	12.7	12.8	12.4
Economics	1.6	2.3	2.6	4.4	4.2	2.9	2.1	0.8	4.0	2.3	3.5	2.5	1.6	2.2	2.7	4.2	4.1	2.8
Other social sciences	3.8	3.2	4.5	4.3	4.5	4.1	3.8	4.2	7.8	5.1	7.2	5.9	3.8	3.3	4.9	4.4	5.0	4.4
BEHAVIORAL SCIENCE TOTAL	6.0	6.9	7.6	7.3	7.4	7.0	7.7	8.1	10.8	9.6	10.9	9.6	6.2	7.1	8.1	7.7	8.2	7.5
Humanities	2.2	1.4	2.5	3.3	4.3	2.7	1.9	2.2	3.8	4.3	4.8	3.6	2.1	1.6	2.8	3.5	4.5	2.9
Professions	1.0	1.2	1.9	1.5	1.8	1.5	1.9	2.3	2.1	4.6	4.6	3.2	1.1	1.3	1.9	1.9	2.2	1.7
Education	0.8	1.0	1.7	1.9	2.2	1.6	1.3	1.2	1.7	2.5	3.4	2.2	0.9	1.0	1.7	2.1	2.5	1.7
NONSCIENCE TOTAL	1.4	1.2	2.0	2.3	2.9	2.0	1.6	1.7	2.6	3.4	4.0	2.9	1.4	1.3	2.1	2.6	3.2	2.2
SCIENCE TOTAL	14.0	16.3	21.4	24.3	23.1	19.5	17.5	21.9	26.9	26.6	26.2	24.3	14.2	16.7	21.9	24.5	23.5	19.9
GRAND TOTAL	9.9	11.3	14.7	16.3	15.4	13.4	8.5	10.6	13.1	13.1	13.4	12.1	9.8	11.2	14.5	15.8	15.0	13.2

SOURCE: NRC, Commission on Human Resources.

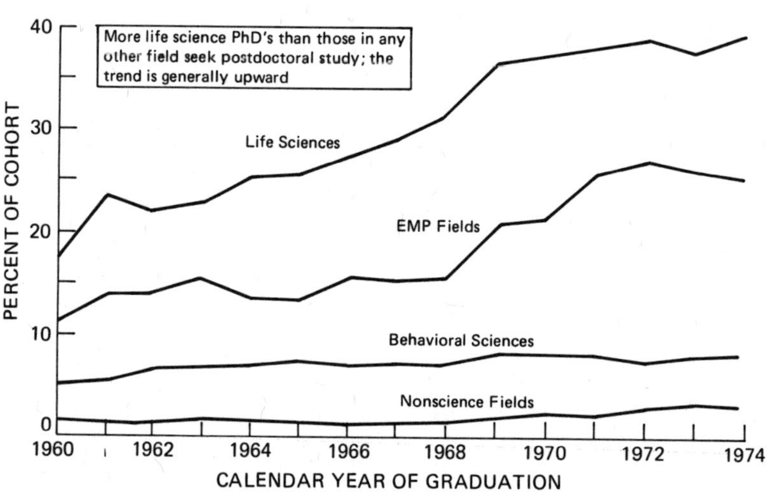

FIGURE 52 Field differences in proportions of PhD's planning postdoctoral study.

THE ACADEMIC MARKET

Traditionally, the employment for the new PhD has been in the academic world. There have been exceptions of long standing, however; chemists, for example, have for a long time sought and found employment in industry. The academic market, however, has been quite unable to absorb the enormous numbers of PhD's graduating in the late 1960's and early 1970's, particularly as the population wave of postwar babies has moved beyond the college age. It is apparent that nontraditional employment must absorb an increasing percentage of the new PhD's, unless there is a decrease in their numbers. The present indications are for some stabilization above 30,000 per year, and projections of future production vary extensively. It is informative, as a starting point for consideration of this question, to consider the factual data regarding the experience of the PhD's of the period since 1960.

In the pages that follow regarding employment, the new PhD's who plan to enter postdoctoral training are excluded, as are those who did not have definite plans. This discussion refers solely to those who, on the Survey of Earned Doctorates, said they planned to enter immediate employment. Table 30 shows, in percentage terms, the proportion of this group in each field who entered academic employment in each of five cohorts with greater detail regarding recent years. The first cohort is 1960-1964; the second 1965-1968; the remaining three cohorts are biennial, covering the last 6 years, with a summary for the entire 15-year period. Data are given separately for men, for women, and for the combined total.

In examining Table 30, it is apparent that in all but two fields--physics and engineering--the percent entering academic employment went up from 1960 to the early 1970's, when it declined, first gradually, then more steeply. In physics and engineering, the academic market has declined more or less regularly for 15 years. The general trend is similar for all fields, although the percent entering academic jobs varies markedly. The trend is similar, also, for men and women--it expresses a quite pervasive phenomenon. It should be noted, in interpreting this table, that these figures represent the percent of all those seeking immediate employment and exclude those who plan to take postdoctoral training, or who are uncertain regarding their future plans.

The data for the entire 15-year period, comparing fields and sexes, is summarized in Table 31, which shows the percent, of those who seek immediate employment after the doctorate, who plan on entering academic jobs. The bottom line provides the proportions for all fields combined and shows that, of the men seeking employment, 59.7 percent were headed for academe, while for the women the proportion was higher, 70.2 percent. The field with the highest academic percentage--humanities--has 88.2 percent for the men and 85.3 percent for the women. In the physical sciences and engineering, the proportions are below 50 percent, except for women in physics (59.7 percent) and in earth sciences (57.7 percent). Women are relatively few in the physical science fields, where industrial employment is relatively high and the proportion of women physical scientists in industry is very low, so they seek teaching jobs in the academic world much

TABLE 30
PERCENTAGE OF PhD's ENTERING EMPLOYMENT, BY FIELD AND SEX, WHO TAKE ACADEMIC JOBS IN EACH OF FIVE COHORTS FROM 1960 TO 1974*

	Men						Women						Both Sexes Combined					
Field of Doctorate	1960-1964	1965-1968	1969-1970	1971-1972	1973-1974	Total, 1960-1974	1960-1964	1965-1968	1969-1970	1971-1972	1973-1974	Total, 1960-1974	1960-1964	1965-1968	1969-1970	1971-1972	1973-1974	Total, 1960-1974
Mathematics	68.6	74.5	81.8	81.7	72.7	75.9	78.1	78.7	95.7	84.6	74.9	81.8	69.2	74.7	82.7	81.9	72.9	76.3
Physics	48.3	47.6	43.9	45.5	33.7	45.4	51.2	58.0	70.0	68.6	51.0	59.7	48.4	47.9	44.6	46.2	34.4	45.7
Chemistry	22.9	26.0	29.7	35.7	23.9	26.6	39.7	45.4	62.6	61.0	37.0	48.4	23.7	27.2	32.2	37.8	25.2	28.1
Earth sciences	38.5	45.8	52.3	51.6	41.8	45.4	50.0	50.0	56.0	73.7	59.0	57.7	38.7	45.9	52.4	52.1	42.7	45.7
Engineering	39.7	34.3	32.6	32.0	25.6	33.2	31.0	24.1	54.2	54.5	53.6	45.7	39.7	34.2	32.7	32.1	26.0	33.3
EMP TOTAL	40.1	41.2	42.3	44.3	35.9	40.9	51.1	55.9	73.4	70.9	56.7	61.0	40.4	41.6	43.3	45.3	37.0	41.6
Agricultural sciences	43.5	44.3	59.7	54.5	49.7	49.5	42.3	41.9	61.5	73.9	60.3	58.3	43.5	44.2	59.7	55.0	50.1	49.7
Medical sciences	47.2	47.5	58.4	60.8	53.8	52.7	50.0	59.0	69.8	64.9	65.6	63.2	47.4	48.7	60.0	61.4	56.5	54.0
Biosciences	56.0	58.5	70.7	65.6	57.3	60.8	66.1	61.8	77.5	73.9	66.2	68.1	57.2	59.0	71.7	67.1	58.8	61.9
LIFE SCIENCE TOTAL	51.2	53.2	65.7	61.2	54.2	56.3	63.8	60.9	75.5	72.7	65.6	66.9	52.3	54.1	66.7	62.6	55.8	57.5
Psychology	46.4	58.0	63.4	56.9	48.7	54.4	47.0	48.0	55.7	54.7	49.4	50.9	46.5	55.8	61.5	56.3	48.9	53.5
Economics	62.1	64.5	77.0	72.0	69.2	68.0	59.3	62.5	72.7	71.0	77.6	69.2	62.0	64.4	76.7	71.9	69.8	68.1
Other social sciences	71.6	78.0	85.9	85.6	78.8	80.2	66.3	77.6	87.1	81.9	80.5	79.7	71.1	77.9	86.0	85.0	79.1	80.2
BEHAVIORAL SCIENCE TOTAL	59.0	67.2	75.8	73.1	66.3	68.1	53.4	58.7	67.0	66.6	63.5	62.4	58.3	66.0	74.4	71.9	65.7	67.1
SCIENCE TOTAL	47.4	50.0	56.1	57.0	50.4	51.8	56.0	58.8	70.3	68.7	62.9	63.3	48.0	50.6	57.4	58.2	52.2	52.9
Humanities	87.2	88.6	94.1	91.1	80.6	88.2	84.0	84.2	91.4	89.5	79.6	85.3	86.7	87.7	93.4	90.7	80.3	87.6
Professions	68.1	73.8	84.1	79.8	75.9	66.2	66.9	72.1	80.4	72.4	79.3	74.2	67.9	73.6	83.6	78.8	76.3	76.0
Education	56.8	61.0	67.5	60.1	47.6	58.6	64.2	66.1	74.1	68.4	59.2	65.8	58.2	62.0	68.8	62.0	50.7	60.1
NONSCIENCE TOTAL	70.3	73.3	78.7	72.9	62.4	71.5	71.8	74.1	81.7	76.9	68.5	74.2	70.5	73.5	79.3	73.8	64.0	72.0
GRAND TOTAL	55.5	58.7	65.3	63.9	55.8	59.7	65.7	68.3	77.6	74.1	66.5	70.2	56.6	59.8	67.0	65.6	58.0	61.2

*This table excludes postdoctorals and those without definite plans.

SOURCE: NRC, Commission on Human Resources.

TABLE 31
THE ACADEMIC MARKET AS A PERCENTAGE OF TOTAL EMPLOYMENT DESTINATIONS, PhD's OF 1960-1974, BY SEX

Field of Doctorate	Men	Women	Both Sexes
Mathematics	75.9	81.8	76.3
Physics	45.4	59.7	45.7
Chemistry	26.6	48.4	28.1
Earth sciences	45.4	57.7	45.7
Engineering	33.2	45.7	33.3
EMP TOTAL	40.9	61.0	41.6
Agricultural sciences	49.5	58.3	49.7
Medical sciences	52.7	63.2	54.0
Biosciences	60.8	68.1	61.9
LIFE SCIENCES TOTAL	56.3	66.9	57.5
Psychology	54.4	50.9	53.5
Economics	68.0	69.2	68.1
Social sciences	80.2	79.7	80.2
BEHAVIORAL SCIENCES TOTAL	68.1	62.4	67.1
SCIENCE TOTAL	51.8	63.3	52.9
Humanities	88.2	85.3	87.6
Professions	76.2	74.2	76.0
Education	58.6	65.8	60.1
NONSCIENCE TOTAL	71.5	74.2	72.0
GRAND TOTAL	59.7	70.2	61.2

SOURCE: NRC, Commission on Human Resources.

more frequently than men do. Within the EMP group, mathematics stands out in its academic orientation (75.9 percent for the men and 81.8 percent for the women). In this respect, it belongs more with the humanities than with the physical sciences.

In the life sciences, except for men in the agricultural sciences, the academic percentages are above the 50 percent line and systematically higher for women than for men. The behavioral sciences are primarily academic also, and the sex differences are small. In psychology, the academic percentage is only slightly over 50, since many of these people are employed in clinics and hospitals, either public or nonprofit, or are self-employed as clinicians. The nonscience fields are strongly academic, although in education a significant portion of doctorate holders are in the public school systems, especially men in administrative roles.

NONACADEMIC EMPLOYMENT

The data for all categories of employer, for those whose plans at PhD were immediate employment, are given in Table 32. This table includes the cases shown in Table 30 but adds the other employer categories: business and industry, U.S. government, state and local government, nonprofit organizations, and other (including unknown).

Turning first to the final figures at the bottom of the table, where the totals for all fields are given, it is instructive to note that the largest nonacademic category is the most vague: "other and unknown." The curve of this category is a mirror image of that for academic employment and apparently reflects the increasing uncertainty in recent years, even for those who plan to seek immediate employment, as to what sort of jobs they will find. This is particularly true for the women, who have the greatest difficulty finding suitable employment and who, in other studies, show a higher unemployment rate than do men.[4]

Turning to the more explicit employer categories, one notes that for men "business and industry" is by far the largest nonacademic category and that this percentage, which held rather steady through the 1960's, dropped dramatically in the 1971-1972 period and then regained some lost ground in the most recent biennium. The combined-sex data are shown, by fiscal year, in Figure 53. For both men and women, none of the other categories accounts for more than 5 percent of employment. For both men and women, the U.S. government as an employer lost, in percentage terms, during the 1960's; it has gained somewhat since but is not back to the level of the early 1960's. State and local government employment has been on the increase for both sexes since the late 1960's, as has the nonprofit category for men; for women there has been little change in the nonprofit category. All of these figures are for the entire PhD group combined; examination of the separate fields will indicate the extent to which these trends are maintained throughout.

[4]Commission on Human Resources, *Doctoral Scientists and Engineers in the United States, 1973 Profile* (Washington, D.C. NAS, 1974).

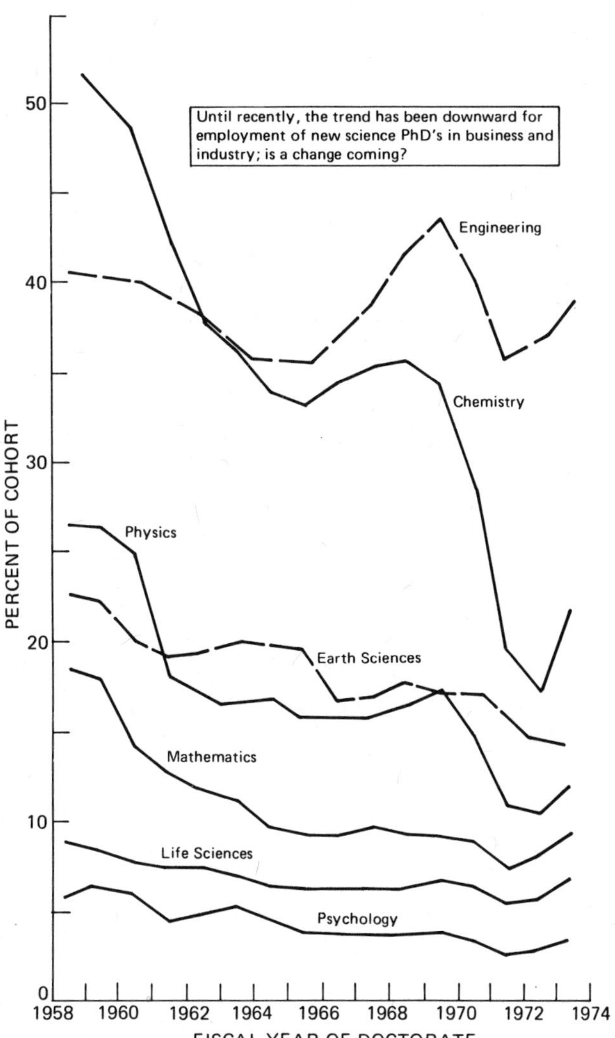

SOURCE: NRC, Commission on Human Resources

FIGURE 53 Post-PhD plans for employment in business and industry (2-year moving average).

TABLE 32
EMPLOYER CATEGORIES FOR 1960-1974 PhD's PLANNING IMMEDIATE EMPLOYMENT: MEN, WOMEN, AND COMBINED SEXES, BY FIELD OF DOCTORATE

	Men						Women						Total					
	1960-1964	1965-1968	1969-1970	1971-1972	1973-1974	Total, 1960-1974	1960-1964	1965-1968	1969-1970	1971-1972	1973-1974	Total, 1960-1974	1960-1964	1965-1968	1969-1970	1971-1972	1973-1974	Total, 1960-1974
MATHEMATICS																		
COLL/UNIV	68.6	74.5	81.8	81.7	72.7	75.9	78.1	78.7	95.7	84.6	74.9	81.8	69.2	74.7	82.7	81.9	72.9	76.3
BUS/IND	14.1	11.1	11.7	8.8	13.4	11.7	5.3	3.0	2.2	5.1	8.4	5.0	13.6	10.6	11.0	8.5	12.8	11.2
U.S. GOVT	3.4	2.8	2.0	3.8	4.3	3.2		.6		1.9	3.0	1.3	3.2	2.6	1.9	3.7	4.2	3.1
US ST/LOC GOV	.3	.1	.3	.2	.2	.2					.5	.1	.3	.1	.3	.2	.3	.2
NON-PROFIT	2.9	1.9	2.1	1.2	1.3	1.8	1.8	1.8		.6	1.5	1.2	2.8	1.9	1.9	1.1	1.3	1.8
OTHER OR UNK	10.8	9.7	2.1	4.4	8.1	7.2	14.9	16.0	2.2	7.7	11.8	10.6	11.0	10.1	2.1	4.6	8.5	7.4
TOTAL EMPL	100.0	100.0	100.0	100.0	100.0	100.0	100.0	100.0	100.0	100.0	100.0	100.0	100.0	100.0	100.0	100.0	100.0	100.0
PHYSICS																		
COLL/UNIV	48.3	47.6	43.9	45.5	33.7	45.4	51.2	58.0	70.0	68.6	51.0	59.7	48.4	47.9	44.6	46.2	34.4	45.7
BUS/IND	25.1	23.3	31.7	21.6	31.2	25.8	14.0	4.5	6.0	7.8	17.6	9.2	25.0	22.9	31.0	21.1	30.7	25.3
U.S. GOVT	8.0	10.8	9.7	17.0	16.8	11.4	4.7	4.5	4.0	5.9	5.9	4.9	8.0	10.6	9.6	16.6	16.4	11.3
US ST/LOC GOV	.3	.2	1.4	.3	.3	.5							.2	.2	1.4	.3	.3	.4
NON-PROFIT	5.0	3.2	5.0	2.9	2.9	3.9			4.0			.7	4.9	3.1	5.0	2.8	2.8	3.8
OTHER OR UNK	13.2	14.9	8.3	12.8	15.0	13.1	30.2	33.0	16.0	17.6	25.5	25.4	13.5	15.3	8.5	12.9	15.5	13.4
TOTAL EMPL	100.0	100.0	100.0	100.0	100.0	100.0	100.0	100.0	100.0	100.0	100.0	100.0	100.0	100.0	100.0	100.0	100.0	100.0
CHEMISTRY																		
COLL/UNIV	22.9	26.0	29.7	35.7	23.9	26.6	39.7	45.4	62.6	61.0	37.0	48.4	23.7	27.2	32.2	37.8	25.2	28.1
BUS/IND	58.9	56.5	59.8	45.0	58.7	56.6	27.4	20.9	20.0	19.5	38.2	24.8	57.3	54.2	56.8	42.8	56.6	54.4
U.S. GOVT	4.0	4.1	3.5	6.2	5.2	4.3	6.4	2.1	4.2	4.5	3.6	4.1	4.1	3.9	3.6	6.1	5.1	4.3
US ST/LOC GOV	.3	.4	.8	1.9	1.0	.7			1.1		.6	.3	.3	.3	.8	1.7	1.0	.7
NON PROFIT	2.3	1.7	2.2	2.0	1.8	2.0	2.3	2.8	2.1	1.9	1.8	2.3	2.3	1.7	2.2	2.0	1.8	2.0
OTHER OR UNK	11.5	11.4	4.0	9.2	9.3	9.7	24.2	28.7	10.0	13.0	18.8	20.2	12.2	12.5	4.5	9.5	10.3	10.4
TOTAL EMPL	100.0	100.0	100.0	100.0	100.0	100.0	100.0	100.0	100.0	100.0	100.0	100.0	100.0	100.0	100.0	100.0	100.0	100.0
EARTH SCIS																		
COLL/UNIV	38.5	45.8	52.3	51.6	41.8	45.4	50.0	50.0	56.0	73.7	59.0	57.7	38.7	45.9	52.4	52.1	42.7	45.7
BUS/IND	23.1	21.7	25.2	21.6	24.2	22.9		3.6	4.0	10.5	20.5	9.8	22.8	21.4	24.5	21.4	24.1	22.6
U.S. GOVT	14.1	13.1	9.4	11.9	14.6	12.8		21.4	16.0	10.5		9.8	14.0	13.2	9.7	11.8	13.9	12.7
US ST/LOC GOV	2.4	2.1	3.4	3.6	4.7	3.0			8.0			1.6	2.4	2.1	3.6	3.5	4.4	3.0
NON-PROFIT	3.0	2.0	2.5	1.6	1.7	2.2			8.0		2.6	2.4	3.0	1.9	2.6	1.5	1.8	2.2
OTHER OR UNK	18.8	15.3	7.3	9.7	12.9	13.6	50.0	25.0	8.0	5.3	17.9	18.7	19.1	15.5	7.3	9.6	13.2	13.8
TOTAL EMPL	100.0	100.0	100.0	100.0	100.0	100.0	100.0	100.0	100.0	100.0	100.0	100.0	100.0	100.0	100.0	100.0	100.0	100.0
ENGINEERING																		
COLL/UNIV	39.7	34.3	32.6	32.0	25.6	33.2	31.0	24.1	54.2	54.5	53.6	45.7	39.7	34.2	32.7	32.1	26.0	33.3
BUS/IND	42.1	43.6	51.0	46.0	54.0	46.8	24.1	37.9	29.2	21.2	24.6	26.6	42.0	43.6	50.9	45.9	53.6	46.7
U.S. GOVT	3.1	6.1	6.0	10.2	9.3	6.7	6.9	3.4	4.2	9.1	11.6	8.2	3.1	6.1	6.0	10.2	9.3	6.8
US ST/LOC GOV	.2	.3	1.1	1.0	.9	.7					1.4	.5	.2	.3	1.1	1.0	1.0	.7
NON-PROFIT	3.5	3.7	3.7	2.6	3.3	3.4	3.4	3.4		3.0	1.4	2.2	3.5	3.7	3.7	2.6	3.2	3.4
OTHER OR UNK	11.3	12.0	5.6	8.3	6.9	9.2	34.5	31.0	12.5	12.1	7.2	16.8	11.4	12.1	5.6	8.3	6.9	9.2
TOTAL EMPL	100.0	100.0	100.0	100.0	100.0	100.0	100.0	100.0	100.0	100.0	100.0	100.0	100.0	100.0	100.0	100.0	100.0	100.0
EMP TOTAL																		
COLL/UNIV	40.1	41.2	42.3	44.3	35.9	40.9	51.1	55.9	73.4	70.9	56.7	61.0	40.4	41.6	43.3	45.3	37.0	41.6
BUS/IND	38.8	36.9	42.5	34.4	42.5	38.7	18.9	13.4	12.1	12.3	21.6	15.8	38.3	36.2	41.5	33.7	41.4	37.9
U.S. GOVT	5.1	6.5	5.6	9.5	9.1	6.9	4.3	3.0	3.5	4.4	4.4	3.9	5.1	6.4	5.6	9.3	8.9	6.8
US ST/LOC GOV	.4	.4	1.1	1.1	1.0	.7			.9		.6	.3	.4	.4	1.1	1.0	1.0	.7
NON-PROFIT	3.4	2.8	3.3	2.2	2.5	2.9	1.9	2.0	1.9	1.2	1.5	1.7	3.3	2.8	3.2	2.2	2.5	2.8
OTHER OR UNK	12.2	12.3	5.2	8.4	8.9	9.9	23.7	25.7	8.2	11.1	15.2	17.3	12.5	12.6	5.3	8.5	9.2	10.1
TOTAL EMPL	100.0	100.0	100.0	100.0	100.0	100.0	100.0	100.0	100.0	100.0	100.0	100.0	100.0	100.0	100.0	100.0	100.0	100.0
AGRIC SCIS																		
COLL/UNIV	43.5	44.3	59.7	54.5	49.7	49.5	42.3	41.9	61.5	73.9	60.3	58.3	43.5	44.2	59.7	55.0	50.1	49.7
BUS/IND	9.5	9.8	14.8	12.6	17.7	12.5		12.9	15.4	2.2	19.0	10.7	9.4	9.9	14.8	12.3	17.8	12.4
U.S. GOVT	12.9	12.7	7.7	10.8	8.9	10.9	3.8	3.2		6.5	8.6	5.3	12.8	12.5	7.6	10.7	8.9	10.8
US ST/LOC GOV	1.7	1.6	4.2	2.1	2.5	2.3							1.7	1.6	4.2	2.0	2.5	2.3
NON-PROFIT	1.0	1.1	1.8	2.3	2.5	1.7		3.2		6.5		2.1	1.0	1.1	1.8	2.4	2.5	1.7
OTHER OR UNK	31.4	30.6	11.8	17.7	18.5	23.1	53.8	38.7	23.1	10.9	12.1	23.5	31.7	30.7	12.0	17.6	18.3	23.1
TOTAL EMPL	100.0	100.0	100.0	100.0	100.0	100.0	100.0	100.0	100.0	100.0	100.0	100.0	100.0	100.0	100.0	100.0	100.0	100.0
MEDICAL SCIS																		
COLL/UNIV	47.2	47.5	58.4	60.8	53.8	52.7	50.0	59.0	69.8	64.9	65.6	63.2	47.4	48.7	60.0	61.4	56.5	54.0
BUS/IND	19.6	19.4	16.7	15.6	19.4	18.3	7.7	5.7	4.7	4.1	7.0	5.8	18.8	17.9	15.0	14.0	16.6	16.6
U.S. GOVT	6.3	5.8	7.3	7.0	6.8	6.5	9.6	4.8	3.5	4.1	6.4	5.4	6.6	5.7	6.8	6.6	6.7	6.4
US ST/LOC GOV	2.8	3.8	4.9	3.1	6.0	4.0		8.6	4.7	5.2	5.1	5.2	2.6	4.3	4.8	3.4	5.8	4.1
NON-PROFIT	4.4	3.9	3.6	4.8	7.2	4.6	5.8	3.8	8.1	14.4	7.0	7.8	4.5	3.9	4.2	6.1	7.1	5.1
OTHER OR UNK	19.7	19.7	9.2	8.8	6.8	13.9	26.9	18.1	9.3	7.2	8.9	12.5	20.2	19.5	9.2	8.6	7.3	13.7
TOTAL EMPL	100.0	100.0	100.0	100.0	100.0	100.0	100.0	100.0	100.0	100.0	100.0	100.0	100.0	100.0	100.0	100.0	100.0	100.0
BIOSCIENCES																		
COLL/UNIV	56.0	58.5	70.7	65.6	57.3	60.8	66.1	61.8	77.5	73.9	66.2	68.1	57.2	59.0	71.7	67.1	58.8	61.9
BUS/IND	9.8	8.2	10.8	8.9	13.3	9.9	2.7	2.5	3.1	3.7	4.8	3.3	8.9	7.3	9.7	8.0	11.8	8.9
U.S. GOVT	9.2	9.3	5.5	8.0	8.1	8.3	4.5	4.2	3.1	4.0	3.2	3.9	8.7	8.6	5.1	7.3	7.2	7.6
US ST/LOC GOV	2.1	1.7	3.0	3.2	3.6	2.5	1.8	.8	2.9	1.1	2.2	1.6	2.0	1.5	3.0	2.9	3.3	2.4
NON-PROFIT	3.5	3.8	3.4	4.2	4.5	3.8	5.6	6.5	3.8	5.0	4.8	5.3	3.8	4.2	3.4	4.3	4.6	4.1
OTHER OR UNK	19.4	18.5	6.7	10.1	13.3	14.7	19.2	24.1	9.6	12.3	18.7	17.7	19.4	19.3	7.2	10.5	14.2	15.2
TOTAL EMPL	100.0	100.0	100.0	100.0	100.0	100.0	100.0	100.0	100.0	100.0	100.0	100.0	100.0	100.0	100.0	100.0	100.0	100.0
LIFE SCI TOT																		
COLL/UNIV	51.2	53.2	65.7	61.2	54.2	56.3	63.8	60.9	75.5	72.7	65.6	66.9	52.3	54.1	66.7	62.6	55.8	57.5
BUS/IND	10.7	9.9	12.8	11.0	15.6	11.6	3.0	3.2	3.9	3.6	6.5	4.0	10.1	9.2	11.8	10.1	14.3	10.8
U.S. GOVT	10.0	9.9	6.4	8.8	8.2	8.9	4.9	4.2	3.0	4.2	4.4	4.2	9.6	9.2	6.0	8.3	7.7	8.4
US ST/LOC GOV	2.0	1.9	3.6	2.8	3.5	2.6	1.6	1.7	3.0	1.6	2.7	2.1	2.0	1.9	3.5	2.7	3.4	2.6
NON-PROFIT	2.8	3.0	2.9	3.6	4.1	3.2	5.4	6.1	4.3	6.4	4.9	5.5	3.1	3.4	3.0	3.9	4.2	3.5
OTHER OR UNK	23.1	22.0	8.7	12.6	14.4	17.3	21.3	23.9	10.2	11.5	16.0	17.3	23.0	22.2	8.8	12.4	14.6	17.3
TOTAL EMPL	100.0	100.0	100.0	100.0	100.0	100.0	100.0	100.0	100.0	100.0	100.0	100.0	100.0	100.0	100.0	100.0	100.0	100.0
PSYCHOLOGY																		
COLL/UNIV	46.4	58.0	63.4	56.9	48.7	54.4	47.0	48.0	55.7	54.7	49.4	50.9	46.5	55.8	61.5	56.3	48.9	53.5
BUS/IND	7.0	5.0	5.5	3.6	5.1	5.3	1.4	2.0	1.3	2.4	2.5	2.0	6.0	4.4	4.4	3.3	4.3	4.5
U.S. GOVT	10.0	5.5	3.3	4.7	4.6	5.8	5.7	3.8	2.8	3.5	3.2	3.7	9.2	5.1	3.2	4.4	4.2	5.3
US ST/LOC GOV	13.8	12.2	12.0	15.9	14.1	13.6	10.5	11.8	15.3	11.6	14.0	12.8	13.2	12.2	12.8	14.7	14.1	13.4
NON-PROFIT	9.4	8.2	8.9	9.3	14.0	9.9	11.1	12.2	11.9	11.5	13.5	12.2	9.7	9.0	9.6	9.9	13.9	10.5
OTHER OR UNK	13.4	11.1	6.9	9.7	13.4	11.1	24.3	22.2	13.0	16.3	17.4	18.5	15.5	13.5	8.4	11.4	14.6	12.9
TOTAL EMPL	100.0	100.0	100.0	100.0	100.0	100.0	100.0	100.0	100.0	100.0	100.0	100.0	100.0	100.0	100.0	100.0	100.0	100.0

TABLE 32 Continued

	Men						Women						Total					
	1960-1964	1965-1968	1969-1970	1971-1972	1973-1974	Total, 1960-1974	1960-1964	1965-1968	1969-1970	1971-1972	1973-1974	Total, 1960-1974	1960-1964	1965-1968	1969-1970	1971-1972	1973-1974	Total, 1960-1974
ECON &-METRC																		
COLL/UNIV	62.1	64.5	77.0	72.0	69.2	68.0	59.3	62.5	72.7	71.0	77.6	69.2	62.0	64.4	76.7	71.9	69.8	68.1
BUS/IND	5.9	5.0	5.2	6.0	6.5	5.7	2.3	5.4	5.7	8.1	3.2	5.0	5.8	5.0	5.2	6.2	6.2	5.6
U.S. GOVT	8.6	7.3	5.3	8.0	8.0	7.5	9.3	8.0	6.8	5.6	8.8	7.7	8.6	7.3	5.4	7.8	8.0	7.5
US ST/LOC GOV	.9	.7	1.9	1.2	2.2	1.3	1.2		2.3	.8	.8	.9	1.0	.7	1.9	1.1	2.1	1.3
NON-PROFIT	4.1	3.6	4.7	4.2	3.9	4.0	7.0	.9	6.8	7.3	2.4	4.7	4.3	3.4	4.8	4.5	3.8	4.1
OTHER OR UNK	18.3	18.9	5.9	8.6	10.3	13.5	20.9	23.2	5.7	7.3	7.2	12.5	18.4	19.1	5.9	8.5	10.0	13.4
TOTAL EMPL	100.0	100.0	100.0	100.0	100.0	100.0	100.0	100.0	100.0	100.0	100.0	100.0	100.0	100.0	100.0	100.0	100.0	100.0
OTHER SOC SCIS																		
COLL/UNIV	71.6	78.0	85.9	85.6	78.8	80.2	66.3	77.6	87.1	81.9	80.5	79.7	71.1	77.9	86.0	85.0	79.1	80.2
BUS/IND	1.8	1.8	3.2	2.1	2.9	2.4	1.0	1.0	1.9	1.1	1.3	1.3	1.7	1.7	3.0	2.0	2.6	2.2
U.S. GOVT	5.4	3.0	1.8	2.6	3.1	3.1	2.9	2.2	.7	1.7	2.0	1.9	5.1	2.9	1.7	2.5	2.9	2.9
US ST/LOC GOV	2.0	1.7	1.9	1.6	2.9	2.0	3.8	1.0	2.4	3.2	2.3	2.5	2.2	1.6	2.0	1.9	2.8	2.1
NON-PROFIT	3.5	2.9	3.0	2.9	3.5	3.2	5.4	3.2	3.6	4.3	4.1	4.1	3.7	2.9	3.1	3.2	3.6	3.3
OTHER OR UNK	15.7	12.6	4.2	5.1	8.7	9.1	20.5	14.9	4.3	7.8	9.8	10.6	16.2	12.9	4.2	5.5	8.9	9.3
TOTAL EMPL	100.0	100.0	100.0	100.0	100.0	100.0	100.0	100.0	100.0	100.0	100.0	100.0	100.0	100.0	100.0	100.0	100.0	100.0
BEHAV SC TOT																		
COLL/UNIV	59.0	67.2	75.8	73.1	66.3	68.1	53.4	58.7	67.0	66.6	63.5	62.4	58.3	66.0	74.4	71.9	65.7	67.1
BUS/IND	5.0	3.8	4.5	3.4	4.3	4.2	1.4	1.9	1.8	2.3	2.0	1.9	4.5	3.5	4.0	3.2	3.8	3.8
U.S. GOVT	8.1	5.0	3.1	4.4	4.6	5.1	5.2	3.6	2.4	3.0	3.0	3.3	7.7	4.8	3.0	4.1	4.2	4.8
US ST/LOC GOV	6.4	5.3	5.6	6.4	6.8	6.1	7.9	7.4	10.2	7.5	8.5	8.3	6.6	5.6	6.3	6.6	7.2	6.5
NON-PROFIT	6.0	5.0	5.5	5.4	7.3	5.8	9.2	8.4	8.9	8.3	9.1	8.8	6.4	5.5	6.1	5.9	7.7	6.3
OTHER OR UNK	15.5	13.7	5.5	7.4	10.7	10.8	23.0	19.9	9.7	12.3	13.8	15.2	16.4	14.6	6.2	8.3	11.4	11.5
TOTAL EMPL	100.0	100.0	100.0	100.0	100.0	100.0	100.0	100.0	100.0	100.0	100.0	100.0	100.0	100.0	100.0	100.0	100.0	100.0
SCIENCE TOTAL																		
COLL/UNIV	47.4	50.0	56.1	57.0	50.4	51.8	56.0	58.8	70.3	68.7	62.9	63.3	48.0	50.6	57.4	58.2	52.2	52.9
BUS/IND	23.8	23.3	26.1	19.7	23.5	23.3	5.3	4.5	4.3	4.1	5.9	4.8	22.5	21.9	24.2	18.1	21.1	21.6
U.S. GOVT	7.0	6.8	5.1	7.7	7.3	6.8	4.9	3.7	2.8	3.5	3.5	3.6	6.9	6.6	4.9	7.3	6.8	6.5
US ST/LOC GOV	2.3	1.9	2.8	3.1	3.6	2.6	4.5	4.2	6.7	5.0	6.2	5.3	2.5	2.1	3.2	3.3	3.9	2.9
NON-PROFIT	3.9	3.4	3.8	3.5	4.6	3.8	6.7	6.5	6.4	6.8	7.1	6.7	4.1	3.6	4.1	3.9	4.9	4.1
OTHER OR UNK	15.6	14.6	6.0	8.9	10.6	11.7	22.6	22.3	9.5	11.9	14.4	16.1	16.0	15.2	6.3	9.2	11.2	12.1
TOTAL EMPL	100.0	100.0	100.0	100.0	100.0	100.0	100.0	100.0	100.0	100.0	100.0	100.0	100.0	100.0	100.0	100.0	100.0	100.0
HUMANITIES																		
COLL/UNIV	87.2	88.6	94.1	91.1	80.6	88.2	84.0	84.2	91.4	89.5	79.6	85.3	86.7	87.7	93.4	90.7	80.3	87.6
BUS/IND	.8	.8	.8	.9	2.1	1.1	.4	.3	.4	.7	1.9	.9	.7	.7	.7	.9	2.0	1.0
U.S. GOVT	1.3	.8	.5	.9	1.4	1.0	.5	.5	.5	.7	.6	.6	1.2	.8	.5	.9	1.2	.9
US ST/LOC GOV	.3	.3	.3	.5	.8	.4	.1	.4	.4	.1	.5	.3	.3	.4	.3	.4	.7	.4
NON-PROFIT	1.7	1.5	1.3	1.4	2.6	1.7	1.7	1.8	.6	1.1	1.5	1.3	1.7	1.5	1.2	1.3	2.3	1.6
OTHER OR UNK	8.7	8.0	3.1	5.2	12.6	7.6	13.3	12.8	6.8	7.8	15.8	11.6	9.4	8.9	3.9	5.9	13.6	8.5
TOTAL EMPL	100.0	100.0	100.0	100.0	100.0	100.0	100.0	100.0	100.0	100.0	100.0	100.0	100.0	100.0	100.0	100.0	100.0	100.0
PROFESSIONS																		
COLL/UNIV	68.1	73.8	84.1	79.8	75.9	76.2	66.9	72.1	80.4	72.4	79.3	74.2	67.9	73.6	83.6	78.8	76.3	76.0
BUS/IND	4.4	5.0	4.6	5.2	6.0	5.1	.7	1.5	1.2	2.7	1.5	1.5	4.0	4.6	4.2	4.9	5.4	4.6
U.S. GOVT	1.3	1.1	1.9	2.3	2.8	1.9	2.5	1.5	3.1	3.3	2.7	2.6	1.5	1.1	2.1	2.4	2.8	1.9
US ST/LOC GOV	.5	.7	.7	1.1	1.1	.8	2.5	1.2	4.6	2.1	.9	2.1	.8	.8	1.2	1.2	1.1	1.0
NON-PROFIT	11.3	7.4	4.6	7.6	9.6	8.1	6.5	5.0	5.4	8.6	7.1	6.6	10.7	7.2	4.7	7.8	9.3	7.9
OTHER OR UNK	14.4	12.0	4.1	4.0	4.6	7.9	20.9	18.8	5.4	11.0	8.6	13.0	15.2	12.8	4.3	4.9	5.1	8.5
TOTAL EMPL	100.0	100.0	100.0	100.0	100.0	100.0	100.0	100.0	100.0	100.0	100.0	100.0	100.0	100.0	100.0	100.0	100.0	100.0
EDUCATION																		
COLL/UNIV	56.8	61.0	67.5	60.1	47.6	58.6	64.2	66.1	74.1	68.4	59.2	65.8	58.2	62.0	68.8	62.0	50.7	60.1
BUS/IND	.8	.9	.9	.9	1.2	.9	.3	.6	.7	.6	1.2	.7	.7	.8	.8	.8	1.2	.9
U.S. GOVT	1.3	1.0	.9	1.4	1.8	1.3	.6	1.1	.8	1.1	1.5	1.1	1.2	1.0	.9	1.3	1.7	1.3
US ST/LOC GOV	3.7	3.3	5.5	5.9	8.4	5.4	2.7	2.4	4.1	4.2	5.8	4.0	3.5	3.2	5.2	5.5	7.7	5.1
NON-PROFIT	2.8	3.1	2.9	3.6	4.1	3.3	3.3	3.5	3.8	3.6	3.7	3.6	2.9	3.2	3.1	3.6	4.0	3.4
OTHER OR UNK	34.6	30.6	22.3	28.0	36.8	30.5	28.9	26.3	16.5	22.2	28.7	24.8	33.5	29.8	21.1	26.7	34.7	29.2
TOTAL EMPL	100.0	100.0	100.0	100.0	100.0	100.0	100.0	100.0	100.0	100.0	100.0	100.0	100.0	100.0	100.0	100.0	100.0	100.0
NON-SCI TOT																		
COLL/UNIV	70.3	73.3	78.7	72.9	62.4	71.5	71.8	74.1	81.7	76.9	68.5	74.2	70.5	73.5	79.3	73.8	64.0	72.0
BUS/IND	1.2	1.3	1.3	1.5	2.1	1.5	.4	.5	.6	.8	1.5	.8	1.1	1.2	1.2	1.3	1.9	1.3
U.S. GOVT	1.3	1.0	.9	1.4	1.8	1.3	.7	.9	.9	1.1	1.2	1.0	1.2	.9	.9	1.3	1.6	1.2
US ST/LOC GOV	2.0	1.9	3.1	3.5	4.9	3.0	1.7	1.5	2.6	2.5	3.4	2.4	1.9	1.8	3.0	3.3	4.5	2.9
NON-PROFIT	3.4	3.0	2.6	3.4	4.2	3.3	3.0	2.9	2.6	2.9	3.0	2.9	3.3	3.0	2.6	3.3	3.9	3.2
OTHER OR UNK	21.9	19.6	13.4	17.4	24.6	19.4	22.5	20.1	11.8	15.9	22.4	18.7	22.0	19.7	13.1	17.1	24.0	19.3
TOTAL EMPL	100.0	100.0	100.0	100.0	100.0	100.0	100.0	100.0	100.0	100.0	100.0	100.0	100.0	100.0	100.0	100.0	100.0	100.0
GRAND TOTAL																		
COLL/UNIV	55.5	58.7	65.3	63.9	55.8	59.7	65.7	68.3	77.6	74.1	66.5	70.2	56.6	59.8	67.0	65.6	58.0	61.2
BUS/IND	15.8	15.1	16.1	11.7	13.9	14.6	2.2	2.1	1.9	1.9	3.1	2.3	14.3	13.5	14.1	10.1	11.7	12.8
U.S. GOVT	5.0	4.6	3.4	4.9	4.8	4.6	2.3	1.9	1.5	1.9	2.0	2.0	4.7	4.3	3.1	4.4	4.3	4.2
US ST/LOC GOV	2.2	1.9	2.9	3.3	4.2	2.8	2.8	2.5	4.0	3.3	4.4	3.5	2.3	2.0	3.1	3.3	4.2	2.9
NON-PROFIT	3.7	3.2	3.3	3.5	4.4	3.6	4.4	4.2	3.9	4.3	4.4	4.3	3.8	3.4	3.4	3.6	4.4	3.7
OTHER OR UNK	17.8	16.5	9.0	12.7	16.9	14.8	22.5	21.0	11.0	14.5	19.6	17.8	18.3	17.0	9.3	13.0	17.4	15.2
TOTAL EMPL	100.0	100.0	100.0	100.0	100.0	100.0	100.0	100.0	100.0	100.0	100.0	100.0	100.0	100.0	100.0	100.0	100.0	100.0

SOURCE: NRC, Commission on Human Resources.

TRENDS IN POST-PhD PLANS

Up to this point, we have looked separately at postdoctoral education, at academic employment, and at nonacademic employment as they figure in the plans for the immediate future of the new PhD's. It is helpful to put these data together into a consistent picture. The table below summarizes very briefly, for the entire 1960-1974 period, the plans for employment, further education, or other activity, by sex and summary field, to illustrate field differences. Table 33 gives data by individual years.

	Men				Women			
	Postdoctoral Study	Employment	Other	Unknown	Postdoctoral Study	Employment	Other	Unknown
EMP Fields	19.7	72.4	3.2	4.7	27.3	63.3	2.3	7.1
Life Sciences	31.3	62.2	2.2	4.3	42.4	49.1	2.0	6.5
Behavioral Sciences	7.0	85.2	2.3	5.5	9.6	82.0	2.0	6.4
Nonscience	2.0	92.0	0.9	5.1	2.9	88.3	2.0	6.8
Grand Total	13.4	79.6	2.1	4.9	12.2	79.2	2.0	6.7

TABLE 33
FIFTEEN-YEAR TREND IN POSTDOCTORAL STUDY, EMPLOYMENT, AND OTHER ACTIVITY, BY FIELD AND SEX, PhD's OF 1960-1974

	1960	1961	1962	1963	1964	1965	1966	1967	1968	1969	1970	1971	1972	1973	1974	Total, 1960-1974
Men																
EMP fields																
Postdoctoral study	11.1	13.4	13.7	15.4	14.4	14.2	15.8	14.9	15.4	20.5	21.2	25.9	27.1	26.0	25.3	19.7
Employment	85.1	81.6	80.7	76.3	78.8	77.8	76.8	78.8	77.5	72.9	71.5	64.9	63.5	64.5	62.7	72.4
Other	2.0	2.8	2.8	3.1	3.2	3.5	3.3	3.6	3.6	3.3	3.2	3.3	3.6	3.1	2.7	3.2
Unknown	1.8	2.3	2.8	5.2	3.5	4.5	4.1	2.7	3.7	3.4	4.1	5.8	5.8	6.4	9.3	4.7
Life sciences																
Postdoctoral study	16.5	22.7	21.1	22.0	24.8	24.6	26.4	27.9	30.4	35.6	35.9	36.6	38.0	35.7	37.4	31.3
Employment	79.8	73.9	74.6	72.9	69.8	71.1	68.2	66.7	63.1	58.6	57.2	55.4	54.5	55.8	53.0	62.2
Other	2.1	1.7	1.9	2.1	2.8	1.6	2.1	2.9	3.4	2.3	2.7	2.0	1.8	1.7	1.6	2.2
Unknown	1.6	1.7	2.4	3.0	2.6	2.7	3.3	2.5	3.1	3.5	4.2	6.0	5.7	6.7	8.0	4.3
Behavioral sciences																
Postdoctoral study	4.8	4.7	7.1	6.6	6.4	7.2	6.6	6.8	7.0	7.8	7.4	7.5	7.1	7.2	7.5	7.0
Employment	90.9	90.5	86.0	86.6	87.0	85.9	85.4	87.4	86.1	85.1	85.8	83.9	84.4	84.2	80.8	85.2
Other	1.9	2.2	1.8	2.6	1.9	2.3	2.5	2.3	2.3	2.9	2.1	2.8	1.9	1.8	2.0	2.3
Unknown	2.4	2.7	5.1	4.2	4.7	4.6	5.4	3.5	4.6	4.2	4.6	5.8	6.7	6.8	9.7	5.5
Science total																
Postdoctoral study	11.0	13.6	14.1	14.9	15.2	15.2	16.3	16.1	17.1	21.3	21.5	24.0	24.5	23.0	23.1	19.5
Employment	85.1	81.8	80.4	77.9	78.3	77.9	76.6	77.9	76.0	72.2	71.5	67.2	66.7	68.0	65.6	73.0
Other	2.0	2.4	2.3	2.8	2.8	2.8	2.9	3.1	3.1	2.9	2.8	2.9	2.7	2.4	2.2	2.7
Unknown	1.9	2.2	3.2	4.4	3.6	4.1	4.2	2.8	3.8	3.6	4.3	5.9	6.0	6.6	9.1	4.8
Nonscience total																
Postdoctoral study	1.2	1.3	1.3	1.6	1.4	1.1	1.0	1.1	1.5	1.9	2.1	2.0	2.6	3.1	2.7	2.0
Employment	95.4	95.1	93.5	93.7	93.4	94.2	93.4	94.7	92.4	92.5	92.3	91.4	90.9	89.8	87.7	92.0
Other	0.8	0.6	0.7	0.7	0.9	0.6	0.9	1.0	1.0	1.0	1.2	1.2	1.1	0.9	0.9	0.9
Unknown	2.6	3.0	4.5	4.0	4.2	4.1	4.7	3.2	5.2	4.7	4.5	5.4	5.4	6.2	8.7	5.1
GRAND TOTAL																
Postdoctoral study	7.9	9.6	10.1	10.7	10.8	10.7	11.3	11.2	11.9	14.8	14.6	16.2	16.4	15.3	15.5	13.4
Employment	88.4	86.2	84.5	82.9	83.2	83.1	82.1	83.4	81.5	79.0	78.8	75.9	75.8	76.4	73.9	79.6
Other	1.6	1.8	1.8	2.1	2.2	2.1	2.2	2.4	2.4	2.3	2.2	2.3	2.1	1.9	1.7	2.1
Unknown	2.1	2.5	3.6	4.3	3.8	4.1	4.4	2.9	4.2	4.0	4.3	5.7	5.8	6.4	8.9	4.9
Women																
EMP fields																
Postdoctoral study	15.8	25.2	23.8	24.2	14.0	22.6	23.6	21.4	21.8	31.3	26.9	32.8	34.7	29.5	30.7	27.3
Employment	71.7	68.0	67.6	67.2	79.1	65.5	70.0	72.6	70.5	61.3	63.0	56.6	53.4	61.6	57.5	63.3
Other	3.9	4.9	2.9	2.3	2.9	3.4	1.5	3.2	2.3	1.3	3.3	1.6	2.6	1.4	1.8	2.3
Unknown	9.2	1.9	5.7	6.3	4.1	8.5	4.9	2.8	5.5	6.3	6.8	8.7	9.3	7.6	10.0	7.1
Life sciences																
Postdoctoral study	23.6	31.2	28.6	29.4	30.7	33.4	34.1	37.2	39.6	46.3	46.4	45.4	47.4	46.7	51.5	42.4
Employment	71.6	64.0	64.8	60.0	62.8	62.2	58.3	56.6	54.4	45.1	46.8	42.7	44.7	43.9	35.9	49.1
Other	2.7	1.6	4.4	3.8	3.0	1.4	2.5	2.4	2.7	2.6	1.4	2.0	1.3	1.2	1.0	2.0
Unknown	2.0	3.2	2.2	6.8	3.5	3.0	5.1	3.8	3.3	6.0	5.4	9.9	6.6	8.2	11.6	6.5
Behavioral Sciences																
Postdoctoral study	6.7	10.7	4.5	7.2	9.1	8.7	7.3	8.8	7.6	10.9	10.7	10.5	8.8	10.8	11.0	9.6
Employment	84.4	80.6	87.3	84.3	82.9	83.6	85.2	84.0	83.1	82.9	83.0	81.3	82.0	81.6	77.9	82.0
Other	4.0	5.5	5.3	5.2	2.4	3.1	2.3	2.6	2.2	1.7	1.4	2.4	1.4	1.2	0.9	2.0
Unknown	4.9	3.2	2.9	3.3	5.6	4.6	5.3	4.6	7.1	4.5	4.9	5.8	7.9	6.4	10.2	6.4
Science total																
Postdoctoral study	13.8	20.5	16.6	18.3	17.5	21.0	21.3	22.1	22.8	27.7	26.2	26.8	26.4	25.7	26.7	24.3
Employment	78.0	72.5	75.7	72.5	75.2	71.6	71.4	71.3	69.5	65.0	66.6	63.2	64.4	65.9	61.6	67.1
Other	3.6	4.1	4.5	4.2	2.8	2.5	2.2	2.7	2.4	1.9	1.8	2.2	1.6	1.2	1.1	2.1
Unknown	4.7	3.0	3.2	5.1	4.5	4.9	5.1	3.9	5.3	5.4	5.4	7.8	7.7	7.2	10.6	6.6
Nonscience total																
Postdoctoral study	1.6	1.6	1.1	1.7	2.0	1.5	1.4	2.0	1.8	2.1	3.0	3.2	3.5	4.2	3.9	2.9
Employment	91.5	92.7	92.0	92.0	90.5	88.6	91.0	92.7	90.6	89.9	89.7	87.5	86.8	86.3	83.6	88.3
Other	3.8	3.3	2.7	2.3	2.6	2.3	1.5	2.2	3.0	1.8	1.6	2.3	1.5	1.5	1.8	2.0
Unknown	3.1	2.5	4.2	4.1	4.9	7.5	6.1	3.2	4.6	6.1	5.7	7.0	8.2	8.0	10.8	6.8
GRAND TOTAL																
Postdoctoral study	6.6	10.2	7.7	9.0	8.8	9.7	10.2	11.1	11.0	13.6	12.8	13.3	12.9	13.3	13.5	12.2
Employment	85.9	83.5	85.0	83.3	83.9	81.5	82.2	83.0	81.3	78.8	80.0	77.2	77.6	77.7	74.3	79.2
Other	3.7	3.6	3.5	3.6	2.7	2.4	1.8	2.4	2.7	1.8	1.7	2.1	1.6	1.4	1.5	2.0
Unknown	3.8	2.7	3.8	4.5	4.7	6.4	5.7	3.5	4.9	5.8	5.6	7.3	8.0	7.6	10.7	6.7

SOURCE: NRC, Commission on Human Resources.

These data are provided in much greater detail, by graduation cohort and by the component fields of the summarized field groups above, in Table 34, and the trends, by individual years, are shown graphically for the four summary fields shown above, in Figures 54 through 57. It may be most useful, however, to begin with the data shown above, for the grand total of all fields combined. About 4 out of 5 new PhD's plan to enter employment immediately, and about 1 in 8 plan further training. Almost 1 in 20 of the men, and somewhat more of the women, are uncertain of their plans, and about 1 in 50 have plans not encompassed in the categories given above.

The field differences shown above are striking but even so tend to mask the differences among the more specific component fields. As shown above, about 20 percent of the men in the EMP fields and over 30 percent in the life sciences plan further training. For women the proportions are markedly higher--perhaps a reflection of the greater degree of difficulty they have in finding suitable employment, which is also reflected in the column marked "unknown." In the behavioral sciences, the proportions are lower: 7 percent for the men and almost 10 percent for the women. In the nonscience fields the proportions are still lower, about 2 percent for the men and 3 percent for the women. These field differences, and sex differences also, are mirrored in the fractions that plan immediate employment: the percentages range from 92 percent for men in the nonscience fields to less than 50 percent for women in the life sciences. It is well to keep these general differences in mind while looking at the time trends shown in Figures 54 through 57 for the four general fields shown above.

In the EMP fields, the proportion seeking postdoctoral training increased slightly but gradually, during the 1960's, as the proportion planning immediate employment slowly decreased. Then, at the end of the 1960's, the change quickened; the number going into postdoctoral training increased rapidly, the proportion entering employment went down, and the uncertainty factor rose. In the last 2 years shown, 1973 and 1974, the proportion going into postdoctoral training decreased, for the first time in a decade, as employment steadied. It must be emphasized that these trends are for the general field as a whole; in each of the component fields the changes have been somewhat different, as indicated by the data of Table 29, with somewhat coarser time intervals.

In the life sciences, the trend to postdoctoral study, as seen earlier in Figure 52, has been much stronger than in the EMP fields, and the decrease in immediate employment after the doctorate has been sharper. With the exception of a single year (1972) there has been a steady upward trend in the proportion who are uncertain as to their plans at the time of completing the Survey of Earned Doctorates. And, as for the EMP fields, there are widely divergent trends within the life sciences group. In the biosciences, for example, the proportion seeking further training has approached 50 percent for the men and exceeded that point for the women. This huge number seeking postdoctoral positions strongly suggests, even in the absence of other data, that what is involved here is something more than a desire for advanced training: we are witnessing a "holding pattern" for those who cannot immediately find suitable employment. Within the medical sciences, the peak in postdoctoral training apparently was passed by 1973, for both men and women. In the agricultural sciences, the postdoctoral training segment was never very high; it must be remembered that a substantial portion of this field is of foreign origin and return to their own countries to take up employment.

In the behavioral sciences, although the postdoctoral proportion was never very high, the differences among the component fields is still large; in psychology, the largest field, the percentages have ranged from 10 percent to 14 percent; in the other fields, it has been a minor fraction of that amount. In any case, the proportion has remained rather steady, in contrast to the rapid increase in the natural sciences. In the humanities the proportion has increased but from a very low base, and in the other nonscience fields the percentage has remained very low, while in all of the nonscience fields immediate employment has been the expectation of over 90 percent of the graduates until the last 2 years and has been only slightly less in the most recent data.

TABLE 34
POSTDOCTORAL PLANS, BY FIELD, SEX, AND COHORT: PhD's OF 1960-1974

	Men						Women						Total					
	1960-1964	1965-1968	1969-1970	1971-1972	1973-1974	Total, 1960-1974	1960-1964	1965-1968	1969-1970	1971-1972	1973-1974	Total, 1960-1974	1960-1964	1965-1968	1969-1970	1971-1972	1973-1974	Total, 1960-1974
MATHEMATICS																		
POSTDOC STUDY	8.5	6.3	8.3	9.2	8.9	8.1	5.4	4.1	4.4	12.5	7.4	7.0	8.3	6.2	8.1	9.4	8.8	8.0
EMPLOYMENT	85.5	87.5	85.5	82.3	81.6	84.7	87.7	85.8	87.4	81.3	83.9	84.9	85.7	87.4	85.6	82.2	81.8	84.7
MILITARY SVC	2.0	1.8	2.0	2.5	1.4	1.9							1.8	1.7	1.8	2.3	1.2	1.8
OTHER PLANS	.1	.2	.2	.2	.2	.2	3.1	3.0	2.5	2.6	3.3	2.9	.3	.4	.3	.3	.5	.4
UNKNOWN	3.9	4.1	4.0	5.9	7.9	5.1	3.8	7.1	5.7	3.6	5.4	5.2	3.9	4.3	4.1	5.7	7.6	5.1
TOTAL	100.0	100.0	100.0	100.0	100.0	100.0	100.0	100.0	100.0	100.0	100.0	100.0	100.0	100.0	100.0	100.0	100.0	100.0
PHYSICS																		
POSTDOC STUDY	16.6	23.7	37.1	42.8	44.4	31.3	8.6	16.8	41.7	42.9	44.8	33.1	16.5	23.6	37.2	42.8	44.4	31.4
EMPLOYMENT	76.0	68.3	53.8	45.9	43.3	59.3	74.1	73.9	52.1	45.5	40.8	55.5	75.9	68.5	53.7	45.8	43.2	59.2
MILITARY SVC	2.9	2.8	2.4	2.1	3.0	2.6							2.8	2.7	2.3	2.1	2.9	2.6
OTHER PLANS	.2	.1	.3	.3	.3	.2	3.4	.8		2.7		1.2	.2	.1	.3	.3	.3	.2
UNKNOWN	4.4	5.0	6.4	9.0	9.0	6.5	13.8	8.4	6.3	8.9	14.4	10.2	4.5	5.1	6.4	9.0	9.2	6.6
TOTAL	100.0	100.0	100.0	100.0	100.0	100.0	100.0	100.0	100.0	100.0	100.0	100.0	100.0	100.0	100.0	100.0	100.0	100.0
CHEMISTRY																		
POSTDOC STUDY	25.0	29.7	36.7	49.6	46.4	35.4	29.1	33.5	37.9	45.4	45.0	38.1	25.2	30.0	36.8	49.3	46.3	35.6
EMPLOYMENT	70.3	64.1	57.5	42.2	44.7	58.2	63.7	60.5	51.8	41.8	43.7	52.5	69.9	63.9	57.0	42.2	44.6	57.7
MILITARY SVC	1.9	3.2	2.4	2.8	1.9	2.5				.3		.1	1.8	2.9	2.2	2.6	1.7	2.3
OTHER PLANS	.1	.1	.1	.2	.1	.1	3.2	2.4	2.7	1.6	1.3	2.2	.2	.2	.3	.3	.2	.3
UNKNOWN	2.8	3.0	3.3	5.2	6.9	3.9	4.1	3.6	7.6	10.9	10.1	7.1	2.9	3.0	3.6	5.7	7.2	4.1
TOTAL	100.0	100.0	100.0	100.0	100.0	100.0	100.0	100.0	100.0	100.0	100.0	100.0	100.0	100.0	100.0	100.0	100.0	100.0
EARTH SCIS																		
POSTDOC STUDY	8.2	11.7	20.6	21.5	21.8	15.9	11.1	0.8	28.9	34.2	23.2	22.8	8.2	11.6	20.9	21.9	21.8	16.0
EMPLOYMENT	85.3	81.7	73.5	71.2	68.7	77.0	66.7	82.4	65.8	50.0	69.6	66.8	85.1	81.7	73.2	70.5	68.8	76.8
MILITARY SVC	1.8	2.5	2.4	2.8	1.8	2.3							1.8	2.4	2.3	2.7	1.7	2.2
OTHER PLANS	.1		.1	.1	.2	.1	11.1	2.9	2.6	2.6		2.7	.2	.1	.2	.2	.2	.2
UNKNOWN	4.6	4.1	3.4	4.5	7.5	4.8	11.1	5.9	2.6	13.2	7.1	7.6	4.7	4.2	3.4	4.8	7.5	4.9
TOTAL	100.0	100.0	100.0	100.0	100.0	100.0	100.0	100.0	100.0	100.0	100.0	100.0	100.0	100.0	100.0	100.0	100.0	100.0
ENGINEERING																		
POSTDOC STUDY	4.9	5.2	8.3	12.9	13.1	8.6	11.8	8.3	7.1	4.8	11.8	9.3	4.9	5.3	8.3	12.9	13.1	8.6
EMPLOYMENT	88.4	87.0	84.6	77.6	75.1	83.0	85.3	80.6	85.7	78.6	81.2	81.8	88.4	86.9	84.6	77.6	75.2	83.0
MILITARY SVC	4.0	4.3	4.1	4.3	3.8	4.1							4.0	4.3	4.0	4.3	3.7	4.1
OTHER PLANS	.1	.1	.2	.3	.1	.1		8.3	3.6	2.4	1.2	2.7	.1	.1	.2	.3	.1	.2
UNKNOWN	2.6	3.4	2.8	4.9	7.9	4.2	2.9	2.8	3.6	14.3	5.9	6.2	2.6	3.4	2.8	4.9	7.8	4.2
TOTAL	100.0	100.0	100.0	100.0	100.0	100.0	100.0	100.0	100.0	100.0	100.0	100.0	100.0	100.0	100.0	100.0	100.0	100.0
EMP TOTAL																		
POSTDOC STUDY	13.8	15.1	20.9	26.5	25.6	19.7	20.2	22.3	28.9	33.8	30.1	27.3	14.0	15.3	21.2	26.8	25.9	20.0
EMPLOYMENT	80.1	77.7	72.1	64.2	63.6	72.4	71.4	70.0	62.2	54.9	59.5	63.3	79.8	77.5	71.8	63.8	63.4	72.1
MILITARY SVC	2.8	3.3	3.0	3.2	2.8	3.1				.1			2.7	3.2	2.9	3.1	2.6	2.9
OTHER PLANS	.1	.1	.2	.2	.2	.1	3.3	2.6	2.3	2.1	1.6	2.3	.2	.2	.3	.3	.2	.2
UNKNOWN	3.3	3.7	3.8	5.8	7.8	4.7	5.1	5.2	6.5	9.0	8.8	7.0	3.3	3.8	3.9	5.9	7.9	4.8
TOTAL	100.0	100.0	100.0	100.0	100.0	100.0	100.0	100.0	100.0	100.0	100.0	100.0	100.0	100.0	100.0	100.0	100.0	100.0
AGRIC SCIS																		
POSTDOC STUDY	7.2	9.2	12.0	14.4	14.9	11.3	12.5	17.9	27.9	26.8	24.7	23.4	7.3	9.4	12.3	14.8	15.3	11.6
EMPLOYMENT	89.8	87.0	82.5	79.9	78.8	83.9	81.3	79.5	60.5	64.8	62.4	67.3	89.7	86.8	82.0	79.4	78.1	83.5
MILITARY SVC	1.1	1.3	2.3	1.0	.6	1.2							1.0	1.3	2.3	.9	.6	1.2
OTHER PLANS	.1	.2	.2	.2	.2	.2			2.3	1.4	3.2	1.8	.1	.2	.2	.2	.3	.2
UNKNOWN	1.8	2.3	3.1	4.5	5.5	3.4	6.3	2.6	9.3	7.0	9.7	7.6	1.8	2.3	3.2	4.6	5.7	3.5
TOTAL	100.0	100.0	100.0	100.0	100.0	100.0	100.0	100.0	100.0	100.0	100.0	100.0	100.0	100.0	100.0	100.0	100.0	100.0
MEDICAL SCIS																		
POSTDOC STUDY	16.8	22.4	29.5	31.7	30.1	25.9	19.4	25.2	27.6	34.5	24.4	26.8	17.0	22.7	29.2	32.1	28.9	26.1
EMPLOYMENT	77.2	70.5	61.9	56.5	56.1	64.7	72.2	69.5	64.2	57.7	62.8	64.1	76.8	70.4	62.2	56.6	57.5	64.6
MILITARY SVC	3.4	3.2	2.8	3.0	3.1	3.1	1.4			.6	.4	.4	3.3	2.9	2.4	2.6	2.5	2.7
OTHER PLANS	.1	.7				.2	4.2	2.6	.7	.6	.8	1.4	.4	.9	.1	.1	.2	.4
UNKNOWN	2.6	3.2	5.8	8.8	10.7	6.1	2.8	2.6	7.5	6.5	11.6	7.2	2.6	3.1	6.0	8.5	10.9	6.2
TOTAL	100.0	100.0	100.0	100.0	100.0	100.0	100.0	100.0	100.0	100.0	100.0	100.0	100.0	100.0	100.0	100.0	100.0	100.0
BIOSCIENCES																		
POSTDOC STUDY	28.0	34.3	45.1	46.6	46.0	39.4	30.4	38.2	49.5	49.0	54.9	45.2	28.3	34.9	45.8	47.1	48.0	40.4
EMPLOYMENT	67.2	60.0	48.7	45.5	44.8	54.0	62.8	55.4	43.1	40.9	34.5	46.4	66.6	59.2	47.8	44.7	42.6	52.7
MILITARY SVC	2.1	2.4	2.3	1.8	1.6	2.1	.1				.1		1.8	2.0	1.9	1.5	1.3	1.7
OTHER PLANS	.2	.3	.1	.2	.1	.2	3.0	2.4	2.1	1.7	.8	1.9	.6	.7	.5	.5	.3	.5
UNKNOWN	2.5	3.0	3.8	5.8	7.5	4.4	3.8	3.9	5.3	8.5	9.6	6.4	2.6	3.2	4.1	6.3	7.9	4.7
TOTAL	100.0	100.0	100.0	100.0	100.0	100.0	100.0	100.0	100.0	100.0	100.0	100.0	100.0	100.0	100.0	100.0	100.0	100.0
LIFE SCI TOT																		
POSTDOC STUDY	21.7	27.6	35.8	37.3	36.6	31.3	29.0	36.6	46.3	46.4	49.1	42.4	22.4	28.7	37.2	38.7	38.8	32.8
EMPLOYMENT	73.9	67.0	57.9	54.9	54.4	62.2	64.1	57.3	46.0	43.7	39.9	49.1	72.9	65.7	56.3	53.3	51.8	60.4
MILITARY SVC	2.0	2.3	2.3	1.7	1.5	2.0	.2			.1	.2	.1	1.8	2.0	2.0	1.5	1.3	1.7
OTHER PLANS	.2	.3	.1	.2	.1	.2	3.0	2.4	2.0	1.6	1.0	1.9	.5	.6	.4	.4	.3	.4
UNKNOWN	2.3	2.9	3.9	5.9	7.4	4.3	3.8	3.8	5.7	8.2	9.9	6.6	2.4	3.0	4.1	6.2	7.8	4.6
TOTAL	100.0	100.0	100.0	100.0	100.0	100.0	100.0	100.0	100.0	100.0	100.0	100.0	100.0	100.0	100.0	100.0	100.0	100.0
PSYCHOLOGY																		
POSTDOC STUDY	10.4	13.2	13.4	12.4	12.2	12.3	10.0	10.9	13.1	13.4	14.2	12.6	10.3	12.7	13.3	12.7	12.8	12.4
EMPLOYMENT	84.2	80.3	80.3	78.1	77.0	80.0	82.7	82.0	81.3	78.2	76.5	79.7	83.9	80.6	80.6	78.1	76.8	79.9
MILITARY SVC	2.6	3.1	2.7	3.2	3.1	2.9	.1			.1	.2	.1	2.1	2.4	2.1	2.4	2.2	2.2
OTHER PLANS	.3	.1	.2	.5	.4	.3	4.0	2.0	1.3	1.8	.9	1.8	1.0	.5	.5	.9	.5	.7
UNKNOWN	2.5	3.3	3.4	5.9	7.3	4.5	3.2	5.1	4.3	6.4	8.3	5.9	2.7	3.7	3.6	6.0	7.6	4.8
TOTAL	100.0	100.0	100.0	100.0	100.0	100.0	100.0	100.0	100.0	100.0	100.0	100.0	100.0	100.0	100.0	100.0	100.0	100.0
ECON &-METRC																		
POSTDOC STUDY	1.6	2.3	2.6	4.4	4.2	2.9	2.1	.8	4.0	2.3	3.5	2.5	1.6	2.2	2.7	4.2	4.1	2.8
EMPLOYMENT	93.0	90.7	89.5	88.7	88.4	90.3	88.7	90.3	88.0	94.7	87.4	89.9	92.8	90.7	89.4	89.2	88.4	90.3
MILITARY SVC	1.2	1.5	2.4	1.0	.5	1.3							1.2	1.4	2.3	1.0	.4	1.2
OTHER PLANS		.1		.1	.2	.1	3.1	4.0	1.0	1.5	1.4	2.2	.2	.3	.1	.2	.3	.2
UNKNOWN	4.2	5.4	5.5	5.8	6.7	5.4	6.2	4.8	7.0	1.5	7.7	5.4	4.3	5.4	5.6	5.5	6.8	5.4
TOTAL	100.0	100.0	100.0	100.0	100.0	100.0	100.0	100.0	100.0	100.0	100.0	100.0	100.0	100.0	100.0	100.0	100.0	100.0

TABLE 34 Continued

	Men						Women						Total					
	1960-1964	1965-1968	1969-1970	1971-1972	1973-1974	Total, 1960-1974	1960-1964	1965-1968	1969-1970	1971-1972	1973-1974	Total, 1960-1974	1960-1964	1965-1968	1969-1970	1971-1972	1973-1974	Total, 1960-1974
OTHER SOC SCIS																		
POSTDOC STUDY	3.8	3.2	4.5	4.3	4.5	4.1	3.8	4.2	7.8	5.1	7.2	5.9	3.8	3.3	4.9	4.4	5.0	4.4
EMPLOYMENT	89.0	89.6	88.5	87.2	84.8	87.7	85.2	86.1	85.1	84.5	83.2	84.5	88.6	89.2	88.0	86.7	84.5	87.2
MILITARY SVC	1.6	1.8	2.0	1.6	.9	1.5	.3			.1		.1	1.5	1.6	1.8	1.3	.7	1.3
OTHER PLANS	.1	.2	.1	.2	.2	.2	5.5	3.1	2.0	1.7	1.0	2.2	.7	.6	.4	.4	.4	.5
UNKNOWN	5.4	5.2	4.9	6.8	9.6	6.6	5.2	6.6	5.1	8.6	8.6	7.4	5.4	5.4	4.9	7.1	9.4	6.7
TOTAL	100.0	100.0	100.0	100.0	100.0	100.0	100.0	100.0	100.0	100.0	100.0	100.0	100.0	100.0	100.0	100.0	100.0	100.0
BEHAV SC TOT																		
POSTDOC STUDY	6.0	6.9	7.6	7.3	7.4	7.0	7.7	8.1	10.8	9.6	10.9	9.6	6.2	7.1	8.1	7.7	8.2	7.5
EMPLOYMENT	88.0	86.2	85.5	84.1	82.5	85.2	83.9	83.9	82.9	81.6	79.6	82.0	87.5	85.9	85.1	83.7	81.8	84.7
MILITARY SVC	1.9	2.2	2.4	2.1	1.7	2.0	.2			.1	.1	.1	1.7	1.9	2.0	1.7	1.3	1.7
OTHER PLANS	.2	.2	.1	.3	.3	.2	4.3	2.5	1.5	1.8	.9	2.0	.7	.5	.3	.6	.4	.5
UNKNOWN	3.9	4.5	4.4	6.2	8.3	5.5	4.0	5.6	4.7	6.9	8.4	6.4	3.9	4.7	4.5	6.4	8.3	5.7
TOTAL	100.0	100.0	100.0	100.0	100.0	100.0	100.0	100.0	100.0	100.0	100.0	100.0	100.0	100.0	100.0	100.0	100.0	100.0
SCIENCE TOTAL																		
POSTDOC STUDY	14.0	16.3	21.4	24.3	23.1	19.5	17.5	21.9	26.9	26.6	26.2	24.3	14.2	16.7	21.9	24.5	23.5	19.9
EMPLOYMENT	80.4	77.0	71.8	67.0	66.8	73.0	74.6	70.8	65.8	63.8	63.7	67.1	79.9	76.5	71.2	66.6	66.3	72.4
MILITARY SVC	2.4	2.8	2.7	2.6	2.1	2.5	.1			.1	.1	.1	2.2	2.6	2.5	2.3	1.8	2.3
OTHER PLANS	.1	.2	.2	.2	.2	.2	3.6	2.5	1.9	1.8	1.0	2.0	.4	.4	.3	.4	.3	.4
UNKNOWN	3.2	3.7	3.9	5.9	7.8	4.8	4.1	4.8	5.4	7.7	8.9	6.6	3.3	3.8	4.1	6.1	8.0	5.0
TOTAL	100.0	100.0	100.0	100.0	100.0	100.0	100.0	100.0	100.0	100.0	100.0	100.0	100.0	100.0	100.0	100.0	100.0	100.0
HUMANITIES																		
POSTDOC STUDY	2.2	1.4	2.5	3.3	4.3	2.7	1.9	2.2	3.8	4.3	4.8	3.6	2.1	1.6	2.8	3.5	4.5	2.9
EMPLOYMENT	92.1	92.6	90.7	88.1	85.7	90.0	87.6	89.2	86.6	83.0	81.1	84.9	91.4	91.9	89.7	86.7	84.3	88.8
MILITARY SVC	.7	1.0	.9	.8	.5	.8							.6	.8	.7	.6	.3	.6
OTHER PLANS	.3	.2	.2	.2	.3	.2	5.3	3.3	2.7	2.8	2.2	3.0	1.1	.8	.8	.9	.9	.9
UNKNOWN	4.7	4.7	5.7	7.6	9.2	6.3	5.3	5.2	6.9	9.9	11.9	8.4	4.8	4.8	6.0	8.2	10.0	6.8
TOTAL	100.0	100.0	100.0	100.0	100.0	100.0	100.0	100.0	100.0	100.0	100.0	100.0	100.0	100.0	100.0	100.0	100.0	100.0
PROFESSIONS																		
POSTDOC STUDY	1.0	1.2	1.9	1.5	1.8	1.5	1.9	2.3	2.1	4.6	4.6	3.2	1.1	1.3	1.9	1.9	2.2	1.7
EMPLOYMENT	92.3	89.4	87.4	89.4	87.4	89.1	89.1	86.5	89.0	86.4	86.4	87.3	91.9	89.0	87.6	89.0	87.3	88.9
MILITARY SVC	1.3	1.8	2.9	2.9	2.2	2.2	.3	.3	.3			.2	1.1	1.6	2.6	2.6	1.9	2.0
OTHER PLANS		.1	.1	.2	.2	.2	2.9	3.1	.7	1.8	1.3	2.0	.4	.5	.2	.4	.4	.4
UNKNOWN	5.4	7.6	7.6	6.0	8.4	7.0	5.8	7.9	7.9	7.2	7.7	7.3	5.4	7.6	7.7	6.1	8.3	7.1
TOTAL	100.0	100.0	100.0	100.0	100.0	100.0	100.0	100.0	100.0	100.0	100.0	100.0	100.0	100.0	100.0	100.0	100.0	100.0
EDUCATION																		
POSTDOC STUDY	.8	1.0	1.7	1.9	2.2	1.6	1.3	1.2	1.7	2.5	3.4	2.2	.9	1.0	1.7	2.1	2.5	1.7
EMPLOYMENT	96.3	95.5	94.8	93.5	91.2	94.2	95.1	92.9	92.6	90.5	87.9	91.2	96.1	95.0	94.3	92.8	90.3	93.5
MILITARY SVC	.4	.3	.4	.6	.5	.4		.1	.2	.1	.1	.1	.3	.3	.4	.4	.4	.4
OTHER PLANS	.1		.1	.2	.2	.1	1.0	1.2	.7	1.0	1.1	1.0	.3	.3	.2	.4	.4	.3
UNKNOWN	2.4	3.1	3.0	3.8	5.9	3.7	2.5	4.7	4.7	5.9	7.5	5.5	2.4	3.4	3.4	4.3	6.4	4.1
TOTAL	100.0	100.0	100.0	100.0	100.0	100.0	100.0	100.0	100.0	100.0	100.0	100.0	100.0	100.0	100.0	100.0	100.0	100.0
NON-SCI TOT																		
POSTDOC STUDY	1.4	1.2	2.0	2.3	2.9	2.0	1.6	1.7	2.6	3.4	4.0	2.9	1.4	1.3	2.1	2.6	3.2	2.2
EMPLOYMENT	94.1	93.6	92.4	91.1	88.8	92.0	91.7	90.8	89.8	87.1	84.9	88.3	93.7	93.1	91.9	90.2	87.7	91.2
MILITARY SVC	.6	.8	.9	.9	.7	.8		.1	.1		.1	.1	.5	.6	.8	.7	.5	.6
OTHER PLANS	.1	.1	.1	.2	.2	.2	2.8	2.3	1.6	1.8	1.6	1.9	.6	.5	.4	.6	.6	.5
UNKNOWN	3.7	4.3	4.6	5.4	7.4	5.1	3.9	5.1	5.9	7.7	9.4	6.8	3.7	4.5	4.8	5.9	7.9	5.5
TOTAL	100.0	100.0	100.0	100.0	100.0	100.0	100.0	100.0	100.0	100.0	100.0	100.0	100.0	100.0	100.0	100.0	100.0	100.0
GRAND TOTAL																		
POSTDOC STUDY	9.9	11.3	14.7	16.3	15.4	13.4	8.5	10.6	13.1	13.1	13.4	12.1	9.8	11.2	14.5	15.8	15.0	13.2
EMPLOYMENT	84.7	82.5	78.9	75.8	75.2	79.6	84.2	82.0	79.4	77.4	75.9	79.2	84.7	82.4	79.0	76.1	75.3	79.5
MILITARY SVC	1.8	2.2	2.1	2.0	1.6	1.9	.1		.1	.1	.1	.1	1.6	1.9	1.8	1.7	1.3	1.7
OTHER PLANS	.1	.2	.1	.2	.2	.2	3.2	2.3	1.7	1.8	1.3	2.0	.5	.4	.4	.5	.4	.4
UNKNOWN	3.4	3.9	4.2	5.7	7.7	4.9	4.0	5.0	5.7	7.7	9.2	6.7	3.4	4.0	4.4	6.0	8.0	5.2
TOTAL	100.0	100.0	100.0	100.0	100.0	100.0	100.0	100.0	100.0	100.0	100.0	100.0	100.0	100.0	100.0	100.0	100.0	100.0

SOURCE: NRC, Commission on Human Resources.

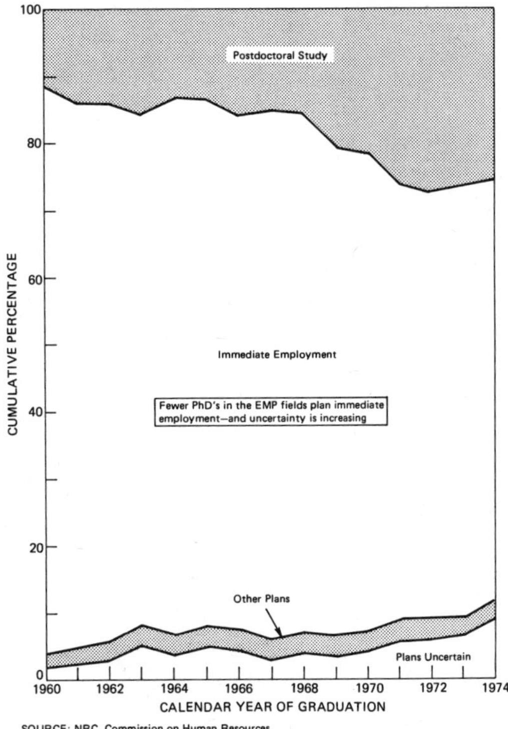

FIGURE 54 Plans for postdoctoral study, employment, or other activity: EMP fields.

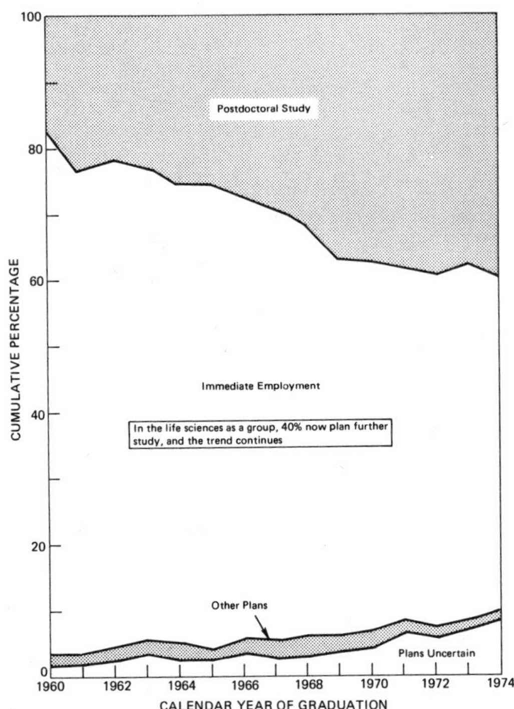

FIGURE 55 Plans for postdoctoral study, employment, or other activity: life sciences.

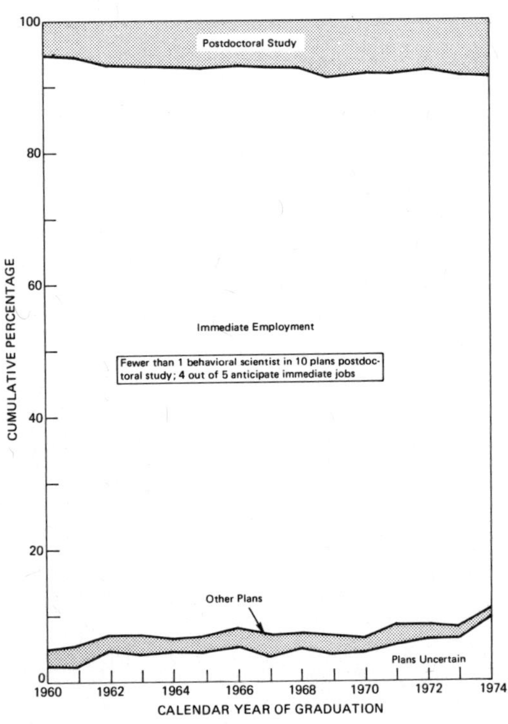

FIGURE 56 Plans for postdoctoral study, employment, or other activity: behavioral sciences.

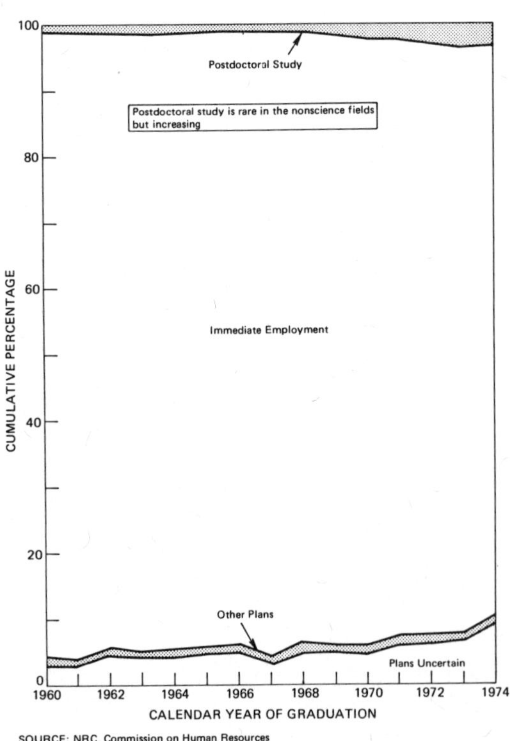

FIGURE 57 Plans for postdoctoral study, employment, or other activity: the nonscience fields.

TABLE 35
PERCENTAGE DISTRIBUTION OF REGIONAL ORIGINS AND DESTINATIONS AT THREE CAREER STAGES, PhD's OF 1960-1974

	Men			Women			Total		
	BA	PhD	Post-PhD	BA	PhD	Post-PhD	BA	PhD	Post-PhD
A. Percent from each U.S. region, foreign, and unknown source; Post-PhD destinations									
New England	8.2	8.7	5.7	8.8	9.2	6.0	8.3	8.8	5.8
Middle Atlantic	17.4	18.1	13.6	21.2	22.8	15.0	18.0	18.7	13.8
East North Central	17.6	23.8	13.6	18.0	22.5	12.5	17.7	23.6	13.4
West North Central	9.1	8.8	5.7	7.8	6.9	4.6	8.9	8.5	5.6
South Atlantic	7.9	10.7	11.2	9.4	11.6	10.0	8.1	10.9	11.0
East South Central	3.7	3.2	3.4	4.1	3.3	3.0	3.8	3.2	3.4
West South Central	6.7	7.2	5.6	7.2	6.7	5.0	6.8	7.0	5.6
Mountain	4.6	5.6	4.2	3.0	4.3	2.9	4.3	5.4	4.0
Pacific	9.7	14.1	10.8	9.2	12.6	9.6	9.6	13.9	10.6
U.S. Total	84.9	100.0	73.9	88.8	100.0	68.5	85.4	100.0	73.1
Foreign	14.1	--	8.3	10.3	--	5.4	13.6	--	7.9
Unknown	1.0	--	17.8	0.9	--	26.2	1.0	--	19.0
GRAND TOTAL	100.0	--	100.0	100.0	--	100.0	100.0	--	100.0
B. Percentage distributions with foreign and unknown excluded									
New England	9.6	8.7	7.7	9.9	9.2	8.8	9.7	8.8	7.9
Middle Atlantic	20.5	18.1	18.4	23.9	22.8	21.9	21.1	18.7	18.8
East North Central	20.7	23.8	18.4	20.3	22.5	18.2	20.7	23.6	18.3
West North Central	10.7	8.8	7.7	8.8	6.9	6.7	10.4	8.5	7.6
South Atlantic	9.4	10.7	15.2	10.5	11.3	14.6	9.5	10.9	15.1
East South Central	4.4	3.2	4.6	4.6	3.3	4.4	4.4	3.2	4.7
West South Central	7.9	7.0	7.6	8.1	6.7	7.3	8.0	7.0	7.6
Mountain	5.4	5.6	5.7	3.4	4.3	4.2	4.9	5.4	5.4
Pacific	11.4	14.1	14.6	10.4	12.6	14.0	11.2	13.9	14.5
TOTAL	100.0	100.0	100.0	100.0	100.0	100.0	100.0	100.0	100.0

SOURCE: NRC, Commission on Human Resources.

POST-PhD GEOGRAPHIC DESTINATIONS

The baccalaureate origins of PhD's are explored in more detail in the chapter dealing with institutional characteristics. Origins have a bearing on the matter of post-PhD plans, because to a great extent the graduates tend to remain in, or return to, their regions of origin. (See Figure 47, page 68 for the states in each region.) It is therefore instructive to examine the regional distribution (including foreign areas as a single region) at three career stages: baccalaureate, doctorate, and postdoctorate levels. The necessary data are shown in Table 35, which is presented in two portions: Part A presents the raw percentage distributions, including the percent from non-U.S. sources and unknown sources and similar percentages for foreign and unknown destinations. In Part B, the foreign and unknown origins and destinations have been excluded, showing the regional changes within the United States alone. Each part of the table is instructive in its own right, and data are presented separately for men, for women, and for both sexes combined.

It will be noted in Part A that 14.1 percent of the men and 10.3 percent of the women among the 1960-1974 PhD's come from foreign countries. For about 1 percent of each group the baccalaureate origin is unknown. At the postgraduation level, however, these proportions change drastically: 8.3 percent of the men and 5.4 percent of the women plan on foreign destinations after the doctorate. A much larger proportion do not know, when they complete the Doctorate Survey form, where they will be going. The "destination unknown" percentages are 17.8 percent for the men and 26.2 percent for the women. It is known that the degree of uncertainty is much greater for those of foreign citizenship, but it is impossible at this stage to ascertain just what proportion of those from non-U.S. sources will eventually go abroad and what proportion will stay in the United States. The data as tabled indicate a net flow into the United States of almost half of the foreign origin total. Follow-up some time later would probably show that this net figure has diminished. The uncertainties recommend that we look at the U.S. data separately, excluding those who plan foreign destinations and those who are uncertain as to their destinations. These data are provided in Part B of Table 35.

The data for men and for women in Part B are roughly similar, although there are interesting differences. Looking first at the combined data in the three columns at the right of the page, we can note the net shifts from stage to stage in the regional distribution of the PhD's. Beginning with New England, we see a net drain at each level, from 9.7 percent of the U.S. total at the BA level to 8.8 percent at the PhD level and 7.9 percent at the post-PhD level. The Middle Atlantic States lose slightly between the undergraduate and graduate levels but hold steady at the post-PhD stage. The East North Central States gain at the doctorate level but suffer a net loss at the employment stage. The West North Central States, like New England, lose progressively throughout the three stages. The South Atlantic States gain rather dramatically from stage to stage. At the employment stage, it is important to remember that Washington, D.C., is in the South Atlantic region--and a great many PhD's are employed in Washington. The East South Central States, rather weak at the PhD level, come back for a net gain at the employment level; the West South Central States gain back almost as many as the proportion of baccalaureates they produce. The Rocky Mountain States gain a bit at the PhD level and hold the gain at the employment stage. The Pacific Coast, like the South Atlantic, gains progressively throughout the three stages. To summarize briefly, the Northeast and the Midwest lose, between the undergraduate and post-PhD stages, while the South and the West gain. It may be significant that this general trend is characteristic not only of PhD's but of the population as a whole over the same period. Further data and detail by states and by institutions of origin will be found in Chapter 4.

REGIONAL INTERCHANGES

Following PhD graduation, people move from region to region for a number of reasons. Some undertake postdoctoral training, some enter academic employment, and some enter employment in nonacademic jobs. The regional interchanges, for those who plan to undertake each of these three types of activities, are shown in Table 36 in percentage terms. The regions of PhD graduation are shown in the rows, the post-PhD destinations in the columns. There are three rows for each region of graduation. The first row gives the destinations, in percentage terms, for those who undertake postdoctoral training. The second row shows the regional distribution of destinations

TABLE 36
REGIONAL INTERCHANGES AFTER THE DOCTORATE: PERCENTAGE DISTRIBUTIONS, BY REGION OF DESTINATION, FOR PhD's OF 1960-1974 SEEKING TRAINING AND EMPLOYMENT IN ACADEME OR ELSEWHERE

	Region of Post-PhD Destination											
Region of PhD	New England	Middle Atlantic	East North Central	West North Central	South Atlantic	East South Central	West South Central	Mountain	Pacific	U.S. Total	Foreign	Unknown
New England												
Postdoctoral study	*34.4*	10.8	5.7	1.6	7.2	0.5	1.3	1.9	11.3	74.7	16.8	8.5
Academic employment	*36.7*	14.3	9.7	2.9	6.7	1.4	2.0	1.7	7.5	83.0	5.5	11.5
Nonacademic employment	*27.7*	14.4	3.7	1.1	8.9	0.6	1.5	1.5	5.1	64.4	13.6	22.0
Middle Atlantic												
Postdoctoral study	8.1	*39.5*	7.7	1.6	7.0	0.8	1.6	1.6	8.2	76.2	13.4	10.5
Academic employment	6.8	*45.8*	8.9	2.4	7.5	1.6	2.0	1.5	5.2	81.8	5.5	12.7
Nonacademic employment	4.2	*49.9*	3.8	0.7	7.5	0.6	1.1	1.0	3.4	72.1	10.4	17.5
East North Central												
Postdoctoral study	6.9	9.8	*34.6*	3.4	7.4	1.3	2.3	2.3	10.3	78.3	12.9	8.9
Academic employment	3.9	8.8	*37.2*	6.5	8.3	3.6	3.8	3.3	6.8	82.4	5.4	12.3
Nonacademic employment	2.3	9.9	*33.9*	2.5	8.1	1.4	2.2	1.8	5.4	67.4	13.1	19.4
West North Central												
Postdoctoral study	5.1	9.3	12.4	*28.0*	7.9	2.0	3.2	2.7	8.9	79.5	10.2	10.3
Academic employment	2.4	4.9	16.4	*33.8*	6.1	3.3	5.5	4.6	6.0	82.9	4.5	12.6
Nonacademic employment	1.4	6.2	10.2	*29.0*	6.8	1.4	4.1	2.4	4.9	66.3	12.3	21.5
South Atlantic												
Postdoctoral study	6.4	9.3	7.6	2.9	*37.6*	2.6	3.6	2.1	7.0	79.2	9.9	10.8
Academic employment	3.1	7.8	7.5	3.1	*45.0*	7.4	4.7	1.6	3.5	83.7	3.7	12.6
Nonacademic employment	2.0	7.8	3.7	1.1	*49.3*	2.6	2.4	1.0	2.6	72.5	8.3	19.2
East South Central												
Postdoctoral study	3.9	7.2	7.8	4.8	14.2	*30.7*	6.1	2.3	6.2	83.1	7.3	9.6
Academic employment	0.9	2.1	6.3	3.4	18.0	*41.6*	10.0	1.1	1.6	85.0	2.0	13.0
Nonacademic employment	0.8	4.5	4.8	1.8	17.4	*39.1*	5.6	1.0	1.8	76.8	5.1	18.1
West South Central												
Postdoctoral study	4.6	7.1	8.0	3.3	7.5	2.1	*34.7*	2.1	7.0	76.3	9.0	14.7
Academic employment	1.1	2.7	6.2	7.3	7.5	6.8	*43.6*	3.2	4.0	82.3	2.9	14.8
Nonacademic employment	0.8	3.0	3.0	3.3	6.0	3.1	*43.7*	2.6	3.8	69.5	7.9	22.6
Mountain												
Postdoctoral study	4.9	8.1	9.5	4.1	8.0	1.1	3.7	*24.6*	11.5	75.4	10.8	13.8
Academic employment	1.6	3.5	9.5	10.3	4.4	2.1	6.1	*29.1*	12.3	78.8	4.3	16.9
Nonacademic employment	0.9	3.8	4.7	4.2	4.4	0.7	3.7	*34.7*	12.5	69.6	7.6	22.8
Pacific												
Postdoctoral study	7.0	8.2	6.8	2.0	5.5	0.5	1.7	2.4	*40.2*	74.4	16.4	9.2
Academic employment	3.9	6.4	8.6	4.0	4.1	1.1	2.8	6.5	*43.8*	81.3	7.2	11.5
Nonacademic employment	1.4	5.5	2.6	1.0	4.7	0.4	1.2	2.5	*47.7*	67.0	15.0	18.0
Total												
Postdoctoral study	9.6	14.6	13.6	4.5	10.5	2.0	4.2	3.0	14.8	*76.9*	13.0	10.1
Academic employment	6.4	13.9	16.4	7.6	11.3	4.7	6.9	4.5	10.7	*82.3*	5.0	12.7
Nonacademic employment	4.2	16.1	11.0	4.0	12.0	2.4	4.9	3.8	10.7	*69.1*	11.3	19.6

SOURCE: NRC, Commission on Human Resources.

of those who plan to enter academic jobs, the third row of those planning nonacademic employment. The destinations, shown in the columns, include the nine census regions of the United States, with a column for the U.S. total. In addition, the total going to foreign countries is given, as is the percentage whose destination is unknown. The final set of rows, at the bottom of the table, provides a general summary for the United States as a whole, and these percentages furnish a kind of norm that may be used to compare the regions. The diagonal entries, showing those who remain in their region of doctorate, are italicized for particular attention. In each region, a plurality--but never a majority--remain in the PhD region, for each of the three types of activities with which the table is concerned.

POSTDOCTORAL EDUCATION REGIONS

Regarding the people who undertake postdoctoral training--whether called fellowships, traineeships, associateships, or whatever--the plurality who remain in their PhD regions for further training varies considerably. The percentages range from 24.6 percent for the Rocky Mountain States and 28 percent for the West North Central States to 39.5 percent for the Middle Atlantic region and 40.2 percent for the Pacific Coast--a rough reflection of the availability of postdoctoral training sources in the several regions. The graduates of the several regions vary, too, in the extent to which they go abroad for postdoctoral training. These percentages vary from 16.8 percent for New England and 16.4 percent for the Pacific region to 7.3 percent for those who graduate in the East South Central States, as shown by the next-to-last column on the right of Table 36. The proportion undertaking postdoctoral training in the United States is an approximate complement of the figure for those going abroad, except for the influence of those whose region of training is unknown, as shown in the final column at the right. Summing across all regions of graduation, we see in the row third from the bottom, that the regions vary greatly as destinations for postdoctoral training. The most-sought regions are the Pacific Coast and the Middle Atlantic States, closely followed by the East North Central region and foreign countries. The West North Central, the Deep South, and the Mountain States rank low as areas for further training.

ACADEMIC EMPLOYMENT REGIONS

The second set of rows in Table 36 concerns those who plan to enter academic employment. Again, there are marked regional variations, whether the regions are considered in terms of the extent to which they are general destinations for such employment, the proportions in each region remaining there for such jobs, or the percent who go into academic employment outside the United States. In the Middle and South Atlantic regions, 45 percent or more remain in the same region for academic employment; in the Mountain States only 29 percent do so. Of the graduates of New England and Middle Atlantic universities who plan to enter academic jobs, 5.5 percent will go abroad; the percentage is only slightly less (5.4 percent) for the East North Central States and much higher (7.2 percent) for the Pacific region. By contrast, the percentages are very low for the East South Central region (2.0 percent) and the West South Central region (2.9 percent). At the bottom of the page, where the U.S. summary data are given, we see that of the national total of those entering academe, 16.4 percent will go to East North Central colleges and universities, 13.9 percent to Middle Atlantic schools, and 10.7 percent to Pacific Coast institutions. These three regions are large in population, of course, and one would expect them to be high on any such index. But the rank orders of the regions vary according to the type of post-PhD activity concerned. The Pacific region is first in postdoctoral training but fourth in academic employment. The East North Central region is first in academic employment but third in postdoctoral training; the Middle Atlantic region is second for both of these types of activities.

NONACADEMIC EMPLOYMENT REGIONS

The final set of rows in Table 36 concerns nonacademic employment--an area that must be expected to become increasingly important in the future, since academic employment tends to stabilize. Here the regional variations are quite different from those for training or academic jobs. The Middle Atlantic States rank first, no doubt because of the extent of technically oriented industry and the employment of PhD's by these states and by nonprofit organizations centered in the major cities of this area. The South Atlantic region comes up to second position probably because of the heavy employment of PhD's by the U.S. government in Washington, D.C., and by many other organizations with headquarters there. Not far behind is the East North Central region--another area of extensive industrialization and urban concentration.

VALIDATION OF PLANS AT GRADUATION

Plans at PhD graduation were the basis for the analyses that have been reported in this chapter. The plans were those stated on the Survey of Earned Doctorates form, usually completed shortly before graduation. The validity of the analyses depends upon these statements and raises the question as to whether the students about to graduate know with a high degree of certainty what their actual situation will be in the following year. The validity of these statements has been examined, and the results are reported below.

TECHNIQUE OF FOLLOW-UP

The Comprehensive Roster of Doctoral Scientists and Engineers makes biennial surveys of a sample of PhD's from the DRF. The sample is carefully

TABLE 37
PERCENTAGE DISTRIBUTION, BY FIELD GROUP, OF 1973 ACTIVITY FOR 1972 PhD's WHO PLANNED POSTDOCTORAL TRAINING AFTER GRADUATION

Field Group	Men				Women			
	Postdoctoral Training	Employed		Not Employed	Postdoctoral Training	Employed		Not Employed
		Full-Time	Part-Time			Full-Time	Part-Time	
EMP fields	61.2	36.7	1.1	1.0	57.1	28.6	14.3	--
Life sciences	68.8	29.4	0.9	0.9	78.0	20.9	--	1.1
Behavioral sciences	20.2	71.9	--	7.9	35.5	51.6	12.9	--
TOTAL, SCIENCES	61.1	36.5	1.0	1.4	65.3	28.7	5.3	0.7

SOURCE: NRC, Commission on Human Resources.

stratified by year of doctorate, field of doctorate, and sex. Each cell in the three-dimensional table made up by these three variables is sampled in inverse proportion to the number of cases in the cell, and the sample is weighted so as to reproduce the original number. Cells with very few cases are included *in toto*; cells with high frequencies have a smaller proportion of cases--but a larger total number--included in the sample. The object of the sampling scheme is to insure that relatively sparse fields--or other groups, such as women--are represented by numbers sufficient to permit analysis. If all individuals in a cell are included, each case will have a weight of 1. If only 10 percent are included, each will have a weight of 10. Across all cases in the population, a sampling ratio of 1 to 6 was approximated; in the biosciences, because of the interest in more detailed data in this area, a minimum sampling ratio of 1 in 4 was used. Because not all individuals in the sample respond to the follow-up questionnaire, a further weight was applied to each case, so that the respondent group could be "blown up" to represent the original population, on the assumption that the respondents were a representative sample of all cases in the base population. Studies made to date indicate that this latter assumption holds to a degree sufficient to permit highly valid analyses. This, then, was the system of follow-up used in the validation study reported below.

VALIDATION OF PLANS FOR TRAINING

When the 1972 PhD's were followed up via the sampling scheme described above, one of the first questions to be examined was whether those who planned to take postdoctoral training were actually holding postdoctoral appointments at the time of follow-up. Here the results were a bit ambiguous apparently because of time phase relationships. The Doctorate Survey questionnaires are customarily completed some time prior to graduation--it may be several months in some cases. Graduation is defined in terms of the formal commencement date. When followed up, the earliest response date possible for the 1973 respondents was April of 1973. In practice, it was frequently later, since the follow-up process, for those who did not respond immediately, extended through the summer. Thus there was considerable opportunity for many who had planned training to have completed it and to have entered regular jobs. In some cases, no doubt, the training took less than a year and was terminated when a suitable job turned up. Whatever the reasons, the data, by field and sex, for the 1972 PhD's, followed up in 1973, are given in Table 37.

It is apparent from Table 37 that the majority of both men and women who had said that they planned to take postdoctoral training were actually engaged in such training in the following year, but that a substantial number, if they had undertaken such training, had already left it for regular employment. The percentages are different for the two sexes, more women than men remaining in training status. This is to be expected if, as other data show, the women have experienced more difficulty in obtaining jobs. The data of the above table, showing a larger proportion of women in part-time jobs, tend to bear out this interpretation. The largest differences, however, are among the fields; in the behavioral sciences only a small minority of those planning postdoctoral training were actually so engaged at the time of follow-up.

TABLE 38
PERCENTAGE DISTRIBUTION, BY FIELD GROUP, OF 1973 ACTIVITY FOR 1972 PhD's WHO PLANNED IMMEDIATE EMPLOYMENT AFTER GRADUATION

	Men				Women			
		Employed				Employed		
Field Group	Postdoctoral Training	Full-Time	Part-Time	Not Employed	Postdoctoral Training	Full-Time	Part-Time	Not Employed
EMP fields	1.6	96.5	0.1	1.8	1.8	83.6	14.6	--
Life sciences	2.4	96.0	1.6	--	8.5	79.7	6.8	5.1
Behavioral sciences	0.3	99.1	--	0.6	1.9	87.3	10.8	--
TOTAL, SCIENCES	1.1	97.4	0.1	1.4	2.8	85.8	10.7	0.7

SOURCE: NRC, Commission on Human Resources.

VALIDATION OF PLANS FOR EMPLOYMENT

When those who said on the Doctorate Survey that they intended to enter employment rather than training were followed up, the results, by sex and for the same field groups as those shown in Table 37, were as shown in Table 38.

In Table 38 the agreement between Doctorate Survey expectations and actual experience as shown a year later on follow-up is very good. Of the men expecting to be employed, 97.4 percent are so employed; of the women, 85.8 percent are employed full time and 10.7 percent part-time, for a total of 96.5 percent. To expect a higher level of agreement would in fact be unrealistic.

4

Institutional Characteristics

We have seen, in previous chapters, the growth in numbers of PhD's and something of their backgrounds, personal characteristics, educational and employment plans, and even a bit about the extent to which these plans have been realized. But what of the institutions from which these people come? How many institutions currently grant the PhD degree? How has this number changed over time? What is the geographic distribution of these institutions and the corresponding changes in the numbers of PhD's from various parts of the country? Is it possible to present not only the numbers of persons who attain degrees from each of the schools but also some generalized institutional characteristics? This chapter will seek to answer these questions. The highlights of the chapter follow.

HIGHLIGHTS

- There were, in 1974, 307 institutions granting the doctorate--up from 61 in the 1920-1924 period, 107 in 1940-1944, and 208 in 1960-1964. This is an accelerating curve with no present evidence of leveling off.
- More than half of the PhD degrees granted over the 55-year period since 1920 were granted by institutions in the business prior to 1920. Those institutions beginning PhD production in the 1920's account for another one-fifth of the total, leaving almost one-fourth for the institutions beginning PhD output in 1930 or later.
- The proportion of PhD's being granted annually by the older institutions has been dropping dramatically as the newer institutions pick up speed. Those beginning doctorate production in the 1930's, 1940's, 1950's, and 1960's are now almost equal in output, and those beginning in the 1970's are rising rapidly.
- In geographic terms, the Northeast is "oldest" in terms of doctorate origins and remains the dominant region, now nearly matched by the Midwest. The output of the western schools (the Pacific Coast and Rocky Mountain States) has risen very rapidly since World War II but has almost been overtaken by the even more rapid rise of output of the southern institutions, which had almost no PhD output in 1920.
- Individual PhD-granting institutions are described by the characteristics of their graduates, as well as by geographic location and numbers of doctorates produced. A set of institutional descriptors is provided, together with statistical norms whereby each institution can compare itself with the generality of other PhD-granting institutions.
- Sex ratios; field mix; percent of PhD's of foreign baccalaureate origin; percent with BA's from the same PhD institution (an in-breeding index); time lapse between baccalaureate and doctorate, by field; and post-PhD plans for further study or employment are among the presently available institutional descriptors. Additional descriptors could readily be derived from the data of the DRF. Analogous descriptors for institutions of baccalaureate origin of PhD's could also be derived.
- For convenient reference to the detailed tables of institutional characteristics, an alphabetical list of PhD institutions is provided in Table 44, with rank orders of institutional size in terms of numbers of graduates--male, female, and total. These rank orders are the key to additional tables in which the schools are presented in the order of the numbers of their PhD graduates.
- Baccalaureate origins of doctorate recipients are given in terms of the total number of PhD's from 1920 to 1974, with baccalaureate degrees from each institution and, for the larger BA sources, by field group and time period. Regional and state summaries of baccalaureate origins data are given.

TABLE 39
NUMBER OF DOCTORATE-GRANTING INSTITUTIONS IN THE UNITED STATES BY 5-YEAR PERIODS, 1920-1974, BY FIELD OF DOCTORATE

	Time Period										
Field	1920-1924	1925-1929	1930-1934	1935-1939	1940-1944	1945-1949	1950-1954	1955-1959	1960-1964	1965-1969	1970-1974
Mathematics	22	33	43	45	47	49	71	74	91	127	159
Physics	28	37	46	55	55	54	74	84	114	150	167
Chemistry	43	47	66	76	74	84	100	112	143	171	194
Earth sciences	24	24	37	38	39	38	50	59	74	96	121
Engineering	19	24	32	37	37	49	63	75	97	127	151
Life sciences	42	57	65	70	74	81	99	122	144	178	224
Psychology	28	31	43	46	49	53	77	88	112	149	183
Social sciences	30	45	51	54	58	63	79	92	104	128	166
Humanities and professions	41	53	64	71	77	85	96	113	134	172	212
Education	34	44	53	58	60	67	86	99	116	138	173
TOTAL	61	75	87	102	107	126	142	171	208	244	307

SOURCE: NRC, Commission on Human Resources.

GROWTH IN NUMBER OF PhD-GRANTING SCHOOLS[1]

Table 39 shows the number of institutions of higher education in the United States that have granted doctorate degrees in various fields, by 5-year time periods since 1924. The bottom line of Table 39 shows the total number of such institutions granting doctorates in any field. The final number on this line is 307 institutions granting degrees in 1974. Because there were a few other institutions which have granted doctorates at some earlier time but which were not represented in the 1970-1974 period, a total of 315 institutions will be shown in other tables. Where there have been splits and mergers of institutions, it is the current institutional arrangements (as of 1974) which determine the count. Thus Case-Western Reserve, for example, is shown as a single school, although for most of the 1920-1974 period it represented two separate institutions.

The data of Table 39 are shown graphically in Figure 58 insofar as they lend themselves to graphic presentation. The top line in Figure 58 shows the total of all institutions, all fields combined. It is noteworthy that this curve bends upward--i.e., the slope increases as a function

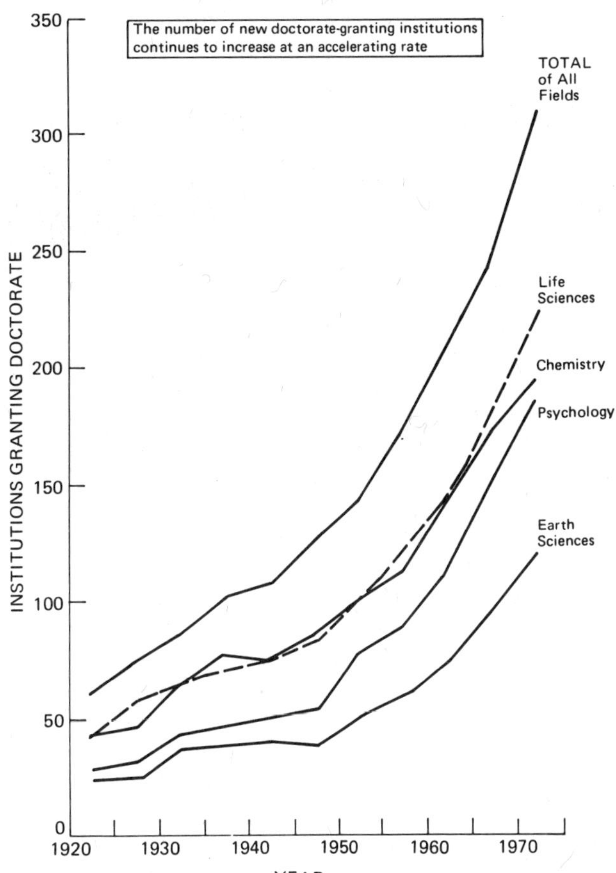

SOURCE: NRC, Commission on Human Resources

FIGURE 58 Growth in numbers of PhD-granting institutions.

[1]The number of doctorate-granting institutions to be included in any list is in part a matter of definition. Separate campuses exist for many of the larger institutions. In some cases they are administratively independent; in other cases they are part of a single administration. In addition, there are many medical schools that grant PhD degrees as well as MD degrees. In some cases these are an integral part of the university administration; in some cases they are independent or quasi-independent. The problem of setting up unambiguous criteria for determining which are independent institutions and which are integral parts of larger organizations has proved to be a refractory one. In the present case, the problem has been solved by including as separate all organizations, including medical schools, that maintain a separate relationship in the DRF. It is always possible to combine the several parts into a single whole; the reverse is not possible once the tabulations have been made. The reader may wish, for reasons of his own, to combine some of the institutions recorded separately in this book. The only significant changes in the tabulations would occur where rank orders according to numbers of degrees granted are concerned: the inevitable result of combining would be to move an institution upward in the rank orders and to change the rank number of institutions lower in the list, lowering the total number of institutional ranks.

of time rather than linearly. Presumably, a point will be reached where the entry of new institutions into the doctorate-granting group will cease to increase so rapidly; the curve would then straighten out and bend over to show a decreasing growth rate. But that time has not yet come.

Curves for several of the science fields are shown separately, with the life science and chemistry curves crossing and recrossing each other. In the most recent period, however, it appears that the growth in number of institutions granting PhD's in chemistry has slackened somewhat, while the number of schools granting doctorates in the life sciences has continued to boom. The fourth curve in Figure 58 is that for schools granting psychology doctorates, and this curve, too, has a positive acceleration. The bottom curve in this set, depicting the earth sciences, also has a positive acceleration, although not as markedly as has psychology or the life science group. All of the other curves, representing institutions granting doctorates in other disciplines, would fall within the area between the life science curve and that for the earth sciences, and all show positive acceleration.

This report does not attempt to assess the question of how many institutions should be in the doctorate-granting category. It is apparent, however, that institutional plans for a PhD program are developed on a long-term basis, and institutions which undertook such plans during the 1960's, when there was a "bull market" for PhD's, are showing results into the 1970's. A tapering off of such expansion plans would have a considerable time lag and could not be expected to show in the data of the DRF for some years to come.

INSTITUTIONS GROUPED BY DECADE OF FIRST PhD

The entry of new institutions into the doctorate-granting group is shown in Table 40 in terms of the number of doctorate degrees granted by 10-year periods by institutions in each successive group to enter this category. That is, the first column represents those schools that were granting doctorates before 1920; the second column indicates those that began to grant doctorates in the 1920's, and so on, to the next-to-last column, which represents those schools that granted their first doctorates in 1970 or later. The final column shows the total number of degrees granted in each 5-year period by all institutions, summing across the institutional categories. For each 5-year period, the percentage of all degrees granted by schools in each category is shown. Figure 59 shows the accumulative total of all doctorates granted over the entire 1920-1974 period, divided into proportions from each institutional group--the data from the bottom line in Table 40. It is apparent in both the table and the graph that the earliest institutional group (pre-1920's) is responsible for the vast majority of the total, the 1920's group for a little over one-fifth, and all the other schools for the approximate one-fifth remaining.

The growth rates of institutions in the several categories have not all been the same. Figure 60 shows the growth in number of doctorates granted by each of the institutional categories defined in terms of the decade in which they first began granting doctorate degrees. This is a graph of the numerical data of Table 40. It should be noted that the vertical scale in Figure 60 is logarithmic; a straight line on this chart would represent a logarithmic growth rate, inasmuch as the time dimension, on the horizontal axis, is linear. The top curve, representing the pre-1920 institutions, begins at about 4,000 degrees per 5-year period and climbs to over 70,000 in the 1970-1974 period. All of the other curves, of course, start from zero (which cannot be shown on a logarithmic scale), and each successive curve shows a higher growth rate. Thus the "1920's" group appears to be approaching the "pre-1920's" group, and the subsequent groups appear to be converging rapidly toward a level of about 15,000 per 5-year period or about 3,000 PhD's per year.

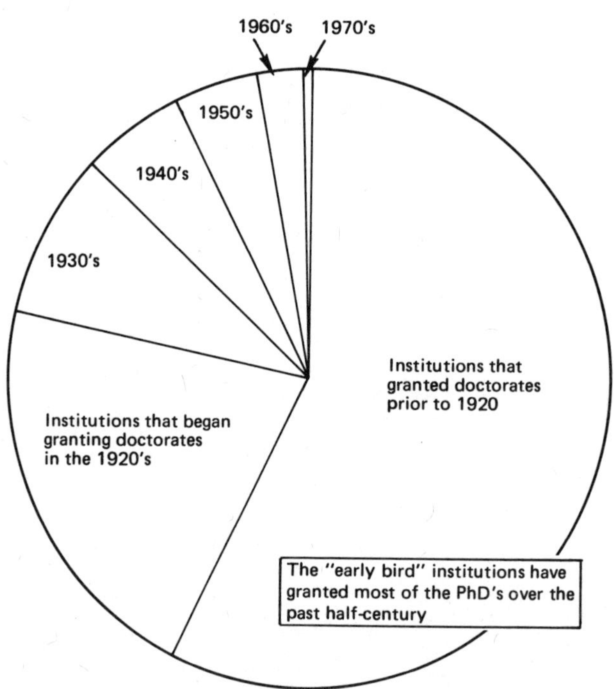

SOURCE: NRC, Commission on Human Resources

FIGURE 59 Proportions of 1920-1974 PhD's granted by institutional groups.

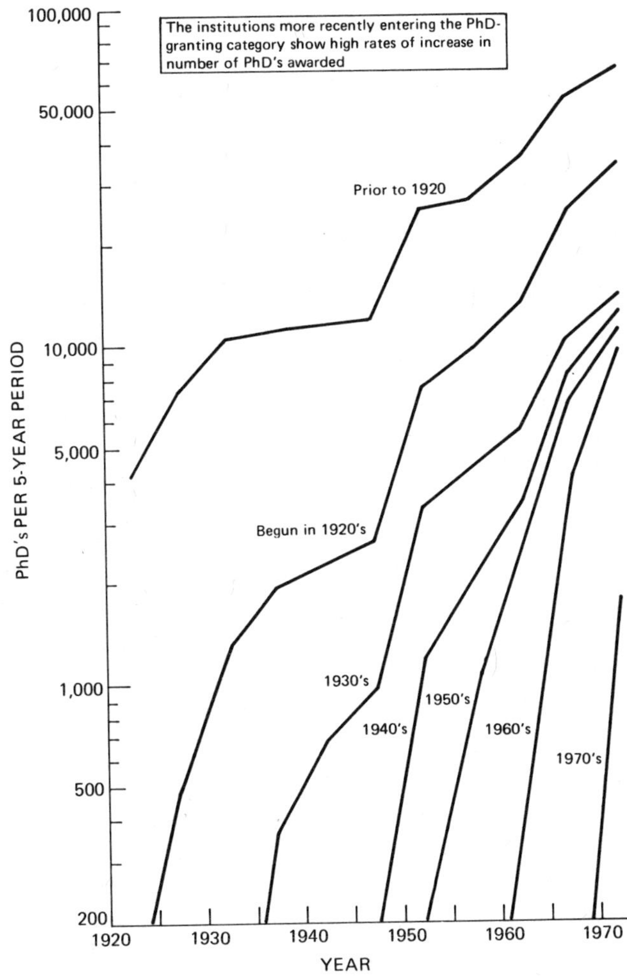

SOURCE: NRC, Commission on Human Resources

FIGURE 60 Doctorates granted by institutional groups.

TABLE 40
PROPORTION OF TOTAL PhD's PRODUCED BY INSTITUTIONAL GROUP BY TIME PERIOD, 1920-1974

Five-Year Period		Year First PhD Granted: Before 1920	1920's	1930's	1940's	1950's	1960's	1970's	TOTAL
1920-	N	4,077	122						4,199
1924	%	97.1	2.9						100.0
1925-	N	7,222	510						7,732
1929	%	93.4	6.6						100.0
1930-	N	10,640	1,283	51					11,974
1934	%	88.9	10.7	0.4					100.0
1935-	N	11,290	2,037	367					13,694
1939	%	82.4	14.9	2.7					100.0
1940-	N	11,610	2,342	745	24				14,721
1944	%	78.9	15.9	5.1	0.2				100.0
1945-	N	21,852	2,758	1,105	184				25,899
1949	%	84.4	10.7	4.3	0.7				100.0
1950-	N	26,037	7,818	3,422	1,199	193			38,669
1954	%	67.3	22.2	8.9	3.1	0.5			100.0
1955-	N	27,144	9,759	4,323	2,118	894			44,238
1959	%	61.4	22.1	9.8	4.8	2.0			100.0
1960-	N	35,390	13,882	5,738	3,374	2,468	413		61,265
1964	%	57.8	22.7	9.4	5.5	4.0	0.7		100.0
1965-	N	53,615	25,974	10,775	7,795	6,737	3,975		109,071
1969	%	49.2	23.8	9.9	7.3	6.2	3.6		100.0
1970-	N	70,887	38,696	16,031	13,469	12,357	11,979	1,889	165,308
1974	%	42.9	23.4	9.7	8.2	7.5	7.3	1.1	100.0
TOTAL,	N	279,764	105,181	42,557	28,363	22,649	16,367	1,889	496,770
1920-1974	%	56.3	21.2	8.6	5.7	4.7	3.3	0.4	100.0

N = number of PhD's.
Percentages may not total to 100.0 because of rounding.

SOURCE: NRC, Commission on Human Resources.

CHANGES IN SHARES FOR INSTITUTIONAL GROUPS

The same data, in percentage terms from Table 40, are shown graphically in Figure 61. Here we see the proportions of the total in each 5-year period granted by institutions in each decade group. While the pre-1920 group is clearly still dominate, its share has declined sharply and almost continuously since the early 1920's. The exception, in the period immediately after World War II, is of particular interest. The institutions in this group had strong graduate departments with well-established doctorate programs and were not overwhelmed by the influx of large numbers of World War II veterans at the undergraduate level to the extent that the other institutions were. Hence, for a brief period, their share in the total doctorate output went up, only to return shortly to its long-term decline. The obverse of this incident, the temporarily declining share of the PhD output in the other institutions, is shown by dips in the curves for the schools entering the PhD picture in the 1920's and 1930's. The later groups, 1940's and 1950's, by definition could not show such a decline, but do show a rapid spurt in the succeeding years. It is possibly of significance that the shares for the 1920's and 1930's groups declined very slightly in the most recent 5-year period, although the total number of their graduates, as for the pre-1920 schools, continued to grow.

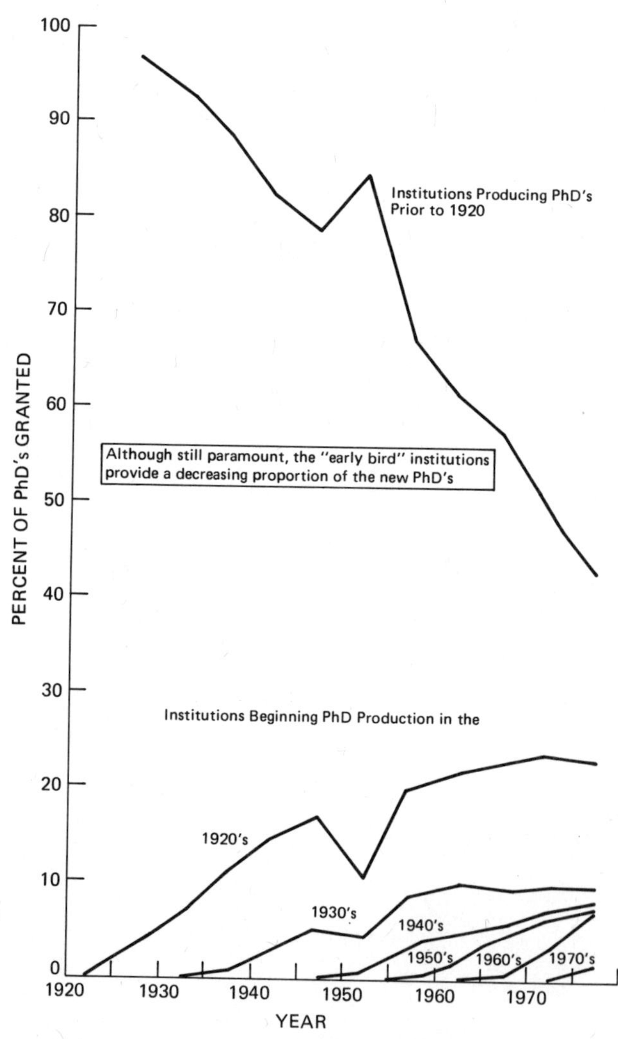

SOURCE: NRC, Commission on Human Resources

FIGURE 61 Varying institutional shares in doctorates granted.

THE GEOGRAPHY OF DOCTORATE OUTPUT

Table 41 shows the PhD output data in geographic terms, the number and proportions of the total granted in each 5-year period, by institutions in each of the nine census regions of the country. For purposes of graphical simplification, these nine regions have been grouped, in Figure 62, into four general areas: the Northeast, the Midwest, the West, and the South. The Northeast, as defined here, includes the East Coast from Maine to the Potomac River, thus including the District of Columbia at its southern extreme. The Midwest includes both the East North Central and West North Central regions, principally the Great Lakes area and the Great Plains. The South includes all of the area below the Potomac and Ohio rivers, and as far west as Texas. The West includes the Rocky Mountains, Pacific Coast, and outlying areas. Here again we see a convergence of the curves similar to that represented by the institutions grouped in terms of date of entry into the PhD-granting set. The correspondence, of course, is not merely incidental. In the earlier days, the PhD-granting schools were highly concentrated in the North and Northeast; the growth in numbers of doctorate-granting schools has come largely in the South and the West. The same data have been shown in a different fashion in Figure 63, in which the area of each graph is proportional to the total number of degrees granted in that area, in each decade

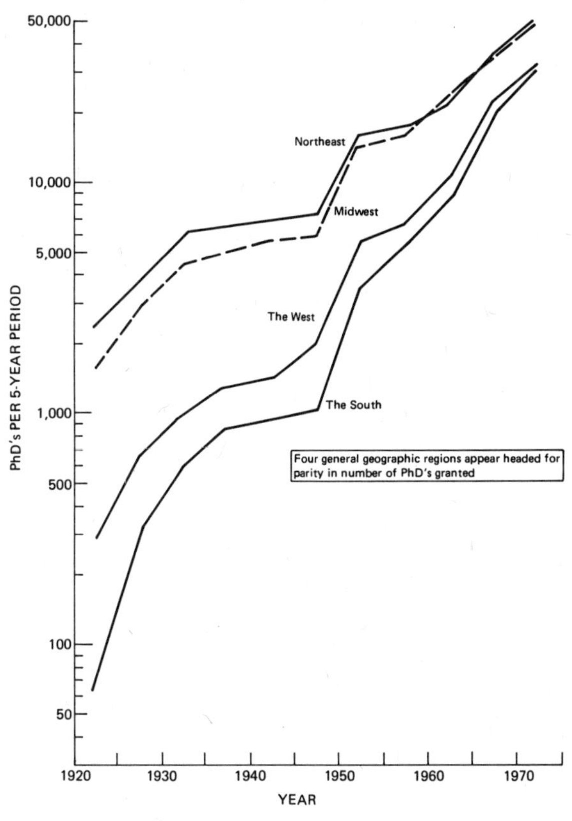

FIGURE 62 Doctorates granted in four geographic areas.

TABLE 41
DOCTORATE OUTPUT BY CENSUS REGION BY 5-YEAR PERIODS, 1920-1974

Region		1920-1924	1925-1929	1930-1934	1935-1939	1940-1944	1945-1949	1950-1954	1955-1959	1960-1964	1965-1969	1970-1974	Total
New England	N	741	1,116	1,742	1,973	1,849	2,127	4,322	4,625	6,207	9,704	13,611	48,017
	%	17.6	14.4	14.5	14.4	12.6	13.4	11.2	10.5	10.1	8.9	8.2	9.9
Middle	N	1,182	2,106	3,293	3,718	3,950	4,167	9,576	10,433	13,008	20,312	29,627	101,372
Atlantic	%	28.1	27.2	27.5	27.1	26.8	26.2	24.8	23.6	21.2	18.6	17.9	20.8
East North	N	1,191	2,199	3,237	3,557	4,124	4,363	10,549	11,559	15,941	25,455	37,855	120,030
Central	%	28.4	28.4	27.0	26.0	28.0	27.4	27.3	26.1	26.0	23.3	22.8	24.6
West North	N	314	749	1,244	1,501	1,588	1,525	3,841	4,041	5,556	9,343	13,743	43,445
Central	%	7.5	9.7	10.4	11.0	10.8	9.6	9.9	9.1	9.1	8.6	8.3	8.9
South	N	458	791	1,139	1,202	1,280	1,216	2,932	3,830	5,501	11,502	19,480	49,331
Atlantic	%	10.9	10.2	9.5	8.8	8.7	7.6	7.6	8.7	9.0	10.5	11.8	10.1
East South	N	20	66	154	171	167	131	597	897	1,455	3,343	5,965	12,966
Central	%	0.5	0.9	1.3	1.2	1.1	0.8	1.5	2.0	2.4	3.1	3.6	2.7
West South	N	9	46	147	254	333	402	1,404	2,164	3,394	7,715	12,383	28,251
Central	%	0.2	0.6	1.2	1.9	2.3	2.5	3.6	4.9	5.5	7.1	7.5	5.8
Mountain	N	10	21	54	89	121	194	856	1,189	2,232	5,875	10,065	20,706
	%	0.2	0.3	0.5	0.6	0.8	1.2	2.2	2.7	3.6	5.4	6.1	4.2
Pacific	N	274	642	967	1,233	1,312	1,779	4,594	5,502	7,972	16,024	23,018	63,317
	%	6.5	8.3	8.1	9.0	8.9	11.2	11.9	12.4	13.0	14.7	13.9	13.0
U.S. TOTAL	N	4,199	7,736	11,977	13,698	14,724	15,904	38,671	44,240	61,266	109,273	165,747	487,435
	%	100.0	100.0	100.0	100.0	100.0	100.0	100.0	100.0	100.0	100.0	100.0	100.0
Summary into Four Areas*													
Northeast	N	2,347	3,888	5,885	6,454	6,645	7,021	15,451	16,864	21,387	34,088	49,501	169,531
	%	55.9	50.3	49.1	47.1	45.1	44.2	40.0	38.1	34.9	31.2	29.9	34.8
Midwest	N	1,505	2,948	4,481	5,058	5,712	5,888	14,390	15,600	21,497	34,798	51,598	163,475
	%	35.8	38.1	37.4	36.9	38.8	37.0	37.2	35.3	35.1	31.8	31.1	33.5
South	N	63	237	590	864	934	1,022	3,380	5,085	8,178	18,488	31,565	70,400
	%	1.5	3.1	4.9	6.3	6.3	6.4	8.7	11.5	13.4	16.9	19.0	14.4
West	N	284	663	1,021	1,322	1,433	1,973	5,450	6,691	10,204	21,899	33,083	84,023
	%	6.8	8.6	8.5	9.7	9.7	12.4	14.1	15.1	16.7	20.0	20.0	17.2

*For definitions of areas, see pages 100-101.
N = number.

SOURCE: NRC, Commission on Human Resources.

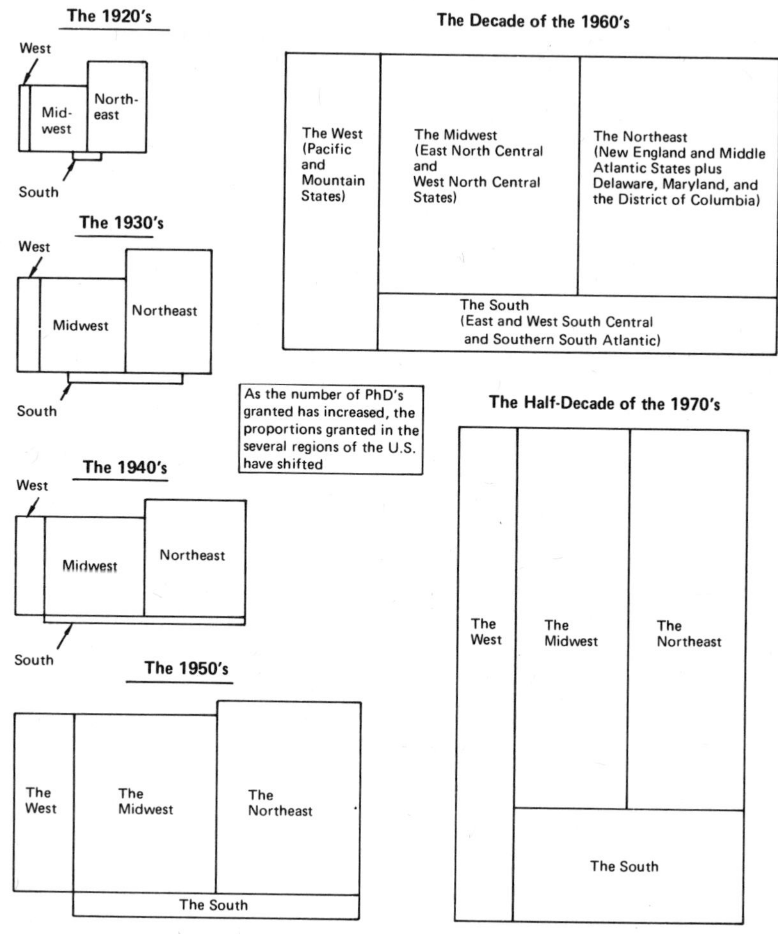

SOURCE: NRC, Commission on Human Resources

FIGURE 63 Diagrams of PhD growth in four geographic areas.

interval. The four general geographic areas are arranged to correspond roughly to their actual geographic position as shown on a typical map. Thus the South is at the bottom, the West at the left, the Northeast at the right and above, and the Midwest in a middle position. The growth in doctorate output, both for the country as a whole and for each of the general areas, is shown for each decade, except, of course, for the 1970's, where only a half-decade of output has yet occurred. Throughout this period, as shown in both Figures 62 and 63, the growth of institutions in the South is most spectacular and that of those in the West only slightly less so. The West, which produced only about 300 PhD's in the early 1920's, increased in each half-decade, although not always at the same pace, being slowed, as was each section, by the 1930's depression and then by World War II. The West gained rather steadily on the northeastern and midwestern sections, until in the most recent period it produced about two-thirds as many as the leading sections of the country. Dramatic as these gains have been, however, they are out-paced by the growth rate of the South, especially in the period since the end of World War II. From a beginning of fewer than 100 doctorates in the early 1920's, the South has increased its contribution to 20 percent of the total in the most recent 5-year period--almost equaling the West. The growth suggests that the South will overtake the West soon.

THE STATES IN EACH AREA

The census regions represented in each of the four general areas are noted in Figure 63. The individual states within each census region, and hence within each of the four general areas, are given below:

Northeast

Region 1 New England: Maine, New Hampshire, Vermont, Massachusetts, Rhode Island, Connecticut.

Region 2 Middle Atlantic States: New York, New Jersey, Pennsylvania.

Region 5 Northern half of South Atlantic region: Delaware, Maryland, District of Columbia.

Midwest

Region 3 East North Central States: Ohio, Indiana, Illinois, Michigan, Wisconsin.

Region 4 West North Central States: Minnesota, Iowa, Missouri, North Dakota, South Dakota, Nebraska, Kansas.

West

Region 8 Rocky Mountain States: Montana, Idaho, Wyoming, Colorado, New Mexico, Arizona, Utah, Nevada.

Region 9 Pacific and Insular States: Washington, Oregon, California, Alaska, Hawaii, Virgin Islands, Puerto Rico.

South

Region 5 Southern portion of South Atlantic region: Virginia, West Virginia, North Carolina, South Carolina, Georgia, Florida.

Region 6 East South Central States: Kentucky, Tennessee, Alabama, Mississippi.

Region 7 West South Central States: Arkansas, Louisiana, Oklahoma, Texas.

INSTITUTIONAL CHARACTERISTICS

The existence of a wide range of individual characteristics within the PhD population is well known and has been described in Chapter 2. Whatever the characteristic being considered, even within field or sex groups, individuals differ greatly. Age at doctorate, time spent in graduate school, migration from baccalaureate to doctorate institution, career plans, career realizations--all of these vary tremendously. However wide these individual variations, the question is open as to whether there are substantial institutional differences. It is conceivable that even a wide range of individual differences would average out for institutions, so that school averages would vary but slightly. To check on this possibility, institutional averages and percentages were computed for a number of characteristics, and these are the data of the remainder of this chapter. It is recognized that these characteristics represent but a very limited and partial set from the possible array of human characteristics. This set, however, makes a start at using individual characteristics to describe institutions. An array of institutional statistics, percentages in the case of some variables, means for others, provides a kind of profile of the institution. When these profiles are examined, a rich variety of patterns becomes apparent. Table 42 presents the profiles.

What Characteristics Describe the Institution?

One of the simplest descriptors is the number of PhD's granted, or the percentage of all U.S. PhD's granted by a given institution. For the purpose of the present profiles, all data have been limited to the degrees that were granted during the period from 1958 (when the Doctorate Survey was instituted) to 1974. The sole exception is the date of the earliest doctorate for that institution in the DRF (1920 for the pre-1920 institutions and those which began in 1920). (Only the last two digits of the year are printed; thus 20 indicates 1920, etc.) The rank order of the school among all U.S. institutions, in terms of the total number of 1958-1974 PhD's, is the second descriptor, followed by the total number itself. The fourth profile point is percentage of women among the school's PhD graduates. The fifth is percent of its graduates whose baccalaureate degrees were earned in foreign countries. The sixth point is the percent of the institutions's PhD's who took their baccalaureates from the PhD institution itself--a measure of inbreeding.

The field mix of the PhD's granted by the individual institution is the basis for the next series of profile points. Percentages are given for five general field groups: (1) EMP fields, (2) bio-behavioral sciences, (3) humanities, (4) professions, and (5) education. The next set of profile points indicates the mean time lapse from baccalaureate to doctorate, for the institution's graduates, by sex and field. The breakout by sex is important because there are quite distinct sex differences. The women take longer to graduate, although they are, on the average, younger at the time of baccalaureate and, as shown earlier, have come from better-educated family backgrounds and have earned higher marks in high school and on scholastic aptitude tests. Whatever the reasons for the sex differences, they are given for each of the field groups. The fields are grouped in accordance with a finding of rather similar BA-PhD time lapses. They are the same set as given above to show the proportions of field mix: EMP fields, bio-behavioral sciences, humanities, professions, and education.

The final set of institutional indices concern the plans of the graduates for post-PhD careers. They show (1) the proportion planning postdoctoral training, either as fellows, trainees, or research associates; (2) the proportion planning academic employment in the year following graduation; (3) the proportion planning to enter nonacademic employment; and (4) the percentage with uncertain plans.

Table 42 shows the institutional profiles for the leading 90 doctorate-granting institutions. Profiles for the remaining institutions with sufficient numbers of graduates to warrant computation of such profiles are given in Appendix A.

A list of the variables in the profile, with their names as given in Table 42 and a brief description, follows:

1. Year of first PhD: the date of the earliest DRF record for the institution.
2. Rank among PhD schools: rank among the entire 315, based on N in column 3.
3. Total PhD's, 1958-1974: the PhD degrees in all fields, 1958-1974.
4. Per 1,000 U.S. Total 1958-1974.
5. Percentage of women: percentage of 1958-1974 PhD's for this school who were women.

TABLE 42
INSTITUTIONAL PROFILES

	PhD Institutions in Rank Order	Year of First PhD	Rank among PhD Schools	Total PhD's, 1958-1974	PhD's per 1,000 U.S. Total, 1958-1974	Percentage of Women	Percent with Foreign BA's	Percent with BA's from School of PhD	Percent Distribution by Field Groups: Percent in EMP Fields	Percent in Bio/ Behavioral Fields	Percent in Humanities	Percent in Professions	Percent in Education	BA-to-PhD Time Lapse, by Sex and Field Group: EMP Fields Males	EMP Fields Females	Bio/ Behavioral Sciences Males	Bio/ Behavioral Sciences Females	Humanities Males	Humanities Females	Professions Males	Professions Females	Education Males	Education Females	Percentage Distribution of Plans at PhD Graduation: Postdoctoral Training	Academic Employment	Nonacademic Employment	Plans Uncertain
35440	WISCONSIN,U-MADISON	20	1	10587	29.9	12.5	17.1	14.2	26.1	38.1	19.6	3.5	12.6	7.2	7.1	8.0	8.6	9.4	11.0	9.7	14.3	12.1	14.3	14.1	49.3	24.6	12.0
93440	CALIF, U-BERKELEY	20	2	10438	29.4	13.1	18.8	18.1	39.4	32.9	12.3	2.5	9.1	7.0	6.6	8.9	10.0	10.2	11.3	11.0	15.1	14.8	15.9	14.7	40.1	23.9	21.3
33474	ILL, U, URBANA-CHAMP	20	3	10088	28.5	11.4	17.6	14.2	38.3	30.7	12.1	4.8	14.1	6.9	7.0	7.9	7.8	9.6	11.2	10.6	13.0	11.7	13.8	12.9	48.2	29.0	9.9
34454	MICHIGAN, UNIV OF	20	4	8961	25.3	14.7	13.3	16.9	29.8	32.9	18.2	4.4	14.8	8.1	8.4	8.7	9.2	10.4	12.5	11.3	17.7	13.5	16.5	9.1	51.2	25.3	14.4
14444	HARVARD UNIV/MA	20	5	8574	24.2	15.8	13.7	11.6	22.6	30.0	28.1	9.0	10.2	6.8	8.3	8.3	8.8	9.4	9.9	11.9	12.8	12.5	13.4	12.5	47.2	20.9	19.4
21460	COLUMBIA UNIV/NY	20	6	7916	22.3	23.4	12.9	9.9	23.3	34.1	31.8	7.8	2.9	7.8	8.0	10.8	11.1	12.0	12.6	13.8	22.1	13.7	16.4	9.1	48.6	20.6	21.7
31480	OHIO STATE UNIV	20	7	7803	22.0	14.1	12.1	18.0	26.6	31.1	12.3	6.0	24.0	8.2	8.2	8.8	9.9	10.3	11.2	10.7	14.9	12.2	14.5	7.6	50.3	28.7	13.4
21562	NEW YORK UNIVERSITY	20	8	7375	20.8	22.8	8.8	13.4	20.0	31.5	19.5	5.6	23.3	9.2	8.6	12.3	14.0	12.5	14.1	14.8	16.9	16.9	19.3	5.0	35.9	27.7	31.3
34452	MICHIGAN STATE UNIV	25	9	7080	20.0	10.6	14.5	12.3	17.8	40.3	8.8	5.5	27.7	7.5	7.1	8.5	10.1	11.0	12.4	10.5	16.9	12.7	15.6	8.3	53.8	26.6	11.3
41430	MINNESOTA,U-MINNEAPL	20	10	7039	19.9	12.3	18.4	22.2	22.2	45.7	13.8	3.9	14.5	7.5	7.8	9.4	10.3	11.4	14.9	11.7	16.1	13.4	15.2	10.9	50.2	26.9	12.0
32430	INDIANA U BLOOMNGTON	20	11	6865	19.4	16.6	11.5	9.5	10.4	21.8	22.7	6.9	38.2	7.0	7.3	8.3	8.6	10.5	12.4	9.4	15.4	13.0	15.6	8.3	62.3	18.6	10.8
93646	STANFORD UNIV/CA	20	12	6691	18.9	11.2	15.5	9.5	48.3	19.7	15.8	3.6	12.6	7.6	6.5	8.2	7.7	9.8	10.8	9.7	11.1	13.6	16.2	13.9	42.9	32.7	10.5
32450	PURDUE UNIVERSITY/IN	28	13	6365	18.0	8.2	14.7	13.9	44.0	42.1	2.5	2.7	7.4	7.4	7.3	7.5	8.6	8.8	10.1	7.4	12.7	10.8	13.6	11.3	39.5	37.4	11.8
93440F	CALIF,U-LOS ANGELES	37	14	6329	17.9	17.5	13.2	25.6	29.7	33.1	16.1	4.4	16.7	8.7	8.8	8.6	9.9	10.6	12.5	10.9	12.5	15.5	17.1	15.2	42.6	27.2	15.0
21473	CORNELL UNIV/NY	20	15	5995	16.9	11.8	24.5	9.2	34.2	43.9	12.9	2.3	6.8	6.7	6.8	8.3	9.1	8.6	9.0	9.0	13.7	13.7	16.4	14.5	44.9	30.6	9.9
33423	CHICAGO, UNIV OF/IL	20	16	5542	15.6	15.8	15.8	14.2	20.9	40.8	20.1	9.7	8.2	6.9	7.2	8.6	10.4	10.7	12.0	13.2	21.6	13.2	16.2	12.7	49.5	16.9	20.9
14471	MASS INST TECHNOLOGY	20	17	5516	15.6	4.2	20.8	22.5	81.3	14.8	1.6	2.3	.0	6.2	5.9	7.1	7.1	6.3	6.5	7.8				16.1	26.4	38.1	19.4
74510	TEXAS, U-AUSTIN	20	18	5448	15.4	14.9	10.8	24.0	34.3	26.8	17.2	5.3	16.4	8.1	8.2	8.2	9.1	10.8	12.5	11.4	17.7	13.5	14.9	10.9	49.9	24.9	14.2
16460	YALE UNIVERSITY/CT	20	19	4960	14.0	16.8	14.5	9.2	27.5	29.3	35.3	7.7	.2	6.4	6.8	7.2	8.0	7.9	7.8	10.6	12.2	14.5	22.0	16.1	52.5	19.3	12.1
93642	SOUTHERN CALIF, U OF	27	20	4875	13.8	16.6	9.7	10.1	14.4	22.9	16.4	7.1	39.1	9.7	8.8	11.7	12.2	13.6	14.6	15.1	19.2	16.6	17.0	6.0	37.7	34.7	21.6
23521	PENNSYLVANIA, U OF	20	21	4864	13.7	16.5	19.2	10.1	31.2	33.9	24.2	4.3	6.5	8.0	7.6	9.2	9.1	11.0	11.5	11.5	21.8	16.9	18.7	13.9	44.9	28.5	12.7
23510	PENN STATE UNIV	26	22	4820	13.6	11.1	11.1	15.3	36.5	26.1	7.2	3.5	26.8	7.8	9.5	8.0	9.4	8.9	11.3	8.6	14.6	13.3	15.8	9.9	43.6	29.4	17.0
91433	WASHINGTON, U OF	20	23	4488	12.7	11.8	14.1	17.4	33.8	33.9	19.4	5.6	7.1	7.7	7.8	8.2	9.1	10.3	11.1	11.3	13.5	14.0	16.7	16.5	45.5	24.3	13.7
33518	NORTHWESTERN UNIV/IL	22	24	4418	12.5	14.9	14.0	8.6	35.2	25.1	21.6	6.8	11.2	6.8	6.4	7.4	8.6	10.3	12.8	10.7	12.9	11.8	14.6	10.9	49.9	26.9	12.2
42422	IOWA, UNIVERSITY OF	20	25	4372	12.3	12.5	9.0	11.7	20.4	27.2	22.2	6.0	24.3	7.3	8.1	7.5	8.4	10.9	13.3	12.1	12.5	12.1	13.4	8.5	60.0	18.8	12.7
52429	MARYLAND, UNIV OF	20	26	3829	10.8	16.5	11.7	11.5	34.4	33.1	8.4	1.3	22.8	8.7	7.8	9.1	11.8	11.5	14.1	8.7	10.6	13.8	17.0	11.7	36.1	37.9	14.3
23530	PITTSBURGH, UNIV OF	20	27	3804	10.7	19.0	13.9	14.9	24.0	29.4	12.5	5.1	29.0	8.6	9.3	9.1	10.3	10.5	12.4	13.0	16.4	13.7	15.9	10.4	43.7	32.5	13.4
42421	IOWA STATE UNIV	20	28	3730	10.5	5.5	16.1	17.4	46.0	46.7	.0	.9	6.5	7.2	8.8	8.2	9.3				14.7	13.2	14.2	11.5	41.6	37.1	9.8
21460F	COLUMBIA-TCHRS C/NY	35	29	3385	9.5	35.6	6.4	2.3	.0	.0	.0	.0	99.9				31.0			23.0		14.8	18.3	1.2	45.3	34.4	19.1
22443	PRINCETON UNIV/NJ	20	30	3352	9.5	3.3	18.2	5.0	49.8	21.8	26.2	2.1	.0	5.8	5.5	7.3	7.5	7.8	7.1	10.4	16.0	5.0		17.0	48.7	26.3	8.0
56450	NC, U OF-CHAPEL HILL	21	31	3336	9.4	17.3	8.6	11.5	17.9	39.0	29.5	3.4	10.2	7.2	7.3	8.8	10.5	10.6	12.8	11.1	13.7	13.5	16.7	12.5	56.7	17.1	13.6
43440	MISSOURI,U-COLUMBIA	20	32	3274	9.2	8.9	11.8	17.7	18.6	37.8	13.2	4.9	25.4	8.2	9.9	9.1	9.9	10.5	11.9	12.1	14.4	11.7	14.6	7.6	56.3	22.4	13.7
59420	FLORIDA, UNIV OF	34	33	3257	9.2	12.0	12.3	19.1	31.5	34.1	8.7	3.2	22.6	7.4	7.8	8.6	8.4	9.5	13.5	11.1	11.6	12.3	16.3	10.6	45.1	30.9	13.4
59420F	FLORIDA STATE UNIV	52	34	3160	8.9	18.9	6.9	12.4	17.2	23.7	15.4	5.6	38.1	7.4	6.3	8.2	9.8	11.3	12.2	11.2	16.0	12.2	13.9	9.9	56.8	21.7	11.5
22447	RUTGERS UNIV/NJ	20	35	3151	8.9	16.7	10.7	17.1	25.6	42.5	10.2	1.5	20.2	8.2	8.8	8.4	9.8	10.0	12.5	12.1	13.5	15.0	17.1	12.0	38.0	34.6	15.5
31412	CASE WESTRN RSRVE/OH	28	36	3091	8.7	15.7	13.9	16.9	47.4	22.1	13.8	5.3	11.3	7.5	7.9	8.6	10.4	11.8	14.2	14.3	18.9	15.7	18.0	14.4	33.3	39.1	13.2
92430	OREGON, UNIV OF	26	37	2963	8.4	14.5	11.6	8.3	11.9	31.9	13.4	4.3	38.6	6.8	8.6	8.1	10.0	10.1	11.9	10.9	15.0	12.4	15.7	10.6	53.4	22.0	14.0
84407	COLORADO,U-BOULDER	21	38	2957	8.3	14.7	11.0	12.1	33.9	31.2	15.4	4.2	15.3	8.1	7.7	9.0	10.3	11.9	13.0	10.0	11.0	14.5	16.1	12.4	49.6	24.9	13.1
21622	SYRACUSE UNIV/NY	21	39	2905	8.2	13.0	12.3	12.3	24.1	35.6	11.2	3.6	25.4	8.7	8.7	9.7	11.6	11.4	15.6	11.1	15.1	12.8	16.1	8.9	50.9	26.9	13.4
47431	KANSAS, UNIV OF	20	40	2810	7.9	13.7	10.1	15.1	28.1	36.0	14.0	2.0	20.0	7.3	6.5	8.4	10.5	9.7	11.8	8.3	11.4	12.7	13.9	12.1	47.3	27.7	13.0
52426	JOHNS HOPKINS U/MD	20	41	2729	7.7	14.5	14.9	9.3	35.1	42.2	20.2	.4	1.9	7.8	7.9	7.8	8.5	8.0	9.5	14.8		11.3	13.9	19.1	40.9	22.0	18.1
14421	BOSTON UNIVERSITY/MA	20	42	2630	7.4	26.7	9.5	12.1	8.0	27.1	17.2	11.6	36.0	9.8	9.9	10.4	11.3	12.4	14.6	13.3	15.2	14.1	16.6	6.9	44.8	29.5	18.8
73426	OKLAHOMA, U OF	29	43	2614	7.4	13.3	8.5	16.8	23.1	34.8	11.2	3.8	27.2	8.9	10.0	9.1	10.7	11.1	12.1	10.5	6.4	14.0	18.1	9.1	51.9	27.3	11.7
56416	DUKE UNIVERSITY/NC	28	44	2584	7.3	13.1	10.6	5.7	21.0	41.9	21.0	6.2	9.7	6.3	7.0	7.7	8.1	8.8	10.2	11.1	12.0	12.9	14.4	17.3	48.1	22.3	12.2
46414	NEBRASKA, U-LINCOLN	20	45	2483	7.0	10.3	8.4	17.9	15.9	33.2	11.8	3.0	36.0	7.6	8.3	9.4	12.0	11.0	11.3	11.7	14.3	14.3	16.4	8.5	52.1	27.3	12.1

87410	UTAH, UNIV OF	47	46	2464	7.0	9.7	9.5	33.8	33.8	29.7	9.1	2.2	25.2	7.5	6.4	8.8	11.6	11.6	13.3	12.3	4.0	12.8	16.2	9.1	33.5	31.9	25.5
62460	TENN, U-KNOXVILLE	37	47	2461	6.9	12.5	7.6	14.7	28.4	37.3	5.9	.9	27.5	8.5	6.6	8.2	9.5	10.5	13.1	9.3	9.7	12.8	14.5	10.4	46.1	32.8	10.6
73425	OKLAHOMA STATE UNIV	42	48	2378	6.7	9.4	10.9	19.0	31.5	31.9	1.2	.5	34.9	9.3	9.0	8.8	8.4	10.3	18.0	9.2		13.5	16.4	6.2	52.4	30.4	11.0
34482	WAYNE STATE UNIV/MI	48	49	2366	6.7	19.2	10.7	27.1	21.2	25.1	10.9	1.4	41.3	8.0	8.8	8.6	11.5	11.3	13.9	10.2	14.0	14.7	18.2	9.1	38.7	35.4	16.8
21610I	SUNY AT BUFFALO	35	50	2356	6.6	13.0	16.7	16.6	22.1	35.0	12.8	2.0	28.0	8.6	11.8	8.2	8.1	9.4	9.7	10.8	11.0	13.3	16.8	17.3	41.8	24.6	16.3
72410	LA ST UNIV & A&M C	35	51	2345	6.6	11.2	12.5	18.1	26.7	40.0	15.0	6.4	11.9	7.9	9.4	9.2	9.5	11.3	14.8	9.3	12.9	14.7	16.9	7.1	54.4	23.7	14.8
74503	TEXAS A&M UNIVERSITY	40	52	2328	6.6	3.7	16.2	19.7	41.7	41.9	.9	.6	14.9	9.4	10.3	9.8	10.9	11.4	14.1	12.0		12.4	17.3	7.4	45.7	32.9	13.9
53410	CATHOLIC U AMER/DC	20	53	2259	6.4	25.8	13.5	9.3	23.8	21.1	20.0	17.3	17.7	10.6	10.3	10.8	12.7	12.9	14.6	12.7	20.3	14.2	15.0	5.0	41.2	37.6	16.2
58432	GEORGIA, UNIV OF	40	54	2241	6.3	16.7	7.5	17.3	10.1	39.7	11.5	3.0	35.7	7.5	8.2	8.6	9.0	9.5	13.7	10.5	21.0	12.2	16.7	8.6	54.8	22.4	14.2
21583	ROCHESTER,UNIV OF/NY	25	55	2140	6.0	14.6	18.0	8.6	36.0	32.4	21.7	.6	9.3	7.0	7.3	8.1	7.7	10.2	11.7	10.4		12.5	15.8	20.9	41.8	24.2	13.1
86401	ARIZONA, UNIV OF	22	56	2096	5.9	11.1	6.1	12.0	35.7	37.8	8.1	1.1	17.3	9.1	8.3	8.6	11.5	11.3	15.3	8.6		14.3	17.8	9.5	41.7	31.5	17.3
54446	VIRGINIA, UNIV OF	20	57	2070	5.8	11.9	7.9	9.6	32.8	20.4	20.7	1.4	24.7	7.3	7.1	7.6	8.0	8.1	11.6	12.2	13.0	13.5	15.2	11.2	50.7	25.5	12.6
93440A	CALIF, U-DAVIS	49	58	1998	5.6	8.0	31.9	13.0	24.8	69.5	5.5	.2	.1	7.8	7.3	8.0	8.3	8.1	9.0	11.3		12.0		22.7	31.9	30.6	14.8
92430D	OREGON STATE UNIV	35	59	1979	5.6	6.0	16.6	7.9	33.1	51.4	.1	.9	14.4	9.2	9.8	9.0	9.9	16.0	13.0	11.6	20.0	14.2	17.2	12.3	39.7	33.6	14.4
56450C	NC STATE U-RALEIGH	47	60	1934	5.5	5.4	22.0	17.4	36.2	52.7	.0	.1	11.0	8.6	9.9	9.0	10.9			10.0		14.9	20.3	9.9	38.9	37.6	13.6
14490	MASS, U OF-AMHERST	22	61	1925	5.4	16.0	15.0	7.9	23.7	35.8	9.9	1.8	28.8	7.7	7.7	7.8	8.9	10.2	11.7	9.6	6.0	11.4	12.6	13.5	40.7	29.4	16.4
84422	NORTHERN COLORADO,U	34	62	1804	5.1	13.9	5.2	6.0	1.7	1.0	.1	.3	96.9	11.6	6.3	10.6	11.0	5.0	9.0	13.2	23.0	12.6	15.7	.9	55.5	32.2	11.5
16410	CONNECTICUT, UNIV OF	49	63	1790	5.0	14.0	8.7	13.0	24.2	33.7	11.2	.3	30.6	9.2	7.8	8.6	11.0	10.2	12.5	8.5	17.5	14.7	15.7	9.4	43.6	32.7	14.2
43477	WASHINGTON UNIV/MO	20	64	1733	4.9	16.4	15.7	16.8	37.7	35.4	13.7	6.8	6.3	8.3	7.4	7.6	9.1	9.5	11.3	11.8	19.6	14.4	17.9	17.0	43.5	28.0	11.5
15401	BROWN UNIVERSITY/RI	20	65	1684	4.8	13.5	20.2	4.8	48.2	25.5	25.3	.9	.0	6.8	7.9	7.4	7.7	8.7	9.9	8.7				15.6	44.6	20.5	19.4
93425	CAL INST TECHNOLOGY	20	66	1642	4.6	3.1	20.0	11.8	89.2	10.6	.0	.2	.0	6.2	6.2	6.1	6.7			8.3				33.7	20.4	34.5	11.3
91432	WASHINGTON STATE U	29	67	1596	4.5	6.6	13.4	9.5	19.5	53.3	4.1	.1	23.0	8.1	6.6	8.9	8.9	9.8	12.0	12.0	18.0	14.5	14.2	9.9	43.0	27.9	19.2
23548	TEMPLE UNIVERSITY/PA	25	68	1586	4.5	15.7	5.4	22.2	12.6	24.8	6.0	6.3	50.3	10.7	11.2	8.5	11.2	12.2	13.9	16.1	11.8	15.7	17.8	6.6	35.8	42.1	15.6
23422	CARNEGIE-MELLON U/PA	20	69	1540	4.3	3.8	18.4	25.8	81.8	7.9	5.8	4.1	.4	7.0	6.6	6.9	5.5	11.7	13.1	7.9		13.0	21.0	8.4	26.6	41.8	23.2
72435	TULANE U OF LA	24	70	1502	4.2	18.3	10.2	8.4	22.1	44.3	30.6	2.8	.1	7.2	7.2	8.5	8.7	9.9	10.7	11.7	21.1		4.0	13.3	52.8	18.4	15.4
43465	ST LOUIS UNIV/MO	28	71	1493	4.2	27.9	9.3	16.3	17.7	27.1	27.1	3.5	24.5	9.5	10.1	9.2	11.3	11.6	12.6	13.8	12.0	14.3	16.6	8.6	49.4	29.4	12.7
21487	FORDHAM UNIV/NY	20	72	1492	4.2	33.4	10.0	10.5	11.5	31.1	31.3	4.0	22.1	8.2	11.7	10.4	12.9	14.1	15.1	13.7	16.9	16.2	16.9	5.2	51.9	27.9	14.9
63403	ALABAMA, UNIVER OF	52	73	1490	4.2	19.9	3.5	22.3	18.9	18.0	7.0	10.3	45.8	8.9	9.1	8.6	10.9	12.2	16.0	11.7	14.9	12.8	14.9	3.7	56.6	24.3	15.4
86400	ARIZONA STATE UNIV	54	74	1457	4.1	16.1	2.7	15.4	21.8	16.3	2.8	5.7	53.3	8.3	8.0	7.9	10.6	11.6	15.1	11.2	11.0	14.0	16.0	6.5	42.3	32.7	18.5
32447	NOTRE DAME, U OF/IN	20	75	1450	4.1	13.4	14.6	14.9	50.1	21.1	22.9	.7	5.2	6.9	10.5	9.7	12.2	9.9	12.1	11.7	15.5	13.9	13.8	14.5	48.5	25.9	11.2
61420	KENTUCKY, UNIV OF	30	76	1447	4.1	14.0	9.5	13.0	21.1	45.7	13.3	1.0	18.7	7.4	10.0	8.4	10.9	10.9	12.7	10.3		13.8	15.9	9.1	55.2	22.5	13.3
62474	VANDERBILT UNIV/TN	20	77	1432	4.0	11.0	10.5	8.8	27.2	37.2	26.7	8.9	.0	7.2	6.5	8.0	8.7	10.3	12.9	12.9	21.3			16.6	51.0	21.8	10.5
31417	CINCINNATI, U OF/OH	20	78	1403	4.0	14.0	12.8	18.6	40.0	31.8	13.8	2.1	12.3	8.7	8.5	8.5	10.3	10.4	11.7	9.3		13.7	16.1	14.8	37.6	33.1	14.5
47430	KANSAS STATE UNIV	33	79	1373	3.9	8.1	24.2	13.8	31.8	55.2	3.4	.9	8.6	7.9	10.4	8.9	10.1	10.8	10.6	7.0	10.8	13.1	13.4	12.5	40.3	31.9	15.2
53419	GEO WASHINGTON U/DC	20	80	1341	3.8	19.6	8.5	12.6	13.9	36.6	8.2	15.7	25.5	12.0	11.1	12.1	13.1	14.9	14.4	15.7	15.5	17.2	20.9	6.7	26.0	50.3	17.1
85411	NEW MEXICO, UNIV OF	47	81	1310	3.7	16.8	7.9	14.7	30.8	14.2	25.5	.1	29.5	9.4	7.5	8.5	9.5	11.5	13.9	14.0		12.2	15.9	6.0	48.3	29.5	16.2
33543	SOUTHERN ILL UNIV	59	82	1272	3.6	12.7	11.4	15.2	5.4	36.6	17.3	5.9	34.7	7.0	10.0	8.8	10.4	9.8	10.6	13.0	15.1	12.0	13.2	6.1	60.9	18.5	14.5
21580	RENSSELAER POLY I/NY	20	83	1221	3.4	3.5	17.2	27.3	93.4	4.2	.4	2.0	.0	7.9	9.0	8.6	11.8	6.5	24.3	10.7				12.6	18.4	57.6	11.4
71406	ARKANSAS,U-FAYETTVLE	53	84	1195	3.4	10.0	4.6	14.0	20.8	17.1	6.9	13.1	42.1	7.6	7.5	9.3	12.0	11.4	15.0	9.6	8.2	13.5	17.2	6.3	60.8	18.7	14.2
84406	COLORADO STATE UNIV	55	85	1186	3.3	4.3	21.3	13.7	36.5	58.6	.0	.3	4.6	9.6	5.8	8.6	10.6			8.5	29.0	12.5	18.3	12.2	41.7	34.7	11.3
74441	HOUSTON, U OF/TX	47	86	1144	3.2	19.0	10.6	17.4	28.3	35.1	.8	1.4	34.4	8.3	9.3	8.8	12.3	12.3	16.6	11.9	16.0	16.0	17.2	11.5	35.1	35.7	17.7
74473	RICE UNIVERSITY/TX	20	87	1143	3.2	9.8	15.7	21.6	73.2	10.2	16.3	.2	.0	6.3	5.6	6.8	10.1	7.6	10.2	9.5				19.0	28.2	34.8	18.0
21576	POLYTECHNIC INST NY	35	88	1120	3.2	2.8	22.9	20.0	99.7	.2	.0	.0	.0	9.8	9.7	15.0								11.3	19.5	56.2	13.1
84411	DENVER, UNIV OF/CO	44	89	1095	3.1	17.3	5.7	8.9	12.1	24.3	28.7	5.2	29.7	10.7	14.3	9.3	11.7	13.4	17.2	12.3	15.8	14.7	19.0	2.9	53.4	29.8	13.9
54443	VA POLY INST&STATE U	42	90	1089	3.1	4.7	15.4	16.4	57.7	38.9	.0	.1	3.3	8.9	8.9	7.9	9.3			6.0		14.0	11.9	10.2	36.5	41.2	12.0

SOURCE: NRC, Commission on Human Resources.

6. Percent with foreign BA's: percent whose baccalaureate degrees were non-U.S.
7. Percent with BA's from school of PhD: a measure of institutional in-breeding.

Variables 8-12 provide a percentage distribution of PhD's among five field groups:

8. Percent in EMP fields: fields of engineering, mathematics, and physical sciences.
9. Percent in bio-behavioral fields: life sciences, psychology, and social sciences.
10. Percent in humanities: all humanities fields combined.
11. Percent in professions: miscellaneous business and professional fields.
12. Percent in education: EdD's and PhD's in education.

Variables 13-22 provide baccalaureate-to-doctorate time lapse in years, by field group and sex:

13, 14. Males and females in EMP fields.
15, 16. Males and females in bio-behavioral fields.
17, 18. Males and females in humanities fields.
19, 20. Males and females in professional fields.
21, 22. Males and females in education.

Variables 23-26 provide a percentage distribution of plans at PhD graduation as given on the Doctorate Survey--percentage with each type of plan for postgraduation year:

23. Postdoctoral training: those planning on fellowships, traineeships, associateships.
24. Academic employment: those expecting to be employed by colleges and universities.
25. Nonacademic employment: those expecting all other categories of employment.
26. Plans uncertain: those who did not know, when they completed the Survey of Earned Doctorates, what they would be doing in the coming year.

To use Table 42, one may begin with the leading institution and consider what the data say about it. The condensed statistical description which the table provides may thus be translated into a verbal description that carries more immediate meaning. A similar translation can, of course, be provided in a similar manner for all of the other institutions in the list. The "translation" for the University of Wisconsin at Madison follows.

The University of Wisconsin was graduating PhD's before 1920, and over the past 17 years has produced more PhD's (10,587) than any other institution in the country, ranking it first among PhD schools. This 10,587 is equal to 29.9 per thousand (2.99 percent) of the total U.S. production during the 1958-1974 period. Of this total, 12.5 percent were women, and 17.1 had their undergraduate training in foreign countries. About one in seven (14.2 percent) took their undergraduate as well as graduate training in Madison. Of the total, 26.1 percent took doctorates in the EMP fields; 38.1 percent in the life or behavioral science fields; 19.6 percent in the humanities; 3.5 percent in the professions; and 12.6 percent in education. Data on baccalaureate-to-doctorate time lapse shows that in the EMP fields the men took, on the average, 7.2 years, and the women, 7.1 years. In the bio-behavioral fields the corresponding time lapses were 8.0 years for the men and 8.6 years for the women. In the humanities it was 9.4 years for the men and 11.0 years for the women; in the professions it was 9.7 years and 14.3 years, while in education it was 12.1 years for the men and 14.3 for the women. Of the total of all 1958-1974 PhD's, 14.1 percent planned at the time of graduation to take postdoctoral training; 49.3 percent planned on entering academic employment; 24.6 percent planned on entering nonacademic employment, and 12.0 percent were uncertain of their plans at the time they completed the Survey of Earned Doctorates form.

TABLE 43
A FRAME OF REFERENCE FOR THE DATA OF THE INSTITUTIONAL PROFILES

Variable	Name of Variable	Mean	Standard Deviation	Percentiles 25	50	75
5	Percent women	14.49	8.67	10.01	14.14	18.26
6	Percent foreign BA	12.50	7.21	6.53	12.55	17.35
7	Percent BA-PhD institution	14.27	7.23	9.95	14.22	18.49
8	Percent EMP	31.08	20.27	17.68	26.54	37.54
9	Percent bio/behavioral sciences	34.07	14.46	24.74	33.46	41.80
10	Percent humanities	15.05	9.73	7.22	14.21	21.15
11	Percent professions	5.34	2.86	2.01	4.98	7.94
12	Percent education	27.05	20.16	13.56	23.43	34.21
13	Time lapse, EMP, male	8.03	1.23	7.17	7.83	8.71
14	Time lapse, EMP, female	7.98	1.37	7.01	7.80	8.86
15	Time lapse, bio/behavioral, male	8.67	1.42	7.89	8.49	9.29
16	Time lapse, bio/behavioral, female	10.07	2.05	8.59	9.86	11.12
17	Time lapse, humanities, male	10.66	1.74	9.48	10.58	11.65
18	Time lapse, humanities, female	12.26	2.02	11.09	12.16	13.65
19	Time lapse, professions, male	11.44	2.05	10.17	11.30	12.60
20	Time lapse, professions, female*	18.27	7.31	14.00	16.04	18.40
21	Time lapse, education, male	13.59	1.49	12.55	13.50	14.48
22	Time lapse, education, female	16.47	3.53	14.90	16.11	17.18
23	Percent postdoctoral study	11.01	6.79	5.00	10.85	16.14
24	Percent academic employment	44.19	10.81	36.59	44.85	52.45
25	Percent nonacademic employment	28.74	9.13	22.31	27.56	34.77
26	Percent plans uncertain	16.31	5.13	12.54	15.63	18.73

*This norm was based on only 34 institutions and hence is not as stable as the others. There is, moreover, a highly skewed distribution, as indicated by the relation of mean and median.

SOURCE: NRC, Commission on Human Resources.

A FRAME OF REFERENCE FOR INSTITUTIONAL DATA

A similar paragraph could be written about each of the 90 institutions listed in Table 42; the numerical data provide a convenient condensation, and one that permits ready comparison with other institutions on the list. A somewhat different kind of comparison, and one that is more comprehensive, is provided by the data of Table 43, which give institutional norms, i.e., means, standard deviations, and percentiles. In Table 43 we have a frame of reference that includes all institutions large enough to provide reliable statistical data about themselves. It is a statistical "norm table," based on the 145 largest PhD-granting institutions. Every institution that produced, over this 17-year period, 330 or more PhD's (i.e., every school that produced as much as 1 in 1,000 of the total) was included in the calculation of this table. It provides the mean, the standard deviation, and the 25th, 50th, and 75th percentile points (based on the institutional means or percentages) for each of the characteristics listed above, from variable 5 (percentage of women) to variable 26 (percent uncertain of post-PhD plans).

The reason for limiting the normative base to the group of 145 leading institutions, rather than including all 307 institutions, is that the variability of percentages based on small numbers can produce quite unrealistic statistics and meaningless information. The decision was made that, because of the fractionation of the total number of graduates of an institution by field, sex, and origin, that a minimum PhD total of 330 would be used as an overall cutoff point. In addition, for any given variable, a mean or a percentage based on fewer than 16 cases would not be included in the norm computation. The result is that this reference frame is based on only rather reliable data points but still shows very wide institutional variations, as given in the norms presented in Table 43.

Some comments may be in order regarding the statistics of Table 43, apart from their application to individual institutions. Any table of norms, by definition, furnishes a partial description of the status of a system--in this case the graduate education system of the United States. Only a few of the parameters of this educational system can be reflected in these norms. Additional parameters might be developed in a similar manner, i.e., based on the characteristics or experiences or aspirations of the graduates. Still other parameters would require very different approaches. It is with a full recognition of the limited range of data available here that the following comments are offered.

The wide disparity in the percentage of women among the doctorate-granting institutions is apparent from the first entry in Table 43. On the average, the institutions have 14.5 percent female PhD graduates, but one-fourth of the institutions have fewer than 10 percent, while another fourth have over 18 percent women PhD graduates. An even wider difference is apparent with respect to the non-U.S. undergraduate origins of the PhD's. One-fourth of the schools have fewer than 6.5 percent PhD's of foreign origin, while at the other extreme, one-fourth have over 17 percent. The "in-breeding index," the seventh characteristic in the norm table, varies from just under 10 percent for the lower quartile to 18.5 percent for the upper quartile point. Similar differences are apparent in the percentages in the several field groups. In the EMP fields, the first and third institutional quartile points are 17.7 percent and 37.5 percent; in the bio-behavioral fields, 24.7 percent and 41.8 percent; in the humanities, 7.2 percent and 21.2 percent; in the professions, 2 percent and 7.9 percent; and in education, 13.6 percent and 34.2 percent. Even with this limited range of variables, a highly varied mosaic of institutional differences begins to emerge.

When we turn to the baccalaureate-to-doctorate time lapse figures, here presented by sex within field groups that are relatively homogeneous with respect to time lapse data, we see another but less variable set of institutional norms. The controls on field and sex obviously moderate institutional variability but do not abolish it by any means. In the EMP fields the institutional mean for men is slightly higher than that for women--the only case in which the difference goes in that direction. In all fields, the standard deviations are greater for women. This means that, with respect to the BA-to-PhD time lapse, institutional variations are greater for women than for men. As seen earlier with respect to the individual data, the BA-to-PhD time lapse is more variable for women and generally longer; here the institutional variations are seen also to be greater in the case of the rate of women's progress through graduate education.

The final set of norms refers to plans at PhD, as shown by the Survey of Earned Doctorates. Here again, wide differences among the institutions appear. Some of this variation is based on the fact that institutions vary in field mix, as described above. Fields vary tremendously in the extent to which their PhD's seek postdoctoral training or employment in academic versus non-academic jobs. And yet, even granting the influence of field mix, the attitude or orientation in the graduate schools with respect to post-PhD careers must vary greatly in order to produce such widely varying norms as those shown here.

AN ALPHABETICAL LIST

From statistical data about institutional characteristics to numerical data about individual institutions is but a step. The data in Table 42 were presented with the institutions in rank order, in terms of the total number of PhD's produced. For many purposes of comparison, this is advantageous. However, to locate a given institution in an extensive table, it is frequently easier if the order is alphabetical rather than given in terms of rank orders. Just such an alphabetical listing is given in Table 44. The data given for each institution include the number of men, number of women, and total number of both sexes to whom the institution has awarded doctorates over the entire 1920-1974 period. With each of these numbers is given the rank of the institution, by sex and by total number, for this period. By reference to these rank orders, the institutions may readily be located in other tables.

TABLE 44
ALPHABETICAL LISTING OF PhD-GRANTING INSTITUTIONS, WITH NUMBERS OF PhD's AND RANK ORDERS,* BY SEX AND TOTAL, 1920-1974

	Male		Female		Both Sexes	
	Number	Rank	Number	Rank	Number	Rank
ADELPHI UNIV/NY	222	157	88	114	310	151
AIR FORCE I TECH/OH	21	252			21	260
AKRON, U OF/OH	218	158	27	162	245	163
ALABAMA, UNIVER OF	1259	82	303	59	1562	79
ALABAMA,U-BIRMINGHAM	59	211	16	179	75	209
ALABAMA,U-HUNTSVILLE	3	299			3	302
ALASKA, UNIV OF	73	202	2	248	75	209
ALFRED UNIVERSITY/NY	56	215			56	221
AMERICAN UNIV/DC	1214	85	182	84	1396	85
AQUINAS INST/IA	43	222	2	248	45	232
ARIZONA STATE UNIV	1230	84	234	74	1464	82
ARIZONA, UNIV OF	1931	62	237	70	2168	62
ARKANSAS,U-FAYETTVLE	1130	90	125	93	1255	91
ARK U-MED SCIENCES	15	264	8	205	23	258
ARKANSAS,U-LTLE ROCK	2	302			2	306
ATLANTA UNIV/GA	11	275	5	223	16	270
AUBURN UNIVERSITY/AL	755	104	119	96	874	105
BALL STATE UNIV/IN	389	130	82	119	471	131
BAYLOR COLL MED/TX	35	233	11	194	46	231
BAYLOR UNIV/TX	317	142	57	134	374	139
BOSTON COLLEGE/MA	338	136	193	82	531	127
BOSTON UNIVERSITY/MA	2708	45	848	25	3556	41
BOWLING GREEN S U/OH	231	155	31	156	262	158
BRANDEIS UNIV/MA	736	105	211	79	947	99
BRIGHAM YOUNG U/UT	675	113	58	133	733	114
BROWN UNIVERSITY/RI	2094	58	299	60	2393	59
BRYN MAWR COLL/PA	120	182	588	35	708	119
CAL INST TECHNOLOGY	2773	44	55	137	2828	50
CALIF, U-BERKELEY	13535	2	1897	5	15432	4
CALIF, U-DAVIS	1990	60	164	85	2154	63
CALIF,U-IRVINE	279	148	68	130	347	144
CALIF,U-LOS ANGELES	6297	20	1232	14	7529	19
CALIF,U-RIVERSIDE	781	103	79	123	860	107
CALIF, U-SAN DIEGO	786	102	106	107	892	103
CAL, U-SAN FRANCISCO	243	153	83	118	326	147
CALIF,U-SANTA BARB	689	110	71	126	760	113
CALIF,U-SANTA CRUZ	68	206	24	167	92	202
CARNEGIE-MELLON U/PA	1923	63	67	131	1990	69
CASE WESTRN RSRVE/OH	3299	36	594	34	3893	36
CATHOLIC U AMER/DC	3068	40	1133	17	4201	34
CHICAGO, UNIV OF/IL	10170	8	1891	6	12061	8
CINCINNATI, U OF/OH	1729	68	265	67	1994	68
CUNY-GRAD SCH&U CTR	552	120	275	65	827	108
CLAREMNT GRAD SCH/CA	818	100	133	92	951	98
CLARK UNIVERSITY/MA	692	109	121	94	813	109
CLARKSON C TECH/NY	124	180	5	223	129	187
CLEMSON UNIV/SC	345	135	14	186	359	143
COLORADO SCH MINES	264	151	1	262	265	157
COLORADO STATE UNIV	1138	89	52	138	1190	93
COLORADO,U-BOULDER	3174	38	529	38	3703	38
COLUMBIA UNIV/NY	12193	5	3409	1	15602	2
COLUMBIA-TCHRS C/NY	4187	30	1839	7	6026	25
CONNECTICUT, UNIV OF	1676	71	268	66	1944	71
COOPER UNION/NY	11	275	1	262	12	280
CORNELL UNIV/NY	9691	10	1262	13	10953	10
CORNELL U MED C/NY	21	252	26	163	47	229
CREIGHTON UNIV/NE	5	296	1	262	6	297
DALLAS THEOL SEM/TX	18	258			18	264
DALLAS, UNIV OF/TX	6	290			6	297
DARTMOUTH COLLEGE/NH	158	173	11	194	169	177
DAYTON, U OF/OH	6	290	1	262	7	292
DELAWARE, UNIV OF	900	97	70	127	970	97
DENVER, UNIV OF/CO	1197	86	232	75	1429	84
DEPAUL UNIVERSITY/IL	23	246	2	248	25	254
DETROIT, U OF/MI	93	192	8	205	101	199

	Male		Female		Both Sexes	
	Number	Rank	Number	Rank	Number	Rank
DRAKE UNIV/IA	6	290	3	239	9	287
DREW UNIVERSITY/NJ	237	154	11	194	248	162
DREXEL UNIVERSITY/PA	164	172	4	233	168	178
DROPSIE UNIV/PA	200	164	5	223	205	170
DUKE UNIVERSITY/NC	3148	39	453	41	3601	40
DUQUESNE UNIV/PA	151	175	22	169	173	176
EAST TENN STATE UNIV	10	280	1	262	11	283
EAST TEXAS STATE U	309	143	74	125	383	137
EMORY UNIV/GA	703	108	189	83	892	103
FAIRLEIGH DICKN U/NJ	18	258	2	248	20	263
FLORIDA, UNIV OF	3332	35	427	44	3759	37
FLORIDA ATLANTIC U	19	255	10	199	29	250
FLORIDA STATE UNIV	2698	46	611	32	3309	43
SOUTH FLORIDA,U OF	22	249	5	223	27	253
FORDHAM UNIV/NY	1657	72	939	24	2596	54
FULLER THEOL SEM/CA	44	220	1	262	45	232
GEO PEABODY COLL/TN	1292	81	230	77	1522	81
GEO WASHINGTON U/DC	1431	77	344	50	1775	75
GEORGETOWN UNIV/DC	1141	88	199	81	1340	88
GEORGIA INST TECH	794	101	5	223	799	111
GEORGIA STATE UNIV	204	163	78	124	282	156
GEORGIA, UNIV OF	1911	64	377	48	2288	61
GLDN GT BAPT THEO/CA	2	302			2	306
GRAD THEOL UNION/CA	88	196	3	239	91	203
HAHNEMANN MED C/PA	71	203	8	205	79	207
HARTFORD SEM FDN/CT	35	233	3	239	38	240
HARVARD UNIV/MA	13436	3	2011	3	15447	3
HAWAII, UNIV OF	620	115	91	113	711	118
HLTH SCI U-CHI MD/IL	16	262	2	248	18	264
HEBREW UNION COLL/OH	111	187	2	248	113	193
HEBREW UNION COLL/CA	14	265			14	274
HEBREW UNION COLL/NY	9	282	1	262	10	286
HOFSTRA UNIV/NY	92	193	38	151	130	185
HOUSTON, U OF/TX	1035	95	236	71	1271	90
HOWARD UNIVERSITY/DC	206	162	45	144	251	161
IDAHO STATE UNIV	25	243	11	194	36	244
IDAHO, UNIV OF	384	131	33	152	417	134
ILLINOIS INST TECH	1118	91	86	116	1204	92
ILLINOIS ST U-NORMAL	127	178	12	192	139	180
ILL, U, URBANA-CHAMP	13357	4	1539	9	14896	5
ILL, U-COLL MEDICINE	138	177	46	142	184	173
ILLINOIS,U-CHIGO CIR	90	195	13	190	103	197
INDIANA STATE UNIV	77	201	20	173	97	200
INDIANA U BLOOMNGTON	7245	17	1342	12	8587	14
INDIANA UNIV OF PA	13	266	1	262	14	274
INST PAPER CHEM/WI	325	140			325	148
IOWA STATE UNIV	5407	24	319	53	5726	26
IOWA, UNIVERSITY OF	6681	18	1015	20	7696	18
JEWISH THEO SEM AMER	127	178	6	218	133	182
JOHNS HOPKINS U/MD	4659	29	761	27	5420	29
JULLIARD SCHOOL/NY	12	270	2	248	14	274
KANSAS STATE UNIV	1430	78	118	99	1548	80
KANSAS, UNIV OF	3057	41	434	43	3491	42
KENT STATE UNIV/OH	513	123	116	102	629	123
KENTUCKY, UNIV OF	1527	75	232	75	1759	76
LAMAR UNIVERSITY/TX	3	299			3	302
LEHIGH UNIVERSITY/PA	1099	94	80	120	1179	94
LOMA LINDA UNIV/CA	24	244	4	233	28	251
LIU-BROOKLYN CTR/NY	11	275	7	209	18	264
LA ST UNIV & A&M C	2538	50	315	56	2853	49
LA ST U, S MED-N ORL	18	258	7	209	25	254
LSU, SCH MED-SHRVPRT	1	308			1	310
LOUISIANA TECH UNIV	20	254	1	262	21	260
LOUISVILLE, U OF/KY	272	149	40	149	312	150
LOYOLA U CHICAGO/IL	676	112	218	78	894	102

TABLE 44 Continued

	Male Number	Male Rank	Female Number	Female Rank	Both Sexes Number	Both Sexes Rank
LOYOLA UNIVERSITY/LA	2	302			2	306
MAINE, U-ORONO	212	159	16	179	228	165
MARQUETTE UNIV/WI	305	145	103	109	408	136
MARYLAND, UNIV OF	4040	31	704	29	4744	31
MARYLAND,U, SCH MED	13	266	3	239	16	270
MASS COLL PHARMACY	33	235	5	223	38	240
MASS INST TECHNOLOGY	7819	14	293	63	8112	16
LOWELL, UNIV OF/MA	27	241	1	262	28	251
MASS, U OF-AMHERST	1790	65	317	55	2107	64
MCNEESE STATE U/LA	31	236	10	199	41	236
MEDICAL COLL GEORGIA	38	232	6	218	44	234
MED COLL PENSYLVANIA	10	280	7	209	17	267
MED COLL WISCONSIN	6	290	1	262	7	292
MED UNIV SO CAROLINA	41	225	3	239	44	234
MED N J-N J MED SCH	12	270	1	262	13	277
MEMPHIS STATE U/TN	106	188	26	163	132	183
MIAMI UNIVERSITY/OH	146	176	16	179	162	179
MIAMI, UNIV OF/FL	579	118	150	90	729	115
MICHIGAN STATE UNIV	7266	16	818	26	8084	17
MICHIGAN TECH UNIV	41	225			41	236
MICHIGAN, UNIV OF	11532	6	1787	8	13319	6
MIDDLE TENN STATE U	9	282	6	218	15	272
MIDDLEBURY COLL/VT	41	225	28	159	69	213
MIDWST BAPT T SEM/MO	6	290			6	297
MINNESOTA,U-MINNEAPL	9705	9	1226	15	10931	11
MISSISSIPPI STATE U	524	121	57	134	581	126
MISSISSIPPI, UNIV OF	593	117	104	108	697	120
MISSISSIPPI U-MED CT	53	216	7	209	60	218
MISSOURI,U-COLUMBIA	3972	32	387	47	4359	33
MISSOURI,U-KANS CITY	177	168	45	144	222	166
MISSOURI,U-ROLLA	359	133	4	233	363	141
MONTANA STATE UNIV	412	128	25	166	437	133
MONTANA, UNIV OF	266	150	21	170	287	155
NAVAL POSTGRAD S/CA	69	205			69	213
NEBRASKA, U-LINCOLN	2948	42	312	57	3260	44
NEVADA, UNIV OF	114	186	16	179	130	185
NEW HAMPSHIRE, U OF	335	137	40	149	375	138
NEW JERSEY INST TECH	58	213			58	219
N MEXICO HIGHLANDS U	3	299			3	302
N MEX I MINING&TECH	39	230	2	248	41	236
NEW MEXICO STATE U	331	139	29	158	360	142
NEW MEXICO, UNIV OF	1158	87	236	71	1394	86
N ORLN BAPT T SEM/LA	170	170	5	223	175	174
NEW SCH SOC RSCH/NY	362	132	99	110	461	132
NEW YORK LAW SCHOOL	31	236	1	262	32	248
NEW YORK MEDICAL COL	43	222	6	218	49	226
NEW YORK UNIVERSITY	9311	11	2472	2	11783	9
NC, U OF-CHAPEL HILL	3914	33	728	28	4642	32
NC CENTRAL UNIV	2	302	2	248	4	301
NC STATE U-RALEIGH	1975	61	108	106	2083	65
NC, U OF-GREENSBORO	48	218	80	120	128	188
NORTH DAKOTA ST UNIV	209	160	6	218	215	169
NORTH DAKOTA, U OF	635	114	59	132	694	121
N TEXAS STATE UNIV	736	105	162	87	898	101
NE LOUISIANA UNIV	27	241	10	199	37	242
NORTHEASTERN U/MA	196	165	23	168	219	167
NORTHERN ARIZONA U	8	285	1	262	9	287
NTHRN BAPT THEOL/IL	120	182	2	248	122	190
NORTHERN COLORADO,U	1759	67	280	64	2039	66
NORTHERN ILL UNIV	324	141	87	115	411	135
NORWESTRN ST UNIV LA	22	249	15	185	37	242
NORTHWESTERN UNIV/IL	5624	23	944	22	6568	22
NOTRE DAME, U OF/IN	1694	70	240	69	1934	72
NOVA UNIVERSITY/FL	13	266	2	248	15	272
OCCIDENTAL COLL/CA	19	255	14	186	33	246
OHIO STATE UNIV	10681	7	1486	10	12167	7
OHIO UNIVERSITY	682	111	93	112	775	112
OKLAHOMA STATE UNIV	2328	54	235	73	2563	56
OKLAHOMA, U OF	2588	48	398	45	2986	46
OLD DOMINION UNIV/VA	1	308			1	310
OREGON, UNIV OF	2776	43	468	40	3244	45
OREGON U-SCH MED	31	236	4	233	35	245
OREGON STATE UNIV	2234	56	142	91	2376	60
PORTLAND STATE U/OR	4	297	3	239	7	292
PACIFIC, U OF/CA	172	169	32	153	204	171
PEABODY I OF BALT/MD	9	282	3	239	12	280
PENN STATE UNIV	5774	22	684	30	6458	23
PENNSYLVANIA, U OF	6307	19	1185	16	7492	20
PHILA C PHARM&SCI/PA	83	198	4	233	87	204
PHILLIPS UNIV/OK	8	285			8	291
PITTSBURGH, UNIV OF	4672	28	942	23	5614	28
POLYTECHNIC INST NY	1548	74	42	148	1590	78
PORTLAND, UNIV OF/OR	165	171	28	159	193	172
PRINCETN THEO SEM/NJ	92	193	2	248	94	201
PRINCETON UNIV/NJ	5197	26	112	105	5309	30
PROVIDENCE COLL/RI	11	275			11	283
PUERTO RICO, UNIV OF	19	255	14	186	33	246
PURDUE UNIVERSITY/IN	7734	15	611	32	8345	15
REDLANDS, U OF/CA	8	285	1	262	9	287
RENSSELAER POLY I/NY	1393	80	44	146	1437	83
RHODE ISLAND, U OF	347	134	26	163	373	140
RICE UNIVERSITY/TX	1235	83	121	94	1356	87
ROCHESTER,UNIV OF/NY	2517	51	398	45	2915	47
ROCKEFELLER UNIV/NY	223	156	32	153	255	159
RUTGERS UNIV/NJ	3347	34	573	36	3920	35
RUTGERS U-NEWARK/NJ	4	297	2	248	6	297
ST BONAVENTURE U/NY	46	219	12	192	58	219
ST JOHNS UNIV/NY	518	122	163	86	681	122
ST LOUIS UNIV/MO	1446	76	530	37	1976	70
ST MARYS COLLEGE/IN	1	308	69	128	70	212
ST MARYS SEM & U/MD	17	261			17	267
ST STEPHEN'S COLL/MA	1	308			1	310
SAM HOUSTON ST U/TX	7	289			7	292
SANTA CLARA, U OF/CA	28	240	2	248	30	249
SETON HALL UNIV/NJ	61	210	5	223	66	215
SMITH COLLEGE/MA	24	244	32	153	56	221
SOUTH CAROLINA, U OF	607	116	116	102	723	116
S DAKOTA S MINE&TECH	12	270			12	280
SOUTH DAKOTA STATE U	118	184	3	239	121	191
SOUTH DAKOTA, U OF	307	144	30	157	337	146
SO BAPT THEOL SEM/KY	52	217	1	262	53	223
SOUTHERN CALIF, U OF	5347	25	996	21	6343	24
SOUTHERN ILL UNIV	1110	92	162	87	1272	89
STHRN METHODIST U/TX	286	147	16	179	302	153
SOUTHERN MISS, U OF	510	124	118	99	628	124
SW BAPT THEOL SEM/TX	122	181	1	262	123	189
SOWESTERN LA, U OF	23	246	1	262	24	256
SPRINGFIELD COLL/MA	83	198	20	173	103	197
STANFORD UNIV/CA	8392	12	1095	18	9487	12
SUNY AT ALBANY	422	127	80	120	502	130
SUNY AT BINGHAMTON	83	198	21	170	104	195
SUNY AT BUFFALO	2271	55	338	51	2609	53
SUNY AT STONY BROOK	439	126	69	128	508	128
SUNY DOWNSTAT MD CTR	85	197	19	176	104	195
SUNY UPSTATE MED CTR	64	208	14	186	78	208
STEVENS INST TECH/NJ	300	146	7	209	307	152
SYRACUSE UNIV/NY	3201	37	438	42	3639	39
SUNY ENVR SCI FSTRY	334	138	7	209	341	145
TEMPLE UNIVERSITY/PA	1713	69	294	62	2007	67
TENNESSEE TECH U	2	302	1	262	3	302
TENN, U-KNOXVILLE	2442	53	330	52	2772	52
TENN,U CTR HTH SCI	59	211	4	233	63	217
TEXAS A&M UNIVERSITY	2457	52	86	116	2543	57
TEXAS CHRISTIAN UNIV	253	152	46	142	299	154
TEXAS TECH UNIV	711	107	96	111	807	110
TEXAS, U-AUSTIN	6258	21	1019	19	7277	21
TEXAS,U-ARLINGTON	23	246	1	262	24	256
TEXAS,U-DALLAS	8	285	1	262	9	287
TEX U MED BR-GALVSTN	39	230	10	199	49	226
TEXAS, U-HOUSTON	64	208	16	179	80	206

TABLE 44 Continued

	Male Number	Male Rank	Female Number	Female Rank	Both Sexes Number	Both Sexes Rank
TEX U HLTH SCI-S ANT	12	270	5	223	17	267
TEX U HTH SCI-DALLAS	29	239	11	194	40	239
TEXAS WOMANS UNIV	2	302	319	53	321	149
THOMAS JEFFRSON U/PA	40	228	7	209	47	229
T JEF U-JEF MED C/PA	96	191	18	178	114	192
TOLEDO, UNIV OF/OH	208	161	44	146	252	160
TUFTS UNIVERSITY/MA	492	125	119	96	611	125
TULANE U OF LA	1406	79	299	60	1705	77
TULSA, UNIV OF/OK	189	167	51	140	240	164
UNION THEOL SEM/NY	71	203	10	199	81	205
UNION THEOL SEM/VA	11	275			11	283
UNION UNIVERSITY/NY	44	220	7	209	51	225
UNION-ALBANY MED/NY	12	270	1	262	13	277
U S INTERNATL U/CA	390	129	117	101	507	129
UTAH, UNIV OF	2571	49	248	68	2819	51
UTAH STATE UNIV	827	99	47	141	874	105
VANDERBILT UNIV/TN	1643	73	201	80	1844	74
VERMONT, U OF	195	166	21	170	216	168
VILLANOVA UNIV/PA	16	262	5	223	21	260
VA COMMONWEALTH UNIV	1	308	1	262	2	306
VA COMONWLTH U MED C	104	189	28	159	132	183
VA POLY INST&STATE U	1105	93	52	138	1157	95
VIRGINIA, UNIV OF	2593	47	309	58	2902	48
WAKE FOREST UNIV/NC	42	224	7	209	49	226
WAKE F-B GRAY MED/NC	1	308			1	310
WASHINGTON STATE U	1787	66	119	96	1906	73
WASHINGTON UNIV/MO	2046	59	375	49	2421	58
WASHINGTON, U OF	5055	27	648	31	5703	27
WAYNE STATE UNIV/MI	2105	57	479	39	2584	55
WESLEYAN UNIV/CT	57	214	9	204	66	215
WEST VIRGINIA UNIV	971	96	115	104	1086	96
WSTRN CONS BAPT S/OR	1	308			1	310
WESTERN MICHIGAN U	155	174	20	173	175	174
WESTMINSTR THEO S/PA	13	266			13	277
WICHITA ST UNIV/KS	6	290	1	262	7	292
WILLIAM & MARY, C/VA	67	207	8	205	75	209
WISCONSIN,U-MADISON	14971	1	1958	4	16929	1
WISCONSIN,U-MILWAUKE	117	185	19	176	136	181
WOODSTOCK COLL/NY	22	249			22	259
WORCESTER POLY I/MA	103	190	3	239	106	194
WYOMING, UNIV OF	851	98	57	134	908	100
YALE UNIVERSITY/CT	8037	13	1423	11	9460	13
YESHIVA UNIV/NY	562	119	154	89	716	117
YESHIVA-EINST MED/NY	40	228	13	190	53	223

*The word "rank," where used in this report, is used in the statistical sense of "order according to a statistical characteristic" (e.g., the number of doctorates granted); its use is not intended to imply degree of eminence or excellence.

SOURCE: NRC, Commission on Human Resources.

TABLE 45A

ONE HUNDRED PhD-GRANTING INSTITUTIONS, LARGEST IN NUMBER OF 1920-1974 PhD's: NATURAL SCIENCES, SUBTOTALS, AND GRAND TOTAL OF ALL FIELDS

Doctoral Institution	Rank	Grand Total	Physics	Chemistry	Earth Sciences	Total, Physical Sciences	Mathematics	Engineering	Total EMP	Basic Medical Sciences	Other Biological Sciences	Total Biological Sciences	Medical Sciences	Agricultural Sciences	Environmental Sciences	Life Sciences
WISCONSIN,U-MADISON	1	16929	643	1714	421	2778	601	1097	4476	1539	1379	2918	465	1378	16	4777
COLUMBIA UNIV/NY	2	15602	708	1189	483	2380	316	833	3529	534	440	974	166	3		1143
HARVARD UNIV/MA	3	15447	1107	974	384	2465	639	336	3440	570	736	1306	176	9	11	1502
CALIF,U-BERKELEY	4	15432	1397	1406	333	3136	794	1840	5770	1082	1401	2483	143	324	12	2962
ILL,U,URBANA-CHAMP	5	14896	790	2309	289	3388	608	2147	6143	972	814	1786	179	885	3	2853
MICHIGAN,UNIV OF	6	13319	686	887	292	1865	563	1781	4209	571	918	1489	334	243	37	2103
OHIO STATE UNIV	7	12167	522	1412	203	2137	234	1155	3526	595	768	1363	228	603	1	2195
CHICAGO,UNIV OF/IL	8	12061	781	1060	363	2204	566	1	2771	748	696	1444	225	1		1670
NEW YORK UNIVERSITY	9	11783	414	586	126	1126	525	579	2230	385	311	696	117	3	4	820
CORNELL UNIV/NY	10	10953	838	989	126	1953	362	1049	3364	767	1370	2137	142	1335	12	3626
MINNESOTA,U-MINNEAPL	11	10931	298	859	147	1304	273	891	2468	986	814	1800	604	924	5	3333
STANFORD UNIV/CA	12	9487	520	562	393	1475	476	2081	4032	352	345	697	40	14	1	752
YALE UNIVERSITY/CT	13	9460	723	861	227	1811	254	489	2554	513	436	949	177	143		1269
INDIANA U BLOOMINGTON	14	8587	293	518	122	933	170		1103	350	329	679	63			742
PURDUE UNIVERSITY/IN	15	8345	364	1414	16	1794	342	1772	3908	626	484	1110	377	672	7	2166
MASS INST TECHNOLOGY	16	8112	1183	1499	420	3102	520	3278	6900	283	79	362	14	15		391
MICHIGAN STATE UNIV	17	8084	197	535	74	806	201	468	1475	518	418	936	65	1065	6	2072
IOWA, UNIVERSITY OF	18	7696	199	702	147	1048	196	390	1634	346	374	720	221	2	1	944
CALIF,U-LOS ANGELES	19	7529	412	492	272	1176	357	743	2276	515	459	974	154	49	4	1181
PENNSYLVANIA, U OF	20	7492	399	670	10	1079	243	726	2048	549	255	804	223	4	1	1032
TEXAS, U-AUSTIN	21	7277	410	714	161	1285	305	854	2444	402	434	836	33	1		870
NORTHWESTERN UNIV/IL	22	6568	200	745	82	1027	176	961	2164	344	142	486	99		2	587
PENN STATE UNIV	23	6458	393	871	382	1646	154	687	2487	364	211	575	3	381	3	962
SOUTHERN CALIF, U OF	24	6343	95	198	57	350	83	390	823	275	107	382	37		2	421
COLUMBIA-TCHRS C/NY	25	6026								2		2				2
IOWA STATE UNIV	26	5726	312	1008	33	1353	248	891	2492	553	716	1269	71	941	2	2283
WASHINGTON, U OF	27	5703	301	645	244	1190	226	505	1921	347	286	633	151	189	4	977
PITTSBURGH, UNIV OF	28	5614	249	552	35	836	177	372	1385	301	220	521	161		4	686
JOHNS HOPKINS U/MD	29	5420	435	604	226	1265	137	548	1950	583	396	979	436	2	25	1442
PRINCETON UNIV/NJ	30	5309	629	655	291	1575	472	620	2667	123	103	226	1		2	229
MARYLAND, UNIV OF	31	4744	497	497	11	1005	220	401	1626	345	299	644	91	400	2	1137
NC, U OF-CHAPEL HILL	32	4642	166	462	78	706	223	23	952	205	223	428	221	13	15	677
MISSOURI,U-COLUMBIA	33	4359	129	263	82	474	97	284	855	268	238	506	50	456	1	1013
CATHOLIC U AMER/DC	34	4201	296	187	3	486	108	157	751	106	122	228	12	1		241
RUTGERS UNIV/NJ	35	3920	160	424	41	625	122	245	992	540	440	980	28	430	9	1447
CASE WESTRN RSRVE/OH	36	3893	293	598	24	915	189	688	1792	258	66	324	35			359
FLORIDA, UNIV OF	37	3759	149	433	2	584	103	493	1180	114	214	328	115	266	16	725
COLORADO,U-BOULDER	38	3703	319	405	121	845	131	264	1240	198	143	341	58			399
SYRACUSE UNIV/NY	39	3639	199	206	41	446	143	300	889	149	109	258	2	23		283
DUKE UNIVERSITY	40	3601	262	322	3	587	126	105	818	312	333	645	22	121		788
BOSTON UNIVERSITY/MA	41	3556	99	111	40	250	37		287	220	39	259	81			340
KANSAS, UNIV OF	42	3491	132	530	83	745	91	198	1034	304	310	614	41	1	4	660
FLORIDA STATE UNIV	43	3309	145	226	100	471	98	4	573	88	90	178	2	2		182
NEBRASKA, U-LINCOLN	44	3260	73	338	32	443	70	55	568	133	234	367	28	262		657
OREGON, UNIV OF	45	3244	94	149	21	264	142		406	165	68	233	10			243
OKLAHOMA, U OF	46	2986	113	123	96	332	71	296	699	205	205	410	108	1	16	535
ROCHESTER,UNIV OF/NY	47	2915	421	379	27	827	79	144	1050	426	122	548	83			631
VIRGINIA, UNIV OF	48	2902	348	330	5	683	131	210	1024	81	132	213	7	1	2	223
LA ST UNIV & A&M C	49	2853	133	279	112	524	99	144	767	120	219	339	10	315		664
CAL INST TECHNOLOGY	50	2828	711	551	191	1453	193	878	2524	210	77	287	1	2	4	294
UTAH, UNIV OF	51	2819	124	273	123	520	91	396	1007	169	149	318	63	1		382
TENN, U-KNOXVILLE	52	2772	206	239	27	472	87	264	823	187	216	403	43	127	1	574
SUNY AT BUFFALO	53	2609	91	281	4	376	61	154	591	288	42	330	96	1		427
FORDHAM UNIV/NY	54	2596	58	237	4	299	4		303	134	111	245			1	246
WAYNE STATE UNIV/MI	55	2584	70	382		452	81	54	587	207	25	232	13			245
OKLAHOMA STATE UNIV	56	2563	69	146	2	217	81	496	794	117	246	363	7	235		605
TEXAS A&M UNIVERSITY	57	2543	119	201	175	495	63	480	1038	193	304	497	31	449	2	979
WASHINGTON UNIV/MO	58	2421	222	182	55	459	99	334	892	166	208	374	35	6	5	420
BROWN UNIVERSITY/RI	59	2393	286	363	48	697	333	166	1196	124	111	235	5	1		241
OREGON STATE UNIV	60	2376	65	294	139	498	126	159	783	252	414	666	23	461		1150
GEORGIA, UNIV OF	61	2288	25	131	7	163	75		238	145	202	347	29	153	1	530
ARIZONA, UNIV OF	62	2168	120	153	216	489	51	247	787	128	179	307	10	145	6	468
CALIF, U-DAVIS	63	2154	74	210	16	300	36	174	510	415	638	1053	115	284	1	1453
MASS, U OF-AMHERST	64	2107	45	264	12	321	41	124	486	167	174	341	3	126		470
NC STATE U-RALEIGH	65	2083	55	62	5	122	120	496	738	121	316	437	2	434		873
NORTHERN COLORADO,U	66	2039	1	6		7	23		30	1	7	8				8
TEMPLE UNIVERSITY/PA	67	2007	92	143		235	16		251	94	18	112	51			163
CINCINNATI, U OF/OH	68	1994	116	351	53	520	82	235	837	175	61	236	98	1	10	345
CARNEGIE-MELLON U/PA	69	1990	287	318	1	606	177	914	1697	1	1	2				2
ST LOUIS UNIV/MO	70	1976	107	135	76	318	84		402	196	42	238	26			264
CONNECTICUT, UNIV OF	71	1944	89	196	3	288	23	173	484	121	102	223	96	18	2	339
NOTRE DAME, U OF/IN	72	1934	208	504		712	146	217	1075	78	76	154	5	1	3	163
WASHINGTON STATE U	73	1906	79	155	22	256	74	40	370	107	209	316	60	322		698
VANDERBILT UNIV/TN	74	1844	154	196		350	37	95	482	164	60	224	56		4	284
GEO WASHINGTON U/DC	75	1775	27	61	29	117	62	74	253	225	84	309	65	2	1	377
KENTUCKY, UNIV OF	76	1759	77	134		211	104	60	375	96	48	144	14	153		311
TULANE U OF LA	77	1705	45	137	14	196	111	88	395	268	87	355	127			482
POLYTECHNIC INST NY	78	1590	153	647		800	63	723	1586	1		1				1
ALABAMA, UNIVER OF	79	1562	56	86		142	60	94	296	47	41	88	6			94
KANSAS STATE UNIV	80	1548	59	255	1	315	40	147	502	173	247	420	36	274		730
GEO PEABODY COLL/TN	81	1522		4	1	5	59		64		3	3		2		5
ARIZONA STATE UNIV	82	1464	42	82	5	129	38	151	318	17	64	81				81
RENSSELAER POLY I/NY	83	1437	211	310	34	555	101	700	1356	24	4	28			8	36
DENVER, UNIV OF/CO	84	1429	21	9	3	33	6	94	133							
AMERICAN UNIV/DC	85	1396	42	47		89	16	5	110	6	2	8	2	2		12
NEW MEXICO, UNIV OF	86	1394	59	98	39	196	72	162	430	23	36	59	7			66
RICE UNIVERSITY/TX	87	1356	279	192	109	580	116	312	1008	60	36	96	6			102
GEORGETOWN UNIV/DC	88	1340	95	193		288	13		301	188	22	210	49	1		260
SOUTHERN ILL UNIV	89	1272	7	45	2	54	14	1	69	45	61	106	2	1		109
HOUSTON, U OF/TX	90	1271	31	91		122	49	153	324	58	14	72	1			73

TABLE 45A Continued

Doctoral Institution		Grand Total	Physics	Chemistry	Earth Sciences	Total, Physical Sciences	Mathematics	Engineering	Total EMP	Basic Medical Sciences	Other Biological Sciences	Total Biological Sciences	Medical Sciences	Agricultural Sciences	Environmental Sciences	Life Sciences
ARKANSAS,U-FAYETTVLE	91	1255	28	149		177	19	67	263	35	34	69	7	24		100
ILLINOIS INST TECH	92	1204	109	216	1	326	91	490	907	58	7	65				65
COLORADO STATE UNIV	93	1190	32	58	64	154	36	246	436	146	159	305	43	197	8	553
LEHIGH UNIVERSITY/PA	94	1179	109	166	32	307	89	455	851	29	24	53	2			55
VA POLY INST&STATE U	95	1157	72	93	35	200	113	368	681	95	123	218	1	148	2	369
WEST VIRGINIA UNIV	96	1086	39	117	22	178	4	140	322	124	68	192	42	70		304
DELAWARE, UNIV OF	97	970	46	371	1	418	35	238	691	36	52	88	2	15		105
CLAREMNT GRAD SCH/CA	98	951					4		4	1	27	28				28
BRANDEIS UNIV/MA	99	947	100	77		177	66	1	244	116	15	131				131
WYOMING, UNIV OF	100	908	57	61	51	169	21	26	216	33	56	89		83	1	173

SOURCE: NRC, Commission on Human Resources.

INSTITUTIONS ARRANGED IN ORDER OF SIZE

Several tables from this point on are arranged in order of size, defined as the total number of PhD's granted over the 1920-1974 period. The first of these, Table 45 (A and B), provides detailed data regarding the leading 100 institutions. The fields of PhD of their graduates are here presented in considerable detail, corresponding to the fields shown in Table 2 (A and B) in Chapter 1--there given by year, with 5-year summaries, for the entire United States. In Table 45A, the institutions' graduates are shown for the natural science fields; in Table 45B, the same data are shown for the behavioral sciences; the total of all sciences; the several nonscience fields, with subtotals; and the total for all sciences combined. Most of the institutions have too few PhD graduates to warrant this degree of detail; for the remaining schools a condensed set of fields is provided in Appendix B. For those whose research may require the finer detail for all institutions, the data may be obtained from the Commission on Human Resources. For other research purposes, state and regional data may be required; these are given in Appendix C and Appendix D, with the same field sets as for the 100 leading schools. The states are arranged by census regions, and the regional summaries are given at the bottom of the table, followed by a row for the entire United States.

Using the alphabetical listing in Table 44 as a guide, one may locate any given institution in Appendix E, which gives a much more detailed breakout of the data, by field group, by sex, and by time period. A grand total, combining all fields and both sexes, is given in the column at the far right, and rank orders based on these totals are given at the left, immediately following the institution name. The time periods for these totals, and ranks based on them, are 1920-1959, 1960-1969, and 1970-1974. This division of time periods produces three data sets roughly equivalent in terms of numbers of PhD's and places greatest emphasis on the most recent period, where the least information has been available heretofore. Below the totals for the entire 1920-1974 period, for each field group by sex, are given percentage figures, showing the proportion of the U.S. total produced, in that column, by each given institution.

Examining the first entry--Wisconsin again--we see that in the 1920-1959 period that institution produced 7,044 PhD's, ranking it third in the nation. Of these 7,044, 6,356 were men and 687 were women. (In one case, field and sex are not available.) Of the men, 1,514 were in the physical sciences and mathematics, 310 in engineering, and so on across the page. During the 1960's, Wisconsin produced 5,403 PhD's, ranking it second in the nation, and in the 1970's it produced 4,482, ranking it first. Over the whole time period, it produced 16,929 PhD's, again a national first. In the physical sciences, Wisconsin's 3,245 male PhD's comprised 3.4 percent of the U.S. total; in engineering, 1,091 men comprised 2.4 percent of that field's male total, etc., across to the grand total, which includes 3.5 percent of the U.S. total for the 1920-1974 period. In a similar manner, each institution's production may be examined, by time period, by field, and by sex grouping.

Going down the page in Appendix E, we find Columbia ranked second for the entire 1920-1974 period. In the earliest period, it had been first; in the 1960's, sixth; and in the 1970's, thirteenth in the nation. Harvard was third in the 1920-1959 period, fourth in the 1960's, and seventh in the 1970's, for an overall rank of third. The University of California at Berkeley was fifth, then first, then second, for an overall rank of fourth, followed by the University of Illinois, Urbana, ranking respectively sixth, third, third, and fifth. Going on down the list, it will be apparent that the public institutions have grown in size more rapidly than have the private ones, thus generally tending to move upward in the rank order over time, while the private institutions tend to move downward. A constant output would thus lead to a declining proportion of the total. A state and regional summary of these data is provided in Appendix F.

TABLE 45B

ONE HUNDRED PhD-GRANTING INSTITUTIONS LARGEST IN NUMBER OF 1920-1974 PhD's: BEHAVIORAL SCIENCES AND NONSCIENCE FIELDS, WITH SUBTOTALS FOR SCIENCE AND NONSCIENCE FIELDS

										Language and Literature							
Doctoral Institution	Rank	Psychology	Economics	Anthropology and Sociology	Political Science and Public Admin.	Other Social Sciences	Total, Behavioral Sciences	Total, Sciences	History	American	Foreign	Other Humanities	Humanities, Total	Education	Professions	Unknown Field	Total, Nonsciences
WISCONSIN,U-MADISON	1	465	947	436	284	254	2386	11639	1041	873	667	589	3170	1690	393	37	5290
COLUMBIA UNIV/NY	2	1169	832	781	713	135	3630	8302	1271	1120	1159	864	4414	1883	984	19	7300
HARVARD UNIV/MA	3	576	1235	633	831	103	3378	8320	1381	916	948	1338	4583	1304	1224	16	7127
CALIF,U-BERKELEY	4	630	757	509	395	257	2548	11280	760	463	517	348	2088	1399	265	400	4152
ILL,U,URBANA-CHAMP	5	634	592	186	236	164	1812	10808	331	564	482	469	1846	1669	560	13	4088
MICHIGAN,UNIV OF	6	1175	338	369	289	228	2399	8711	423	611	464	885	2383	1748	453	24	4608
OHIO STATE UNIV	7	1001	369	305	116	158	1949	7670	343	285	258	544	1430	2489	566	12	4497
CHICAGO,UNIV OF/IL	8	944	544	917	588	242	3235	7676	714	551	556	457	2278	859	1171	77	4385
NEW YORK UNIVERSITY	9	1211	332	228	476	164	2411	5461	362	538	428	547	1875	3656	765	26	6322
CORNELL UNIV/NY	10	376	512	436	184	102	1610	8600	301	419	259	457	1436	682	210	25	2353
MINNESOTA,U-MINNEAPL	11	1045	436	296	263	166	2206	8007	378	362	177	426	1343	1284	294	3	2924
STANFORD UNIV/CA	12	495	283	167	206	76	1227	6011	391	411	342	362	1506	1701	251	18	3476
YALE UNIVERSITY/CT	13	418	352	326	319	27	1442	5265	567	900	776	755	2998	371	816	10	4195
INDIANA U BLOOMINGTON	14	392	233	180	265	97	1167	3012	375	402	328	700	1805	3232	521	17	5575
PURDUE UNIVERSITY/IN	15	846	331	94	11	51	1333	7407	4	53	1	132	190	488	174	86	938
MASS INST TECHNOLOGY	16	63	377	1	109	39	589	7880			2	84	86		124	22	232
MICHIGAN STATE UNIV	17	566	277	232	90	232	1397	4944	133	164	62	292	651	2098	367	24	3140
IOWA, UNIVERSITY OF	18	772	179	119	201	126	1397	3975	272	439	195	876	1782	1549	387	3	3721
CALIF,U-LOS ANGELES	19	596	133	278	192	154	1353	4810	361	239	280	312	1192	1248	275	4	2719
PENNSYLVANIA, U OF	20	314	582	297	264	218	1675	4755	472	668	443	371	1954	562	198	23	2737
TEXAS, U-AUSTIN	21	578	179	123	118	47	1045	4359	352	420	238	296	1306	1242	366	4	2918
NORTHWESTERN UNIV/IL	22	395	215	238	186	135	1169	3920	246	349	188	711	1494	763	387	4	2648
PENN STATE UNIV	23	419	99	120	43	96	777	4226	66	156	52	135	409	1634	172	17	2232
SOUTHERN CALIF, U OF	24	412	187	181	281	76	1137	2381	213	177	204	543	1137	2395	418	12	3962
COLUMBIA-TCHRS C/NY	25	4					4	6						6018	2		6020
IOWA STATE UNIV	26	88	391	93		44	616	5391						287	46	2	335
WASHINGTON, U OF	27	305	123	236	148	169	981	3879	235	368	248	213	1064	476	269	15	1824
PITTSBURGH, UNIV OF	28	385	189	158	124	71	927	2998	116	220	173	193	702	1707	199	8	2616
JOHNS HOPKINS U/MD	29	207	172	56	275	59	769	4161	258	208	419	217	1102	135	11	11	1259
PRINCETON UNIV/NJ	30	220	268	78	308	30	904	3800	291	355	451	335	1432	1	71	5	1509
MARYLAND, UNIV OF	31	288	107	51	122	38	606	3369	126	126	69	43	364	960	51		1375
NC, U OF-CHAPEL HILL	32	316	177	262	203	71	1029	2658	362	462	389	216	1429	438	113	4	1984
MISSOURI,U-COLUMBIA	33	226	112	148	75	18	579	2447	172	117	90	138	517	1202	191	2	1912
CATHOLIC U AMER/DC	34	292	89	206	32	5	624	1616	238	148	300	356	1042	598	940	5	2585
RUTGERS UNIV/NJ	35	181	76	27	52	37	373	2812	114	111	90	18	333	728	40	7	1108
CASE WESTRN RSRVE/OH	36	395	41	62	26	35	559	2710	149	200	103	139	591	423	139	30	1183
FLORIDA, UNIV OF	37	276	108	57	71	55	567	2472	80	154	39	65	338	841	106	2	1287
COLORADO,U-BOULDER	38	284	157	147	95	36	719	2358	168	139	153	88	548	672	124	1	1345
SYRACUSE UNIV/NY	39	327	136	96	288	242	1089	2261	106	123	44	126	399	869	101	9	1378
DUKE UNIVERSITY	40	260	196	91	173	5	725	2331	328	270	66	91	755	287	221	7	1270
BOSTON UNIVERSITY/MA	41	398	28	77	32	21	556	1183	165	148	33	335	681	1166	525	1	2373
KANSAS, UNIV OF	42	372	55	65	62	71	625	2319	110	101	110	110	431	684	54	3	1172
FLORIDA STATE UNIV	43	316	37	122	62	80	617	1372	75	114	78	246	513	1239	179	6	1937
NEBRASKA, U-LINCOLN	44	239	90	68	48	70	515	1740	114	173	34	52	373	1067	80		1520
OREGON, UNIV OF	45	296	100	197	104	55	752	1401	87	166	49	112	414	1303	125	1	1843
OKLAHOMA, U OF	46	263	83	1	69	44	460	1694	146	95	39	60	340	853	98	1	1292
ROCHESTER,UNIV OF/NY	47	281	65	17	28	1	392	2073	114	100	17	400	631	198	12	1	842
VIRGINIA, UNIV OF	48	93	200	22	119	1	435	1682	235	239	81	68	623	566	30	1	1220
LA ST UNIV & A&M C	49	175	82	117	11	70	455	1886	88	119	74	182	463	339	165		967
CAL INST TECHNOLOGY	50	5					5	2823								5	5
UTAH, UNIV OF	51	308	36	59	43	14	460	1849	41	96	28	85	250	667	52	1	970
TENN, U-KNOXVILLE	52	306	45	35	36	33	455	1852	28	120	5	4	157	739	22	2	920
SUNY AT BUFFALO	53	250	50	82	35	18	435	1453	43	128	37	101	309	796	50	1	1156
FORDHAM UNIV/NY	54	322	60	83	79	1	545	1094	191	192	151	371	905	532	61	4	1502
WAYNE STATE UNIV/MI	55	251	57	46	11	13	378	1210	30	80	24	124	258	1081	33	2	1374
OKLAHOMA STATE UNIV	56	86	95	32	1	13	227	1626	23	6			29	895	13		937
TEXAS A&M UNIVERSITY	57	7	81	2		54	144	2161	1	18		1	20	347	11	4	382
WASHINGTON UNIV/MO	58	266	80	131	50	5	532	1844	55	69	73	92	289	168	117	3	577
BROWN UNIVERSITY/RI	59	150	97	57	44	16	364	1801	96	192	135	134	557	5	29	1	592
OREGON STATE UNIV	60	4	36	3		24	67	2000	2				2	353	9	12	376
GEORGIA, UNIV OF	61	222	20	51	38	34	365	1133	154	46	20	40	260	827	67	1	1155
ARIZONA, UNIV OF	62	153	26	105	58	5	347	1602	40	33	61	37	171	372	22	1	566
CALIF, U-DAVIS	63	17	21	25	11	3	77	2040	26	66	13	5	110	1		3	114
MASS, U OF-AMHERST	64	223	31	54	58	5	371	1327	25	104	40	21	190	554	33	3	780
NC STATE U-RALEIGH	65	29	167	18		44	258	1869						212		2	214
NORTHERN COLORADO,U	66	4				6	10	48		2			2	1983	6		1991
TEMPLE UNIVERSITY/PA	67	219	12	15	16	3	265	679	16	46	2	34	98	1008	221	1	1328
CINCINNATI, U OF/OH	68	156	38	11	22	21	248	1430	30	61	101	75	267	265	30	2	564
CARNEGIE-MELLON U/PA	69	58	57		1	14	130	1829	35	18		37	90	6	63	2	161
ST LOUIS UNIV/MO	70	139	67	69	24	13	312	978	199	108	86	149	542	396	59	1	998
CONNECTICUT, UNIV OF	71	220	35	24	37	10	326	1149	39	100	52	9	200	589	6		795
NOTRE DAME, U OF/IN	72	14	49	66	73	6	208	1446	101	158	2	132	393	84	11		488
WASHINGTON STATE U	73	155	57	129	12	6	359	1427	36	27		9	72	405	2		479
VANDERBILT UNIV/TN	74	191	94	63	28		376	1142	154	222	98	85	559		142	1	702
GEO WASHINGTON U/DC	75	160	75	3	88	23	349	979	64	34	34	10	142	429	225		796
KENTUCKY, UNIV OF	76	205	101	80	64	10	460	1146	103	68	60	7	238	358	15	2	613
TULANE U OF LA	77	101	58	70	47	1	277	1154	121	135	134	117	507	1	42	1	551
POLYTECHNIC INST NY	78					2	2	1589								1	1
ALABAMA, UNIVER OF	79	133	34		19	7	193	583	55	39	16	4	114	698	167		979
KANSAS STATE UNIV	80	53	62			23	138	1370	17	30			47	118	12	1	178
GEO PEABODY COLL/TN	81	218	7	4	1	8	238	307	47	80	13	40	180	1031	2	2	1215
ARIZONA STATE UNIV	82	144		7	4	2	157	556	1	32	4	4	41	784	83		908
RENSSELAER POLY I/NY	83	1	5			9	15	1407		1		4	5		22	3	30
DENVER, UNIV OF/CO	84	244	1	8	60	49	362	495	41	132	2	245	420	456	58		934
AMERICAN UNIV/DC	85	80	137	48	498	28	791	913	105	6	1	12	124	221	131	7	483
NEW MEXICO, UNIV OF	86	78	5	31	7	15	136	632	132	141	64	38	375	386		1	762
RICE UNIVERSITY/TX	87	5	32	5	2	3	47	1157	45	69	64	18	196		2	1	199
GEORGETOWN UNIV/DC	88		83	4	201	14	302	863	241	6	50	155	452	1	20	4	477
SOUTHERN ILL UNIV	89	168	40	50	70	29	357	535	3	37		180	220	442	75		737
HOUSTON, U OF/TX	90	324	41	1	2		368	765	1	8			9	481	16		506

TABLE 45B Continued

Doctoral Institution	Rank	Psychology	Economics	Anthropology and Sociology	Political Science and Public Admin.	Other Social Sciences	Total, Behavioral Sciences	Total, Sciences	History	Language and Literature: American	Language and Literature: Foreign	Other Humanities	Humanities, Total	Education	Professions	Unknown Field	Total, Nonsciences
ARKANSAS,U-FAYETTVLE	91	42	67				109	472	1	69	8	10	88	538	156	1	783
ILLINOIS INST TECH	92	204	5			1	210	1182				5	5		16	1	22
COLORADO STATE UNIV	93	82	35	13		13	143	1132						55	2	1	58
LEHIGH UNIVERSITY/PA	94	19	12				31	937	18	25		4	47	190	2	3	242
VA POLY INST&STATE U	95		30	1	1	38	70	1120						36		1	37
WEST VIRGINIA UNIV	96	92	23		15		130	756	37	1		20	58	272			330
DELAWARE, UNIV OF	97	70				5	75	871	37	30		9	76	21		2	99
CLAREMNT GRAD SCH/CA	98	155	82	1	218	16	472	504	57	60	6	59	182	191	74		447
BRANDEIS UNIV/MA	99	50		65	6	25	146	521	82	97	37	72	288		138		426
WYOMING, UNIV OF	100	40					40	429	5				5	474			479

SOURCE: NRC, Commission on Human Resources.

GRADUATE STUDENT RECRUITMENT PATTERNS

An aspect of the graduate education process that has a considerable degree of inherent interest is the pattern of student recruitment for doctoral education. Two aspects of this recruitment process were provided in the institutional profiles of Table 42--the extent to which each PhD-granting institution recruited its own baccalaureate graduates and the percent from foreign BA sources. More detail on this same question is provided in Table 46. (Because of the extensive space requirements, only the first page of the table is shown here for illustrative purposes; the entire table is available from the Commission on Human Resources for researchers interested in this degree of detail.) The information provided is as follows for each of two time periods, 1920-1959 and 1960-1974: (1) the number of the institution's PhD's who graduated from the same institution at the baccalaureate level; (2) the number whose baccalaureates were from another institution in the same state; (3) the number whose BA's were from another state in the same census region; (4) the number whose BA's were from other regions in the United States; and (5) the number whose baccalaureates were awarded outside the United States. The data are given separately for each sex and for both sexes combined. Two types of percentage figures are given: (1) the percent by sex within each origin group and (2) the percentage each origin group is of the total. It is hoped that these data may be useful for institutions for self-study purposes. To provide something by way of a normative framework, state and regional summaries, using the same format, are also available.

A summary of the data regarding the graduate student recruitment patterns for the entire United States is given below and shown graphically in Figure 64.

	PhD's Earning Baccalaureate Degrees in:				
	PhD Insti-tution	Other School in Same State	Other State in Same Region	Other Region in United States	Outside United States
1920-1959					
Males	20.7	14.8	11.5	44.5	8.7
Females	16.3	19.9	10.7	47.5	5.7
Total	20.1	15.4	11.4	44.8	8.3
1960-1974					
Males	14.6	16.0	12.2	42.9	14.3
Females	13.0	21.1	11.5	44.0	10.4
Total	14.4	16.8	12.1	43.1	13.7

Examination of these data shows that there have been important changes over time, principally in the categories of foreign origins and of those earning baccalaureates and doctorates at the same institution. The proportions from the other sources have changed only marginally from the earlier to the more recent time period. The sex differences have maintained the same pattern, although changing somewhat over time. Fewer women, proportionately, take BA and PhD degrees at the same institution, but more of them come from other institutions in the same state. A smaller proportion of women than men move from one state to another in the same region, but more move to other regions for the doctorate. A smaller proportion come from foreign countries than is true for men. The data shown graphically in Figure 64 are for the total of both sexes combined. The area shown in each circle is drawn in proportion to the total number of PhD's granted in each time period, so that the entire area within the outer circle represents the total U.S. PhD production over the 55-year period.

TABLE 46
GRADUATE STUDENT RECRUITING PATTERNS OF PhD-GRANTING INSTITUTIONS IN TWO TIME PERIODS, 1920-1959 AND 1960-1974

Doctoral Institutions, by Sex			1920-1959 Itself	1920-1959 Other Institutions in State	1920-1959 Other States in Region	1920-1959 Other Regions in United States	1920-1959 Foreign BA	1920-1959 Total	1960-1974 Itself	1960-1974 Other Institutions in State	1960-1974 Other States in Region	1960-1974 Other Regions in United States	1960-1974 Foreign BA	1960-1974 Total	Unknown BA Institutions	Grand Total
WISCONSIN,U-MADISON	1	N H														
MALE		N	1473	356	1016	2781	705	6331	1232	624	1288	3875	1542	8561	79	14971
		H	23.3	5.6	16.0	43.9	11.1	42.3	14.4	7.3	15.0	45.3	18.0	57.2	.5	
		V1	5.4	1.8	6.7	4.7	6.1	4.8	3.0	1.4	3.7	3.2	3.8	3.0	1.9	3.6
FEMALE		N	127	33	125	350	48	683	136	91	243	631	165	1266	9	1958
		H	18.6	4.8	18.3	51.2	7.0	34.9	10.7	7.2	19.2	49.8	13.0	64.7	.5	
		V2	4.4	.9	6.6	4.1	4.8	3.8	2.2	.9	4.4	3.0	3.3	2.6	1.4	3.0
TOTAL		N	1600	389	1141	3131	753	7014	1368	715	1531	4506	1707	9827	88	16929
		H	22.8	5.5	16.3	44.6	10.7	41.4	13.9	7.3	15.6	45.9	17.4	58.0	.5	
		V3	5.3	1.7	6.7	4.7	6.0	4.7	2.9	1.3	3.8	3.1	3.7	3.0	1.9	3.5
COLUMBIA UNIV/NY	2	N H														
MALE		N	879	1496	519	3144	609	6647	626	1170	420	1925	774	4915	631	12193
		H	13.2	22.5	7.8	47.3	9.2	54.5	12.7	23.8	8.5	39.2	15.7	40.3	5.2	
		V1	3.2	7.7	3.4	5.3	5.3	5.0	1.5	2.6	1.2	1.6	1.9	1.7	15.5	2.9
FEMALE		N	116	549	91	782	85	1623	67	680	112	609	169	1637	149	3409
		H	7.1	33.8	5.6	48.2	5.2	47.6	4.1	41.5	6.8	37.2	10.3	48.0	4.4	
		V2	4.0	15.5	4.8	9.2	8.4	9.1	1.1	6.7	2.0	2.9	3.4	3.4	22.7	5.1
TOTAL		N	995	2045	610	3926	694	8270	693	1850	532	2534	943	6552	780	15602
		H	12.0	24.7	7.4	47.5	8.4	53.0	10.6	28.2	8.1	38.7	14.4	42.0	5.0	
		V3	3.3	8.9	3.6	5.8	5.6	5.5	1.5	3.3	1.3	1.8	2.1	2.0	16.5	3.2
HARVARD UNIV/MA	3	N H														
MALE		N	1350	560	598	3503	743	6754	888	642	561	3508	956	6555	127	13436
		H	20.0	8.3	8.9	51.9	11.0	50.3	13.5	9.8	8.6	53.5	14.6	48.8	.9	
		V1	4.9	2.9	3.9	6.0	6.5	5.1	2.1	1.4	1.6	2.9	2.4	2.3	3.1	3.2
FEMALE		N	3	278	30	342	84	737	6	406	46	670	129	1257	17	2011
		H	.4	37.7	4.1	46.4	11.4	36.6	.5	32.3	3.7	53.3	10.3	62.5	.8	
		V2	.1	7.8	1.6	4.0	8.3	4.1	.1	4.0	.8	3.2	2.6	2.6	2.6	3.0
TOTAL		N	1353	838	628	3845	827	7491	894	1048	607	4178	1085	7812	144	15447
		H	18.1	11.2	8.4	51.3	11.0	48.5	11.4	13.4	7.8	53.5	13.9	50.6	.9	
		V3	4.5	3.6	3.7	5.7	6.6	5.0	1.9	1.9	1.5	2.9	2.4	2.3	3.0	3.2
CALIF,U-BERKELEY	4	N H														
MALE		N	1750	578	220	1935	487	4970	1475	1005	281	3435	1737	7933	632	13535
		H	35.2	11.6	4.4	38.9	9.8	36.7	18.6	12.7	3.5	43.3	21.9	58.6	4.7	
		V1	6.4	3.0	1.5	3.3	4.2	3.8	3.6	2.2	.8	2.8	4.3	2.8	15.5	3.2
FEMALE		N	185	65	32	256	44	582	253	159	43	606	161	1222	93	1897
		H	31.8	11.2	5.5	44.0	7.6	30.7	20.7	13.0	3.5	49.6	13.2	64.4	4.9	
		V2	6.3	1.8	1.7	3.0	4.4	3.3	4.1	1.6	.8	2.9	3.2	2.6	14.2	2.9
TOTAL		N	1935	643	252	2191	531	5552	1728	1164	324	4041	1898	9155	725	15432
		H	34.9	11.6	4.5	39.5	9.6	36.0	18.9	12.7	3.5	44.1	20.7	59.3	4.7	
		V3	6.4	2.8	1.5	3.3	4.3	3.7	3.6	2.1	.8	2.8	4.2	2.8	15.3	3.2
ILL,U,URBANA-CHAMP	5	N H														
MALE		N	973	614	723	2262	467	5039	1197	831	1151	3579	1523	8281	37	13357
		H	19.3	12.2	14.3	44.9	9.3	37.7	14.5	10.0	13.9	43.2	18.4	62.0	.3	
		V1	3.6	3.1	4.8	3.8	4.1	3.8	2.9	1.8	3.3	2.9	3.7	2.9	.9	3.2
FEMALE		N	76	84	45	206	32	443	130	144	145	501	173	1093	3	1539
		H	17.2	19.0	10.2	46.5	7.2	28.8	11.9	13.2	13.3	45.8	15.8	71.0	.2	
		V2	2.6	2.4	2.4	2.4	3.2	2.5	2.1	1.4	2.6	2.4	3.5	2.3	.5	2.3
TOTAL		N	1049	698	768	2468	499	5482	1327	975	1296	4080	1696	9374	40	14896
		H	19.1	12.7	14.0	45.0	9.1	36.8	14.2	10.4	13.8	43.5	18.1	62.9	.3	
		V3	3.5	3.0	4.5	3.7	4.0	3.7	2.8	1.7	3.2	2.8	3.7	2.8	.8	3.1
MICHIGAN,UNIV OF	6	N H														
MALE		N	1105	573	607	1700	397	4382	1213	865	1087	2951	986	7102	48	11532
		H	25.2	13.1	13.9	38.8	9.1	38.0	17.1	12.2	15.3	41.6	13.9	61.6	.4	
		V1	4.0	2.9	4.0	2.9	3.5	3.3	2.9	1.9	3.1	2.4	2.4	2.5	1.2	2.7
FEMALE		N	104	53	80	234	65	536	198	170	186	556	138	1248	3	1787
		H	19.4	9.9	14.9	43.7	12.1	30.0	15.9	13.6	14.9	44.6	11.1	69.8	.2	
		V2	3.6	1.5	4.2	2.8	6.4	3.0	3.2	1.7	3.4	2.6	2.8	2.6	.5	2.7
TOTAL		N	1209	626	687	1934	462	4918	1411	1035	1273	3507	1124	8350	51	13319
		H	24.6	12.7	14.0	39.3	9.4	36.9	16.9	12.4	15.2	42.0	13.5	62.7	.4	
		V3	4.0	2.7	4.0	2.9	3.7	3.3	3.0	1.9	3.2	2.4	2.5	2.5	1.1	2.7
OHIO STATE UNIV	7	N H														
MALE		N	883	1045	487	1744	267	4426	1126	1149	679	2457	787	6198	57	10681
		H	20.0	23.6	11.0	39.4	6.0	41.4	18.2	18.5	11.0	39.6	12.7	58.0	.5	
		V1	3.2	5.4	3.2	3.0	2.3	3.3	2.7	2.5	2.0	2.0	1.9	2.2	1.4	2.5
FEMALE		N	106	101	39	183	8	437	173	212	118	447	98	1048	1	1486
		H	24.3	23.1	8.9	41.9	1.8	29.4	16.5	20.2	11.3	42.7	9.4	70.5	.1	
		V2	3.6	2.8	2.0	2.2	.8	2.4	2.8	2.1	2.1	2.1	2.0	2.2	.2	2.2
TOTAL		N	989	1146	526	1927	275	4863	1299	1361	797	2904	885	7246	58	12167
		H	20.3	23.6	10.8	39.6	5.7	40.0	17.9	18.8	11.0	40.1	12.2	59.6	.5	
		V3	3.3	5.0	3.1	2.9	2.2	3.2	2.7	2.4	2.0	2.0	1.9	2.2	1.2	2.5

N = number; H = horizontal percentage; V1 = percent of total males; V2 = percent of total females; V3 = percent of grand total.

SOURCE: NRC, Commission on Human Resources.

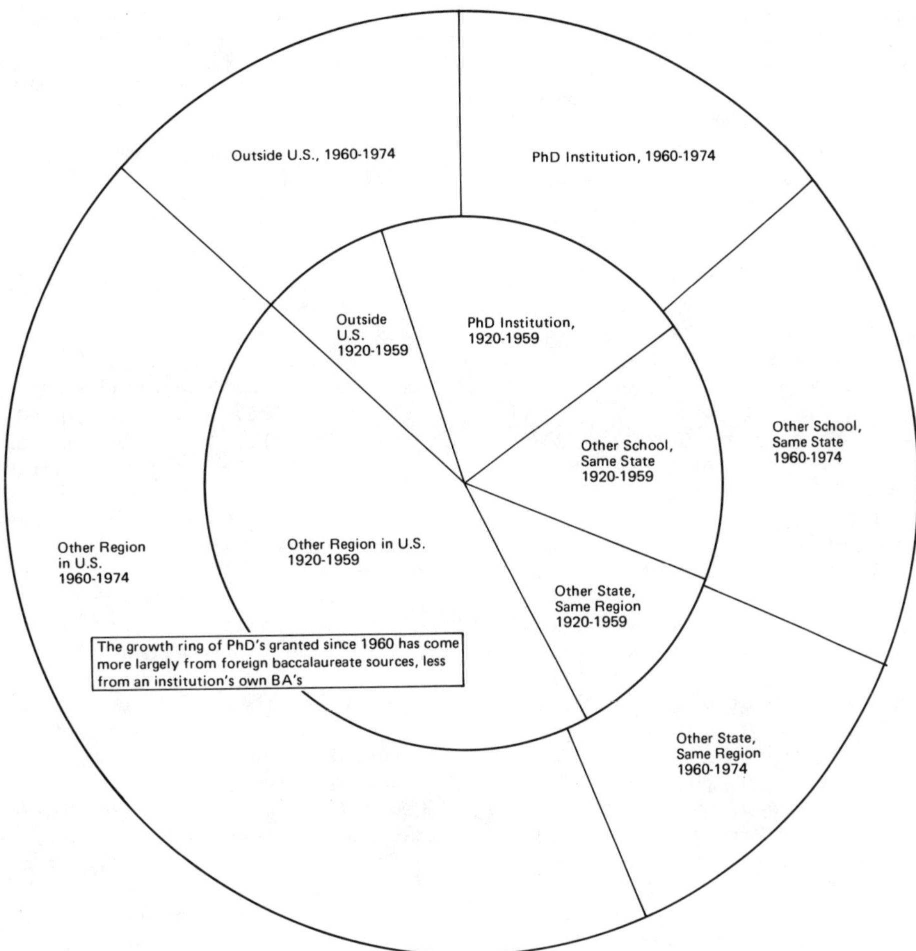

SOURCE: NRC, Commission on Human Resources

FIGURE 64 Graduate student recruitment patterns in two time periods.

BACCALAUREATE ORIGINS OF PhD's

Historically, a great deal of interest has centered on the matter of the baccalaureate origins of PhD's and particularly on the institutions at which the PhD's earned their first degrees. The earliest publication in the series of which this book is seventh was entitled, *Baccalaureate Origins of the Science Doctorates Awarded in the United States 1936-1945*. With the advent of the Survey of Earned Doctorates, and an increase in the amount of detailed information regarding PhD's, the emphasis shifted, and other aspects became more prominent. Yet the interest in the baccalaureate institutions remained and finds expression in the tables that follow.

Largest Baccalaureate Origins Institutions

The number of baccalaureate-granting institutions whose alumni receive PhD's has increased over time, as the number of doctorate holders has increased. As of the compilation of this book, there were almost 1,600 institutions in the United States in this category and many hundreds in other countries. In Appendix G the 633 U.S. institutions largest in number of PhD alumni are listed in rank order of total number of their doctorate-holding alumni (1920-1974 PhD's only). Included in the rank-ordered list of 633 are only the institutions that granted baccalaureates to more than 100 eventual PhD's. For each institution the table provides the number of alumni and the rank of the institutions, based on this number. These data are given for males, for females, and for both sexes combined. Most of the leading schools in this list are also PhD-granting, as there are few large institutions that do not grant the doctorate. And yet, among the high-ranking institutions there are some which do not, such as Oberlin (thirty-second), Swarthmore (sixty-ninth), Amherst (eighty-third), DePauw (ninety-fourth), and San Jose State (ninety-sixth). Beyond this point, ties become so frequent, and the number of institutions tied at the same rank is so large, that ranking begins to lose its meaning.

An Alphabetical List

Essentially the same data as given in Appendix G are provided in Appendix H, but here the listing is alphabetical, to provide data on all the schools whose graduates eventually attained the doctorate degree.

STATE AND REGIONAL DATA

For comparison with PhD graduations, data providing state and regional baccalaureate origins figures by time period and by sex, for seven fields and the total of all fields, is shown in Appendix I. Each state's and each region's contribution per 1,000 U.S. total is shown, to furnish a convenient frame of reference.

Foreign Origins

Foreign countries of baccalaureate origin are listed in Appendix J, with rank orders, by sex and for the two sexes combined. Some of the names of countries in this list afford problems. China is an example. All persons of known mainland origin are so listed, although most of them graduated from Chinese universities before the Communist revolution. Very few have come from the mainland since 1950. Taiwan has sent 5,843, as shown on the list. There are, in addition, 841 Chinese whose precise origin could not be ascertained. They are listed under China (unspecified). It is obvious that the rank orders of the countries are affected by these ambiguities, and the use of rank data requires careful attention to this problem. Another such problem is Pakistan. Prior to the division of the country in 1971, there was no problem, but the state of Bangladesh means that the graduates of East Pakistan universities must be accounted for separately from Pakistan. They have, insofar as possible, been credited to Bangladesh, even though they graduated before that state came into existence. Another example is Russia, here entered under the old name rather than under USSR. The reason is that most, if not all the PhD's from that area, either graduated before the Russian revolution in 1917, or came from the Baltic states of Esthonia, Latvia, and Lithuania during the period between World War I and World War II when those countries were independent. Few U.S. PhD's came from USSR universities.

A regional summary of foreign origins, providing data by geographic area, regardless of political changes that have intervened, is provided in Appendix K. Here we have a time series, comparable to that provided for PhD's in Appendix E. The proportions which each region represents are expressed in the number per thousand among all foreign origin PhD's and the number per thousand grand total.

APPENDIX A
FINE FIELD CLASSIFICATION OF PhD's GRANTED, 1920-1974, WITH ANNUAL DATA FOR 1970-1974 BY SEX AND TOTAL

	Both Sexes							Men							Women						
PhD Fields	Total, 1920-1974	1960-1969	1970	1971	1972	1973	1974	Total, 1920-1974	1960-1969	1970	1971	1972	1973	1974	Total, 1920-1974	1960-1969	1970	1971	1972	1973	1974
GRAND TOTAL	487435	170539	31489	33163	34458	33472	33165	421072	150413	27111	28178	28735	27101	26380	66363	20126	4378	4985	5723	6371	6785
MATH TOTAL	17331	6782	1282	1274	1341	1215	1155	16044	6392	1186	1188	1235	1090	1038	1287	390	96	86	106	125	117
000+070 ALGEBR	2107	1126	211	190	158	141	111	1898	1033	184	173	138	115	94	209	93	27	17	20	26	17
010 ANALYSIS	3171	1693	261	266	259	212	188	2980	1605	242	252	245	189	171	191	88	19	14	14	23	17
020 GEOMETRY	477	228	41	34	34	33	33	427	211	37	30	31	29	29	50	17	4	4	3	4	4
030 LOGIC	376	196	34	38	38	27	27	344	183	33	34	32	23	24	32	13	1	4	6	4	3
040 NO. THEORY	363	193	23	39	31	34	22	316	169	20	32	28	30	18	47	24	3	7	3	4	4
050 PROBABIL	1816	901	88	119	193	130	171	1694	854	79	110	175	117	155	122	47	9	9	18	13	16
060 TOPOLOGY	1392	725	135	134	119	114	96	1308	691	126	128	108	100	87	84	34	9	6	11	14	9
080 COMP THEOR	1184	287	147	146	194	229	181	1126	282	144	139	182	213	166	58	5	3	7	12	16	15
082 OPER RES	55				2	7	46	53				2	7	44	2						2
085 APPL MATH	1719	873	143	111	134	133	115	1655	844	135	109	132	125	111	64	29	8	2	2	8	4
098 MATH, GEN	1775	304	109	106	103	109	118	1576	282	98	95	92	103	102	199	22	11	11	11	6	16
099 MATH, OTH	2896	256	90	91	76	46	47	2667	238	88	86	70	39	37	229	18	2	5	6	7	10
ASTR&PHY TOTAL	26717	10342	1715	1743	1697	1412	1360	25952	10117	1667	1689	1639	1359	1288	765	225	48	54	58	53	72
100 A + APHYS	821	432						732	404						89	28					
101 ASTRONOMY	359	51	62	57	63	61	65	331	47	60	53	59	56	56	28	4	2	4	4	5	9
102 ASTROPHYS	424	86	63	60	78	57	80	402	79	58	56	75	57	77	22	7	5	4	3		3
110 ATOM & MOL	1965	1078	144	136	161	107	133	1924	1058	140	134	156	105	127	41	20	4	2	5	2	6
120 ELECTROMAG	371	236	19	14	13	11	12	366	233	19	14	13	11	11	5	3					1
130 MECHANICS	111	66	4	8	5	7	4	109	66	4	8	4	6	4	2				1	1	
132 ACOUSTICS	216	102	19	21	17	13	11	215	102	19	21	16	13	11	1				1		
134 FLUIDS	411	282	24	28	18	33	24	399	273	24	27	18	32	23	12	9		1		1	1
135 PLASMA	479	92	86	93	92	55	61	473	92	85	93	87	55	61	6		1		5		
136 OPTICS	275	109	24	30	32	25	37	272	107	24	30	32	25	36	3	2					1
138 THERMAL	210	130	15	18	21	14	12	201	125	15	17	20	12	12	9	5		1	1	2	
140+145 PHYS	2888	1643	273	250	239	164	132	2804	1608	262	240	231	156	123	84	35	11	10	8	8	9
150 NUCL STRUC	2940	1648	243	222	232	146	136	2880	1623	234	217	229	140	132	60	25	9	5	3	6	4
160 SOLID STAT	4969	2656	425	431	398	388	340	4848	2613	414	420	385	372	321	121	43	11	11	13	16	19
170 THEORETICL	559	243						550	240						9	3					
198 PHYS, GEN	3239	655	152	167	171	193	190	3128	634	150	159	166	185	177	111	21	2	8	5	8	13
199 PHYS, OTH	6480	833	162	208	157	138	123	6318	813	159	200	148	134	117	162	20	3	8	9	4	6
CHEM TOTAL	46747	15101	2284	2248	2007	1831	1800	43747	14114	2094	2059	1828	1644	1609	3000	987	190	189	179	187	191
200 ANALYTICAL	2240	1086	165	173	137	161	133	2098	1014	153	165	125	151	125	142	72	12	8	12	10	8
210 INORGANIC	3477	1680	282	311	306	215	228	3159	1544	255	281	276	179	196	318	136	27	30	30	36	32
220 ORGANIC	12637	6183	859	826	699	643	593	11885	5831	801	763	652	599	544	752	352	58	63	47	44	49
230 NUCLEAR	432	287	27	38	25	25	30	408	272	27	33	23	25	28	24	15		5	2		2
240 PHYSICAL	8340	4080	564	510	476	429	403	7729	3796	516	462	428	379	353	611	284	48	48	48	50	50
250 THEORETICL	620	307	78	69	54	56	55	554	282	70	58	49	49	46	66	25	8	11	5	7	9
260 AGRI+FOOD	950	438	75	40	15	13	7	872	411	62	35	12	10	7	78	27	13	5	3	3	
270 PHARM'LS	1062	489	56	66	51	52	72	1003	470	52	60	44	45	64	59	19	4	6	7	7	8
275 POLYMER	58				1	18	39	55				1	18	36	3						3
298 CHEM, GEN	4209	312	86	111	138	152	196	3865	279	73	105	125	133	176	344	33	13	6	13	19	20
299 CHEM, OTH	12722	239	92	104	105	67	44	12119	215	85	97	93	56	34	603	24	7	7	12	11	10

APPENDIX A Continued

PhD Fields	Both Sexes							Men							Women						
	Total, 1920-1974	1960-1969	1970	1971	1972	1973	1974	Total, 1920-1974	1960-1969	1970	1971	1972	1973	1974	Total, 1920-1974	1960-1969	1970	1971	1972	1973	1974
EARTH SC TOTAL	9761	3647	534	564	636	575	574	9475	3575	516	547	615	547	546	286	72	18	17	21	28	28
300 MIN,PET,GE	929	738						904	718						25	20					
301 MINERALOGY	327	70	52	53	64	43	45	308	64	48	51	60	42	43	19	6	4	2	4	1	2
305 GEOCHEM	283	63	40	46	45	38	51	268	60	38	43	43	35	49	15	3	2	3	2	3	2
310 STRATIGRAP	1032	572	63	60	56	51	50	1015	569	61	58	53	48	49	17	3	2	2	3	3	1
320 PALEONTOL	597	355	34	37	41	47	30	568	346	31	35	39	40	28	29	9	3	2	2	7	2
330 STRUC GEOL	330	194	19	30	20	21	19	322	190	19	28	19	21	18	8	4		2	1		1
340 GEOPHYSICS	889	324	74	69	75	77	88	874	322	74	66	73	76	83	15	2		3	2	1	5
350 GEOMORPH	267	119	22	21	22	27	22	260	115	22	21	22	27	20	7	4					2
360 HYDROLOGY	185	72	24	21	22	30	15	183	71	24	21	22	29	15	2	1				1	
370 OCEANOGRPH	730	292	60	66	93	79	79	706	287	57	66	91	71	75	24	5	3		2	8	4
380 METEOROLGY	810	324	61	64	80	55	55	795	318	60	63	79	53	53	15	6	1	1	1	2	2
390+391 AP GEO	451	265	19	30	38	26	28	449	263	19	30	38	26	28	2	2					
395 FUEL TECH	84	29	14	12	6	13	10	81	28	13	12	6	13	9	3	1	1				1
398 EARTH, GEN	2483	129	25	32	36	42	51	2405	124	24	32	33	42	49	78	5	1		3		2
399 EARTH, OTH	364	101	27	23	38	26	31	337	100	26	21	37	24	27	27	1	1	2	1	2	4
ENGR TOTAL	45463	19965	3603	3654	3493	3259	3039	45204	19883	3587	3634	3471	3215	2998	259	82	16	20	22	44	41
400 AERONAUTIC	2202	1009	218	182	182	175	136	2183	1002	215	181	181	174	132	19	7	3	1	1	1	4
410 AGRICULTUR	707	297	55	73	72	68	41	705	297	55	73	72	67	40	2					1	1
415 BIOMEDICAL	393	48	63	69	81	71	61	386	48	63	69	78	69	59	7				3	2	2
420 CIVIL	4256	2011	350	378	371	349	313	4235	2004	348	377	370	342	311	21	7	2	1	1	7	2
430 CHEMICAL	6969	3059	444	437	386	397	394	6928	3041	442	435	383	391	387	41	18	2	2	3	6	7
435 CERAMIC	619	315	46	41	23	31	26	611	312	46	41	22	28	26	8	3			1	3	
437 COMPUTER	40						40	37						37	3						3
440 ELECTRICAL	8889	4126	743	777	698	634	568	8854	4114	743	772	693	631	561	35	12		5	5	3	7
445 ELECTRONIC	1647	976	152	117	132	83	87	1639	973	150	115	131	83	87	8	3	2	2	1		
450 INDUSTRIAL	1165	495	132	142	119	111	92	1155	491	130	142	119	108	91	10	4	2			3	1
455 NUCLEAR	753	162	124	123	122	124	98	748	162	123	122	121	123	97	5		1	1	1	1	1
460 ENG MECH	2742	1569	220	215	205	177	169	2727	1561	220	215	204	174	166	15	8			1	3	3
465 ENG PHYS	1032	787	41	45	36	35	15	1025	785	40	44	36	33	15	7	2	1	1		2	
470 MECHANICAL	5165	2373	418	427	404	363	362	5149	2371	417	425	403	361	355	16	2	1	2	1	2	7
475 METALLURGY	3323	1502	221	217	163	137	126	3304	1495	220	214	162	134	126	19	7	1	3	1	3	
476 SYS DESIGN	21						21	21						21							
478 OPER RES	330			26	73	130	101	325			26	72	127	100	5				1	3	1
479 FUEL TECH	31				3	7	21	31				3	7	21							
480 SANITARY	703	382	57	41	63	40	35	700	380	57	41	63	39	35	3	2				1	
485+497 T&MS E	496	30	39	72	111	125	111	486	30	39	72	110	123	111	10				1	2	
486 MINING	68	14	12	15	17	7	3	68	14	12	15	17	7	3							
498 ENG, GEN	402	133	43	35	31	44	58	401	132	43	35	31	44	58	1	1					
499 ENG, OTH	3510	677	225	222	201	151	161	3486	671	224	220	200	150	159	24	6	1	2	1	1	2
LIFE SCI TOTAL	81316	27759	4883	5224	5264	4937	5013	70830	24505	4251	4466	4449	4042	4125	10486	3254	632	758	815	895	888
589 ENVIRON SC	319			29	69	105	116	289			29	60	94	106	30				9	11	10
AGR SCI SUBTOT	16284	5780	1012	1109	1064	1002	1083	15945	5690	988	1075	1027	954	1038	339	90	24	34	37	48	45
500 AGRONOMY	4159	1589	208	187	128	159	136	4126	1582	204	183	126	155	134	33	7	4	4	2	4	2
501 AGRI ECON	982	135	133	180	183	174	174	966	135	133	178	175	170	172	16			2	8	4	2
502 ANIMAL HUS	2525	1232	121	84	63	20	19	2492	1211	121	82	61	20	19	33	21		2	2		
503 FOOD SCI	484	53	53	84	91	98	105	421	51	48	70	84	77	91	63	2	5	14	7	21	14
504 WILDLIFE	630	247	46	57	50	57	51	620	245	45	57	49	54	50	10	2	1		1	3	1
505 FORESTRY	1223	491	82	79	80	72	81	1220	490	82	79	80	72	79	3	1					2
506 HORTICULT	1772	591	88	76	72	41	76	1730	577	83	75	70	40	72	42	14	5	1	2	1	4
507 SOIL SCI	466	56	38	77	106	94	95	457	55	36	74	105	92	95	9	1	2	3	1	2	
510 ANIMAL SCI	397	1		42	82	125	147	374			41	80	117	136	23	1		1	2	8	11
511 PHYTOPATH	2207	898	108	108	103	84	117	2128	868	104	104	95	79	111	79	30	4	4	8	5	6
518 AGRI, GEN	188	46	3	2	5	7	6	187	45	3	2	5	7	6	1	1					
519 AGRI,OTHER	1251	441	132	133	101	71	76	1224	431	129	130	97	71	73	27	10	3	3	4		3

PhD Fields	Both Sexes Total, 1920-1974	Both Sexes 1960-1969	Both Sexes 1970	Both Sexes 1971	Both Sexes 1972	Both Sexes 1973	Both Sexes 1974	Men Total, 1920-1974	Men 1960-1969	Men 1970	Men 1971	Men 1972	Men 1973	Men 1974	Women Total, 1920-1974	Women 1960-1969	Women 1970	Women 1971	Women 1972	Women 1973	Women 1974
MED SCI SUBTOT	8396	2862	544	607	604	583	611	7394	2579	470	529	514	454	490	1002	283	74	78	90	129	121
520 MED & SURG	651	120	4	11	5	6	5	616	119	4	10	5	6	5	35	1		1			
522 PUB HEALTH	1422	429	107	61	83	110	107	1144	353	85	49	62	72	70	278	76	22	12	21	38	37
523 VET MED	577	297	47	46	30	32	34	564	292	46	46	28	30	31	13	5	1		2	2	3
524 HOSP ADMIN	83	33	13	10	8	7	6	79	32	12	10	7	7	6	4	1	1		1		
527 PARASITOL	59				10	25	24	48				7	21	20	11				3	4	4
534 PATHOLOGY	882	334	58	85	74	79	81	809	316	55	76	70	67	76	73	18	3	9	4	12	5
536 PHARMACOL	2648	994	156	180	194	153	183	2354	891	136	161	167	123	152	294	103	20	19	27	30	31
537 PHARMACY	1025	379	47	66	76	71	66	967	356	46	62	73	68	60	58	23	1	4	3	3	6
538 MED SC,GEN	123	33	23	17	17	17	16	102	29	20	15	15	11	12	21	4	3	2	2	6	4
521+525+539	926	243	89	131	107	83	89	711	191	66	100	80	49	58	215	52	23	31	27	34	31
BIO SCI SUBTOT	56317	19117	3327	3479	3527	3247	3203	47202	16236	2793	2833	2848	2540	2491	9115	2881	534	646	679	707	712
540 BIOCHEM	10864	4136	608	655	639	621	606	9003	3390	512	533	524	478	458	1861	746	96	122	115	143	148
542 BIOPHYSICS	1415	641	101	99	132	100	133	1291	587	92	86	120	90	121	124	54	9	13	12	10	12
544 BIOMETRICS	419	192	49	31	35	34	35	348	164	42	26	27	28	26	71	28	7	5	8	6	9
545 ANATOMY	2074	720	121	173	146	131	114	1674	592	97	137	101	107	89	400	128	24	36	45	24	25
546 CYTOLOGY	489	257	56	56	38	42	36	318	182	35	26	21	22	30	171	75	21	30	17	20	6
547 EMBRYOLOGY	402	231	45	35	35	24	23	276	158	32	26	24	17	13	126	73	13	9	11	7	10
548 IMMUNOLOGY	165			7	29	63	66	123			4	21	48	50	42			3	8	15	16
550 BOTANY	5539	1439	173	227	205	177	167	4629	1233	145	193	161	146	133	910	206	28	34	44	31	34
560 ECOLOGY	1310	519	114	131	140	145	150	1207	498	105	117	129	127	133	103	21	9	14	11	18	17
562 HYDROBIOL	248	108	20	32	18	16	10	235	104	19	29	16	16	10	13	4	1	3	2		
564 MICROBIOL	7543	2720	424	387	434	376	343	6158	2231	345	303	339	274	251	1385	489	79	84	95	102	92
565 PHYS P+A	2349	274						1999	244						350	30					
566 ANIM PHYS	3529	1752	380	344	359	339	338	2982	1498	325	289	303	272	280	547	254	55	55	56	67	58
567 PLANT PHYS	1080	596	89	93	80	86	76	965	538	82	84	68	67	69	115	58	7	9	12	19	7
569 ZOOLOGY	8101	2335	390	353	366	271	259	6906	2016	346	306	302	220	211	1195	319	44	47	64	51	48
570 GENETICS	2766	1102	157	153	158	118	145	2356	932	122	120	127	90	103	410	170	35	33	31	28	42
571 ENTOMOLOGY	3684	1259	199	237	184	178	171	3500	1199	190	224	172	164	160	184	60	9	13	12	14	11
572 MOLEC BIOL	787	134	88	134	159	124	148	567	103	67	91	119	88	99	220	31	21	43	40	36	49
578 BIO SC,GEN	1481	262	139	160	161	198	179	1168	208	110	116	125	157	122	313	54	29	44	36	41	57
568+579 OTHER	2072	440	174	172	209	204	204	1497	359	127	123	149	129	133	575	81	47	49	60	75	71
PSYCH TOTAL	32855	11501	2119	2181	2386	2512	2741	25391	9089	1604	1630	1747	1729	1899	7464	2412	515	551	639	783	842
600 CLINICAL	8687	3824	616	656	732	733	802	6586	2932	457	488	541	502	565	2101	892	159	168	191	231	237
610 COUN+GUID	1793	702	121	163	179	191	227	1362	566	90	117	127	134	156	431	136	31	46	52	57	71
620 DEVEL+GER	1346	380	103	121	148	161	168	698	204	58	60	75	77	78	648	176	45	61	73	84	90
630 EDUCATIONL	1936	566	103	111	114	124	133	1457	405	72	86	72	82	85	479	161	31	25	42	42	48
635 SCHOOL PSY	641	198	62	76	99	101	99	434	146	43	56	64	63	56	207	52	19	20	35	38	43
640 E,C,P	3076	379						2661	323						415	56					
641 EXPERIMNTL	3936	2098	403	377	325	353	363	3209	1775	326	297	250	266	279	727	323	77	80	75	87	84
642 COMPARATIV	234	123	22	18	23	22	26	198	106	19	15	20	18	20	36	17	3	3	3	4	6
643 PHYSIOLOG	1201	567	143	117	114	136	120	956	484	112	85	97	95	79	245	83	31	32	17	41	41
650 INDUSTRIAL	957	465	72	50	72	85	61	902	446	65	50	67	76	56	55	19	7		5	9	5
660 PERSONALTY	588	309	48	42	52	63	58	438	245	36	28	30	45	44	150	64	12	14	22	18	14
670 PSYCHOMET	404	192	27	25	28	28	23	347	166	24	22	22	23	18	57	26	3	3	6	5	5
680 SOCIAL	2488	1074	175	179	209	203	225	1919	837	133	132	164	143	163	569	237	42	47	45	60	62
698 PSYCH, GEN	4626	426	140	134	125	173	291	3529	301	107	104	94	123	196	1097	125	33	30	31	50	95
646+699 OTHER	942	198	84	112	166	139	145	695	153	62	90	124	82	104	247	45	22	22	42	57	41

APPENDIX A Continued

Both Sexes

PhD Fields	Total, 1920–1974	1960–1969	1970	1971	1972	1973	1974
SOC SCI TOTAL	46029	14950	2901	3260	3493	3575	3592
700 ANTHROPOL	3394	1077	229	258	294	356	388
708 COMMUNIC'N	753			75	176	228	274
710 SOCIOLOGY	8628	2681	556	625	610	661	643
720 ECONOMICS	15837	5512	817	837	950	877	880
725 ECONOMET	448	217	25	27	41	24	24
727 STATISTICS	602	186	133	115	73	46	49
740 GEOGRAPHY	2495	729	166	169	190	214	203
745 AREA STUDY	429	125	77	63	28	32	39
750 POLITCL SC	10030	3268	600	750	805	788	740
755 INTL RELAT	1812	739	119	143	120	128	117
770 URBAN PLAN	252		13	41	57	55	85
798 SOC SC,GEN	278	71	21	24	29	35	34
799 SOC SC,OTH	1071	345	145	133	120	131	116
HUM&PROF TOTAL	92488	30661	5725	5959	6676	6790	6564
OTH HUM SUBTOT	44527	14880	2546	2665	3012	3132	2980
800 ART,FIN+AP	865	423					
801 ART, APPL	36	4	9	4	9	7	3
802 ART,HIST	642	91	105	90	102	118	136
803 HIST, GEN	11455	4702					
804 AMER HIST	2798	504	438	475	453	484	444
805 EURO HIST	2158	367	322	360	408	348	353
806 HIST, OTH	1972	335	319	270	341	358	347
807 SCI HIST	146		13	38	34	31	30
808 AMER STUDY	27						27
830 MUSIC	3386	1250	183	202	268	386	354
831 SPEECH,DR	4831	2181	243	248	271	201	121
832 ARCHEOLOGY	366	101	13	19	12	28	22
833+880+881	6197	1911	248	292	383	359	366
834 PHILOSOPHY	6105	1926	379	366	371	412	398
835 LINGUISTIC	1971	801	150	167	179	190	187
878 A & H, GEN	470	55	20	17	17	20	25
879 A & H, OTH	1102	229	104	117	164	190	167
LANG&LIT SBTOT	34014	10840	2023	2171	2382	2418	2288
810 ENG & AMER	11782	5303					
811 AMERICAN	1419	214	213	228	241	279	244
812 ENGLISH	6604	1141	1014	1057	1172	1131	1089
821 GERMAN	1576	718	155	164	188	189	160
822 RUSSIAN	416	159	36	48	46	70	57
823 FRENCH	2177	913	238	238	247	288	251
824 SPAN+PORT	1930	802	179	219	247	227	253
826 ITALIAN	164	58	16	21	19	35	15
827 CLASSICAL	2448	714	91	110	96	96	85
829 OTH LANGS	5498	818	81	86	126	103	134

Men

PhD Fields	Total, 1920–1974	1960–1969	1970	1971	1972	1973	1974
SOC SCI TOTAL	40753	13522	2577	2819	2979	2990	2919
700 ANTHROPOL	2551	837	174	190	200	249	262
708 COMMUNIC'N	580			63	138	182	197
710 SOCIOLOGY	6961	2216	446	502	463	486	448
720 ECONOMICS	14923	5246	772	778	880	818	798
725 ECONOMET	429	208	24	25	41	24	22
727 STATISTICS	565	174	126	111	65	44	45
740 GEOGRAPHY	2318	691	155	154	176	200	193
745 AREA STUDY	368	105	73	51	23	26	32
750 POLITCL SC	9078	2996	540	655	709	688	619
755 INTL RELAT	1624	665	107	129	108	106	106
770 URBAN PLAN	232		13	39	49	49	81
798 SOC SC,GEN	228	64	17	16	26	27	22
799 SOC SC,OTH	896	320	130	106	101	91	94
HUM&PROF TOTAL	73803	25142	4508	4625	5079	4972	4761
OTH HUM SUBTOT	37785	12947	2128	2235	2449	2489	2299
800 ART,FIN+AP	628	293					
801 ART, APPL	26	2	6	2	8	7	1
802 ART,HIST	349	59	55	49	47	63	76
803 HIST, GEN	9950	4188					
804 AMER HIST	2425	456	386	415	392	423	353
805 EURO HIST	1793	302	274	315	336	291	275
806 HIST, OTH	1649	297	267	231	273	303	276
807 SCI HIST	113		12	30	30	19	22
808 AMER STUDY	22						22
830 MUSIC	2860	1078	155	165	218	301	288
831 SPEECH,DR	3988	1846	197	196	212	148	85
832 ARCHEOLOGY	227	68	9	11	4	17	9
833+880+881	5860	1810	239	277	354	333	337
834 PHILOSOPHY	5322	1708	328	325	327	347	336
835 LINGUISTIC	1447	620	112	122	127	121	116
878 A & H, GEN	392	43	16	14	9	11	17
879 A & H, OTH	734	177	72	83	112	105	86
LANG&LIT SBTOT	24036	8002	1363	1430	1533	1428	1345
810 ENG & AMER	9067	4073					
811 AMERICAN	969	154	149	154	172	190	150
812 ENGLISH	4318	820	689	710	759	686	654
821 GERMAN	1052	529	104	104	125	106	82
822 RUSSIAN	275	109	26	35	28	39	38
823 FRENCH	1140	549	132	119	117	112	110
824 SPAN+PORT	1255	553	116	136	154	142	152
826 ITALIAN	108	40	10	14	13	23	8
827 CLASSICAL	1786	579	72	84	68	61	57
829 OTH LANGS	4066	596	65	74	97	69	94

Women

PhD Fields	Total, 1920–1974	1960–1969	1970	1971	1972	1973	1974
SOC SCI TOTAL	5276	1428	324	441	514	585	673
700 ANTHROPOL	843	240	55	68	94	107	126
708 COMMUNIC'N	173			12	38	46	77
710 SOCIOLOGY	1667	465	110	123	147	175	195
720 ECONOMICS	914	266	45	59	70	59	82
725 ECONOMET	19	9	1	2			2
727 STATISTICS	37	12	7	4	8	2	4
740 GEOGRAPHY	177	38	11	15	14	14	10
745 AREA STUDY	61	20	4	12	5	6	7
750 POLITCL SC	952	272	60	95	96	100	121
755 INTL RELAT	188	74	12	14	12	22	11
770 URBAN PLAN	20			2	8	6	4
798 SOC SC,GEN	50	7	4	8	3	8	12
799 SOC SC,OTH	175	25	15	27	19	40	22
HUM&PROF TOTAL	18685	5519	1217	1334	1597	1818	1803
OTH HUM SUBTOT	6742	1933	418	430	563	643	681
800 ART,FIN+AP	237	130					
801 ART, APPL	10	2	3	2	1		2
802 ART,HIST	293	32	50	41	55	55	60
803 HIST, GEN	1505	514					
804 AMER HIST	373	48	52	60	61	61	91
805 EURO HIST	365	65	48	45	72	57	78
806 HIST, OTH	323	38	52	39	68	55	71
807 SCI HIST	33		1	8	4	12	8
808 AMER STUDY	5						5
830 MUSIC	526	172	28	37	50	85	66
831 SPEECH,DR	843	335	46	52	59	53	36
832 ARCHEOLOGY	139	33	4	8	8	11	13
833+880+881	337	101	9	15	29	26	29
834 PHILOSOPHY	783	218	51	41	44	65	62
835 LINGUISTIC	524	181	38	45	52	69	71
878 A & H, GEN	78	12	4	3	8	9	8
879 A & H, OTH	368	52	32	34	52	85	81
LANG&LIT SBTOT	9978	2838	660	741	849	990	943
810 ENG & AMER	2715	1230					
811 AMERICAN	450	60	64	74	69	89	94
812 ENGLISH	2286	321	325	347	413	445	435
821 GERMAN	524	189	51	60	63	83	78
822 RUSSIAN	141	50	10	13	18	31	19
823 FRENCH	1037	364	106	119	130	176	141
824 SPAN+PORT	675	249	63	83	93	85	101
826 ITALIAN	56	18	6	7	6	12	7
827 CLASSICAL	662	135	19	26	28	35	28
829 OTH LANGS	1432	222	16	12	29	34	40

PhD Fields	Both Sexes Total, 1920-1974	1960-1969	1970	1971	1972	1973	1974	Men Total, 1920-1974	1960-1969	1970	1971	1972	1973	1974	Women Total, 1920-1974	1960-1969	1970	1971	1972	1973	1974
PROF FLD SBTOT	13947	4941	1156	1123	1282	1240	1296	11982	4193	1017	960	1097	1055	1117	1965	748	139	163	185	185	179
882 BUS ADMIN	8423	3173	673	687	809	791	846	8174	3091	663	668	789	755	814	249	82	10	19	20	36	32
883 HOME EC	806	391	42	45	33	54	41	53	16	3	6	3	9	6	753	375	39	39	30	45	35
884 JOURNALISM	457	243	31	29	26	26	14	419	222	29	25	25	22	13	38	21	2	4	1	4	1
885 SP+HEAR SC	856	112	172	150	169	133	120	609	88	137	108	111	88	77	247	24	35	42	58	45	43
886 LAW, JURIS	1383	288	33	25	47	35	18	1323	279	33	25	43	32	18	60	9			4	3	
887 SOC WORK	1161	507	122	113	116	106	120	769	321	86	78	77	74	88	392	186	36	35	39	32	32
888 ARCHITECT	56	25						52	25						4						
891 LIBRARY SC	591	176	43	52	68	66	54	397	126	30	29	36	49	36	194	50	13	23	32	17	18
897 PROF, OTH	214	26	40	22	14	29	83	186	25	36	21	13	26	65	28	1	4	1	1	3	18
EDUC TOTAL	87523	29373	6305	6898	7318	7331	7219	68827	23655	4994	5386	5566	5484	5111	18696	5718	1311	1512	1752	1847	2108
900 FOUNDATION	3048	1598	275	311	303	302	255	2329	1235	212	242	233	227	177	719	363	63	69	70	75	78
908 ELEM EDUC	3385	1877	289	311	334	318	252	1888	1131	165	172	154	150	113	1497	746	124	139	180	168	139
909 SEC EDUC	2790	1616	248	211	259	235	208	2275	1342	216	178	189	187	151	515	274	32	33	70	48	57
910 EDUC PSYCH	4340	1923	497	457	460	479	456	2993	1389	337	312	314	307	280	1347	534	160	145	146	172	176
918 HIGHER ED	1888	55	142	218	336	562	575	1524	46	116	181	270	436	475	364	9	26	37	66	126	100
919 ADULT EDUC	589	21	68	108	99	137	156	473	20	54	85	77	119	118	116	1	14	23	22	18	38
920 EDUC MEAS	954	380	113	125	129	109	95	776	324	96	101	104	79	69	178	56	17	24	25	30	26
929 CURRICULUM	2417	56	123	221	430	776	811	1611	39	81	143	295	553	500	806	17	42	78	135	223	311
930 ED ADMIN	16086	8392	1542	1657	1636	1400	1367	14646	7688	1425	1516	1493	1251	1183	1440	704	117	141	143	149	184
940 GUID+COUNS	6598	3049	693	777	728	673	667	5077	2430	538	600	539	500	459	1521	619	155	177	189	173	208
950 SPECIAL ED	2649	1230	254	279	304	287	292	1843	913	180	199	189	193	166	806	317	74	80	115	94	126
960 A-V MEDIA	857	317	119	117	122	92	90	750	280	114	102	105	81	68	107	37	5	15	17	11	22
TCH FLD SUBTOT	14784	6764	1497	1654	1717	1514	1431	11177	5247	1133	1249	1305	1107	1001	3607	1517	364	405	412	407	430
970 AGRICULTUR	529	348	39	51	41	22	27	521	341	39	50	41	22	27	8	7		1			
972 ART	500	213	55	64	56	61	49	349	154	37	46	43	40	28	151	59	18	18	13	21	21
974 BUSINESS	913	437	84	105	90	92	92	634	313	56	72	63	63	56	279	124	28	33	27	29	36
976 ENGLISH	790	341	75	99	104	83	86	539	252	47	68	68	57	46	251	89	28	31	36	26	40
978 FORGN LANG	241	80	43	30	34	26	28	162	58	31	20	20	20	13	79	22	12	10	14	6	15
980 HOME EC	351	172	36	33	32	41	37	12	6		1	1	1	3	339	166	36	32	31	40	34
982 INDUS ARTS	684	325	84	89	63	65	54	680	325	84	88	61	64	54	4			1	2	1	
984 MATH	1211	556	140	142	148	118	105	996	468	113	120	125	86	82	215	88	27	22	23	32	23
986 MUSIC	1205	599	113	130	118	124	110	1022	524	97	103	100	94	93	183	75	16	27	18	30	17
988 PHYS ED	3772	1716	375	406	429	363	334	2731	1255	278	303	313	267	232	1041	461	97	103	116	96	102
990 SCIENCE ED	1949	1069	179	200	218	152	122	1582	840	159	159	191	125	100	367	229	20	41	27	27	22
992 SOC SCI ED	657	307	67	75	79	70	54	535	248	56	66	63	57	41	122	59	11	9	16	13	13
994 VOC EDUC	884	222	76	94	126	172	191	801	212	69	88	118	149	162	83	10	7	6	8	23	29
993,996 OTHER	1098	379	131	136	179	125	142	613	251	67	65	98	62	64	485	128	64	71	81	63	78
998 EDUC, GEN	25609	1605	205	222	208	298	404	20459	1208	156	158	149	205	271	5150	397	49	64	59	93	133
999 EDUC,OTH	1529	490	240	230	253	149	160	1006	363	171	148	150	89	80	523	127	69	82	103	60	80
899 OTH FIELDS	540	256	49	29	30	20	18	461	233	44	23	24	17	15	79	23	5	6	6	3	3
UNKNOWN	665	202	89	129	117	15	90	585	186	83	112	103	12	71	80	16	6	17	14	3	19

SOURCE: NRC, Commission on Human Resources.

APPENDIX B
SMALLER DOCTORATE-GRANTING INSTITUTIONS, BY GENERAL FIELDS, 1920-1974 PhD's

Doctoral Institution	Rank	PhD Field: Mathematics	Physics	Chemistry	Earth Sciences	Engineering	Life Sciences	Psychology	Social Sciences	Humanities	Professions	Unknown	Total
N TEXAS STATE UNIV	101	1	20	33			50	15	6	86	59	628	898
LOYOLA U CHICAGO/IL	102			49			173	243	14	187	2	226	894
CALIF, U-SAN DIEGO	103	43	196	86	138	81	185	47	19	96		1	892
EMORY UNIV/GA	103	31	6	112			165	104	77	315	79	3	892
AUBURN UNIVERSITY/AL	105	77	23	32		83	247	20	1	49		342	874
UTAH STATE UNIV	105		23	42	6	109	341	43	28		4	278	874
CALIF,U-RIVERSIDE	107	65	119	106	24		360	44	73	67		2	860
CUNY-GRAD SCH&U CTR	108	50	38	73		72	101	189	67	178	56	3	827
CLARK UNIVERSITY/MA	109	8	14	117	4		30	185	351	85		19	813
TEXAS TECH UNIV	110	44	22	33	13	96	34	162	20	125	72	186	807
GEORGIA INST TECH	111	33	93	178	2	490				3			799
OHIO UNIVERSITY	112	4	73	81		15	9	84	53	199	31	226	775
CALIF,U-SANTA BARB	113	46	45	121	28	51	120	31	110	185		23	760
BRIGHAM YOUNG U/UT	114		52	53	13	14	54	60	21	46	23	397	733
MIAMI, UNIV OF/FL	115	22	19	30	33	5	228	113	12	67		200	729
SOUTH CAROLINA, U OF	116	26	26	105	12	32	52	93	27	187	19	144	723
YESHIVA UNIV/NY	117	58	50	10	1		39	283	6	90	44	135	716
HAWAII, UNIV OF	118	2	18	76	43	17	323	62	94	63	1	12	711
BRYN MAWR COLL/PA	119	18	18	48	23	1	54	52	70	389	26	9	708
MISSISSIPPI, UNIV OF	120	11	6	68		12	147	46	23	45	27	312	697
NORTH DAKOTA, U OF	121			38	23	2	110	99	6	14	2	400	694
ST JOHNS UNIV/NY	122		8	60			96	120	28	224	2	143	681
KENT STATE UNIV/OH	123	5	16	51			38	94	27	153	53	192	629
SOUTHERN MISS, U OF	124			21			21	91	17	37	12	429	628
TUFTS UNIVERSITY/MA	125	1	44	40		17	117	41	270	71	10		611
MISSISSIPPI STATE U	126	1	4	15		54	233	18	57	47	42	110	581
BOSTON COLLDEGE/MA	127		24	40			27	57	81	119	3	180	531
SUNY AT STONY BROOK	128	66	124	58	8	62	47	76	14	53			508
U S INTERNATL U/CA	129	1			1			336	18	10	1	140	507
SUNY AT ALBANY	130	9	28	36	18		28	44	60	42	1	236	502
BALL STATE UNIV/IN	131							1	3	32		435	471
NEW SCH SOC RSCH/NY	132							127	295	37		2	461
MONTANA STATE UNIV	133	27	12	55		93	148		25		1	76	437
IDAHO, UNIV OF	134	13	16	54	22	34	95	1	16	10		156	417
NORTHERN ILL UNIV	135			16			2	24	15	45		309	411
MARQUETTE UNIV/WI	136	3	3	20		46	96	9	6	88	41	96	408
EAST TEXAS STATE U	137							10		19		354	383
NEW HAMPSHIRE, U OF	138	14	30	129		4	159	24	8	6		1	375
BAYLOR UNIV/TX	139		9	54			122	60		22	6	101	374
RHODE ISLAND, U OF	140	6	6	66	64	69	142	14	5	1			373
MISSOURI,U-ROLLA	141	29	52	29	33	218	1		1				363
NEW MEXICO STATE U	142	75	53	25		73	21					113	360
CLEMSON UNIV/SC	143	32	48	74		87	105		7		5	1	359
CALIF,U-IRVINE	144	24	29	37		29	104	31	33	55	5		347
SUNY ENVR SCI FRSTRY	145		1	110		21	193		11	4		1	341
SOUTH DAKOTA, U OF	146			15			43	59				220	337
CAL, U-SAN FRANCISCO	147			86			223	9	5	3			326
INST PAPER CHEM/WI	148		22	258		40	4			1			325
TEXAS WOMANS UNIV	149			10		7	56	8	2	17	88	133	321
LOUISVILLE, U OF/KY	150		2	111		26	116	44		10		3	312
ADELPHI UNIV/NY	151	29	15	39			2	220				5	310
STEVENS INST TECH/NJ	152	44	87	58		115		1		1		1	307
STHRN METHODIST U/TX	153	42	5		23	148			63	4	17		302
TEXAS CHRISTIAN UNIV	154	42	36	30				84	1	106			299
MONTANA, UNIV OF	155	4		9	26		55	66	6	4		117	287
GEORGIA STATE UNIV	156	1					1	51	25	2	109	93	282
COLORADO SCH MINES	157	3	4	6	126	124			2				265
BOWLING GREEN S U/OH	158						26	48	18	117	12	41	262
ROCKEFELLER UNIV/NY	159	8	14	7			218	5		3			255
TOLEDO, UNIV OF/OH	160	12	12	13		20	4	9		11		171	252
HOWARD UNIVERSITY/DC	161		27	63			99	2	27	32		1	251
DREW UNIVERSITY/NJ	162							2	4	25	217		248
AKRON, U OF/OH	163		1	127		21		12		1		83	245
TULSA, UNIV OF/OK	164				8	22				22		188	240
MAINE, U-ORONO	165		7	30		21	63	42		28		37	228
MISSOURI,U-KANS CITY	166	9		26			10	9	15	62		91	222
NORTHEASTERN U/MA	167	13	42	62		74	13	13	2				219
VERMONT, U OF	168	2	13	58		11	95	37					216
NORTH DAKOTA ST UNIV	169			78			137						215
DROPSIE UNIV/PA	170								10	99	58	38	205

APPENDIX B Continued

Doctoral Institution	Rank	Mathematics	Physics	Chemistry	Earth Sciences	Engineering	Life Sciences	Psychology	Social Sciences	Humanities	Professions	Unknown	Total
		PhD Field											
PACIFIC, U OF/CA	171			48			14	4	4	28		106	204
PORTLAND, UNIV OF/OR	172							132				61	193
ILL, U-COLL MEDICINE	173			25		3	156						184
N ORLN BAPT T SEM/LA	174									12	95	68	175
WESTERN MICHIGAN U	174	12		12	1		5		19			126	175
DUQUESNE UNIV/PA	176			47			16	46		62	1	1	173
DARTMOUTH COLLEGE/NH	177	45	26	11	12	31	33	10	1				169
DREXEL UNIVERSITY/PA	178	7	19	23		93	20	2	1	1	2		168
MIAMI UNIVERSITY/OH	179			1	6		12	21	7	22	1	92	162
ILLINOIS ST U-NORMAL	180						22					117	139
WISCONSIN,U-MILWAUKE	181	27	17	5	1		7	30	20	15		14	136
JEWISH THEO SEM AMER	182									24	96	13	133
MEMPHIS STATE U/TN.	183			17			3	22		1		89	132
VA COMONWLTH U MED C	183			23			109						132
HOFSTRA UNIV/NY	185							81				49	130
NEVADA, UNIV OF	185		18	19	22	1	6	48		16			130
CLARKSON C TECH/NY	187	10	25	57		37							129
NC, U OF-GREENSBORO	188						2	27		2	34	63	128
SW BAPT THEOL SEM/TX	189									11	86	26	123
NTHRN BAPT THEOL/IL	190										122		122
SOUTH DAKOTA STATE U	191			7		5	89		20				121
T JEF U-JEF MED C/PA	192					1	113						114
HEBREW UNION COLL/OH	193							1	2	44	65	1	113
WORCESTER POLY I/MA	194		20	24		62							106
SUNY AT BINGHAMTON	195	9	6	10	11		2	3	17	45		1	104
SUNY DOWNSTAT MD CTR	195						104						104
ILLINOIS,U-CHIGO CIR	197	13	6	23		30	2	12	9	8			103
SPRINGFIELD COLL/MA	197											103	103
DETROIT, U OF/MI	199			46		33	5	8		9			101
INDIANA STATE UNIV	200				1		6	16	12			62	97
PRINCETN THEO SEM/NJ	201							2	1	6	84	1	94
CALIF,U-SANTA CRUZ	202	2	15	14	8		18	6		29			92
GRAD THEOL UNION/CA	203							2	2	20	66	1	91
PHILA C PHARM&SCI/PA	204			12			75						87
UNION THEOL SEM/NY	205									19	62		81
TEXAS, U-HOUSTON	206	1					78		1				80
HAHNEMANN MED C/PA	207			1			78						79
SUNY UPSTATE MED CTR	208			1			74					3	78
ALABAMA,U-BIRMINGHAM	209			1			74						75
ALASKA, UNIV OF	209		19		39	2	15						75
WILLIAM & MARY,C/VA	209		29		13		8			5		20	75
ST MARYS COLLEGE/IN	212										70		70
MIDDLEBURY COLL/VT	213									69			69
NAVAL POSTGRAD S/CA	213	3	21	2	2	40						1	69
SETON HALL UNIV/NJ	215			62			4						66
WESLEYAN UNIV/CT	215	18	5	14			11			18			66
TENN,U CTR HTH SCI	217			5			58						63
MISSISSIPPI,U, S MED	218						59				1		60
NEW JERSEY INST TECH	219			1		56	1						58
ST BONAVENTURE U/NY	219						36		1	21			58
ALFRED UNIVERSITY/NY	221		5	7	1	43							56
SMITH COLLEGE/MA	221		1	1			9	1		5	39		56
SO BAPT THEOL SEM/KY	223									6	37	10	53
YESHIVA-EINST MED/NY	223						52					1	53
UNION UNIVERSITY/NY	225	1				13	37						51
NEW YORK MEDICAL COL	226						49						49
TEXAS,U,MED BR-GLVST	226						49						49
WAKE FOREST UNIV/NC	226						49						49
CORNELL U MED C/NY	229						47						47
THOMAS JEFFRSON U/PA	229		4				43						47
BAYLOR COLL MED/TX	231						45				1		46
AQUINAS INST/IA	232									12	29	4	45
FULLER THEOL SEM/CA	232							40			5		45
MEDICAL COLL GEORGIA	234						44						44
MED UNIV SO CAROLINA	234			4			40						44
MCNEESE STATE U/LA	236											41	41
MICHIGAN TECH UNIV	236			9	5	25	2						41
N MEX I MINING&TECH	236		11		30								41
TEXAS U-SWSTRN MED S	239						27	13					40
HARTFORD SEM FDN/CT	240							3	4	14	15	2	38

APPENDIX B Continued

Doctoral Institution	Rank	Mathematics	Physics	Chemistry	Earth Sciences	Engineering	Life Sciences	Psychology	Social Sciences	Humanities	Professions	Unknown	Total
		PhD Field											
MASS COLL PHARMACY	240			15			23						38
NE LOUISIANA UNIV	242						1					36	37
NORWESTRN ST UNIV LA	242											37	37
IDAHO STATE UNIV	244	11					6		7	11		1	36
OREGON U-SCH MED	245						29	6					35
OCCIDENTAL COLL/CA	246									33			33
PUERTO RICO, UNIV OF	246			8			2			23			33
NEW YORK LAW SCHOOL	248										32		32
SANTA CLARA, U OF/CA	249		1			13					16		30
FLORIDA ATLANTIC U	250											29	29
LOMA LINDA UNIV/CA	251	1		1			26						28
LOWELL, UNIV OF/MA	251		9	19									28
SOUTH FLORIDA, U OF	253			4		1	11	3				8	27
DEPAUL UNIVERSITY/IL	254							8		17			25
LA ST U, S MED-N ORL	254						25						25
SOWESTERN LA, U OF	256	8					5		3	5		3	24
TEXAS,U-ARLINGTON	256					23		1					24
ARKANSAS, U, SCH MED	258		1				22						23
WOODSTOCK COLL/NY	259										22		22
AIR FORCE I TECH/OH	260	1	5			15							21
LOUISIANA TECH UNIV	260	4				5			1		11		21
VILLANOVA UNIV/PA	260			17			4						21
FAIRLEIGH DICKN U/NJ	263											20	20
CHICAGO MED SCH/IL	264						18						18
DALLAS THEOL SEM/TX	264									1	16	1	18
LIU-BROOKLYN CTR/NY	264							17				1	18
MED COLL PENSYLVANIA	267						17						17
ST MARYS SEM & U/MD	267									2	15		17
TEXAS,U MED SN ANTON	267						17						17
ATLANTA UNIV/GA	270						8	3				5	16
MARYLAND,U, SCH MED	270			2			14						16
MIDDLE TENN STATE U	272									7		8	15
NOVA UNIVERSITY/FL	272				2			9				4	15
HEBREW UNION COLL/CA	274									3	11		14
INDIANA UNIV OF PA	274									3		11	14
JULLIARD SCHOOL/NY	274									14			14
MED N J-N J MED SCH	277						13						13
UNION-ALBANY MED/NY	277						13						13
WESTMINSTR THEO S/PA	277									1	12		13
COOPER UNION/NY	280		1	1		10							12
PEABODY I OF BALT/MD	280									11		1	12
S DAKOTA S MINE&TECH	280				7	5							12
EAST TENN STATE UNIV	283											11	11
PROVIDENCE COLL/RI	283			11									11
UNION THEOL SEM/VA	283										11		11
HEBREW UNION COLL/NY	286									4	6		10
DRAKE UNIV/IA	287											9	9
NORTHERN ARIZONA U	287						1					8	9
REDLANDS, U OF/CA	287								1	8			9
TEXAS,U-DALLAS	287		3		5		1						9
PHILLIPS UNIV/OK	291									4	4		8
DAYTON, U OF/OH	292						7						7
MED COLL WISCONSIN	292						7						7
PORTLAND STATE U/OR	292					3	2	1	1				7
SAM HOUSTON ST U/TX	292								6		1		7
WICHITA ST UNIV/KS	292									1	3	3	7
CREIGHTON UNIV/NE	297						6						6
DALLAS, UNIV OF/TX	297								4	2			6
MIDWST BAPT T SEM/MO	297									1	5		6
RUTGERS U-NEWARK/NJ	297			3			3						6
NC CENTRAL UNIV	301											4	4
ALABAMA,U-HUNTSVILLE	302					3							3
LAMAR UNIVERSITY/TX	302					3							3
N MEXICO HIGHLANDS U	302			1			2						3
TENNESSEE TECH U	302					3							3
ARKANSAS,U-LTLE ROCK	306					1				1			2
GLDN GT BAPT THEO/CA	306										2		2
LOYOLA UNIVERSITY/LA	306			1								1	2
VA COMMONWEALTH UN&V	306			1				1					2
LSU, SCH MED-SHRVPRT	310						1						1
OLD DOMINION UNIV/VA	310					1							1
ST STEPHENS COLL/MA	310									1			1
WAKE F-B GRAY MED/NC	310						1						1
WSTRN CONS BAPT S/OR	310									1			1

SOURCE: NRC, Commission on Human Resources.

APPENDIX C
STATE AND REGIONAL SUMMARIES OF FIELDS OF PhD's, 1920-1974, IN THE NATURAL SCIENCES

	Grand Total	Physics	Chemistry	Earth Sciences	Total, Physical Sciences	Mathematics	Engineering	Total EMP	Basic Medical Sciences	Other Biological Sciences	Total Biological Sciences	Medical Sciences	Agricultural Sciences	Environmental Sciences	Life Sciences Total
MAINE	228	7	30		37		21	58	7	25	32		31		63
NEW HAMPSHIRE	544	56	140	12	208	59	35	302	69	98	167	5	20		192
VERMONT	285	13	58		71	2	11	84	51	23	74	19	2		95
MASSACHUSETTS	32675	2688	3243	860	6791	1325	3892	12008	1483	1093	2576	315	151	11	3053
RHODE ISLAND	2777	292	440	112	844	339	235	1418	168	154	322	46	15		383
CONNECTICUT	11508	817	1071	230	2118	295	662	3075	640	543	1183	273	161	2	1619
NEW YORK	64945	3408	5293	884	9585	1894	4740	16219	3336	2745	6081	747	1499	26	8353
NEW JERSEY	10041	876	1203	332	2411	638	1036	4085	676	546	1222	33	430	12	1697
PENNSYLVANIA	26386	1570	2868	483	4921	881	3249	9051	1580	764	2344	569	385	22	3320
OHIO	20520	1038	2634	286	3958	527	2149	6634	1078	940	2018	362	604	11	2995
INDIANA	19504	865	2436	139	3440	658	1989	6087	1057	892	1949	445	673	10	3077
ILLINOIS	37897	1893	4488	737	7118	1468	3633	12219	2417	1740	4157	608	887	5	5657
MICHIGAN	24304	953	1871	372	3196	857	2361	6414	1307	1362	2669	412	1308	43	4432
WISCONSIN	17805	685	1997	422	3104	631	1183	4918	1600	1398	2998	498	1379	16	4891
MINNESOTA	10931	298	859	147	1304	273	891	2468	986	814	1800	604	924	5	3333
IOWA	13476	511	1710	180	2401	444	1281	4126	899	1090	1989	292	943	3	3227
MISSOURI	9347	510	635	246	1391	318	836	2545	631	488	1119	121	462	6	1708
NORTH DAKOTA	909		116	23	139		2	141	100	78	178	3	66		247
SOUTH DAKOTA	470		22	7	29		10	39	30	33	63	3	66		132
NEBRASKA	3266	73	338	32	443	70	55	568	138	234	372	29	262		663
KANSAS	5046	191	785	84	1060	131	345	1536	477	557	1034	77	275	4	1390
DELAWARE	970	46	371	1	418	35	238	691	36	52	88	2	15		105
MARYLAND	10209	932	1103	237	2272	357	949	3578	936	695	1631	533	402	27	2593
DIST. OF COL.	8963	487	551	32	1070	199	236	1505	548	280	828	154	6	1	989
VIRGINIA	4280	449	447	53	949	244	579	1772	247	267	514	42	149	4	709
WEST VIRGINIA	1086	39	117	22	178	4	140	322	124	68	192	42	70		304
NORTH CAROLINA	10508	483	846	86	1415	469	624	2508	671	881	1552	255	568	15	2390
SOUTH CAROLINA	1126	74	183	12	269	58	119	446	39	93	132	24	37	4	197
GEORGIA	4321	124	421	9	554	140	490	1184	278	259	537	57	153	1	748
FLORIDA	7868	313	693	137	1143	223	503	1869	312	424	736	122	272	16	1146
KENTUCKY	2124	79	245		324	104	86	514	162	83	245	29	153		427
TENNESSEE	6362	360	461	28	849	183	362	1394	392	279	671	119	129	5	924
ALABAMA	2514	79	119		198	137	180	515	153	140	293	23	99		415
MISSISSIPPI	1966	10	104		114	12	66	192	134	126	260	88	112		460
ARKANSAS	1280	29	149		178	19	68	265	57	34	91	7	24		122
LOUISIANA	4921	178	417	126	721	222	237	1180	413	309	722	141	315		1178
OKLAHOMA	5797	182	269	106	557	152	814	1523	322	451	773	115	236	16	1140
TEXAS	16253	934	1358	486	2778	663	2076	5517	1009	901	1910	136	454	3	2503
MONTANA	724	12	64	26	102	31	93	226	47	105	152		50	1	203
IDAHO	453	16	54	22	92	24	34	150	15	36	51		50		101
WYOMING	908	57	61	51	169	21	26	216	33	56	89		83	1	173
COLORADO	8626	377	484	314	1175	199	728	2102	345	309	654	101	197	8	960
NEW MEXICO	1798	123	124	69	316	147	235	698	30	50	80	8	1		89
ARIZONA	3641	162	235	221	618	89	398	1105	145	243	388	11	145	6	550
UTAH	4426	199	368	142	709	91	519	1319	233	323	556	69	152		777
NEVADA	130	18	19	22	59		1	60	2	4	6				6
GUAM															
WASHINGTON	7609	380	800	266	1446	300	545	2291	454	495	949	211	511	4	1675
OREGON	5856	159	443	160	762	268	162	1192	441	482	923	38	461	2	1424
CALIFORNIA	49033	3635	3920	1463	9018	2128	6320	17466	3233	3494	6727	598	789	27	8141
ALASKA	75	19		39	58		2	60	11	3	14			1	15
HAWAII	711	18	76	43	137	2	17	156	63	141	204	10	108	1	323
PUERTO RICO	33		8		8			8	2		2				2
NEW ENGLAND	48017	3873	4982	1214	10069	2020	4856	16945	2418	1936	4354	658	380	13	5405
MIDDLE ATLANTIC	101372	5854	9364	1699	16917	3413	9025	29355	5592	4055	9647	1349	2314	60	13370
EAST NORTH CENTRAL	120030	5434	13426	1956	20816	4141	11315	36272	7459	6332	13791	2325	4851	85	21052
WEST NORTH CENTRAL	43445	1583	4465	719	6767	1236	3420	11423	3261	3294	6555	1129	2998	18	10700
SOUTH ATLANTIC	49331	2947	4732	589	8268	1729	3878	13875	3191	3019	6210	1231	1672	68	9181
EAST SOUTH CENTRAL	12966	528	929	28	1485	436	694	2615	841	628	1469	259	493	5	2226
WEST SOUTH CENTRAL	28251	1323	2193	718	4234	1056	3195	8485	1801	1695	3496	399	1029	19	4943
MOUNTAIN	20706	964	1409	867	3240	602	2034	5876	850	1126	1976	189	678	16	2859
PACIFIC AND INSULAR	63317	4211	5247	1971	11429	2698	7046	21173	4204	4615	8819	857	1869	35	11580

SOURCE: NRC, Commission on Human Resources.

APPENDIX D
STATE AND REGIONAL SUMMARIES OF FIELDS OF PhD's, 1920-1974, IN BEHAVIORAL SCIENCES AND NONSCIENCE FIELDS

	Psychology	Economics	Anthropology and Sociology	Political Science and Public Admin.	Other Social Sciences	Total, Behavioral Sciences	Total, Sciences	History	Language and Literature		Other Humanities	Humanities, Total	Education	Professions	Unknown Field	Total, Nonsciences
									American	Foreign						
MAINE	42					42	163	28				28	37			65
NEW HAMPSHIRE	34	1	7		1	43	537	1	5			6			1	7
VERMONT	37					37	216			68	1	69				69
MASSACHUSETTS	1607	1870	846	1277	441	6041	21102	1778	1321	1115	1892	6106	3326	2096	45	11573
RHODE ISLAND	164	102	57	44	16	383	2184	96	193	135	134	558	5	29	1	593
CONNECTICUT	641	387	353	356	38	1775	6469	608	1000	828	794	3230	962	837	10	5039
NEW YORK	5106	2170	1892	1937	692	11797	36369	2653	2841	2197	3036	10727	15212	2528	109	28576
NEW JERSEY	406	344	110	360	67	1287	7069	409	472	541	373	1795	750	412	15	2972
PENNSYLVANIA	1514	964	619	469	420	3986	16357	814	1215	860	965	3854	5161	954	60	10029
OHIO	1821	451	379	184	297	3132	12761	614	826	479	914	2833	3982	897	47	7759
INDIANA	1269	613	340	349	169	2740	11904	508	613	331	968	2420	4301	776	103	7600
ILLINOIS	2632	1407	1414	1084	571	7108	24984	1392	1613	1236	1859	6100	4385	2333	95	12913
MICHIGAN	2000	672	666	390	473	4201	15047	586	864	550	1301	3301	5053	853	50	9257
WISCONSIN	504	950	445	291	261	2451	12260	1049	906	672	646	3273	1800	434	38	5545
MINNESOTA	1045	436	296	263	166	2206	8007	378	362	177	426	1343	1284	294	3	2924
IOWA	860	570	212	201	170	2013	9366	272	439	195	888	1794	1845	462	9	4110
MISSOURI	640	261	350	150	47	1448	5701	427	294	249	440	1410	1857	372	7	3646
NORTH DAKOTA	99		3	2	1	105	493	8	6			14	400	2		416
SOUTH DAKOTA	59	6	14			79	250						220			220
NEBRASKA	239	90	68	48	70	515	1746	114	173	34	52	373	1067	80		1520
KANSAS	425	117	65	62	94	763	3689	127	131	110	111	479	805	69	4	1357
DELAWARE	70				5	75	871	37	30		9	76	21		2	99
MARYLAND	495	279	107	397	97	1375	7546	385	334	489	271	1479	1096	77	11	2663
DIST. OF COL.	534	385	262	840	74	2095	4589	665	207	386	534	1792	1249	1316	17	4374
VIRGINIA	94	230	23	120	39	506	2987	240	239	81	68	628	622	41	2	1293
WEST VIRGINIA	92	23		15		130	756	37	1		20	58	272			330
NORTH CAROLINA	632	540	371	376	120	2039	6937	690	734	455	307	2186	1004	368	13	3571
SOUTH CAROLINA	93	20		14		127	770	63	104		20	187	143	24	2	356
GEORGIA	380	44	95	65	41	625	2557	244	132	53	148	577	928	255	4	1764
FLORIDA	717	146	179	140	139	1321	4336	155	279	131	352	917	2321	285	9	3532
KENTUCKY	249	101	80	64	10	504	1445	104	77	60	13	254	369	52	4	679
TENNESSEE	737	146	102	65	41	1091	3409	234	425	116	129	904	1878	166	5	2953
ALABAMA	153	35		19	7	214	1144	57	83	16	7	163	1040	167		1370
MISSISSIPPI	155	33	43	14	7	252	904	73	40		16	129	851	82		1062
ARKANSAS	42	67				109	496	1	69	8	10	88	538	156	2	784
LOUISIANA	276	141	187	58	74	736	3094	214	256	208	309	987	521	313	6	1827
OKLAHOMA	349	178	33	70	57	687	3350	169	123	39	64	395	1936	115	1	2447
TEXAS	1267	364	153	143	133	2060	10080	523	667	306	423	1919	3499	741	14	6173
MONTANA	66	24	6		1	97	526	4				4	193	1		198
IDAHO	1			23		24	275	10	11			21	157			178
WYOMING	40					40	429	5				5	474			479
COLORADO	614	195	168	155	104	1236	4298	209	273	155	333	970	3166	190	2	4328
NEW MEXICO	78	5	31	7	15	136	923	132	141	64	38	375	499		1	875
ARIZONA	297	26	112	62	7	504	2159	41	65	65	41	212	1162	105	3	1482
UTAH	411	46	82	43	30	612	2708	56	96	37	107	296	1342	79	1	1718
NEVADA	48					48	114	2	14			16				16
GUAM																
WASHINGTON	460	180	365	160	175	1340	5306	271	395	248	222	1136	881	271	15	2303
OREGON	439	136	200	104	80	959	3575	89	166	49	113	417	1716	134	14	2281
CALIFORNIA	2860	1519	1254	1384	617	7634	33241	1942	1570	1448	1782	6742	7181	1389	480	15792
ALASKA							75									
HAWAII	62	11	33	37	13	156	635	15			48	63	12	1		76
PUERTO RICO							10			18	5	23				23
NEW ENGLAND	2525	2360	1263	1677	496	8321	30671	2511	2519	2146	2821	9997	4330	2962	57	17346
MIDDLE ATLANTIC	7026	3478	2621	2766	1179	17070	59795	3876	4528	3598	4374	16376	21123	3894	184	41577
EAST NORTH CENTRAL	8226	4093	3244	2298	1771	19632	76956	4149	4822	3268	5688	17927	19521	5293	333	43074
WEST NORTH CENTRAL	3367	1480	1008	726	548	7129	29252	1326	1405	765	1917	5413	7478	1279	23	14193
SOUTH ATLANTIC	3107	1667	1037	1967	515	8293	31349	2516	2060	1595	1729	7900	7656	2366	60	17982
EAST SOUTH CENTRAL	1294	315	225	162	65	2061	6902	468	625	192	165	1450	4138	467	9	6064
WEST SOUTH CENTRAL	1934	750	373	271	264	3592	17020	907	1115	561	806	3389	6494	1325	23	11231
MOUNTAIN	1555	296	399	290	157	2697	11432	459	600	321	519	1899	6993	375	7	9274
PACIFIC AND INSULAR	3821	1846	1852	1685	885	10089	42842	2317	2131	1763	2170	8381	9790	1795	509	20475

SOURCE: NRC, Commission on Human Resources.

APPENDIX E
ONE HUNDRED PhD-GRANTING INSTITUTIONS LARGEST IN NUMBERS OF PhD's, 1920-1974, BY SEX AND FIELD GROUP, WITH TOTALS AND RANK ORDERS BY TIME PERIOD

Institution	Rank	Men: Physical Sciences	Engineering	Life Sciences	Behavioral Sciences	Humanities	Professions	Education	Total	Women: Physical Sciences	Engineering	Life Sciences	Behavioral Sciences	Humanities	Professions	Education	Total	Unknown Field	Grand Total
WISCONSIN,U-MADISON																			
1920-1959	3	1514	310	2235	948	940	59	348	6356	48	2	225	69	263	10	69	687	1	7044
1960-1969	2	1043	431	1276	622	799	121	512	4821	51	1	132	62	183	38	107	581	1	5403
1970-1974	1	688	350	784	557	753	146	507	3790	35	3	125	128	232	19	147	690	2	4482
TOTAL 1920-1974	1	3245	1091	4295	2127	2492	326	1367	14967	134	6	482	259	678	67	323	1958	4	16929
PER 1000 TOTAL		34.4	24.4	60.0	32.2	44.4	18.8	19.9	35.5	25.5	23.3	46.6	20.0	41.1	29.9	17.7	29.9	6.6	34.4
COLUMBIA UNIV/NY																			
1920-1959	1	1369	306	508	1317	1637	377	1238	6758	178	1	181	339	467	39	444	1651	1	8410
1960-1969	6	688	341	201	908	1027	278	84	3528	58	3	100	283	384	73	51	952	4	4484
1970-1974	13	366	181	89	507	569	150	39	1903	37	1	64	276	330	67	27	803	2	2708
TOTAL 1920-1974	2	2423	828	798	2732	3233	805	1361	12189	273	5	345	898	1181	179	522	3406	7	15602
PER 1000 TOTAL		25.5	18.8	11.1	41.1	57.7	46.6	19.9	29.9	51.1	19.9	32.2	70.0	72.2	78.8	27.7	51.1	10.0	32.2
HARVARD UNIV/MA																			
1920-1959	2	1430	170	643	1565	2098	499	439	6845	76	1	121	190	276	10	67	745		7590
1960-1969	4	966	109	309	806	1073	442	341	4052	50	1	100	139	258	6	90	645	2	4699
1970-1974	7	548	55	242	540	638	252	260	2537	34		87	138	240	15	107	621		3158
TOTAL 1920-1974	3	2944	334	1194	2911	3809	1193	1040	13434	160	2	308	467	774	31	264	2011	2	15447
PER 1000 TOTAL		30.0	7.7	16.6	44.4	67.7	68.8	15.5	31.1	30.0	7.7	29.9	36.6	47.7	13.3	14.4	30.0	3.3	31.1
CALIF, U-BERKELEY																			
1920-1959	5	1568	206	1266	774	739	7	413	4973	82		160	105	139	6	91	583		5556
1960-1969	1	1511	900	758	788	560	95	426	5042	69	4	144	150	110	11	112	600	146	5788
1970-1974	2	650	725	494	567	365	125	235	3162	50	5	140	164	175	21	122	677	249	4088
TOTAL 1920-1974	4	3729	1831	2518	2129	1664	227	1074	13177	201	9	444	419	424	38	325	1860	395	15432
PER 1000 TOTAL		39.9	40.0	35.5	32.2	29.9	13.3	15.5	31.1	37.7	34.4	42.2	32.2	25.5	16.6	17.7	28.8	594.4	31.1
ILL, U, URBANA-CHAMP																			
1920-1959	6	1949	506	1059	592	559	109	268	5043	103	1	102	38	143	10	47	444		5487
1960-1969	3	1158	1051	931	524	493	219	529	4914	69	5	109	62	124	16	92	477	1	5392
1970-1974	3	671	581	555	483	364	179	566	3399	46	3	97	113	163	27	167	617	1	4017
TOTAL 1920-1974	5	3778	2138	2545	1599	1416	507	1363	13356	218	9	308	213	430	53	306	1538	2	14896
PER 1000 TOTAL		39.9	47.7	35.5	24.4	25.5	29.9	19.9	31.1	40.0	34.4	29.9	16.6	26.6	23.3	16.6	23.3	3.3	30.0
MICHIGAN, UNIV OF																			
1920-1959	9	1073	571	855	671	731	101	389	4392	74	3	136	105	120	6	92	536	1	4929
1960-1969	5	779	762	530	704	655	161	469	4077	41	1	98	127	145	15	115	543		4620
1970-1974	4	433	440	392	617	525	147	506	3062	28	4	92	175	207	23	177	707	1	3770
TOTAL 1920-1974	6	2285	1773	1777	1992	1911	409	1364	11531	143	8	326	407	472	44	384	1786	2	13319
PER 1000 TOTAL		24.4	39.9	25.5	30.0	33.3	23.3	19.9	27.7	26.6	30.0	31.1	31.1	28.8	19.9	20.0	26.6	3.3	27.7
OHIO STATE UNIV																			
1920-1959	11	1225	321	996	768	448	110	568	4436	40	3	68	96	82	17	131	437	1	4874
1960-1969	7	657	482	583	486	418	163	646	3440	26	1	55	83	67	65	133	430		3870
1970-1974	5	388	347	432	401	326	155	749	2804	35	1	61	115	89	56	262	619		3423
TOTAL 1920-1974	7	2270	1150	2011	1655	1192	428	1963	10680	101	5	184	294	238	138	526	1486	1	12167
PER 1000 TOTAL		23.3	25.5	28.8	25.5	21.1	24.4	28.8	25.5	18.8	19.9	17.7	23.3	14.4	60.0	28.8	22.2	1.1	25.5
CHICAGO, UNIV OF/IL																			
1920-1959	4	1552		879	1510	973	573	352	5879	138	1	221	251	263	104	81	1071	2	6952
1960-1969	17	622		283	704	387	268	202	2470	41		59	135	68	29	59	391	2	2863
1970-1974	18	385		185	496	443	175	119	1804	32		43	139	144	22	46	427	15	2246
TOTAL 1920-1974	8	2559		1347	2710	1803	1016	673	10153	211	1	323	525	475	155	186	1889	19	12061
PER 1000 TOTAL		26.6		19.9	41.1	32.2	58.8	9.9	24.4	39.9	3.3	30.0	41.1	28.8	68.8	9.9	28.8	28.8	24.4
NEW YORK UNIVERSITY																			
1920-1959	8	727	80	242	660	383	370	1581	4053	45		61	137	122	23	511	901		4954
1960-1969	8	517	256	170	699	507	196	707	3054	40	1	69	205	179	19	263	779	1	3834
1970-1974	9	291	240	163	521	443	143	397	2199	31	2	115	189	241	14	197	789	7	2995
TOTAL 1920-1974	9	1535	576	575	1880	1333	709	2685	9306	116	3	245	531	542	56	971	2469	8	11783
PER 1000 TOTAL		16.6	12.2	8.8	28.8	23.3	40.0	39.9	22.2	21.1	11.1	23.3	41.1	33.3	24.4	51.1	37.7	12.2	24.4
CORNELL UNIV/NY																			
1920-1959	7	1068	298	1863	641	538	56	270	4746	54	2	216	85	158	36	39	594		5340
1960-1969	15	602	434	832	400	320	37	212	2841	32	2	96	65	61	33	34	323		3164
1970-1974	15	519	310	555	331	255	37	93	2103	40	3	64	88	104	11	34	345	1	2449
TOTAL 1920-1974	10	2189	1042	3250	1372	1113	130	575	9690	126	7	376	238	323	80	107	1262	1	10953
PER 1000 TOTAL		23.3	23.3	45.5	20.0	19.9	7.7	8.8	23.3	23.3	27.7	35.5	18.8	19.9	35.5	5.5	19.9	1.1	22.2
MINNESOTA,U-MINNEAPL																			
1920-1959	12	762	224	1609	737	360	24	248	3964	34		90	129	78	10	61	402		4366
1960-1969	9	465	376	982	603	413	116	398	3354	23	3	55	97	74	10	89	351		3705
1970-1974	10	259	284	535	493	325	117	372	2385	34	4	62	147	93	17	116	473	2	2860
TOTAL 1920-1974	11	1486	884	3126	1833	1098	257	1018	9703	91	7	207	373	245	37	266	1226	2	10931
PER 1000 TOTAL		15.5	19.9	44.4	27.7	19.9	14.4	14.4	23.3	17.7	27.7	19.9	29.9	14.4	16.6	14.4	18.8	3.3	22.2
STANFORD UNIV/CA																			
1920-1959	14	589	324	293	353	394	37	795	2787	30		37	45	110		153	375		3162
1960-1969	10	752	1027	175	366	442	111	373	3257	31	6	46	73	98	3	77	334		3591
1970-1974	12	521	716	151	314	312	96	233	2345	28	8	50	76	150	4	70	386	3	2734
TOTAL 1920-1974	12	1862	2067	619	1033	1148	244	1401	8389	89	14	133	194	358	7	300	1095	3	9487
PER 1000 TOTAL		19.9	45.5	8.8	15.5	20.0	14.4	20.0	20.0	16.6	54.4	12.2	15.5	21.1	3.3	16.6	16.6	4.4	19.9
YALE UNIVERSITY/CT																			
1920-1959	10	1002	241	561	548	1124	472	315	4263	71		161	88	234	15	53	623		4886
1960-1969	19	593	162	231	413	731	247	1	2384	31		82	70	222	8		413		2797
1970-1974	27	334	84	170	257	469	71	2	1390	34	2	64	66	218	3		387		1777
TOTAL 1920-1974	13	1929	487	962	1218	2324	790	318	8037	136	2	307	224	674	26	53	1423		9460
PER 1000 TOTAL		20.0	10.0	13.3	18.8	41.1	45.5	4.4	19.9	25.5	7.7	29.9	17.7	41.1	11.1	2.2	21.1		19.9
INDIANA U BLOOMNGTON																			
1920-1959	25	410		168	274	254	91	629	1827	20		29	33	51	3	115	252		2079
1960-1969	11	389		251	397	625	234	1076	2983	18		42	68	129	8	253	518		3501
1970-1974	8	252		205	341	537	165	933	2434	14		47	54	209	20	226	572	1	3007
TOTAL 1920-1974	14	1051		624	1012	1416	490	2638	7244	52		118	155	389	31	594	1342	1	8587
PER 1000 TOTAL		11.1		8.8	15.5	25.5	28.8	38.8	17.7	9.9		11.1	12.2	23.3	13.3	31.1	20.0	1.1	17.7
PURDUE UNIVERSITY/IN																			
1920-1959	20	850	399	562	394	39	2	28	2274	26	2	31	40	1	9	1	110		2384
1960-1969	13	733	809	859	471	73	34	144	3128	33	2	52	45	5	24	28	189	3	3320
1970-1974	14	480	555	597	312	41	75	207	2267	14	5	65	71	31	30	80	296	78	2641
TOTAL 1920-1974	15	2063	1763	2018	1177	153	111	379	7669	73	9	148	156	37	63	109	595	81	8345
PER 1000 TOTAL		21.1	39.9	28.8	17.7	2.2	6.6	5.5	18.8	13.3	34.4	14.4	12.2	2.2	27.7	5.5	9.9	121.1	17.7
MASS INST TECHNOLOGY																			
1920-1959	16	1588	1103	93	94	1	13		2893	52	3	8	2		2		67		2960
1960-1969	16	1163	1386	132	253	32	61		3040	46	8	11	26	2			93	5	3138
1970-1974	22	730	772	104	187	37	48		1881	43	6	43	27	14			133		2014
TOTAL 1920-1974	16	3481	3261	329	534	70	122		7814	141	17	62	55	16	2		293	5	8112
PER 1000 TOTAL		36.6	72.2	4.4	8.8	1.1	7.7		18.8	26.6	65.5	5.5	4.4	1.1	0.0		4.4	7.7	16.6
MICHIGAN STATE UNIV																			
1920-1959	32	202	76	569	178	28	2	164	1219	9		24	14	8	1	34	90	4	1313
1960-1969	12	400	237	767	572	287	155	785	3218	15	1	35	45	34	25	115	271		3489
1970-1974	6	353	154	626	491	233	164	802	2825	28		51	97	61	20	198	457		3282
TOTAL 1920-1974	17	955	467	1962	1241	548	321	1751	7262	52	1	110	156	103	46	347	818	4	8084
PER 1000 TOTAL		10.0	10.0	27.7	18.8	9.9	18.8	25.5	17.7	9.9	3.3	10.0	12.2	6.6	20.0	18.8	12.2	6.6	16.6

APPENDIX E Continued

Institution	Rank	Men								Women									
		Physical Sciences	Engineering	Life Sciences	Behavioral Sciences	Humanities	Professions	Education	Total	Physical Sciences	Engineering	Life Sciences	Behavioral Sciences	Humanities	Professions	Education	Total	Unknown Field	Grand Total
IOWA, UNIVERSITY OF																			
1920-1959	13	634	134	388	631	748	132	429	3096	28	1	75	131	130	5	130	500		3596
1960-1969	22	331	137	236	296	456	139	416	2012	10	1	25	42	44	6	129	257		2269
1970-1974	26	228	115	190	259	329	95	355	1573	13	2	30	38	75	10	90	258		1831
TOTAL 1920-1974	18	1193	386	814	1186	1533	366	1200	6681	51	4	130	211	249	21	349	1015		7696
PER 1000 TOTAL		12.2	8.8	11.1	17.7	27.7	20.0	17.7	15.5	9.9	15.5	12.2	16.6	15.5	9.9	18.8	15.5		15.5
CALIF,U-LOS ANGELES																			
1920-1959	29	440	54	234	248	181	3	184	1344	15		28	34	33	1	46	157		1501
1960-1969	14	614	318	441	442	327	149	413	2704	29	4	80	103	134	2	132	484	2	3190
1970-1974	11	402	362	297	397	346	115	327	2247	33	5	101	129	171	5	146	590	1	2838
TOTAL 1920-1974	19	1456	734	972	1087	854	267	924	6295	77	9	209	266	338	8	324	1231	3	7529
PER 1000 TOTAL		15.5	16.6	13.3	16.6	15.5	15.5	13.3	15.5	14.4	34.4	19.9	20.0	20.0	3.3	17.7	18.8	4.4	15.5
PENNSYLVANIA, U OF																			
1920-1959	17	507	80	429	585	701	21	210	2533	21		95	76	171	3	57	423	3	2959
1960-1969	20	443	383	214	458	502	49	111	2170	36	1	69	45	128	27	29	335		2505
1970-1974	21	265	261	165	407	302	88	105	1601	50	1	60	104	150	10	50	427		2028
TOTAL 1920-1974	20	1215	724	808	1450	1505	158	426	6304	107	2	224	225	449	40	136	1185	3	7492
PER 1000 TOTAL		12.2	16.6	11.1	21.1	26.6	9.9	6.6	15.5	20.0	7.7	21.1	17.7	27.7	17.7	7.7	17.7	4.4	15.5
TEXAS, U-AUSTIN																			
1920-1959	23	550	117	226	275	333	87	324	1912	13		33	29	94	7	57	233		2145
1960-1969	18	608	421	322	324	355	145	323	2498	27	2	74	39	101	9	84	336		2834
1970-1974	17	362	314	167	299	295	106	301	1848	30		48	79	128	12	153	450		2298
TOTAL 1920-1974	21	1520	852	715	898	983	338	948	6258	70	2	155	147	323	28	294	1019		7277
PER 1000 TOTAL		16.6	18.8	10.0	13.3	17.7	19.9	13.3	14.4	13.3	7.7	14.4	11.1	19.9	12.2	15.5	15.5		14.4
NORTHWESTERN UNIV/IL																			
1920-1959	19	521	139	230	351	507	96	218	2070	24		50	60	104	4	76	318		2388
1960-1969	24	349	470	130	312	429	103	173	1968	20	1	32	67	90	8	43	261		2229
1970-1974	23	262	345	95	284	266	156	176	1586	27	6	42	95	98	20	77	365		1951
TOTAL 1920-1974	22	1132	954	463	947	1202	355	567	5624	71	7	124	222	292	32	196	944		6568
PER 1000 TOTAL		11.1	21.1	6.6	14.4	21.1	20.0	8.8	13.3	13.3	27.7	11.1	17.7	17.7	14.4	10.0	14.4		13.3
PENN STATE UNIV																			
1920-1959	27	623	178	286	213	66	1	362	1730	29	1	25	32	9	19	58	173		1903
1960-1969	21	671	279	331	223	116	23	533	2185	21		22	31	31	33	95	234	1	2420
1970-1974	19	428	229	261	227	137	77	494	1858	28		37	51	50	19	92	277		2135
TOTAL 1920-1974	23	1722	686	878	663	319	101	1389	5773	78	1	84	114	90	71	245	684	1	6458
PER 1000 TOTAL		18.8	15.5	12.2	10.0	5.5	5.5	20.0	13.3	14.4	3.3	8.8	8.8	5.5	31.1	13.3	10.0	1.1	13.3
SOUTHERN CALIF, U OF																			
1920-1959	28	131	10	142	327	326	97	515	1549	4		23	37	65	2	91	222		1771
1960-1969	23	134	149	130	321	356	133	684	1915	6		14	68	84	18	147	337		2252
1970-1974	16	139	228	96	315	215	132	755	1881	19	3	16	69	91	36	203	437	2	2320
TOTAL 1920-1974	24	404	387	368	963	897	362	1954	5345	29	3	53	174	240	56	441	996	2	6343
PER 1000 TOTAL		4.4	8.8	5.5	14.4	15.5	20.0	28.8	12.2	5.5	11.1	5.5	13.3	14.4	24.4	23.3	15.5	3.3	13.3
COLUMBIA-TCHRS C/NY																			
1920-1959	15			1	2			2312	2315			1	1		1	755	758		3073
1960-1969	28						1	1251	1252				1			629	630		1882
1970-1974	54							620	620							451	451		1071
TOTAL 1920-1974	25			1	2		1	4183	4187			1	2		1	1835	1839		6026
PER 1000 TOTAL				0.0	0.0		0.0	60.0	10.0			0.0	0.0		0.0	98.8	27.7		12.2
IOWA STATE UNIV																			
1920-1959	21	660	184	1072	153		2	44	2115	36		58	6		16	8	124	1	2240
1960-1969	26	582	465	673	239			74	2033	17	2	30	18		19	15	101		2134
1970-1974	39	293	240	429	176			120	1258	13		21	24		9	26	94		1352
TOTAL 1920-1974	26	1535	889	2174	568		2	238	5406	66	2	109	48		44	49	319	1	5726
PER 1000 TOTAL		16.6	19.9	30.0	8.8		0.0	3.3	12.2	12.2	7.7	10.0	3.3		19.9	2.2	4.4	1.1	11.1
WASHINGTON, U OF																			
1920-1959	30	434	47	233	241	198	25	148	1329	14		31	20	41		29	135		1464
1960-1969	25	550	223	331	316	369	136	88	2013	20		41	46	64	5	16	192	1	2206
1970-1974	20	370	234	283	284	301	92	140	1707	28	1	58	74	91	11	55	318	8	2033
TOTAL 1920-1974	27	1354	504	847	841	868	253	376	5049	62	1	130	140	196	16	100	645	9	5703
PER 1000 TOTAL		14.4	11.1	12.2	12.2	15.5	14.4	5.5	12.2	11.1	3.3	12.2	11.1	11.1	7.7	5.5	9.9	13.3	11.1
PITTSBURGH, UNIV OF																			
1920-1959	26	436	71	180	284	181	15	598	1765	14		42	51	61		70	238		2003
1960-1969	29	318	189	201	228	178	60	276	1452	15		45	43	57	11	68	239		1691
1970-1974	25	212	111	159	250	149	90	479	1455	18	1	59	71	76	23	216	465		1920
TOTAL 1920-1974	28	966	371	540	762	508	165	1353	4672	47	1	146	165	194	34	354	942		5614
PER 1000 TOTAL		10.0	8.8	7.7	11.1	9.9	9.9	19.9	11.1	8.8	3.3	13.3	13.3	11.1	15.5	18.8	14.4		11.1
JOHNS HOPKINS U/MD																			
1920-1959	18	792	212	687	278	454	9	45	2478	46		118	51	128		42	385		2863
1960-1969	37	325	213	292	173	235	2	18	1261	22	1	47	25	50		6	151		1412
1970-1974	50	201	117	233	180	168		15	916	16	5	65	62	67		9	224	5	1145
TOTAL 1920-1974	29	1318	542	1212	631	857	11	78	4655	84	6	230	138	245		57	760	5	5420
PER 1000 TOTAL		13.3	12.2	17.7	9.9	15.5	0.0	1.1	11.1	15.5	23.3	21.1	10.0	14.4		3.3	11.1	7.7	11.1
PRINCETON UNIV/NJ																			
1920-1959	22	1023	81	110	353	609	5		2181				2				2	1	2184
1960-1969	27	655	336	62	323	456	44		1877			3	2	9	1		15	2	1894
1970-1974	45	353	199	49	201	311	21	1	1135	16	4	5	23	47			95	1	1231
TOTAL 1920-1974	30	2031	616	221	877	1376	70	1	5193	16	4	8	27	56	1		112	4	5309
PER 1000 TOTAL		21.1	13.3	3.3	13.3	24.4	4.4	0.0	12.2	3.3	15.5	0.0	2.2	3.3	0.0		1.1	6.6	10.0
MARYLAND, UNIV OF																			
1920-1959	37	327	36	437	87	36	2	92	1017	11		28	10	15		33	97		1114
1960-1969	30	442	165	361	181	98	7	249	1503	18		40	21	30	2	74	185		1688
1970-1974	24	397	198	224	227	112	30	332	1520	30	2	47	80	73	10	180	422		1942
TOTAL 1920-1974	31	1166	399	1022	495	246	39	673	4040	59	2	115	111	118	12	287	704		4744
PER 1000 TOTAL		12.2	8.8	14.4	7.7	4.4	2.2	9.9	9.9	11.1	7.7	11.1	8.8	7.7	5.5	15.5	10.0		9.9
NC, U OF-CHAPEL HILL																			
1920-1959	31	377	2	119	265	422	3	104	1292	15		23	41	78		13	170	1	1463
1960-1969	34	303	9	182	284	359	54	142	1336	12		43	44	77	1	34	211		1547
1970-1974	30	209	11	248	328	332	53	105	1286	13	1	62	67	161	2	40	346		1632
TOTAL 1920-1974	32	889	22	549	877	1113	110	351	3914	40	1	128	152	316	3	87	727	1	4642
PER 1000 TOTAL		9.9	0.0	7.7	13.3	19.9	6.6	5.5	9.9	7.7	3.3	12.2	11.1	19.9	1.1	4.4	11.1	1.1	9.9
MISSOURI,U-COLUMBIA																			
1920-1959	35	228	47	285	78	80	28	389	1135	11		24	4	28	6	35	108		1243
1960-1969	35	193	86	327	202	160	39	365	1373	4		12	16	41	6	29	108		1481
1970-1974	29	128	149	339	238	169	97	343	1463	7	2	26	41	39	15	41	171	1	1635
TOTAL 1920-1974	33	549	282	951	518	409	164	1097	3971	22	2	62	61	108	27	105	387	1	4359
PER 1000 TOTAL		5.5	6.6	13.3	7.7	7.7	9.9	15.5	9.9	4.4	7.7	5.5	4.4	6.6	11.1	5.5	5.5	1.1	8.8
CATHOLIC U AMER/DC																			
1920-1959	24	191	7	56	227	334	572	119	1507	52		44	91	291	18	94	591		2098
1960-1969	45	178	59	62	118	136	195	119	868	21		34	50	95	35	93	329		1197
1970-1974	62	142	90	26	97	133	95	109	692	10	1	19	41	53	25	64	213	1	906
TOTAL 1920-1974	34	511	156	144	442	603	862	347	3067	83	1	97	182	439	78	251	1133	1	4201
PER 1000 TOTAL		5.5	3.3	2.2	6.6	10.0	49.9	5.5	7.7	15.5	3.3	9.9	14.4	26.6	34.4	13.3	17.7	1.1	8.8

APPENDIX E Continued

		Men								Women									
Institution	Rank	Physical Sciences	Engineering	Life Sciences	Behavioral Sciences	Humanities	Professions	Education	Total	Physical Sciences	Engineering	Life Sciences	Behavioral Sciences	Humanities	Professions	Education	Total	Unknown Field	Grand Total
RUTGERS UNIV/NJ																			
1920-1959	39	187	38	520	21	15		99	880	5	2	35	1			17	60		940
1960-1969	33	336	92	477	108	96	18	208	1338	15	1	70	28	23	6	67	210		1548
1970-1974	35	182	111	280	166	137	11	238	1128	22	1	65	49	62	5	99	303	1	1432
TOTAL 1920-1974	35	705	241	1277	295	248	29	545	3346	42	4	170	78	85	11	183	573	1	3920
PER 1000 TOTAL		7.7	5.5	18.8	4.4	4.4	1.1	7.7	8.8	7.7	15.5	16.6	6.6	5.5	4.4	9.9	8.8	1.1	8.8
CASE WESTRN RSRVE/OH																			
1920-1959	40	303	68	106	122	136	3	72	810	9		21	26	46	4	17	123		933
1960-1969	31	434	350	101	166	147	43	181	1434	19		29	54	43	20	45	213		1647
1970-1974	41	318	269	73	137	131	52	62	1055	21	1	29	54	88	17	46	258		1313
TOTAL 1920-1974	36	1055	687	280	425	414	98	315	3299	49	1	79	134	177	41	108	594		3893
PER 1000 TOTAL		11.1	15.5	4.4	6.6	7.7	5.5	4.4	7.7	9.9	3.3	7.7	10.0	10.0	18.8	5.5	9.9		8.8
FLORIDA, UNIV OF																			
1920-1959	50	169	16	160	78	66	4	111	605	8		6	4	15		16	49		654
1960-1969	32	282	252	270	231	127	41	269	1473	16	1	25	22	31		72	167		1640
1970-1974	32	202	222	243	187	71	52	277	1254	10	2	21	45	28	9	96	211		1465
TOTAL 1920-1974	37	653	490	673	496	264	97	657	3332	34	3	52	71	74	9	184	427		3759
PER 1000 TOTAL		6.6	10.0	9.9	7.7	4.4	5.5	9.9	7.7	6.6	11.1	5.5	5.5	4.4	4.4	9.9	6.6		7.7
COLORADO,U-BOULDER																			
1920-1959	45	245	18	115	77	80		217	752	14		27	8	25		31	105		857
1960-1969	36	447	129	107	244	168	37	174	1306	19		23	35	45	2	44	168		1474
1970-1974	38	240	116	97	281	158	78	145	1116	11	1	30	74	72	7	61	256		1372
TOTAL 1920-1974	38	932	263	319	602	406	115	536	3174	44	1	80	117	142	9	136	529		3703
PER 1000 TOTAL		9.9	5.5	4.4	9.9	7.7	6.6	7.7	7.7	8.8	3.3	7.7	9.9	8.8	4.4	7.7	8.8		7.7
SYRACUSE UNIV/NY																			
1920-1959	44	183	36	105	271	79	4	136	814	8		10	16	12	1	31	78		892
1960-1969	42	208	153	74	352	127	21	259	1194	12	1	7	34	28	8	40	130		1324
1970-1974	36	164	109	72	343	115	59	322	1192	14	1	15	73	38	8	81	230	1	1423
TOTAL 1920-1974	39	555	298	251	966	321	84	717	3200	34	2	32	123	78	17	152	438	1	3639
PER 1000 TOTAL		5.5	6.6	3.3	14.4	5.5	4.4	10.0	7.7	6.6	7.7	3.3	9.9	4.4	7.7	8.8	6.6	1.1	7.7
DUKE UNIVERSITY/NC																			
1920-1959	36	297		224	211	190	75	40	1037	15		41	28	43	1	5	133		1170
1960-1969	40	237	40	248	233	238	104	105	1205	10		44	22	28	3	16	123	6	1334
1970-1974	53	134	65	183	183	207	37	90	899	20		48	48	49	1	31	197	1	1097
TOTAL 1920-1974	40	668	105	655	627	635	216	235	3141	45		133	98	120	5	52	453	7	3601
PER 1000 TOTAL		7.7	2.2	9.9	9.9	11.1	12.2	3.3	7.7	8.8		12.2	7.7	7.7	2.2	2.2	6.6	10.0	7.7
BOSTON UNIVERSITY/MA																			
1920-1959	38	80		76	119	208	234	201	918	8		16	16	53	11	80	184		1102
1960-1969	43	101		80	169	207	190	271	1018	10		50	62	46	9	114	291		1309
1970-1974	50	72		73	107	120	79	320	771	16		45	83	47	2	180	373	1	1145
TOTAL 1920-1974	41	253		229	395	535	503	792	2707	34		111	161	146	22	374	848	1	3556
PER 1000 TOTAL		2.2		3.3	6.6	9.9	28.8	11.1	6.6	6.6		10.0	12.2	8.8	9.9	20.0	12.2	1.1	7.7
KANSAS, UNIV OF																			
1920-1959	46	259	8	167	116	42		145	738	11		25	15	9		9	69		807
1960-1969	40	348	98	222	165	138	3	246	1222	14	1	24	17	26		30	112		1334
1970-1974	40	191	91	190	228	156	38	203	1097	13		32	84	60	13	51	253		1350
TOTAL 1920-1974	42	798	197	579	509	336	41	594	3057	38	1	81	116	95	13	90	434		3491
PER 1000 TOTAL		8.8	4.4	8.8	7.7	6.6	2.2	8.8	7.7	7.7	3.3	7.7	9.9	5.5	5.5	4.4	6.6		7.7
FLORIDA STATE UNIV																			
1920-1959	81	52		24	54	36	4	48	218			3	4	3	9	8	27		245
1960-1969	39	246		71	224	163	19	394	1121	12		3	32	41	41	99	229		1350
1970-1974	28	249	4	70	250	184	81	520	1359	10		11	53	86	25	170	355		1714
TOTAL 1920-1974	43	547	4	165	528	383	104	962	2698	22		17	89	130	75	277	611		3309
PER 1000 TOTAL		5.5	0.0	2.2	8.8	6.6	5.5	14.4	6.6	4.4		1.1	7.7	7.7	33.3	14.4	9.9		6.6
NEBRASKA, U-LINCOLN																			
1920-1959	43	179		189	174	78	6	204	830	5		7	22	14		16	64		894
1960-1969	46	156	21	207	134	95	23	440	1076	7		11	13	18	2	46	97		1173
1970-1974	47	159	32	221	149	126	48	307	1042	7	2	22	23	42	1	54	151		1193
TOTAL 1920-1974	44	494	53	617	457	299	77	951	2948	19	2	40	58	74	3	116	312		3260
PER 1000 TOTAL		5.5	1.1	8.8	6.6	5.5	4.4	13.3	7.7	3.3	7.7	3.3	4.4	4.4	1.1	6.6	4.4		6.6
OREGON, UNIV OF																			
1920-1959	70	62		28	36	21		171	318	3		10	5	3		26	47		365
1960-1969	38	185		97	278	126	44	489	1219	10		20	26	20	1	63	140		1359
1970-1974	31	140		70	324	178	77	450	1239	6		18	83	66	3	104	281		1520
TOTAL 1920-1974	45	387		195	638	325	121	1110	2776	19		48	114	89	4	193	468		3244
PER 1000 TOTAL		4.4		2.2	9.9	5.5	6.6	16.6	6.6	3.3		4.4	8.8	5.5	1.1	10.0	7.7		6.6
OKLAHOMA, U OF																			
1920-1959	60	103	7	65	42	43		150	410	2		11	5	15		34	67		477
1960-1969	44	163	170	184	168	144	21	305	1155	4		22	18	18	3	71	136		1291
1970-1974	46	127	116	216	195	84	69	215	1023	4	3	37	32	36	5	78	195		1218
TOTAL 1920-1974	46	393	293	465	405	271	90	670	2588	10	3	70	55	69	8	183	398		2986
PER 1000 TOTAL		4.4	6.6	6.6	6.6	4.4	5.5	9.9	6.6	1.1	11.1	6.6	4.4	4.4	3.3	9.9	6.6		6.6
ROCHESTER,UNIV OF/NY																			
1920-1959	41	333	3	240	78	171			825	13		49	15	26			103		928
1960-1969	53	284	72	143	113	184		61	858	24		34	12	37		13	120		978
1970-1974	58	237	68	133	142	156	12	86	834	15	1	32	32	57		38	175		1009
TOTAL 1920-1974	47	854	143	516	333	511	12	147	2517	52	1	115	59	120		51	398		2915
PER 1000 TOTAL		9.9	3.3	7.7	5.5	9.9	0.0	2.2	6.6	9.9	3.3	11.1	4.4	7.7		2.2	6.6		6.6
VIRGINIA, UNIV OF																			
1920-1959	42	370	1	81	146	185	1	64	848	7		18	8	27		7	67		915
1960-1969	57	238	76	32	159	155	7	171	838	13		15	8	16		34	86		924
1970-1974	55	176	132	60	92	201	20	225	906	10	1	17	22	39	2	65	156	1	1063
TOTAL 1920-1974	48	784	209	173	397	541	28	460	2592	30	1	50	38	82	2	106	309	1	2902
PER 1000 TOTAL		8.8	4.4	2.2	6.6	9.9	1.1	6.6	6.6	5.5	3.3	4.4	3.3	5.5	0.0	5.5	4.4	1.1	6.6
LA ST UNIV & A&M C																			
1920-1959	52	146	22	138	95	90	18	63	572	4		12	6	31	2	9	64		636
1960-1969	48	257	53	278	173	126	66	98	1051	7	1	11	16	41	5	23	104		1155
1970-1974	56	189	68	201	137	134	64	122	915	20		24	28	41	10	24	147		1062
TOTAL 1920-1974	49	592	143	617	405	350	148	283	2538	31	1	47	50	113	17	56	315		2853
PER 1000 TOTAL		6.6	3.3	8.8	6.6	6.6	8.8	4.4	6.6	5.5	3.3	4.4	3.3	6.6	7.7	3.3	4.4		5.5
CAL INST TECHNOLOGY																			
1920-1959	33	795	350	136					1281	3		1					4	1	1286
1960-1969	54	510	353	73	3				940	11	4	5					20		960
1970-1974	88	314	167	67					551	13	4	12	2				31		582
TOTAL 1920-1974	50	1619	870	276	3				2772	27	8	18	2				55	1	2828
PER 1000 TOTAL		17.7	19.9	3.3	0.0				6.6	5.5	30.0	1.1	0.0				0.0	1.1	5.5
UTAH, UNIV OF																			
1920-1959	63	147	66	74	71	34		53	445	2		3	4	2		3	14		459
1960-1969	50	268	181	152	143	69	12	189	1015	9		10	23	10		33	85		1100
1970-1974	43	180	149	131	181	108	39	323	1111	5		12	38	27	1	66	149		1260
TOTAL 1920-1974	51	595	396	357	395	211	51	565	2571	16		25	65	39	1	102	248		2819
PER 1000 TOTAL		6.6	8.8	5.5	6.6	3.3	2.2	8.8	6.6	3.3		2.2	5.5	2.2	0.0	5.5	3.3		5.5

APPENDIX E Continued

Institution	Rank	Men: Physical Sciences	Men: Engineering	Men: Life Sciences	Men: Behavioral Sciences	Men: Humanities	Men: Professions	Men: Education	Men: Total	Women: Physical Sciences	Women: Engineering	Women: Life Sciences	Women: Behavioral Sciences	Women: Humanities	Women: Professions	Women: Education	Women: Total	Unknown Field	Grand Total
TENN, U-KNOXVILLE																			
1920-1959	66	128	17	65	61	10		89	371	5		10	4	5		5	29		400
1960-1969	51	240	109	213	139	38	1	234	974	6		27	3	17	7	51	112		1086
1970-1974	42	167	138	225	227	58	8	274	1097	13		34	21	29	6	86	189		1286
TOTAL 1920-1974	52	535	264	503	427	106	9	597	2442	24		71	28	51	13	142	330		2772
PER 1000 TOTAL		5.5	5.5	7.7	6.6	1.1	0.0	8.8	5.5	4.4		6.6	2.2	3.3	5.5	7.7	5.5		5.5
SUNY AT BUFFALO																			
1920-1959	71	80		22	38	9	4	126	279	3		5	3	1		28	40		319
1960-1969	62	166	42	131	133	62	9	196	739	4		20	23	11		31	89		828
1970-1974	33	172	110	210	196	187	35	342	1252	12	2	39	42	39	2	73	209	1	1462
TOTAL 1920-1974	53	418	152	363	367	258	48	664	2270	19	2	64	68	51	2	132	338	1	2609
PER 1000 TOTAL		4.4	3.3	5.5	5.5	4.4	2.2	9.9	5.5	3.3	7.7	6.6	5.5	3.3	0.0	7.7	5.5	1.1	5.5
FORDHAM UNIV/NY																			
1920-1959	34	130		98	173	252	2	105	761	18		37	85	230		113	484		1245
1960-1969	71	82		51	85	148	4	72	442	22		21	59	78	1	74	255		697
1970-1974	80	42		26	100	146	43	95	452	9		13	43	51	11	73	200	2	654
TOTAL 1920-1974	54	254		175	358	546	49	272	1655	49		71	187	359	12	260	939	2	2596
PER 1000 TOTAL		2.2		2.2	5.5	9.9	2.2	4.4	3.3	9.9		6.6	14.4	21.1	5.5	13.3	14.4	3.3	5.5
WAYNE STATE UNIV/MI																			
1920-1959	74	110		27	4	4		120	265	5		6	1			27	39		304
1960-1969	49	225	24	76	130	129	5	341	931	17	1	30	41	28		98	215		1146
1970-1974	52	161	29	82	156	69	22	389	908	15		24	46	28	6	106	225	1	1134
TCTAL 1920-1974	55	496	53	185	290	202	27	850	2104	37	1	60	88	56	6	231	479	1	2584
PER 1000 TOTAL		5.5	1.1	2.2	4.4	3.3	1.1	12.2	5.5	6.6	3.3	5.5	6.6	3.3	2.2	12.2	7.7	1.1	5.5
OKLAHOMA STATE UNIV																			
1920-1959	80	49	19	03	9			73	233			1	1			13	15		248
1960-1969	47	152	284	277	98			274	1085	3	1	9	4			55	72		1157
1970-1974	48	92	191	224	99	26	13	365	1010	2	1	11	16	3		115	148		1158
TOTAL 1920-1974	56	293	494	584	206	26	13	712	2328	5	2	21	21	3		183	235		2563
PER 1000 TOTAL		3.3	10.0	8.8	3.3	0.0	0.0	10.0	5.5	0.0	7.7	2.2	1.1	0.0		9.9	3.3		5.5
TEXAS A&M UNIVERSITY																			
1920-1959	73	57	41	195	12				305										305
1960-1969	52	237	229	376	39			93	975	5		3				3	11		986
1970-1974	44	244	210	393	88	10	11	218	1177	15		12	5	10		33	75		1252
TOTAL 1920-1974	57	538	480	964	139	10	11	311	2457	20		15	5	10		36	86		2543
PER 1000 TOTAL		5.5	10.0	13.3	2.2	0.0	0.0	4.4	5.5	3.3		1.1	0.0	0.0		1.1	1.1		5.5
WASHINGTON UNIV/MO																			
1920-1959	48	217	47	179	115	45	1	57	661	4		49	21	12	1	10	98		759
1960-1969	65	183	136	62	155	68	49	50	703	8	1	24	40	24	8	10	115		818
1970-1974	65	138	149	70	148	100	48	27	681	8	1	36	53	40	10	14	162	1	844
TOTAL 1920-1974	58	538	332	311	418	213	98	134	2045	20	2	109	114	76	19	34	375	1	2421
PER 1000 TOTAL		5.5	7.7	4.4	6.6	3.3	5.5	1.1	4.4	3.3	7.7	10.0	8.8	4.4	8.8	1.1	5.5	1.1	5.5
BROWN UNIVERSITY/RI																			
1920-1959	47	408	6	83	70	128	13	4	712	15		28	9	26	1	1	80		792
1960-1969	64	317	88	56	124	139	6		730	10		27	18	33	1		89		819
1970-1974	69	262	72	32	120	157	8		651	18		15	23	74			130	1	782
TOTAL 1920-1974	59	987	166	171	314	424	27	4	2093	43		70	50	133	2	1	299	1	2393
PER 1000 TOTAL		10.0	3.3	2.2	4.4	7.7	1.1	0.0	5.5	8.8		6.6	3.3	8.8	0.0	0.0	4.4	1.1	4.4
OREGON STATE UNIV																			
1920-1959	62	130	15	234	5			62	446	2		7			1	15	25		471
1960-1969	56	255	68	447	33		2	70	880	15		22	1		3	8	49		929
1970-1974	60	211	76	417	24	1	2	170	906	11		23	4	1	1	28	68	2	976
TOTAL 1920-1974	60	596	159	1098	62	1	4	302	2232	28		52	5	1	5	51	142	2	2376
PER 1000 TOTAL		6.6	3.3	15.5	0.0	0.0	0.0	4.4	5.5	5.5		5.5	0.0	0.0	2.2	2.2	2.2	3.3	4.4
GEORGIA, UNIV OF																			
1920-1959	113	12		12	1	4		30	59			1				5	6		65
1960-1969	67	81		201	81	87	8	188	646	2		17	10	14		83	126	1	773
1970-1974	34	136		268	223	126	58	394	1205	7		31	50	29	1	127	245		1450
TOTAL 1920-1974	61	229		481	305	217	66	612	1910	9		49	60	43	1	215	377	1	2288
PER 1000 TOTAL		2.2		6.6	4.4	3.3	3.3	8.8	4.4	1.1		4.4	4.4	2.2	0.0	11.1	5.5	1.1	4.4
ARIZONA, UNIV OF																			
1920-1959	99	48	1	18	11	4		15	97			3	1			2	6		103
1960-1969	59	242	125	189	121	48		110	835	4		12	15	11		32	74		909
1970-1974	49	235	119	227	159	81	22	155	999	11	2	19	40	27		58	157		1156
TOTAL 1920-1974	62	525	245	434	291	133	22	280	1931	15	2	34	56	38		92	237		2168
PER 1000 TOTAL		5.5	5.5	6.6	4.4	2.2	1.1	4.4	4.4	2.2	7.7	3.3	4.4	2.2		4.4	3.3		4.4
CALIF, U-DAVIS																			
1920-1959	84	23		197					220	1		6					7		227
1960-1969	58	141	62	617	11	25		1	858	5	1	45	3	6			60		918
1970-1974	58	159	109	532	49	61			912	7	2	56	14	18			97		1009
TOTAL 1920-1974	63	323	171	1346	60	86		1	1990	13	3	107	17	24			164		2154
PER 1000 TOTAL		3.3	3.3	19.9	0.0	1.1		0.0	4.4	2.2	11.1	10.0	1.1	1.1			2.2		4.4
MASS, U OF-AMHERST																			
1920-1959	88	36		145	16				197	3		6					10		207
1960-1969	85	118	13	112	137	21		34	435	18		20	25	5		3	71		506
1970-1974	37	173	109	163	155	124	33	400	1158	14	2	24	38	40		117	236		1394
TOTAL 1920-1974	64	327	122	420	308	145	33	434	1790	35	2	50	63	45		120	317		2107
PER 1000 TOTAL		3.3	2.2	5.5	4.4	2.2	1.1	6.6	4.4	6.6	7.7	4.4	4.4	2.2		6.6	4.4		4.4
NC STATE U-RALEIGH																			
1920-1959	86	22	29	131	27				209	1		1	2				4		213
1960-1969	60	106	209	371	102			20	810	1	1	11	2			6	21		831
1970-1974	57	106	252	324	115			159	956	6	5	35	10			27	83		1039
TOTAL 1920-1974	65	234	490	826	244			179	1975	8	6	47	14			33	108		2083
PER 1000 TOTAL		2.2	10.0	11.1	3.3			2.2	4.4	1.1	23.3	4.4	1.1			1.1	1.1		4.4
NORTHERN COLORADO,U																			
1920-1959	75							248	248							43	43		291
1960-1969	55				2			845	847							105	105		952
1970-1974	68	27		7	7	1	5	617	664	3		1	1	1	1	125	132		796
TOTAL 1920-1974	66	27		7	9	1	5	1710	1759	3		1	1	1	1	273	280		2039
PER 1000 TOTAL		0.0		0.0	0.0	0.0	0.0	24.4	4.4	0.0		0.0	0.0	0.0	0.0	14.4	4.4		4.4
TEMPLE UNIVERSITY/PA																			
1920-1959	57	59		14	35	3	136	206	453	5		1	4			39	49	1	503
1960-1969	76	99		51	82	12	46	266	556	2		10	17	2		55	86		642
1970-1974	64	79		72	107	60	35	350	703	7		15	20	21	4	92	159		862
TOTAL 1920-1974	67	237		137	224	75	217	822	1712	14		26	41	23	4	186	294	1	2007
PER 1000 TOTAL		2.2		1.1	3.3	1.1	12.2	11.1	4.4	2.2		2.2	3.3	1.1	1.1	9.9	4.4	1.1	4.4
CINCINNATI, U OF/OH																			
1920-1959	51	240	46	105	35	65		76	568	11	1	21	3	13		19	69		637
1960-1969	77	208	80	98	70	60	1	41	558	18		9	10	15		18	70		628
1970-1974	74	112	106	97	102	80	29	77	603	13	2	15	28	34		34	126		729
TOTAL 1920-1974	68	560	232	300	207	205	30	194	1729	42	3	45	41	62		71	265		1994
PER 1000 TOTAL		5.5	5.5	4.4	3.3	3.3	1.1	2.2	4.4	7.7	11.1	4.4	3.3	3.3		3.3	4.4		4.4

APPENDIX E Continued

Institution	Rank	Men: Physical Sciences	Men: Engineering	Men: Life Sciences	Men: Behavioral Sciences	Men: Humanities	Men: Professions	Men: Education	Men: Total	Women: Physical Sciences	Women: Engineering	Women: Life Sciences	Women: Behavioral Sciences	Women: Humanities	Women: Professions	Women: Education	Women: Total	Unknown Field	Grand Total
CARNEGIE-MELLON U/PA																			
1920-1959	56	273	239		16		4		532	10			1				11		543
1960-1969	61	295	412		50	15	37		810	16	2			1			19		829
1970-1974	84	181	260	2	61	51	22	3	580	8	1		2	23		3	37	1	618
TOTAL 1920-1974	69	749	911	2	127	66	63	3	1922	34	3		3	24		3	67	1	1990
PER 1000 TOTAL		7.7	20.0	0.0	1.1	1.1	3.3	0.0	4.4	6.6	11.1		0.0	1.1		0.0	1.1	1.1	4.4
ST LOUIS UNIV/MO																			
1920-1959	54	141		102	55	101	11	14	424	26		11	18	57	1	23	136		560
1960-1969	75	115		63	76	111	14	64	443	16		18	32	83		55	204		647
1970-1974	73	95		51	91	134	32	175	579	9		19	40	56	1	65	190		769
TOTAL 1920-1974	70	351		216	222	346	57	253	1446	51		48	90	196	2	143	530		1976
PER 1000 TOTAL		3.3		3.3	3.3	6.6	3.3	3.3	3.3	9.9		4.4	7.7	11.1	0.0	7.7	8.8		4.4
CONNECTICUT, UNIV OF																			
1920-1959	82	63		45	39		1	65	213	4		4	10			8	26		239
1960-1969	62	121	79	132	116	70		218	736	4		20	24	12	1	31	92		828
1970-1974	63	110	93	114	109	87	3	211	727	9	1	24	28	31	1	56	150		877
TOTAL 1920-1974	71	294	172	291	264	157	4	494	1676	17	1	48	62	43	2	95	268		1944
PER 1000 TOTAL		3.3	3.3	4.4	4.4	2.2	0.0	7.7	4.4	3.3	3.3	4.4	4.4	2.2	0.0	5.5	4.4		4.4
NOTRE DAME, U OF/IN																			
1920-1959	53	346	24	36	29	62	1	10	508	27		6	3	17		2	55		563
1960-1969	71	268	85	41	50	129		22	595	32		16	9	37		8	102		697
1970-1974	78	176	108	50	102	115	6	34	591	9		14	15	33	4	8	83		674
TOTAL 1920-1974	72	790	217	127	181	306	7	66	1694	68		36	27	87	4	18	240		1934
PER 1000 TOTAL		8.8	4.4	1.1	2.2	5.5	0.0	1.1	4.4	12.2		3.3	2.2	5.5	1.1	1.1	3.3		4.4
WASHINGTON STATE U																			
1920-1959	68	68		202	37	6		47	360			8	3			4	15		375
1960-1969	68	146	9	241	103	27		190	716	4		9	11	6	1	13	44		760
1970-1974	72	111	31	223	185	28	1	132	711	1		15	20	5		19	60		771
TOTAL 1920-1974	73	325	40	666	325	61	1	369	1787	5		32	34	11	1	36	119		1906
PER 1000 TOTAL		3.3	0.0	9.9	4.4	1.1	0.0	5.5	4.4	0.0		3.3	2.2	0.0	0.0	1.1	1.1		3.3
VANDERBILT UNIV/TN																			
1920-1959	58	116		54	79	165	30		444	2		16	1	29	1		49		493
1960-1969	69	169	37	80	140	141	74		641	3		19	21	23	1		67	1	709
1970-1974	82	90	57	94	120	161	35		557	7	1	21	15	40	1		85		642
TOTAL 1920-1974	74	375	94	228	339	467	139		1642	12	1	56	37	92	3		201	1	1844
PER 1000 TOTAL		3.3	2.2	3.3	5.5	8.8	8.8		3.3	2.2	3.3	5.5	2.2	5.5	1.1		3.3	1.1	3.3
GEO WASHINGTON U/DC																			
1920-1959	59	66	3	144	63	32	19	71	398	2		40	15	4	2	26	89		487
1960-1969	83	39	29	90	82	26	63	106	435	4		17	26	6	1	27	81		516
1970-1974	71	61	42	53	119	40	139	144	598	7		33	44	34	1	55	174		772
TOTAL 1920-1974	75	166	74	287	264	98	221	321	1431	13		90	85	44	4	108	344		1775
PER 1000 TOTAL		1.1	1.1	4.4	4.4	1.1	12.2	4.4	3.3	2.2		8.8	6.6	2.2	1.1	5.5	5.5		3.3
KENTUCKY, UNIV OF																			
1920-1959	67	76	5	8	114	42		94	340	4		1	12	11		8	36		376
1960-1969	74	110	3	116	175	64		111	579	11		12	21	16		17	77		656
1970-1974	75	106	52	151	125	70	15	88	607	8		23	13	35		40	119	1	727
TOTAL 1920-1974	76	292	60	275	414	176	15	293	1526	23		36	46	62		65	232	1	1759
PER 1000 TOTAL		3.3	1.1	3.3	6.6	3.3	0.0	4.4	3.3	4.4		3.3	3.3	3.3		3.3	3.3	1.1	3.3
TULANE U OF LA																			
1920-1959	78	76		72	30	44			222	4		14	4	15			37		259
1960-1969	65	121	50	197	111	205	10		694	18		37	12	57			124		818
1970-1974	83	80	38	120	92	134	25		489	8		42	28	52	7	1	138	1	628
TOTAL 1920-1974	77	277	88	389	233	383	35		1405	30		93	44	124	7	1	299	1	1705
PER 1000 TOTAL		2.2	1.1	5.5	3.3	6.6	2.2		3.3	5.5		8.8	3.3	7.7	3.3	0.0	4.4	1.1	3.3
POLYTECHNIC INST NY																			
1920-1959	55	346	186	1					533	12							12		545
1960-1969	78	303	297						600	15	3						18		618
1970-1974	113	176	236		2				414	11	1						12	1	427
TOTAL 1920-1974	78	825	719	1	2				1547	38	4						42	1	1590
PER 1000 TOTAL		8.8	15.5	0.0	0.0				3.3	7.7	15.5						0.0	1.1	3.3
ALABAMA, UNIVER OF																			
1920-1959	102	22		15	4	8	19	24	92	1		3		1	1	2	8		100
1960-1969	73	84	49	46	84	40	82	185	570	7	2	10	17	12	3	63	114		684
1970-1974	70	78	43	17	72	31	58	298	597	10		3	16	22	4	126	181		778
TOTAL 1920-1974	79	184	92	78	160	79	159	507	1259	18	2	16	33	35	8	191	303		1562
PER 1000 TOTAL		1.1	2.2	1.1	2.2	1.1	9.9	7.7	3.3	3.3	7.7	1.1	2.2	2.2	3.3	10.0	4.4		3.3
KANSAS STATE UNIV																			
1920-1959	85	76	1	139					216	1		8					9		225
1960-1969	79	145	68	291	57	10			572	7		15	4	1	7		34		606
1970-1974	76	118	77	249	72	30		96	642	8	1	28	5	6	5	22	75		717
TOTAL 1920-1974	80	339	146	679	129	40		96	1430	16	1	51	9	7	12	22	118		1548
PER 1000 TOTAL		3.3	3.3	9.9	2.2	0.0		1.1	3.3	3.3	3.3	4.4	0.0	0.0	5.5	1.1	1.1		3.3
GEO PEABODY COLL/TN																			
1920-1959	49	25		5	66	74	1	468	640	4			11	18	1	43	77		717
1960-1969	93	9			56	49		263	377				15	4		55	74	1	452
1970-1974	122	24			68	25		157	274	2			22	10		45	79		353
TOTAL 1920-1974	81	58		5	190	148	1	888	1291	6			48	32	1	143	230	1	1522
PER 1000 TOTAL		0.0		0.0	2.2	2.2	0.0	12.2	3.3	1.1			3.3	1.1	0.0	7.7	3.3	1.1	3.3
ARIZONA STATE UNIV																			
1920-1959	136							14	14							1	1		15
1960-1969	83	76	57	25	48	10	10	231	457	6		4	4	3	1	41	59		516
1970-1974	61	81	94	39	80	14	71	380	759	4		13	25	14	1	117	174		933
TOTAL 1920-1974	82	157	151	64	128	24	81	625	1230	10		17	29	17	2	159	234		1464
PER 1000 TOTAL		1.1	3.3	0.0	1.1	0.0	4.4	9.9	2.2	1.1		1.1	2.2	1.1	0.0	8.8	3.3		3.3
RENSSELAER POLY I/NY																			
1920-1959	77	141	122						263	2							2		265
1960-1969	70	312	347	5	2		10		678	18	3	3					24		702
1970-1974	103	173	226	26	12	2	12		452	10	2	2	1	3			18		470
TOTAL 1920-1974	83	626	695	31	14	2	22		1393	30	5	5	1	3			44		1437
PER 1000 TOTAL		6.6	15.5	0.0	0.0	0.0	1.1		3.3	5.5	19.9	0.0	0.0	0.0			0.0		2.2
DENVER, UNIV OF/CO																			
1920-1959	65				121	113	1	138	373				15	20	1	20	56		429
1960-1969	82	11	44		82	160	2	151	450	2			20	32		29	83		533
1970-1974	104	24	50		91	70	44	95	374	2			33	25	10	23	93		467
TOTAL 1920-1974	84	35	94		294	343	47	384	1197	4			68	77	11	72	232		1429
PER 1000 TOTAL		0.0	2.2		4.4	6.6	2.2	5.5	2.2	0.0			5.5	4.4	4.4	3.3	3.3		2.2
AMERICAN UNIV/DC																			
1920-1959	69	23	4	9	218	40	28	13	341	1		1	15	7	2	5	32		373
1960-1969	87	9			314	39	37	47	446				35	4		18	57		503
1970-1974	94	61	1	2	176	26	61	100	427	11			33	8	3	38	93		520
TOTAL 1920-1974	85	93	5	11	708	105	126	160	1214	12		1	83	19	5	61	182		1396
PER 1000 TOTAL		1.1	0.0	0.0	10.0	1.1	7.7	2.2	2.2	2.2		0.0	6.6	1.1	2.2	3.3	2.2		2.2

APPENDIX E Continued

Institution	Rank	Men								Women									
		Physical Sciences	Engineering	Life Sciences	Behavioral Sciences	Humanities	Professions	Education	Total	Physical Sciences	Engineering	Life Sciences	Behavioral Sciences	Humanities	Professions	Education	Total	Unknown Field	Grand Total
NEW MEXICO, UNIV OF																			
1920-1959	97	35		9	10	38			92	2		1	1	17			21		113
1960-1969	91	108	75	15	27	96		86	408	6			2	21		22	51		459
1970-1974	66	111	87	33	72	151		204	658	6		8	24	52		74	164		822
TOTAL 1920-1974	86	254	162	57	109	285		290	1158	14		9	27	90		96	236		1394
PER 1000 TOTAL		2.2	3.3	0.0	1.1	5.5		4.4	2.2	2.2		0.0	2.2	5.5		5.5	3.3		2.2
RICE UNIVERSITY/TX																			
1920-1959	79	200	6	31	1	8			246	2		3		6			11		257
1960-1969	81	267	145	30	12	55	1		510	3	1	6	1	23			34		544
1970-1974	91	212	160	25	25	55	1		478	12		7	8	49			76	1	555
TOTAL 1920-1974	87	679	311	86	38	118	2		1234	17	1	16	9	78			121	1	1356
PER 1000 TOTAL		7.7	6.6	1.1	0.0	2.2	0.0		2.2	3.3	3.3	1.1	0.0	4.4			1.1	1.1	2.2
GEORGETOWN UNIV/DC																			
1920-1959	61	113		83	107	114	17	1	439	13		10	4	9			36		475
1960-1969	94	79		70	106	122	2		379	12		17	7	34			70		449
1970-1974	115	73		54	67	128	1		323	11		26	11	45			93		416
TOTAL 1920-1974	88	265		207	280	364	20	1	1141	36		53	22	88			199		1340
PER 1000 TOTAL		2.2		2.2	4.4	6.6	1.1	0.0	2.2	6.6		5.5	1.1	5.5			3.3		2.2
SOUTHERN ILL UNIV																			
1920-1959	169					1			1										1
1960-1969	92	15		46	122	83	13	125	404			2	15	10	4	18	49		453
1970-1974	67	49	1	53	203	110	50	239	705	4		8	17	16	8	60	113		818
TOTAL 1920-1974	89	64	1	99	325	194	63	364	1110	4		10	32	26	12	78	162		1272
PER 1000 TOTAL		0.0	0.0	1.1	4.4	3.3	3.3	5.5	2.2	0.0		1.1	2.2	1.1	5.5	4.4	2.2		2.2
HOUSTON, U OF/TX																			
1920-1959	90				54			88	142				6			18	24		166
1960-1969	96	47	46	17	140			112	362	5		1	25			42	73		435
1970-1974	79	108	107	47	104	3	15	147	531	11		8	39	6	1	74	139		670
TOTAL 1920-1974	90	155	153	64	298	3	15	347	1035	16		9	70	6	1	134	236		1271
PER 1000 TOTAL		1.1	3.3	0.0	4.4	0.0	0.0	5.5	2.2	3.3		0.0	5.5	0.0	0.0	7.7	3.3		2.2
ARKANSAS,U-FAYETTVLE																			
1920-1959	106	19		4	4	3		50	80	1				6		3	10		90
1960-1969	80	86	22	35	45	33	62	240	524			3	2	14	1	30	50		574
1970-1974	86	82	45	52	51	24	88	184	526	8		6	7	8	5	31	65		591
TOTAL 1920-1974	91	187	67	91	100	60	150	474	1130	9		9	9	28	6	64	125		1255
PER 1000 TOTAL		2.2	1.1	1.1	1.1	1.1	8.8	6.6	2.2	1.1		0.0	0.0	1.1	2.2	3.3	1.1		2.2
ILLINOIS INST TECH																			
1920-1959	75	132	118	7	24		2		284	1	2	2	2				7		291
1960-1969	86	171	223	22	51		3		470	10	2	9	12		1		34		504
1970-1974	116	92	142	19	99	3	9		364	11	3	6	22	2	1		45		409
TOTAL 1920-1974	92	395	483	48	174	3	14		1118	22	7	17	36	2	2		86		1204
PER 1000 TOTAL		4.4	10.0	0.0	2.2	0.0	0.0		2.2	4.4	27.7	1.1	2.2	0.0	0.0		1.1		2.2
COLORADO STATE UNIV																			
1920-1959	143	1	7	3					11			1					1		12
1960-1969	88	76	107	243	43			8	478			4	3			1	8		486
1970-1974	77	110	131	286	85		1	36	649	3	1	16	12		1	10	43		692
TOTAL 1920-1974	93	187	245	532	128		1	44	1138	3	1	21	15		1	11	52		1190
PER 1000 TOTAL		2.2	5.5	7.7	1.1		0.0	0.0	2.2	0.0	3.3	2.2	1.1		0.0	0.0	0.0		2.2
LEHIGH UNIVERSITY/PA																			
1920-1959	83	122	83	10		7			222	2		4					6		228
1960-1969	88	164	210	17	9	18		45	466	2	1	3		2		12	20		486
1970-1974	106	98	159	18	19	17	1	99	411	8	2	3	3	3	1	34	54		465
TOTAL 1920-1974	94	384	452	45	28	42	1	144	1099	12	3	10	3	5	1	46	80		1179
PER 1000 TOTAL		4.4	10.0	0.0	0.0	0.0	0.0	2.2	2.2	2.2	11.1	1.1	0.0	0.0	0.0	2.2	1.1		2.2
VA POLY INST&STATE U																			
1920-1959	103	39	36	20					95			1					1		96
1960-1969	90	143	154	150	18				466	5		7					12		478
1970-1974	87	118	177	179	48			22	544	8	1	12	4			14	39		583
TOTAL 1920-1974	95	300	367	349	66			22	1105	13	1	20	4			14	52		1157
PER 1000 TOTAL		3.3	8.8	4.4	1.1			0.0	2.2	2.2	3.3	1.1	0.0			0.0	0.0		2.2
WEST VIRGINIA UNIV																			
1920-1959	92	52	22	46		12		5	137	1				2			3		140
1960-1969	101	64	57	107	24	12		63	327	3		15	6	1		17	42		369
1970-1974	89	62	61	123	84	27		150	507			13	16	4		37	70		577
TOTAL 1920-1974	96	178	140	276	108	51		218	971	4		28	22	7		54	115		1086
PER 1000 TOTAL		1.1	3.3	3.3	1.1	0.0		3.3	2.2	0.0		2.2	1.1	0.0		2.2	1.1		2.2
DELAWARE, UNIV OF																			
1920-1959	87	148	56	3					207	2							2		209
1960-1969	98	163	108	48	29	20		6	376	4	1	6	6	2		2	21		397
1970-1974	120	129	72	39	30	41		6	317	7	1	9	10	13		7	47		364
TOTAL 1920-1974	97	440	236	90	59	61		12	900	13	2	15	16	15		9	70		970
PER 1000 TOTAL		4.4	5.5	1.1	0.0	1.1		0.0	2.2	2.2	7.7	1.1	1.1	0.0		0.0	1.1		2.2
CLAREMNT GRAD SCH/CA																			
1920-1959	115			5	25	9	1	11	51				4	4		1	9		60
1960-1969	97			16	174	74	37	47	348			1	25	13	3	10	52		400
1970-1974	98	4		4	211	71	32	97	419			2	33	11	1	25	72		491
TOTAL 1920-1974	98	4		25	410	154	70	155	818			3	62	28	4	36	133		951
PER 1000 TOTAL		0.0		0.0	6.6	2.2	4.4	2.2	1.1			0.0	4.4	1.1	1.1	1.1	2.2		2.2
BRANDEIS UNIV/MA																			
1920-1959	146			1	3	6			10					1			1		11
1960-1969	95	117	1	52	48	83	63		364	11		23	9	28	10		81		445
1970-1974	98	101		44	54	113	50		362	14		11	32	57	15		129		491
TOTAL 1920-1974	99	218	1	97	105	202	113		736	25		34	41	86	25		211		947
PER 1000 TOTAL		2.2	0.0	1.1	1.1	3.3	6.6		1.1	4.4		3.3	3.3	5.5	11.1		3.3		1.1
WYOMING, UNIV OF																			
1920-1959	95	15		15	1			84	115	2						3	5		120
1960-1969	103	55	8	60	5			209	337	1		3	2			18	24		361
1970-1974	113	111	17	90	31	4		146	399	6	1	5	1	1		14	28		427
TOTAL 1920-1974	100	181	25	165	37	4		439	851	9	1	8	3	1		35	57		908
PER 1000 TOTAL		1.1	0.0	2.2	0.0	0.0		6.6	2.2	1.1	3.3	0.0	0.0	0.0		1.1	0.0		1.1

SOURCE: NRC, Commission on Human Resources.

APPENDIX F
STATE AND REGIONAL SUMMARY OF NUMBERS OF PhD's, 1920-1974, BY SEX, FIELD, AND TIME PERIOD, BY GEOGRAPHIC AREAS

		Men								Women									
	Rank	Physical Sciences	Engineering	Life Sciences	Behavioral Sciences	Humanities	Professions	Education	Total	Physical Sciences	Engineering	Life Sciences	Behavioral Sciences	Humanities	Professions	Education	Total	Unknown Field	Grand Total
MAINE																			
1960-1969	49	21	7	19	10	8		1	66	1		3	1				5		71
1970-1974	49	14	14	36	27	20		35	146	1		5	4			1	11		157
TOTAL 1920-1974	49	35	21	55	37	28		36	212	2		8	5			1	16		228
PER 1000 TOTAL		0.4	0.5	0.8	0.6	0.5		0.5	0.5	0.4		0.8	0.4			0.1	0.2		0.5
NEW HAMPSHIRE																			
1920-1959	45	7		10					17	1							1		18
1960-1969	45	119	11	75					205	8		11					19	1	225
1970-1974	46	123	24	85	36	2			270	9		11	7	4			31		301
TOTAL 1920-1974	45	249	35	170	36	2			492	18		22	7	4			51	1	544
PER 1000 TOTAL		2.6	0.8	2.4	0.5	0.0			1.2	3.4		2.1	0.5	0.2			0.8	1.5	1.1
VERMONT																			
1920-1959	43			1		17			18					9			9		27
1960-1969	48	31		35	4	11			81	2		2	1	7			12		93
1970-1974	48	39	11	45	29	13			137	1		12	3	12			28		165
TOTAL 1920-1974	48	70	11	81	33	41			236	3		14	4	28			49		285
PER 1000 TOTAL		0.7	0.2	1.1	0.5	0.7			0.6	0.6		1.3	0.3	1.7			0.7		0.6
MASSACHUSETTS																			
1920-1959	4	3215	1273	987	2120	2381	749	666	11396	141	4	160	262	381	25	159	1137		12533
1960-1969	4	2639	1579	755	1668	1445	769	722	9596	148	9	228	313	347	31	252	1329	7	10932
1970-1974	4	1813	1018	684	1298	1103	478	1078	7478	160	9	239	380	449	44	449	1731	1	9210
TOTAL 1920-1974	4	7667	3870	2426	5086	4929	1996	2466	28470	449	22	627	955	1177	100	860	4197	8	32675
PER 1000 TOTAL		80.5	85.6	34.3	76.9	87.5	114.2	35.8	67.7	84.1	84.9	59.8	75.0	71.7	44.0	46.0	63.3	12.0	67.0
RHODE ISLAND																			
1920-1959	28	408	6	83	70	128	13	4	712	15		28	9	26	1	1	80		792
1960-1969	33	380	106	104	124	139	6		859	12		33	18	33	1		97		956
1970-1974	35	342	123	110	139	158	8		880	26		25	23	74			148	1	1029
TOTAL 1920-1974	32	1130	235	297	333	425	27	4	2451	53		86	50	133	2	1	325	1	2777
PER 1000 TOTAL		11.9	5.2	4.2	5.0	7.5	1.5	0.1	5.8	9.9		8.2	3.9	8.1	0.9	0.1	4.9	1.5	5.7
CONNECTICUT																			
1920-1959	10	1065	241	606	587	1124	473	380	4476	75		165	98	234	15	61	649		5125
1960-1969	15	723	241	363	529	801	247	219	3129	35		102	94	234	9	31	505		3634
1970-1974	21	470	177	292	372	584	87	215	2200	45	3	91	95	253	6	56	549		2749
TOTAL 1920-1974	12	2258	659	1261	1488	2509	807	814	9805	155	3	358	287	721	30	148	1703		11508
PER 1000 TOTAL		23.7	14.6	17.8	22.5	44.5	46.2	11.8	23.3	29.0	11.6	34.1	22.5	43.9	13.2	7.9	25.7		23.6
NEW YORK																			
1920-1959	1	4399	1043	3134	3341	3147	932	5792	21817	333	3	563	719	1049	100	1924	4700	1	26518
1960-1969	1	3480	2018	2018	3064	2520	655	2990	16757	241	14	421	837	821	140	1182	3659	12	20428
1970-1974	1	2782	1648	1740	2810	2173	566	2268	14005	244	14	477	1026	1017	135	1056	3971	23	17999
TOTAL 1920-1974	1	10661	4709	6892	9215	7840	2153	11050	52579	818	31	1461	2582	2887	375	4162	12330	36	64945
PER 1000 TOTAL		112.0	104.2	97.3	139.3	139.2	123.1	160.5	125.0	153.2	119.7	139.3	202.7	175.9	165.1	222.6	186.0	54.1	133.2
NEW JERSEY																			
1920-1959	15	1212	121	630	377	629	98	99	3166	5	2	35	3		1	17	63	1	3230
1960-1969	12	1121	502	547	433	562	188	208	3566	19	2	75	30	32	14	67	239	2	3807
1970-1974	17	647	404	339	372	461	104	257	2588	45	5	71	72	111	7	102	413	3	3004
TOTAL 1920-1974	16	2980	1027	1516	1182	1652	390	564	9320	69	9	181	105	143	22	186	715	6	10041
PER 1000 TOTAL		31.3	22.7	21.4	17.9	29.3	22.3	8.2	22.2	12.9	34.7	17.3	8.2	8.7	9.7	9.9	10.8	9.0	20.6
PENNSYLVANIA																			
1920-1959	5	2039	651	996	1139	1024	222	1391	7463	137	2	189	212	414	25	226	1205	9	8677
1960-1969	6	2041	1488	944	1087	898	235	1246	7964	106	4	187	168	315	80	259	1120	1	9085
1970-1974	5	1343	1098	798	1101	794	329	1549	7031	[illegible]	6	206	279	409	63	490	1592	1	8624
TOTAL 1920-1974	5	5423	3237	2738	3327	2716	786	4186	22458	[illegible]	12	582	659	1138	168	975	3917	11	26386
PER 1000 TOTAL		57.0	71.6	38.7	50.3	48.2	45.0	60.8	53.4	71.0	46.3	55.5	51.7	69.3	73.9	52.2	59.1	16.5	54.1
OHIO																			
1920-1959	8	1774	435	1207	927	657	142	716	5859	60	4	110	125	143	21	167	631	1	6491
1960-1969	8	1469	917	794	769	785	236	1043	6030	66	1	94	164	149	85	224	786		6816
1970-1974	8	1034	788	677	906	832	331	1366	5954	82	4	113	241	267	82	466	1258	1	7213
TOTAL 1920-1974	7	4277	2140	2678	2602	2274	709	3125	17843	208	9	317	530	559	188	857	2675	2	20520
PER 1000 TOTAL		44.9	47.3	37.8	39.3	40.4	40.6	45.4	42.4	39.0	34.7	30.2	41.6	34.1	82.7	45.8	40.4	3.0	42.1
INDIANA																			
1920-1959	11	1606	423	766	697	355	94	667	4609	73	2	66	76	69	63	118	468		5077
1960-1969	7	1390	894	1152	920	840	269	1354	6835	83	2	110	123	173	50	315	856	3	7694
1970-1974	9	909	663	856	781	708	246	1466	5630	37	5	127	143	275	54	381	1024	79	6733
TOTAL 1920-1974	8	3905	1980	2774	2398	1903	609	3487	17074	193	9	303	342	517	167	814	2348	82	19504
PER 1000 TOTAL		41.0	43.8	39.2	36.3	33.8	34.8	50.7	40.6	36.2	34.7	28.9	26.8	31.5	73.5	43.5	35.4	123.3	40.0
ILLINOIS																			
1920-1959	2	4158	763	2218	2511	2066	890	861	13509	267	4	378	359	522	121	216	1879	2	15390
1960-1969	3	2346	1744	1473	1810	1436	617	1167	10608	140	8	221	320	316	58	260	1323	3	11934
1970-1974	3	1543	1102	1119	1689	1290	569	1443	8758	132	12	248	419	470	78	438	1799	16	10573
TOTAL 1920-1974	3	8047	3609	4810	6010	4792	2076	3471	32875	539	24	847	1098	1308	257	914	5001	21	37897
PER 1000 TOTAL		84.5	79.8	67.9	90.9	85.1	118.7	50.4	78.2	101.0	92.7	80.8	86.2	79.7	113.1	48.9	75.4	31.6	77.7
MICHIGAN																			
1920-1959	7	1385	647	1451	853	763	103	673	5876	88	3	166	120	128	7	153	665	5	6546
1960-1969	5	1413	1037	1375	1407	1072	321	1598	8256	74	3	163	213	207	40	329	1031		9287
1970-1974	6	1017	667	1109	1287	831	333	1806	7054	76	4	168	321	300	49	494	1415	2	8471
TOTAL 1920-1974	6	3815	2351	3935	3547	2666	757	4077	21186	238	10	497	654	635	96	976	3111	7	24304
PER 1000 TOTAL		40.1	52.0	55.6	53.6	47.3	43.3	59.2	50.4	44.6	38.6	47.4	51.3	38.7	42.3	52.2	46.9	10.5	49.9
WISCONSIN																			
1920-1959	6	1679	324	2239	955	951	59	354	6563	51	2	227	69	275	10	76	711	1	7275
1960-1969	10	1146	463	1328	626	816	132	528	5057	51	1	142	62	189	45	110	607	1	5665
1970-1974	10	772	389	822	601	790	160	561	4100	36	4	133	138	252	28	171	763	2	4865
TOTAL 1920-1974	9	3597	1176	4389	2182	2557	351	1443	15720	138	7	502	269	716	83	357	2081	4	17805
PER 1000 TOTAL		37.8	26.0	62.0	33.0	45.4	20.1	21.0	37.4	25.[illegible]	27.0	47.9	21.1	43.6	36.5	19.1	31.4	6.0	36.5
MINNESOTA																			
1920-1959	12	762	224	1609	737	360	24	248	3964	34		90	129	78	10	61	402		4366
1960-1969	14	465	376	982	603	413	116	398	3354	23	3	55	97	74	10	89	351		3705
1970-1974	18	259	284	535	493	325	117	372	2385	34	4	62	147	93	17	116	473	2	2860
TOTAL 1920-1974	13	1486	884	3126	1833	1098	257	1018	9703	91	7	207	373	245	37	266	1226	2	10931
PER 1000 TOTAL		15.6	19.6	44.1	27.7	19.5	14.7	14.8	23.1	17.0	27.0	19.7	29.3	14.9	16.3	14.2	18.5	3.0	22.4
IOWA																			
1920-1959	9	1294	318	1460	784	748	134	473	5211	64	1	133	137	130	21	138	624	1	5836
1960-1969	11	913	602	909	535	462	143	490	4055	27	3	55	60	44	25	144	358	4	4417
1970-1974	15	521	355	619	435	334	119	481	2866	26	2	51	62	76	20	119	357		3223
TOTAL 1920-1974	11	2728	1275	2988	1754	1544	396	1444	12132	117	6	239	259	250	66	401	1339	5	13476
PER 1000 TOTAL		28.7	28.2	42.2	26.5	27.4	22.6	21.0	28.9	21.9	23.2	22.8	20.3	15.2	29.0	21.4	20.2	7.5	27.6
MISSOURI																			
1920-1959	18	586	94	566	248	226	40	462	2222	41		84	43	97	8	70	344		2566
1960-1969	18	540	286	455	439	360	102	504	2688	28	1	54	89	148	14	97	431		3119
1970-1974	13	486	451	467	486	441	182	579	3094	28	4	82	143	138	26	145	566	2	3662
TOTAL 1920-1974	17	1612	831	1488	1173	1027	324	1545	8004	97	5	220	275	383	48	312	1341	2	9347
PER 1000 TOTAL		16.9	18.4	21.0	17.7	18.2	18.5	22.4	19.0	18.2	19.3	21.0	21.6	23.3	21.1	16.7	20.2	3.0	19.2

APPENDIX F Continued

	Rank	Men								Women									
		Physical Sciences	Engineering	Life Sciences	Behavioral Sciences	Humanities	Professions	Education	Total	Physical Sciences	Engineering	Life Sciences	Behavioral Sciences	Humanities	Professions	Education	Total	Unknown Field	Grand Total
NORTH DAKOTA																			
1920-1959	39	1	2	5	25	4	1	62	100				1			2	3		103
1960-1969	42	48		84	42	2		145	321	4		4	2			8	18		339
1970-1974	40	86		151	31	5		150	423			3	4	3	1	33	44		467
TOTAL 1920-1974	41	135	2	240	98	11	1	357	844	4		7	7	3	1	43	65		909
PER 1000 TOTAL		1.4	0.0	3.4	1.5	0.2	0.1	5.2	2.0	0.7		0.7	0.5	0.2	0.4	2.3	1.0		1.9
SOUTH DAKOTA																			
1920-1959	47			2	1			2	5							1	1		6
1960-1969	46	9		64	19			103	195				1			6	7		202
1970-1974	47	20	10	63	48			96	237			3	10			12	25		262
TOTAL 1920-1974	46	29	10	129	68			201	437			3	11			19	33		470
PER 1000 TOTAL		0.3	0.2	1.8	1.0			2.9	1.0			0.3	0.9			1.0	0.5		1.0
NEBRASKA																			
1920-1959	26	179		189	174	78	6	204	830	5		7	22	14		16	64		894
1960-1969	31	156	21	207	134	95	23	440	1076	7		11	13	18	2	46	97		1173
1970-1974	33	159	32	226	149	126	48	307	1047	7	2	23	23	42	1	54	152		1199
TOTAL 1920-1974	31	494	53	622	457	299	77	951	2953	19	2	41	58	74	3	116	313		3266
PER 1000 TOTAL		5.2	1.2	8.8	6.9	5.3	4.4	13.8	7.0	3.6	7.7	3.9	4.6	4.5	1.3	6.2	4.7		6.7
KANSAS																			
1920-1959	22	335	9	306	116	42		145	954	12		33	15	9		9	78		1032
1960-1969	26	493	166	513	222	149	3	249	1798	21	1	39	21	27	7	30	146		1944
1970-1974	28	309	168	439	300	186	40	299	1741	21	1	60	89	66	19	73	329		2070
TOTAL 1920-1974	25	1137	343	1258	638	377	43	693	4493	54	2	132	125	102	26	112	553		5046
PER 1000 TOTAL		11.9	7.6	17.8	9.6	6.7	2.5	10.1	10.7	10.1	7.7	12.6	9.8	6.2	11.4	6.0	8.3		10.4
DELAWARE																			
1920-1959	33	148	56	3					207	2							2		209
1960-1969	39	163	108	48	29	20		6	376	4	1	6	6	2		2	21		397
1970-1974	44	129	72	39	30	41		6	317	7	1	9	10	13		7	47		364
TOTAL 1920-1974	40	440	236	90	59	61		12	900	13	2	15	16	15		9	70		970
PER 1000 TOTAL		4.6	5.2	1.3	0.9	1.1		0.2	2.1	2.4	7.7	1.4	1.3	0.9		0.5	1.1		2.0
MARYLAND																			
1920-1959	13	1119	248	1124	365	492	20	137	3506	57		146	61	143		75	482		3988
1960-1969	19	767	378	653	354	336	9	267	2767	40	1	87	46	81	2	80	337		3104
1970-1974	16	600	315	468	407	286	36	347	2461	46	7	115	142	141	10	190	651	5	3117
TOTAL 1920-1974	15	2486	941	2245	1126	1114	65	751	8734	143	8	348	249	365	12	345	1470	5	10209
PER 1000 TOTAL		26.1	20.8	31.7	17.0	19.8	3.7	10.9	20.8	26.8	30.9	33.2	19.5	22.2	5.3	18.5	22.2	7.5	20.9
DISTRICT OF COLUMBIA																			
1920-1959	14	398	14	292	615	520	636	204	2690	68		95	125	311	22	125	748		3438
1960-1969	21	344	88	247	623	325	297	272	2197	38		76	118	139	36	138	546		2743
1970-1974	20	378	133	183	482	346	296	353	2171	43	1	96	132	151	29	157	609	2	2782
TOTAL 1920-1974	18	1120	235	722	1720	1191	1229	829	7058	149	1	267	375	601	87	420	1903	2	8963
PER 1000 TOTAL		11.8	5.2	10.2	26.0	21.1	70.3	12.0	16.8	27.9	3.9	25.5	29.4	36.6	38.3	22.5	28.7	3.0	18.4
VIRGINIA																			
1920-1959	23	412	37	109	146	185	1	64	954	7		21	8	27		7	70		1024
1960-1969	29	401	230	217	177	155	7	171	1359	18		27	8	16		34	103		1462
1970-1974	30	331	310	288	140	205	31	263	1568	24	2	47	27	40	2	83	225	1	1794
TOTAL 1920-1974	29	1144	577	614	463	545	39	498	3881	49	2	95	43	83	2	124	398	1	4280
PER 1000 TOTAL		12.0	12.8	8.7	7.0	9.7	2.2	7.2	9.2	9.2	7.7	9.1	3.4	5.1	0.9	6.6	6.0	1.5	8.8
WEST VIRGINIA																			
1920-1959	35	52	22	46		12		5	137	1				2			3		140
1960-1969	40	64	57	107	24	12		63	327	3		15	6	1		17	42		369
1970-1974	39	62	61	123	84	27		150	507			13	16	4		37	70		577
TOTAL 1920-1974	39	178	140	276	108	51		218	971	4		28	22	7		54	115		1086
PER 1000 TOTAL		1.9	3.1	3.9	1.6	0.9		3.2	2.3	0.7		2.7	1.7	0.4		2.9	1.7		2.2
NORTH CAROLINA																			
1920-1959	17	696	31	474	503	612	78	146	2540	31		65	71	121	1	19	308	1	2849
1960-1969	13	646	258	815	620	597	159	267	3367	23	1	99	69	105	11	61	369	6	3742
1970-1974	11	449	328	784	639	539	98	379	3216	39	6	153	137	212	21	132	700	1	3917
TOTAL 1920-1974	14	1791	617	2073	1762	1748	335	792	9123	93	7	317	277	438	33	212	1377	8	10508
PER 1000 TOTAL		18.8	13.6	29.3	26.6	31.0	19.2	11.5	21.7	17.4	27.0	30.2	21.7	26.7	14.5	11.3	20.8	12.0	21.6
SOUTH CAROLINA																			
1920-1959	41	10		10		14		10	44	1		1		6		4	12		56
1960-1969	38	156	41	71	29	40	5	27	369	6		5	5	12		7	35	1	405
1970-1974	37	144	78	97	85	89	19	66	578	10		13	8	26		29	86	1	665
TOTAL 1920-1974	38	310	119	178	114	143	24	103	991	17		19	13	44		40	133	2	1126
PER 1000 TOTAL		3.3	2.6	2.5	1.7	2.5	1.4	1.5	2.4	3.2		1.8	1.0	2.7		2.1	2.0	3.0	2.3
GEORGIA																			
1920-1959	32	75	40	40	9	30	1	30	225	3		8		4		5	20		245
1960-1969	28	257	215	274	145	184	70	188	1333	13		40	25	42	5	83	208	1	1542
1970-1974	23	326	234	338	340	236	174	452	2102	20	1	48	106	81	5	170	432		2534
TOTAL 1920-1974	28	658	489	652	494	450	245	670	3660	36	1	96	131	127	10	258	660	1	4321
PER 1000 TOTAL		6.9	10.8	9.2	7.5	8.0	14.0	9.7	8.7	6.7	3.9	9.2	10.3	7.7	4.4	13.8	10.0	1.5	8.9
FLORIDA																			
1920-1959	24	221	16	184	132	102	8	159	823	8		9	8	18	9	24	76		899
1960-1969	17	567	252	433	489	296	60	702	2805	31	1	36	61	78	41	185	434		3239
1970-1974	12	517	232	431	507	297	133	917	3035	22	2	53	124	126	34	334	695		3730
TOTAL 1920-1974	20	1305	500	1048	1128	695	201	1778	6663	61	3	98	193	222	84	543	1205		7868
PER 1000 TOTAL		13.7	11.1	14.8	17.1	12.3	11.5	25.8	15.8	11.4	11.6	9.3	15.1	13.5	37.0	29.0	18.2		16.1
KENTUCKY																			
1920-1959	31	101	6	10	114	42	1	94	369	6		1	12	11		8	38		407
1960-1969	34	172	17	177	189	65		111	731	12		20	23	17		18	90		821
1970-1974	36	126	63	183	148	80	51	97	748	11		36	18	39		41	145	3	896
TOTAL 1920-1974	34	399	86	370	451	187	52	302	1848	29		57	53	67		67	273	3	2124
PER 1000 TOTAL		4.2	1.9	5.2	6.8	3.3	3.0	4.4	4.4	5.4		5.4	4.2	4.1		3.6	4.1	4.5	4.4
TENNESSEE																			
1920-1959	21	269	17	124	206	249	31	557	1455	11		26	16	52	2	48	155		1610
1960-1969	24	418	146	293	336	228	75	507	2003	9		46	39	44	8	108	255	2	2260
1970-1974	25	302	197	375	433	248	43	505	2103	23	2	60	61	83	7	153	389		2492
TOTAL 1920-1974	22	989	360	792	975	725	149	1569	5561	43	2	132	116	179	17	309	799	2	6362
PER 1000 TOTAL		10.4	8.0	11.2	14.7	12.9	8.5	22.8	13.2	8.1	7.7	12.6	9.1	10.9	7.5	16.5	12.1	3.0	13.1
ALABAMA																			
1920-1959	34	27		31	4	8	19	43	132	2		3		1	1	4	11		143
1960-1969	32	145	87	159	84	48	82	298	903	11	2	15	17	13	3	84	145		1048
1970-1974	31	135	91	176	88	54	58	439	1041	15		31	21	39	4	172	282		1323
TOTAL 1920-1974	33	307	178	366	176	110	159	780	2076	28	2	49	38	53	8	260	438		2514
PER 1000 TOTAL		3.2	3.9	5.2	2.7	2.0	9.1	11.3	4.9	5.2	7.7	4.7	3.0	3.2	3.5	13.9	6.6		5.2
MISSISSIPPI																			
1920-1959	42			13				28	41							2	2		43
1960-1969	35	57	17	159	56	41	13	234	577	2		16	9	14	3	48	92		669
1970-1974	32	63	48	249	163	52	61	426	1062	4	1	23	24	22	5	113	192		1254
TOTAL 1920-1974	35	120	65	421	219	93	74	688	1680	6	1	39	33	36	8	163	286		1966
PER 1000 TOTAL		1.3	1.4	5.9	3.3	1.7	4.2	10.0	4.0	1.1	3.9	3.7	2.6	2.2	3.5	8.7	4.3		4.0

APPENDIX F Continued

	Rank	Men								Women									
		Physical Sciences	Engineering	Life Sciences	Behavioral Sciences	Humanities	Professions	Education	Total	Physical Sciences	Engineering	Life Sciences	Behavioral Sciences	Humanities	Professions	Education	Total	Unknown Field	Grand Total
ARKANSAS																			
1920–1959	40	19		4	4	3		50	80	1				6		3	10		90
1960–1969	37	86	22	35	45	33	62	240	524			3	2	14	1	30	50		574
1970–1974	38	83	46	66	51	24	88	184	543	8		14	7	8	5	31	73		616
TOTAL 1920–1974	37	188	68	105	100	60	150	474	1147	9		17	9	28	6	64	133		1280
PER 1000 TOTAL		2.0	1.5	1.5	1.5	1.1	8.6	6.9	2.7	1.7		1.6	0.7	1.7	2.6	3.4	2.0		2.6
LOUISIANA																			
1920–1959	25	222	22	210	125	134	18	63	794	8		26	10	46	2	9	101		895
1960–1969	25	378	103	475	284	333	122	118	1813	25	1	48	28	98	6	27	233		2046
1970–1974	29	282	111	346	233	282	147	244	1645	28		73	56	94	18	60	329	6	1980
TOTAL 1920–1974	26	882	236	1031	642	749	287	425	4252	61	1	147	94	238	26	96	663	6	4921
PER 1000 TOTAL		9.3	5.2	14.6	9.7	13.3	16.4	6.2	10.1	11.4	3.9	14.0	7.4	14.5	11.4	5.1	10.0	9.0	10.1
OKLAHOMA																			
1920–1959	29	152	26	148	51	43		232	652	2		12	6	15		50	85		737
1960–1969	22	316	454	461	266	144	21	645	2307	7	1	31	22	18	3	148	230		2537
1970–1974	24	226	329	440	294	126	86	652	2154	6	4	48	48	49	5	209	369		2523
TOTAL 1920–1974	24	694	809	1049	611	313	107	1529	5113	15	5	91	76	82	8	407	684		5797
PER 1000 TOTAL		7.3	17.9	14.8	9.2	5.6	6.1	22.2	12.2	2.8	19.3	8.7	6.0	5.0	3.5	21.8	10.3		11.9
TEXAS																			
1920–1959	16	822	164	462	346	360	87	477	2718	17	7	49	35	103	18	90	319		3037
1960–1969	9	1286	887	809	644	493	162	949	5231	52	3	116	80	154	66	247	721		5952
1970–1974	7	1172	1013	895	778	549	363	1238	6015	92	2	172	177	260	45	498	1248	1	7264
TOTAL 1920–1974	10	3280	2064	2166	1768	1402	612	2664	13964	161	12	337	292	517	129	835	2288	1	16253
PER 1000 TOTAL		34.4	45.7	30.6	26.7	24.9	35.0	38.7	33.2	30.2	46.3	32.1	22.9	31.5	56.8	44.7	34.5	1.5	33.3
MONTANA																			
1920–1959	44	4	7	3				5	19										19
1960–1969	43	53	48	77	32		1	61	272	3		8	2			5	18		290
1970–1974	43	70	38	111	58	4		106	387	3		4	5			16	28		415
TOTAL 1920–1974	43	127	93	191	90	4	1	172	678	6		12	7			21	46		724
PER 1000 TOTAL		1.3	2.1	2.7	1.4	0.1	0.1	2.5	1.6	1.1		1.1	0.5			1.1	0.7		1.5
IDAHO																			
1960–1969	47	40	9	27	5	6		44	131	2		1	1			7	11		142
1970–1974	45	71	25	68	15	8		91	278	3		5	3	7		15	33		311
TOTAL 1920–1974	47	111	34	95	20	14		135	409	5		6	4	7		22	44		453
PER 1000 TOTAL		1.2	0.8	1.3	0.3	0.2		2.0	1.0	0.9		0.6	0.3	0.4		1.2	0.7		0.9
WYOMING																			
1920–1959	36	15		15	1			84	115	2						3	5		120
1960–1969	41	55	8	60	5			209	337	1		3	2			18	24		361
1970–1974	42	111	17	90	31	4		146	399	6	1	5	1	1		14	28		427
TOTAL 1920–1974	42	181	25	165	37	4		439	851	9	1	8	3	1		35	57		908
PER 1000 TOTAL		1.9	0.6	2.3	0.6	0.1		6.4	2.0	1.7	3.9	0.8	0.2	0.1		1.9	0.9		1.9
COLORADO																			
1920–1959	20	289	55	118	198	193	1	603	1457	14		28	23	45	1	94	205		1662
1960–1969	16	582	326	350	371	328	39	1178	3175	21		27	58	77	2	179	364		3539
1970–1974	14	448	345	390	466	229	128	893	2900	20	2	47	120	98	19	219	525		3425
TOTAL 1920–1974	19	1319	726	858	1035	750	168	2674	7532	55	2	102	201	220	22	492	1094		8626
PER 1000 TOTAL		13.9	16.1	12.1	15.6	13.3	9.6	38.9	17.9	10.3	7.7	9.7	15.8	13.4	9.7	26.3	16.5		17.7
NEW MEXICO																			
1920–1959	38	36		9	10	38			93	2		1	1	17			21		114
1960–1969	36	207	112	18	27	96		116	577	9			2	21		24	56		633
1970–1974	34	199	123	50	72	151		266	861	10		11	24	52		93	190		1051
TOTAL 1920–1974	36	442	235	77	109	285		382	1531	21		12	27	90		117	267		1798
PER 1000 TOTAL		4.6	5.2	1.1	1.6	5.1		5.6	3.6	3.9		1.1	2.1	5.5		6.3	4.0		3.7
ARIZONA																			
1920–1959	37	48	1	18	11	4		29	111			3	1			3	7		118
1960–1969	30	318	182	214	169	58	10	341	1292	10		16	19	14	1	73	133		1425
1970–1974	27	316	213	266	239	95	93	541	1764	15	2	33	65	41	1	175	332	2	2098
TOTAL 1920–1974	30	682	396	498	419	157	103	911	3167	25	2	52	85	55	2	251	472	2	3641
PER 1000 TOTAL		7.2	8.8	7.0	6.3	2.8	5.9	13.2	7.5	4.7	7.7	5.0	6.7	3.4	0.9	13.4	7.1	3.0	7.5
UTAH																			
1920–1959	30	147	73	100	72	34		61	487	2		3	4	2		3	14		501
1960–1969	27	363	224	320	172	81	24	368	1553	12		19	30	11	3	51	126		1679
1970–1974	26	268	221	312	291	138	50	753	2033	8	1	23	43	30	2	106	213		2246
TOTAL 1920–1974	27	778	518	732	535	253	74	1182	4073	22	1	45	77	43	5	160	353		4426
PER 1000 TOTAL		8.2	11.5	10.3	8.1	4.5	4.2	17.2	9.7	4.1	3.9	4.3	6.0	2.6	2.2	8.6	5.3		9.1
NEVADA																			
1960–1969	50	20			14	2			36				2				2		38
1970–1974	50	39	1	6	24	8			78				8	6			14		92
TOTAL 1920–1974	50	59	1	6	38	10			114				10	6			16		130
PER 1000 TOTAL		0.6	0.0	0.1	0.6	0.2			0.3				0.8	0.4			0.2		0.3
WASHINGTON																			
1920–1959	19	502	47	435	278	204	25	195	1689	14		39	23	41		33	150		1839
1960–1969	20	696	232	572	419	396	136	278	2729	24		50	57	70	6	29	236	1	2966
1970–1974	19	481	265	506	469	329	93	272	2418	29	1	73	94	96	11	74	378	8	2804
TOTAL 1920–1974	21	1679	544	1513	1166	929	254	745	6836	67	1	162	174	207	17	136	764	9	7609
PER 1000 TOTAL		17.6	12.0	21.4	17.6	16.5	14.5	10.8	16.3	12.6	3.9	15.4	13.7	12.6	7.5	7.3	11.5	13.5	15.6
OREGON																			
1920–1959	27	192	15	262	54	21		235	779	5		17	5	3	1	41	72		851
1960–1969	23	440	68	544	350	126	46	598	2177	25		42	35	20	4	77	203		2380
1970–1974	22	351	79	512	414	180	79	632	2252	17		47	101	67	4	133	370	3	2625
TOTAL 1920–1974	23	983	162	1318	818	327	125	1465	5208	47		106	141	90	9	251	645	3	5856
PER 1000 TOTAL		10.3	3.6	18.6	12.4	5.8	7.1	21.3	12.4	8.8		10.1	11.1	5.5	4.0	13.4	9.7	4.5	12.0
CALIFORNIA																			
1920–1959	3	3546	945	2274	1734	1663	147	1921	12233	135		255	225	351	9	383	1358	1	13592
1960–1969	2	4184	2854	2562	2179	1862	541	1991	16205	175	19	375	434	469	37	488	1997	157	18359
1970–1974	2	2903	2474	2169	2428	1670	583	1790	14029	203	28	506	634	727	72	608	2779	274	17082
TOTAL 1920–1974	2	10633	6273	7005	6341	5195	1271	5702	42467	513	47	1136	1293	1547	118	1479	6134	432	49033
PER 1000 TOTAL		111.7	138.8	98.9	95.9	92.2	72.7	82.8	101.0	96.1	181.5	108.3	101.5	94.3	51.9	79.1	92.5	649.6	100.6
ALASKA																			
1920–1959	48	4							4										4
1960–1969	51	26	1	2					29			1					1		30
1970–1974	51	27	1	12					40	1							1		41
TOTAL 1920–1974	51	57	2	14					73	1		1					2		75
PER 1000 TOTAL		0.6	0.0	0.2					0.2	0.2		0.1					0.0		0.2
HAWAII																			
1920–1959	46	6		9					15			2					2		17
1960–1969	44	48	1	130	29	19		1	228	2		16	7	1		1	27		255
1970–1974	41	80	16	147	94	34	1	5	377	3		19	26	9		5	62		439
TOTAL 1920–1974	44	134	17	286	123	53	1	6	620	5		37	33	10		6	91		711
PER 1000 TOTAL		1.4	0.4	4.0	1.9	0.9	0.1	0.1	1.5	0.9		3.5	2.6	0.6		0.3	1.4		1.5

APPENDIX F Continued

		Men								Women									
	Rank	Physical Sciences	Engineering	Life Sciences	Behavioral Sciences	Humanities	Professions	Education	Total	Physical Sciences	Engineering	Life Sciences	Behavioral Sciences	Humanities	Professions	Education	Total	Unknown Field	Grand Total
PUERTO RICO																			
1960–1969	52					1			1					5			5		6
1970–1974	52	7		1		10			18	1		1		7			9		27
TOTAL 1920–1974	52	7		1		11			19	1		1		12			14		33
PER 1000 TOTAL		0.1		0.0		0.2			0.0	0.2		0.1		0.7			0.2		0.1
NEW ENGLAND																			
1920–1959	3	4695	1520	1687	2777	3650	1235	1050	16619	232	4	353	369	650	41	221	1876		18495
1960–1969	5	3913	1944	1351	2335	2404	1022	942	13936	206	9	379	427	621	41	283	1967	8	15911
1970–1974	6	2801	1367	1252	1901	1880	573	1328	11111	242	12	383	512	792	50	506	2498	2	13611
TOTAL 1920–1974	5	11409	4831	4290	7013	7934	2830	3320	41666	680	25	1115	1308	2063	132	1010	6341	10	48017
PER 1000 TOTAL		119.8	106.9	60.6	106.0	140.9	161.9	48.2	99.1	127.4	96.5	106.3	102.7	125.7	58.1	54.0	95.7	15.0	98.5
MIDDLE ATLANTIC																			
1920–1959	2	7650	1815	4760	4857	4800	1252	7282	32446	475	7	787	934	1463	126	2167	5968	11	38425
1960–1969	2	6642	4008	3509	4584	3980	1078	4444	28287	366	20	683	1035	1168	234	1508	5018	15	33320
1970–1974	2	4772	3150	2877	4283	3428	999	4074	23624	425	25	754	1377	1537	205	1648	5976	27	29627
TOTAL 1920–1974	2	19064	8973	11146	13724	12208	3329	15800	84357	1266	52	2224	3346	4168	565	5323	16962	53	101372
PER 1000 TOTAL		200.2	198.5	157.4	207.5	216.8	190.4	229.6	200.6	237.2	200.8	212.1	262.6	253.9	248.7	284.7	255.9	79.7	208.0
EAST NORTH CENTRAL																			
1920–1959	1	10602	2592	7881	5943	4792	1288	3271	36416	539	15	947	749	1137	222	730	4354	9	40779
1960–1969	1	7764	5055	6122	5532	4949	1575	5690	36786	414	15	730	882	1034	278	1238	4603	7	41396
1970–1974	1	5275	3609	4583	5264	4451	1639	6642	31496	363	29	789	1262	1564	291	1950	6259	100	37855
TOTAL 1920–1974	1	23641	11256	18586	16739	14192	4502	15603	104698	1316	59	2466	2893	3735	791	3918	15216	116	120030
PER 1000 TOTAL		248.3	249.0	262.4	253.1	252.0	257.5	226.7	249.0	246.5	227.8	235.2	227.1	227.6	348.2	209.6	229.6	174.4	246.2
WEST NORTH CENTRAL																			
1920–1959	5	3157	647	4137	2085	1458	205	1596	13286	156	1	347	347	328	39	297	1516	1	14803
1960–1969	6	2624	1451	3214	1994	1481	387	2329	13487	110	8	218	283	311	58	420	1408	4	14899
1970–1974	5	1840	1300	2500	1942	1417	506	2284	11793	116	13	284	478	418	84	552	1946	4	13743
TOTAL 1920–1974	6	7621	3398	9851	6021	4356	1098	6209	38566	382	22	849	1108	1057	181	1269	4870	9	43445
PER 1000 TOTAL		80.0	75.2	139.1	91.0	77.3	62.8	90.2	91.7	71.6	84.9	81.0	87.0	64.4	79.7	67.9	73.5	13.5	89.1
SOUTH ATLANTIC																			
1920–1959	6	3131	464	2282	1770	1967	744	755	11126	178		345	273	632	32	259	1721	1	12848
1960–1969	4	3365	1627	2865	2490	1965	607	1963	14900	176	4	391	344	476	95	607	2095	8	17003
1970–1974	4	2936	1763	2751	2714	2066	787	2933	15955	211	20	547	702	794	101	1139	3515	10	19480
TOTAL 1920–1974	4	9432	3854	7898	6974	5998	2138	5651	41981	565	24	1283	1319	1902	228	2005	7331	19	49331
PER 1000 TOTAL		99.1	.85.3	111.5	105.4	106.5	122.3	82.1	99.8	105.8	92.7	122.4	103.5	115.9	100.4	107.2	110.6	28.6	101.2
EAST SOUTH CENTRAL																			
1920–1959	9	397	23	178	324	299	51	722	1997	19		30	28	64	3	62	206		2203
1960–1969	9	792	267	788	665	382	170	1150	4214	34	2	97	88	88	14	258	582	2	4798
1970–1974	9	626	399	983	832	434	213	1467	4954	53	3	150	124	183	16	479	1008	3	5965
TOTAL 1920–1974	9	1815	689	1949	1821	1115	434	3339	11165	106	5	277	240	335	33	799	1796	5	12966
PER 1000 TOTAL		19.1	15.2	27.5	27.5	19.8	24.8	48.5	26.6	19.9	19.3	26.4	18.8	20.4	14.5	42.7	27.1	7.5	26.6
WEST SOUTH CENTRAL																			
1920–1959	7	1215	212	824	526	540	105	822	4244	28	7	87	51	170	20	152	515		4759
1960–1969	7	2066	1466	1780	1239	1003	367	1952	9875	84	5	198	132	284	76	452	1234		11109
1970–1974	7	1763	1499	1747	1356	981	684	2318	10357	134	6	307	288	411	73	798	2019	7	12383
TOTAL 1920–1974	7	5044	3177	4351	3121	2524	1156	5092	24476	246	18	592	471	865	169	1402	3768	7	28251
PER 1000 TOTAL		53.0	70.3	61.4	47.2	44.8	66.1	74.0	58.2	46.1	69.5	56.5	37.0	52.7	74.4	75.0	56.8	10.5	58.0
MOUNTAIN																			
1920–1959	8	539	136	263	292	269	1	782	2282	20		35	29	64	1	103	252		2534
1960–1969	8	1638	909	1066	795	571	74	2317	7373	58		74	116	123	6	357	734		8107
1970–1974	8	1522	983	1293	1196	637	271	2796	8700	65	6	128	269	235	22	638	1363	2	10065
TOTAL 1920–1974	8	3699	2028	2622	2283	1477	346	5895	18355	143	6	237	414	422	29	1098	2349	2	20706
PER 1000 TOTAL		38.8	44.9	37.0	34.5	26.2	19.8	85.6	43.7	26.8	23.2	22.6	32.5	25.7	12.8	58.7	35.4	3.0	42.5
PACIFIC AND INSULAR																			
1920–1959	4	4250	1007	2980	2066	1888	172	2351	14720	154		313	253	395	10	457	1582	1	16303
1960–1969	3	5394	3156	3810	2977	2404	723	2868	21369	226	19	484	533	565	47	595	2469	158	23996
1970–1974	3	3849	2835	3347	3405	2223	756	2699	19134	254	29	646	855	906	87	820	3599	285	23018
TOTAL 1920–1974	3	13493	6998	10137	8448	6515	1651	7918	55223	634	48	1443	1641	1866	144	1872	7650	444	63317
PER 1000 TOTAL		141.7	154.8	143.1	127.7	115.7	94.4	115.0	131.3	118.8	185.3	137.6	128.8	113.7	63.4	100.1	115.4	667.7	129.9

SOURCE: NRC, Commission on Human Resources.

APPENDIX G
LARGEST BACCALAUREATE ORIGINS INSTITUTIONS, RANKED BY NUMBER OF 1920-1974 PhD's AMONG THEIR ALUMNI

	Male		Female		Both Sexes	
	Number	Rank	Number	Rank	Number	Rank
CALIF, U-BERKELEY	7117	1	1071	2	8188	1
CUNY-CITY COLLEGE	6526	2	362	32	6888	2
ILL, U, URBANA-CHAMP	6076	3	667	16	6743	3
WISCONSIN,U-MADISON	5344	5	737	12	6081	4
MICHIGAN, UNIV OF	5071	6	938	4	6009	5
HARVARD UNIV/MA	5830	4	21	493	5851	6
MINNESOTA,U-MINNEAPL	4707	7	789	7	5496	7
CORNELL UNIV/NY	4265	9	745	10	5010	8
MASS INST TECHNOLOGY	4670	8	68	189	4738	9
CALIF,U-LOS ANGELES	3971	10	738	11	4709	10
CHICAGO, UNIV OF/IL	3865	11	821	6	4686	11
OHIO STATE UNIV	3842	12	572	19	4414	12
COLUMBIA UNIV/NY	3715	13	468	22	4183	13
NEW YORK UNIVERSITY	3417	16	721	14	4138	14
TEXAS, U-AUSTIN	3381	17	664	17	4045	15
CUNY-BROOKLYN COLL	3240	18	774	8	4014	16
PENN STATE UNIV	3465	15	330	37	3795	17
YALE UNIVERSITY/CT	3481	14	10	724	3491	18
WASHINGTON, U OF	2918	20	421	26	3339	19
STANFORD UNIV/CA	2817	21	520	21	3337	20
PURDUE UNIVERSITY/IN	3005	19	209	56	3214	21
MICHIGAN STATE UNIV	2580	23	330	37	2910	22
RUTGERS UNIV/NJ	2393	25	370	30	2763	23
IOWA STATE UNIV	2523	24	172	67	2695	24
PRINCETON UNIV/NJ	2670	22	2	1035	2672	25
PENNSYLVANIA, U OF	2230	27	441	24	2671	26
NORTHWESTERN UNIV/IL	2136	29	441	24	2577	27
UTAH, UNIV OF	2339	26	212	55	2551	28
MISSOURI,U-COLUMBIA	2189	28	309	40	2498	29
INDIANA U BLOOMNGTON	2064	31	397	28	2461	30
NEBRASKA, U-LINCOLN	2062	32	294	42	2356	31
OBERLIN COLLEGE/OH	1905	36	449	23	2354	32
IOWA, UNIVERSITY OF	1978	33	340	34	2318	33
BRIGHAM YOUNG U/UT	2136	29	99	133	2235	34
KANSAS, UNIV OF	1917	35	282	44	2199	35
FLORIDA, UNIV OF	1936	34	169	68	2105	36
WAYNE STATE UNIV/MI	1740	39	335	35	2075	37
CASE WESTRN RSRVE/OH	1754	38	259	46	2013	38
COLORADO,U-BOULDER	1704	41	309	40	2013	38
PITTSBURGH, UNIV OF	1594	46	362	32	1956	40
SYRACUSE UNIV/NY	1618	45	323	39	1941	41
MARYLAND, UNIV OF	1585	47	215	54	1800	42
OKLAHOMA STATE UNIV	1650	42	133	97	1783	43
DARTMOUTH COLLEGE/NH	1771	37	2	1035	1773	44
OKLAHOMA, U OF	1531	50	224	51	1755	45
NC, U OF-CHAPEL HILL	1564	48	155	73	1719	46
CAL INST TECHNOLOGY	1709	40	2	1035	1711	47
BROWN UNIVERSITY/RI	1447	52	253	47	1700	48
ROCHESTER,UNIV OF/NY	1414	54	273	45	1687	49
RENSSELAER POLY I/NY	1633	43	9	755	1642	50
NOTRE DAME, U OF/IN	1621	44	19	531	1640	51
BOSTON UNIVERSITY/MA	1213	63	403	27	1616	52
CUNY-HUNTER COLLEGE	403	210	1206	1	1609	53
JOHNS HOPKINS U/MD	1551	49	58	223	1609	53
LA ST UNIV & A&M C	1417	53	190	60	1607	55
UTAH STATE UNIV	1500	51	65	192	1565	56
CUNY-QUEENS COLL	1139	69	386	29	1525	57
TEMPLE UNIVERSITY/PA	1282	59	242	49	1524	58
CARNEGIE-MELLON U/PA	1411	55	102	129	1513	59
KANSAS STATE UNIV	1367	57	145	87	1512	60
WASHINGTON UNIV/MO	1264	60	246	48	1510	61
SOUTHERN CALIF, U OF	1221	62	207	58	1428	62
OREGON STATE UNIV	1307	58	92	145	1399	63
CINCINNATI, U OF/OH	1202	64	179	64	1381	64
TEXAS A&M UNIVERSITY	1370	56	6	855	1376	65
MASS, U OF-AMHERST	1241	61	131	101	1372	66
FORDHAM UNIV/NY	1193	65	177	65	1370	67
DUKE UNIVERSITY/NC	1115	71	231	50	1346	68
SWARTHMORE COLL/PA	968	89	363	31	1331	69
CATHOLIC U AMER/DC	1090	76	219	52	1309	70
SUNY AT BUFFALO	1118	70	187	62	1305	71
KENTUCKY, UNIV OF	1147	68	152	77	1299	72
GEORGIA, UNIV OF	1095	75	173	66	1268	73
MIAMI UNIVERSITY/OH	1104	74	152	77	1256	74
RICE UNIVERSITY/TX	1109	73	142	89	1251	75
WASHINGTON STATE U	1152	67	96	138	1248	76
TENN, U-KNOXVILLE	1081	77	150	79	1231	77
WEST VIRGINIA UNIV	1110	72	121	106	1231	77
OREGON, UNIV OF	1037	81	190	60	1227	79
CONNECTICUT, UNIV OF	1077	78	114	117	1191	80
SOUTHERN ILL UNIV	1064	79	123	104	1187	81
ALABAMA, UNIVER OF	987	88	198	59	1185	82
AMHERST COLLEGE/MA	1156	66			1156	83
ARIZONA, UNIV OF	988	87	148	82	1136	84
GEO WASHINGTON U/DC	925	95	208	57	1133	85
FLORIDA STATE UNIV	776	112	332	36	1108	86
N TEXAS STATE UNIV	947	91	158	71	1105	87
COLORADO STATE UNIV	1029	82	64	195	1093	88
ARKANSAS,U-FAYETTVLE	956	90	126	103	1082	89
OHIO UNIVERSITY	931	94	146	85	1077	90
VIRGINIA, UNIV OF	1044	80	29	379	1073	91
BOSTON COLLEGE/MA	994	86	55	234	1049	92
ST LOUIS UNIV/MO	892	101	146	85	1038	93
DEPAUW UNIVERSITY/IN	934	93	103	126	1037	94
NC STATE U-RALEIGH	1021	83	12	670	1033	95
SAN JOSE STATE U/CA	905	98	113	118	1018	96
BAYLOR UNIV/TX	865	103	153	76	1018	96
AUBURN UNIVERSITY/AL	945	92	60	214	1005	98
GEORGIA INST TECH	998	85	4	935	1002	99
TEXAS TECH UNIV	900	100	102	129	1002	99
LEHIGH UNIVERSITY/PA	1000	84			1000	101
DENVER, UNIV OF/CO	839	104	155	73	994	102
POMONA COLLEGE/CA	803	108	156	72	959	103
TUFTS UNIVERSITY/MA	830	107	120	108	950	104
COLUMBIA-BARNARD/NY	3	1188	945	3	948	105
SAN DIEGO STATE U/CA	839	104	93	142	932	106
POLYTECHNIC INST NY	921	96	4	935	925	107
VA POLY INST&STATE U	901	99	15	607	916	108
WESLEYAN UNIV/CT	912	97	2	1035	914	109
REED COLLEGE/OR	766	114	147	84	913	110
ILLINOIS INST TECH	880	102	22	472	902	111
IDAHO, UNIV OF	833	106	57	227	890	112
NEW MEXICO, UNIV OF	774	113	115	115	889	113
WELLESLEY COLLEGE/MA	4	1141	885	5	889	113
MIAMI, UNIV OF/FL	741	118	132	98	873	115
CARLETON COLLEGE/MN	717	123	149	80	866	116
NORTHERN IOWA, U OF	721	122	137	93	858	117
WOOSTER, COLL OF/OH	725	120	129	102	854	118
VANDERBILT UNIV/TN	726	119	113	118	839	119
EMORY UNIV/GA	760	115	79	164	839	119
MAINE, U-ORONO	752	116	85	156	837	121
MISSISSIPPI STATE U	800	110	33	350	833	122
NEW HAMPSHIRE, U OF	750	117	79	164	829	123
WESTERN MICHIGAN U	725	120	103	126	828	124
WHEATON COLLEGE/IL	715	124	108	122	823	125
MARQUETTE UNIV/WI	682	132	140	91	822	126
KENT STATE UNIV/OH	696	129	119	109	815	127
LOYOLA U CHICAGO/IL	710	125	101	131	811	128
WILLIAMS COLLEGE/MA	802	109	1	1101	803	129
OHIO WESLEYAN UNIV	674	135	121	106	795	130
STHRN METHODIST U/TX	675	134	115	115	790	131
CALIF,U-SANTA BARB	701	127	88	149	789	132
UNION UNIVERSITY/NY	785	111	2	1035	787	133
RADCLIFFE COLL/MA	3	1188	751	9	754	134
TULANE U OF LA	689	131	62	201	751	135
ST OLAF COLLEGE/MN	678	133	69	185	747	136
SMITH COLLEGE/MA	3	1188	737	12	740	137
ANTIOCH COLLEGE/OH	590	147	148	82	738	138
MANHATTAN COLLEGE/NY	697	128	27	400	724	139
ST JOHNS UNIV/NY	561	156	161	69	722	140

APPENDIX G Continued

	Male		Female		Both Sexes	
	Number	Rank	Number	Rank	Number	Rank
ARIZONA STATE UNIV	608	142	109	120	717	141
NORTHERN COLORADO,U	628	139	87	154	715	142
SAN FRANCISC ST U/CA	612	140	99	133	711	143
FRNKLN&MARSHAL C/PA	707	126	1	1101	708	144
MONTANA STATE UNIV	664	136	42	293	706	145
SUNY AT ALBANY	570	153	136	95	706	145
CALIF, U-DAVIS	634	138	65	192	699	147
HAVERFORD COLL/PA	690	130			690	148
ILLINOIS ST U-NORMAL	566	154	119	109	685	149
VASSAR COLLEGE/NY	7	1062	678	15	685	149
WILLIAM & MARY, C/VA	550	159	119	109	669	151
MT HOLYOKE COLL/MA	3	1188	659	18	662	152
MONTANA, UNIV OF	585	149	64	195	649	153
LAFAYETTE COLLEGE/PA	638	137	1	1101	639	154
EMPORIA KAN ST COLL	556	157	77	168	633	155
GRINNELL COLLEGE/IA	537	163	95	139	632	156
DREXEL UNIVERSITY/PA	605	143	25	425	630	157
WYOMING, UNIV OF	579	152	42	293	621	158
INDIANA STATE UNIV	516	170	103	126	619	159
OCCIDENTAL COLL/CA	544	161	74	174	618	160
NORTHEASTERN U/MA	591	146	26	412	617	161
CALVIN COLLEGE/MI	590	147	23	460	613	162
BUCKNELL UNIV/PA	507	174	104	125	611	163
US NAVAL ACADEMY/MD	611	141			611	163
CLEMSON UNIV/SC	595	145	7	821	602	165
DELAWARE, UNIV OF	531	165	70	181	601	166
BOWDOIN COLLEGE/ME	599	144			599	167
BOWLING GREEN S U/OH	496	178	98	137	594	168
BALL STATE UNIV/IN	503	175	88	149	591	169
RHODE ISLAND, U OF	542	162	49	263	591	169
GEORGETOWN UNIV/DC	553	158	37	322	590	171
NORTHERN ILL UNIV	514	171	73	175	587	172
US MILITARY ACADEMY	585	149			585	173
COLGATE U/NY	580	151			580	174
DETROIT, U OF/MI	526	167	51	256	577	175
HOLY CROSS, C OF/MA	566	154			566	176
BRYN MAWR COLL/PA	4	1141	560	20	564	177
HOUSTON, U OF/TX	446	189	116	112	562	178
VERMONT, U OF	477	184	79	164	556	179
HOPE COLLEGE/MI	524	169	30	367	554	180
SOUTH DAKOTA STATE U	526	167	24	440	550	181
NORTH DAKOTA, U OF	499	177	51	256	550	181
WAKE FOREST UNIV/NC	510	173	39	309	549	183
SOUTH CAROLINA, U OF	488	182	59	219	547	184
DAVIDSON COLLEGE/NC	547	160			547	184
DAYTON, U OF/OH	503	175	37	322	540	186
HAWAII, UNIV OF	445	190	93	142	538	187
CLARK UNIVERSITY/MA	492	180	45	279	537	188
COOPER UNION/NY	531	165	5	888	536	189
WABASH COLLEGE/IN	534	164			534	190
KANS ST C PITTSBURG	477	184	52	248	529	191
CAL ST U,LOS ANGELES	436	195	89	147	525	192
CAL ST U, FRESNO	490	181	33	350	523	193
PUERTO RICO, UNIV OF	383	216	137	93	520	194
SW MISSOURI ST UNIV	454	188	62	201	516	195
MIDDLEBURY COLL/VT	425	198	90	146	515	196
MISSOURI,U-ROLLA	513	172	1	1101	514	197
TEXAS CHRISTIAN UNIV	430	197	81	160	511	198
NORTH DAKOTA ST UNIV	483	183	28	390	511	198
DENISON UNIV/OH	423	201	88	149	511	198
WICHITA ST UNIV/KS	462	187	47	271	509	201
ALLEGHENY COLLEGE/PA	442	191	66	191	508	202
LOUISVILLE, U OF/KY	441	192	61	206	502	203
RICHMOND, U OF/VA	441	192	61	206	502	203
BRANDEIS UNIV/MA	346	245	155	73	501	205
HAMILTON COLLEGE/NY	494	179			494	206
CALIF,U-RIVERSIDE	440	194	54	236	494	206
EASTERN MICHIGAN U	415	204	76	170	491	208
CAL ST U, LONG BEACH	425	198	61	206	486	209
LAWRENCE UNIV/WI	387	214	95	139	482	210
YESHIVA UNIV/NY	470	186	8	786	478	211
DUQUESNE UNIV/PA	389	212	88	149	477	212
MISSISSIPPI, UNIV OF	420	202	53	242	473	213
HOWARD UNIVERSITY/DC	334	252	136	95	470	214
VILLANOVA UNIV/PA	431	196	39	309	470	214

	Male		Female		Both Sexes	
	Number	Rank	Number	Rank	Number	Rank
REDLANDS, U OF/CA	424	200	41	295	465	216
BATES COLLEGE/ME	407	206	54	236	461	217
GETTYSBURG COLL/PA	419	203	41	295	460	218
ROOSEVELT UNIV/IL	389	212	69	185	458	219
BEREA COLLEGE/KY	404	208	53	242	457	220
DRAKE UNIV/IA	393	211	61	206	454	221
DEPAUL UNIVERSITY/IL	354	237	99	133	453	222
EARLHAM COLLEGE/IN	381	217	61	206	442	223
EAST TEXAS STATE U	357	235	81	160	438	224
VALPARAISO UNIV/IN	379	218	58	223	437	225
AUGUSTANA COLL/IL	406	207	30	367	436	226
LOUISIANA TECH UNIV	375	220	60	214	435	227
KNOX COLLEGE/IL	387	214	48	268	435	227
CTRL MISSOURI ST U	371	222	62	201	433	229
AKRON, U OF/OH	370	223	56	230	426	230
SOWESTERN LA, U OF	362	230	59	219	421	231
SOUTHERN MISS, U OF	349	242	71	179	420	232
CENTRAL MICHIGAN U	369	225	48	268	417	233
TOLEDO, UNIV OF/OH	360	232	56	230	416	234
KALAMAZOO COLLEGE/MI	375	220	38	315	413	235
PROVIDENCE COLL/RI	404	208	8	786	412	236
TRINITY COLLEGE/CT	409	205	1	1101	410	237
BELOIT COLLEGE/WI	347	244	62	201	409	238
EASTERN ILL UNIV	370	223	37	322	407	239
INDIANA UNIV OF PA	351	239	52	248	403	240
WESTERN KENTUCKY U	351	239	50	260	401	241
SETON HALL UNIV/NJ	356	236	38	315	394	242
HOFSTRA UNIV/NY	334	252	60	214	394	242
BUTLER UNIV/IN	329	255	63	200	392	244
CORNELL COLLEGE/IA	353	238	38	315	391	245
MEMPHIS STATE U/TN	310	270	72	176	382	246
XAVIER UNIV/OH	365	226	15	607	380	247
GONZAGA UNIV/WA	358	234	22	472	380	247
COLORADO COLLEGE	311	269	69	185	380	247
MUHLENBERG COLL/PA	363	229	16	584	379	250
BRADLEY UNIV/IL	345	246	33	350	378	251
NEW MEXICO STATE U	360	232	17	563	377	253
WILLAMETTE UNIV/OR	337	251	40	303	377	253
WORCESTER POLY I/MA	377	219			377	253
ALBION COLLEGE/MI	341	248	35	336	376	256
ABILENE CHRIST U/TX	349	242	26	412	375	257
SPRINGFIELD COLL/MA	364	227	8	786	372	258
MISSISSIPPI COLLEGE	342	247	30	367	372	258
LONG ISLAND U-UNK/NY	350	241	21	493	371	260
MURRAY STATE UNIV/KY	331	254	38	315	369	261
WITTENBERG UNIV/OH	316	265	49	263	365	262
LA SALLE COLLEGE/PA	364	227			364	263
BIRMNGHAM-STHRN C/AL	304	273	59	219	363	264
SOUTH DAKOTA, U OF	321	260	41	295	362	265
MANCHESTER COLL/IN	338	250	24	440	362	265
WASHINGTON&LEE U/VA	361	231			361	267
NEBRASKA,U-OMAHA	320	262	40	303	360	268
SE MISSOURI ST UNIV	325	258	32	360	357	269
JUNIATA COLLEGE/PA	323	259	34	344	357	269
WESTERN ILLINOIS U	326	257	30	367	356	271
MACALESTER COLL/MN	294	278	61	206	355	272
ALFRED UNIVERSITY/NY	328	256	27	400	355	272
MONTCLAIR ST COLL/NJ	280	288	75	171	355	272
SUNY COLL BUFFALO	266	296	88	149	354	275
DICKINSON COLL/PA	310	270	41	295	351	276
NE MISSOURI STATE U	303	275	47	271	350	277
MICHIGAN TECH UNIV	341	248	4	935	345	278
CONCORDIA-MORHEAD/MN	310	270	32	360	342	279
GEO PEABODY COLL/TN	229	340	109	120	338	280
WHITMAN COLLEGE/WA	294	278	43	287	337	281
FURMAN UNIV/SC	304	273	32	360	336	282
MISSOURI,U-KANS CITY	282	284	52	248	334	283
LUTHER COLLEGE/IA	314	267	14	625	328	284
CANISIUS COLLEGE/NY	316	265	12	670	328	284
FT HAYS KANSAS ST C	297	277	26	412	323	286
MARSHALL UNIV/WV	267	294	54	236	321	287
ST THOMAS, C OF/MN	321	260			321	287
WESTERN WASH STATE C	290	280	30	367	320	289
SCRANTON, U OF/PA	320	262			320	289
AMERICAN UNIV/DC	247	319	72	176	319	291

APPENDIX G Continued

	Male		Female		Both Sexes	
	Number	Rank	Number	Rank	Number	Rank
TULSA, UNIV OF/OK	281	286	37	322	318	292
NEBRASKA WESLEYAN U	281	286	33	350	314	293
WEST CHESTER ST C/PA	275	291	37	322	312	294
KENYON COLLEGE/OH	312	268			312	294
MUSKINGUM COLLEGE/OH	264	298	45	279	309	296
ST JOSEPHS COLL/PA	302	276	3	972	305	297
SUNY AT BINGHAMTON	259	304	45	279	304	298
ST LAWRENCE UNIV/NY	262	301	41	295	303	299
BALDWIN-WALLACE C/OH	264	298	37	322	301	300
COLBY COLLEGE/ME	256	308	43	287	299	301
CREIGHTON UNIV/NE	235	335	64	195	299	301
NORWESTRN ST UNIV LA	234	336	64	195	298	303
WHITTIER COLLEGE/CA	252	312	44	285	296	304
JOHN CARROLL UNIV/OH	290	280	4	935	294	305
NORTH CENTRAL C/IL	271	292	22	472	293	306
LEBANON VALLEY C/PA	264	298	27	400	291	307
URSINUS COLLEGE/PA	245	321	46	274	291	307
HAMLINE UNIV/MN	265	297	26	412	291	307
WASH&JEFFERSON C/PA	290	280			290	310
CAL ST U, SACRAMENTO	251	313	39	309	290	310
MILLSAPS COLLEGE/MS	261	302	29	379	290	310
STETSON UNIV/FL	221	349	69	185	290	310
HIRAM COLLEGE/OH	259	304	30	367	289	314
ST JOHNS UNIV/MN	287	283			287	315
MARIETTA COLLEGE/OH	254	311	32	360	286	316
GOUCHER COLLEGE/MD	2	1252	284	43	286	316
SW TEXAS STATE UNIV	236	334	49	263	285	318
NEVADA, UNIV OF	256	308	27	400	283	319
ADELPHI UNIV/NY	182	398	101	131	283	319
HOBART&WM SMITH C/NY	249	316	34	344	283	319
STEVENS INST TECH/NJ	282	284			282	322
COLUMBIA-TCHRS C/NY	122	522	160	70	282	322
ST PETERS COLL/NJ	280	288	1	1101	281	324
CENTRAL STATE U/OK	223	345	56	230	279	325
ST MARYS COLLEGE/MN	278	290	1	1101	279	325
CAL ST U, CHICO	258	306	20	514	278	327
ST BONAVENTURE U/NY	260	303	18	548	278	327
CAL POL S U-SL OBISP	269	293	6	855	275	329
LORAS COLLEGE/IA	258	306	17	563	275	329
ST. CLOUD STATE U/MN	248	318	27	400	275	329
DREW UNIVERSITY/NJ	240	326	33	350	273	332
SAMFORD UNIV/AL	233	337	40	303	273	332
PARK COLLEGE/MO	239	328	33	350	272	334
SAM HOUSTON ST U/TX	239	328	31	366	270	335
LAMAR UNIVERSITY/TX	245	321	25	425	270	335
WILLIAM JEWELL C/MO	244	324	24	440	268	337
GUSTAV ADOLPHUS C/MN	245	321	22	472	267	338
CLARKSON C TECH/NY	267	294			267	338
PHILA C PHARM&SCI/PA	251	313	14	625	265	340
PACIFIC, U OF/CA	237	331	26	412	263	341
MONMOUTH COLLEGE/IL	240	326	22	472	262	342
CAPITAL UNIV/OH	241	325	20	514	261	343
GOSHEN COLLEGE/IN	238	330	22	472	260	344
KEARNEY ST COLL/NE	231	338	27	400	258	345
MANKATO STATE U/MN	237	331	20	514	257	346
WISCONSIN,U-L CROSSE	225	344	32	360	257	346
COE COLLEGE/IA	222	347	35	336	257	346
SOWESTERN MEMPHIS/TN	230	339	26	412	256	349
COLORADO SCH MINES	255	310	1	1101	256	349
WEST TEXAS STATE U	211	357	40	303	251	351
WOFFORD COLLEGE/SC	250	315			250	352
WISCONSIN,U-RIVR FLS	237	331	13	644	250	352
SOUTH, UNIV OF/TN	249	316			249	354
CALIF STATE COLL/PA	226	343	23	460	249	354
MARYVILLE COLLEGE/TN	209	361	39	309	248	356
ST VINCENT COLL/PA	247	319			247	357
YOUNGSTOWN ST U/OH	204	364	39	309	243	358
CENTRAL METH COLL/MO	219	351	22	472	241	359
PORTLAND STATE U/OR	210	360	30	367	240	360
LOYOLA COLLEGE/MD	218	353	21	493	239	361
EAST CAROLINA U/NC	193	381	46	274	239	361
WASHBURN U TOPEKA/KS	201	369	38	315	239	361
SUNY COLL OSWEGO	219	351	20	514	239	361
SUNY COLL CORTLAND	193	381	45	279	238	365
GROVE CITY COLL/PA	211	357	26	412	237	366

	Male		Female		Both Sexes	
	Number	Rank	Number	Rank	Number	Rank
NW MISSOURI STATE U	199	374	36	331	235	367
SAN FRANCSCO,U OF/CA	223	345	12	670	235	367
LOYOLA UNIVERSITY/LA	195	378	38	315	233	369
IDAHO STATE UNIV	215	355	18	548	233	369
WISCONSIN,U-MILWAUKE	203	366	30	367	233	369
EASTERN WASH STATE C	213	356	19	531	232	372
SPRING HILL COLL/AL	222	347	10	724	232	372
EASTERN KENTUCKY U	204	364	26	412	230	374
HASTINGS COLLEGE/NE	218	353	12	670	230	374
MOREHOUSE COLL/GA	229	340			229	376
NEW JERSEY INST TECH	227	342	2	1035	229	376
WESTMINSTER COLL/PA	202	368	25	425	227	378
GENEVA COLLEGE/PA	196	376	30	367	226	379
WESTERN MARYLAND COL	191	387	35	336	226	379
PUGET SOUND, U OF/WA	205	363	21	493	226	379
S F AUSTIN ST U/TX	194	379	28	390	222	382
MERCER UNIV/GA	199	374	23	460	222	382
CENTRAL CONN ST COLL	194	379	28	390	222	382
OTTERBEIN COLLEGE/OH	200	372	21	493	221	385
ILLINOIS WESLEYAN U	201	369	20	514	221	385
VIRGINIA MILITARY I	220	350			220	387
TENNESSEE TECH U	201	369	19	531	220	387
TEXAS WOMANS UNIV	2	1252	218	53	220	387
LEWIS & CLARK C/OR	193	381	26	412	219	390
ANDREWS UNIV/MI	193	381	25	425	218	391
CENTRAL WASH STATE C	207	362	10	724	217	392
SLIPPERY ROCK S C/PA	193	381	23	460	216	393
TRINITY UNIV/TX	177	411	38	315	215	394
SANTA CLARA, U OF/CA	203	366	9	755	212	395
WISCONSIN,U-WHITWATR	187	389	25	425	212	395
BENEDICTINE COLL/KS	159	448	53	242	212	395
CENTRAL ARKANSAS, U	178	407	33	350	211	398
S DAKOTA S MINE&TECH	211	357			211	398
BAKER UNIV/KS	189	388	21	493	210	400
WISCONSIN,U-E CLAIRE	187	389	21	493	208	401
MT UNION COLLEGE/OH	179	402	28	390	207	402
CAL ST U, NORTHRIDGE	178	407	29	379	207	402
HOUGHTON COLL/NY	181	399	26	412	207	402
TRENTON ST COLL/NJ	156	451	49	263	205	405
OKLAHOMA BAPT UNIV	179	402	26	412	205	405
HENDRIX COLLEGE/AR	176	415	29	379	205	405
EAST TENN STATE UNIV	179	402	25	425	204	408
GREENVILLE COLL/IL	184	395	20	514	204	408
WISCONSIN,U-STEVN PT	185	392	18	548	203	410
SOUTHWESTERN COLL/KS	185	392	18	548	203	410
RANDOLPH-MACON C/VA	196	376	6	855	202	412
MIDDLE TENN STATE U	178	407	24	440	202	412
ASBURY COLLEGE/KY	173	421	28	390	201	414
MILLERSVILLE ST C/PA	177	411	24	440	201	414
TEXAS A&I UNIVERSITY	177	411	24	440	201	414
SOWESTERN OKLA ST U	172	422	29	379	201	414
PHILLIPS UNIV/OK	183	397	18	548	201	414
ALBRIGHT COLLEGE/PA	187	389	14	625	201	414
AUGUSTANA COLL/SD	177	411	23	460	200	420
SOUTHEASTERN LA U	176	415	24	440	200	420
CITADEL, THE/SC	200	372			200	420
APPLACHIAN ST U/NC	167	433	33	350	200	420
ARKANSAS STATE UNIV	185	392	14	625	199	424
WISCONSIN,U-PLATTVIL	178	407	21	493	199	424
RIPON COLLEGE/WI	179	402	19	531	198	426
HARDING COLLEGE/AR	184	395	14	625	198	426
WISCONSIN,U-OSHKOSH	176	415	20	514	196	428
DRURY COLLEGE/MO	174	420	22	472	196	428
CARSON-NEWMAN C/TN	171	428	23	460	194	430
HEIDELBERG COLL/OH	169	431	24	440	193	431
IONA COLLEGE/NY	193	381			193	431
NOEASTERN OKLA ST U	172	422	21	493	193	431
WAYNE ST COLL/NE	179	402	13	644	192	434
SEATTLE UNIV/WA	155	454	36	331	191	435
HARDIN-SIMMONS U/TX	163	439	27	400	190	436
LOYOLA MARYMONT U/CA	181	399	9	755	190	436
SHIPPENSBURG ST C/PA	172	422	17	563	189	438
CARROLL COLLEGE/WI	172	422	17	563	189	438
MORNINGSIDE COLL/IA	164	438	24	440	188	440
MILLIKIN UNIV/IL	160	447	28	390	188	440

APPENDIX G Continued

	Male		Female		Both Sexes	
	Number	Rank	Number	Rank	Number	Rank
DAVID LIPSCOMB C/TN	176	415	12	670	188	440
BETHANY COLLEGE/WV	172	422	16	584	188	440
FAIRLEIGH DICKN U/NJ	170	430	17	563	187	444
CENTRAL UNIV/IA	172	422	14	625	186	445
E CENTRAL STATE C/OK	162	443	23	460	185	446
NC, U OF-GREENSBORO	3	1188	181	63	184	447
BLOOMSBURG ST COL/PA	166	436	18	548	184	447
PACIFIC LTHRN U/WA	168	432	16	584	184	447
SOUTHESTRN OKLA ST U	150	463	34	344	184	447
FLORIDA SOUTHERN C	149	467	32	360	181	451
CONCORD THEO SEM/MO	181	399			181	451
OHIO NORTHERN UNIV	166	436	15	607	181	451
LINFIELD COLLEGE/OR	163	439	17	563	180	454
HANOVER COLLEGE/IN	157	449	22	472	179	455
CONCORDIA TCHRS C/IL	171	428	8	786	179	455
SUNY COLL FREDONIA	167	433	12	670	179	455
WAGNER COLLEGE/NY	155	454	23	460	178	458
LEMOYNE COLLEGE/NY	156	451	22	472	178	458
SIMPSON COLLEGE/IA	162	443	16	584	178	458
WISC, U-STOUT	161	446	17	563	178	458
SOUTHWESTERN U/TX	163	439	15	607	178	458
NORTHERN MICHIGAN U	150	463	27	400	177	463
ROCKHURST COLLEGE/MO	176	415	1	1101	177	463
FISK UNIVERSITY/TN	116	536	61	206	177	463
VIRGINIA STATE COLL	134	493	41	295	175	466
TENN, U-CHATTANOOGA	140	481	35	336	175	466
SOUTH FLORIDA,U OF	151	460	24	440	175	466
HAMPTON INSTITUTE/VA	125	516	49	263	174	469
WALLA WALLA COLL/WA	162	443	11	698	173	470
ST MARYS UNIV/TX	167	433	5	888	172	471
AUSTIN COLLEGE/TX	154	456	17	563	171	472
CENTENARY COLL/LA	141	478	30	367	171	472
EVANSVILLE, U OF/IN	153	457	18	548	171	472
BETHEL COLL/KS	163	439	8	786	171	472
GEORGETOWN COLL/KY	152	458	16	584	168	476
SEATTLE PACIFIC C/WA	151	460	16	584	167	477
SUNY COLL BROCKPORT	143	474	24	440	167	477
AMER INTERNATL C/MA	150	463	16	584	166	479
SUNY AT STONY BROOK	137	486	28	390	165	480
OUACHITA BAPT U/AR	152	458	12	670	164	481
PEPPERDINE UNIV/CA	147	470	16	584	163	482
HUMBOLDT STATE U/CA	157	449	6	855	163	482
MOORHEAD STATE U/MN	147	470	15	607	162	484
WEST VA WESLEYAN C	151	460	10	724	161	485
ALMA COLLEGE/MI	148	469	12	670	160	486
LAKE FOREST COLL/IL	126	513	34	344	160	486
KUTZTOWN ST COLL/PA	143	474	15	607	158	488
UNION COLLEGE/NE	139	483	19	531	158	488
TROY STATE UNIV/AL	134	493	24	440	158	488
BRIDGEWATER COLL/VA	142	476	15	607	157	491
HAMPDEN-SYDNEY C/VA	156	451			156	492
OKLAHOMA CITY UNIV	135	491	21	493	156	492
ST AMBROSE COLL/IA	140	481	16	584	156	492
TUSKEGEE INST/AL	109	553	46	274	155	495
PACIFIC UNION C/CA	141	478	14	625	155	495
IDAHO, COLLEGE OF	129	505	25	425	154	497
UPSALA COLLEGE/NJ	131	498	23	460	154	497
NORTHERN ST COLL/SD	136	489	17	563	153	499
NIAGARA UNIV/NY	147	470	5	888	152	500
EASTERN NEW MEXICO U	137	486	14	625	151	501
GEORGIA SOUTHERN C	130	501	21	493	151	501
AGNES SCOTT COLL/GA	1	1328	149	80	150	503
PORTLAND, UNIV OF/OR	141	478	9	755	150	503
FAIRFIELD UNIV/CT	150	463			150	503
SUNY ENVR SCI FSTRY	149	467			149	506
SOUTHERN UNIV/LA	112	544	37	322	149	506
FLORIDA AG & MECH U	110	549	39	309	149	506
PERU ST COLL/NE	139	483	10	724	149	506
LOWELL, UNIV OF/MA	130	501	17	563	147	510
CLARION STATE C/PA	138	485	9	755	147	510
SIMMONS COLLEGE/MA	2	1252	144	88	146	512
SIENA COLLEGE/NY	146	473			146	512
ELMHURST COLLEGE/IL	136	489	10	724	146	512
CLEVELAND ST UNIV/OH	131	498	13	644	144	515
TAYLOR UNIVERSITY/IN	133	496	11	698	144	515
TRINITY COLLEGE/DC	2	1252	141	90	143	517
NORTHERN ARIZONA U	127	512	16	584	143	517
TRANSYLVANIA U/KY	121	524	21	493	142	519
CENTRE COLL KENTUCKY	126	513	16	584	142	519
WARTBURG COLL/IA	137	486	5	888	142	519
THIEL COLLEGE/PA	130	501	12	670	142	519
E STROUDSBURG SC/PA	120	526	22	472	142	519
EDINBORO ST COLL/PA	129	505	13	644	142	519
COLUMBIA U-COL C/NY	142	476			142	519
OTTAWA UNIVERSITY/KS	129	505	12	670	141	526
ILLINOIS COLLEGE	126	513	15	607	141	526
GEORGIA STATE UNIV	105	564	36	331	141	526
EMORY & HENRY C/VA	128	509	13	644	141	526
NEW ROCHELLE, COLL	1	1328	139	92	140	530
ROLLINS COLLEGE/FL	113	543	26	412	139	531
WISCONSIN,U-SUPERIOR	128	509	11	698	139	531
MC PHERSON COLLEGE/KS	131	498	8	786	139	531
LOUISIANA COLLEGE	123	519	15	607	138	534
ST FRANCIS COLL/NY	135	491	3	972	138	534
ST NORBERT COLL/WI	128	509	9	755	137	536
WHITWORTH COLL/WA	124	518	12	670	136	537
HARVEY MUDD COLL/CA	133	496	3	972	136	537
BRIDGEWATER ST C/MA	105	564	30	367	135	539
LYNCHBURG COLLEGE/VA	123	519	12	670	135	539
NOWESTERN OKLA ST U	118	531	16	584	134	541
LOCK HAVEN ST C/PA	119	530	15	607	134	541
CONNECTICUT COLLEGE	2	1252	132	98	134	541
WESTMINSTER COLL/MO	134	493			134	541
CARTHAGE COLL/WI	122	522	11	698	133	545
FRANKLIN C INDIANA	114	539	19	531	133	545
BETHANY-NAZRENE C/OK	118	531	15	607	133	545
RANDOLPH-MACN WOM/VA	1	1328	132	98	133	545
WESTERN ST COLL COLO	123	519	10	724	133	545
ST MARYS COLL CALIF	130	501			130	550
HENDERSON ST U/ARK	114	539	15	607	129	551
JACKSONVILLE ST U/AL	105	564	24	440	129	551
WAYNESBURG COLL/PA	111	546	18	548	129	551
KINGS COLLEGE/PA	129	505			129	551
BEMIDJI STATE U/MN	117	534	11	698	128	555
CHARLESTON, C OF/SC	120	526	8	786	128	555
GUILFORD COLL/NC	116	536	12	670	128	555
TENNESSEE STATE UNIV	102	575	25	425	127	558
TOWSON ST COLL/MD	103	572	24	440	127	558
DOANE COLLEGE/NE	121	524	6	855	127	558
ROSE-HULMAN TECH/IN	125	516			125	561
WILKES COLLEGE/PA	110	549	15	607	125	561
BELLARMINE COLL/KY	106	560	19	531	125	561
IOWA WESLEYAN COLL	109	553	15	607	124	564
AUGSBURG COLLEGE/MN	110	549	13	644	123	565
ST JOSEPHS COLL/IN	120	526	3	972	123	565
BOB JONES UNIV/SC	106	560	17	563	123	565
MT ST VINCENT,COL/NY	1	1328	122	105	123	565
YANKTON COLLEGE/SD	109	553	13	644	122	569
JAMESTOWN COLLEGE/ND	114	539	8	786	122	569
COLUMBIA UNION C/MD	107	559	14	625	121	571
BRIDGEPORT, U OF/CT	104	570	17	563	121	571
SUNY COLL GENESEO	102	575	19	531	121	571
ST ANSELMS COLL/NH	117	534	4	935	121	571
ST MARYS SEM & U/MD	120	526			120	575
NC AG & TECH ST U	106	560	14	625	120	575
NC CENTRAL UNIV	91	605	29	379	120	575
SUSQUEHANNA UNIV/PA	99	582	20	514	119	578
MIDLAND LTHRN C/NE	109	553	10	724	119	578
MASS COLL PHARMACY	116	536	3	972	119	578
SUNY COLL NEW PALTZ	101	579	17	563	118	581
ELIZABETHTOWN C/PA	111	546	7	821	118	581
MANHATTANVILLE C/NY	2	1252	116	112	118	581
ILL BENEDICTINE COLL	118	531			118	581
MOREHEAD STATE U/KY	106	560	12	670	118	581
MORGAN STATE UNIV/MD	92	602	25	425	117	586
DUBUQUE, UNIV OF/IA	108	558	9	755	117	586
INDIANA CENTRAL UNIV	105	564	11	698	116	588
CONCORD COLLEGE/WV	94	598	22	472	116	588
DELTA STATE UNIV/MS	95	593	21	493	116	588
TULANE U-NEWCMB C/LA			116	112	116	588

APPENDIX G Continued

	Male		Female		Both Sexes	
	Number	Rank	Number	Rank	Number	Rank
SOUTHERN CONN ST COL	94	598	22	472	116	588
ESTRN NAZARENE C/MA	99	582	16	584	115	593
HOWARD PAYNE COLL/TX	96	588	19	531	115	593
WINONA STATE UNIV/MN	109	553	6	855	115	593
NORTH ALABAMA, UNIV	101	579	13	644	114	596
LINCOLN UNIV/PA	114	539			114	596
BARD COLLEGE/NY	94	598	20	514	114	596
ST MICHAELS COLL/VT	112	544	1	1101	113	599
REGIS COLLEGE/CO	110	549	3	972	113	599
UNION UNIVERSITY/TN	104	570	8	786	112	601
ROANOKE COLLEGE/VA	99	582	13	644	112	601
BLUFFTON COLLEGE/OH	102	575	10	724	112	601
ADAMS STATE COLL/CO	105	564	6	855	111	605
GANNON COLLEGE/PA	111	546			111	605
TEXAS,U-ARLINGTON	100	581	10	724	110	607
ST JOHNS COLLEGE/MD	103	572	7	821	110	607
PRINCIPIA COLLEGE/IL	90	608	20	514	110	607
VALLEY CITY ST C/ND	102	575	7	821	109	610
MACMURRAY COLLEGE/IL	45	771	64	195	109	610
PRAIRIE VIEW A&M/TX	85	623	24	440	109	610
DAKOTA WESLEYAN U/SD	95	593	13	644	108	613
MUNDELEIN COLLEGE/IL			108	122	108	613
SUNY COLL ONEONTA	81	633	27	400	108	613
AUSTIN PEAY ST U/TN	98	586	10	724	108	613
MANSFIELD ST COLL/PA	96	588	11	698	107	617
WILSON COLLEGE/PA			107	124	107	617
WILMINGTON COLL/OH	95	593	11	698	106	619
CHADRON ST COLL/NE	96	588	10	724	106	619
MORAVIAN COLLEGE/PA	98	586	8	786	106	619
ANDERSON COLLEGE/IN	96	588	9	755	105	622
LENOIR-RHYNE COLL/NC	93	601	12	670	105	622
WEST VIRGINIA ST C	79	646	25	425	104	625
ST. JOSEPH SEMNRY/NY	103	572	1	1101	104	625
RHODE ISLAND COLLEGE	69	682	35	336	104	625
ITHACA COLLEGE/NY	86	617	17	563	103	628
EMMANUEL COLLEGE/MA	4	1141	99	133	103	628
THOMAS MORE COLL/KY	80	640	23	460	103	628
WESTMAR COLLEGE/IA	95	593	8	786	103	628
FRIENDS UNIV/KS	89	610	14	625	103	628
TEXAS, U-EL PASO	80	640	23	460	103	628
FAIRMONT STATE C/WV	89	610	13	644	102	634
CATAWBA COLLEGE/NC	89	610	13	644	102	634
MCMURRAY COLLEGE/TX	91	605	10	724	101	636
WSTRN CAROLINA U/NC	84	626	17	563	101	636
D C TEACHERS COLLEGE	65	693	36	331	101	636
TARKIO COLLEGE/MO	96	588	5	888	101	636
HARTWICK COLLEGE/NY	90	608	11	698	101	636
PRATT INSTITUTE/NY	95	593	5	888	100	641
SUNY COLL POTSDAM	86	617	14	625	100	641
GENERAL MOTORS I/MI	99	582			99	643
HARRIS TCHRS COLL/MO	56	724	43	287	99	643
WASHINGTON COLL/MD	85	623	13	644	98	645
CONCORDIA TCHRS C/NE	91	605	7	821	98	645
BERRY COLLEGE/GA	86	617	12	670	98	645
GLASSBORO ST COLL/NJ	77	651	20	514	97	648
FITCHBERG ST COLL/M	89	610	7	821	96	649
OREGON COLL OF EDUC	84	626	12	670	96	649
PACIFIC UNIV/OR	85	623	10	724	95	651
MIDWESTERN UNIV/TX	86	617	9	755	95	651
MINOT STATE COLL/ND	83	629	12	670	95	651
ASHLAND COLLEGE/OH	87	615	7	821	94	654
MARYGROVE COLLEGE/MI			94	141	94	654
VIRGINIA UNION UNIV	75	656	19	531	94	654
PRESBYTERIAN COLL/SC	92	602	2	1035	94	654
MILLS COLLEGE/CA	1	1328	93	142	94	654

	Male		Female		Both Sexes	
	Number	Rank	Number	Rank	Number	Rank
ST FRANCIS COLL/PA	86	617	8	786	94	654
LYCOMING COLLEGE/PA	81	633	13	644	94	654
POINT LOMA COLL/CA	82	630	11	698	93	661
SUL ROSS STATE U/TX	82	630	11	698	93	661
ALABAMA STATE UNIV	79	646	14	625	93	661
GLENVILLE ST COLL/WV	81	633	12	670	93	661
WEST LIBERTY ST C/WV	84	626	9	755	93	661
ROCKFORD COLLEGE/IL	32	843	61	206	93	661
ERSKINE COLLEGE/SC	73	662	19	531	92	667
CAL ST POLY-POMONA	87	615	5	888	92	667
QUINCY COLLEGE/IL	80	640	11	698	91	669
AQUINAS COLLEGE/MI	71	666	20	514	91	669
N MEXICO HIGHLANDS U	81	633	9	755	90	671
TALLADEGA COLLEGE/AL	65	693	25	425	90	671
SETON HILL COLL/PA	1	1328	89	147	90	671
JULLIARD SCHOOL/NY	71	666	19	531	90	671
MERRIMACK COLLEGE/MA	80	640	9	755	89	676
NE LOUISIANA UNIV	71	666	18	548	89	676
USAF ACADEMY/CO	89	610			89	676
LINCOLN UNIV/MO	71	666	18	548	89	676
BETHANY COLL/KS	81	633	7	821	88	681
MINNESOTA,U-DULUTH	80	640	8	786	88	681
MONTEVALLO, U OF/AL	22	908	65	192	87	683
ARKANSAS, U-PINE BLU	65	693	21	493	86	684
ST CATHERINE,C OF/MN			86	155	86	684
MT ST MARYS COLL/MD	86	617			86	684
BUENA VISTA COLL/IA	79	646	6	855	85	687
GORDON COLLEGE/MA	79	646	6	855	85	687
HILLSDALE COLLEGE/MI	67	688	17	563	84	689
STERLING COLLEGE/KS	76	655	8	786	84	689
CENTRAL STATE U/OH	72	664	12	670	84	689
WINTHROP COLLEGE/SC			84	157	84	689
MISS UNIV WOMEN	3	1188	80	162	83	693
GEORGIA COLLEGE	1	1328	82	159	83	693
BLACKBURN COLLEGE/IL	74	658	9	755	83	693
ST MARYS COLLEGE/IN			83	158	83	693
TABOR COLLEGE/KS	82	630	1	1101	83	693
ILLINOIS,U-CHIGO CIR	70	673	13	644	83	693
CARROLL COLLEGE/MT	80	640	3	972	83	693
HURON COLLEGE/SD	74	658	8	786	82	700
TEXAS WESLEYAN COLL	61	705	21	493	82	700
ST JOSEPHS COLL/NY	2	1252	80	162	82	700
ROCHESTER I TECH/NY	77	651	4	935	81	703
KEAN COLL NEW JERSEY	53	729	28	390	81	703
CLAREMONT MENS C/CA	81	633			81	703
NW NAZARENE COLL/ID	71	666	9	755	80	706
ARKANSAS,U-MONTICELO	73	662	7	821	80	706
NEW ORLEANS,U OF/LA	69	682	11	698	80	706
WILLIAM PENN COLL/IA	66	689	14	625	80	706
MISSOURI VALLEY C/MO	74	658	6	855	80	706
OLIVET COLLEGE/MI	75	656	4	935	79	711
MARION COLLEGE/IN	70	673	9	755	79	711
ADRIAN COLLEGE/MI	70	673	9	755	79	711
MORRIS HARVEY C/WV	70	673	9	755	79	711
HUNTINGDON COLL/AL	45	771	34	344	79	711
CHATHAM COLLEGE/PA			79	164	79	711
WOODSTOCK COLL/NY	79	646			79	711
TAMPA, UNIV OF/FL	70	673	8	786	78	719
KING COLLEGE/TN	70	673	8	786	78	719
OLD DOMINION UNIV/VA	65	693	13	644	78	719
ROSARY COLLEGE/IL	1	1328	77	168	78	719
OAKLAND UNIV/MI	66	689	11	698	77	723
KANSAS WESLEYAN	70	673	7	821	77	723
ST JOHN FISHER C/NY	77	651			77	723
SARAH LAWRENCE C/NY	2	1252	75	171	77	723

SOURCE: NRC, Commission on Human Resources.

APPENDIX H
ALPHABETIC LISTING OF INSTITUTIONS OF BACCALAUREATE ORIGIN OF 1920-1974 PhD's, WITH INSTITUTIONAL RANKS BY SEX

	Male		Female		Both Sexes	
	Number	Rank	Number	Rank	Number	Rank
ABILENE CHRIST U/TX	349	242	26	412	375	257
ACAD NEW CHURCH/PA	2	1252			2	1418
ADAMS STATE COLL/CO	105	564	6	855	111	605
ADELPHI UNIV/NY	182	398	101	131	283	319
ADRIAN COLLEGE/MI	70	673	9	755	79	711
AGNES SCOTT COLL/GA	1	1328	149	80	150	503
AIR FORCE I TECH/OH	9	1038			9	1206
AKRON, U OF/OH	370	223	56	230	426	230
ALABAMA AG&MECH U	36	828	11	698	47	867
ALABAMA CHRISTIAN C	1	1328			1	1482
ALABAMA STATE UNIV	79	646	14	625	93	661
ALABAMA, UNIVER OF	987	88	198	59	1185	82
ALABAMA,U-BIRMINGHAM	2	1252	1	1101	3	1361
ALABAMA,U-HUNTSVILLE	3	1188			3	1361
ALASKA METHODIST U	6	1080	1	1101	7	1246
ALASKA, UNIV OF	70	673	6	855	76	729
ALBANY STATE COLL/GA	12	1004	4	935	16	1124
ALBERTUS MAGNUS C/CT	1	1328	46	274	47	867
ALBION COLLEGE/MI	341	248	35	336	376	256
ALBRIGHT COLLEGE/PA	187	389	14	625	201	414
ALBUQUERQUE,U OF/NM	13	993	6	855	19	1089
ALCORN STATE U/MS	46	764	7	821	53	825
ALDERSN BROADUS C/WV	24	890	7	821	31	964
ALFRED UNIVERSITY/NY	328	256	27	400	355	272
ALLEGHENY COLLEGE/PA	442	191	66	191	508	202
ALLEN UNIVERSITY/SC	13	993	8	786	21	1068
ALLNTWN C ST FRAN/PA	1	1328			1	1482
ALLIANCE COLLEGE/PA	13	993			13	1152
ALMA COLLEGE/MI	148	469	12	670	160	486
ALMA WHITE COLL/NJ	3	1188			3	1361
ALVERNIA COLLEGE/PA			1	1101	1	1482
ALVERNO COLLEGE/WI			46	274	46	874
AM BAPT SEM W-BER/CA	1	1328			1	1482
AM BAPT SEM W-COV/CA	2	1252			2	1418
AMER CONSERV MUS/IL	30	851	8	786	38	921
AMER INTERNATL C/MA	150	463	16	584	166	479
AMERICAN UNIV/DC	247	319	72	176	319	291
AMHERST COLLEGE/MA	1156	66			1156	83
ANDERSON COLLEGE/IN	96	588	9	755	105	622
ANDVR NEW THEOL S/MA	4	1141			4	1321
ANDREWS UNIV/MI	193	381	25	425	218	391
ANGELO STATE UNIV/TX	7	1062	2	1035	9	1206
ANNA MARIA COLL/MA			9	755	9	1206
ANNHURST COLLEGE/CT			8	786	8	1221
ANTIOCH COLLEGE/OH	590	147	148	82	738	138
ANTIOCH EAST/MD			1	1101	1	1482
AQUINAS COLLEGE/MI	71	666	20	514	91	669
AQUINAS INST/IA	12	1004			12	1159
ARIZONA STATE UNIV	608	142	109	120	717	141
ARIZONA, UNIV OF	988	87	148	82	1136	84
ARKANSAS BAPTIST C	1	1328			1	1482
ARKANSAS COLLEGE	34	837	6	855	40	911
ARKANSAS POLY COLL	70	673	3	972	73	741
ARKANSAS STATE UNIV	185	392	14	625	199	424
ARKANSAS,U-FAYETTVLE	956	90	126	103	1082	89
ARKANSAS,U-LTLE ROCK	25	883	9	755	34	946
ARKANSAS,U-MONTICELO	73	662	7	821	80	706
ARKANSAS, U-PINE BLU	65	693	21	493	86	684
ARMSTRONG COLLEGE/CA	3	1188	1	1101	4	1321
ARMSTRONG STATE C/GA	2	1252	1	1101	3	1361
ASBURY COLLEGE/KY	173	421	28	390	201	414
ASBURY THEOL SEM/KY	2	1252			2	1418
ASHLAND COLLEGE/OH	87	615	7	821	94	654
ASSUMPTION COLL/MA	62	702			62	777
ASSUMPTION FRIARY/MN	3	1188			3	1361
ASSUMPTION SEM/TX	2	1252			2	1418
ATHENAEUM OF OHIO	48	755	10	724	58	794
ATHENS COLLEGE/AL	18	947	5	888	23	1048
ATLANTA COLL ART/GA	1	1328			1	1482
ATLANTA LAW SCH/GA			1	1101	1	1482
ATLANTA UNIV/GA	10	1027			10	1192
ATLANTIC CHRSTN C/NC	62	702	8	786	70	753
ATLANTIC UNION C/MA	57	721	8	786	65	766
AUBURN UNIVERSITY/AL	945	92	60	214	1005	98
AUGSBURG COLLEGE/MN	110	549	13	644	123	565
AUGUSTA COLLEGE/GA	9	1038	3	972	12	1159
AUGUSTANA COLL/IL	406	207	30	367	436	226
AUGUSTANA COLL/SD	177	411	23	460	200	420
AURORA COLLEGE/IL	49	747	3	972	52	833
AUSTIN COLLEGE/TX	154	456	17	563	171	472
AUSTIN PEAY ST U/TN	98	586	10	724	108	613
AUSTIN PRSBY THEO/TX	1	1328			1	1482
AVILA COLLEGE/MO			11	698	11	1175
AZUSA PACIFIC C/CA	18	947	1	1101	19	1089
BABSON COLLEGE/MA	10	1027			10	1192
BAKER UNIV/KS	189	388	21	493	210	400
BALDWIN-WALLACE C/OH	264	298	37	322	301	300
BALL STATE UNIV/IN	503	175	88	149	591	169
BALTIMORE,UNIV OF/MD	8	1049			8	1221
BANGOR THEOL SEM/ME	3	1188			3	1361
BAPTIST BIBLE C PENN	13	993	2	1035	15	1132
BARAT COLLEGE/IL			35	336	35	938
BARBER-SCOTIA C/NC			2	1035	2	1418
BARD COLLEGE/NY	94	598	20	514	114	596
BARRINGTON COLL/RI	24	890	3	972	27	999
BARRY COLLEGE/FL			17	563	17	1111
BATES COLLEGE/ME	407	206	54	236	461	217
BAYLOR COLL MED/TX	2	1252			2	1418
BAYLOR UNIV/TX	865	103	153	76	1018	96
BEAVER COLLEGE/PA			27	400	27	999
BELHAVEN COLLEGE/MS	10	1027	9	755	19	1089
BELLARMINE COLL/KY	106	560	19	531	125	561
BELMONT ABBEY C/NC	16	964	3	972	19	1089
BELMONT COLLEGE/TN	18	947	3	972	21	1068
BELOIT COLLEGE/WI	347	244	62	201	409	238
BEMIDJI STATE U/MN	117	534	11	698	128	555
BENEDICT COLLEGE/SC	19	939	3	972	22	1057
BENEDICTINE COLL/KS	159	448	53	242	212	395
BENJMN FRANKLIN U/DC	1	1328			1	1482
BENNETT COLLEGE/NC			18	548	18	1101
BENNINGTON COLL/VT			40	303	40	911
BEREA COLLEGE/KY	404	208	53	242	457	220
BERKSHRE CHRIST C/MA	4	1141			4	1321
BERRY COLLEGE/GA	86	617	12	670	98	645
BETHANY BIBLE C/CA	4	1141			4	1321
BETHANY COLL/KS	81	633	7	821	88	681
BETHANY COLLEGE/WV	172	422	16	584	188	440
BETHANY-NAZRENE C/OK	118	531	15	607	133	545
BETHANY THEOL SEM/IL			1	1101	1	1482
BETHEL COLLEGE/IN	16	964	1	1101	17	1111
BETHEL COLL/KS	163	439	8	786	171	472
BETHEL COLLEGE/MN	15	973			15	1132
BETHEL SEMINARY/MN	36	828	1	1101	37	927
BETHEL COLLEGE/TN	45	771	3	972	48	862
BETHUNE-COOKMAN C/FL	24	890	6	855	30	972
BIOLA COLLEGE/CA	22	908	3	972	25	1022
BIRMNGHAM-STHRN C/AL	304	273	59	219	363	264
BISCAYNE COLLEGE/FL	1	1328			1	1482
BISHOP COLLEGE/TX	23	902	13	644	36	933
BLACK HILLS ST C/SD	61	705	6	855	67	760
BLACKBURN COLLEGE/IL	74	658	9	755	83	693
BLOOMFIELD COLL/NJ	16	964	1	1101	17	1111
BLOOMSBURG ST COL/PA	166	436	18	548	184	447
BLUE MOUNTAIN C/MS	2	1252	28	390	30	972
BLUEFIELD ST COLL/WV	14	981	5	888	19	1089
BLUFFTON COLLEGE/OH	102	575	10	724	112	601
BOB JONES UNIV/SC	106	560	17	563	123	565
BOISE STATE UNIV/ID	5	1106	3	972	8	1221
BORROMEO COL OF OHIO	7	1062	1	1101	8	1221

APPENDIX H Continued

	Male		Female		Both Sexes	
	Number	Rank	Number	Rank	Number	Rank
BOSTON COLLEGE/MA	994	86	55	234	1049	92
BOSTON CONSRV MUS/MA	4	1141	2	1035	6	1269
BOSTON UNIVERSITY/MA	1213	63	403	27	1616	52
BOWDOIN COLLEGE/ME	599	144			599	167
BOWIE ST COLL/MD	1	1328	1	1101	2	1418
BOWLING GREEN S U/OH	496	178	98	137	594	168
BRADLEY UNIV/IL	345	246	33	350	378	251
BRANDEIS UNIV/MA	346	245	155	73	501	205
BRENAU COLLEGE/GA	1	1328	13	644	14	1141
BRESCIA COLLEGE/KY	11	1014	6	855	17	1111
BRIAR CLIFF COLL/IA	1	1328	15	607	16	1124
BRIDGEPORT, U OF/CT	104	570	17	563	121	571
BRIDGEWATER COLL/VA	142	476	15	607	157	491
BRIGHAM YOUNG U/UT	2136	29	99	133	2235	34
BRIGHAM YOUNG,HAWAII	3	1188			3	1361
BROOKLYN LAW SCHOOL	19	939	2	1035	21	1068
BROWN UNIVERSITY/RI	1447	52	253	47	1700	48
BRYAN COLLEGE/TN	24	890	3	972	27	999
BRYANT COLLEGE/RI	19	939	3	972	22	1057
BRYN MAWR COLL/PA	4	1141	560	20	564	177
BUCKNELL UNIV/PA	507	174	104	125	611	163
BUENA VISTA COLL/IA	79	646	6	855	85	687
BUTLER UNIV/IN	329	255	63	200	392	244
CABRINI COLLEGE/PA			1	1101	1	1482
CALDWELL COLL/NJ			14	625	14	1141
CALIF BAPTIST COLL	4	1141			4	1321
CAL C ARTS & CRAFTS	5	1106	1	1101	6	1269
CAL INST TECHNOLOGY	1709	40	2	1035	1711	47
CALIF INST ARTS	4	1141			4	1321
CALIF LUTHERAN COLL	12	1004			12	1159
CALIF MARITIME ACAD	3	1188			3	1361
CALIF STATE COLL/PA	226	343	23	460	249	354
CAL POL S U-SL OBISP	269	293	6	855	275	329
CAL ST C DOMINGUEZ H	2	1252	1	1101	3	1361
CAL ST COLL, SONOMA	22	908	3	972	25	1022
CAL ST C STANISLAUS	9	1038			9	1206
CAL ST POLY-POMONA	87	615	5	888	92	667
CAL ST U, CHICO	258	306	20	514	278	327
CAL ST U, FRESNO	490	181	33	350	523	193
CAL ST U, FULLERTON	60	711	12	670	72	745
CAL ST U, HAYWARD	50	744	8	786	58	794
HUMBOLDT STATE U/CA	157	449	6	855	163	482
CAL ST U, LONG BEACH	425	198	61	206	486	209
CAL ST U,LOS ANGELES	436	195	89	147	525	192
CAL ST U, NORTHRIDGE	178	407	29	379	207	402
CAL ST U, SACRAMENTO	251	313	39	309	290	310
CAL ST C,S BERNRDINO	4	1141	3	972	7	1246
SAN DIEGO STATE U/CA	839	104	93	142	932	106
SAN FRANCISC ST U/CA	612	140	99	133	711	143
SAN JOSE STATE U/CA	905	98	113	118	1018	96
CALIFORNIA ST U-UNK	3	1188			3	1361
CALIF, U-BERKELEY	7117	1	1071	2	8188	1
CALIF, U-DAVIS	634	138	65	192	699	147
CALIF,U-DAVIS,S MED	1	1328			1	1482
CALIF,U-IRVINE	43	785	9	755	52	833
CAL,U-IRVINE,COLL MD	1	1328			1	1482
CALIF,U-LOS ANGELES	3971	10	738	11	4709	10
CALIF,U-RIVERSIDE	440	194	54	236	494	206
CALIF, U-SAN DIEGO	28	860	5	888	33	952
CAL, U-SAN FRANCISCO	2	1252	1	1101	3	1361
CALIF,U,SAN FRAN MED			4	935	4	1321
CALIF,U-SANTA BARB	701	127	88	149	789	132
CALIF,U-SANTA CRUZ	25	883	8	786	33	952
CALIFORNIA, U-UNK	18	947	7	821	25	1022
CALUMET COLLEGE/IN	2	1252	1	1101	3	1361
CALVARY BIBLE C/MO	6	1080			6	1269
CALVIN COLLEGE/MI	590	147	23	460	613	162
CALVIN THEOL SEM/MI	4	1141			4	1321
CAMERON UNIV/OKLA	1	1328			1	1482
CAMPBELL COLLEGE/NC	11	1014			11	1175
CAMPBELLSVILLE C/KY	9	1038	2	1035	11	1175
CANISIUS COLLEGE/NY	316	265	12	670	328	284
CAPITAL UNIV/OH	241	325	20	514	261	343
CAPITOL I OF TECH/MD	1	1328			1	1482
CARDINAL GLENON C/MO	27	865			27	999
CARDINL STRITCH C/WI			18	548	18	1101
CARLETON COLLEGE/MN	717	123	149	80	866	116
CARLOW COLLEGE/PA			48	268	48	862
CARNEGIE-MELLON U/PA	1411	55	102	129	1513	59
CARROLL COLLEGE/MT	80	640	3	972	83	693
CARROLL COLLEGE/WI	172	422	17	563	189	438
CARSON-NEWMAN C/TN	171	428	23	460	194	430
CARTHAGE COLL/WI	122	522	11	698	133	545
CASE WESTRN RSRVE/OH	1754	38	259	46	2013	38
CASTLETON ST COLL/VT	8	1049	4	935	12	1159
CATAWBA COLLEGE/NC	89	610	13	644	102	634
CATHED C IM CONCP/NY	55	727			55	807
CATHOLIC U AMER/DC	1090	76	219	52	1309	70
CATHOLIC UNIV P.R.	3	1188	6	855	9	1206
CEDAR CREST COLL/PA	1	1328	16	584	17	1111
CEDARVILLE COLL/OH	22	908	3	972	25	1022
CENTENARY COLL/LA	141	478	30	367	171	472
CENTRAL ARKANSAS, U	178	407	33	350	211	398
CTRL BAPT THEOL S/KS	1	1328			1	1482
CENTRAL BIBLE C/MO	16	964	3	972	19	1089
CENTRAL UNIV/IA	172	422	14	625	186	445
CENTRAL CONN ST COLL	194	379	28	390	222	382
CENTRAL METH COLL/MO	219	351	22	472	241	359
CENTRAL MICHIGAN U	369	225	48	268	417	233
CTRL MISSOURI ST U	371	222	62	201	433	229
CENTRAL STATE U/OH	72	664	12	670	84	689
CENTRAL STATE U/OK	223	345	56	230	279	325
CENTRAL WASH STATE C	207	362	10	724	217	392
CENTRL WESLEYAN C/SC	7	1062	1	1101	8	1221
CENTRE COLL KENTUCKY	126	513	16	584	142	519
CHADRON ST COLL/NE	96	588	10	724	106	619
CHAMINADE C HONOLULU	1	1328	4	935	5	1293
CHAPMAN COLLEGE/CA	58	716	5	888	63	771
CHARLESTON, C OF/SC	120	526	8	786	128	555
CHATHAM COLLEGE/PA			79	164	79	711
CHESTNUT HILL C/PA			54	236	54	816
CHEYNEY ST COLL/PA	25	883	10	724	35	938
CHG ACAD FINE ART/IL	1	1328			1	1482
CHICAGO CONS COLL/IL	6	1080	2	1035	8	1221
CHICAGO STATE U/IL	29	856	9	755	38	921
CHICAGO TECH COLL/IL	1	1328			1	1482
CHICAGO THEOL SEM/IL	2	1252			2	1418
CHICAGO, UNIV OF/IL	3865	11	821	6	4686	11
CHRISTN BROTHRS C/TN	37	823			37	927
CHRISTN THEOL SEM/IN	2	1252			2	1418
CINCIN BIBLE COLL/OH	24	890	1	1101	25	1022
CINCINNATI, U OF/OH	1202	64	179	64	1381	64
CITADEL, THE/SC	200	372			200	420
CUNY-BERNRD BARUCH C	21	919	3	972	24	1035
CUNY-BROOKLYN COLL	3240	18	774	8	4014	16
CUNY-CITY COLLEGE	6526	2	362	32	6888	2
CUNY-HUNTER COLLEGE	403	210	1206	1	1609	53
CUNY-JOHN JAY COLL	2	1252			2	1418
CUNY-HRBERT LEHMAN C	8	1049	3	972	11	1175
CUNY-QUEENS COLL	1139	69	386	29	1525	57
CUNY-UNKNOWN	7	1062	1	1101	8	1221
CLAFLIN COLLEGE/SC	16	964	1	1101	17	1111
CLAREMNT GRAD SCH/CA	1	1328			1	1482
CLAREMONT MENS C/CA	81	633			81	703
HARVEY MUDD COLL/CA	133	496	3	972	136	537
PITZER COLLEGE/CA	1	1328	5	888	6	1269
POMONA COLLEGE/CA	803	108	156	72	959	103
SCRIPPS COLLEGE/CA	2	1252	19	531	21	1068
CLARION STATE C/PA	138	485	9	755	147	510
CLARK COLLEGE/GA	46	764	13	644	59	786
CLARK UNIVERSITY/MA	492	180	45	279	537	188
CLARKE COLLEGE/IA			59	219	59	786
CLARKSON C TECH/NY	267	294			267	338
CLEMSON UNIV/SC	595	145	7	821	602	165
CLEVELAND INST MUSIC	14	981	2	1035	16	1124
CLEVELAND ST UNIV/OH	131	498	13	644	144	515
COE COLLEGE/IA	222	347	35	336	257	346
COKER COLLEGE/SC	2	1252	16	584	18	1101
COLBY COLLEGE/ME	256	308	43	287	299	301
COLBY-SAWYER C/NH	1	1328			1	1482

APPENDIX H Continued

	Male Number	Male Rank	Female Number	Female Rank	Both Sexes Number	Both Sexes Rank
COLG RCH-BEX-CROZ/NY	5	1106	1	1101	6	1269
COLGATE U/NY	580	151			580	174
COLORADO COLLEGE	311	269	69	185	380	247
COLORADO SCH MINES	255	310	1	1101	256	349
COLORADO STATE UNIV	1029	82	64	195	1093	88
COLORADO,U-BOULDER	1704	41	309	40	2013	38
COLO,U-COLO SPRINGS	2	1252			2	1418
COLO,U-DENVER CTR			3	972	3	1361
COLORADO WOMEN'S COL			5	888	5	1293
COLUMBIA BIBLE C/SC	13	993	7	821	20	1081
COLUMBIA COLLEGE/IL	9	1038			9	1206
COLUMBIA COLLEGE/SC	1	1328	17	563	18	1101
COLMBIA THEOL SEM/GA	1	1328			1	1482
COLUMBIA UNION C/MD	107	559	14	625	121	571
COLUMBIA UNIV/NY	3715	13	468	22	4183	13
COLUMBIA-BARNARD/NY	3	1188	945	3	948	105
COLUMBIA U-COL C/NY	142	476			142	519
COLUMBIA-PHARM C/NY	4	1141			4	1321
COLUMBIA-TCHRS C/NY	122	522	160	70	282	322
COMBS COLL MUSIC/PA	1	1328			1	1482
CONCEPTION SEM C/MO	26	877			26	1014
CONCORD COLLEGE/WV	94	598	22	472	116	588
CONCORDIA-MORHEAD/MN	310	270	32	360	342	279
CONCORDIA SR COLL/IN	53	729			53	825
CONCORDIA TCHRS C/IL	171	428	8	786	179	455
CONCORDIA TCHRS C/NE	91	605	7	821	98	645
CONCORDIA THEOL S/IL	11	1014			11	1175
CONCORD THEO SEM/MO	181	399			181	451
CONNECTICUT COLLEGE	2	1252	132	98	134	541
CONNECTICUT, UNIV OF	1077	78	114	117	1191	80
CONVERSE COLLEGE/SC	4	1141	29	379	33	952
COOPER UNION/NY	531	165	5	888	536	189
COPPIN ST COLL/MD	4	1141	4	935	8	1221
CORNELL COLLEGE/IA	353	238	38	315	391	245
CORNELL UNIV/NY	4265	9	745	10	5010	8
CORNELL U MED C/NY			1	1101	1	1482
COVENANT COLL/TN	3	1188			3	1361
CREIGHTON UNIV/NE	235	335	64	195	299	301
CROSER HOUSE STUD/IN	1	1328			1	1482
CULVER-STOCKTON C/MO	68	687	6	855	74	738
CUMBERLAND COLL/KY	8	1049	2	1035	10	1192
CUMBERLAND COLL TENN	2	1252			2	1418
CURRY COLLEGE/MA	6	1080			6	1269
CURTIS I OF MUSIC/PA	10	1027			10	1192
DAKOTA ST COLL/SD	39	808	2	1035	41	904
DAKOTA WESLEYAN U/SD	95	593	13	644	108	613
DALLAS, UNIV OF/TX	27	865	5	888	32	958
DANA COLLEGE/NE	57	721	1	1101	58	794
DARTMOUTH COLLEGE/NH	1771	37	2	1035	1773	44
DAVID LIPSCOMB C/TN	176	415	12	670	188	440
DAVIDSON COLLEGE/NC	547	160			547	184
DAVIS & ELKINS C/WV	57	721	5	888	62	777
DAYTON, U OF/OH	503	175	37	322	540	186
DEFIANCE COLLEGE/OH	49	747	5	888	54	816
DELAWARE STATE COLL	12	1004			12	1159
DELAWARE, UNIV OF	531	165	70	181	601	166
DELAWARE VALLEY C/PA	71	666			71	749
DELTA STATE UNIV/MS	95	593	21	493	116	588
DENISON UNIV/OH	423	201	88	149	511	198
DENVER, UNIV OF/CO	839	104	155	73	994	102
DEPAUL UNIVERSITY/IL	354	237	99	133	453	222
DEPAUW UNIVERSITY/IN	934	93	103	126	1037	94
DETROIT BIBLE C/MI	5	1106			5	1293
DETROIT COLL OF LAW	1	1328			1	1482
DETROIT C MUSIC S/MI	3	1188	1	1101	4	1321
DETROIT I TECH/MI	31	845			31	964
DETROIT, U OF/MI	526	167	51	256	577	175
DICKINSON COLL/PA	310	270	41	295	351	276
DICKINSON ST COLL/ND	48	755	3	972	51	847
DILLARD UNIV/LA	46	764	13	644	59	786
D C TEACHERS COLLEGE	65	693	36	331	101	636
DIVINE WORD COLL/IA	4	1141			4	1321
DOANE COLLEGE/NE	121	524	6	855	127	558
DOMIN C SAN RAFEL/CA			25	425	25	1022
DOMNCN HOUSE STD/DC			1	1101	1	1482
DON BOSCO COLLEGE/NJ	17	954			17	1111
DORDT COLLEGE/IA	7	1062	1	1101	8	1221
DOWLING COLLEGE/NY	5	1106	1	1101	6	1269
DR MARTIN LUTHR C/MN	2	1252			2	1418
DRAKE UNIV/IA	393	211	61	206	454	221
DREW UNIVERSITY/NJ	240	326	33	350	273	332
DREXEL UNIVERSITY/PA	605	143	25	425	630	157
DROPSIE UNIV/PA	1	1328			1	1482
DRURY COLLEGE/MO	174	420	22	472	196	428
DUBUQUE, UNIV OF/IA	108	558	9	755	117	586
DUKE UNIVERSITY/NC	1115	71	231	50	1346	68
DUNS SCOTUS COLL/MI	27	865	1	1101	28	987
DUQUESNE UNIV/PA	389	212	88	149	477	212
DYOUVILLE COLLEGE/NY			50	260	50	852
DYKE COLLEGE/OH	1	1328			1	1482
EARLHAM COLLEGE/IN	381	217	61	206	442	223
E CENTRAL STATE C/OK	162	443	23	460	185	446
E STROUDSBURG SC/PA	120	526	22	472	142	519
EAST TENN STATE UNIV	179	402	25	425	204	408
EAST TEXAS BAPTIST C	35	834	6	855	41	904
EAST TEXAS STATE U	357	235	81	160	438	224
ESTRN BAPT THEO S/PA	20	927			20	1081
EASTERN COLLEGE/PA	36	828	3	972	39	917
EASTERN CONN ST COLL	16	964	9	755	25	1022
EASTERN ILL UNIV	370	223	37	322	407	239
EASTERN KENTUCKY U	204	364	26	412	230	374
ESTRN MENNONITE C/VA	61	705	5	888	66	765
EASTERN MICHIGAN U	415	204	76	170	491	208
EASTERN MONTANA COLL	42	792	2	1035	44	884
ESTRN NAZARENE C/MA	99	582	16	584	115	593
EASTERN NEW MEXICO U	137	486	14	625	151	501
EASTERN WASH STATE C	213	356	19	531	232	372
ECKERD COLLEGE/FL	37	823	12	670	49	857
EDEN THEOL SEM/MO	3	1188			3	1361
EDGECLIFF COLLEGE/OH			19	531	19	1089
EDGEWOOD COLL/WI			11	698	11	1175
EDINBORO ST COLL/PA	129	505	13	644	142	519
EDWARD WATERS C/FL	4	1141			4	1321
ELIZABETHTOWN C/PA	111	546	7	821	118	581
ELMHURST COLLEGE/IL	136	489	10	724	146	512
ELMIRA COLLEGE/NY	2	1252	50	260	52	833
ELON COLLEGE/NC	66	689	7	821	73	741
EMBRY-RIDDLE U/FL	1	1328			1	1482
EMERSON COLLEGE/MA	47	760	15	607	62	777
EMMANUEL COLLEGE/MA	4	1141	99	133	103	628
EMORY & HENRY C/VA	128	509	13	644	141	526
EMORY UNIV/GA	760	115	79	164	839	119
EMPORIA KAN ST COLL	556	157	77	168	633	155
EPISCPL DIV SCH/MA	5	1106			5	1293
ERSKINE COLLEGE/SC	73	662	19	531	92	667
EUREKA COLLEGE/IL	48	755	7	821	55	807
EVANGEL COLLEGE/MO	19	939	2	1035	21	1068
EVANSVILLE, U OF/IN	153	457	18	548	171	472
FAIRFIELD UNIV/CT	150	463			150	503
FAIRLEIGH DICKN U/NJ	170	430	17	563	187	444
FAIRLGH D-MADISON/NJ	4	1141	1	1101	5	1293
FAIRLGH D-TEANECK/NJ	20	927	4	935	24	1035
FAIRMONT STATE C/WV	89	610	13	644	102	634
FAITH THEOL SEM/PA	1	1328			1	1482
FEDERAL CITY COLL/DC	1	1328			1	1482
FELICIAN COLLEGE/NJ			1	1101	1	1482
FERRIS ST COLL/MI	56	724	3	972	59	786
FINDLAY COLLEGE/OH	52	734	4	935	56	804
FISK UNIVERSITY/TN	116	536	61	206	177	463
FLORIDA INST TECH	1	1328			1	1482
FLORIDA MEMORIAL C	6	1080	2	1035	8	1221
FLORIDA SOUTHERN C	149	467	32	360	181	451
FLORIDA, UNIV OF	1936	34	169	68	2105	36
FLORIDA AG & MECH U	110	549	39	309	149	506
FLORIDA ATLANTIC U	53	729	9	755	62	777
FLORIDA INTERNAT U	1	1328			1	1482
FLORIDA STATE UNIV	776	112	332	36	1108	86
SOUTH FLORIDA,U OF	151	460	24	440	175	466
NEW COLLEGE/FL	11	1014	5	888	16	1124
SOUTH FLA,U ST PETE			1	1101	1	1482

APPENDIX H Continued

	Male Number	Male Rank	Female Number	Female Rank	Both Sexes Number	Both Sexes Rank
WEST FLORIDA, U OF	2	1252	2	1035	4	1321
ST U FLORIDA-UNKNOWN	1	1328			1	1482
FONTBONNE COLLEGE/MO			58	223	58	794
FORDHAM UNIV/NY	1193	65	177	65	1370	67
FT HAYS KANSAS ST C	297	277	26	412	323	286
FT LAUDRDL C BS&F/FL	1	1328			1	1482
FT LEWIS COLLEGE/CO	20	927			20	1081
FT VALLEY ST COLL/GA	36	828	16	584	52	833
FT WAYNE BIBLE C/IN	17	954	1	1101	18	1101
FT WRIGHT COLL/WA			12	670	12	1159
FRNKLN&MARSHAL C/PA	707	126	1	1101	708	144
FRANKLIN C INDIANA	114	539	19	531	133	545
FRANKLIN UNIV/OH	3	1188			3	1361
FREE WILL BAPT C/TN	6	1080			6	1269
FRIENDS BIBLE C/KS	1	1328			1	1482
FRIENDS UNIV/KS	89	610	14	625	103	628
FROSTBURG ST COLL/MD	45	771	7	821	52	833
FULLER THEOL SEM/CA	2	1252			2	1418
FURMAN UNIV/SC	304	273	32	360	336	282
GALLAUDET COLLEGE/DC	17	954	1	1101	18	1101
GANNON COLLEGE/PA	111	546			111	605
GARRET-EVN THEO S/IL	2	1252			2	1418
GENERAL MOTORS I/MI	99	582			99	643
GENERAL THEOL SEM/NY	3	1188			3	1361
GENEVA COLLEGE/PA	196	376	30	367	226	379
GEORGE FOX COLL/OR	19	939	3	972	22	1057
GEORGE MASON U/VA	1	1328			1	1482
GEO PEABODY COLL/TN	229	340	109	120	338	280
GEO WASHINGTON U/DC	925	95	208	57	1133	85
GEORGE WILLIAMS C/IL	60	711	3	972	63	771
GEORGETOWN COLL/KY	152	458	16	584	168	476
GEORGETOWN UNIV/DC	553	158	37	322	590	171
GEORGIA COLLEGE	1	1328	82	159	83	693
GEORGIA INST TECH	998	85	4	935	1002	99
GEORGIA SOUTHERN C	130	501	21	493	151	501
GEORGIA STATE UNIV	105	564	36	331	141	526
GEORGIA, UNIV OF	1095	75	173	66	1268	73
GEORGIAN COURT C/NJ			33	350	33	952
GETTYSBURG COLL/PA	419	203	41	295	460	218
GLASSBORO ST COLL/NJ	77	651	20	514	97	648
GLENVILLE ST COLL/WV	81	633	12	670	93	661
GODDARD COLLEGE/VT	23	902	2	1035	25	1022
GOLDEN GATE UNIV/CA	7	1062	1	1101	8	1221
GONZAGA UNIV/WA	358	234	22	472	380	247
GORDON COLLEGE/MA	79	646	6	855	85	687
GOSHEN COLLEGE/IN	238	330	22	472	260	344
GOUCHER COLLEGE/MD	2	1252	284	43	286	316
GRACE BIBLE INST/NE	4	1141			4	1321
GRACE THEOL SEM&C/IN	6	1080			6	1269
GRACELAND COLL/IA	28	860	3	972	31	964
GRAMBLING ST UN/LA	20	927	11	698	31	964
GRAND CANYON COLL/AZ	14	981	1	1101	15	1132
GR RAPIDS BAPT C/MI	3	1188			3	1361
GRAND VALLEY ST C/MI	6	1080	2	1035	8	1221
GRATZ COLLEGE/PA	5	1106	1	1101	6	1269
GREAT FALLS, C OF/MT	26	877	18	548	44	884
GREENSBORO COLL/NC	15	973	19	531	34	946
GREENVILLE COLL/IL	184	395	20	514	204	408
GRINNELL COLLEGE/IA	537	163	95	139	632	156
GROVE CITY COLL/PA	211	357	26	412	237	366
GUAM, UNIV OF	4	1141	2	1035	6	1269
GUILFORD COLL/NC	116	536	12	670	128	555
GUSTAV ADOLPHUS C/MN	245	321	22	472	267	338
GWYNEDD-MERCY C/PA			3	972	3	1361
HAHNEMANN MED C/PA	3	1188			3	1361
HAMILTON COLLEGE/NY	494	179			494	206
HAMLINE UNIV/MN	265	297	26	412	291	307
HAMPDEN C PHARMCY/MA	2	1252	1	1101	3	1361
HAMPDEN-SYDNEY C/VA	156	451			156	492
HAMPTON INSTITUTE/VA	125	516	49	263	174	469
HANOVER COLLEGE/IN	157	449	22	472	179	455
HARDIN-SIMMONS U/TX	163	439	27	400	190	436
HARDING COLLEGE/AR	184	395	14	625	198	426
HARRIS TCHRS COLL/MO	56	724	43	287	99	643
HART GRD CTR-RPI/CT	1	1328			1	1482

	Male Number	Male Rank	Female Number	Female Rank	Both Sexes Number	Both Sexes Rank
HARTFORD SEM FDN/CT	5	1106	2	1035	7	1246
HARTFORD, UNIV OF/CT	46	764	8	786	54	816
HARTWICK COLLEGE/NY	90	608	11	698	101	636
HARVARD UNIV/MA	5830	4	21	493	5851	6
RADCLIFFE COLL/MA	3	1188	751	9	754	134
HASTINGS COLLEGE/NE	218	353	12	670	230	374
HAVERFORD COLL/PA	690	130			690	148
HAWAII PACIFIC COLL	2	1252			2	1418
HAWAII, UNIV OF	445	190	93	142	538	187
HEALD ENGR COLL/CA	6	1080			6	1269
HEBREW COLLEGE/MA	21	919	7	821	28	987
HEBREW UNION COLL/OH	18	947			18	1101
HEBREW UNION COLL/CA	1	1328			1	1482
HEBREW UNION COLL/NY	5	1106			5	1293
HEIDELBERG COLL/OH	169	431	24	440	193	431
HELLENIC C/MA	3	1188			3	1361
HENDERSON ST U/ARK	114	539	15	607	129	551
HENDRIX COLLEGE/AR	176	415	29	379	205	405
HIGH POINT COLL/NC	45	771	7	821	52	833
HILLSDALE COLLEGE/MI	67	688	17	563	84	689
HIRAM COLLEGE/OH	259	304	30	367	289	314
HOBART&WM SMITH C/NY	249	316	34	344	283	319
HOFSTRA UNIV/NY	334	252	60	214	394	242
HOLLINS COLLEGE/VA			43	287	43	891
HOLY CROSS, C OF/MA	566	154			566	176
HOLY FAMILY COLL/PA			5	888	5	1293
HOLY NAMES COLL/CA			36	331	36	933
HOLY REDEEMER C/WI	9	1038			9	1206
HOOD COLLEGE/MD			37	322	37	927
HOPE COLLEGE/MI	524	169	30	367	554	180
HOUGHTON COLL/NY	181	399	26	412	207	402
HOUSTON BAPT UNIV/TX	2	1252			2	1418
HOUSTON CONSV MUS/TX	1	1328			1	1482
HOUSTON, U OF/TX	446	189	116	112	562	178
HOWARD PAYNE COLL/TX	96	588	19	531	115	593
HOWARD UNIVERSITY/DC	334	252	136	95	470	214
HUNTINGDON COLL/AL	45	771	34	344	79	711
HUNTINGTON COLL/IN	34	837	1	1101	35	938
HURON COLLEGE/SD	74	658	8	786	82	700
HUSSON COLLEGE/ME	1	1328			1	1482
HUSTON-TILLOTSN C/TX	33	840	11	698	44	884
IDAHO, COLLEGE OF	129	505	25	425	154	497
IDAHO STATE UNIV	215	355	18	548	233	369
IDAHO, UNIV OF	833	106	57	227	890	112
ILL BENEDICTINE COLL	118	531			118	581
ILLINOIS COLLEGE	126	513	15	607	141	526
ILL COLL OPTOMETRY	6	1080			6	1269
ILLINOIS INST TECH	880	102	22	472	902	111
ILLINOIS ST U-NORMAL	566	154	119	109	685	149
ILL, U, URBANA-CHAMP	6076	3	667	16	6743	3
ILL, U-COLL MEDICINE	20	927	5	888	25	1022
ILLINOIS,U-CHIGO CIR	70	673	13	644	83	693
ILLINOIS WESLEYAN U	201	369	20	514	221	385
IMMACULATA COLL/PA			53	242	53	825
IMMAC CONCPTN SEM/NJ	7	1062			7	1246
IMMAC CONCPTN SEM/NY	3	1188			3	1361
IMMAC HEART COLL/CA	2	1252	75	171	77	723
INCARNATE WORD C/TX	2	1252	43	287	45	878
INDIANA CENTRAL UNIV	105	564	11	698	116	588
INDIANA INST OF TECH	43	785			43	891
INDIANA STATE UNIV	516	170	103	126	619	159
INDIANA U BLOOMNGTON	2064	31	397	28	2461	30
INDIANA U-NORTHWEST	1	1328			1	1482
INDIANA U-SOUTH BEND	1	1328			1	1482
IND U-PURDUE INDNPLS	1	1328	1	1101	2	1418
IND U-PRDUE MED, IND	1	1328	1	1101	2	1418
IND U-PRDUE FT WAYNE	4	1141			4	1321
INDIANA UNIV OF PA	351	239	52	248	403	240
I AMER U-SAN GERM/PR	35	834	11	698	46	874
I AMERICAN U PR-UNK			1	1101	1	1482
I-DENOM THEOL CTR/GA			1	1101	1	1482
IONA COLLEGE/NY	193	381			193	431
IOWA STATE UNIV	2523	24	172	67	2695	24
IOWA, UNIVERSITY OF	1978	33	340	34	2318	33
IOWA WESLEYAN COLL	109	553	15	607	124	564

APPENDIX H Continued

	Male		Female		Both Sexes	
	Number	Rank	Number	Rank	Number	Rank
ITHACA COLLEGE/NY	86	617	17	563	103	628
JACKSON STATE U/MS	37	823	16	584	53	825
JACKSONVILLE ST U/AL	105	564	24	440	129	551
JACKSONVILLE UNIV/FL	33	840	7	821	40	911
JAMESTOWN COLLEGE/ND	114	539	8	786	122	569
JARVIS CHRISTAN C/TX	4	1141	4	935	8	1221
JERSEY CITY ST C/NJ	44	782	20	514	64	768
JEWISH THEO SEM AMER	30	851	2	1035	32	958
JOHN BROWN UNIV/AR	31	845	3	972	34	946
JOHN CARROLL UNIV/OH	290	280	4	935	294	305
J MARSHALL LAW/IL	2	1252			2	1418
JOHN WESLEY COLL/MI	9	1038			9	1206
JOHNS HOPKINS U/MD	1551	49	58	223	1609	53
JOHNSON BIBLE C/TN	19	939			19	1089
JOHNSON C SMITH U/NC	56	724	6	855	62	777
JOHNSON ST COLL/VT	4	1141	2	1035	6	1269
JUDSON COLLEGE/AL			14	625	14	1141
JUDSON COLLEGE/IL	2	1252	2	1035	4	1321
JULLIARD SCHOOL/NY	71	666	19	531	90	671
JUNIATA COLLEGE/PA	323	259	34	344	357	269
KALAMAZOO COLLEGE/MI	375	220	38	315	413	235
KANS CTY ART INST/MO	4	1141			4	1321
KANSAS NEWMAN COLL	1	1328	4	935	5	1293
KANS ST C PITTSBURG	477	184	52	248	529	191
KANSAS STATE UNIV	1367	57	145	87	1512	60
KANSAS, UNIV OF	1917	35	282	44	2199	35
KANSAS, U, SCH MED	1	1328	1	1101	2	1418
KANSAS WESLEYAN	70	673	7	821	77	723
KEAN COLL NEW JERSEY	53	729	28	390	81	703
KEARNEY ST COLL/NE	231	338	27	400	258	345
KENRICK SEMINARY/MO	7	1062			7	1246
KENT STATE UNIV/OH	696	129	119	109	815	127
KENTUCKY CHRISTIAN C	6	1080	1	1101	7	1246
KENTUCKY STATE UNIV	35	834	13	644	48	862
KENTUCKY, UNIV OF	1147	68	152	77	1299	72
KENTUCKY WESLEYAN C	54	728	9	755	63	771
KENYON COLLEGE/OH	312	268			312	294
KEUKA COLLEGE/NY			24	440	24	1035
KING COLLEGE/TN	70	673	8	786	78	719
KINGS COLLEGE/PA	129	505			129	551
KINGS COLLEGE,THE/NY	27	865	2	1035	29	979
KIRKSVL C OSTEO&S/MO	1	1328			1	1482
KNOX COLLEGE/IL	387	214	48	268	435	227
KNOXVILLE COLL/TN	39	808	5	888	44	884
KUTZTOWN ST COLL/PA	143	474	15	607	158	488
LA GRANGE COLL/GA	20	927	13	644	33	952
LA ROCHE COLLEGE/PA			1	1101	1	1482
LA SALLE COLLEGE/PA	364	227			364	263
LA VERNE COLL/CA	69	682	7	821	76	729
LADYCLIFF COLLEGE/NY			10	724	10	1192
LAFAYETTE COLLEGE/PA	638	137	1	1101	639	154
LAKE ERIE COLLEGE/OH			24	440	24	1035
LAKE FOREST COLL/IL	126	513	34	344	160	486
LAKELAND COLL/WI	46	764	3	972	49	857
LAMAR UNIVERSITY/TX	245	321	25	425	270	335
LAMBUTH COLLEGE/TN	43	785	5	888	48	862
LANDER COLLEGE/SC	3	1188	5	888	8	1221
LANE COLLEGE/TN	17	954	5	888	22	1057
LANGSTON UNIV/OK	45	771	24	440	69	757
LAWRENCE I TECH/MI	21	919			21	1068
LAWRENCE UNIV/WI	387	214	95	139	482	210
LEBANON VALLEY C/PA	264	298	27	400	291	307
LEE COLLEGE/TN	4	1141			4	1321
LEHIGH UNIVERSITY/PA	1000	84			1000	101
LEMOYNE COLLEGE/NY	156	451	22	472	178	458
LEMOYNE-OWEN COLL/TN	16	964	8	786	24	1035
LENOIR-RHYNE COLL/NC	93	601	12	670	105	622
LESLEY COLLEGE/MA			3	972	3	1361
LETOURNEAU COLL/TX	7	1062			7	1246
LEWIS & CLARK C/OR	193	381	26	412	219	390
LEWIS UNIVERSITY/IL	49	747	2	1035	51	847
LIMESTONE COLLEGE/SC	3	1188	10	724	13	1152
LINCOLN CHRISTN C/IL	12	1004	1	1101	13	1152
LINCOLN MEM UNIV/TN	69	682	1	1101	70	753
LINCOLN UNIV/MO	71	666	18	548	89	676

	Male		Female		Both Sexes	
	Number	Rank	Number	Rank	Number	Rank
LINCOLN UNIV/PA	114	539			114	596
LINDENWOOD COLLS/MO	2	1252	21	493	23	1048
LINFIELD COLLEGE/OR	163	439	17	563	180	454
LIVINGSTON UNIV/AL	44	782	10	724	54	816
LIVINGSTONE COLL/NC	27	865	11	698	38	921
LOCK HAVEN ST C/PA	119	530	15	607	134	541
LOMA LINDA UNIV/CA	15	973	7	821	22	1057
LOMA LIN-LA SIERA/CA	61	705	7	821	68	759
LONE MOUNTAIN C/CA			44	285	44	884
LIU-BROOKLYN CTR/NY	45	771	7	821	52	833
LIU-BKLYN C PHAR/NY	15	973	1	1101	16	1124
LIU-C W POST CTR/NY	39	808	4	935	43	891
LIU-SOUTHAMPTON C/NY	3	1188			3	1361
LONG ISLAND U-UNK/NY	350	241	21	493	371	260
LONGWOOD COLLEGE/VA	2	1252	29	379	31	964
LORAS COLLEGE/IA	258	306	17	563	275	329
LORETTO HEIGHTS C/CO			27	400	27	999
LOUISIANA COLLEGE	123	519	15	607	138	534
LA ST UNIV & A&M C	1417	53	190	60	1607	55
LA ST U, S MED-N ORL			1	1101	1	1482
NEW ORLEANS,U OF/LA	69	682	11	698	80	706
LOUISIANA TECH UNIV	375	220	60	214	435	227
LOUISVL PRSBY T S/KY	2	1252			2	1418
LOUISVILLE, U OF/KY	441	192	61	206	502	203
LOYOLA COLLEGE/MD	218	353	21	493	239	361
LOYOLA MARYMONT U/CA	181	399	9	755	190	436
LOYOLA U CHICAGO/IL	710	125	101	131	811	128
LOYOLA UNIVERSITY/LA	195	378	38	315	233	369
LUTHER COLLEGE/IA	314	267	14	625	328	284
LUTHRN SCH THEOL/IL	9	1038	1	1101	10	1192
LTHRN T SEM-GETTY/PA	1	1328			1	1482
LTHRN T SEM-PHILA/PA	3	1188			3	1361
LYCOMING COLLEGE/PA	81	633	13	644	94	654
LYNCHBURG COLLEGE/VA	123	519	12	670	135	539
LYNDON ST COLL/VT	6	1080	2	1035	8	1221
MACALESTER COLL/MN	294	278	61	206	355	272
MACMURRAY COLLEGE/IL	45	771	64	195	109	610
MADISON COLLEGE/VA	14	981	45	279	59	786
MADONNA COLLEGE/MI			12	670	12	1159
MAINE MARITIME ACAD	3	1188			3	1361
MAINE, U-ORONO	752	116	85	156	837	121
MAINE, U-FARMINGTON	19	939	5	888	24	1035
MAINE, U-MACHIAS	4	1141			4	1321
MAINE, U-PRTLND-GORH	43	785	7	821	50	852
MAINE, U-PRESQUE IS	1	1328			1	1482
MALONE COLLEGE/OH	21	919	2	1035	23	1048
MANCHESTER COLL/IN	338	250	24	440	362	265
MANHATTAN CHRISTN/KS	6	1080			6	1269
MANHATTAN COLLEGE/NY	697	128	27	400	724	139
MANHATTAN SCH MUS/NY	26	877	3	972	29	979
MANHATTANVILLE C/NY	2	1252	116	112	118	581
MANKATO STATE U/MN	237	331	20	514	257	346
MANNES COLL MUSIC/NY	4	1141			4	1321
MANSFIELD ST COLL/PA	96	588	11	698	107	617
MARIAN COLLEGE/IN	22	908	19	531	41	904
MARIAN C FONDULAC/WI			10	724	10	1192
MARIETTA COLLEGE/OH	254	311	32	360	286	316
MARION COLLEGE/IN	70	673	9	755	79	711
MARIST COLLEGE/NY	58	716			58	794
MARLBORO COLLEGE/VT	2	1252			2	1418
MARQUETTE UNIV/WI	682	132	140	91	822	126
MARS HILL COLLEGE/NC	5	1106	3	972	8	1221
MARSHALL UNIV/WV	267	294	54	236	321	287
MARY BALDWIN COLL/VA			23	460	23	1048
MARY COLLEGE/ND			1	1101	1	1482
M HARDIN-BAYLOR C/TX	1	1328	29	379	30	972
MARY IMMACULATE,C/CT			1	1101	1	1482
MARY IMMACULT SEM/PA	14	981			14	1141
MARY WASHINGTON C/VA	2	1252	57	227	59	786
MARYCREST COLLEGE/IA			25	425	25	1022
MARYGROVE COLLEGE/MI			94	141	94	654
MARYKNOLL SEM/NY	14	981			14	1141
MD INST, COLL OF ART	4	1141	1	1101	5	1293
MARYLAND, UNIV OF	1585	47	215	54	1800	42
MARYLAND,U, SCH MED	4	1141	1	1101	5	1293

APPENDIX H Continued

	Male		Female		Both Sexes	
	Number	Rank	Number	Rank	Number	Rank
MARYLAND,U-BALT CITY	2	1252			2	1418
MARYLAND,U-BALT CNTY	1	1328			1	1482
MARYLAND,U-E SHORE	16	964	1	1101	17	1111
MARYLAND, U-OVERSEAS	1	1328			1	1482
MARYLAND, U-UNKNOWN	1	1328			1	1482
MARYLHURST ED CTR/OR			30	367	30	972
MARY MANSE COLL/OH			12	670	12	1159
MARYMOUNT COLL/KS			28	390	28	987
MARYMOUNT COLLEGE/NY			72	176	72	745
MARYMNT MNHTTN C/NY			21	493	21	1068
MARYVILLE COLL/MO	1	1328	21	493	22	1057
MARYVILLE COLLEGE/TN	209	361	39	309	248	356
MARYWOOD COLLEGE/PA			52	248	52	833
MASS COLL OPTOMETRY	3	1188			3	1361
MASS COLL PHARMACY	116	536	3	972	119	578
MASS INST TECHNOLOGY	4670	8	68	189	4738	9
BOSTON ST COLL/MA	38	816	35	336	73	741
BRIDGEWATER ST C/MA	105	564	30	367	135	539
FITCHBERG ST COLL/M	89	610	7	821	96	649
FRAMINGHAM ST C/MA	1	1328	22	472	23	1048
LOWELL, UNIV OF/MA	130	501	17	563	147	510
MASS COLLEGE OF ART	24	890	4	935	28	987
MASS MARITIME ACAD	5	1106			5	1293
NORTH ADAMS ST C/MA	22	908	6	855	28	987
SALEM STATE COLL/MA	52	734	22	472	74	738
WESTFIELD ST C/MA	25	883	4	935	29	979
WORCHESTER ST C/MA	31	845	20	514	51	847
MASS ST COLL-UNKNOWN	1	1328			1	1482
MASS, U OF-AMHERST	1241	61	131	101	1372	66
MASS, U-BOSTON	5	1106			5	1293
MAYVILLE ST COLL/ND	43	785	4	935	47	867
MCCORMICK THEOL S/IL	4	1141			4	1321
MCKENDREE COLLEGE/IL	52	734	4	935	56	804
MCMURRAY COLLEGE/TX	91	605	10	724	101	636
MCNEESE STATE U/LA	66	689	10	724	76	729
MCPHERSON COLLEGE/KS	131	498	8	786	139	531
MDVL-LOMBRD THEOL/IL	2	1252			2	1418
MEDAILLE COLLEGE/NY	1	1328	13	644	14	1141
MEDICAL COLL GEORGIA			2	1035	2	1418
MED COLL PENSYLVANIA			3	972	3	1361
MED UNIV SO CAROLINA	6	1080			6	1269
MEHARRY MED COLL/TN			2	1035	2	1418
MEMPHIS STATE U/TN	310	270	72	176	382	246
MENLO COLLEGE/CA	1	1328			1	1482
MERCER UNIV/GA	199	374	23	460	222	382
MERCER U-SO PHRM/GA	2	1252			2	1418
MERCY COLLEGE/NY	1	1328	1	1101	2	1418
MERCY C DETROIT/MI	1	1328	20	514	21	1068
MERCYHURST COLL/PA	1	1328	25	425	26	1014
MEREDITH COLLEGE/NC			51	256	51	847
MERRIMACK COLLEGE/MA	80	640	9	755	89	676
MESSIAH COLLEGE/PA	22	908	5	888	27	999
METHODIST COLLEGE/NC	4	1141			4	1321
METROPOLITAN ST C/CO			1	1101	1	1482
MIAMI UNIVERSITY/OH	1104	74	152	77	1256	74
MIAMI, UNIV OF/FL	741	118	132	98	873	115
MICHIGAN STATE UNIV	2580	23	330	37	2910	22
MICHIGAN TECH UNIV	341	248	4	935	345	278
MICHIGAN, UNIV OF	5071	6	938	4	6009	5
MICHIGAN,U-DEARBORN	15	973			15	1132
MICHIGAN, U-FLINT	20	927	5	888	25	1022
MIDDLE TENN STATE U	178	407	24	440	202	412
MIDDLEBURY COLL/VT	425	198	90	146	515	196
MIDLAND LTHRN C/NE	109	553	10	724	119	578
MIDWST BAPT T SEM/MO			1	1101	1	1482
MIDWESTERN UNIV/TX	86	617	9	755	95	651
MILES COLLEGE/AL	17	954	5	888	22	1057
MILLERSVILLE ST C/PA	177	411	24	440	201	414
MILLIGAN COLLEGE/TN	42	792	3	972	45	878
MILLIKIN UNIV/IL	160	447	28	390	188	440
MILLS COLLEGE/CA	1	1328	93	142	94	654
MILLSAPS COLLEGE/MS	261	302	29	379	290	310
MILTON COLLEGE/WI	41	800	4	935	45	878
MILWAUKEE SCH ENGR	31	845			31	964
MINNEAPLIS C ART&DES	1	1328			1	1482
MINN BIBLE COLLEGE	5	1106			5	1293
MINNESOTA,U-MINNEAPL	4707	7	789	7	5496	7
MINN, U, C MED SCI	1	1328	1	1101	2	1418
MINNESOTA,U-DULUTH	80	640	8	786	88	681
MINNESOTA, U-MORRIS	11	1014	2	1035	13	1152
MINOT STATE COLL/ND	83	629	12	670	95	651
MISERICORDIA, C/PA			35	336	35	938
MISSISSIPPI COLLEGE	342	247	30	367	372	258
MISSISSIPPI INDUST C	3	1188	3	972	6	1269
MISSISSIPPI STATE U	800	110	33	350	833	122
MISS UNIV WOMEN	3	1188	80	162	83	693
MISSISSIPPI, UNIV OF	420	202	53	242	473	213
MISSISSIPPI U-MED CT			1	1101	1	1482
MISSISSIPPI VALLY SU	9	1038	2	1035	11	1175
MISSOURI STHRN ST C	2	1252			2	1418
MISSOURI,U-COLUMBIA	2189	28	309	40	2498	29
MISSOURI,U-KANS CITY	282	284	52	248	334	283
MISSOURI,U-KC MED S	1	1328			1	1482
MISSOURI,U-ROLLA	513	172	1	1101	514	197
MISSOURI,U-ST LOUIS	17	954	5	888	22	1057
MISSOURI VALLEY C/MO	74	658	6	855	80	706
MOBILE COLLEGE/AL	3	1188			3	1361
MOLLOY COLLEGE/NY			3	972	3	1361
MONMOUTH COLLEGE/IL	240	326	22	472	262	342
MONMOUTH COLLEGE/NJ	45	771	8	786	53	825
MONT C MINRL SC&TECH	49	747			49	857
MONTANA STATE UNIV	664	136	42	293	706	145
MONTANA, UNIV OF	585	149	64	195	649	153
MONTCLAIR ST COLL/NJ	280	288	75	171	355	272
MONTERY I FRGN ST/CA	2	1252	1	1101	3	1361
MONTEVALLO, U OF/AL	22	908	65	192	87	683
MOORHEAD STATE U/MN	147	470	15	607	162	484
MORAVIAN COLLEGE/PA	98	586	8	786	106	619
MOREHEAD STATE U/KY	106	560	12	670	118	581
MOREHOUSE COLL/GA	229	340			229	376
MORGAN STATE UNIV/MD	92	602	25	425	117	586
MORNINGSIDE COLL/IA	164	438	24	440	188	440
MORRIS BROWN COLL/GA	15	973	11	698	26	1014
MORRIS COLLEGE/SC	4	1141	3	972	7	1246
MORRIS HARVEY C/WV	70	673	9	755	79	711
MT ANGEL SEMINARY/OR	8	1049	1	1101	9	1206
MT HOLYOKE COLL/MA	3	1188	659	18	662	152
MT MARTY COLL/SD			16	584	16	1124
MT MARY COLL/WI	1	1328	40	303	41	904
MT MERCY COLLEGE/IA			1	1101	1	1482
MT ST ALPHONS SEM/NY	4	1141			4	1321
MT ST JOS ON OHIO, C	1	1328	33	350	34	946
MT ST MARY COLL/NH			12	670	12	1159
MT ST MARY COLL/NY			1	1101	1	1482
MT ST MARYS COLL/CA	3	1188	51	256	54	816
MT ST MARYS COLL/MD	86	617			86	684
MT ST VINCENT,COL/NY	1	1328	122	105	123	565
MT UNION COLLEGE/OH	179	402	28	390	207	402
MUHLENBERG COLL/PA	363	229	16	584	379	250
MULTNOMAH S BIBLE/OR	3	1188			3	1361
MUNDELEIN COLLEGE/IL			108	122	108	613
MURRAY STATE UNIV/KY	331	254	38	315	369	261
MUS&ART U ST LOUI/MO	1	1328			1	1482
MUSKINGUM COLLEGE/OH	264	298	45	279	309	296
NASHOTAH HOUSE/WI	1	1328			1	1482
NASSON COLLEGE/ME	12	1004			12	1159
NATL COLL EDUC/IL	1	1328	19	531	20	1081
NATL C EDUC-URBAN/IL			3	972	3	1361
NAVAL POSTGRAD S/CA	10	1027			10	1192
NAZARETH COLL/MI			18	548	18	1101
NAZARETH C ROCHTR/NY			41	295	41	904
NEBRASKA, U-LINCOLN	2062	32	294	42	2356	31
NEBRASKA,U-OMAHA	320	262	40	303	360	268
NEBRASKA WESLEYAN U	281	286	33	350	314	293
NER ISRAEL RABBIN/MD	5	1106			5	1293
NEVADA, UNIV OF	256	308	27	400	283	319
NEVADA,U-LAS VEGAS	7	1062			7	1246
NEW BRUNS THEOL S/NJ			1	1101	1	1482
NEW ENGLAND COLL/NH	5	1106	2	1035	7	1246
NEW ENGL CONS MUS/MA	38	816	4	935	42	896

APPENDIX H Continued

	Male		Female		Both Sexes	
	Number	Rank	Number	Rank	Number	Rank
NEW ENGL SCH LAW/MA	2	1252			2	1418
NEW HAMPSHIRE, U OF	750	117	79	164	829	123
NH, U-KEENE ST COLL	46	764	4	935	50	852
NH, U-PLYMOUTH ST C	31	845	4	935	35	938
NEW HAVEN U/CONN	7	1062	1	1101	8	1221
NEW JERSEY INST TECH	227	342	2	1035	229	376
N MEXICO HIGHLANDS U	81	633	9	755	90	671
N MEX I MINING&TECH	64	700	3	972	67	760
NEW MEX MILTARY INST	1	1328			1	1482
NEW MEXICO STATE U	360	232	17	563	377	253
NEW MEXICO, UNIV OF	774	113	115	115	889	113
N ORLN BAPT T SEM/LA	1	1328			1	1482
NEW ROCHELLE, COLL	1	1328	139	92	140	530
NEW SCH SOC RSCH/NY	52	734	22	472	74	738
NEW SUBIACO ABBEY/AR	1	1328			1	1482
NY INST TECHNOLOGY	1	1328			1	1482
NY I TECH-CITY CAMP	1	1328			1	1482
NEW YORK LAW SCHOOL	3	1188			3	1361
NEW YORK MEDICAL COL	1	1328	1	1101	2	1418
NY THEOLOGICAL SEM	3	1188			3	1361
NEW YORK UNIVERSITY	3417	16	721	14	4138	14
NEWBERRY COLLEGE/SC	49	747	7	821	56	804
NIAGARA UNIV/NY	147	470	5	888	152	500
NICHOLLS STATE U/LA	20	927			20	1081
NORFOLK STATE C/VA	10	1027	5	888	15	1132
NORTH ALABAMA, UNIV	101	579	13	644	114	596
NC, U OF-CHAPEL HILL	1564	48	155	73	1719	46
APPLACHIAN ST U/NC	167	433	33	350	200	420
EAST CAROLINA U/NC	193	381	46	274	239	361
ELIZ CITY ST U/NC	8	1049	3	972	11	1175
FAYETTEVILLE S U/NC	11	1014	8	786	19	1089
NC AG & TECH ST U	106	560	14	625	120	575
NC CENTRAL UNIV	91	605	29	379	120	575
NC STATE U-RALEIGH	1021	83	12	670	1033	95
NC, U OF-ASHEVILLE	5	1106	1	1101	6	1269
NC, U OF-CHARLOTTE	11	1014			11	1175
NC, U OF-GREENSBORO	3	1188	181	63	184	447
NC, U OF-WILMINGTON	6	1080	1	1101	7	1246
PEMBROKE ST U/NC	14	981	2	1035	16	1124
WSTRN CAROLINA U/NC	84	626	17	563	101	636
WINSTN-SALEM S U/NC	18	947	9	755	27	999
NC WESLEYAN COLLEGE	5	1106			5	1293
N CENTRAL BIBLE C/MN	2	1252			2	1418
NORTH CENTRAL C/IL	271	292	22	472	293	306
NORTH DAKOTA ST UNIV	483	183	28	390	511	198
NORTH DAKOTA, U OF	499	177	51	256	550	181
NORTH GEORGIA COLL	48	755	6	855	54	816
N PARK C&THEOL S/IL	49	747	10	724	59	786
N TEXAS STATE UNIV	947	91	158	71	1105	87
NE LOUISIANA UNIV	71	666	18	548	89	676
NE MISSOURI STATE U	303	275	47	271	350	277
NORTHEASTERN ILL U	6	1080	2	1035	8	1221
NOEASTERN OKLA ST U	172	422	21	493	193	431
NORTHEASTERN U/MA	591	146	26	412	617	161
NE U-BOSTON BOUVE/MA			6	855	6	1269
NORTHERN ARIZONA U	127	512	16	584	143	517
NTHRN BAPT THEOL/IL	12	1004			12	1159
NORTHERN COLORADO,U	628	139	87	154	715	142
NORTHERN ILL UNIV	514	171	73	175	587	172
NORTHERN IOWA, U OF	721	122	137	93	858	117
NTHRN KENTUCKY ST C	2	1252			2	1418
NORTHERN MICHIGAN U	150	463	27	400	177	463
NORTHERN MONTANA COL	14	981			14	1141
NORTHERN ST COLL/SD	136	489	17	563	153	499
NORTHLAND COLL/WI	43	785	4	935	47	867
NORTHROP UNIV/CA	11	1014			11	1175
NW CHRISTIAN COLL/OR	27	865			27	999
NORTHWEST COLL/WA	2	1252			2	1418
NW MISSOURI STATE U	199	374	36	331	235	367
NW NAZARENE COLL/ID	71	666	9	755	80	706
NORTHWESTERN COLL/IA	8	1049			8	1221
NORTHWESTERN COLL/MN	1	1328			1	1482
NORTHWESTERN COLL/WI	39	808	3	972	42	896
NW LTHRN THEOL S/MN	1	1328	1	1101	2	1418
NOWESTERN OKLA ST U	118	531	16	584	134	541

	Male		Female		Both Sexes	
	Number	Rank	Number	Rank	Number	Rank
NORWESTRN ST UNIV LA	234	336	64	195	298	303
NORTHWESTERN UNIV/IL	2136	29	441	24	2577	27
NOWSTRN U-MED SCH/IL	3	1188			3	1361
NORWICH UNIV/VT	58	716			58	794
NOTRE DAME COLL/MO			12	670	12	1159
NOTRE DAME COLL/NH			2	1035	2	1418
NOTRE DAME COLL/OH			41	295	41	904
NOTRE DAME, C OF/CA	1	1328	6	855	7	1246
NOTRE DAME MD, C OF			52	248	52	833
NT DM SM-GRD S T/LA	13	993			13	1152
NOTRE DAME, U OF/IN	1621	44	19	531	1640	51
NYACK COLLEGE/NY	20	927	3	972	23	1048
OAKLAND CITY COLL/IN	53	729	2	1035	55	807
OAKLAND UNIV/MI	66	689	11	698	77	723
OAKWOOD COLLEGE/AL	13	993	5	888	18	1101
OBERLIN COLLEGE/OH	1905	36	449	23	2354	32
OBLATE COLLEGE/DC	3	1188			3	1361
OBLATE COLL OF SW/TX	2	1252			2	1418
OCCIDENTAL COLL/CA	544	161	74	174	618	160
OGLETHORPE UNIV/GA	53	729	16	584	69	757
OHIO DOMINICAN COLL	1	1328	52	248	53	825
OHIO NORTHERN UNIV	166	436	15	607	181	451
OHIO STATE UNIV	3842	12	572	19	4414	12
OHIO UNIVERSITY	931	94	146	85	1077	90
OHIO WESLEYAN UNIV	674	135	121	106	795	130
OKLAHOMA BAPT UNIV	179	402	26	412	205	405
OKLAHOMA CHRISTIAN C	20	927	1	1101	21	1068
OKLAHOMA CITY UNIV	135	491	21	493	156	492
OKLAHOMA PANHND ST U	65	693	7	821	72	745
OKLAHOMA STATE UNIV	1650	42	133	97	1783	43
OKLAHOMA, U OF	1531	50	224	51	1755	45
OLD DOMINION UNIV/VA	65	693	13	644	78	719
OLIVET COLLEGE/MI	75	656	4	935	79	711
OLIVET NAZARENE C/IL	71	666	5	888	76	729
ORAL ROBERTS UNIV/OK	1	1328	1	1101	2	1418
OREGON, UNIV OF	1037	81	190	60	1227	79
OREGON U-SCH MED	1	1328			1	1482
EASTERN ORE ST COLL	60	711	5	888	65	766
OREGON COLL OF EDUC	84	626	12	670	96	649
OREGON STATE UNIV	1307	58	92	145	1399	63
PORTLAND STATE U/OR	210	360	30	367	240	360
STHRN ORE ST COLL	65	693	6	855	71	749
OSTEOP MD&SURG, C/IA	1	1328			1	1482
OTTAWA UNIVERSITY/KS	129	505	12	670	141	526
OTTERBEIN COLLEGE/OH	200	372	21	493	221	385
OUACHITA BAPT U/AR	152	458	12	670	164	481
OUR LADY HOLY CR/LA			2	1035	2	1418
OUR LADY LASALETT/MA	3	1188			3	1361
OUR LADY ELMS, C/MA			22	472	22	1057
OUR LADY LAKE UN/TX	4	1141	60	214	64	768
OZARK BIBLE C/MO	5	1106			5	1293
OZARKS, COLL OF/AR	46	764	9	755	55	807
PACE UNIVERSITY/NY	31	845	5	888	36	933
PACIFIC CHRSTAN C/CA	5	1106			5	1293
PACIFIC COLLEGE/CA	4	1141			4	1321
PACIFIC LTHRN U/WA	168	432	16	584	184	447
PACIFIC UNION C/CA	141	478	14	625	155	495
PACIFIC UNIV/OR	85	623	10	724	95	651
PACIFIC, U OF/CA	237	331	26	412	263	341
PAINE COLLEGE/GA	22	908	5	888	27	999
PAN AMERICAN UNIV/TX	28	860	6	855	34	946
PARK COLLEGE/MO	239	328	33	350	272	334
PARKS,ST LOUIS U/IL	33	840			33	952
PAUL QUINN COLL/TX	2	1252	1	1101	3	1361
PEABODY I OF BALT/MD	18	947	5	888	23	1048
PENN COLL OPTOMETRY	1	1328			1	1482
PENN STATE UNIV	3465	15	330	37	3795	17
PENNSYLVANIA, U OF	2230	27	441	24	2671	26
PEPPERDINE UNIV/CA	147	470	16	584	163	482
PEPPERDINE-MALIBU/CA	1	1328			1	1482
PERU ST COLL/NE	139	483	10	724	149	506
PFEIFFER COLLEGE/NC	43	785	7	821	50	852
PHILA COLL OF ART/PA	6	1080	1	1101	7	1246
PHILA COLL BIBLE/PA	9	1038			9	1206
PHILA C PHARM&SCI/PA	251	313	14	625	265	340

APPENDIX H Continued

	Male		Female		Both Sexes	
	Number	Rank	Number	Rank	Number	Rank
PHIL C TEXTIL&SCI/PA	13	993	1	1101	14	1141
PHILA MUSICAL ACADMY	5	1106			5	1293
PHILANDER SMITH C/AR	27	865	8	786	35	938
PHILLIPS UNIV/OK	183	397	18	548	201	414
PIEDMONT COLLEGE/GA	24	890	4	935	28	987
PIKEVILLE COLLEGE/KY	5	1106	1	1101	6	1269
PITSBRG THEOL SEM/PA	4	1141			4	1321
PITTSBURGH, UNIV OF	1594	46	362	32	1956	40
POINT LOMA COLL/CA	82	630	11	698	93	661
POLYTECHNIC INST NY	921	96	4	935	925	107
PONT C JOSEPHINUM/OH	25	883			25	1022
PORTLAND, UNIV OF/OR	141	478	9	755	150	503
PRATT INSTITUTE/NY	95	593	5	888	100	641
PRESBYTERIAN COLL/SC	92	602	2	1035	94	654
PRSBY S CHRIST ED/VA			1	1101	1	1482
PRINCETN THEO SEM/NJ	1	1328			1	1482
PRINCETON UNIV/NJ	2670	22	2	1035	2672	25
PRINCIPIA COLLEGE/IL	90	608	20	514	110	607
PROVIDENCE COLL/RI	404	208	8	786	412	236
PUERTO RICO, UNIV OF	383	216	137	93	520	194
PUERTO R,U-MAYAGUEZ	8	1049	1	1101	9	1206
PUERTO RICO, U-UNK	1	1328			1	1482
PUGET SOUND, U OF/WA	205	363	21	493	226	379
PURDUE UNIVERSITY/IN	3005	19	209	56	3214	21
QUEEN HOLY ROSARY/CA			1	1101	1	1482
QUEENS COLLEGE/NC	3	1188	22	472	25	1022
QUINCY COLLEGE/IL	80	640	11	698	91	669
QUINNIPIAC COLL/CT	1	1328	2	1035	3	1361
RADFORD COLLEGE/VA	5	1106	27	400	32	958
RANDOLPH-MACON C/VA	196	376	6	855	202	412
RANDOLPH-MACN WOM/VA	1	1328	132	98	133	545
REDLANDS, U OF/CA	424	200	41	295	465	216
REED COLLEGE/OR	766	114	147	84	913	110
REGIS COLLEGE/CO	110	549	3	972	113	599
REGIS COLLEGE/MA	1	1328	70	181	71	749
RENSSELAER POLY I/NY	1633	43	9	755	1642	50
RHODE ISLAND COLLEGE	69	682	35	336	104	625
RHODE ISLND S DESIGN	14	981	5	888	19	1089
RHODE ISLAND, U OF	542	162	49	263	591	169
RICE UNIVERSITY/TX	1109	73	142	89	1251	75
RICHMOND, U OF/VA	441	192	61	206	502	203
RICKER COLLEGE/ME	7	1062	1	1101	8	1221
RICKS COLLEGE/ID	4	1141	1	1101	5	1293
RIDER COLLEGE/NJ	48	755	7	821	55	807
RIO GRANDE COLL/OH	20	927	1	1101	21	1068
RIPON COLLEGE/WI	179	402	19	531	198	426
RIVIER COLLEGE/NH			17	563	17	1111
ROANOKE COLLEGE/VA	99	582	13	644	112	601
ROBERTS WESLYAN C/NY	22	908	2	1035	24	1035
ROCHESTER I TECH/NY	77	651	4	935	81	703
ROCHESTER,UNIV OF/NY	1414	54	273	45	1687	49
ROCKFORD COLLEGE/IL	32	843	61	206	93	661
ROCKHURST COLLEGE/MO	176	415	1	1101	177	463
ROCKMONT COLLEGE/CO	7	1062			7	1246
ROCKY MOUNTAIN C/MT	36	828			36	933
ROLLINS COLLEGE/FL	113	543	26	412	139	531
ROOSEVELT UNIV/IL	389	212	69	185	458	219
ROSARY COLLEGE/IL	1	1328	77	168	78	719
ROSARY HILL COLL/NY			11	698	11	1175
ROSE-HULMAN TECH/IN	125	516			125	561
ROSEMONT COLLEGE/PA			47	271	47	867
RUSSELL SAGE COLL/NY	3	1188	45	279	48	862
RUST COLLEGE/MS	11	1014	6	855	17	1111
RUTGERS UNIV/NJ	2393	25	370	30	2763	23
RUTGERS U-CAMDEN/NJ	10	1027			10	1192
RUTGERS U-NEWARK/NJ	21	919	7	821	28	987
SACRED HEART,C OF/PR			8	786	8	1221
SACRED HEART SEM/MI	42	792			42	896
SAGINAW VALY ST C/NJ	1	1328			1	1482
ST ALBERTS COLL/CA	2	1252			2	1418
ST ALPHONSUS COLL/CT	1	1328			1	1482
ST AMBROSE COLL/IA	140	481	16	584	156	492
ST ANDREWS PRBY C/NC	6	1080	18	548	24	1035
ST ANSELMS COLL/NH	117	534	4	935	121	571
ST ANTHONY FRIARY/NH	1	1328			1	1482

	Male		Female		Both Sexes	
	Number	Rank	Number	Rank	Number	Rank
ST AUGUSTINES C/NC	22	908	4	935	26	1014
ST BASILS COLLEGE/CT	1	1328			1	1482
ST BENEDICT, C OF/MN			37	322	37	927
ST BERNARDS SEM/NY	41	800			41	904
ST BONAVENTURE U/NY	260	303	18	548	278	327
ST CATHERINE,C OF/MN			86	155	86	684
ST CHAS BORMC SEM/PA	42	792			42	896
ST. CLOUD STATE U/MN	248	318	27	400	275	329
ST EDWARDS UNIV/TX	52	734			52	833
ST ELIZABETH,C OF/NJ	1	1328	71	179	72	745
ST FIDELIS COLL/PA	6	1080			6	1269
ST FRANCIS COLL/IN	5	1106	15	607	20	1081
ST FRANCIS COLL/ME	14	981			14	1141
ST FRANCIS COLL/NY	135	491	3	972	138	534
ST FRANCIS COLL/PA	86	617	8	786	94	654
ST FRANCIS, C OF/IL			24	440	24	1035
ST FRAN DESALES C/WI	40	805			40	911
ST HYACINTH C&SEM/MA	1	1328			1	1482
ST JOHN FISHER C/NY	77	651			77	723
ST JOHNS COLLEGE/CA	21	919			21	1068
ST JOHN C CLEVELD/OH	3	1188	21	493	24	1035
ST JOHNS COLLEGE/MD	103	572	7	821	110	607
ST JOHNS COLLEGE/NM	1	1328			1	1482
ST JOHNS SEMINARY/MA	39	808	1	1101	40	911
ST JOHNS UNIV/MN	287	283			287	315
ST JOHNS UNIV/NY	561	156	161	69	722	140
ST JOS CAP SEM-CP/IN	2	1252			2	1418
ST JOSEPH COLLEGE/CT	1	1328	29	379	30	972
ST JOSEPHS COLL/IN	120	526	3	972	123	565
ST JOSEPHS COLL/ME			11	698	11	1175
ST JOSEPHS COLL/NY	2	1252	80	162	82	700
ST JOSEPHS COLL/PA	302	276	3	972	305	297
ST. JOSEPH SEMNRY/NY	103	572	1	1101	104	625
ST LAWRENCE UNIV/NY	262	301	41	295	303	299
ST LEO COLLEGE/FL	1	1328			1	1482
ST LOUIS CONS MUS/MO	10	1027	1	1101	11	1175
ST LOUIS C PHARM/MO	38	816			38	921
ST LOUIS UNIV/MO	892	101	146	85	1038	93
ST MARTINS COLL/WA	34	837	2	1035	36	933
ST MARY COLLEGE/KS	2	1252	29	379	31	964
ST MARY, COLL OF/NE			10	724	10	1192
ST MARY LAKE SEM/IL	60	711	1	1101	61	782
ST MARY OF PLAINS/KS	7	1062	2	1035	9	1206
ST MARY WOODS C/IN	1	1328	56	230	57	801
ST MARY SEMINARY/OH	1	1328			1	1482
ST MARYS COLLEGE/IN			83	158	83	693
ST MARYS COLLEGE/MI	10	1027			10	1192
ST MARYS COLLEGE/MN	278	290	1	1101	279	325
ST MARYS COLL CALIF	130	501			130	550
ST MARYS COLL OF MD	4	1141			4	1321
ST MARY C SEM/KY	12	1004			12	1159
ST MARYS DOM COLL/LA			22	472	22	1057
ST MARYS SEMINARY/CT	17	954			17	1111
ST MARYS SEM & U/MD	120	526			120	575
ST MARYS SEMINARY/MO	27	865	1	1101	28	987
ST MARYS UNIV/TX	167	433	5	888	172	471
ST MEINRAD COLLEG/IN	61	705			61	782
ST MICHAELS COLL/VT	112	544	1	1101	113	599
ST MICHL PASS MON/NJ	4	1141			4	1321
ST NORBERT COLL/WI	128	509	9	755	137	536
ST OLAF COLLEGE/MN	678	133	69	185	747	136
ST PATRICKS COLL/CA	39	808			39	917
ST PAUL BIBLE C/MN	2	1252			2	1418
ST PAUL SEMINARY/MN	44	782			44	884
ST PAULS COLLEGE/VA	7	1062	3	972	10	1192
ST PETERS COLL/NJ	280	288	1	1101	281	324
ST. PIUS X SEMNRY/KY	1	1328			1	1482
ST ROSE, COLL OF/NY			54	236	54	816
ST SCHOLASTICA, C/MN	1	1328	34	344	35	938
ST TERESA, C OF/MN			70	181	70	753
ST THOM AQUINAS C/NY			4	935	4	1321
ST THOMAS, C OF/MN	321	260			321	287
ST THOMAS SEM/CO	13	993			13	1152
ST THOMAS, U OF/TX	58	716	5	888	63	771
ST VINCENT COLL/PA	247	319			247	357

APPENDIX H Continued

	Male		Female		Both Sexes	
	Number	Rank	Number	Rank	Number	Rank
ST XAVIER COLLEGE/IL			54	236	54	816
SALEM COLLEGE/NC	1	1328	22	472	23	1048
SALEM COLLEGE/WV	30	851	2	1035	32	958
SALISBURY ST COLL/MD	15	973			15	1132
SALVE REGINA COLL/RI			10	724	10	1192
SAM HOUSTON ST U/TX	239	328	31	366	270	335
SAMFORD UNIV/AL	233	337	40	303	273	332
SAN DIEGO,UNIV OF/CA	14	981	10	724	24	1035
SAN FRAN ART I C/CA			1	1101	1	1482
SAN FRAN THEOL S/CA	2	1252			2	1418
SAN FRANCSCO,U OF/CA	223	345	12	670	235	367
SAN JOSE BIBLE C/CA	4	1141			4	1321
SANTA CLARA, U OF/CA	203	366	9	755	212	395
SANTA FE, COLL OF/NM	26	877	1	1101	27	999
SARAH LAWRENCE C/NY	2	1252	75	171	77	723
SAVANNAH ST COLL/GA	29	856	13	644	42	896
SCARRITT COLL/TN	3	1188	4	935	7	1246
SCHOOL OF OZARKS/MO	2	1252			2	1418
SCH ART&GDMN DRMA/IL	25	883	9	755	34	946
SCI & ARTS OKLA,UNIV			55	234	55	807
SCRANTON, U OF/PA	320	262			320	289
SEATTLE PACIFIC C/WA	151	460	16	584	167	477
SEATTLE UNIV/WA	155	454	36	331	191	435
SEM OUR LADY PROV/RI	6	1080			6	1269
SETON HALL UNIV/NJ	356	236	38	315	394	242
SETON HILL COLL/PA	1	1328	89	147	90	671
SHAW UNIVERSITY/NC	28	860	14	625	42	896
SHENANDOAH COLL/VA	8	1049	1	1101	9	1206
SHEPHERD COLLEGE/WV	47	760	2	1035	49	857
SHERWOOD MUSIC S/IL	2	1252			2	1418
SHIMER COLLEGE/IL	38	816	4	935	42	896
SHIPPENSBURG ST C/PA	172	422	17	563	189	438
SHORTER COLLEGE/GA	13	993	15	607	28	987
SIENA COLLEGE/NY	146	473			146	512
SIENA HEIGHTS C/MI			58	223	58	794
SILVER LAKE COLL/WI			7	821	7	1246
SIMMONS COLLEGE/MA	2	1252	144	88	146	512
SIMPSON COLLEGE/CA	5	1106			5	1293
SIMPSON COLLEGE/IA	162	443	16	584	178	458
SIOUX FALLS COLL/SD	62	702	8	786	70	753
SKIDMORE COLLEGE/NY	1	1328	62	201	63	771
SLIPPERY ROCK S C/PA	193	381	23	460	216	393
SMITH COLLEGE/MA	3	1188	737	12	740	137
SOUTH ALABAMA, U	13	993	2	1035	15	1132
SO CAROLINA STATE C	52	734	21	493	73	741
SOUTH CAROLINA, U OF	488	182	59	219	547	184
S DAKOTA S MINE&TECH	211	357			211	398
SOUTH DAKOTA STATE U	526	167	24	440	550	181
SOUTH DAKOTA, U OF	321	260	41	295	362	265
SO DAK,U-SPRINGFIELD	24	890	4	935	28	987
SOUTH, UNIV OF/TN	249	316			249	354
SE MISSOURI ST UNIV	325	258	32	360	357	269
SOEASTERN BIBLE C/AL	3	1188			3	1361
S-EASTERN BIBLE C/FL	1	1328			1	1482
SOUTHEASTERN LA U	176	415	24	440	200	420
SE MASS U-N DARTMOTH	50	744	2	1035	52	833
SE MASS U-NEW BEDFRD	1	1328			1	1482
SOUTHESTRN OKLA ST U	150	463	34	344	184	447
SOUTHEASTERN UNIV/DC	5	1106			5	1293
SO BAPT THEOL SEM/KY	4	1141	1	1101	5	1293
STHRN BENEDICT C/AL	21	919	3	972	24	1035
SOUTHERN CALIF COLL	7	1062			7	1246
STHRN CAL OPTOMETRY	3	1188			3	1361
SOUTHERN CALIF, U OF	1221	62	207	58	1428	62
STHRN C FINE ARTS/TX	1	1328			1	1482
STHRN C OPTOMETRY/TN	2	1252			2	1418
SOUTHERN COLO, UNIV	24	890	2	1035	26	1014
SOUTHERN CONN ST COL	94	598	22	472	116	588
SOUTHERN ILL UNIV	1064	79	123	104	1187	81
SO ILL U/EDWARDSVILL	24	890	5	888	29	979
STHRN ILLINOIS U-UNK	3	1188			3	1361
STHRN METHODIST U/TX	675	134	115	115	790	131
STHRN MISSIONRY C/TN	37	823	2	1035	39	917
SOUTHERN MISS, U OF	349	242	71	179	420	232
SOUTHERN STATE C/AR	49	747	10	724	59	786

	Male		Female		Both Sexes	
	Number	Rank	Number	Rank	Number	Rank
SOUTHERN UNIV/LA	112	544	37	322	149	506
STHRN U-N ORLEANS/LA	1	1328			1	1482
SOUTHWEST BAPT C/MO	5	1106			5	1293
SW MISSOURI ST UNIV	454	188	62	201	516	195
SW TEXAS STATE UNIV	236	334	49	263	285	318
SW ASMBLIES GOD C/TX	11	1014	1	1101	12	1159
SOWESTERN MEMPHIS/TN	230	339	26	412	256	349
SW BAPT THEOL SEM/TX	2	1252			2	1418
SOUTHWESTERN COLL/KS	185	392	18	548	203	410
SOWESTERN LA, U OF	362	230	59	219	421	231
SOWESTERN OKLA ST U	172	422	29	379	201	414
SOUTHWESTERN U/CA	1	1328			1	1482
SOUTHWESTERN U/TX	163	439	15	607	178	458
SPALDING COLL/KY			52	248	52	833
SPELMAN COLLEGE/GA			57	227	57	801
SPERTUS C JUDAICA/IL	2	1252			2	1418
SPRING ARBOR COLL/MI	5	1106			5	1293
SPRING HILL COLL/AL	222	347	10	724	232	372
SPRINGFIELD COLL/MA	364	227	8	786	372	258
STANFORD UNIV/CA	2817	21	520	21	3337	20
SUNY AT ALBANY	570	153	136	95	706	145
SUNY AT BINGHAMTON	259	304	45	279	304	298
SUNY AT BUFFALO	1118	70	187	62	1305	71
SUNY BUFFALO HTH SCI	1	1328			1	1482
SUNY AT STONY BROOK	137	486	28	390	165	480
SUNY ST BRK HTH SCI	1	1328			1	1482
SUNY COLL BROCKPORT	143	474	24	440	167	477
SUNY COLL BUFFALO	266	296	88	149	354	275
SUNY COLL CORTLAND	193	381	45	279	238	365
SUNY COLL FREDONIA	167	433	12	670	179	455
SUNY COLL GENESEO	102	575	19	531	121	571
SUNY COLL NEW PALTZ	101	579	17	563	118	581
SUNY COLL ONEONTA	81	633	27	400	108	613
SUNY COLL OSWEGO	219	351	20	514	239	361
SUNY COLL PLATTSBURG	60	711	16	584	76	729
SUNY COLL POTSDAM	86	617	14	625	100	641
SUNY DOWNSTAT MD CTR	1	1328			1	1482
SUNY MARITIME COLL	23	902			23	1048
SUNY BRANCH UNK/NY	1	1328			1	1482
S F AUSTIN ST U/TX	194	379	28	390	222	382
STEPHENS COLLEGE/MO			2	1035	2	1418
STERLING COLLEGE/KS	76	655	8	786	84	689
STETSON UNIV/FL	221	349	69	185	290	310
STEUBENVILLE,C OF/OH	32	843	6	855	38	921
STEVENS INST TECH/NJ	282	284			282	322
STILLMAN COLLEGE/AL	6	1080	3	972	9	1206
STONEHILL COLLEGE/MA	51	741	12	670	63	771
SUFFOLK UNIV/MA	65	693	6	855	71	749
SUL ROSS STATE U/TX	82	630	11	698	93	661
SULPICIAN SEM NW/WA	15	973			15	1132
SUSQUEHANNA UNIV/PA	99	582	20	514	119	578
SWARTHMORE COLL/PA	968	89	363	31	1331	69
SWEET BRIAR COLL/VA	1	1328	53	242	54	816
SYRACUSE UNIV/NY	1618	45	323	39	1941	41
SYRACUSE U-UTICA/NY	23	902	6	855	29	979
SUNY ENVR SCI FSTRY	149	467			149	506
TABOR COLLEGE/KS	82	630	1	1101	83	693
TALLADEGA COLLEGE/AL	65	693	25	425	90	671
TAMPA, UNIV OF/FL	70	673	8	786	78	719
TARKIO COLLEGE/MO	96	588	5	888	101	636
TAYLOR UNIVERSITY/IN	133	496	11	698	144	515
TEMPLE UNIVERSITY/PA	1282	59	242	49	1524	58
TENNESSEE STATE UNIV	102	575	25	425	127	558
TENNESSEE TECH U	201	369	19	531	220	387
TENN TEMPLE SCHOOLS	25	883	2	1035	27	999
TENN, U-KNOXVILLE	1081	77	150	79	1231	77
TENN,U CTR HTH SCI	5	1106	2	1035	7	1246
TENN, U-CHATTANOOGA	140	481	35	336	175	466
TENN, U-MARTIN	26	877	3	972	29	979
TENN WESLEYAN COLL	17	954	2	1035	19	1089
TEXAS A&I UNIVERSITY	177	411	24	440	201	414
TEXAS A&M UNIVERSITY	1370	56	6	855	1376	65
PRAIRIE VIEW A&M/TX	85	623	24	440	109	610
TARLETON STATE U/TX	17	954	1	1101	18	1101
TEXAS CHRISTIAN UNIV	430	197	81	160	511	198

APPENDIX H Continued

	Male		Female		Both Sexes	
	Number	Rank	Number	Rank	Number	Rank
TEXAS COLLEGE	22	908	4	935	26	1014
TEXAS LUTHERAN COLL	47	760	5	888	52	833
TEXAS SOUTHERN UNIV	38	816	9	755	47	867
TEXAS TECH UNIV	900	100	102	129	1002	99
TEXAS, U-AUSTIN	3381	17	664	17	4045	15
TEXAS,U-ARLINGTON	100	581	10	724	110	607
TEXAS, U-EL PASO	80	640	23	460	103	628
TEX U MED BR-GALVSTN			2	1035	2	1418
TEXAS WESLEYAN COLL	61	705	21	493	82	700
TEXAS WOMANS UNIV	2	1252	218	53	220	387
THEOL SEM RE EPIS/PA	3	1188			3	1361
THIEL COLLEGE/PA	130	501	12	670	142	519
T JEF U-JEF MED C/PA	4	1141			4	1321
THOMAS MORE COLL/KY	80	640	23	460	103	628
TIFFIN UNIV/OH	1	1328			1	1482
TIFT COLLEGE/GA			17	563	17	1111
TOCCOA FLS BLE I/GA	3	1188	1	1101	4	1321
TOLEDO, UNIV OF/OH	360	232	56	230	416	234
TOUGALOO COLLEGE/MS	39	808	13	644	52	833
TOWSON ST COLL/MD	103	572	24	440	127	558
TRANSYLVANIA U/KY	121	524	21	493	142	519
TRENTON ST COLL/NJ	156	451	49	263	205	405
TREVECCA NZRENE C/TN	19	939	2	1035	21	1068
TRI-STATE UNIV/IN	42	792			42	896
TRINITY CHRISTN C/IL	1	1328			1	1482
TRINITY COLLEGE/CT	409	205	1	1101	410	237
TRINITY COLLEGE/DC	2	1252	141	90	143	517
TRINITY COLLEGE/IL	6	1080	1	1101	7	1246
TRINITY COLLEGE/VT			9	755	9	1206
TRINITY UNIV/TX	177	411	38	315	215	394
TROY STATE UNIV/AL	134	493	24	440	158	488
TUFTS UNIVERSITY/MA	830	107	120	108	950	104
TULANE U OF LA	689	131	62	201	751	135
TULANE U-NEWCMB C/LA			116	112	116	588
TULSA, UNIV OF/OK	281	286	37	322	318	292
TUSCULUM COLLEGE/TN	49	747	4	935	53	825
TUSKEGEE INST/AL	109	553	46	274	155	495
UNION COLLEGE/KY	51	741	6	855	57	801
UNION COLLEGE/NE	139	483	19	531	158	488
UNION THEOL SEM/NY	4	1141			4	1321
UNION UNIVERSITY/NY	785	111	2	1035	787	133
UNION-ALBANY MED/NY			1	1101	1	1482
UNION UNIVERSITY/TN	104	570	8	786	112	601
USAF ACADEMY/CO	89	610			89	676
US COAST GUARD ACAD	45	771			45	878
U S INTERNATL U/CA	29	856	8	786	37	927
US MERCHANT MAR ACAD	77	651			77	723
US MILITARY ACADEMY	585	149			585	173
US NAVAL ACADEMY/MD	611	141			611	163
UNITED THEOL SEM/OH	1	1328			1	1482
UNITED WESLEYAN C/PA	3	1188			3	1361
UPPER IOWA UNIVERSTY	74	658	2	1035	76	729
UPSALA COLLEGE/NJ	131	498	23	460	154	497
URSINUS COLLEGE/PA	245	321	46	274	291	307
URSULINE COLL/OH			22	472	22	1057
UTAH, UNIV OF	2339	26	212	55	2551	28
SOUTHERN UTAH ST C	36	828	1	1101	37	927
UTAH STATE UNIV	1500	51	65	192	1565	56
WEBER STATE COLL/UT	61	705	3	972	64	768
UTAH HGR ED SYST-UNK	1	1328			1	1482
VALDOSTA STATE C/GA	20	927	11	698	31	964
VALLEY CITY ST C/ND	102	575	7	821	109	610
VALPARAISO UNIV/IN	379	218	58	223	437	225
VANDERBILT UNIV/TN	726	119	113	118	839	119
VANDERCOOK C MUS/IL	2	1252			2	1418
VASSAR COLLEGE/NY	7	1062	678	15	685	149
VENNARD COLLEGE/IA	3	1188	1	1101	4	1321
VERMONT, U OF	477	184	79	164	556	179
VILLA MARIA COLL/PA			20	514	20	1081
VILLANOVA UNIV/PA	431	196	39	309	470	214
VIRGINIA COLLEGE	1	1328			1	1482
VA COMMONWEALTH UNIV	45	771	16	584	61	782
VA COMONWLTH U MED C	23	902	7	821	30	972
VIRGINIA MILITARY I	220	350			220	387
VA POLY INST&STATE U	901	99	15	607	916	108
VIRGINIA STATE COLL	134	493	41	295	175	466
VIRGINIA UNION UNIV	75	656	19	531	94	654
VIRGINIA, UNIV OF	1044	80	29	379	1073	91
VIRGINIA, U-UNKNOWN	1	1328			1	1482
VITERBO COLLEGE/WI			20	514	20	1081
VOORHEES COLLEGE/SC			1	1101	1	1482
WABASH COLLEGE/IN	534	164			534	190
WADHAMS HALL/NY	3	1188			3	1361
WAGNER COLLEGE/NY	155	454	23	460	178	458
WAKE FOREST UNIV/NC	510	173	39	309	549	183
WALLA WALLA COLL/WA	162	443	11	698	173	470
WALSH COLLEGE/OH	5	1106			5	1293
WARNER PACIFIC C/OR	8	1049			8	1221
WARREN WILSON C/NC	1	1328			1	1482
WARTBURG COLL/IA	137	486	5	888	142	519
WARTBURG THEO SEM/IA	2	1252			2	1418
WASHBURN U TOPEKA/KS	201	369	38	315	239	361
WASH&JEFFERSON C/PA	290	280			290	310
WASHINGTON&LEE U/VA	361	231			361	267
WASHINGTN BIBLE C/MD	2	1252			2	1418
WASHINGTON COLL/MD	85	623	13	644	98	645
WASHINGTON STATE U	1152	67	96	138	1248	76
WASH THEOL COALTN/MD	1	1328			1	1482
WASHINGTON UNIV/MO	1264	60	246	48	1510	61
WASHINGTON, U OF	2918	20	421	26	3339	19
WAYLAND BAPT COLL/TX	40	805	5	888	45	878
WAYNE ST COLL/NE	179	402	13	644	192	434
WAYNE STATE UNIV/MI	1740	39	335	35	2075	37
WAYNESBURG COLL/PA	111	546	18	548	129	551
WEBB I NAVAL ARCH/NY	45	771	1	1101	46	874
WEBSTER COLLEGE/MO			53	242	53	825
WELLESLEY COLLEGE/MA	4	1141	885	5	889	113
WELLS COLLEGE/NY			67	190	67	760
WESLEYAN COLLEGE/GA	6	1080	43	287	49	857
WESLEYAN UNIV/CT	912	97	2	1035	914	109
WEST CHESTER ST C/PA	275	291	37	322	312	294
WEST GEORGIA COLLEGE	21	919	3	972	24	1035
WEST LIBERTY ST C/WV	84	626	9	755	93	661
WEST TEXAS STATE U	211	357	40	303	251	351
WEST VA INST OF TECH	42	792	3	972	45	878
WEST VIRGINIA ST C	79	646	25	425	104	625
WEST VIRGINIA UNIV	1110	72	121	106	1231	77
WEST VA WESLEYAN C	151	460	10	724	161	485
WSTRN BAPT BIBL C/OR	2	1252			2	1418
WESTERN CONN ST COLL	29	856	10	724	39	917
WESTERN ILLINOIS U	326	257	30	367	356	271
WESTERN KENTUCKY U	351	239	50	260	401	241
WESTERN MARYLAND COL	191	387	35	336	226	379
WESTERN MICHIGAN U	725	120	103	126	828	124
WESTERN MONTANA COLL	30	851	2	1035	32	958
WSTRN NEW ENGL C/MA	5	1106			5	1293
WESTERN NEW MEXICO U	38	816	5	888	43	891
WESTERN ST COLL COLO	123	519	10	724	133	545
WESTERN WASH STATE C	290	280	30	367	320	289
WESTMAR COLLEGE/IA	95	593	8	786	103	628
WSTMINSTR CHOIR C/NJ	27	865			27	999
WESTMINSTER COLL/MO	134	493			134	541
WESTMINSTER COLL/PA	202	368	25	425	227	378
WESTMINSTER COLL/UT	27	865	1	1101	28	987
WESTMONT COLLEGE/CA	72	664	4	935	76	729
WHEATON COLLEGE/IL	715	124	108	122	823	125
WHEATON COLLEGE/MA	5	1106	70	181	75	737
WHEELING COLLEGE/WV	40	805	6	855	46	874
WHEELOCK COLLEGE/MA			11	698	11	1175
WHITE PLAINS, COL/NY			21	493	21	1068
WHITMAN COLLEGE/WA	294	278	43	287	337	281
WHITTIER COLLEGE/CA	252	312	44	285	296	304
WHITWORTH COLL/WA	124	518	12	670	136	537
WICHITA ST UNIV/KS	462	187	47	271	509	201
WIDENER C/PA	38	816			38	921
WILBERFORCE UNIV/OH	41	800	14	625	55	807
WILEY COLLEGE/TX	42	792	8	786	50	852
WILKES COLLEGE/PA	110	549	15	607	125	561
WILLAMETTE UNIV/OR	337	251	40	303	377	253
WILLIAM & MARY, C/VA	550	159	119	109	669	151

APPENDIX H Continued

	Male		Female		Both Sexes	
	Number	Rank	Number	Rank	Number	Rank
WM CAREY COLL/MS	30	851	5	888	35	938
WILLIAM JEWELL C/MO	244	324	24	440	268	337
WM MITCHELL C LAW/MN	4	1141			4	1321
WM PATERSON C OF NJ	50	744	17	563	67	760
WILLIAM PENN COLL/IA	66	689	14	625	80	706
WILLIAMS COLLEGE/MA	802	109	1	1101	803	129
WILMINGTON COLL/OH	95	593	11	698	106	619
WILSON COLLEGE/PA			107	124	107	617
WINDHAM COLLEGE/VT	1	1328			1	1482
WINONA STATE UNIV/MN	109	553	6	855	115	593
WINTHROP COLLEGE/SC			84	157	84	689
WISC COLL CONSERVTRY	3	1188			3	1361
WISCONSIN,U-MADISON	5344	5	737	12	6081	4
WISCONSIN,U-E CLAIRE	187	389	21	493	208	401
WISCONSIN,U-L CROSSE	225	344	32	360	257	346
WISCONSIN,U-MILWAUKE	203	366	30	367	233	369
WISCONSIN,U-OSHKOSH	176	415	20	514	196	428
WISC, U-PARKSIDE	1	1328			1	1482
WISCONSIN,U-PLATTVIL	178	407	21	493	199	424
WISCONSIN,U-RIVR FLS	237	331	13	644	250	352
WISCONSIN,U-STEVN PT	185	392	18	548	203	410
WISC, U-STOUT	161	446	17	563	178	458
WISCONSIN,U-SUPERIOR	128	509	11	698	139	531
WISCONSIN,U-WHITWATR	187	389	25	425	212	395
WITTENBERG UNIV/OH	316	265	49	263	365	262
WOFFORD COLLEGE/SC	250	315			250	352
WOODBURY UNIV/CA	4	1141			4	1321
WOODSTOCK COLL/NY	79	646			79	711
WOOSTER, COLL OF/OH	725	120	129	102	854	118
WORCESTER POLY I/MA	377	219			377	253
WRIGHT STATE UNIV/OH	10	1027	1	1101	11	1175
WYOMING, UNIV OF	579	152	42	293	621	158
XAVIER UNIV/OH	365	226	15	607	380	247
XAVIER UNIV/LA	51	741	16	584	67	760
YALE UNIVERSITY/CT	3481	14	10	724	3491	18
YANKTON COLLEGE/SD	109	553	13	644	122	569
YESHIVA UNIV/NY	470	186	8	786	478	211
YESHIVA U-STERN C/NY			2	1035	2	1418
YESHIVA-YESHIVA C/NY	12	1004			12	1159
YOUNGSTOWN ST U/OH	204	364	39	309	243	358

SOURCE: NRC, Commission on Human Resources.

APPENDIX I
BACCALAUREATE ORIGINS OF 1920-1974 PhD's: STATE AND REGIONAL SUMMARY, BY GEOGRAPHIC AREA

	Rank	Men: Physical Sciences	Men: Engineering	Men: Life Sciences	Men: Behavioral Sciences	Men: Humanities	Men: Professions	Men: Education	Men: Total	Women: Physical Sciences	Women: Engineering	Women: Life Sciences	Women: Behavioral Sciences	Women: Humanities	Women: Professions	Women: Education	Women: Total	Unknown Field	Grand Total
MAINE																			
1920-1959	37	185	14	182	102	160	33	117	793	5		14	6	25		15	65		858
1960-1969	39	154	37	139	106	146	20	102	705	5		10	10	14	4	20	63	1	769
1970-1974	41	96	32	130	107	124	13	123	626	3		13	10	23	2	27	78	1	705
TOTAL 1920-1974	39	435	83	451	315	430	66	342	2124	13		37	26	62	6	62	206	2	2332
PER 1000 U.S. TOTAL		5.3	2.5	7.8	5.4	8.3	4.4	5.2	5.8	3.0		4.1	2.2	4.2	3.0	3.5	3.4	21.5	5.5
NEW HAMPSHIRE																			
1920-1959	32	285	20	195	164	208	27	109	1008	2		14	6	9		3	34		1042
1960-1969	34	244	53	167	164	192	36	115	971	4		9	7	5	1	8	34		1005
1970-1974	39	145	48	93	149	165	32	116	748	2		10	6	13	1	26	58		806
TOTAL 1920-1974	35	674	121	455	477	565	95	340	2727	8		33	19	27	2	37	126		2853
PER 1000 U.S. TOTAL		8.1	3.6	7.9	8.2	10.9	6.4	5.2	7.5	1.8		3.7	1.6	1.8	1.0	2.1	2.1		6.7
VERMONT																			
1920-1959	43	115	9	73	57	59	8	53	374	5		12	10	15	1	12	55		429
1960-1969	46	92	22	98	66	63	7	48	397	5		12	17	24	6	19	83		480
1970-1974	46	56	14	83	61	60	6	64	345	7		15	14	32	3	20	91		436
TOTAL 1920-1974	46	263	45	254	184	182	21	165	1116	17		39	41	71	10	51	229		1345
PER 1000 U.S. TOTAL		3.2	1.3	4.4	3.2	3.5	1.4	2.5	3.1	3.9		4.3	3.5	4.8	5.0	2.9	3.8		3.2
MASSACHUSETTS																			
1920-1959	5	2313	551	931	1063	1433	227	625	7145	213	2	322	284	503	29	219	1573		8718
1960-1969	4	2350	1181	776	1104	1284	242	670	7618	145	5	245	272	426	32	240	1366	5	8989
1970-1974	4	1536	787	682	1125	1075	252	821	6283	125	7	261	456	604	30	357	1841	8	8132
TOTAL 1920-1974	5	6199	2519	2389	3292	3792	721	2116	21046	483	14	828	1012	1533	91	816	4780	13	25839
PER 1000 U.S. TOTAL		74.9	75.2	41.2	56.5	73.4	48.2	32.4	57.7	111.2	95.9	92.2	86.5	103.1	45.6	46.3	80.0	139.8	60.9
RHODE ISLAND																			
1920-1959	35	272	23	194	107	122	32	57	807	15		34	15	25	1	13	103		910
1960-1969	35	280	74	163	128	129	23	72	870	6		22	33	29	2	26	118		988
1970-1974	35	207	57	123	151	151	28	130	848	11		23	35	55	2	33	159	1	1008
TOTAL 1920-1974	33	759	154	480	386	402	83	259	2525	32		79	83	109	5	72	380	1	2906
PER 1000 U.S. TOTAL		9.2	4.6	8.3	6.6	7.8	5.6	4.0	6.9	7.4		8.8	7.1	7.3	2.5	4.1	6.4	10.8	6.8
CONNECTICUT																			
1920-1959	15	658	130	359	394	683	80	194	2498	8	1	23	20	22	2	29	105		2603
1960-1969	18	527	185	292	434	538	94	232	2307	13		29	29	34	2	36	143		2450
1970-1974	24	282	96	201	387	459	70	291	1790	4	1	34	44	51	7	57	198	1	1989
TOTAL 1920-1974	18	1467	411	852	1215	1680	244	717	6595	25	2	86	93	107	11	122	446	1	7042
PER 1000 U.S. TOTAL		17.7	12.3	14.7	20.8	32.5	16.3	11.0	18.1	5.8	13.7	9.6	8.0	7.2	5.5	6.9	7.5	10.8	16.6
NEW YORK																			
1920-1959	1	4220	1011	2106	2578	2188	494	2284	14883	339	6	449	588	808	61	807	3059		17942
1960-1969	1	4082	2204	1750	2978	2265	460	2054	15822	217	12	439	798	753	80	718	3022	5	18849
1970-1974	1	2652	1439	1466	2600	2032	458	2041	12701	225	12	472	941	1011	94	912	3671	13	16385
TOTAL 1920-1974	1	10954	4654	5322	8156	6485	1412	6379	43406	781	30	1360	2327	2572	235	2437	9752	18	53176
PER 1000 U.S. TOTAL		132.3	138.9	91.9	139.9	125.5	94.5	97.7	119.0	179.8	205.5	151.4	199.0	173.0	117.9	138.2	163.3	193.5	125.2
NEW JERSEY																			
1920-1959	16	646	118	411	329	505	68	287	2364	14	1	34	22	35	4	75	185		2549
1960-1969	14	704	347	371	386	489	95	362	2759	20	1	43	50	35	7	104	260	1	3020
1970-1974	13	547	279	320	410	438	78	460	2533	21	2	50	82	92	11	139	397	7	2937
TOTAL 1920-1974	14	1897	744	1102	1125	1432	241	1109	7656	55	4	127	154	162	22	318	842	8	8506
PER 1000 U.S. TOTAL		22.9	22.2	19.0	19.3	27.7	16.1	17.0	21.0	12.7	27.4	14.1	13.2	10.9	11.0	18.0	14.1	86.0	20.0
PENNSYLVANIA																			
1920-1959	3	2488	553	1330	1265	1148	275	1489	8550	124	1	205	228	360	25	255	1199	5	9754
1960-1969	3	2179	1211	1174	1188	966	278	1455	8461	122	1	222	208	318	48	277	1196		9657
1970-1974	3	1546	827	1129	1174	936	320	1778	7717	138	3	243	330	425	43	528	1711		9428
TOTAL 1920-1974	3	6213	2591	3633	3627	3050	873	4722	24728	384	5	670	766	1103	116	1060	4106	5	28839
PER 1000 U.S. TOTAL		75.0	77.3	62.7	62.2	59.0	58.4	72.3	67.8	88.4	34.2	74.6	65.5	74.2	58.2	60.1	68.8	53.8	67.9
OHIO																			
1920-1959	6	2184	341	1169	1256	1163	270	981	7368	89	2	170	194	247	30	225	957		8325
1960-1969	6	1656	675	867	1123	1033	337	1153	6869	72	1	165	231	203	44	279	995		7864
1970-1974	6	1077	496	753	1045	830	332	1230	5772	71		180	330	313	55	470	1419		7191
TOTAL 1920-1974	6	4917	1512	2789	3424	3026	939	3364	20009	232	3	515	755	763	129	974	3371		23380
PER 1000 U.S. TOTAL		59.4	45.1	48.1	58.7	58.6	62.8	51.5	54.8	53.4	20.5	57.3	64.6	51.3	64.7	55.2	56.5		55.1
INDIANA																			
1920-1959	8	1110	339	757	517	572	162	641	4100	43	1	71	45	113	22	87	384		4484
1960-1969	9	894	737	636	555	509	253	841	4434	27		47	70	86	24	183	437	1	4872
1970-1974	9	575	491	537	564	513	216	908	3806	29	3	77	115	131	30	228	614		4420
TOTAL 1920-1974	9	2579	1567	1930	1636	1594	631	2390	12340	99	4	195	230	330	76	498	1435	1	13776
PER 1000 U.S. TOTAL		31.2	46.8	33.3	28.1	30.9	42.2	36.6	33.8	22.8	27.4	21.7	19.7	22.2	38.1	28.2	24.0	10.8	32.4
ILLINOIS																			
1920-1959	2	2645	448	1443	1513	1273	358	1044	8729	135	2	223	227	329	50	302	1268	1	9998
1960-1969	5	1637	868	1052	1250	1033	300	1297	7446	87	2	123	237	262	29	301	1044	1	8491
1970-1974	5	1054	520	832	1133	859	319	1427	6148	70	4	156	294	338	44	426	1334	5	7487
TOTAL 1920-1974	4	5336	1836	3327	3896	3165	977	3768	22323	292	8	502	758	929	123	1029	3646	7	25976
PER 1000 U.S. TOTAL		64.5	54.8	57.4	66.8	61.3	65.4	57.7	61.2	67.2	54.8	55.9	64.8	62.5	61.7	58.3	61.1	75.3	61.2
MICHIGAN																			
1920-1959	7	1247	382	937	681	651	110	614	4624	58		98	100	103	15	132	507		5131
1960-1969	8	1047	761	793	777	759	188	1052	5385	58	3	108	150	148	28	248	744		6129
1970-1974	8	769	528	628	854	598	221	1189	4790	62	8	135	259	228	33	372	1098	1	5889
TOTAL 1920-1974	7	3063	1671	2358	2312	2008	519	2855	14799	178	11	341	509	479	76	752	2349	1	17149
PER 1000 U.S. TOTAL		37.0	49.9	40.7	39.7	38.9	34.7	43.7	40.6	41.0	75.3	38.0	43.5	32.2	38.1	42.6	39.3	10.8	40.4
WISCONSIN																			
1920-1959	10	804	196	888	575	479	103	581	3626	30	3	98	75	125	10	111	452		4078
1960-1969	11	586	329	571	431	359	118	656	3054	26		62	70	98	19	158	435	1	3490
1970-1974	10	496	243	452	487	366	128	666	2841	30	4	90	121	134	24	184	589	2	3432
TOTAL 1920-1974	10	1886	768	1911	1493	1204	349	1903	9521	86	7	250	266	357	53	453	1476	3	11000
PER 1000 U.S. TOTAL		22.8	22.9	33.0	25.6	23.3	23.3	29.1	26.1	19.8	47.9	27.8	22.7	24.0	26.6	25.7	24.7	32.3	25.9
MINNESOTA																			
1920-1959	12	808	172	773	533	392	123	438	3239	40		86	97	131	13	125	492		3731
1960-1969	10	722	238	624	471	485	153	630	3326	35	1	55	85	110	12	138	436		3762
1970-1974	11	484	160	443	486	417	136	615	2742	34		66	128	147	23	156	554	2	3298
TOTAL 1920-1974	11	2014	570	1840	1490	1294	412	1683	9307	109	1	207	310	388	48	419	1482	2	10791
PER 1000 U.S. TOTAL		24.3	17.0	31.8	25.6	25.0	27.6	25.8	25.5	25.1	6.8	23.0	26.5	26.1	24.1	23.8	24.8	21.5	25.4
IOWA																			
1920-1959	11	844	188	721	603	494	160	547	3559	44		73	71	121	13	145	467		4026
1960-1969	13	543	335	542	427	327	116	641	2935	10	1	42	40	58	21	124	296		3231
1970-1974	14	386	203	421	370	259	107	600	2350	17		59	69	83	24	145	397	1	2748
TOTAL 1920-1974	13	1773	726	1684	1400	1080	383	1788	8844	71	1	174	180	262	58	414	1160	1	10005
PER 1000 U.S. TOTAL		21.4	21.7	29.1	24.0	20.9	25.6	27.4	24.2	16.3	6.8	19.4	15.4	17.6	29.1	23.5	19.4	10.8	23.6
MISSOURI																			
1920-1959	13	795	153	475	475	511	130	705	3245	36	1	68	49	121	14	132	421		3666
1960-1969	12	596	357	395	427	433	136	681	3028	22	1	46	72	109	14	144	408	1	3437
1970-1974	12	408	305	302	361	343	124	672	2518	27	1	55	101	126	22	216	548	2	3068
TOTAL 1920-1974	12	1799	815	1172	1263	1287	390	2058	8791	85	3	169	222	356	50	492	1377	3	10171
PER 1000 U.S. TOTAL		21.7	24.3	20.2	21.7	24.9	26.1	31.5	24.1	19.6	20.5	18.8	19.0	23.9	25.1	27.9	23.1	32.3	24.0

APPENDIX I Continued

	Rank	Men								Women									
		Physical Sciences	Engineering	Life Sciences	Behavioral Sciences	Humanities	Professions	Education	Total	Physical Sciences	Engineering	Life Sciences	Behavioral Sciences	Humanities	Professions	Education	Total	Unknown Field	Grand Total
NORTH DAKOTA																			
1920-1959	42	99	19	103	74	34	9	104	442	2		6	6	6	1	10	31		473
1960-1969	45	79	44	107	55	28	9	154	477	4		8	3	5	5	8	33		510
1970-1974	43	79	36	101	42	10	20	203	491	3		7	7	8	7	20	52		543
TOTAL 1920-1974	44	257	99	311	171	72	38	461	1410	9		21	16	19	13	38	116		1526
PER 1000 U.S. TOTAL		3.1	3.0	5.4	2.9	1.4	2.5	7.1	3.9	2.1		2.3	1.4	1.3	6.5	2.2	1.9		3.6
SOUTH DAKOTA																			
1920-1959	38	174	31	154	79	65	13	113	629	7		12	2	20	3	10	54		683
1960-1969	41	110	73	137	80	63	29	168	662	3		4	4	8	2	23	44		706
1970-1974	42	91	37	102	70	44	14	189	547	5		13	11	19	1	28	77		624
TOTAL 1920-1974	41	375	141	393	229	172	56	470	1838	15		29	17	47	6	61	175		2013
PER 1000 U.S. TOTAL		4.5	4.2	6.8	3.9	3.3	3.7	7.2	5.0	3.5		3.2	1.5	3.2	3.0	3.5	2.9		4.7
NEBRASKA																			
1920-1959	21	362	31	382	286	186	57	363	1667	15		33	38	64	6	85	241		1908
1960-1969	29	178	94	249	173	179	42	568	1483	13		21	18	34	10	69	165		1648
1970-1974	31	155	67	217	144	132	63	416	1195	8	1	18	29	40	6	74	176	1	1372
TOTAL 1920-1974	28	695	192	848	603	497	162	1347	4345	36	1	72	85	138	22	228	582	1	4928
PER 1000 U.S. TOTAL		8.4	5.7	14.6	10.3	9.6	10.8	20.6	11.9	8.3	6.8	8.0	7.3	9.3	11.0	12.9	9.7	10.8	11.6
KANSAS																			
1920-1959	14	551	94	548	386	265	101	509	2454	31	1	62	51	88	10	74	317		2771
1960-1969	15	427	251	446	302	274	75	566	2341	13		33	32	40	28	88	235		2576
1970-1974	18	297	183	319	294	235	97	529	1955	16		42	70	66	12	144	351		2306
TOTAL 1920-1974	15	1275	528	1313	982	774	273	1604	6750	60	1	137	153	194	50	306	903		7653
PER 1000 U.S. TOTAL		15.4	15.8	22.7	16.8	15.0	18.3	24.6	18.5	13.8	6.8	15.3	13.1	13.0	25.1	17.3	15.1		18.0
DELAWARE																			
1920-1959	49	34	14	29	13	18	2	7	117			1	1	6		4	12		129
1960-1969	47	46	51	57	24	13	4	18	213	3		6	4	5	1	3	22		235
1970-1974	47	47	45	53	26	16	6	20	214	4		5	4	8	2	13	36		250
TOTAL 1920-1974	48	127	110	139	63	47	12	45	544	7		12	9	19	3	20	70		614
PER 1000 U.S. TOTAL		1.5	3.3	2.4	1.1	0.9	0.8	0.7	1.5	1.6		1.3	0.8	1.3	1.5	1.1	1.2		1.4
MARYLAND																			
1920-1959	20	496	169	355	186	225	44	151	1626	44		82	33	69	4	65	297		1923
1960-1969	23	340	289	326	263	210	70	220	1723	16		36	44	52	5	65	218		1941
1970-1974	25	272	242	227	286	227	100	294	1650	18		62	60	73	17	89	319		1969
TOTAL 1920-1974	23	1108	700	908	735	662	214	665	4999	78		180	137	194	26	219	834		5833
PER 1000 U.S. TOTAL		13.4	20.9	15.7	12.6	12.8	14.3	10.2	13.7	18.0		20.0	11.7	13.0	13.0	12.4	14.0		13.7
DISTRICT OF COLUMBIA																			
1920-1959	24	225	20	165	232	299	417	106	1465	17		47	52	130	13	83	342		1807
1960-1969	32	169	56	91	208	204	72	108	909	16		35	54	57	6	50	218		1127
1970-1974	33	129	59	91	227	194	52	140	892	18	1	57	76	62	11	83	308	2	1202
TOTAL 1920-1974	32	523	135	347	667	697	541	354	3266	51	1	139	182	249	30	216	868	2	4136
PER 1000 U.S. TOTAL		6.3	4.0	6.0	11.4	13.5	36.2	5.4	9.0	11.7	6.8	15.5	15.6	16.7	15.0	12.2	14.5	21.5	9.7
VIRGINIA																			
1920-1959	18	544	83	277	284	373	65	216	1842	27		33	32	74	12	55	233		2075
1960-1969	27	383	213	191	221	244	72	244	1569	21		45	29	53	12	70	231		1800
1970-1974	26	287	204	227	216	231	70	301	1536	26		68	65	90	12	126	388		1924
TOTAL 1920-1974	24	1214	500	695	721	848	207	761	4947	74		146	126	217	36	251	852		5799
PER 1000 U.S. TOTAL		14.7	14.9	12.0	12.4	16.4	13.8	11.7	13.6	17.0		16.3	10.8	14.6	18.1	14.2	14.3		13.7
WEST VIRGINIA																			
1920-1959	36	202	47	208	92	82	24	166	822	7		17	9	13	4	37	87		909
1960-1969	37	178	62	188	104	103	27	164	828	4		19	12	19	4	41	99		927
1970-1974	36	113	65	154	106	71	37	259	806	5		22	17	19	6	67	136	1	943
TOTAL 1920-1974	36	493	174	550	302	256	88	589	2456	16		58	38	51	14	145	322	1	2779
PER 1000 U.S. TOTAL		6.0	5.2	9.5	5.2	5.0	5.9	9.0	6.7	3.7		6.5	3.2	3.4	7.0	8.2	5.4	10.8	6.5
NORTH CAROLINA																			
1920-1959	19	437	63	278	255	383	82	259	1757	16		40	31	65	5	45	202		1959
1960-1969	16	499	218	327	266	366	125	399	2203	17		49	41	87	20	115	329	1	2533
1970-1974	15	364	182	353	300	369	104	561	2234	21	2	73	73	134	19	190	513		2747
TOTAL 1920-1974	16	1300	463	958	821	1118	311	1219	6194	54	2	162	145	286	44	350	1044	1	7239
PER 1000 U.S. TOTAL		15.7	13.8	16.5	14.1	21.6	20.8	18.7	17.0	12.4	13.7	18.0	12.4	19.2	22.1	19.8	17.5	10.8	17.0
SOUTH CAROLINA																			
1920-1959	33	233	40	187	87	179	34	112	872	9		11	11	30	3	30	94		966
1960-1969	38	168	98	110	103	124	44	142	790	4	2	13	4	39	5	44	111		901
1970-1974	38	118	104	102	92	110	45	187	759	12		19	12	43	5	61	152		911
TOTAL 1920-1974	37	519	242	399	282	413	123	441	2421	25	2	43	27	112	13	135	357		2778
PER 1000 U.S. TOTAL		6.3	7.2	6.9	4.8	8.0	8.2	6.8	6.6	5.8	13.7	4.8	2.3	7.5	6.5	7.7	6.0		6.5
GEORGIA																			
1920-1959	29	283	82	208	141	184	52	152	1103	19		30	17	55	7	52	180		1283
1960-1969	28	314	206	238	211	163	85	233	1450	20		39	29	61	15	108	272		1722
1970-1974	27	274	195	234	208	135	124	279	1449	19	2	37	79	78	15	164	396	1	1846
TOTAL 1920-1974	29	871	483	680	560	482	261	664	4002	58	2	106	125	194	37	324	848	1	4851
PER 1000 U.S. TOTAL		10.5	14.4	11.7	9.6	9.3	17.5	10.2	11.0	13.4	13.7	11.8	10.7	13.0	18.6	18.4	14.2	10.8	11.4
FLORIDA																			
1920-1959	34	211	13	202	158	119	13	124	841	10		19	21	26	3	42	121		962
1960-1969	24	273	159	213	314	210	70	368	1609	15		30	53	61	11	98	268		1877
1970-1974	16	290	160	264	379	229	115	561	1998	13	3	42	119	96	13	217	503	1	2502
TOTAL 1920-1974	25	774	332	679	851	558	198	1053	4448	38	3	91	193	183	27	357	892	1	5341
PER 1000 U.S. TOTAL		9.3	9.9	11.7	14.6	10.8	13.2	16.1	12.2	8.7	20.5	10.1	16.5	12.3	13.5	20.2	14.9	10.8	12.6
KENTUCKY																			
1920-1959	28	319	45	252	200	188	62	269	1337	22	1	15	20	47	6	29	140		1477
1960-1969	30	303	87	305	176	164	69	322	1428	18	1	28	33	31	9	78	198		1626
1970-1974	30	193	73	199	144	147	41	387	1185	11	1	43	29	47	14	125	270		1455
TOTAL 1920-1974	30	815	205	756	520	499	172	978	3950	51	3	86	82	125	29	232	608		4558
PER 1000 U.S. TOTAL		9.8	6.1	13.0	8.9	9.7	11.5	15.0	10.8	11.7	20.5	9.6	7.0	8.4	14.5	13.2	10.2		10.7
TENNESSEE																			
1920-1959	25	320	42	210	211	294	51	315	1444	6		39	22	59	8	94	228		1672
1960-1969	21	376	202	298	241	322	86	405	1932	17	1	34	29	47	13	106	247		2179
1970-1974	20	255	160	284	227	257	103	514	1801	11	2	47	51	85	10	149	355	2	2158
TOTAL 1920-1974	20	951	404	792	679	873	240	1234	5177	34	3	120	102	191	31	349	830	2	6009
PER 1000 U.S. TOTAL		11.5	12.1	13.7	11.6	16.9	16.1	18.9	14.2	7.8	20.5	13.4	8.7	12.8	15.5	19.8	13.9	21.5	14.2
ALABAMA																			
1920-1959	31	215	36	193	108	156	37	238	983	4		22	15	32	3	39	115		1098
1960-1969	31	253	125	230	119	149	70	328	1275	10		29	30	42	13	94	218		1493
1970-1974	29	179	119	204	149	137	67	418	1276	15		35	33	61	13	181	338		1614
TOTAL 1920-1974	31	647	280	627	376	442	174	984	3534	29		86	78	135	29	314	671		4205
PER 1000 U.S. TOTAL		7.8	8.4	10.8	6.4	8.6	11.6	15.1	9.7	6.7		9.6	6.7	9.1	14.5	17.8	11.2		9.9
MISSISSIPPI																			
1920-1959	40	149	19	150	81	80	22	98	599	5	1	6	11	18	3	23	67		666
1960-1969	36	140	84	156	94	125	59	199	857	3	1	21	12	36	7	36	116		973
1970-1974	32	124	83	191	111	112	84	302	1007	5		27	30	43	6	114	225	2	1234
TOTAL 1920-1974	34	413	186	497	286	317	165	599	2463	13	2	54	53	97	16	173	408	2	2873
PER 1000 U.S. TOTAL		5.0	5.6	8.6	4.9	6.1	11.0	9.2	6.8	3.0	13.7	6.0	4.5	6.5	8.0	9.8	6.8	21.5	6.8

APPENDIX I Continued

		Men								Women									
	Rank	Physical Sciences	Engineering	Life Sciences	Behavioral Sciences	Humanities	Professions	Education	Total	Physical Sciences	Engineering	Life Sciences	Behavioral Sciences	Humanities	Professions	Education	Total	Unknown Field	Grand Total
ARKANSAS																			
1920-1959	39	141	18	125	75	83	26	146	614	5		13	6	13	5	20	62		676
1960-1969	33	116	72	182	88	97	64	292	912	7		4	7	23	12	51	104		1016
1970-1974	34	96	55	161	88	96	64	300	860	6		12	18	33	4	80	153		1013
TOTAL 1920-1974	38	353	145	468	251	276	154	738	2386	18		29	31	69	21	151	319		2705
PER 1000 U.S. TOTAL		4.3	4.3	8.1	4.3	5.3	10.3	11.3	6.5	4.1		3.2	2.7	4.6	10.5	8.6	5.3		6.4
LOUISIANA																			
1920-1959	30	268	69	232	146	137	35	147	1034	18		29	21	41	9	36	154		1188
1960-1969	26	396	167	291	163	194	94	267	1572	18		38	27	60	14	83	241		1813
1970-1974	23	281	151	268	227	193	99	367	1588	21	1	53	62	88	26	158	408		1996
TOTAL 1920-1974	27	945	387	791	536	524	228	781	4194	57	1	120	110	189	49	277	803		4997
PER 1000 U.S. TOTAL		11.4	11.5	13.7	9.2	10.1	15.3	12.0	11.5	13.1	6.8	13.4	9.4	12.7	24.6	15.7	13.4		11.8
OKLAHOMA																			
1920-1959	27	269	66	306	178	163	46	323	1351	7		21	13	32	4	65	142		1493
1960-1969	19	361	318	420	237	185	81	568	2172	9		31	30	32	10	138	250		2422
1970-1974	22	209	177	316	180	166	98	540	1688	7	3	37	54	58	18	180	357		2045
TOTAL 1920-1974	22	839	561	1042	595	514	225	1431	5211	23	3	89	97	122	32	383	749		5960
PER 1000 U.S. TOTAL		10.1	16.7	18.0	10.2	10.0	15.1	21.9	14.3	5.3	20.5	9.9	8.3	8.2	16.0	21.7	12.5		14.0
TEXAS																			
1920-1959	9	986	237	510	496	558	178	662	3628	41	5	85	61	177	19	154	542		4170
1960-1969	7	1316	760	746	673	645	314	933	5392	52	1	94	98	165	54	278	746		6138
1970-1974	7	942	570	802	770	677	311	1121	5199	78	1	164	198	278	52	458	1231		6430
TOTAL 1920-1974	8	3244	1567	2058	1939	1880	803	2716	14219	171	7	343	357	620	125	890	2519		16738
PER 1000 U.S. TOTAL		39.2	46.8	35.5	33.3	36.4	53.7	41.6	39.0	39.4	47.9	38.2	30.5	41.7	62.7	50.5	42.2		39.4
MONTANA																			
1920-1959	41	196	41	160	40	30	10	53	531	4		14	3	2	1	6	31		562
1960-1969	43	119	64	130	82	34	15	81	526	4	1	17	4	18	3	8	55		581
1970-1974	44	63	46	107	71	49	23	111	470	1		9	9	10	1	15	45	1	516
TOTAL 1920-1974	43	378	151	397	193	113	48	245	1527	9	1	40	16	30	5	29	131	1	1659
PER 1000 U.S. TOTAL		4.6	4.5	6.9	3.3	2.2	3.2	3.8	4.2	2.1	6.8	4.5	1.4	2.0	2.5	1.6	2.2	10.8	3.9
IDAHO																			
1920-1959	44	84	12	153	41	27	7	66	390	3		12		7		7	29		419
1960-1969	44	81	42	134	64	51	16	103	493	2		5	3	8	2	18	38		531
1970-1974	45	58	43	110	43	34	13	114	416	1		6	5	9	3	24	48		464
TOTAL 1920-1974	45	223	97	397	148	112	36	283	1299	6		23	8	24	5	49	115		1414
PER 1000 U.S. TOTAL		2.7	2.9	6.9	2.5	2.2	2.4	4.3	3.6	1.4		2.6	0.7	1.6	2.5	2.8	1.9		3.3
WYOMING																			
1920-1959	47	45	4	57	24	13	3	28	174			2	3	2		3	10		184
1960-1969	47	47	22	70	24	15	7	39	224	1			1		1	8	11		235
1970-1974	50	24	22	63	28	11	8	25	181	2		2	4	3		10	21		202
TOTAL 1920-1974	47	116	48	190	76	39	18	92	579	3		4	8	5	1	21	42		621
PER 1000 U.S. TOTAL		1.4	1.4	3.3	1.3	0.8	1.2	1.4	1.6	0.7		0.4	0.7	0.3	0.5	1.2	0.7		1.5
COLORADO																			
1920-1959	23	373	104	362	234	184	43	309	1609	20		37	42	46	3	63	211		1820
1960-1969	22	371	183	363	286	175	74	434	1891	12	1	26	45	33	12	75	204	1	2096
1970-1974	21	261	174	337	307	179	88	417	1763	13	4	46	92	64	12	96	327		2090
TOTAL 1920-1974	21	1005	461	1062	827	538	205	1160	5263	45	5	109	179	143	27	234	742	1	6006
PER 1000 U.S. TOTAL		12.1	13.8	18.3	14.2	10.4	13.7	17.8	14.4	10.4	34.2	12.1	15.3	9.6	13.5	13.3	12.4	10.8	14.1
NEW MEXICO																			
1920-1959	46	49	25	65	57	45	2	36	279	2		3	7	7	1	6	26		305
1960-1969	42	150	64	82	93	58	14	129	591	4		7	4	15	1	11	43		634
1970-1974	40	118	78	94	87	70	14	168	629	7		15	18	21	3	37	101		730
TOTAL 1920-1974	42	317	167	241	237	173	30	333	1499	13		25	29	43	5	54	170		1669
PER 1000 U.S. TOTAL		3.8	5.0	4.2	4.1	3.3	2.0	5.1	4.1	3.0		2.8	2.5	2.9	2.5	3.1	2.8		3.9
ARIZONA																			
1920-1959	45	90	14	79	63	41	7	67	361	4		8	4	6	1	8	31		392
1960-1969	40	120	70	107	110	66	12	144	630	6		12	11	15	4	31	79		709
1970-1974	37	94	72	133	132	82	37	197	749	5		15	31	29	5	79	164		913
TOTAL 1920-1974	40	304	156	319	305	189	56	408	1740	15		35	46	50	10	118	274		2014
PER 1000 U.S. TOTAL		3.7	4.7	5.5	5.2	3.7	3.7	6.2	4.8	3.5		3.9	3.9	3.4	5.0	6.7	4.6		4.7
UTAH																			
1920-1959	22	377	94	546	302	160	45	244	1770	6		13	16	16	10	24	85		1855
1960-1969	20	356	266	439	354	238	92	527	2273	3		14	28	24	7	46	122		2395
1970-1974	19	214	186	358	390	239	113	558	2059	8		10	36	30	2	94	180		2239
TOTAL 1920-1974	19	947	546	1343	1046	637	250	1329	6102	17		37	80	70	19	164	387		6489
PER 1000 U.S. TOTAL		11.4	16.3	23.2	17.9	12.3	16.7	20.3	16.7	3.9		4.1	6.8	4.7	9.5	9.3	6.5		15.3
NEVADA																			
1920-1959	51	27	4	10	14	9	4	9	77			1		2		1	4		81
1960-1969	51	31	10	21	9	11	2	13	97				4	1	1	1	7		104
1970-1974	51	22	7	16	15	5		23	89	3		2	3	2		6	16		105
TOTAL 1920-1974	51	80	21	47	38	25	6	45	263	3		3	7	5	1	8	27		290
PER 1000 U.S. TOTAL		1.0	0.6	0.8	0.7	0.5	0.4	0.7	0.7	0.7		0.3	0.6	0.3	0.5	0.5	0.5		0.7
GUAM																			
1960-1969	53				1				1										1
1970-1974	53				1			2	3							2	2		5
TOTAL 1920-1974	53				2			2	4							2	2		6
PER 1000 U.S. TOTAL					0.0			0.0	0.0							0.1	0.0		0.0
WASHINGTON																			
1920-1959	17	544	130	405	379	338	61	307	2166	25	1	59	43	45	6	79	258		2424
1960-1969	17	472	232	343	344	310	110	442	2255	16		28	55	55	12	60	226	2	2483
1970-1974	17	331	187	339	386	262	87	439	2033	10		49	65	75	8	75	283		2316
TOTAL 1920-1974	17	1347	549	1087	1109	910	258	1188	6454	51	1	136	163	175	26	214	767	2	7223
PER 1000 U.S. TOTAL		16.3	16.4	18.8	19.0	17.6	17.3	18.2	17.7	11.7	6.8	15.1	13.9	11.8	13.0	12.1	12.8	21.5	17.0
OREGON																			
1920-1959	26	425	41	292	230	159	45	233	1425	17		35	21	32	3	49	158		1583
1960-1969	25	409	109	292	267	183	58	341	1661	20		41	44	33	7	55	201		1862
1970-1974	28	287	63	233	267	182	65	367	1464	16	1	32	66	68	10	76	269		1733
TOTAL 1920-1974	26	1121	213	817	764	524	168	941	4550	53	1	108	131	133	20	180	628		5178
PER 1000 U.S. TOTAL		13.5	6.4	14.1	13.1	10.1	11.2	14.4	12.5	12.2	6.8	12.0	11.2	8.9	10.0	10.2	10.5		12.2
CALIFORNIA																			
1920-1959	4	2372	472	1538	1421	1188	199	1051	8241	80	1	159	193	250	17	259	960		9201
1960-1969	2	2452	1051	1474	1810	1237	300	1434	9782	70	3	199	313	311	28	331	1255	3	11040
1970-1974	2	2003	875	1537	2305	1283	345	1561	9921	98	10	320	562	516	54	451	2013	9	11943
TOTAL 1920-1974	2	6827	2398	4549	5536	3708	844	4046	27944	248	14	678	1068	1077	99	1041	4228	12	32184
PER 1000 U.S. TOTAL		82.5	71.6	78.5	94.9	71.8	56.5	62.0	76.6	57.1	95.9	75.5	91.3	72.4	49.6	59.0	70.8	129.0	75.8
ALASKA																			
1920-1959	52	5	2	1	3	2			13										13
1960-1969	52	12	3	11	6			2	34										34
1970-1974	52	8	3	4	7	1	1	5	29	2			2	1		2	7		36
TOTAL 1920-1974	52	25	8	16	16	3	1	7	76	2			2	1		2	7		83
PER 1000 U.S. TOTAL		0.3	0.2	0.3	0.3	0.1	0.1	0.1	0.2	0.5			0.2	0.1		0.1	0.1		0.2

APPENDIX I Continued

	Rank	Men: Physical Sciences	Men: Engineering	Men: Life Sciences	Men: Behavioral Sciences	Men: Humanities	Men: Professions	Men: Education	Men: Total	Women: Physical Sciences	Women: Engineering	Women: Life Sciences	Women: Behavioral Sciences	Women: Humanities	Women: Professions	Women: Education	Women: Total	Unknown Field	Grand Total
HAWAII																			
1920-1959	50	22	2	43	19	13	2	18	119			4		2		3	9		128
1960-1969	50	23	6	55	26	13	9	21	153	2		7	6	5		13	33		186
1970-1974	48	21	12	51	34	20	6	35	180	4		5	16	10	2	18	55		235
TOTAL 1920-1974	50	66	20	149	79	46	17	74	452	6		16	22	17	2	34	97		549
PER 1000 U.S. TOTAL		0.8	0.6	2.6	1.4	0.9	1.1	1.1	1.2	1.4		1.8	1.9	1.1	1.0	1.9	1.6		1.3
PUERTO RICO																			
1920-1959	48	19	6	53	17	11	2	20	128	2		12	8	4	3	15	44		172
1960-1969	49	19	19	43	23	11	3	21	141	1		16	4	13	5	24	63		204
1970-1974	49	25	26	32	31	21	6	24	166	2		6	10	15	2	24	59		225
TOTAL 1920-1974	49	63	51	128	71	43	11	65	435	5		34	22	32	10	63	166		601
PER 1000 U.S. TOTAL		0.8	1.5	2.2	1.2	0.8	0.7	1.0	1.2	1.2		3.8	1.9	2.2	5.0	3.6	2.8		1.4
NEW ENGLAND																			
1920-1959	4	3828	747	1934	1887	2665	407	1155	12625	248	3	419	341	599	33	291	1935		14560
1960-1969	5	3647	1552	1635	2002	2352	422	1239	12868	178	5	327	368	532	47	349	1807	6	14681
1970-1974	6	2322	1034	1312	1980	2034	401	1545	10640	152	8	356	565	778	45	520	2425	11	13076
TOTAL 1920-1974	5	9797	3333	4881	5869	7051	1230	3939	36133	578	16	1102	1274	1909	125	1160	6167	17	42317
PER 1000 U.S. TOTAL		118.3	99.5	84.2	100.7	136.5	82.3	60.3	99.0	133.1	109.6	122.7	108.9	128.4	62.7	65.8	103.3	182.8	99.7
MIDDLE ATLANTIC																			
1920-1959	2	7354	1682	3847	4172	3841	837	4060	25797	477	8	688	838	1203	90	1137	4443	5	30245
1960-1969	1	6965	3762	3295	4552	3720	833	3871	27042	359	14	704	1056	1106	135	1099	4478	6	31526
1970-1974	1	4745	2545	2915	4184	3406	856	4279	22951	384	17	765	1353	1528	148	1579	5779	20	28750
TOTAL 1920-1974	2	19064	7989	10057	12908	10967	2526	12210	75790	1220	39	2157	3247	3837	373	3815	14700	31	90521
PER 1000 U.S. TOTAL		230.3	238.4	173.6	221.4	212.3	169.0	187.0	207.8	280.9	267.1	240.1	277.6	258.1	187.1	216.3	246.2	333.3	213.2
EAST NORTH CENTRAL																			
1920-1959	1	7990	1706	5194	4542	4138	1003	3861	28447	355	8	660	641	917	127	857	3568	1	32016
1960-1969	2	5820	3370	3919	4136	3693	1196	4999	27188	270	6	505	758	797	144	1169	3655	3	30846
1970-1974	2	3971	2278	3202	4083	3166	1216	5420	23357	262	19	638	1119	1144	186	1680	5054	8	28419
TOTAL 1920-1974	1	17781	7354	12315	12761	10997	3415	14280	78992	887	33	1803	2518	2858	457	3706	12277	12	91281
PER 1000 U.S. TOTAL		214.8	219.5	212.5	218.9	212.9	228.4	218.6	216.5	204.2	226.0	200.7	215.3	192.3	229.2	210.1	205.6	129.0	215.0
WEST NORTH CENTRAL																			
1920-1959	3	3633	688	3156	2436	1947	593	2779	15235	175	2	340	314	551	60	581	2023		17258
1960-1969	3	2655	1392	2500	1935	1789	560	3408	14252	100	3	209	254	364	92	594	1617	1	15870
1970-1974	5	1900	991	1905	1767	1440	561	3224	11798	110	2	260	415	489	95	783	2155	6	13959
TOTAL 1920-1974	3	8188	3071	7561	6138	5176	1714	9411	41285	385	7	809	983	1404	247	1958	5795	7	47087
PER 1000 U.S. TOTAL		98.9	91.7	130.5	105.3	100.2	114.7	144.1	113.2	88.6	47.9	90.1	84.1	94.4	123.9	111.0	97.0	75.3	110.9
SOUTH ATLANTIC																			
1920-1959	6	2665	531	1909	1448	1862	733	1293	10445	149		280	207	468	51	413	1568		12013
1960-1969	6	2370	1352	1741	1714	1637	569	1896	11294	116	2	272	270	434	79	594	1768	1	13063
1970-1974	4	1894	1256	1705	1840	1582	653	2602	11538	136	8	385	505	603	100	1010	2751	5	14294
TOTAL 1920-1974	6	6929	3139	5355	5002	5081	1955	5791	33277	401	10	937	982	1505	230	2017	6087	6	39370
PER 1000 U.S. TOTAL		83.7	93.7	92.4	85.8	98.4	130.8	88.7	91.2	92.3	68.5	104.3	84.0	101.2	115.3	114.4	101.9	64.5	92.7
EAST SOUTH CENTRAL																			
1920-1959	9	1003	142	805	600	718	172	920	4363	37	2	82	68	156	20	185	550		4913
1960-1969	9	1072	498	989	630	760	284	1254	5492	48	3	112	104	156	42	314	779		6271
1970-1974	9	751	435	878	631	653	295	1621	5269	42	3	152	143	236	43	569	1188	4	6461
TOTAL 1920-1974	9	2826	1075	2672	1861	2131	751	3795	15124	127	8	346	315	548	105	1068	2517	4	17645
PER 1000 U.S. TOTAL		34.1	32.1	46.1	31.9	41.3	50.2	58.1	41.5	29.2	54.8	38.5	26.9	36.9	52.7	60.6	42.1	43.0	41.6
WEST SOUTH CENTRAL																			
1920-1959	7	1664	390	1173	895	941	285	1278	6627	71	5	148	101	263	37	275	900		7527
1960-1969	7	2189	1317	1639	1161	1121	553	2060	10048	86	2	167	162	280	90	550	1341		11389
1970-1974	7	1528	953	1547	1265	1132	572	2328	9335	112	4	266	332	457	100	876	2149		11484
TOTAL 1920-1974	7	5381	2660	4359	3321	3194	1410	5666	26010	269	11	581	595	1000	227	1701	4390		30400
PER 1000 U.S. TOTAL		65.0	79.4	75.2	57.0	61.8	94.3	86.8	71.3	61.9	75.3	64.7	50.9	67.3	113.8	96.4	73.5		71.6
MOUNTAIN																			
1920-1959	8	1241	298	1432	775	509	121	812	5191	39		90	75	88	16	118	427		5618
1960-1969	8	1275	721	1346	1022	648	232	1470	6725	32	2	81	100	114	31	198	559	1	7285
1970-1974	8	854	628	1218	1073	669	296	1613	6356	40	4	105	198	168	26	361	902	1	7259
TOTAL 1920-1974	8	3370	1647	3996	2870	1826	649	3895	18272	111	6	276	373	370	73	677	1888	2	20162
PER 1000 U.S. TOTAL		40.7	49.2	69.0	49.2	35.3	43.4	59.6	50.1	25.6	41.1	30.7	31.9	24.9	36.6	38.4	31.6	21.5	47.5
PACIFIC AND INSULAR																			
1920-1959	5	3387	653	2332	2069	1711	309	1629	12092	124	2	269	265	333	29	405	1429		13521
1960-1969	4	3387	1420	2218	2477	1754	480	2261	14027	109	3	291	422	417	52	483	1778	5	15810
1970-1974	3	2675	1166	2196	3031	1769	510	2433	13796	132	11	412	721	685	76	648	2688	9	16493
TOTAL 1920-1974	4	9449	3239	6746	7577	5234	1299	6323	39915	365	16	972	1408	1435	157	1536	5895	14	45824
PER 1000 U.S. TOTAL		114.1	96.7	116.4	130.0	101.3	86.9	96.8	109.4	84.0	109.6	108.2	120.4	96.5	78.7	87.1	98.7	150.5	107.9

SOURCE: NRC, Commission on Human Resources.

APPENDIX J
FOREIGN COUNTRIES OF BACCALAUREATE ORIGIN, ARRANGED IN ORDER OF NUMBER OF U.S. PhD's, BY SEX AND TOTAL

	Male		Female		Both Sexes	
	Number	Rank*	Number	Rank	Number	Rank
Afganistan	29	72			29	74
Algeria	5	98	7	62	12	85
Argentina	360	29	104	13	464	26
Australia	1,137	10	95	15	1,232	11
Austria	231	40	46	26	277	38
Bangladesh	263	37	12	53	275	39
Belgium	342	31	37	33	379	31
Bolivia	16	82	2	73	18	79
Brazil	525	20	41	28	566	20
Bulgaria	10	86	2	73	12	85
Burma	81	61	11	54	92	59
Canada	9,456	1	1,063	1	10,519	1
Chile	354	30	32	35	386	30
China (unspecified)	749	13	92	16	841	14
China (mainland)	1,551	6	103	14	1,654	6
Colombia	257	39	16	45	273	40
Costa Rica	47	67	4	67	51	67
Cuba	132	50	48	23	180	48
Cyprus	1	107			1	107
Czechoslovakia	171	45	15	47	186	47
Denmark	132	50	17	43	149	52
Dominican Republic	5	98			5	99
Ecuador	34	69	3	69	37	71
Egypt	2077	5	165	7	2242	5
El Salvador	6	94			6	96
England	2,253	4	314	5	2,567	4
Ethiopia	83	60	3	69	86	61
Finland	87	57	16	45	103	55
France	781	12	221	6	1,002	12
Germany (unspecified)	265	36	49	22	314	36
Germany (East)	42	68	13	51	55	65
Germany (West)	745	14	151	8	896	13
Ghana	48	66	2	73	50	68
Greece	571	19	40	30	611	19
Guatemala	21	77	2	73	23	77
Guyana	2	104			2	104
Haiti	26	74	2	73	28	75
Honduras	6	94			6	96
Hong Kong	331	32	47	25	378	32
Hungary	260	38	28	38	288	37
Iceland	7	90	1	81	8	92
India	8,484	2	572	3	9,056	2
Indonesia	229	41	14	49	243	41
Iran	607	17	41	28	648	17
Iraq	453	23	22	41	475	25
Ireland (unspecified)	5	98			5	99
Ireland (Republic of)	327	33	17	43	344	33
Ireland (Northern)	51	65	4	67	55	65
Israel	1,163	9	141	9	1,304	10
Italy	398	26	63	19	461	27
Jamaica	30	71	9	58	39	69
Japan	1,437	8	131	10	1,568	8
Jordan	10	86			10	89
Kenya	4	101			4	101
Korea (South)	1,498	7	130	11	1,628	7

	Male		Female		Both Sexes	
	Number	Rank	Number	Rank	Number	Rank
Korea (unspecified)	8	89	1	81	9	90
Lebanon	633	15	68	18	701	16
Lesotho	3	103			3	103
Liberia	22	76	3	69	25	76
Libya	15	83			15	83
Luxembourg			1	81	1	107
Malaysia	56	64	8	61	64	64
Malta	2	104			2	104
Mexico	524	21	22	41	546	22
Morocco	1	106	1	81	2	104
Nepal	17	79	1	81	18	79
Netherlands	374	28	28	38	402	29
New Zealand	434	25	54	20	488	24
Nicaragua	12	84	2	73	14	84
Nigeria	193	43	2	73	195	44
Norway	228	42	15	47	243	41
Pakistan (pre-1971)	180	44	14	49	194	46
Pakistan (post-1971)	581	18	48	23	629	18
Palestine			1	81	1	107
Panama	25	75	5	64	30	73
Papua			1	81	1	107
Paraguay	7	90	2	73	9	90
Peru	151	48	5	64	156	50
Philippines	1006	11	524	4	1530	9
Poland	158	47	43	27	201	43
Portugal	32	70	6	63	38	70
Rhodesia	4	101			4	101
Romania	60	63	9	58	69	63
Russia	128	52	26	40	154	51
South Africa	495	22	40	30	535	23
Sierra Leone	6	94	1	81	7	94
Saudi Arabia	17	79			17	81
Scotland	291	34	39	32	330	34
Senegal	1	106			1	107
Singapore	68	62	10	56	78	62
Spain	291	34	33	34	324	35
Sri Lanka	103	54	9	58	112	54
Sudan, The	90	56			90	60
Sweden	151	48	29	37	180	48
Switzerland	384	27	53	21	437	28
Syria	95	55	3	69	98	56
Taiwan	5,216	3	627	2	5,843	3
Tanzania	7	90			7	94
Thailand	441	24	117	12	558	21
Trinidad & Tobago	10	86	1	81	11	87
Tunisia	17	79			17	81
Turkey	620	16	88	17	708	15
United Arab Emirates	11	85			11	87
Uganda	20	78			20	78
Uruguay	27	73	5	64	32	72
Venezuela	115	53	13	51	128	53
Vietnam, North	6	94			6	96
Vietnam, South	84	58	11	54	95	57
Wales	84	58	10	56	94	58
Yugoslavia	165	46	30	36	195	44
Zaire	7	90	1	81	8	92

*"Rank" is used here in the sense of "order according to a statistical characteristic" (e.g., the number of PhD's granted by U.S. universities) and is not intended to imply degree of eminence or excellence.

SOURCE: NRC, Commission on Human Resources.

APPENDIX K
BACCALAUREATE ORIGINS OF 1920-1974 PhD's: FOREIGN REGIONAL SUMMARY

		Men								Women									
	Rank	Physical Sciences	Engineering	Life Sciences	Behavioral Sciences	Humanities	Professions	Education	Total	Physical Sciences	Engineering	Life Sciences	Behavioral Sciences	Humanities	Professions	Education	Total	Unknown Field	Grand Total
CANADA																			
1920-1959	1	1197	214	1092	496	456	131	237	3823	35		95	49	117	7	42	345	1	4169
1960-1969	3	706	405	652	553	332	175	321	3151	20	2	51	70	63	39	68	313	4	3468
1970-1974	3	444	203	432	512	308	170	397	2473	22		55	104	96	29	97	404	5	2882
TOTAL 1920-1974	3	2347	822	2176	1561	1096	476	955	9447	77	2	201	223	276	75	207	1062	10	10519
PER 1000 FOR'N BA TOT		196.3	71.8	186.7	213.5	262.4	203.5	303.7	181.4	79.9	18.2	144.4	232.5	203.4	293.0	222.1	177.8	370.4	181.1
PER 1000 BA GRD TOTAL		24.6	18.2	30.7	23.6	19.5	27.2	13.9	22.5	14.4	7.7	19.2	17.5	16.8	33.0	11.1	16.0	15.0	21.6
MEXICO AND CENTRAL AMERICA																			
1920-1959	12	18	7	37	9	12	3	4	90				1	2		1	4		94
1960-1969	11	37	33	137	37	21	4	9	279	2	1	6		3	1	2	15		294
1970-1974	12	53	57	78	43	15	7	18	272	1		4	2	7		2	16		288
TOTAL 1920-1974	12	108	97	252	89	48	14	31	641	3	1	10	3	12	1	5	35		676
PER 1000 FOR'N BA TOT		9.0	8.5	21.6	12.2	11.5	6.0	9.9	12.3	3.1	9.1	7.2	3.1	8.8	3.9	5.4	5.9		11.6
PER 1000 BA GRD TOTAL		1.1	2.1	3.6	1.3	0.9	0.8	0.5	1.5	0.6	3.9	1.0	0.2	0.7	0.4	0.3	0.5		1.4
CUBA AND ISLANDS																			
1920-1959	13	5	1	5	1	6			18	1		1	1				3		21
1960-1969	13	8	9	24	22	29	5	4	101	3		3	2	5		3	16		117
1970-1974	14	6	3	18	16	62	4	3	112	2		2	3	32		4	43		155
TOTAL 1920-1974	14	19	13	47	39	97	9	7	231	6		6	6	37		7	62		293
PER 1000 FOR'N BA TOT		1.6	1.1	4.0	5.3	23.2	3.8	2.2	4.4	6.2		4.3	6.3	27.3		7.5	10.4		5.0
PER 1000 BA GRD TOTAL		0.2	0.3	0.7	0.6	1.7	0.5	0.1	0.5	1.1		0.6	0.5	2.3		0.4	0.9		0.6
SOUTH AMERICA																			
1920-1959	10	35	16	68	21	20	4	5	169	1		2	3	3		2	11		180
1960-1969	10	153	120	155	92	34	8	9	572	14	2	16	15	24	1	9	81		653
1970-1974	6	261	216	362	134	54	28	52	1107	24	1	22	27	39	4	14	131		1238
TOTAL 1920-1974	8	449	352	585	247	108	40	66	1848	39	3	40	45	66	5	25	223		2071
PER 1000 FOR'N BA TOT		37.6	30.7	50.2	33.8	25.9	17.1	21.0	35.5	40.5	27.3	28.7	46.9	48.6	19.5	26.8	37.3		35.7
PER 1000 BA GRD TOTAL		4.7	7.8	8.3	3.7	1.9	2.3	1.0	4.4	7.3	11.6	3.8	3.5	4.0	2.2	1.3	3.4		4.2
EUROPE, NORTHERN																			
1920-1959	4	186	129	126	123	142	44	32	782	13		14	14	27	2	6	76		858
1960-1969	4	315	268	275	256	212	70	65	1461	12		37	25	52	9	13	149		1610
1970-1974	4	281	226	225	240	208	91	105	1378	15		46	62	77	4	33	237	1	1616
TOTAL 1920-1974	4	782	623	626	619	562	205	202	3621	40		97	101	156	15	52	462	1	4084
PER 1000 FOR'N BA TOT		65.4	54.4	53.7	84.7	134.5	87.6	64.2	69.5	41.5		69.7	105.3	115.0	58.6	55.8	77.3	37.0	70.3
PER 1000 BA GRD TOTAL		8.2	13.8	8.8	9.4	10.0	11.7	2.9	8.6	7.5		9.3	7.9	9.5	6.6	2.8	7.0	1.5	8.4
EUROPE, CENTRAL																			
1920-1959	7	107	49	63	98	128	34	15	494	5		16	15	41	2	5	84		578
1960-1969	8	163	112	54	98	143	35	17	624	10	3	12	11	64		5	105		729
1970-1974	9	114	114	54	99	128	39	25	573	7		11	26	81	4	4	133		706
TOTAL 1920-1974	9	384	275	171	295	399	108	57	1691	22	3	39	52	186	6	14	322		2013
PER 1000 FOR'N BA TOT		32.1	24.0	14.7	40.3	95.5	46.2	18.1	32.5	22.8	27.3	28.0	54.2	137.1	23.4	15.0	53.9		34.7
PER 1000 BA GRD TOTAL		4.0	6.1	2.4	4.5	7.1	6.2	0.8	4.0	4.1	11.6	3.7	4.1	11.3	2.6	0.7	4.9		4.1
EUROPE, EASTERN																			
1920-1959	9	75	46	66	83	71	31	24	396	6		9	3	12	1	2	33		429
1960-1969	9	173	127	120	86	91	25	20	642	9	2	12	5	31	3	3	65		707
1970-1974	10	125	130	74	72	58	25	14	498	13	7	21	14	35	3	6	99		597
TOTAL 1920-1974	10	373	303	260	241	220	81	58	1536	28	9	42	22	78	7	11	197		1733
PER 1000 FOR'N BA TOT		31.2	26.5	22.3	33.0	52.7	34.6	18.4	29.5	29.0	81.8	30.2	22.9	57.5	27.3	11.8	33.0		29.8
PER 1000 BA GRD TOTAL		3.9	6.7	3.7	3.6	3.9	4.6	0.8	3.7	5.2	34.7	4.0	1.7	4.8	3.1	0.6	3.0		3.6
EUROPE, WESTERN																			
1920-1959	5	154	90	87	75	133	30	8	577	11	1	7	9	55		3	86		663
1960-1969	7	150	210	97	105	126	36	11	736	5	1	18	19	60	1	4	108		844
1970-1974	7	185	274	92	125	140	57	20	893	17	7	16	18	116	2	10	186		1079
TOTAL 1920-1974	6	489	574	276	305	399	123	39	2206	33	9	41	46	231	3	17	380		2586
PER 1000 FOR'N BA TOT		40.9	50.1	23.7	41.7	95.5	52.6	12.4	42.4	34.2	81.8	29.5	48.0	170.2	11.7	18.2	63.6		44.5
PER 1000 BA GRD TOTAL		5.1	12.7	3.9	4.6	7.1	7.0	0.6	5.2	6.2	34.7	3.9	3.6	14.1	1.3	0.9	5.7		5.3
ASIA, EASTERN																			
1920-1959	2	473	553	441	319	97	107	119	2110	31	1	40	22	8	5	27	134		2244
1960-1969	2	1135	1391	632	405	139	92	111	3908	174	17	172	36	32	16	32	480	1	4389
1970-1974	1	1610	1934	954	498	189	129	198	5514	236	19	228	46	56	13	77	675	2	6191
TOTAL 1920-1974	2	3218	3878	2027	1222	425	328	428	11532	441	37	440	104	96	34	136	1289	3	12824
PER 1000 FOR'N BA TOT		269.1	338.6	173.9	167.1	101.7	140.2	136.1	221.4	457.5	336.4	316.1	108.4	70.7	132.8	145.9	215.8	111.1	220.8
PER 1000 BA GRD TOTAL		33.8	85.8	28.6	18.5	7.5	18.8	6.2	27.4	82.6	142.9	42.0	8.2	5.8	15.0	7.3	19.4	4.5	26.3
ASIA, WESTERN																			
1920-1959	3	365	310	623	293	89	74	138	1892	11	1	28	28	5	4	29	106		1998
1960-1969	1	1362	1353	1602	766	205	188	303	5789	63	6	100	81	42	36	86	414	3	6206
1970-1974	2	1105	1920	1175	699	213	260	212	5587	94	18	112	98	67	27	84	500	5	6092
TOTAL 1920-1974	1	2832	3583	3400	1758	507	522	653	13268	168	25	240	207	114	67	199	1020	8	14296
PER 1000 FOR'N BA TOT		236.8	312.9	291.7	240.4	121.4	223.2	207.6	254.7	174.3	227.3	172.4	215.8	84.0	261.7	213.5	170.8	296.3	246.1
PER 1000 BA GRD TOTAL		29.7	79.3	48.0	26.6	9.0	29.9	9.5	31.6	31.5	96.5	22.9	16.2	6.9	29.5	10.6	15.4	12.0	29.3
AUSTRALASIA																			
1920-1959	6	92	36	147	77	32	37	79	500	7		30	17	4	6	49	113		613
1960-1969	5	227	153	362	174	78	69	128	1195	36	5	79	32	32	15	96	295		1490
1970-1974	5	201	133	308	161	73	78	153	1108	40	3	65	48	41	8	75	280	3	1391
TOTAL 1920-1974	5	520	322	817	412	183	184	360	2803	83	8	174	97	77	29	220	688	3	3494
PER 1000 FOR'N BA TOT		43.5	28.1	70.1	56.3	43.8	78.7	114.5	53.8	86.1	72.7	125.0	101.1	56.7	113.3	236.1	115.2	111.1	60.2
PER 1000 BA GRD TOTAL		5.5	7.1	11.5	6.2	3.2	10.5	5.2	6.7	15.5	30.9	16.6	7.6	4.7	12.8	11.8	10.4	4.5	7.2
WEST NORTH AFRICA																			
1920-1959	14	1		1		1		1	4					1			1		5
1960-1969	14	6	1	24	13	10	1	13	68					1		4	5		73
1970-1974	13	18	10	57	68	23	9	36	221			2	1	6		1	10		231
TOTAL 1920-1974	13	25	11	82	81	34	10	50	293			2	1	8		5	16		309
PER 1000 FOR'N BA TOT		2.1	1.0	7.0	11.1	8.1	4.3	15.9	5.6			1.4	1.0	5.9		5.4	2.7		5.3
PER 1000 BA GRD TOTAL		0.3	0.2	1.2	1.2	0.6	0.6	0.7	0.7			0.2	0.1	0.5		0.3	0.2		0.6
EAST NORTH AFRICA																			
1920-1959	8	36	92	193	66	9	25	50	472				2	1		1	4		476
1960-1969	6	143	200	342	150	25	91	97	1051	13	3	34	22	4	8	12	96		1147
1970-1974	8	97	205	194	103	21	85	37	742	8	9	13	18	6	3	11	68		810
TOTAL 1920-1974	7	276	497	729	319	55	201	184	2265	21	12	47	42	11	11	24	168		2433
PER 1000 FOR'N BA TOT		23.1	43.4	62.5	43.6	13.2	85.9	58.5	43.5	21.8	109.1	33.8	43.8	8.1	43.0	25.8	28.1		41.9
PER 1000 BA GRD TOTAL		2.9	11.0	10.3	4.8	1.0	11.5	2.7	5.4	3.9	46.3	4.5	3.3	0.7	4.8	1.3	2.5		5.0
SOUTH AFRICA																			
1920-1959	11	34	19	45	23	2	5	12	140		1	4	1		1	2	9		149
1960-1969	12	44	43	93	39	18	12	16	266	1		3	3	1		1	9		275
1970-1974	11	57	40	69	62	24	21	27	300	2		6	6	8	2	7	31	2	333
TOTAL 1920-1974	11	135	102	207	124	44	38	55	706	3	1	13	10	9	3	10	49	2	757
PER 1000 FOR'N BA TOT		11.3	8.9	17.8	17.0	10.5	16.2	17.5	13.6	3.1	9.1	9.3	10.4	6.6	11.7	10.7	8.2	74.1	13.0
PER 1000 BA GRD TOTAL		1.4	2.3	2.9	1.9	0.8	2.2	0.8	1.7	0.6	3.9	1.2	0.8	0.5	1.3	0.5	0.7	3.0	1.6
TOTAL																			
1920-1959		2778	1562	2994	1684	1198	525	724	11467	121	4	246	165	276	28	169	1009	1	12477
1960-1969		4622	4425	4569	2796	1463	811	1124	19843	362	42	543	321	414	129	338	2151	8	22002
1970-1974		4557	5465	4092	2832	1516	1003	1297	20778	481	64	603	473	667	99	425	2813	18	23609
TOTAL 1920-1974		11957	11452	11655	7312	4177	2339	3145	52088	964	110	1392	959	1357	256	932	5973	27	58088
PER 1000 BA GRD TOTAL		125.6	253.3	164.5	110.5	74.2	133.8	45.7	123.9	180.6	424.7	132.7	75.3	82.7	112.7	49.9	90.1	40.6	119.2

SOURCE: NRC, Commission on Human Resources.

APPENDIX L
FORMS USED FOR DATA COLLECTION

The Doctorate Survey form, completed by each new PhD since 1957, and forwarded to the Commission on Human Resources by the dean of the graduate school, has changed in detail over the 2 decades of its use. However, the major outline has remained constant; the main changes have been to add further details of information as the institutions and other data users have felt the need for more data. The form in use at the time the present book was written is given on the three following pages, together with the specialties list.

The biennial surveys of doctoral scientists and engineers have been accomplished by means of questionnaires sent to a carefully stratified sample of PhD's in the science fields. These questionnaires have also varied somewhat from one survey to the next. The questionnaire form used in the 1975 Survey of Doctoral Scientists and Engineers is given on pages 163-66.

NSF Form 558 1974
OMB No. 99-R0290
Approval Expires June 30, 1976

SURVEY OF EARNED DOCTORATES

This form is to be returned to the GRADUATE DEAN, for forwarding to .... Board on Human-Resource Data and Analyses
Commission on Human Resources
National Research Council
2101 Constitution Avenue, Washington, D. C. 20418

Please print or type.

A. Name in full: .... (9-30)
(Last Name) (First Name) (Middle Name)

Cross Reference: Maiden name or former name legally changed .... (31)

B. Permanent address through which you could always be reached: (Care of, if applicable) ....
....
(Number) (Street) (City)
....
(State) (Zip Code) (Or Country if not U.S.)

C. U.S. Social Security Number: __ __ __ - __ __ - __ __ __ __ (33-41)

D. Date of birth: .... Place of birth: ....
(42-46) (Month) (Day) (Year) (47-48) (State) (Or Country if not U.S.)

E. Sex: 1 ☐ Male 2 ☐ Female (49)

F. Marital status: 1 ☐ Married 2 ☐ Not married (including widowed, divorced) (50)

G. Citizenship: 0 ☐ U.S. native 2 ☐ Non U.S., Immigrant (Permanent Resident)
1 ☐ U.S. naturalized 3 ☐ Non-U.S., Non-Immigrant (Temporary Resident) (51)
If Non-U.S., indicate country of present citizenship .... (52-53)

H. Racial or ethnic group: (Check all that apply.) 0 ☐ White/Caucasian 1 ☐ Black/Negro/Afro-American
2 ☐ American Indian 3 ☐ Spanish-American/Mexican-American/Chicano
4 ☐ Puerto Rican-American 5 ☐ Oriental 6 ☐ Other, specify .... (54-56)

I. Number of dependents:
Do not include yourself. (Dependent = someone receiving at least one half of his or her support from you) .... (57)

EDUCATION

J. High school last attended: .... (58-59)
(School Name) (City) (State)

Year of graduation from high school: .... (60-61)

K. List in the table below all collegiate and graduate institutions you have attended including 2-year colleges. List chronologically, and include your doctoral institution as the last entry.

Institution Name	Location	Years Attended		Major Field (Use Specialties List)		Minor Field	Degree (if any)		
		From	To	Name	Number	Number	Title of Degree	Granted Mo.	Granted Yr.

L. Enter below the title of your doctoral dissertation and the most appropriate classification number and field. If a project report or a musical or literary composition (not a dissertation) is a degree requirement, please check box. ☐ (44)

Title .... Classify using Specialties List
.... Number .... Name of field ....
....

M. Name the department (or interdisciplinary committee, center, institute, etc.) and school or college of the university which supervised your doctoral program: ....
(Department/Institute/Committee/Program) (School)

N. Name of your dissertation adviser: ....
(Last Name) (First Name) (Middle Initial)

continued on next page

Please Do Not Write In This Space

[1] 8
9-30 NA
cr( ) 31 d( ) 32
33-41 SS
42 | 43 44 | 45 46
47 48
49 | 50
51 | 52 53
54 55 56 | 57
HS
58 59 | 60 61
UG
62
63 64 | 65 66
B
67 68 69 70 71 72
73 74 75
76 | 77 78 | n( ) 79
GR
[2] 8
9 10 11 12 13 14
15 16
M
17 18 19 20 21 22
23 24 25
26 | 27 28
29 | 30 31
P
D
32 33 34 35 36 37
38 39 40
41 | 42 43 | 44 | 45
TO
46 47 CE-BA
48 49 BA-GE
50 51 GE-MA
52 53 MA-PHD
54 55 GE-PHD
TI
56 57

APPENDIX L Continued

SURVEY OF EARNED DOCTORATES, Cont.

O. Please check each source from which you received some support during graduate study. Check as many sources as apply.

58 ___ NSF Fellowship
59 ___ NSF Traineeship
60 ___ NIH Fellowship
61 ___ NIH Traineeship
62 ___ NDEA Fellowship
63 ___ Other HEW
64 ___ AEC Fellowship
65 ___ NASA Traineeship
66 ___ GI Bill
67 ___ Other Federal support (specify) ....
68 ___ Woodrow Wilson Fellowship
69 ___ Other U.S. national fellowship (specify) ....
70 ___ University fellowship
71 ___ Teaching Assistantship
72 ___ Research Assistantship
73 ___ Educational fund of industrial or business firm
74 ___ Other institutional funds (specify) ....
75 ___ Own earnings
76 ___ Spouse's earnings
77 ___ Family contributions
78 ___ Loans (NDSL direct)
79 ___ Other loans
80 ___ Other (specify) ....

58 59 60 61 62 63 64 65 66 67 68 69 70 71 72 73 74 75 76 77 78 79 80

P. Please check the space which most fully describes your status during the year immediately preceding the doctorate.

0 ☐ Held fellowship
1 ☐ Held assistantship
2 ☐ Held own research grant
3 ☐ Not employed
4 ☐ Part-time employed

Full-time Employed in: (Other than 0, 1, 2)
5 ☐ College or university, teaching
6 ☐ College or university, non-teaching
7 ☐ Elem. or sec. school, teaching
8 ☐ Elem. or sec. school, non-teaching
9 ☐ Industry or business
(11) ☐ Other (specify) ....

(12) ☐ Any other (specify) .... (9)

Q. U.S. veteran status:
0 ☐ Veteran 1 ☐ On active duty 2 ☐ Non-veteran or not applicable (10)

3
8

POSTGRADUATION PLANS

R. How well defined are your postgraduation plans?
0 ☐ Have signed contract or made definite commitment
1 ☐ Am negotiating with a specific organization, or more than one
2 ☐ Am seeking appointment but have no specific prospects
3 ☐ Other (specify) .... (11)

9 10

S. What are your immediate postgraduation plans?
0 ☐ Postdoctoral fellowship?
1 ☐ Postdoctoral research associateship?
2 ☐ Traineeship?
3 ☐ Other study (specify) ....
4 ☐ Employment? (other than 0, 1, 2, 3)
5 ☐ Military service?
6 ☐ Other (specify) .... (12)

11 12

If you check 0, 1, 2, or 3, please answer "T" and omit "U"

If you checked 4, 5, or 6, please answer "U" and omit "T"

T

T. If you plan to be on a postdoctoral fellowship, associateship, or traineeship —

What is the field of your postdoctoral appointment?
Classify using Specialties List.

Number .... Field .... (13-15)

What is the primary source of support?
0 ☐ U.S. Government
1 ☐ College or university
2 ☐ Private foundation
3 ☐ Nonprofit, other than private foundation
4 ☐ Other (specify) ....
6 ☐ Unknown (16)

13 14 15 16

U

U. If you plan to be employed, enter military service, or other —

What will be the type of employer?
0 ☐ 4-year college or university
1 ☐ Jr. or community college
2 ☐ Elem. or sec. school
3 ☐ Foreign government
4 ☐ U.S. Government
5 ☐ U.S. state or local government
6 ☐ Nonprofit organization
7 ☐ Industry or business
8 ☐ Self-employed
9 ☐ Other (specify) .... (17)

17

Indicate primary work activity with "1" in appropriate box; secondary work activity (if any) with "2" in appropriate box.
0 ☐ Research and development
1 ☐ Teaching
2 ☐ Administration
3 ☐ Professional services to individuals
5 ☐ Other (specify) .... (18-19)

18 19

In what field will you be working?
Please enter number from Specialties List .... (20-22)

20 21 22

V

V. What is the name and address of the organization with which you will be associated?

.... (Name of Organization)

.... (Street) .... (City, State) (Or Country if not U.S.) (23-28)

23 24 25 26 27 28

W

BACKGROUND INFORMATION

W. Please indicate, by circling the highest grade attained, the education of

		Elementary school	High school	College	Graduate		
your father:	none	1 2 3 4 5 6 7 8	9 10 11 12	1 2 3 4	MA, MD PhD	Postdoctoral	(29)
your mother	none	1 2 3 4 5 6 7 8	9 10 11 12	1 2 3 4	MA, MD PhD	Postdoctoral	(30)
	0	1 2 3	4 5	6 7	8 9	(11)	

29 30

Signature .... Date completed .... (31-33)

31 32 33 1 34

APPENDIX L Continued

SPECIALTIES LIST

MATHEMATICS

000 — Algebra
010 — Analysis & Functional Analysis
020 — Geometry
030 — Logic
040 — Number Theory
050 — Probability, Math. Statistics (see also 544, 670, 725, 727, 920)
060 — Topology
080 — Computing Theory & Practice
082 — Operations Research (see also 478)
085 — Applied Mathematics
098 — Mathematics, General
099 — Mathematics, Other*

ASTRONOMY

101 — Astronomy
102 — Astrophysics

PHYSICS

110 — Atomic & Molecular
120 — Electromagnetism
130 — Mechanics
132 — Acoustics
134 — Fluids
135 — Plasma
136 — Optics
138 — Thermal
140 — Elementary Particles
150 — Nuclear Structure
160 — Solid State
198 — Physics, General
199 — Physics, Other*

CHEMISTRY

200 — Analytical
210 — Inorganic
220 — Organic
230 — Nuclear
240 — Physical
250 — Theoretical
260 — Agricultural & Food
270 — Pharmaceutical
275 — Polymer
298 — Chemistry, General
299 — Chemistry, Other*

EARTH SCIENCES

301 — Mineralogy, Petrology
305 — Geochemistry
310 — Stratigraphy, Sedimentation
320 — Paleontology
330 — Structural Geology
341 — Geophysics (Solid Earth)
350 — Geomorph., Glacial Geology
360 — Hydrology
370 — Oceanography
381 — Atmospheric Physics and Chemistry
382 — Atmospheric Dynamics
383 — Atmospheric Sciences, Other*
391 — Applied Geol., Geol. Engr., Econ. Geol.
395 — Fuel Tech., Petrol. Engr. (see also 479)
398 — Earth Sciences, General
399 — Earth Sciences, Other*

ENGINEERING

400 — Aeronautical & Astronautical
410 — Agricultural
415 — Biomedical
420 — Civil
430 — Chemical
435 — Ceramic
437 — Computer
440 — Electrical
445 — Electronics
450 — Industrial
455 — Nuclear
460 — Engineering Mechanics
465 — Engineering Physics
470 — Mechanical
475 — Metallurgy & Phys. Met. Engr.
476 — Systems Design, Systems Science
478 — Operations Research (see also 082)
479 — Fuel Tech., Petrol. Engr. (see also 395)
480 — Sanitary
486 — Mining
497 — Materials Science
498 — Engineering, General
499 — Engineering, Other*

ENVIRONMENTAL SCIENCES

589 — Environmental Sciences*

AGRICULTURAL SCIENCES

500 — Agronomy
501 — Agricultural Economics
502 — Animal Husbandry
503 — Food Science & Technology
504 — Fish & Wildlife
505 — Forestry
506 — Horticulture
507 — Soils & Soil Science
510 — Animal Sciences
511 — Phytopathology
518 — Agriculture, General
519 — Agriculture, Other*

MEDICAL SCIENCES

520 — Medicine & Surgery
522 — Public Health
523 — Veterinary Medicine
524 — Hospital Administration
527 — Parasitology
534 — Pathology
536 — Pharmacology
537 — Pharmacy
538 — Medical Sciences, General
539 — Medical Sciences, Other*

BIOLOGICAL SCIENCES

540 — Biochemistry
542 — Biophysics
544 — Biometrics, Biostatistics (see also 050, 670, 725, 727, 920)
545 — Anatomy
546 — Cytology
547 — Embryology
548 — Immunology
550 — Botany
560 — Ecology
562 — Hydrobiology
564 — Microbiology & Bacteriology
566 — Physiology, Animal
567 — Physiology, Plant
569 — Zoology
570 — Genetics
571 — Entomology
572 — Molecular Biology
576 — Nutrition and/or Dietetics
578 — Biological Sciences, General
579 — Biological Sciences, Other*

PSYCHOLOGY

600 — Clinical
610 — Counseling & Guidance
620 — Developmental & Gerontological
630 — Educational
635 — School Psychology
641 — Experimental
642 — Comparative
643 — Physiological
650 — Industrial & Personnel
660 — Personality
670 — Psychometrics (see also 050, 544, 725, 727, 920)
680 — Social
698 — Psychology, General
699 — Psychology, Other*

SOCIAL SCIENCES

700 — Anthropology
708 — Communications*
710 — Sociology
720 — Economics (see also 501)
725 — Econometrics (see also 050, 544, 670, 727, 920)
727 — Statistics (see also 050, 544, 670, 725, 920)
740 — Geography
745 — Area Studies*
751 — Political Science
752 — Public Administration
755 — International Relations
770 — Urban & Reg. Planning
798 — Social Sciences, General
799 — Social Sciences, Other*

ARTS & HUMANITIES

801 — Art, Applied
802 — Art, History & Criticism
804 — History, American
805 — History, European
806 — History, Other*
807 — History & Philosophy of Science
808 — American Studies
830 — Music
831 — Speech as a Dramatic Art (see also 885)
832 — Archeology
833 — Religion (see also 881)
834 — Philosophy
835 — Linguistics
836 — Comparative Literature
878 — Arts & Humanities, General
879 — Arts & Humanities, Other*

LANGUAGES & LITERATURE

811 — American
812 — English
821 — German
822 — Russian
823 — French
824 — Spanish & Portuguese
826 — Italian
827 — Classical*
829 — Other Languages*

EDUCATION

900 — Foundations: Social, Philosoph.
910 — Educational Psychology
908 — Elementary Educ., General
909 — Secondary Educ., General
918 — Higher Education
919 — Adult Educ. & Extension Educ.
920 — Educ. Meas. & Stat.
929 — Curriculum & Instruction
930 — Educ. Admin. & Superv.
940 — Guid., Couns., & Student Pers.
950 — Special Education (Gifted, Handicapped, etc.)
960 — Audio-Visual Media

TEACHING FIELDS

970 — Agriculture Educ.
972 — Art Educ.
974 — Business Educ.
976 — English Educ.
978 — Foreign Languages Educ.
980 — Home Economics Educ.
982 — Industrial Arts Educ.
984 — Mathematics Educ.
986 — Music Educ.
988 — Phys. Ed., Health, & Recreation
989 — Reading Education
990 — Science Educ.
992 — Social Science Educ.
993 — Speech Education
994 — Vocational Educ.
996 — Other Teaching Fields*

998 — Education, General
999 — Education, Other*

OTHER PROFESSIONAL FIELDS

881 — Theology (see also 833)
882 — Business Administration
883 — Home Economics
884 — Journalism
885 — Speech & Hearing Sciences (see also 831)
886 — Law, Jurisprudence
887 — Social Work
891 — Library & Archival Science
897 — Professional Field, Other*

899 — OTHER FIELDS*

* Identify the specific field in the space provided on the questionnaire.

APPENDIX L Continued

OMB No. 099-R0294

1975 SURVEY OF DOCTORAL SCIENTISTS AND ENGINEERS

CONDUCTED BY THE NATIONAL RESEARCH COUNCIL WITH THE SUPPORT OF THE NATIONAL SCIENCE FOUNDATION

THE ACCOMPANYING LETTER requests your assistance in this biennial survey of doctoral scientists and engineers – including the fields of the natural and social sciences, mathematics, and engineering.

PLEASE READ the instructions for each question carefully and answer by printing your reply or entering an 'X' in the appropriate box.

PLEASE CHECK the pre-printed information to be certain that it is correct and complete.

PLEASE RETURN the completed form in the enclosed envelope to the Commission on Human Resources, JH 638, National Research Council, 2101 Constitution Avenue, N.W., Washington, D.C. 20418.

NOTE: ALL INFORMATION YOU PROVIDE WILL BE TREATED AS CONFIDENTIAL AND USED IN GROUP COMPARISONS FOR RESEARCH PURPOSES ONLY.

Please do not write in this space

1 2-9 ctr # C

10 11

(10)

If your name and address are incorrect, please enter correct information on the lines provided above. Include ZIP CODE.

If there is an alternate address through which you can always be reached, please provide it on the line below.

C/O Number Street City State ZIP CODE (11)

12 13 14 15 16

1. Date of Birth — Mo. Day Year (12-16)

2. State or Foreign Country of Birth (17-18)

3. Citizenship (19) — USA 0☐ Non-USA, specify country 1☐ (20-21)

4. Sex (22) — 1☐ Male 2☐ Female

17 18 19 20 21

22 23

5. Racial/Ethnic Identification (23)
0 ☐ White/Caucasian
1 ☐ Black/Negro/Afro-American
2 ☐ American Indian
3 ☐ Mexican-American/Chicano
4 ☐ Puerto Rican-American
5 ☐ Oriental
6 ☐ Other Asian
7 ☐ Other, specify

B

24 25 26

27 28 29

30 31 32 33 34 35

6. List in the table below all collegiate and graduate degrees, excluding honorary degrees, that have been awarded to you. Please check the pre-printed information, including the number and name of the specialty from the list on page 3, to be certain that it is correct and complete.

Type of Degree	Granted Mo. Yr.	Major Field (Use Specialties List) Name Number	Institution Name City (or campus) & State
Bachelor's			
Master's			
Doctorate			
Other, Specify			

M

36 37 38

39 40 41

42 43 44 45 46 47

D

48 49 50

51 52 53

54 55 56 57 58 59

PLEASE NOTE that in items 7-10 information is requested for both the current year, as of the week of February 9-15, 1975, and last year, as of the week of February 10-16, 1974.

7. What was your employment status as of the periods indicated? (Check only one category in each year.)

	1974	1975
Employed full-time, science or engineering related position	☐	1 ☐
Employed full-time, nonscience or nonengineering related position	☐	2 ☐
Employed part-time, science or engineering related position	☐	3 ☐
Employed part-time, nonscience or nonengineering related position	☐	4 ☐
Postdoctoral appointment (fellowship, traineeship, research associateship, etc.)	☐	5 ☐
Unemployed and seeking employment	☐	6 ☐
Specify number of months unemployed: ______ (66-67)		
Unemployed and not seeking employment	☐	7 ☐
Retired and not employed	☐	8 ☐
Specify year of retirement: ______ (68-69)		
Other, specify: ______	☐	9 ☐
	(64)	(65)

7a. If you were employed full-time during February 9-15, 1975, in a position unrelated to science or engineering, what was the MOST important reason for taking the position?

	1975
Prefer nonscience or nonengineering position	☐ 1
Promoted out of science or engineering position	☐ 2
Pay is better	☐ 3
Locational preference	☐ 4
Science or engineering position not available	☐ 5
Other, specify: ______	☐ 6
	(70)

7b. If you were employed part-time during February 9-15, 1975, were you seeking full-time employment? 1 ☐ Yes 2 ☐ No (71)

O

60 61 62 63

64 65

66 67 68 69

70 71

APPENDIX L Continued

8. Which category below best describes the type of organization of your principal employment OR postdoctoral appointment?

(Check only one category in each year.)

	1974		1975
Business or industry	☐	1	☐
Junior college, 2-year college, technical institute	☐	2	☐
Medical school	☐	3	☐
4-year college or university, other than medical school	☐	4	☐
Elementary or secondary school system	☐	5	☐
Hospital or clinic	☐	6	☐
U.S. military service, active duty, or Commissioned Corps, e.g., USPHS, NOAA	☐	7	☐
U.S. government, civilian employee	☐	8	☐
State government	☐	9	☐
Local or other government, specify: ______	☐	10	☐
International Agency	☐	11	☐
Non-profit organization, other than hospital, clinic, or educational institution	☐	12	☐
Other, specify: ______	☐	13	☐
	(72-73)		(74-75)

9. What were the primary (A) and secondary (B) work activities related to your position?

(Check only one box in each column.)

	1974 A	1974 B		1975 A	1975 B
Management or administration of:					
Research and development	☐	☐	1	☐	☐
Other than research and development	☐	☐	2	☐	☐
Both	☐	☐	3	☐	☐
Basic research	☐	☐	4	☐	☐
Applied research	☐	☐	5	☐	☐
Development of equipment, products, systems, data	☐	☐	6	☐	☐
Design	☐	☐	7	☐	☐
Teaching	☐	☐	8	☐	☐
Report or other technical writing, editing	☐	☐	9	☐	☐
Production	☐	☐	10	☐	☐
Consulting, specify: ______	☐	☐	11	☐	☐
Professional services to individuals	☐	☐	12	☐	☐
Quality control, inspection, testing	☐	☐	13	☐	☐
Sales, marketing, purchasing, estimating	☐	☐	14	☐	☐
Other, specify: ______	☐	☐	15	☐	☐
	(10-13)			(14-17)	

72 73 74 75

2
1 2-9 ctr #

10 11 12 13

14 15 16 17

10. From the Degree and Employment Specialties List on page 4, select and enter both the number and title of the scientific specialty most closely related to your principal employment or postdoctoral appointment. Write in your specialty if it is not on the list.

1974 ______ Number Title of Specialty (18-20)

1975 ______ Number Title of Specialty (21-23)

18 19 20

21 22 23

Please answer items 11 through 13 regarding your employment during the week of February 9-15, 1975.

11. What percent of time did you devote to each of the following activities?

	%	
Management or administration of:		
Research and development	______	(24)
Other than research and development	______	(26)
Both	______	(28)
Basic research	______	(30)
Applied research	______	(32)
Development	______	(34)
Design	______	(36)
Teaching	______	(38)
Consulting	______	(40)
Other, specify: ______	______	(42)
TOT. L	100%	

12. Please give the name of your principal employer (organization, company, etc., or, if self-employed, write "self"), and actual place of employment.

______
Name of Employer (44-49)

______
Number Street

______
City State ZIP Code (50-54)

24 25 26 27 28 29

30 31 32 33 34 35

36 37 38 39 40 41

42 43

44 45 46 47 48 49

50 51 52 53 54

13. What was the basic annual salary* associated with your principal professional employment during the week of February 9-15, 1975? If you were on a postdoctoral appointment (e.g., fellowship, traineeship, research associateship), what was your annual stipend plus allowances?

$______ per year (55-57)

55 56 57

***NOTE:** Basic annual salary is your annual salary before deductions for income tax, social security, retirement, etc., but does not include bonuses, overtime, summer teaching, or other payment for professional work.

If academically employed:

a. Check whether salary was for ☐ 9-10 months **or** ☐ 11-12 months. (58)

b. Did you hold a tenured position during February 9-15, 1975? 0 ☐ Yes 1 ☐ No. (59) **If yes, what year was the tenure granted?** ______ (60-61)

c. What is the rank of your position?

1 ☐ Professor
2 ☐ Associate Professor
3 ☐ Assistant Professor
4 ☐ Instructor
5 ☐ Lecturer
6 ☐ Dean
7 ☐ President or Chancellor
8 ☐ Other, specify: ______
9 ☐ Does not apply
(62)

58

59 60 61

62

APPENDIX L Continued

14. **How many years of professional work experience, including teaching, have you had?** ______________ Year(s) (63-64)

63 64

15. **Have you ever held a postdoctoral appointment?** 0 ☐ Yes 1 ☐ No (65)

65

If yes, list below the time periods of your most recent postdoctoral appointments.

Appointment	Starting Year		Total Months	
Most Recent	______	(66-67)	______	(68-69)
Second Most Recent	______	(70-71)	______	(72-73)
Third Most Recent	______	(74-75)	______	(76-77)

How many other postdoctoral appointments have you held? ______________ (78)

66 67 68 69
70 71 72 73
74 75 76 77
78

3
1 2-9 ctr #

16. **Have you ever been a full-time employee (excluding summer employment) of business or industry since earning your doctorate?**

0 ☐ Yes 1 ☐ No (10)

If yes,

a. **For how many years?**

______________ Year(s) (11-12)

b. **If you were employed by business or industry in February, 1975, check here ☐. If not, how many years ago did you leave your most recent business or industry employment?**

______________ Year(s) (14-15)

17. **Have you ever been a full-time employee (excluding summer employment) of an academic institution or organization since earning your doctorate?**

0 ☐ Yes 1 ☐ No (16)

If yes,

a. **For how many years?**

______________ Year(s) (17-18)

b. **If you were employed by an academic institution or organization in February, 1975, please check here ☐. If not, how many years ago did you leave your most recent academic employment?**

______________ Year(s) (20-21)

18. **Have you ever been a full-time employee (excluding summer employment) of government (federal, state, or local) since earning your doctorate?**

0 ☐ Yes 1 ☐ No (22)

If yes,

a. **For how many years?**

______________ Year(s) (23-24)

b. **If you were employed by government in February, 1975, check here ☐. If not, how many years ago did you leave your most recent government employment?**

______________ Year(s) (26-27)

10 11 12
13 14 15
16 17 18
19 20 21
22 23 24
25 26 27

---

19. **Listed below are selected topics of critical national interest. If you devoted a significant proportion of your professional time to any of these problem areas in February, 1975, please check the box for the one on which you spent the MOST time.**

Education:
1 ☐ Teaching
2 ☐ Other
3 ☐ Health
4 ☐ Defense
5 ☐ Environmental protection, pollution control
6 ☐ Space
7 ☐ Crime prevention and control
8 ☐ Food production and technology
9 ☐ Energy and fuel
10 ☐ Other mineral resources
11 ☐ Community development and services
12 ☐ Housing (planning, design, construction)
13 ☐ Transportation, communications
14 ☐ Other, specify: ______________

(28-29)

28 29

---

20. **Was any of your work in February, 1975, supported or sponsored by U.S. Government funds?**

0 ☐ Yes 1 ☐ No 2 ☐ Don't know (30)

30

If yes, which of the following federal agencies or departments were supporting the work? (Check all that apply.)

31 ☐ NASA
32 ☐ National Science Foundation
33 ☐ Environmental Protection Agency
34 ☐ Energy Research & Development Administration (AEC)
35 ☐ Nuclear Regulatory Commission (AEC)
36 ☐ Agency for International Development
37 ☐ Department of the Interior
38 ☐ National Institutes of Health, HEW
39 ☐ Alcohol, Drug Abuse & Mental Health Administration, HEW
40 ☐ Office of Education, HEW
41 ☐ Other HEW, specify: ______________
42 ☐ Department of Defense
43 ☐ Department of Commerce
44 ☐ Department of Agriculture
45 ☐ Department of Transportation
46 ☐ Department of Justice
47 ☐ Department of Housing and Urban Development
48 ☐ Other agency or department, specify: ______________
49 ☐ Don't know source agency

31 32 33 34
35 36 37 38
39 40 41 42
43 44 45 46
47 48 49

APPENDIX L Continued

DEGREE AND EMPLOYMENT SPECIALTIES LIST

MATHEMATICAL SCIENCES

000 - Algebra
010 - Analysis & Functional Analysis
020 - Geometry
030 - Logic
040 - Number Theory
052 - Probability
055 - Math, Statistics (see also 544, 670, 725, 729)
060 - Topology
080 - Computing Theory & Practice
082 - Operations Research (see also 477)
085 - Applied Mathematics
089 - Combinatorics & Finite Mathematics
091 - Physical Mathematics
098 - Mathematics, General
099 - Mathematics, Other*

ASTRONOMY

101 - Astronomy
102 - Astrophysics

PHYSICS

110 - Atomic & Molecular Physics
120 - Electromagnetism
130 - Mechanics
132 - Acoustics
134 - Fluids
135 - Plasma Physics
136 - Optics
138 - Thermal Physics
140 - Elementary Particles
150 - Nuclear Structure
160 - Solid State
198 - Physics, General
199 - Physics, Other*

CHEMISTRY

200 - Analytical
210 - Inorganic
215 - Synthetic Inorganic & Organometallic
220 - Organic
225 - Synthetic Organic & Natural Products
230 - Nuclear
240 - Physical
245 - Quantum
250 - Theoretical
255 - Structural
260 - Agricultural & Food
265 - Thermodynamics & Material Properties
270 - Pharmaceutical
275 - Polymers
280 - Biochemistry (see also 540)
285 - Chemical Dynamics
298 - Chemistry, General
299 - Chemistry, Other*

EARTH, ENVIRONMENTAL & MARINE SCIENCES

301 - Mineralogy, Petrology
305 - Geochemistry
310 - Stratigraphy, Sedimentation
320 - Paleontology
330 - Structural Geology
341 - Geophysics (Solid Earth)
350 - Geomorph., Glacial Geology
360 - Hydrology
370 - Oceanography
381 - Atmospheric Chemistry & Physics
382 - Atmospheric Dynamics
391 - Applied Geology, Geol. Engr., Econ. Geol.
388 - Environmental Sciences, General
389 - Environmental Sciences, Other*
397 - Marine Sciences, Other*
398 - Earth Sciences, General
399 - Earth Sciences, Other*

ENGINEERING

400 - Aeronautical & Astronautical
410 - Agricultural
415 - Biomedical
420 - Civil
430 - Chemical
435 - Ceramic
440 - Electrical
445 - Electronics
450 - Industrial, Manufacturing
455 - Nuclear
460 - Engineering Mechanics
465 - Engineering Physics
470 - Mechanical
475 - Metallurgy & Phys. Met. Engr.
477 - Operations Research, Systems (see also 082)
479 - Fuel Technology, Petrol Engr.
480 - Sanitary/Environmental
486 - Mining
497 - Materials Science Engr.
498 - Engineering, General
499 - Engineering, Other*

AGRICULTURAL SCIENCES

500 - Agronomy
501 - Agricultural Economics
502 - Animal Husbandry
504 - Fish & Wildlife
505 - Forestry
506 - Horticulture
507 - Soils & Soil Science
510 - Animal Sciences
511 - Phytopathology
517 - Food Science & Technology (see also 573)
518 - Agriculture, General
519 - Agriculture, Other*

MEDICAL SCIENCES

520 - Medicine & Surgery
522 - Public Health
523 - Veterinary Medicine
524 - Hospital Administration
527 - Parasitology
534 - Pathology
536 - Pharmacology
537 - Pharmacy
538 - Medical Sciences, General
539 - Medical Sciences, Other*

BIOLOGICAL SCIENCES

540 - Biochemistry (see also 280)
542 - Biophysics
543 - Biomathematics
544 - Biometrics, Biostatistics (see also 055, 670, 725, 729)
545 - Anatomy
546 - Cytology
547 - Embryology
548 - Immunology
550 - Botany
560 - Ecology
562 - Hydrobiology
564 - Microbiology & Bacteriology
566 - Physiology, Animal
567 - Physiology, Plant
569 - Zoology
570 - Genetics
571 - Entomology
572 - Molecular Biology
573 - Food Science & Technology (see also 517)
574 - Behavior/Ethology
578 - Biological Sciences, General
579 - Biological Sciences, Other*

PSYCHOLOGY

600 - Clinical
610 - Counseling & Guidance
620 - Developmental & Gerontological
630 - Educational
635 - School Psychology
641 - Experimental
642 - Comparative
643 - Physiological
650 - Industrial & Personnel
660 - Personality
670 - Psychometrics (see also 055, 544, 725, 729)
680 - Social
698 - Psychology, General
699 - Psychology, Other*

SOCIAL SCIENCES

700 - Anthropology
703 - Archeology
708 - Communications*
709 - Linguistics
710 - Sociology
720 - Economics (see also 501)
725 - Econometrics (see also 055, 544, 670, 729)
729 - Social Statistics (see also 055, 544, 670, 725)
740 - Geography
745 - Area Studies*
750 - Political Science, Public Administration
755 - International Relations
770 - Urban & Reg. Planning
775 - History & Phil. of Science
798 - Social Sciences, General
799 - Social Sciences, Other*

ARTS & HUMANITIES

841 - Fine & Applied Arts (including Music, Speech, Drama, etc.)
842 - History
843 - Philosophy, Religion, Theology
845 - Languages & Literature
846 - Other Arts and Humanities*

EDUCATION & OTHER PROFESSIONAL FIELDS

938 - Education

882 - Business Administration
883 - Home Economics
884 - Journalism
885 - Speech and Hearing Sciences
886 - Law, Jurisprudence
887 - Social Work
891 - Library & Archival Science
898 - Professional Field, Other*

899 - OTHER FIELDS*

*Identify the specific field in the space provided on the questionnaire.

A Selective Bibliography

The bibliography listed below is not intended to be comprehensive; it selects reports that have a special bearing on doctoral education and that in turn contain references to subsidiary or related studies. Reports listed are some of those prepared by the Office of Scientific Personnel (OSP), predecessor to the Commission on Human Resources, and by organizations working in close conjunction with the Commission or under its administrative unbrella. Those organizations include the Commission on Human Resources and Higher Education (late 1960's), the Board on Human Resources (1970-1974), and the National Board on Graduate Education (NBGE), established in 1971 by the Conference Board of Associated Research Councils.

The bibliography is arranged by topics or series of reports, rather than chronologically or alphabetically, to indicate the interrelationships of reports. There are six groups of reports included:

1. Studies based directly on the DRF.
2. Studies of high school backgrounds, which originated with the DRF.
3. Studies based on the Comprehensive Roster of Doctoral Scientists and Engineers.
4. Studies sponsored by the National Institutes of Health (NIH) or the National Institute of General Medical Sciences (NIGMS), relating primarily to NIH support of students.
5. Miscellaneous OSP/Commission on Human Resources studies, with various sponsors.
6. Studies by the related organizations mentioned above.

STUDIES BASED ON THE DRF

There have been six reports describing the baccalaureate origins of PhD's and the number of doctorate degrees awarded in the United States since 1920. The present report, *A Century of Doctorates*, is the seventh in this series. In addition, a series of annual supplementary reports have been issued since 1967. The following list provides the appropriate references to these studies.

1. *Baccalaureate Origins of the Science Doctorates Awarded in the United States 1936-1945*. NAS, 1948. 93 pages. (out of print)
2. *Baccalaureate Origins of Science Doctorates Awarded in the United States 1936-1950*. NAS, 1955. 158 pages. (out of print)
3. *Baccalaureate Origins of Doctorates in the Arts, Humanities, and Social Sciences Awarded in the United States 1936-1950*. NAS Publication 460, 1956. 131 pages. (out of print)
4. *Doctorate Production in United States Universities, 1936-1956, With Baccalaureate Origins of Doctorates in Sciences, Arts, and Professions*. NAS Publication 582, 1958. 155 pages. (out of print)
5. *Doctorate Production in United States Universities 1920-1962, With Baccalaureate Origins of Doctorates in Sciences, Arts, and Professions*. NAS Publication 1142, 1963. 215 pages. (price $6.00)
6. *Doctorate Recipients from United States Universities 1958-1966*. NAS Publication 1489, 1967. 280 pages. (price $9.75)
7. *A Century of Doctorates*.
8. Annual *Summary Report*, published in each year since 1967. (A set of key tables updating the data of publication 1489, cited above.)

HIGH SCHOOL BACKGROUNDS STUDIES

1. Scientific Manpower Report 3 to the National Science Foundation (NSF) February 1961, by L. R. Harmon. Published in slightly altered

form, in *Science*, March 19, 1961, as "The High School Backgrounds of Science Doctorates."

2. Scientific Manpower Report 4 to NSF, *A Multiple Discriminant Analysis of the High School Background Data for the Doctorates of 1958*, by L. R. Harmon. NAS, 1964.

3. *High School Ability Patterns--A Backward Look From the Doctorate*, by L. R. Harmon. NAS, 1965.

STUDIES BASED ON THE COMPREHENSIVE ROSTER

1. *Doctoral Scientists and Engineers in the United States: 1973 Profile*. The first report of the 1973 survey and results. Commission on Human Resources, NAS, March 1974, 37 pages.

2. *Doctoral Scientists and Engineers in the United States: 1975 Profile*. Commission on Human Resources, NAS, 1976.

3. *Minority Groups Among United States Doctorate Level Scientists, Engineers, and Scholars, 1973*. Commission on Human Resources, NAS, April 1975.

4. *Field Mobility of Doctoral Scientists and Engineers*. Commission on Human Resources, NAS, December 1975.

5. *An Evaluation of the 1973 Survey of Doctoral Scientists and Engineers*. Commission on Human Resources, NAS, November 1976.

6. *Employment Status of PhD Scientists and Engineers 1973 and 1975*. Commission on Human Resources, NAS, 1976.

7. *Characteristics of Doctoral Scientists and Engineers in the United States, 1973*. A report based on the NSF's Manpower Characteristics System Survey of Science Resources Series, NSF 75-312.

8. *Characteristics of Doctoral Scientists and Engineers in the United States, 1973*. Detailed statistical tables (Appendix B to NSF 75-312), NSF 75-312-A.

9. *Characteristics of Doctoral Scientists and Engineers in the United States, 1975*. As for 7 above, based on 1975 data, NSF 77-309.

STUDIES SPONSORED BY NIH AND NIGMS

A. The Career Patterns Reports, in numbered series, prepared by L. R. Harmon:

1. *Profiles of PhD's in the Sciences, Summary Report on Follow-up of Doctorate Cohorts 1935-1960*. NAS Publication 1293, 1965.

2. *Careers of PhD's, Academic versus Nonacademic, a Second Report on Follow-up of Doctoral Cohorts 1935-1960*. NAS Publication 1577, October 1968.

3. *Mobility of PhD's, Before and After the Doctorate, with Associated Economic and Educational Characteristics of States*. NAS Publication 1874, 1971.

B. Studies of persons supported by NIH or NIGMS

1. *Effects of NIGMS Training Programs on Graduate Education in the Biomedical Sciences*. NIH, Department of Health, Education, and Welfare (HEW), 1969.

2. *Postdoctoral Training in the Biomedical Sciences, an Evaluation of NIGMS Postdoctoral Traineeship and Fellowship Programs*. NAS, 1974. Available from the National Technical Information Service, Department of Commerce, PB-231 164/5GA.

3. *Research Training and Career Patterns of Bioscientists: The Training Programs of the National Institutes of Health*. NAS, 1976.

C. Reports of the Committee on a Study of National Needs for Biomedical and Behavioral Research Personnel

1. *Personnel Needs and Training for Biomedical and Behavioral Research 1975 Report*. Commission on Human Resources, NAS, 1975.

2. *Personnel Needs and Training for Biomedical and Behavioral Research 1976 Report*. Commission on Human Resources, NAS, 1976.

MISCELLANEOUS OSP/COMMISSION ON HUMAN RESOURCES STUDIES

1. Special Report LL, for the U.S. Office of Education: *Doctorates in Linguistics and Modern Foreign Languages: Their Numbers, 1957-1961, Education, and Experience*, by L. R. Harmon, October 31, 1963. 37 pages.

2. *The Backgrounds and Early Careers of Engineering Doctorate Recipients*. A report to the Ford Foundation, by Joan G. Creager, May 6, 1968. 50 pages.

3. *The Ford Foundation Forgivable Loans in Support of Graduate Education in Engineering--A Program Evaluation*. A report to the Ford Foundation, by L. R. Harmon, May 1970. 38 pages.

4. *Education and Employment Patterns of Bioscientists--A Statistical Report*. Published by NIH, U.S. Department of HEW, 1971.

5. *The Invisible University: Postdoctoral Education in the United States*. NAS, 1969. Study Director, Richard B. Curtis.

STUDIES BY RELATED ORGANIZATIONS

A. *Human Resources and Higher Education*. Staff report of the Commission on Human Resources and Higher Education, by John K. Folger, Helen S. Astin, and Alan E. Bayer. Russell Sage Foundation, New York, 1970.

B. Studies by the staff of the Board on Human Resources, which antedated the Commission on Human Resources

1. *Does College Matter? Some Evidence on the Impacts of Higher Education*, by Lewis C. Solmon (Ed. with Paul Taubman). Academic Press, New York, 1973.

2. *Women in Doctoral Education: Clues and Puzzles Regarding Institutional Discrimination*, by Lewis C. Solmon. *Research and Higher Education*, Vol. 1, 1973.

C. Studies by the National Board on Graduate Education

1. Technical Report 1. *An Economic Perspective on the Evolution of Graduate Education*, by Stephen P. Dresch, March 1974. 76 pages.

2. Technical Report 2. *Forecasting of the PhD Labor Market: Pitfalls for Policy*, by Richard Freeman and David W. Breneman, April 1974. 50 pages.

3. Technical Report 3. *Graduate School Adjustments to the "New Depression" in Higher Education*, by David W. Breneman, with a Commentary by the National Board on Graduate Education, February 1975. 96 pages.

4. Technical Report 4. *Science Development: An Evaluation Study*, by David E. Drew, June 1975. 182 pages.

5. *Minority Group Participation in Graduate Education*, June 1976. 273 pages.

6. *An Annotated Bibliography on Graduate Education*, 1971-1972, October 1972. 151 pages.

Glossary

BA Any baccalaureate degree; as used here, it includes the bachelor of science degree.

Bio-behavioral field A field group that includes the life sciences, psychology, and the social sciences.

Cohort All those individuals graduating within a given period, which may be a single year or a set of years. Also, it may mean birth cohort, i.e., those born in a given year or over a given period of years.

Comprehensive Roster The Comprehensive Roster of Doctoral Scientists and Engineers, compiled by the Commission on Human Resources and surveyed biennially.

Donor/receptor As used in this report, refers to donor/receptor relationships, defined as field-switching ratios between the baccalaureate and doctorate degrees. Within the PhD population, the ratio of baccalaureate degrees in a given field to doctorate degrees in that field defines whether a field is a "donor" or "receptor" field. If the fraction is greater than 1.00, the field is a donor; if less than 1.00, the field is a receptor. The term also refers to geographic regions, with the same calculation procedure.

DRF Doctorate Records File, a file of names of all PhD's granted in United States universities from 1920 to the present, maintained continually.

Educational level As used here, the eventual grade level attained by an individual, on a scale of grades 1-8 for elementary school, 9-12 for high school, 13-16 for undergraduate education, and arbitrary values assigned to the higher degrees--18 for a master's degree and 20 for the doctorate. Grade level, in this report, refers to aggregates of individuals, and normative terms such as mean, median, or percentiles are typically used.

EMP A field group consisting of engineering, mathematics, and the physical sciences.

Field Defined operationally by the major headings in the *Specialties List* shown on page 162 in Appendix L. The term subfield or fine field, when used, refers to the numbered disciplines shown under these major headings. A set of field titles with slight changes, more suitable for employment specialties in the sciences included in the Comprehensive Roster of Doctoral Scientists and Engineers but with condensations in the arts and humanities fields, is provided on page 166.

Field group An aggregation of several major fields, such as engineering, mathematics, and physical sciences (EMP fields); bio-behavioral fields; and nonscience fields.

Field mix A set of proportions describing the percentages of each field in a set of fields.

Field switching, field shifts Used to describe the movement from one field at the baccalaureate level to a different field at the doctorate level or changes of field after the doctorate is awarded.

Increments to growth As used here, the increments are typically annual percentage increments, i.e., the percentage change from one year to the next. In some tables and graphs, increments are averaged.

Institutional profile A set of numbers describing the institution's characteristics, as outlined in Chapter 4. Characteristics include such things as year in which the institution first awarded the doctorate, the percentage of women among its PhD's, the percentages in various field groups, the time lapse of its

PhD's from baccalaureate to doctorate, etc. See pages 101-4.

Isochron A line of equal time, used here to define the proportion of a given field who graduate at the PhD level a given number of years after the baccalaureate degree. Each isochron defines a given time lapse interval, such as 3 years, 8 years, 20 years, etc.

Moving average A means of smoothing time trend data. If a 2-year moving average is used, it is the midpoint between each successive pair of years; if 3 years is used, the numbers for each set of 3 years are added, and the sum is divided by 3. A center-weighted moving average, as used here, includes data for 4 years, with the 2 middle years' data doubled and the sum divided by 6.

Norm A standard of reference. As used in this book, it is typically a statistical description, in terms of a mean and standard deviation or percentiles. Norms may describe a reference population of individuals or of institutions and may refer to any of a number of characteristics.

Population of PhD's The number of living PhD's in the United States at any given time (as distinct from PhD output). A computer model describes this population by field, sex, and age levels.

Postdoctoral training Training, whether on a fellowship, traineeship, associateship, or other title, in which the main aim is further development of skills and knowledge, rather than regular employment, although the training may include teaching and research production.

Professions As defined in the DRF, these include business administration, journalism, home economics, law, library and archival science, social work, speech and hearing science, and theology.

Regions of U.S. As used here, the nine census regions of the United States, described in terms of the states included on pages 100-101.

Roose-Andersen ratings Ratings of graduate departments, as described in the book *A Rating of Graduate Programs* by Roose and Andersen, published by the American Council on Education, 1970.

Subfields Also referred to as "fine fields." Each of the major fields is subdivided into specialties; the entire set of these specialties, with numbers of PhD's in each subfield, is given in Appendix A.

Tetrad A group or arrangement of 4. Here it is used to describe a 2 × 2 arrangement, the mothers and fathers of male and female PhD's, and refers to the educational levels of these groups of parents.

Subject Index